Latter-day Saint Theology among Christian Theologies

LATTER-DAY SAINT THEOLOGY
AMONG
CHRISTIAN THEOLOGIES

Grant Underwood

WILLIAM B. EERDMANS PUBLISHING COMPANY

GRAND RAPIDS, MICHIGAN

Wm. B. Eerdmans Publishing Co.
2006 44th Street SE, Grand Rapids, MI 49508
www.eerdmans.com

31 30 29 28 27 26 25   1 2 3 4 5 6 7

ISBN 978-0-8028-8440-4

Library of Congress Cataloging-in-Publication Data

A catalog record for this book is available from the Library of Congress.

For "Miss Rice"
and
Mike Campbell

CONTENTS

Foreword by Craig Blomberg   ix

Preface   xv

Note on Nomenclature and Style   xix

List of Abbreviations   xxi

Introduction   1

1. God: Divinity and Trinity   19

2. God: Creation, Providence, and Theodicy   61

3. Christ: His "Person" and Nature   99

4. Christ: His Atoning "Work"   140

5. Anthropology: Humanity as "Royalty Deposed"   177

6. Soteriology: Dimensions of Salvation   216

7. Church: Images, Models, and "Marks"   268

8. Church: Authority, Priesthood, and Ministry   308

9. Sacraments: Theory and Application   351

10. The Eucharist: Savoring the Lord's Supper   395

11. Additional Sacraments: An Abundance of Grace   435

12. Eschatology: The End of the Age and the Afterlife   478

CONTENTS

Afterword   545

Birth and Death Dates of Persons Discussed   549

Bibliography   553

Index of Authors   567

Index of Subjects   582

Index of Scripture   600

FOREWORD

Little did I know in the spring of 1992 that I was embarking on one of the most unexpected yet one of the most rewarding adventures of my academic career: to get to know about and to make good friends with many people from the Church of Jesus Christ of Latter-day Saints. The student body president at Denver Seminary where I was teaching had organized a panel discussion to interact with BYU professor Stephen Robinson's best-selling book *Are Mormons Christians?* and had asked me to be one of the panelists. Thirty-two years later, as I write this foreword, I look back in amazement on the opportunities that correspondence with Robinson and friendship with that student president, the Reverend Greg Vettel Johnson, who has spent his career in ministry in Utah, have created. Robinson and I coauthored a book, *How Wide the Divide? A Mormon and an Evangelical in Conversation*, published by IVP in 1997; I participated for twenty years, from 2000 to 2022 (with a two-year hiatus in 2020–2021 because of the COVID pandemic), in an evangelical-Mormon dialogue group of professors of biblical studies, theology, church history, and related fields; I attended numerous events at BYU and individual sessions at larger conferences throughout North America that focused on some aspect of Mormon studies; and I wrote several articles in both Latter-day Saint and evangelical publications as the outgrowth of my research, my experiences, and what I was learning.

The point persons for the LDS and evangelical contingents in the dialogue were, respectively, Dr. Robert Millet from BYU and Dr. Richard Mouw from Fuller Seminary. Without their indefatigable enthusiasm for our ongoing gatherings, I'm sure things would have fallen apart at some point. But unquestionably in my mind, the third-most-important professor in our cohorts, which averaged about fifteen in semiannual attendance but garnered more than forty individuals who participated at least once over the years, was Dr. Grant Underwood. At the risk of offending a lot of my good friends by not choosing them for this honor, Grant may have been the purest scholar and educator in our illustrious group. He was with us from almost the beginning, and no one else asked as many questions of "the other side" simply to clarify what he thought he was hearing or to ask about implications of what had just been said, and no one else jumped into conversation as often or as helpfully in order to clarify what others on his side were saying or to address what he understood to be the boundaries between acceptable and unacceptable belief or practice in the Church of Jesus Christ of Latter-day Saints.

Grant Underwood is a consummate church historian. His early publication, *The Millenarian World of Early Mormonism*, won a string of awards, and his many subsequent publications pertaining to religious history evidence a similar quality. His PhD came from UCLA, he has been active in the American Academy of Religion, and he has regularly participated in gatherings of scholars that extend well beyond the LDS. The book that you are about to read is the outgrowth of many years of careful study of many different theological perspectives, past and present, and of numerous rounds of revision. Grant embodies one of the foundational goals of a good educator that my professors tried to inculcate in me when I was in college: when you teach about a person or group that is considerably different than yourself or with which you disagree on at least a few important topics, you should present their viewpoints in a way that they would commend as accurate and fair if they were present to hear you. Only then are you entitled to express your agreements and disagreements. That does not mean Grant has succeeded without a single flaw, but it does mean that he has worked very hard at the task.

I have nothing but admiration for Eerdmans in their willingness to publish this book. Of course, they broke fresh ground a number of years ago with Robert Millet's *A Different Jesus? The Christ of Latter-day Saints*. But there are a number of hurdles that outsiders to a group like the LDS have to overcome to read a work like this one well. When I cowrote *How Wide the Divide?* with Stephen Robinson, in addition to a lot of commendation and thanks, I received some quite vitriolic criticism, almost all of it from fellow evangelicals. After a while, I realized that the complaints largely boiled down to one or more of three claims:

1. Robinson sounded too close to evangelical Christianity, so he must be lying about what he believes.
2. If Robinson is telling the truth about what he believes, then he must be a dissident on the verge of being excommunicated.
3. Even if Robinson is telling the truth and his views are acceptable within

the LDS church, Blomberg shouldn't be writing a book of this nature with him. That just confuses people. The only legitimate kind of conversation an evangelical should have with a Mormon, including in print, is one of overt proselytizing.

The first two claims were fairly quickly disproved; the amount of good that the book has produced has convinced most people that the third claim is also invalid. The book actually clarified much more than it confused.

Still, there were some rough edges to Robinson's personality and demeanor that made it hard for some evangelicals and Mormons alike to interact with him. I still recall one of his favorite sayings when he thought someone's position on a topic was logically contradictory: "That's just oxymoronic, and maybe plain moronic!" Grant Underwood couldn't be further removed from that kind of approach. I still chuckle when I recall the time he and a colleague approached the door of the room we were meeting in for one of our dialogue gatherings at exactly the same time, and each tried to defer and hold the door open for the other. "You go first," was followed by "No, you go," and back and forth very courteously until a third professor from BYU grinned and said, "Oh, no. It's a Mormon 'polite-out.' This could last all afternoon!" Grant is just that likable a person. Nor have I ever heard anyone question his impeccable LDS credentials to represent mainstream Mormon thought.

Of course, Underwood has an agenda in this book. Why would anyone ever go to the lengths of the kind of careful historical research and engagement with the literature that he has undertaken without an agenda? He wants to compare and contrast the thinking of the LDS church with a broad cross section of Christian alternatives. He wants to be as accurate as he can be, recognizing that no one can be an expert on all the subdisciplines of church history and theology that he has canvassed. But he believes and therefore wants to show that there is often precedent for the more distinctive Mormon beliefs in previous branches or thinkers of Christendom, sometimes in eras long past. He believes Latter-day Saint beliefs represent a legitimate Christian option, once they are represented fairly and once the breadth of views, of both their theologians and those of other churches, come into full view.

There are fair and unfair ways to critique this book. Fair ways include arguing that a person's or movement's perspective on a topic is not described accurately enough—perhaps boundaries should be drawn either more narrowly or more broadly. Perhaps a perceived parallel between LDS and historic Christian thought is not as close as alleged, or perhaps a difference is not as great as alleged. Maybe the significance of a viewpoint within a larger topic is smaller or greater than what is depicted. These are always judgment calls to a significant degree anyway. Unfair critiques include arguing that a certain perspective can't be true because it is not one that a person has encountered before, unless one is sure that they've encountered everything in the history of Christianity! Act-consequence critiques are also typically on shaky ground: "If I accept *x* is true, then it will lead to *y* or *z*, which I deem unacceptable." Genuine truth-seekers, not to mention anyone who believes in Ephesians 4:15 and "speaking the truth in love," must be committed to determining if *x* is true. If it is, inherent consequences alone cannot be reasons for rejecting it. Of course, in our highly polarized world, perhaps the most common inappropriate critiques are the *ad hominem* or *ad hoc* ones, which simply attack a person or which label a perspective in order to dismiss it, without giving any actual supporting arguments for one's dismissal. Grant's book is exemplary in not doing this. If he has done it somewhere, I missed it, and it would be rare and unintentional.

Underwood is candid in acknowledging he hopes his book will help outsiders to the LDS church see Mormonism as genuinely Christian. A key question not asked often enough by both conversation partners in dialogues like the one in which we participated is: What does it mean to call a movement, a denomination, an institution, or a group of people "Christian"? When I was a college student, I went to a large Christmastime conference of a well-known parachurch organization. One of its breakout session tracks was called "Christianity and the Cults." I was intrigued, and so I went to the first of their three sessions. We were given a handout that indicated that the entire first session was on Roman Catholicism. What the presenters were communicating with their title was that they believed some Catholic doctrines conflicted with Scripture and thus with orthodox, apostolic Christianity, but I knew enough about standard, dictionary definitions of both "Christianity" and "cult" to find the title very bizarre—both misleading and offensive. Today it would be very unusual to find Catholicism discussed under such a heading, whatever one thinks of it. Have evangelicals done something similar with Mormonism? I honestly don't know the answer to the question and am not suggesting one by asking it either.

What I do want to suggest, however, is that a big part of the problem in answering a question like that is that evangelicals have almost entirely focused on what it means for an *individual* to have genuinely Christian faith and not on what it means for an entire movement or institution to be genuinely Christian. I don't ever want to usurp God's role, but if it were left to me, I would have no trouble whatever affirming that Grant Underwood is a wonderful Christian man. I have met other Latter-day Saints about whom I would say the same thing. I have met a few I can't say that about, and quite a few about which I'm just not sure. But the same is true with people who have attended the Baptist churches in which I have spent most of my adult life! Maybe the proportion of people who fall into each category varies, but that doesn't change the principles that a church may not be fully Christian while having some people in it who are, and that a church may be fully Christian while having some people in it who are not.

As a lifelong educator, I would be thrilled if people read this book and came away smiling and saying, "I know so much more about the major doctrines of the Christian faith and the Church of Jesus Christ of Latter-day Saints and about what different individuals and groups of people have believed down through the centuries as well as today." I don't expect there to be anything close to a consensus concerning the significance of the book that appears before you, but if it provokes constructive thought, I will be pleased. If it encourages readers to learn more, to learn how to represent others fairly in all their diversity, and to have a courteous conversation with people not entirely like themselves, the book will have done a great service in our very fractured world. If it causes new reflections not so much about what one needs to do or how one should behave to be thoroughly in line with the Bible in every "jot" or "tittle," but rather about what constitutes a true follower of Jesus, theological warts and all, it will have been worth the reading.

I am reminded of a story that my now late but longtime colleague Dr. Gordon Lewis, professor of theology, philosophy, and apologetics for almost forty years at Denver Seminary, used to like to tell. When he was newly hired in the late 1950s, the Conservative Baptists who had birthed the seminary less than a decade earlier had quite a firebrand fundamentalist for a denominational president. This man had learned that Lewis had dared to suggest in class that while the virgin birth of Christ was an important doctrinal affirmation, he did not think it merited inclusion in a list of the five most fundamental truths of the faith that had to be believed if one was to be saved (a claim of the highly influential series of pamphlets called *The Fundamentals* that were published in the late 1910s). This denominational president proceeded to publicly berate Lewis's notion during a talk he gave at the annual national conference of the Conservative Baptists. A day later, when the president had been asked to share his testimony about becoming a believer, he mentioned that it occurred at age five and that he had an unbroken history of Christian growth from that time on. Accidentally speaking a little louder than he intended to, and sitting in the front row of the auditorium, Lewis turned to Dr. Bruce Shelley, also from the seminary faculty, who was sitting next to him, chuckled, and asked, "Do you think he even knew what a virgin was when he was five years old?" Unfortunately, the speaker heard what Lewis said; fortunately, he just glowered at him without saying anything further! No one needs to repeat the mistake of this church leader.

But enough from me. Please enjoy the course in church history and theology you have before you. Learn, question, debate, reflect, and try to decide what you believe and are committed to. If that happens, good things should result. Dr. Underwood, thank you so much for this labor of love, for giving it your very best shot and for sharing it with a wider audience than just those in your church, even if that means including a few people who aren't always interested in listening and learning, or in being the model of courtesy and friendship that you have been for the nearly twenty-five years that we have known each other.

CRAIG BLOMBERG
Distinguished Professor Emeritus of New Testament,
Denver Seminary, Centennial, Colorado

PREFACE

In an important sense, this book began when I was a high school student in California, and it is dedicated to two individuals who instilled in me a lasting desire to bring my faith into conversation with other religious traditions. I only knew "Miss Rice" by her title, although our yearbook did disclose that the initial of her first name was "S." Miss Rice was one of the most popular English teachers at my high school, a guru of sorts who attracted a devoted band of acolytes who loved to sit lotus position on the checkerboard of carpet squares covering her floor and think big thoughts with her. She offered a course on world religions that was a must-take. I managed to get in. At one point, she asked if I would fill in for a local representative of the Church of Jesus Christ of Latter-day Saints who was to lecture on Mormonism. I accepted with trepidation. I prepared as well as I could, made the presentation, and survived the Q&A with my fellow classmates. The experience was intellectually and spiritually exhilarating, but what really lingers in my memory is the simple, encouraging comment Miss Rice made afterward: "Grant, I think one day you will help many people understand your faith." I hope this book fulfills her intuition.

Mike Campbell was one of my closest high school friends. Both of us were "born-again" Christians in our own way. When I was fifteen, I had experienced a significant awakening to Christ that filled my soul with profound gratitude for his gracious redemption of my own life and stirred within me a passion to learn all I could about his incomparable life and teachings. Mike felt the same. We spent many hours together studying and discussing the pocket-sized Bible I carried with me to school. We visited the famed Calvary Chapel in Costa Mesa to hear the inimitable Pastor Chuck (Smith). Mike and I differed in our reading of the Bible and worshiped at different churches, but I greatly respected his commitment to Christ and his Christlike personality. After graduation, I lost track of Mike (and Miss Rice), easy to do in a day before the Internet and social media, but I have never forgotten them. Our interactions planted deep in my heart a yearning to learn from and about other Christians and make intelligible and attractive my own faith as a member of the Church of Jesus Christ of Latter-day Saints. Wherever you are today, Miss Rice and Mike, I hope this book finds its way into your hands and that you'll consider it a worthy tribute to your formative influence on me.

Because this book culminates many years of interreligious engagement, a list of friends and much-appreciated influencers from other faiths would fill many pages, and to adequately detail their impact on my life would require many more. Among them are fellow laborers in local interfaith councils, professional colleagues at universities, and numerous bright and beloved students. If any of them, too many to mention here by name, read this volume, I hope they will recognize insights gleaned from them and know how grateful I am for our interactions over the years. For influence and friendship going back more than thirty years, special mention must be made of Dr. Richard Mouw, former president of Fuller Theological Seminary; Dr. Richard Hughes, a leading scholar in the Churches of Christ tradition; and Dr. Danel Walker Howe, Pulitzer Prize–winning historian and my *Doktorvater* (PhD supervisor) at UCLA. Each has had a profound and lasting impact on my life as one who models first-rate scholarship and authentic religious faith.

Another longtime friend, Dr. Brian Birch, philosopher and religious studies professor at Utah Valley University, provided the initial impetus for this book. Brian had started work on a similar volume but soon found himself inundated with administrative responsibilities at his university. He invited me to come on board as a coauthor. For several years, I worked on my chapters and benefited from his thoughtful input along the way. Brian's university continued to require his leadership talents, and this prevented him from doing the writing he hoped to do. As time progressed, it also became apparent that each of us had different ideas about the direction and approach the book should take. We parted amicably five years ago, and I went on to finish the volume I had in mind and found in Eerdmans its ideal publisher. I had long contemplated writing a book like this, but Brian's invitation in early 2011 was the catalyst to move forward. Not only am I grateful to him for how his expertise and incisive mind strengthened my writing in the early stages, but I will always recall with fondness the sheer pleasure of our conversations and association together.

Two special groups also deserve an expression of sincere appreciation. First are the several dozen theologians who constituted the Evangelical-Mormon Dialogue that met at least annually for twenty-plus years beginning in the early 2000s. I had the good fortune of being part of this group conceived of and jointly led by Rich Mouw from Fuller and Bob Millet from BYU. It was a most enriching experience to sit for hours with faithful Christians who were also deeply invested in the scholarly enterprise and together probe a wide range of theological topics of importance. Conversation was always candid but courteous, rigorous but respectful. On several occasions, a draft of one of this book's chapters served as the reading for part of the dialogue's daylong discussion. Invariably, the chapter received a thorough vetting, along with a healthy dose of encouragement for the author to press forward with the volume. Thanks are due to everyone in the group for deepening my knowledge, sharpening my perspectives, and refining my writing. All became good friends during our years together. The other group requiring recognition is my students. Numbers of them over the past dozen years or so sat through a course designed around the material in this volume and offered valuable assessments large and small as they completed the RTD (Read the Draft) class assignment for most of the chapters in this book. Other students served helpfully as research assistants during this period, and I am grateful to them for fulfilling a host of responsibilities, ranging from tracking down sources and catching typos to raising important conceptual questions and offering ideas for improvement. To the nearly hundred individuals (mostly students) who populate these two groups, I express appreciation for the part each played in refining this volume. Additionally, special thanks go to my neighbor, Chauncey C. Riddle, distinguished former professor of philosophy and university administrator at Brigham Young University, who, keen-minded as ever at age ninety-six, graciously read every word of the manuscript and offered numerous illuminating comments.

I also wish to express gratitude to Dr. James Ernest, vice president and editor in chief at Eerdmans, for the delightful experience it has been to work with him at all points along the path to publication. Having interacted with a number of editors over the years, none has exceeded James in his combination of professional excellence and pleasant personality. I am grateful also to other members of the Eerdmans "family" for their hospitality and helpfulness—to Anita Eerdmans, president and publisher, for her graciousness and support; to Jenny Hoffman for her outstanding skills as project editor; to Tom Raabe for excellent work as copy editor; and to many others in the Eerdmans team for their support of the book. Appreciation is also expressed to IVP Press for inclusion of parts of a chapter on anthropology I wrote for *Talking Doctrine: Mormons and Evangelicals in Conversation*, edited by Richard J. Mouw and Robert L. Millet (2015); to BYU's Religious Studies Center for portions of a chapter on Christology contributed to *Thou Art the Christ, the Son of the Living God* (2018); and to the *International Journal of Mormon Studies* for parts of a 2009 piece on soteriology (reprinted in abbreviated form in *Element: The Journal of the Society for Mormon Philosophy and Theology*).

A significant debt of gratitude is owed to Brigham Young University for appointment as Richard L. Evans Chair of Religious Understanding, which has provided both time and financial support critical to the completion of this book. Heartfelt thanks also are due to the Carl H. Nelson Foundation for additional financial support. My final acknowledgment and expression of gratitude is arguably the most important of all. This book simply could not have been written without the unflinching and unflagging support of my wife, Sheree. Sheree is every man's dream companion. Her intelligence makes her the perfect conversation partner. As an educated, interested generalist rather than a specialist in the subject, Sheree has been the very kind of reader I am hoping to reach. Moreover, her patience has been generously and ungrudgingly extended not only when long hours have been required to work on this book but when they have been required over and over again for more than a decade! Through it all, her cheerful and loving disposition has lightened my load, lifted my spirts, and enabled me to press on to completion.

Note on Nomenclature and Style

This volume seeks to accommodate both the self-referential preferences of the Church of Jesus Christ of Latter-day Saints and the customary usages of public and academic discourse by alternating the terms used to refer to the church, its members, and its doctrines. Members of the Church of Jesus Christ of Latter-day Saints are here referred to both as "Latter-day Saints" and as "Mormons." The church itself is referenced by its full name or the abbreviated "LDS Church," but not "Mormon church." For the sake of brevity, when referring collectively to the beliefs and practices of the Church of Jesus Christ of Latter-day Saints, "Mormonism" is typically used. When adjectival reference is needed, "Latter-day Saint," "LDS," and "Mormon" are employed interchangeably (e.g., "Latter-day Saint practice" or "Mormon doctrine"). This variety in nomenclature is intended to reflect the sensibilities and referential conventions of all audiences who read the book. Variation also has the added advantage of avoiding cumbersome and tedious repetition.

As is common in books such as this written for the general public, rather than as in-house literature prepared for a particular denomination, ecclesiastical and honorific titles such as "Reverend," "Cardinal," "Bishop," "Father," "Pastor," or "Elder" (for Latter-day Saint leaders) are omitted. Church officials/ministers are initially introduced by their ecclesiastical position and thereafter are referenced by their full name or surname without each time prefacing that name with their title. Thus, while in Catholic devotional literature "Saint Augustine" or "Cardinal Kasper" would be common, here it is "Augustine" or "Walter Kasper." Martin Luther was "Reverend Father Martin Luther" to his followers, and Billy Graham was "Reverend Graham" in church settings. Here, they are "Martin Luther" and "Billy Graham." In these examples, and numerous others like them, no disrespect is meant by not constantly invoking individuals' ecclesiastical (or professorial) titles. Latter-day Saint apostles and prophets are referred to in the same fashion, again with no intention of lessening the esteem in which they are held by the faithful. So, for example, instead of "Elder Dale G. Renlund," one of the church's Twelve Apostles, "Dale Renlund" is used, and with the same implicit respect intended for all church leaders and ministers who are quoted or discussed in this book. Supreme ecclesiastical authorities conventionally referenced even in nonchurch literature by their titles—for example, "Pope Francis" (Catholic), "Patriarch Bartholomew" (Orthodox), "President Nelson" (Latter-day Saint)—constitute the occasional exception. A listing of all persons discussed in the book, with their birth and death dates appended, appears at the end of the book.

In the Church of Jesus Christ of Latter-day Saints, the president, also known as "the prophet," is the senior living apostle (see chapter 8 for a full discussion of the church's hierarchy). As such, he will have served and taught as an apostle for a number of years before acceding to the presidency. When his earlier teachings are cited here, he is introduced as are all the apostles in the manner mentioned above. When quoting his speeches and writings as prophet-president of the church, however, because there is a difference in authoritativeness, he is referred to as "President." Thus, reference to remarks by "President Gordon Hinckley" signals to the reader that the quoted comments were made during the time he served as the church's prophet-president. Remarks by "Gordon Hinckley" come from his earlier apostolic ministry.

In matters of style, Eerdmans generally chooses to follow the Society of Biblical Literature's *Handbook of Style*. This entails decisions about capitalization that are different from what many Christian readers are accustomed to seeing. For instance, reference to Christ's incarnation, passion, crucifixion, resurrection, or atonement all appear in lowercase throughout the book. Pronouns and adjectives referring to members of the Trinity are also not capitalized. None of this is meant to be disrespectful. All books are published under certain stylistic constraints, and this volume is no different. The stylistic choices readers encounter in this book are consistent with the highest professional standards of nondenominational religious publishing. They are not a reflection of either the author's personal religious convictions or his stylistic preferences.

Abbreviations

ANF	*Ante-Nicene Fathers*, ed. Alexander Roberts and James Donaldson, 10 vols. (1885–1887; reprint, Peabody, MA: Hendrickson, 1994).
Aquinas, *Summa Theologiae*	Thomas Aquinas, *Summa Theologiae: Latin Text and English Translation, Introductions, Notes, Appendices, and Glossaries*, ed. Thomas Gilby, 61 vols. (Cambridge: Blackfriars, 1964–1975). The work is divided into four sections: *Prima Pars* (First Part), *Prima Secundae* (First part of the Second Part), *Secunda Secundae* (Second part of the Second Part), and *Tertia Pars* (Third Part). Over the years, these parts have been referenced using different citation styles. In this volume, the Blackfriars method is followed. It adds an "a" or "ae" (from the concluding Latin letters) to the Arabic numerals designating each part. Thus, 2a2ae refers to the *Secunda Secundae. Prima Secundae* is 1a2ae. *Prima Pars* and *Tertia Pars* are, respectively, 1a and 3a. Aquinas further divides his work into questions and articles within questions, here indicated with Arabic numerals. Thus, an example of a full reference would be 2a2ae.35.4.
BEM	*Baptism, Eucharist, and Ministry*, Faith and Order Paper no. 111 (Geneva: World Council of Churches, 1984).
Bible Dictionary	This is published as an appendix in *The Holy Bible . . . Authorized King James Version with Explanatory Notes and Cross References to the Standard*

	Works of The Church of Jesus Christ of Latter-day Saints (Salt Lake City: The Church of Jesus Christ of Latter-day Saints, 2013).
Book of Concord	*Book of Concord: The Confessions of the Evangelical Lutheran Church*, ed. Robert Kolb and Timothy J. Wengert (Minneapolis: Fortress, 2000).
Calvin, *Institutes*	John Calvin, *Institutes of the Christian Religion*, ed. John T. McNeill, trans. Ford Lewis Battles, 2 vols. (1960; reprint, Louisville: WJK, 2006).
CCC	*Catechism of the Catholic Church*, 2nd ed. (Vatican City: Libreria Editrice Vaticana, 1997). Referenced by paragraph number, not page number. Paragraphs in *CCC* are numbered in continuous sequence from beginning to end.
Compendium of Doctrines	*A Compendium of the Doctrines of the Gospel*, ed. Franklin D. Richards and James A. Little (Salt Lake City: Deseret News, 1882).
Conference Report	Proceedings of the multiday general conference held every April and October by the Church of Jesus Christ of Latter-day Saints; each report includes complete transcripts of all addresses by the church's general authorities.
Creeds & Confessions	*Creeds & Confessions of Faith in the Christian Tradition*, ed. Jaroslav Pelikan and Valerie Hotchkiss, 4 vols. (New Haven: Yale University Press, 2003).
D&C	Doctrine and Covenants. The first number in citations is the "section" (i.e., chapter), followed by a colon, and the verse. Thus, 42:56 means section 42, verse 56.
D&C-1835	Doctrine and Covenants, 1st edition, published in 1835, followed by a comma and page reference.
DCC	*The Doctrine and Covenants . . . with an Introduction and Historical and Exegetical Notes*, ed. Hyrum M. Smith and Janne Sjodahl (Liverpool: George F. Richards, 1919); later revised by apostles Joseph Fielding Smith, Harold B. Lee, and Marion G. Romney (Salt Lake City: Deseret Book, 1951) and popularly known as *Doctrine and Covenants Commentary*. The revised edition is cited here.

Denzinger	Heinrich Denzinger, *Compendium of Creeds, Definitions, and Declarations on Matters of Faith and Morals*, ed. Robert Fastiggi and Anne England Nash, trans. Peter Hunermann, 43rd ed. (San Francisco: Ignatius, 2012). Similar to the *CCC*, this volume is referenced by marginal number (generally more than a single paragraph).
Doctrines of Salvation	*Doctrines of Salvation: Sermons and Writings of Joseph Fielding Smith*, comp. Bruce R. McConkie, 3 vols. (Salt Lake City: Bookcraft, 1954–1956).
"The Father and the Son"	"The Father and the Son: A Doctrinal Exposition of the First Presidency and the Twelve," *Improvement Era*, August 1916, 934–42.
GH	*General Handbook: Serving in The Church of Jesus Christ of Latter-day Saints* (Salt Lake City: The Church of Jesus Christ of Latter-day Saints, 2023). Organized and cited by section numbers, as in *CCC* and Denzinger. Citations of earlier editions additionally carry the year of publication in parentheses ahead of the section numbers, as in this example: *GH* (2020) 38.4.2.
Gospel Doctrine	*Gospel Doctrine: Selections from the Sermons and Writings of Joseph F. Smith* (Salt Lake City: Deseret News, 1919).
Gospel Principles	*Gospel Principles* (Salt Lake City: The Church of Jesus Christ of Latter-day Saints, 1978–2011).
Guide to the Scriptures	(Salt Lake City: The Church of Jesus Christ of Latter-day Saints), https://www.churchofjesus christ.org/study/scriptures/gs?lang=eng).
Hymns	*Hymns of The Church of Jesus Christ of Latter-day Saints* (Salt Lake City: The Church of Jesus Christ of Latter-day Saints, 1985).
JDDJ	The Lutheran World Federation and the Roman Catholic Church, *Joint Declaration on the Doctrine of Justification* (Grand Rapids: Eerdmans, 1997).
Journal of Discourses	*Journal of Discourses* [of nineteenth-century LDS apostles and prophets], 26 vols. (Liverpool: F. D. Richards, 1854–1886).

JSP	*The Joseph Smith Papers*, ed. Ronald K. Esplin, Matthew J. Grow, and Matthew C. Godfrey, 27 vols. (Salt Lake City: Church Historian's Press, 2012–2023). The *JSP* are arranged in separate volume series—Documents (D), Journals (J), Revelations and Translations (R), Histories (H), and Administrative Records (A).
McConkie, *Mormon Doctrine*	Bruce R. McConkie, *Mormon Doctrine* (Salt Lake City: Bookcraft, 1958; 2nd rev. ed., Salt Lake City: Bookcraft, 1966).
McGuckin, *Orthodox Church*	John Anthony McGuckin, *The Orthodox Church: An Introduction to Its History, Doctrine, and Spiritual Culture* (Chichester, UK: Wiley-Blackwell, 2008).
NPNF	*Nicene and Post-Nicene Fathers*, ed. Philip Schaff, 14 vols. (1886–1889; reprint, Peabody, MA: Hendrickson, 1994).
NTOB	*Joseph Smith's New Translation of the Bible: Original Manuscripts*, ed. Scott H. Faulring, Kent P. Jackson, and Robert J. Matthews (Provo, UT: BYU Religious Studies Center, 2004).
OED	*Oxford English Dictionary*, 2nd ed., 20 vols. (Oxford: Oxford University Press, 1989).
OHST	*The Oxford Handbook of Sacramental Theology*, ed. Hans Boersma and Matthew Levering (New York: Oxford University Press, 2015).
OSB	*The Orthodox Study Bible*, ed. St. Athanasius Academy of Orthodox Theology (Nashville: Nelson, 2008).
Pratt, *Key to Theology*	Parley P. Pratt, *Key to the Science of Theology* (Liverpool: F. D. Richards, 1855).
Roberts, *Course in Theology*	Brigham Henry Roberts, *The Seventy's Course in Theology*, 5 vols. (Salt Lake City: Deseret News, 1907–1912).
[Scrip] Student Manual	For the college-level courses in its educational curricula, the Church of Jesus Christ of Latter-day Saints publishes "student manuals" containing study aids and explanatory commentary. These manuals are produced by church curricu-

lum committees. Thus, without named authors, they are here cited simply by prefatory reference to the volume of scripture covered and the publication year. So, for example, the *New Testament Student Manual, 211–212* (Salt Lake City: The Church of Jesus Christ of Latter-day Saints, 2018) is cited as *NT Student Manual* (2018). Some manuals carry *Seminary* in the title. "Seminary" is the name of the church's high school–level religious education program.

Talmage, *Jesus the Christ* James E. Talmage, *Jesus the Christ: A Study of the Messiah and His Mission according to Holy Scriptures Both Ancient and Modern* (Salt Lake City: Deseret News, 1915).

Teachings: [Name] *Teachings of Presidents of the Church: [Name of Church President]*, 16 vols. (Salt Lake City: The Church of Jesus Christ of Latter-day Saints, 1997–2020).

True to the Faith *True to the Faith: A Gospel Reference* (Salt Lake City: The Church of Jesus Christ of Latter-day Saints, 2004).

WC "The Westminster Confession of Faith, 1647," in *Creeds & Confessions*, 601–49.

INTRODUCTION

In 2002, Salt Lake City, the world headquarters of the Church of Jesus Christ of Latter-day Saints, hosted the Winter Olympics. This was the first in a series of events in the new century that focused renewed public attention on "the Mormons." In the years that followed, Latter-day Saint support for California's Proposition 8 (recognizing marriage as only between a man and a woman) prompted a national firestorm of controversy, and the *Book of Mormon* musical took Broadway by storm. In 2012, Mitt Romney won the Republican nomination for president of the United States of America. By the second decade of the twenty-first century, Mormons and Mormonism seemed ubiquitous on the public stage.[1] Gone were the days when the only contact most people had with the church was through the well-mannered, neatly dressed young adults sent out to serve as its missionary representatives. The Latter-day Saint faith was also drawing increased attention within academia. More and more religious studies programs at American colleges and universities were discussing Mormonism, and survey courses in American religious history routinely dealt with the topic. Additionally, the early decades of the twenty-first century witnessed the establishment of the first endowed chairs in Mormon studies (at Claremont Graduate University in California, the University of Virginia, and Utah State University), the creation of a Mormon studies unit in the American Academy of Religion, and a flurry of first-rate publications from top trade and university presses. Still, even today, relatively few among the general populace profess to know much about the beliefs and practices of the Church of Jesus Christ of Latter-day Saints or how they relate to Christianity in all its varieties. Providing a detailed, nuanced discussion of such matters is the primary ob-

1. These and other events sometimes described as the arrival on the American scene of the "Mormon moment" are detailed in J. B. Haws, *The Mormon Image in the American Mind: Fifty Years of Public Perception* (New York: Oxford University Press, 2013).

jective of this volume as it seeks to bring Mormon doctrine into conversation with historically prominent strands of Christian theology.

The Church of Jesus Christ of Latter-day Saints, originally known simply as the Church of Christ, was birthed in 1830 in upstate New York. For a decade before that, a young farm boy of ordinary name and unexceptional background—Joseph Smith—experienced a series of visions and received a number of revelations that led to the formal organization of the church. Although only in his twenties and thirties during the church's formative years, Smith came to be regarded by his followers as a "prophet of God," a kind of modern Moses. The audacity of the claim to speak for God, along with the canonical revelations produced in an age when most believed the canon of scripture to be closed, was a primary cause of the persecution that hounded the Latter-day Saints during the church's early years. Such antagonism, sometimes devolving into violent opposition, compelled this "new Israel" to successively abandon homes in New York, Ohio, Missouri, and Illinois, and ultimately flee beyond the boundary of the United States to settle in the Great Basin in what would eventually become Utah and portions of Idaho, Wyoming, Nevada, and Arizona. Smith's life, however, was cut short by assassins in 1844, prior to the Mormon exodus west. At the time, the church numbered in the tens of thousands. A half century later, after decades of determined and successful proselytizing, particularly in Britain and Scandinavia, the church counted several hundred thousand members. Most responded to the church's call to "gather" to the Mormon "Zion" in Utah and the West. Over the next century, the church gradually expanded to other parts of the United States and the world as it switched its emphasis from "gathering" to encouraging converts to remain in their own locales and establish the church there. Especially after the Second World War, international growth accelerated, and by the twenty-first century, church membership numbered more than ten million, over half of which resided outside the United States. Although growth has slowed in recent decades, with the current membership yet to reach twenty million, the church has a presence in more than two hundred countries and territories and translates its literature into hundreds of different languages and dialects.[2] Beyond this very brief overview, it is not the purpose of this book to recount the history of the LDS Church; many other volumes have taken up that task.[3]

2. *Liahona*, November 2021, 117.

3. A bibliographic gold mine is James B. Allen, Ronald W. Walker, and David J. Whittaker, eds., *Studies in Mormon History, 1830–1997: An Indexed Bibliography* (Urbana: University of Illinois Press, 2000). Along with subsequent additions, this exhaustive compilation of

Definitions

A few words about terminology will be helpful. "Theology" is derived from a combination of the Greek *theos* (God) and *logos* (communication, word, expression) and basically means "talk about God" or "study of God." Originally "theology" referred specifically to ideas about God's nature and relationship to the universe. Over time, the word came to be an umbrella term for reflection on the whole array of topics encompassed within Christian belief systems. This is the broad meaning attached to the term in this volume. To some, the theological enterprise may seem arid, arcane, even inconsequential. In reality, Christian theology, as the sustained and systematic attempt by Christian thinkers to answer some of life's deepest questions, is quite relevant and important. From a religious standpoint, theology historically has represented the best efforts of the devout to make the faith intelligible and meaningful to fellow believers. Nearly a thousand years ago, Anselm of Canterbury famously characterized the study of theology as "faith seeking understanding."[4] Whatever readers' backgrounds, they will likely find that the theology discussed in this volume often addresses questions on which they themselves have ruminated.

On the face of it, the definitions of "Christian" and "Christianity" are self-evident. In the broadest sense, anyone who believes in Christ as Savior of the world may be considered a Christian, and Christianity refers to any system of beliefs grounded in the teachings of Jesus Christ. In practice, however, the definitions are contested. One person's Christianity is not that of another. Theologically, what merits the label "Christian" is widely debated. The criteria for deciding what counts as "Christian" vary almost from individual to individual, certainly from tradition to tradition. The reality is that in Christendom there is no universally regarded central authority or supreme court of Christianity

---

thousands of references can be electronically accessed at mormonhistory.byu.edu. Single-volume overviews of Latter-day Saint history vary in purpose and quality. Though dated, still worth consulting is the classic Leonard J. Arrington and Davis Bitton, *The Mormon Experience: A History of the Latter-day Saints*, 2nd ed. (Urbana: University of Illinois Press, 1992). Beginning in 2018, the LDS Church itself started publishing a readable, four-volume history entitled *Saints* that, while designed to be "faith-promoting" for church members, is nonetheless based on the sound historical scholarship of the past half century detailed in mormonhistory.byu.edu.

4. This was the original title of Anselm's influential *Proslogium*. To be sure, as formal Christian theology drawing heavily on philosophy developed its own technical language and complex conceptual universe, it could indeed seem abstruse. Yet, there has always been a pastoral undercurrent to some of the best Christian theology.

to determine such matters. Many consider the Bible as the ultimate arbiter of truth, but the Bible, as any text, is subject to interpretation. Moreover, the New Testament does not provide an explicit creedal or behavioral test of faith, let alone a systematic theology. Lacking such definitive norms, Christians over the centuries have tried to distill their own standards from the scriptural record. In the process, they have constructed categories of "orthodoxy" and "heresy," of "correct" and "false" doctrine, to certify some teachings (and those who espouse them) as genuinely Christian and others as mistaken, even heretical. Sociologists call such activity "boundary maintenance," and it has been taking place within the Christian fold ever since Paul the apostle stigmatized his ministerial rivals in first-century Corinth as "false apostles" (2 Cor. 11:13). This volume, however, does not attempt to adjudicate between "true" and "false" Christianity. A church or doctrine that claims the appellation "Christian" is allowed to own it. "Christian" and "Christianity" are here used in their most capacious senses. Thus, the Church of Jesus Christ of Latter-day Saints and its doctrines are consistently referred to as one among many versions of Christianity. Whether or not Mormon doctrine meets a reader's criteria for acceptable Christian theology is an individual matter, of course, but one that is likely to be influenced by what the reader encounters in this volume.

Many are aware that "Mormon" is an appellation derived from the Book of Mormon. Less well known is that the Church of Jesus Christ of Latter-day Saints is not the only ecclesial body that traces its origins to Joseph Smith and the Book of Mormon. The largest of these additional bodies is the Community of Christ, which numbers several hundred thousand. Other groups are much smaller. Each in its own way considers itself a rightful heir to Smith's mantle and custodian of a true version of his doctrine. Though the history and theology of these churches are fascinating indeed, they are not the subject of this volume.[5] Numerically, members of the Church of Jesus Christ of Latter-day Saints constitute more than 95 percent of all whose religious roots are entwined with Joseph Smith, and they are the group most commonly in view when the term "Mormon" is used. The other churches have tended to avoid the label "Mormon" so as not to be confused with the Church of Jesus Christ of Latter-day Saints.[6]

---

5. For an introduction to these groups and their theologies, see Steven L. Shields, *Divergent Paths of the Restoration: An Encyclopedia of the Smith-Rigdon Movement*, 5th ed., 2 vols. (Salt Lake City: Signature Books, 2021), and Newell G. Bringhurst and John C. Hamer, *Scattering of the Saints: Schism within Mormonism* (Independence, MO: John Whitmer Books, 2007).

6. In contrast, some small groups who perpetuate the practice of polygamy abandoned

Ironically, in its efforts in recent decades to be fully recognized as Christian, the Church of Jesus Christ of Latter-day Saints itself has eschewed the use of the term "Mormon" and its derivatives. The church today prefers that its full name be used and that its members be referred to as "Latter-day Saints." At the same time, academic literature, particularly religious studies, and the media have a long history of using "Mormon(s)" and "Mormonism" to refer to Latter-day Saints and their beliefs and practices. As stated in the prefatory "Note on Nomenclature and Style," in an effort to be sensitive to both patterns of usage, this volume will alternate between "official" church terminology and the customary stylistic practices of public and academic discourse. Incorporating the referential conventions of both Latter-day Saint and academic "communities of discourse" has the added advantage of avoiding cumbersome and tedious repetition. For a more detailed explanation, see the above-mentioned "Note on Nomenclature and Style."

ORGANIZATION

While introductions to Mormonism and the Church of Jesus Christ of Latter-day Saints abound, what has been lacking heretofore is a single volume addressed to non–Latter-day Saints that systematically brings Mormon thought into conversation with main currents of Christian theology. To achieve that objective, this book is organized around the standard, classical subdivisions of theology, its *loci communes*, that begin with "Theology" proper (who God is), move on to "Christology" (who Jesus Christ is), "Anthropology" (who we are), "Soteriology" (how we are saved), "Ecclesiology" (what the church is—its nature, organization, and sacraments), and conclude with "Eschatology" (what the future holds—for human history as well as for individual human lives). Within Christianity, these interrelated but topically distinct "-ologies" address questions asked by generations of Christians and reflect centuries of effort to provide a comprehensive, logically consistent set of plausible answers.

---

by the Church of Jesus Christ of Latter-day Saints at the turn of the twentieth century are mistakenly labeled "Mormon" in the media. Typically, these polygamous groups have not actively resisted the appellation, much to the chagrin of LDS Church leaders. Emphasized church president Gordon Hinckley, "I wish to state categorically that this Church has nothing whatever to do with those practicing polygamy. They are not members of this Church. Most of them have never been members. They are in violation of the civil law. They know they are in violation of the law. They are subject to its penalties. . . . If any of our members are found to be practicing plural marriage, they are excommunicated, the most serious penalty the Church can impose." *Ensign*, November 1988, 71.

Theologians today often refer to the combination of these "-ologies" as "systematic theology."[7] Because these categories have perennially provided both a basic organizational structure and a useful set of doctrinal "maps" for the comprehensive study of Christian theology, it seemed prudent to organize this book in the same fashion. It is a structure that is familiar to students of Christianity and enables wide-ranging comparison of Mormon doctrine with the major topics and issues that have engaged Christian thinkers over the years. Most chapters follow a format in which relevant themes are introduced with an overview of significant Christian reflection on the topic followed by an exploration of Latter-day Saint thought on the subject.

While the standard subdivisions of theology around which this volume is organized provide an analytically helpful way of exploring the breadth of Christian doctrine, a high degree of interconnectedness exists between theology's various subdivisions. Consider, for instance, the book's treatment of soteriology, the doctrine of salvation. While the bulk of the discussion, exploring such fundamental issues as justification and the relationship between grace and works, occurs in chapter 6, other chapters address related matters of vital importance. Thus, any discussion of Christian soteriology must begin by considering the redemptive work of Jesus Christ, examined here in chapter 4. This in turn is dependent on an adequate understanding of the person and nature of Jesus Christ himself, addressed in chapter 3. Most soteriologies, especially that of the Latter-day Saints, hold that Christ in one way or another mediates salvation through the church and its sacraments. Therefore, this important connection receives extended treatment in the book's later chapters (7–11). Finally, as salvation culminates in afterlife glorification, chapter 12, on eschatology, rounds out the discussion of soteriology. This example of topical interconnectedness can be replicated for theology's other subdivisions as well and illustrates the conceptual interdependence inherent in theological study. As a result, the reader will

---

7. The *Oxford Handbook of Systematic Theology* defines systematic theology as the effort to develop "a conceptual articulation of Christian claims about God and everything else in relation to God, characterized by comprehensiveness and coherence. It seeks to present Christian teaching as a unified whole." That this took centuries to achieve may surprise some until it is realized that the books of the New Testament evidence no apparent concern for "systematic order or conceptual regularity" and "do not attempt a comprehensive presentation of Christian teaching." Likewise, "early post-apostolic explications of doctrine, undertaken primarily for purposes of edification or combating heresy, generally adopt some variant of the commentarial or expository genre." John Webster, "Introduction: Systematic Theology," in *The Oxford Handbook of Systematic Theology*, ed. John B. Webster, Kathryn Tanner, and Iain R. Torrance (New York: Oxford University Press, 2007), 2–3.

necessarily encounter a recapitulation of some themes and concepts as the book moves through the full range of Christian and Latter-day Saint theology.

METHOD

Bringing Mormonism into conceptual conversation with other Christian theologies requires a certain degree of "translation." Latter-day Saint theology, both in its conceptualization and in its vocabulary, developed over time with lessening links to the broader Christian tradition. The resulting intellectual isolation was partially due to a conscious effort by Joseph Smith and his associates to bypass the theological reflection of the centuries and go directly to the biblical source. They sought to discern (and restore) through revelation from God foundational principles and practices of the Bible—both from the "primitive" (as in "first," "original") church of the New Testament and from ancient Israel in the Old Testament. As Joseph Smith saw it, there was little need to quench the Saints' theological thirst downstream when they could drink directly from the divine fountain. This biblical "primitivism," along with decades of comparative isolation in the American West, yielded both conceptual distinctiveness and terminological idiosyncrasy in need of translation to be adequately understood by Christians of other faith communities. While some of this work has been done selectively elsewhere, this volume seeks more systematically and with greater depth of engagement to translate LDS theology into the idiom and conceptual universe of historical Christianity.

A few caveats about comparison are in order as the endeavor begins. First, similarity is not identity. No matter how similar certain ideas or practices may seem, they are never identical. Nor does similarity prove that one religion borrowed from another, even when they are proximate in time and space. Parallels do not prove provenance. Similarities grow out of different contexts and carry different connotations. To be avoided is what biblical scholar Samuel Sandmel dubbed "parallelomania."[8] This volume, therefore, does not attempt a "genealogy" of Latter-day Saint thought even if it were possible to pinpoint the source of this or that Mormon doctrine. Comparison is valuable, however, because it can make aspects and tendencies in one faith that might otherwise be overlooked stand out in bold relief. Moreover, human comprehension always requires some degree of generalization and comparison. In the words of cognitive scientist Douglas Hofstadter, "analogy [is] the core of cognition."[9] When

---

8. Samuel Sandmel, "Parallelomania," *Journal of Biblical Literature* 81 (March 1962): 1–13.
9. Douglas R. Hofstadter, "Analogy as the Core of Cognition," in *The Analogical Mind:*

the caveat is remembered that comparisons are approximations, not equations, designed to offer a different angle of vision, then the value of comparative studies such as this can be appreciated and fresh perspectives gained.

In a related vein, this book is not addressed to Latter-day Saints, though they may profit by reading it. It is written to other Christians to make Mormonism intelligible to them in the concepts and vocabulary of traditional Christian theology. Moreover, the book is introductory. It presupposes no prior knowledge of the Church of Jesus Christ of Latter-day Saints, and it does not presume a mastery of Christian theology. It might be thought of as being addressed to the many "armchair" theologians who populate the pews of Christendom, individuals who are interested in Christian theology but have little or no formal training in it. The beginning seminary or divinity school student may also find the volume suitable for his or her purposes. Although the book does engage Christian theology at some of its most technical points, it endeavors to do so in a manner that is clear and comprehensible. As such, technical theological terms and specialized vocabulary, Christian and Latter-day Saint alike, are explained when they first appear. Furthermore, because the book is written for the nonspecialist, it privileges clarity of exposition over novelty of interpretation. The volume is not itself a work of theology seeking to reframe or reconceptualize the doctrine of the Church of Jesus Christ of Latter-day Saints or that of any other church. Consequently, it does not pass judgment on the various theological formulations it discusses. Its purpose is to deepen understanding, not decide theological controversies. Value judgments are left to the reader.[10]

On the other hand, while the theological expressions discussed here are treated with empathy and respect, they are also not promoted. The volume seeks to investigate, not indoctrinate, to analyze, not catechize. Its objective is to probe, not propagate, the theological viewpoints under study. In short, it endeavors to explain, not persuade. Such an approach is more than a commitment to objectivity or an effort to be balanced and fair-minded. It is a commitment to intentionally sympathetic exposition. One may even detect in the book an undertone of what the Swedish Lutheran bishop-scholar Krister

---

Perspectives from Cognitive Science, ed. Dedre Gentner, Keith J. Holyoak, and Boicho N. Kokinovet (Cambridge, MA: MIT Press, 2001), 499–538.

10. The goal, notes religion scholar Stephen Stein, "is not to declare one or another religious group to be 'true' and all others 'false,' but rather to understand the ways these religious communities have functioned in the lives of their members." Stephen J. Stein, *Communities of Dissent: A History of Alternative Religions in America* (New York: Oxford University Press, 2000), 11.

Stendahl called "holy envy"—genuine admiration for the principles and practices of another's faith.[11] To be sure, the author is a practicing Latter-day Saint,
but that reality only enhances his appreciation for the theology produced by
centuries of fellow Christians of faith who, in Anselm's words, have diligently
and devoutly "sought understanding."

Sensitive, sympathetic treatment of different Christian theologies, however,
does not entail uncritical embrace or conversion. What it does require, writes
Robert Orsi, a former president of the American Academy of Religion, is "to
stand in an attitude of open, disciplined, and engaged attentiveness" to another
religion that puts "one's own world in dialogue; to be open is to be vulnerable—to be vulnerable to the disorientation of seriously meeting a different
reality."[12] It is the challenge of understanding people who worship differently,
who conceive of God and God's relations with humanity differently, and who
articulate their religious beliefs in terms and concepts that are unfamiliar.
Readers of this book are invited to approach its sympathetic presentation of
various Christian theologies, including that of the Latter-day Saints, with just
such an openness and vulnerability that can lead to a more accurate, nuanced
understanding of the doctrines discussed.

Sources

Because Mormonism is not a monolith and Christianity certainly is not, it may
be asked, "Which articulations of Mormon doctrine and which versions of
Christian theology are engaged in this volume?" As the Gospel of John whim-
sically remarks regarding the many unrecorded aspects of Jesus's life, so it might
be said of the totality of two millennia of Christian voices—"if they should be
written every one, I suppose that even the world itself could not contain the
books that should be written" (John 21:25). How, then, is this voluminous historical output to be narrowed to a manageable, single-volume treatment? Two
related criteria govern the selection of voices heard in this book—representivity
and influence. What this means for Mormonism is that the Latter-day Saint

11. Stendahl may not have invented the term "holy envy," but it has come to be associ-
ated with him almost exclusively given his long history of irenic advocacy of the concept.
Stendahl mentions his passion for the idea in his lecture "From God's Perspective We Are
All Minorities," *Journal of Religious Pluralism* 2 (1993): 10. Stendahl's ideal is developed at
length in Barbara Brown Taylor, *Holy Envy: Finding God in the Faith of Others* (New York:
HarperOne, 2019).

12. Robert Orsi, "A 'Bit of Judgment,'" in "Four Responses to [Stephen Prothero's] 'Belief
Unbracketed,'" *Harvard Divinity Bulletin* 32 (Fall 2004): 17.

doctrine here discussed is that which the Church of Jesus Christ of Latter-day Saints institutionally promulgates in the twenty-first century and is recognizable to, and presumably embraced by, a majority of the church's members. First and foremost, these criteria are met by focusing on the teachings of the church's top leaders, its "apostles" and "prophets." Their voices are influentially heard twice a year in the church's "general conferences" as they discourse on Latter-day Saint belief and behavior. Subsequently, their conference "talks" are discussed in a variety of settings in weekly church services and are quoted extensively in church curricular materials. Furthermore, the apostles and prophets influence by their ultimate approval a whole range of institutional literature from church handbooks to scriptural "study helps." In short, these leaders, along with other "general authorities" of the church, dominate the institutional articulation of Latter-day Saint doctrine. In an ecclesial body that lacks a cadre of seminary-trained, professional theologians, the general authorities *are* the church's "theologians." They are heard and read by literally millions of Mormons worldwide. As the most influential "meaning makers" of Mormonism, theirs are the voices to which this volume primarily, though not exclusively, attends in its effort to provide the most representative account of Latter-day Saint thought today.

Referring in quotation marks to the church's general authorities as "theologians" merely signals that they are not academically trained in theology. They are not graduates of divinity schools or theological seminaries, and most have not done advanced studies in philosophy. Some may wonder, therefore, whether the apostles and prophets "do" theology or whether the church "has" a theology. If the definition of theology is confined to that which is articulated in the formal language and terms of academic "systematic theology," the answer would generally be no. Here, however, "theology" is understood more broadly in keeping with its root meaning of "talk about God," and Latter-day Saint leaders certainly do that. Mormon theology fundamentally is "preached theology." Yet, as will be apparent throughout this volume, the church's prophets and apostles in their own way and idiom have engaged many of the questions and issues that animate the various component "-ologies" of systematic theology. In this sense, they do "do" theology, and the church does "have" a theology, although Latter-day Saints usually refer to it as "doctrine." This may reflect the fact that "theology" and its derivatives are not found in scripture, whereas "doctrine" does appear, especially in the King James Version (KJV), which is the church's official Bible.[13] It may also represent a subtle, perhaps

13. The specific term "theology" is noticeably less common in LDS discourse. For in-

subconscious, rhetorical move to distinguish the teachings of the Church of Jesus Christ of Latter-day Saints from those of other Christian bodies in the sense that theology is what "they" do. Whatever the reasons, "doctrine," for Latter-day Saints, serves as the functional stand-in for "theology," connoting some of the same formality and weightiness that "theology" can communicate to other Christians.

Christian theology, of course, has never been the sole province of academically trained specialists. Even as late as the sixteenth century, "the doctrinal work of the magisterial [Protestant] reformers recalls earlier modes of expounding Christian teaching, in that it takes the form of extensive biblical commentary or polemical and hortatory works in which doctrine is not so much a discrete interest as an ingredient of practical divinity."[14] To a significant degree, this assessment provides an apt characterization of Mormon theology. For most of the church's relatively young life, Latter-day Saint theology, too, has consisted primarily of scriptural commentary and explication in support of pastoral instruction, polemical debate, or evangelism. In this sense, LDS theology, much like earlier Christian theology, might be characterized broadly as "ecclesial theology," that is, not theology *about* the church (which is ecclesiology), but theology that in all its branches is done *for* the church. That the institutional articulation of LDS doctrine, as with Christian theology in the first centuries, has evidenced little inclination toward formal "systematic theology" does not mean, however, that rational, orderly discussion of the faith is lacking. Augustine of Hippo, the influential early Christian bishop-theologian, topically arranged his *Enchiridion* (handbook) and *On Faith and the Creed* around a version of the Apostles' Creed.[15] Similarly, the prominent Latter-day Saint writer and later apostle, James Talmage, organized one of the most influential LDS doctrinal treatises, *Articles of Faith*, around the church's

---

stance, across the span of nearly two centuries of general conferences, the church's general authorities have used "doctrine" more than nine thousand times and "theology" just over three hundred times. See lds-general-conferences.org.

14. Webster, "Introduction," 4.

15. "According to tradition, *The Apostles' Creed* is the product of the combined effort of the twelve apostles, who were inspired on Pentecost to express their faith, each contributing a line to the statement of belief. This legend, though charming and still believed well into the Reformation era, has no historical basis. The creed is first mentioned by name (*symbolum apostolorum*) in the fourth century . . . [and] the text as we now know it first appears in the early eighth century." *Creeds & Confessions*, 1:667.

canonical thirteen "Articles of Faith."[16] In the twentieth century, other *enchiridions* of Mormon doctrine written by individual general authorities followed, and the church itself has a long history of publishing curricular materials and reference works that present basic doctrines in a rational, organized, albeit introductory, fashion.[17]

To be sure, over the years a sizable Mormon literature has been generated outside the institutional confines of the Church of Jesus Christ of Latter-day Saints in what has been dubbed the "unsponsored sector" of Mormonism. These writings range from the "highbrow" discussions of the faith and philosophically informed ruminations of Latter-day Saint intellectuals to an extensive literature written for popular LDS consumption (the Mormon equivalent of the devotional works that often appear on Christian best-seller lists) and a fecund Mormon folklore embedded in a variety of popular sources.[18] That the

16. Talmage's volume is *Articles of Faith: A Series of Lectures on the Principal Doctrines of the Church of Jesus Christ of Latter-day Saints* (Salt Lake City: Deseret News Press, 1899). Talmage noted in his preface that the church's "First Presidency" (its presiding leadership) had requested him to prepare the lectures to "be published for use in the various educational institutions of the Church" (iv).

17. During a period of doctrinal consolidation and stabilization in the LDS Church from roughly 1880 into the 1930s, a number of important works were published that aimed at providing comprehensive, orderly treatments of Latter-day Saint doctrine. Talmage's *Articles of Faith* was arguably the most influential, going through sixteen printings between 1899 and 1930. Other significant publications from the period include Franklin D. Richards and James A. Little, *Compendium of the Doctrines of the Gospel* (1882–1925; eight editions); Charles Penrose, *Mormon Doctrine, Plain and Simple* (1882–1928; eight editions); B. H. Roberts, *The Gospel: An Exposition of Its First Principles* (1888–1928; seven editions); and John A. Widtsoe, *Rational Theology: As Taught by the Church of Jesus Christ of Latter-day Saints* (1915–1929; four editions). Similarly influential in the mid-twentieth century were *Doctrines of Salvation* (1954–1956), the compiled teachings of Joseph Fielding Smith; and Bruce R. McConkie, *Mormon Doctrine* (1958). Since the 1970s, as the Latter-day Saint population has become more international and multilingual, alongside books individually authored by general authorities, the church has institutionally produced, translated, and disseminated accessible introductory doctrinal reference works such as *Gospel Principles* (1978–2011), *True to the Faith: A Gospel Reference* (2004), and the online series "Topics and Questions."

18. Entrée into the vast literature of the unsponsored sector can be gained by topically searching the sources listed in mormonhistory.byu.edu, browsing the catalogues of Mormon-related presses such as Deseret Book, or consulting independent journals such as *Dialogue: A Journal of Mormon Thought*. Much of the scholarship on Mormonism in the past half century has focused on the church's history and to a degree on historical theology. In addition to book-length treatments published by university and trade presses, the annual meeting of the Mormon History Association and the Association's *Journal of Mormon History* have provided prominent venues for the presentation of such work. For more

parameters of this book do not allow for more than occasional, supplementary inclusion of these voices is not to say that they are either uninteresting or unimportant. They reflect the conceptual fertility of Mormon culture, but they are not its most influential voices. In theological discussions by the general authorities and in the church's institutional literature, independent Mormon voices, whether highbrow or lowbrow, are almost never cited and are familiar to only a relative fraction of the church's membership. In terms of influence and representivity, the author's goal is an imagined conversation between a Christian reader and her Mormon acquaintance in which the Latter-day Saint recognizes the LDS voices quoted and acknowledges the book's presentation of Mormon doctrine as that which is commonly taught in the church today.

The book's focus on current LDS doctrine necessarily leaves to other authors the detailed excavation and reconstruction of Mormon thought from earlier periods in the church's history. Still, attention to historical context and doctrinal development is present in this volume in an introductory fashion as it facilitates the exposition of current church teachings. Generally omitted, though, is discussion of obsolete ideas and intriguing but speculative notions from the Mormon past that the church eventually deemed unsatisfactory and are largely unknown to the generality of Latter-day Saints today. Extensive histories of such aspects of earlier Mormon thought are available elsewhere.[19] That said, because contemporary church doctrine continues to draw upon the teachings of founder Joseph Smith and successive prophets, so does this volume.[20] The focus, though, is on how Smith's expressions are understood

---

philosophically inflected discussions, readers may consult the publications of BYU's Neal A. Maxwell Institute for Religious Scholarship or sample the intermittently published *Element: The Journal of the Society for Mormon Philosophy and Theology.* The first extended treatment of Mormon theology by a Latter-day Saint formally trained in philosophy did not appear until the second half of the twentieth century: Sterling M. McMurrin, *The Philosophical Foundations of Mormon Theology* (Salt Lake City: University of Utah Press, 1959), and *The Theological Foundations of the Mormon Religion* (Salt Lake City: University of Utah Press, 1965). Since then, the number of Latter-day Saints who have pursued advanced degrees in theology or some combination of philosophy and religion, although still relatively small, has increased noticeably. For Mormon folklore, consult the collections at BYU's William A. Wilson Digital Folklore Archive.

19. See the previously noted comprehensive bibliography of Mormon scholarship at mormonhistory.byu.edu.

20. Citations of Joseph Smith's doctrine are taken from *JSP,* the multivolume, critical edition of Joseph Smith's "papers" (his journals, revelations, contemporary reports of his discourses, correspondence, minutes, etc.). The sermons of Smith's nineteenth-century successors are generally quoted from the twenty-six-volume *Journal of Discourses.* The teachings

and deployed today rather than on an attempt to reconstruct his "original intent" or expound 1840s Mormonism. Thus, while the book's treatment of LDS theology has a clear historical flavor, it primarily engages past articulations of doctrine that are still considered theologically serviceable by the church and its prophet-leaders today.

Attention to representativeness and influence also governs the selection of Christian voices heard in this volume. Thus, often quoted are the perennially influential formulations of the so-called fathers of the church from Christianity's formative, patristic (from Latin *pater* for "father") period. In terms of numerical representativeness, Catholic doctrine, which at least theoretically represents the beliefs of nearly half the world's Christians, figures prominently in the book. So does Orthodox theology, which, despite speaking for a quarter of a billion adherents, is sometimes overshadowed by its Western Christian counterparts. Of course, Protestant voices, too, are regularly engaged, both important founding figures such as Martin Luther, John Calvin, or John Wesley and major theological traditions such as Lutheranism, Anglicanism, Methodism, Pentecostalism, and various Baptist traditions. Because this volume is interested in bringing broadly representative formulations of Latter-day Saint doctrine into conversation with majoritarian expositions of Christian thought, it does not address similarities or differences with many minor Christian bodies, although such comparisons are certainly possible and interesting.

Scripture

Scripture is a source category that is integral to the full range of Christian theology and is consistently part of the conversation in this volume. The book proceeds on the basis of the common Christian conviction that "all scripture is given by inspiration of God" (2 Tim. 3:16), and it applies this assumption to LDS scripture as well as to the Bible. The book does not argue with Christians about their belief in God's involvement with scripture, nor does it encumber its pages with constant qualifications such as "alleged author" or "purported revelation." Debates over authorship and myriad other aspects of scriptural criticism have their important place, but this volume is not that place. Of primary concern here is the theological use of scripture, its "reception history," so to speak, not its genesis or redaction history. For present purposes, Christian eisegesis is more important than biblical exegesis.

The Church of Jesus Christ of Latter-day Saints recognizes four volumes of

---

of subsequent church presidents can be found in the sixteen-volume *Teachings of Presidents of the Church*. See the list of abbreviations.

scripture—the Bible, Book of Mormon, Doctrine and Covenants, and Pearl of Great Price. In terms of size, the latter three combined represent just over half the word count of the Bible.[21] From the beginning, Latter-day Saints have respected and relied on the Bible. An index of all passages of scripture cited in the church's general conferences for nearly two hundred years through 2024 reveals that Bible verses have been cited some sixty-seven thousand times, while the combined citation total from the other three volumes of scripture is a little over fifty-seven thousand.[22] Early in the twenty-first century, apostle Russell Ballard remarked, "We believe, revere, and love the Holy Bible. We do have additional sacred scripture . . . but it supports the Bible, never substituting for it."[23] Members of the Church of Jesus Christ of Latter-day Saints have long described the relationship between the Book of Mormon and the Bible by reference to Paul's declaration that "in the mouth of two or three witnesses shall every word be established" (2 Cor. 13:1). Latter-day Saints believe that the Book of Mormon is a second witness to the Bible's teachings. The church underlined this point in the 1980s when it added this subtitle to the Book of Mormon: "Another Testament of Jesus Christ." Orson Spencer, a nineteenth-century Baptist minister once invited to pastor the congregation attended by the governor of Massachusetts, endeavored to explain to the editor of the *Christian Watchman*, a prominent New England Baptist weekly at the time, why he had come to believe the Book of Mormon was "graced with the pen of inspiration." The book, he wrote, has such a "godly bearing, sound morality, and harmony with ancient scriptures" that "the enemy of all righteousness might as well proclaim the dissolution of his own kingdom as to spread the contents of such a volume among men."[24]

The Book of Mormon is a sprawling saga that primarily details the thousand-year, New World history of several groups of people who migrated from the Kingdom of Judah to the Western Hemisphere around 600 BC. At just under six hundred printed pages, the book provides enough historical narrative to give readers a sense of societal ebb and flow, but its chief interest is theological—to restore "plain and precious" truths thought to have been lost at some point in the transmission of biblical texts.[25] Early nineteenth-century

---

21. For purposes of comparison, the Doctrine and Covenants is about two-thirds the length of the New Testament. The New Testament is about two-thirds the length of the Book of Mormon. And the Book of Mormon is less than half the length of the Old Testament.

22. See the "LDS Scripture Citation Index," https://scriptures.byu.edu.

23. M. Russell Ballard, "The Miracle of the Holy Bible," *Ensign*, May 2007, 81.

24. Orson Spencer, *Letters Exhibiting the Most Prominent Doctrines of the Church of Jesus Christ of Latter-day Saints* (Liverpool, 1848), 11–12.

25. The LDS Church's Eighth Article of Faith reads: "We believe the Bible to be the word of God as far as it is translated [transmitted] correctly." See also 1 Nephi 13–14.

America was an era characterized by a cacophony of competing religious voices, all proclaiming that their beliefs were based on the Bible. In the words of noted non-Mormon historian Gordon Wood, the Book of Mormon served to "cut through these controversies. . . . It answered perplexing questions of theology, clarified obscure passages of the Bible, and carried its story into the New World. And it did all this with the assurance of divine authority."[26] Joseph Smith described the Book of Mormon as the translation of an ancient record written on gold plates given to him by a heavenly messenger. Knowing nothing of ancient languages, Smith said his "translation" of the Book of Mormon came by revelation or, as he phrased it in the book's preface, "by the gift and power of God."[27] As New World scripture, the Book of Mormon is regarded by Latter-day Saints as "evidence that God loves all His children in all parts of the world."[28]

Smith dictated two other major "translation-revelations"—his unpublished "New Translation" of the Bible and the Book of Abraham. The "New Translation" of the Bible, like the Book of Mormon, was not a translation in the usual sense of the word. Smith did not know the biblical languages, and thus did not render them in English. Instead, he selectively revised and amplified the KJV wherever he felt inspired to do so.[29] In similar fashion, he also "translated" or discerned by revelation an account of Abraham's earliest years and what Abraham learned from God about the cosmos and its creation. By the time Joseph Smith had finished his "New Translation" of the Bible three years after beginning the project, he had revised some three thousand of the approximately thirty-one thousand verses in the KJV Bible, or about 10 percent of its content. Smith considered his "translation" to be authoritative, accomplished by revelation, and superior to ordinary linguistic decipherment.[30] Broadly characterized, the revisions and expansions in the "New Translation" may be

---

26. Gordon S. Wood, "Evangelical America and Early Mormonism," *New York History* 61 (October 1980): 381.

27. "Preface," Book of Mormon (Palmyra, NY, 1830), [3].

28. https://www.churchofjesuschrist.org/comeuntochrist/believe/book-of-mormon /how-the-bible-and-the-book-of-mormon-work-together.

29. In the 1830s, "translate" could also mean "to interpret" and "to explain" (see Noah Webster, *American Dictionary of the English Language* [1828], s.v. "translate"), which is what is taking place in parts of the "New Translation."

30. For an overview and interpretation, see Grant Underwood, "Joseph Smith's 'New Translation' of the Bible," in *The Bible and the Latter-day Saint Tradition*, ed. Taylor G. Petrey, Cory Crawford, and Eric A. Eliason (Salt Lake City: University of Utah Press, 2023), 47–62.

classified into one or more of three categories: theological clarification, narrative enrichment, and stylistic refinement.[31] Although the Church of Jesus Christ of Latter-day Saints recognizes the supplementary theological value of the "New Translation," it continues to use the KJV as its official Bible. As such, the KJV is the primary version quoted in this book.

Another volume of LDS scripture frequently referenced here is the Doctrine and Covenants. The Doctrine and Covenants is a compilation of over a hundred revelation texts that emanated from Joseph Smith, ranging in length from a paragraph to a dozen or more manuscript pages. As published in the Doctrine and Covenants, each revelation text stands alone as a distinct, numbered "section," originally divided into numbered paragraphs and later into smaller verses.[32] These revelations guided the founding and function of the church and helped establish its doctrine. Lastly, the smallest volume of LDS scripture, a mere tenth the size of the Book of Mormon, is the Pearl of Great Price. The Book of Abraham is included in this volume canonized in 1880, as are excerpts from the "New Translation," highlights from Joseph Smith's history, and the church's Articles of Faith.[33]

With the terms in this book's title—*Latter-day Saint Theology among Christian Theologies*—explained, the book's organizational structure and methodology set forth, and its principal sources identified, the stage is set

---

31. Similar categorizations are found in Robert J. Matthews, *"A Plainer Translation"— Joseph Smith's Translation of the Bible: A History and Commentary* (Provo, UT: BYU Press, 1975); Philip L. Barlow, *Mormons and the Bible: The Place of the Latter-day Saints in American Religion* (New York: Oxford University Press, 1991); and the introductory essays in *NTOB*, the critical edition of the "New Translation" (see the list of abbreviations).

32. In the LDS scriptures and KJV published by the Church of Jesus Christ of Latter-day Saints, notational references to the Doctrine and Covenants use the abbreviation "D&C," a practice followed in this volume. Thus, reference to a passage in the Doctrine and Covenants will be cited like this: "D&C 42:56," where "42" is the section and "56" the verse. The first edition of the Doctrine and Covenants carried the long title *Doctrine and Covenants of the Church of the Latter Day Saints: Carefully Selected from the Revelations of God and Compiled by Joseph Smith Junior, Oliver Cowdery, Sidney Rigdon, Frederick G. Williams, Presiding Elders of Said Church* (Kirtland, OH, 1835). Subsequent revelations were added to later editions. Unless there are significant wording changes from earlier editions, the current edition, which reflects the present section-and-verse configuration, is cited throughout this book. Occasional reference to the first, 1835, edition, which is not versified, will use the abbreviation "D&C-1835," followed by a page number.

33. Unless the wording differs significantly, the "New Translation" portions included in the Pearl of Great Price are here cited as titled in the Pearl of Great Price—"Selections from the Book of Moses" (or simply "Moses") and "Joseph Smith—Matthew."

to commence the volume's interfaith conversation. It begins where Christian theologies often begin—with consideration of "theology" proper. Traditionally, this discussion is divided into two sections—God's nature and God's work. Thus, chapter 1 deals with the nature of God and the Trinity, and chapter 2 explores God's work or relation to the world, focusing on such themes as creation and providence.

1

GOD

Divinity and Trinity

In 2010, the American Academy of Religion bestowed its prestigious Award for Excellence in the Study of Religion: Textual Studies on a book the awards committee called a scholarly "tour de force." In it, the book's author, Benjamin Sommer, professor of Bible and ancient Semitic languages at Jewish Theological Seminary, advanced a particularly provocative thesis about ancient Israelite theology: "The God of the Hebrew Bible has a body."[1] Not that he just *appears* to have a body, but that he actually *has* one. "This must be stated at the outset," emphasized Sommer "because so many people, including many scholars, assume otherwise. The evidence for this simple thesis is overwhelming. So much so that the carnal nature of the biblical God should not occasion surprise." Yet the idea does surprise because for more than two millennia the dominant view has been otherwise. "Ever since Jewish and Christian thinkers began to believe that God is not a physical being," Sommer explained, "many became embarrassed by their own sacred scripture" and endeavored to "minimize, explain away, render metaphorical, or eviscerate the Bible's anthropomorphism."[2] The

---

1. Benjamin D. Sommer, *The Bodies of God and the World of Ancient Israel* (New York: Cambridge University Press, 2009). As the plural title suggests, Sommer argues that ancient Israelites believed that God could "inhabit" other bodies, from temples to trees, while at the same time possessing his own "stable," human-like, corporeal body, generally thought to reside in heaven.

2. Sommer, *The Bodies of God*, 1–5. Sommer's (re)assessment of ancient Hebrew beliefs about God has been shared by a number of other scholars in the twenty-first century. Although Anne K. Knafl, *Forming God: Divine Anthropomorphism in the Pentateuch* (Winona Lake, IN: Eisenbrauns, 2014), sees complexity and diversity in the various pentateuchal sources, she argues that "ancient Israel's deity was in fact deeply anthropomorphic," including notions of God as concretely "corporeal" and "proximate" (275, 257). Also providing nuance is Mark S. Smith, *Where the Gods Are: Spatial Dimensions of Anthropomorphism in the Biblical World* (New Haven: Yale University Press, 2016), who sees accounts of "God's natural 'human' body" primarily confined to Genesis. Supportive of Sommer's conclusions

embarrassment arose as first Judaism and then Christianity was influenced by Platonic philosophy with its powerful emphasis on divine transcendence and its "incessant privileging of the spiritual over the physical."[3] That sense of radical transcendence rendered what Plato called the perfect, unchanging, immaterial "World of Being"—the realm of Ideas or Forms occupied by Deity and distinct from the created, material "World of Becoming"—incompatible with the imperfections and finitude of materiality and corporeality. The result was that an unbridgeable chasm was created between the *infinite* God and the finite created realm, between immaterial Creator and material creation. Consequently, belief in an embodied God had to be discarded and biblical anthropomorphism reinterpreted along now familiar metaphorical lines.[4] Centuries later, this would all be challenged by the Mormon prophet Joseph Smith, who dramatically reclaimed the physicality of God and sought to bridge the unbridgeable chasm between finite and infinite. That, however, is getting ahead of the story. First, the trajectory of philosophically influenced reflection on the nature of God needs to be briefly sketched.

Central to that trajectory was the idea that scriptural depictions of God's corporeality were to be understood as examples of the infinite and immaterial God temporarily making itself comprehensible to finite humans. "Accommodationism" was the label eventually attached to this perspective on biblical anthropomorphism, and from the Hellenistic era onward an accommodationist hermeneutic[5] dominated the reading of embodiment texts in the Bible. A related but slightly different interpretive tack was the emphasis on allegory, prominently associated with such notable early Christian theologians as Origen of Alexandria (in Egypt) and Augustine of Hippo (in North Africa). Augustine's book-length commentary *On Genesis* is typical of this approach. Augustine acknowledged that in scripture "God's eyes are mentioned, and his ears, and lips, and feet," but, he explained, "all those who have a spiritual understanding of the scriptures have learned to take these names as meaning,

---

and even broader in scope is Christoph Markschies's comprehensive *God's Body: Jewish, Christian, and Pagan Images of God* (Waco, TX: Baylor University Press, 2019).

3. Louis Markos, *From Plato to Christ: How Platonic Thought Shaped the Christian Faith* (Downers Grove, IL: IVP Academic, 2021), 124.

4. Knafl stresses "the importance of distinguishing between biblical conceptions and later, theological or philological assertions about divinity" (*Forming God*, 56) and to that end cites Christopher J. Insole, "Anthropomorphism and the Apophatic God," *Modern Theology* 17 (2001): 475–83.

5. "Hermeneutic," from the Greek for "interpretation," refers to one's principles or theory of interpretation.

not parts of the body, but spiritual powers . . . the faithful who have a spiritual understanding do not believe that God is circumscribed in a bodily shape."[6] Still, as one modern scholar has noted, "God without a body was not an easy sell. The notion of the incorporeality of the divine was the fruit of philosophical abstraction. In myth, poetry, and ritual, however, the divine was embodied, if not in images at least in the imagination. Furthermore, the scriptural depiction of a god who acts and intervenes in history did not lend itself to the philosophical notion of incorporeality."[7]

John Cassian, the famous early Christian ascetic, tells the story of the pious fourth-century Egyptian monk "Abba" Serapion, who was confronted by Photinus, a learned deacon from Cappadocia (in what is today Turkey). Photinus reported that many Eastern monks were interpreting Genesis 1:27—"God created man in his own image"—spiritually, not literally. "Serapion was devastated. The loss of a human shape for the image of God left him despairing. Prostrating himself on the ground, he wept and cried out, 'They have taken my God from me and I have now no one to behold, whom to worship and address!'"[8] This concern persisted within the Egyptian monastic community, and several decades later, in 399, serious theological wrangling broke out in Alexandria over the question of God's corporeality. This "anthropomorphite controversy" pitted the monks against their Alexandrian bishop, whose Easter festal letter claimed God was incorporeal. The monks were furious because this challenged their long-standing practice of seeking through their spiritual disciplines a vision of the eternal, preincarnation body of Christ, visible in Old Testament theophanies (appearances of God), and in whose corporeal image, like Serapion, they believed humanity was created.[9]

---

6. Augustine, *On Genesis: A Refutation of the Manichees* 1.17.27–28, ed. and trans. Edmund Hill, Works of Saint Augustine: A Translation for the 21st Century (Hyde Park, NY: New City, 2004), 56–57.

7. Karen Jo Torjesen, "The Enscripturation of Philosophy: The Incorporeality of God in Origen's Exegesis," in *Biblical Interpretation: History, Context, and Reality*, ed. Christine Helmer and Taylor Petrey (Atlanta: Society of Biblical Literature, 2005), 74.

8. Cassian tells this story in his *Conferences* 10.3. The quotation is from Torjesen, "The Enscripturation of Philosophy," 75. Roughly contemporaneous statements that depict Deity as having a divine body, though not a material or anthropomorphic one, are found in the *Pseudo-Clementine Homilies* (i.e., sermons): God "has shape, and He has every limb primarily and solely for beauty's sake, and not for use. For He has not eyes that He may see with them, for He sees on every side" and "He has the most beautiful shape on account of man, that the pure in heart may be able to see Him" (Ps.-Clem. 17.7, in *ANF*, 8:319–20).

9. The "anthropomorphite controversy," as the "Egyptian" contribution to the broader contemporary debate over Origen's teachings, is discussed in Elizabeth Clark, *The Origenist*

The difficult move away from anthropomorphism, which entails more than just divine corporeality, happened neither all at once nor evenly throughout the early centuries of Christianity. For the most part, however, a literal reading of embodiment texts was rare by the 400s.[10] Centuries later, the use of analogy and metaphor to describe Deity was given one of its most influential expositions by Thomas Aquinas in "Question 13—Theological Language" of his masterwork *Summa Theologiae* (which means "summary/compendium of theology").[11] Aquinas discusses three kinds of language—univocal, equivocal, and analogical. Terms used univocally refer to the same thing, to that which is identical (e.g., "I have two *legs*; Jane has two *legs*"). In this case, "legs" may differ in size and shape, but both are the same recognizable part of the human anatomy. Univocally understood, the same is true of moral qualities, in which case to say that God is "loving" or "merciful" communicates essentially the same meaning such terms do in everyday life. Equivocal language, on the other hand, is where the same word refers to two entirely different things (e.g., "I write with a *pen*; a pig lives in a *pen*"). Thus, discussed equivocally, the nature of God's love or mercy may in actuality be dramatically different from what humans assume when thinking univocally based on their experience. Analogy, in Aquinas's view, "lies somewhere between pure equivocation and simple univocity, for the word is neither used in the same sense, as with univocal language, nor in totally different senses, as with equivocation."[12] Thus, for Aquinas, analogy is the best of the inevitably inadequate ways to talk about a transcendent, infinite God. Since God is incomprehensibly superior to humans, the only proper way to speak of him is through faint approximations, through analogy. For Aquinas, there was no univocity when it came to biblical language about God. Once the immateriality and incorporeality of Deity became a given, understanding biblical descriptions of God's body and parts univocally was out of the question. A philosophically inflected metaphysics[13] demanded a hermeneutics of metaphor and analogy.

Controversy: The Cultural Construction of an Early Christian Debate (Princeton: Princeton University Press, 1992), 43–84. Subsequent studies include Paul A. Patterson, *Visions of Christ: The Anthropomorphite Controversy of 399 C.E.* (Tübingen: Mohr Siebeck, 2012), and Markschies, *God's Body*, 231–73. See also Alexander Golitzin, "The Vision of God and the Form of Glory: More Reflections on the Anthropomorphite Controversy of AD 399," in *Abba: The Tradition of Orthodoxy in the West*, ed. Andrew Louth et al. (Crestwood, NY: St. Vladimir's Seminary Press, 2003), 273–97.

10. Yet, Carl W. Griffin and David L. Paulsen, "Augustine and the Corporeality of God," *Harvard Theological Review* 95 (January 2002): 97–118, argue that a type of anthropomorphism persisted even with Augustine.

11. See Aquinas, *Summa Theologiae* 1a.13.1–12, and appendix 4—"Analogy."

12. Aquinas, *Summa Theologiae* 1a.13.5.

13. "Metaphysics" is broadly defined as "the branch of philosophy that deals with the first

Yet for all its strengths in unpacking the richness of biblical language, metaphorical interpretation can become a slippery slope. As with all language, metaphor, too, is rooted in human experience. It helps humans make sense of the world. Yet, finite human experience can only go so far when it comes to understanding God. "For my thoughts are not your thoughts, neither are your ways my ways, saith the LORD. For as the heavens are higher than the earth, so are my ways higher than your ways, and my thoughts than your thoughts" (Isa. 55:8–9). It did not take Christian thinkers long to realize the inadequacy of analogy and metaphor. Superficially satisfying, preliminarily helpful perhaps, but ultimately even analogical language fell short. Some theologians chose not to venture beyond the older *via negativa*. That is, they thought it more fitting to speak of what God is *not*, rather than what he is. Such "apophatic" theology (from the Greek term for negation) stressed that God cannot be encompassed by reasoned, human explanations, including analogies. Although Aquinas favored analogical language as the best of imperfect human attempts to describe God, he acknowledged that God is "greater than all we can say, greater than all we can know" and "transcends all that can be conceived by us."[14] Ultimately, the medieval tendency was to lean toward equivocity. As declared by the Fourth Lateran Council (1215), "Between Creator and creature no similitude can be expressed without implying a greater dissimilitude."[15] This reflected the Augustinian axiom *si comprehendis, non est Deus* (if you comprehend it, it isn't God).[16]

Such apophatic declarations were intended to honor God, highlight his utter transcendence, and keep humans humble, but for some, theologians and laypeople alike, it turned God into an inaccessible mystery. It was not until many centuries later, under the influence of Enlightenment thought, that such

---

principles of things or reality, including questions about being, substance, time and space, causation, change, and identity." In particular, it can refer to discussion of that which "is above or goes beyond the laws of nature; belonging to an operation or agency which is more than or other than physical or natural; supernatural." *OED*, s.v. "metaphysics."

14. Aquinas, *Commentary on [Pseudo-] Dionysius's The Divine Names* 1.3, as quoted in Brian Davies, "Aquinas on What God Is Not," in *Aquinas's* Summa Theologiae: *Critical Essays*, ed. Brian Davies (Lanham, MD: Rowman & Littlefield, 2006), 129.

15. Fourth Lateran Council, "Chapter 2—the False Doctrine of Joachim of Fiore." Denzinger 806.

16. Augustine, *Sermons* 117.3.5. Augustine, however, was speaking of God's essence, not his character. That ultimately God in some sense is incomprehensible is recognized in many religious traditions. A well-known parallel to Augustine's axiom is the opening declaration in the Chinese classic *Tao Te Ching*: "The Tao that can be spoken of is not the eternal Tao; The Name that can be named is not the eternal Name." Paul J. Lin, trans., *A Translation of Lao-tzu's* Tao Te Ching *and Wang Pi's Commentary* (Ann Arbor: University of Michigan Center for Chinese Studies, 1977), 3.

formulations began to be criticized as theological obfuscation, and univocal language about God became more acceptable. The Enlightenment era has been characterized as witnessing the "domestication of transcendence."[17] What was often fingered as the culprit in an overly apophatic, equivocal understanding of God was Greek philosophy. Polymath Blaise Pascal famously distinguished the "God of Abraham, Isaac, and Jacob" from "the God of the philosophers and scholars."[18] By the nineteenth century, when Mormonism was born, univocity was dominant and Platonism was a pariah. In writing to his old comrade John Adams, Thomas Jefferson remarked, "The doctrines which flowed from the lips of Jesus himself are within the comprehension of a child; but thousands of volumes have not yet explained the Platonisms engrafted on them: and for this obvious reason that nonsense can never be explained."[19] Although overstated, such a characterization was common at the time, reinforced by a literal reading of the apostle Paul's warning to "beware lest any man spoil you through philosophy and vain deceit" (Col. 2:8). In nineteenth-century America, the formal, philosophically grounded theology of the past had for a number of popular (and populist) thinkers become exhibit A in the case for the alleged historical corruption of original Christianity.[20]

17. William C. Placher, *The Domestication of Transcendence: How Modern Thinking about God Went Wrong* (Louisville: Westminster John Knox, 1996). An attempt to redress the imbalance between apophatically stressing God's transcendence and the Enlightenment domestication of Deity is Charles Haldon, *A Human-Shaped God: Theology of an Embodied God* (Louisville: Westminster John Knox, 2021).

18. Referenced in Francis Schüssler Fiorenza and Gordon D. Kaufman, "God," in *Critical Terms for Religious Studies*, ed. Mark C. Taylor (Chicago: University of Chicago Press, 1998), 140–41.

19. Jefferson to Adams, July 5, 1814, as quoted in *Jefferson's Extracts from the Gospels: "The Philosophy of Jesus" and "The Life and Morals of Jesus,"* ed. Dickinson W. Adams (Princeton: Princeton University Press, 1983), 359. A century earlier, in his influential *Christianity Not Mysterious* (1696), John Toland similarly contrasted the common sense of ordinary folk with what he considered the obscurantism of the theological establishment: "The uncorrupted Doctrines of *Christianity* are not above [the people's] Reach or Comprehension, but the Gibberish of your *Divinity Schools* they understand not." Philip McGuinness, Alan Harrison, and Richard Kearney, eds., *John Toland's "Christianity Not Mysterious"* (Dublin, Ireland: Lilliput, 1997), 87.

20. E. Brooks Holifield, *Theology in America: Christian Thought from the Age of the Puritans to the Civil War* (New Haven: Yale University Press, 2003), 164. Such a view was popular in various Enlightenment-influenced polemical works of the eighteenth and nineteenth centuries and received more sustained and sophisticated theological exposition in the later nineteenth-century writings of German theologian-historians Albrecht Ritschl and Adolf von Harnack.

LDS Views on Divine Embodiment

In Mormonism, apophaticism gave way to an unusually robust cataphaticism (describing God positively) and a decided leaning toward univocity. One of the "first principles of the Gospel," declared Joseph Smith, is "to know for a certainty the character of God." Therefore, he urged his followers, "I want you all to know God, to be familiar with Him."[21] Mormonism's confident cataphaticism is firmly rooted in Joseph Smith's revelatory and visionary experience. Smith was not a theologian, even less a philosopher; he was, in the view of the Latter-day Saints, a prophet. More than know *about* God, Smith claimed to *know* God. Around 1820, Smith had a foundational experience that came to be known as his "First Vision." He later described it in these words: "I saw a pillar of light exactly over my head above the brightness of the sun, which descended gradually untill it fell upon me. . . . When the light rested upon me I saw two personages (whose brightness and glory defy all description) standing above me in the air. One of them spake unto me calling me by name and said (pointing to the other) 'This is my beloved Son, Hear him.'"[22] This revelatory experience became the basis for the distinctive Mormon doctrine that the Father and Son are not two persons in one being, but separate, individual divine beings or "personages" (the more common LDS term).[23]

Smith's vision of distinct divine personages recalls the account of Stephen the Martyr, who, as recorded in the book of Acts, "being full of the Holy Ghost, looked up stedfastly into heaven, and saw the glory of God, and Jesus standing on the right hand of God, and said, Behold, I see the heavens opened, and the Son of man standing on the right hand of God" (Acts 7:55-56). Whereas generations of Christians have regarded Stephen's experience as one more example of divine "accommodation," Smith came to view the anthropomorphic theophany he experienced not only as demonstrating God's distinctness from the Son but also as evidence of God's essential and permanent corporeality. In time, Smith also taught that the corporeality of God was more than spiritual, that it consisted of glorified, celestial flesh.[24] In a statement that later became

21. *JSP*, D15:345.

22. *JSP*, H1:214.

23. One definition of "personage" is simply "a person," any person. The term, however, is also used to specifically denote "a person of high rank, distinction, or importance; a person of note." *OED*, s.v. "personage." This additional meaning is reflected in the common LDS use of "personage" when referring to heavenly or supernatural persons such as God or angels.

24. Previously, the notion of the Father's *spiritual* corporeality seems to have been assumed. The forepart of the first (1835) edition of the Doctrine and Covenants consisted of

canonical for Latter-day Saints, Joseph Smith proclaimed: "The Father has a body of flesh & bones [not blood] as tangible as mans, the Son also, but the Holy Ghost is a personage of spirit."[25] As unconventional as such views are, the Catholic theologian Stephen Webb discerned a certain logic in them: "If Christ's heavenly, resurrected body is a glory to him, then how is the Son not more than the Father unless, that is, the Father himself is also material in some way? . . . It is precisely this dilemma that forced Joseph Smith to argue that God the Father is embodied, since Smith believed that bodies are a blessing and God the Father does not lack what the Son has."[26]

Toward the end of Joseph Smith's life, in addition to proclaiming these striking ideas about God's body, he taught the even more astonishing doctrine that God not only looked like a glorified, enfleshed man but that, in a sense, he *was* one. "God himself, who sits enthroned in yonder heavens, is a man like unto one of yourselves," declared Smith. "That is the great secret. If the vail was rent to-day, and the great God, who holds this world in its orbit, and upholds all things by his power; if you were to see him to-day, you would see him in all the person, image and very form as a man."[27] If God has a glorified, celestial body of flesh and bone, as Latter-day Saints declare, how did he obtain it? It is widely supposed "that God was God from eternity," declared Smith, but "I will refute that Idea [and] take away the veil so you may see." In reality, "God himself, the Father of us all dwelt on an earth the same as Jesus Christ himself did."[28] This startling statement requires clarification. First, the intent of Smith's remark seems *not* to have been to imply that God was once a fallen, sinful individual like the rest of us, but rather to declare that God and humans are linked "ontologically." "Ontology" is the term philosophers use

---

a series of doctrinal "lectures" or catechisms later referred to collectively as "Lectures on Faith." The fifth lecture included a reference to the Father as "a personage of spirit, glory and power" and the Son as "a personage of tabernacle" (D&C-1835, 53). It may have been the case that seeing in vision two personages "whose brightness and glory defy all description" did not prompt in Joseph Smith an immediate recognition of the Father's *fleshly* corporeality. In any case, Smith's earliest unambiguous statement on record about God having a body of flesh and bone was made in January 1841: "That which is without body or parts is nothing. There is no other God in heaven but that God who has flesh and bones." *JSP*, D7:494.

25. *JSP*, D12:143–44 and J2:326. The canonical statement is D&C 130:22.

26. Stephen H. Webb, *Mormon Christianity* (New York: Oxford University Press, 2013), 195.

27. *JSP*, D14:345.

28. *JSP*, D14:337, 345. Another notetaker at Smith's sermon reported his words thus: God "was once as one of us and was on a planet as Jesus was in the flesh" (329). Later, a close associate summarized Smith's teaching: "God: a man like one of us . . . Not God from all Eternity, Once on a planet with flesh and blood, like Christ" (341).

to refer to the nature of a thing or its essential being. In Greek philosophy (and Christian theologies influenced by it) God was considered ontologically unique, an entirely different order of being or kind of existence that in every way transcended created reality, including humankind. Not so for Latter-day Saints. As Smith's apostolic associate Parley Pratt summarized it, God and man are not "two distinct species" but "one species, one race, one great family."[29]

Replacing the Creator-creature divide with a single ontological continuum of being and affirming a literal family relationship between God and humankind is a dramatic step beyond the traditional Christian concept of a "personal God" with whom humans can have a "relationship." To be sure, for Christians who pray "Our Father," the notion of "father" is one of the most cherished metaphors applied to God. Images of parental love and care are perhaps the closest approximation humans have to the transcendent, supernal love of the One who is described in scripture *as* love (1 John 4:8). Moreover, Christians think of God figuratively as "father" in the sense of having created or brought humanity into existence, just as someone may be considered the "father" of an invention. While Latter-day Saints embrace such concepts, they also regard reference to the heavenly "Father" as more than metaphorical. As detailed at length in chapter 5, Mormons consider all humans to be literal sons and daughters of God, believing that human souls or "spirits" (as Latter-day Saints usually call them) were not created but procreated. Mormons refer to this divine generation of souls, believed to have taken place long before the creation of the earth, as "spirit birth." In this way, a literal kinship connection between humanity and the heavenly Father is established.[30] This is how Latter-

---

29. Pratt, *Key to Theology*, 33. Although early Mormons had no awareness of German idealism, there are some striking parallels. "For Hegel, human beings are reconciled to the Absolute when they come to explicit awareness that they are in fact divine in their nature. Reconciliation, that is, does not involve joining together a previously separated humanity and divinity; human nature and divine nature are not two discrete things. Instead, there is only one nature that is divine-human. . . . In his 1821 *Lectures on the Philosophy of Religion*, Hegel expresses this lofty anthropology as follows: 'Humanity implicitly bears within itself the divine idea, not bearing it within itself like something from somewhere else but *as its own substantial nature*.' His 1824 lectures more straightforwardly maintain that 'divine and human nature are not intrinsically different.'" Mark McInroy, "Deification under the Aegis of Idealism: *Theosis* as Essential Union with God in Ferdinand Christian Baur's Patristic Scholarship" (unpublished paper delivered at the 2023 annual meeting of the American Academy of Religion).

30. For Latter-day Saints, "This doctrine is so basic, so oft stated, and so instinctively simple," noted one LDS Church leader, "that it can seem to be ordinary, when in reality it is among the most extraordinary knowledge we can obtain." Donald L. Hallstrom, "I Am a Child of God," *Ensign*, May 2016, 26. From childhood, Mormon girls and boys learn a

day Saints understand the scriptural designation of humans as "the offspring of God" (Acts 17:28–29) and how they interpret the declaration in Psalm 82:6 that "all of you are children of the most High." Although it is not uncommon for other Christians to refer to human beings in some figurative sense as "God's children," for Latter-day Saints the familial connection is intimate *and* genetic. "If we could see our heavenly Father," declared Brigham Young, Joseph Smith's prophet-successor, we would "see a being similar [in appearance] to our earthly parent, with this difference, our Father in heaven is exalted and glorified." Upon entering God's presence, "He will receive you into His arms, and you will be ready to fall into His embrace and kiss Him, as you would your fathers and friends that have been dead for a score of years."[31]

It is important to clarify that the LDS doctrine of the Father's literal relation to his human "offspring" is not meant to diminish Deity in any way. Explained twentieth-century apostle Hugh B. Brown, "we do not mean to humanize God, but rather to deify man—not as he now is but as he may become. The difference between us is indescribably great, but it is one of degree rather than of kind."[32] Furthermore, Latter-day Saints do not reject such biblical passages as Numbers 23:19 or Hosea 11:9 that declare that God is "not a man." *As* God, he is not a man in the earthbound sense of the word. Because his physical embodiment is envisioned to have occurred countless aeons ago, Mormons do not hesitate to affirm God's everlastingness. Finally, it is worth noting that Latter-day Saints today are cautious about expounding the meaning of Joseph Smith's declaration that God once "dwelt on an earth," especially since Smith never elaborated on it. When asked about the postulate of the Father's predivine, incarnate life, church president Gordon Hinckley simply acknowledged, "I don't know a lot about it, and I don't know that others know a lot about it."[33]

---

beloved LDS children's song entitled "I Am a Child of God." *Children's Songbook of the Church of Jesus Christ of Latter-day Saints* (Salt Lake City: The Church of Jesus Christ of Latter-day Saints, 2000), #1.

31. *Journal of Discourses*, 4:55.

32. Hugh B. Brown, *Conference Report*, April 1956, 105. Donald Macleod, *The Person of Christ: Contours of Christian Theology* (Downers Grove, IL: IVP Academic, 1998), described the qualitative distance between God and humans as the difference between Einstein and a mollusk (210). That acknowledged, Stephen Webb's earlier work *Jesus Christ, Eternal God: Heavenly Flesh and the Metaphysics of Matter* (New York: Oxford University Press, 2012) offers an extended argument in behalf of the proposition that God and humanity are ultimately *not* different in kind and that the glorified Christ represents the *telos* (end point) of humankind's potential.

33. *Time*, August 4, 1997, 56. Brigham Young commented that "many have tried to penetrate to the First Cause of all things; but it would be as easy for . . . a gnat to trace the history

Still, the basic concept continues to be affirmed in church literature today, albeit without elaboration or explanation.[34] In sum, as a result of Joseph Smith's teachings, for Latter-day Saints, the unbridgeable chasm between Creator and human "creatures" has been decisively crossed.[35]

That other Christians might consider the Mormon view of God's relationship to humanity heretical, even blasphemous, is understandable. For centuries, mainstream Christianity has erected its entire theological edifice on the premise of divine otherness, on the foundation of an ultimately apophatic incomparability and incomprehensibility with regard to divinity. Smith, however, built on an entirely different premise and did so boldly because he believed that through his revelatory experiences he had learned the true nature of God. Consequently, neither charges of doctrinal novelty, philosophical inconsistency, or unscripturality fazed him or his followers. As they viewed the matter, Smith's knowledge of God was firsthand, the result of a direct encounter with Deity, and for that reason it was thought to trump centuries of seeing through a glass darkly. "Could you gaze in[to] heaven 5 minute[s]," Smith once declared, "you would know more—than you would by read[ing] all that ever was writt[e]n on the subject."[36] Just as Christian theology has "mystery" as the

---

of man back to his origin as for man to fathom the First Cause of all things, lift the veil of eternity, and reveal the mysteries that have been sought after by philosophers from the beginning." *Journal of Discourses*, 7:284.

34. For example, the statement that God "was once a man like us" appears in every edition of the church publication *Gospel Principles* from the original 1978 edition to the latest 2011 edition (e.g., *Gospel Principles*, 279). It also appears in other recent church curricula such as the *Doctrines of the Gospel Student Manual* (2010), 8, and in the *NT Student Manual* (2018), 33, 529—God "was once as we are now, and is an exalted man."

35. So, too, for a distinct minority of Christian theologians. Trinity College religion professor Edmond Cherbonnier wrote, "The doctrine of creation does not, as is sometimes held, fix a great gulf between two realms of being, the divine and the human. On the contrary, the existence which God bestows upon Adam does not differ in kind from his own. It is therefore misleading to speak of 'discontinuity' between the Creator and his creation. Opposition between men and God there surely is, but it is volitional, not metaphysical." Edmond La Beaume Cherbonnier, "The Logic of Biblical Anthropomorphism," *Harvard Theological Review* 55 (July 1962): 202. David Bentley Hart, *You Are Gods: On Nature and Supernature* (Notre Dame: University of Notre Dame Press, 2022), similarly posits a single metaphysical continuum that erases the ontological distinction between divinity and humanity and nature and supernature.

36. *JSP*, J3:133. Strangely, Smith's statement recalls an episode at the end of Thomas Aquinas's life in which he had an extraordinary experience that caused him to abruptly stop work on his *Summa*. When his astonished secretary asked why, Thomas reportedly replied, "I cannot do any more. Everything I have written seems to me a straw in comparison with

last redoubt in defending its ultimately inexplicable propositions, Mormon theism (doctrine of God), too, has a final defense when challenged on theological, philosophical, or historical grounds. Instead of "it's a divine mystery," LDS theology resorts to "we know it by latter-day revelation." No Christian theology is without its logically indefensible assertions that are taken on faith. What makes the LDS doctrine of God stand out, though, is how it contrasts so dramatically with views espoused in many other Christian theologies.

God's Attributes

It might be wondered, then, given the distinctiveness of Mormon views about God's being, whether they share any of the standard Christian depictions of God's character and attributes. The answer is both yes and no. In the realm of practice, the answer is yes; metaphysically, the answer requires qualification. As a lived religion, Mormonism's predominant orientation is to emphasize the perfection of God's attributes, and to do so in much the same way and even in much the same language as do Christians generally. "In the primitive Christian tradition, such characterizations were given liturgical, homiletic, or catechetical expression, drawing on scriptural language," and "in scripture the primary idiom in which the divine attributes come to expression is doxological [as praise]."[37] Not surprisingly, therefore, most Christians, including Latter-day Saints, encounter discussion of God's superlative attributes as they are extolled in worship or sermon or doctrinal confession, rather than in abstract philosophical discourse. The early "Articles and Covenants" of the Church of Jesus Christ of Latter-day Saints, for instance, contains a confessional declaration that most Christians could affirm: "We know that there is a God in heaven, who is infinite and eternal, from everlasting to everlasting the same unchangeable God, the framer of heaven and earth, and all things which are in them" (D&C 20:17). To be sure, Latter-day Saints over the years have interpreted such characterizations in clarifying and qualifying ways, but the declaration retains its canonical status for church members. So does this revealed prayer: "O Lord God Almighty, hear us in these our petitions, and answer us from heaven, thy holy habitation, where thou sittest enthroned, with glory, honor, power, majesty, might, dominion, truth, justice, judgment, mercy, and an infinity of fulness, from everlasting to everlasting" (D&C 109:77).

---

what I have seen." Quoted in Jean-Pierre Torrell, *Saint Thomas Aquinas*, vol. 1, *The Person and His Work*, rev. ed. (Washington, DC: Catholic University of America Press, 2005), 289.

37. John Webster, "Attributes, Divine," in *Cambridge Dictionary of Christian Theology*, ed. Ian A. McFarland et al. (New York: Cambridge University Press, 2011), 45, 47.

When it comes to whether or not Latter-day Saints affirm God's absolute, infinite attributes, the so-called omni characteristics—*omniscience* (all knowledge), *omnipotence* (all power), and *omnipresence* (everywhere present)—Mormonism's dual answer is more discernible. One might assume, for instance, that the LDS view of God's physical corporeality negates the possibility of affirming divine omnipresence, but this is not so. Latter-day Saints explain God's omnipresence in much the same way that Christians account for the omnipresence of the glorified Christ. Most Christians do not believe that Christ shed his physical, resurrected body upon ascending to heaven. Noted seventeenth-century Reformed theologian Francis Turretin is typical on this point: "Christ went up locally, visibly, and bodily from the earth into the third heaven. . . . There he will remain unto the day of judgment, so that although he is always present with us by his grace and Spirit and Divinity, yet he is no longer with us by the bodily presence of the flesh."[38] Latter-day Saints similarly reason that while the glorified, corporeal Father is physically located in a material heaven, through *his* "grace and spirit and divinity," he is truly omnipresent. "What part of God is omnipresent," asked Joseph Smith in one of his sermons. "It is the Spirit of god which proceeds from him."[39] Thereby he is "in all things, and is through all things, and is round about all things" (D&C 88:41). As Brigham Young taught, "He is present with all his creations through his influence, through his government, spirit and power, but he himself is a personage of tabernacle."[40]

Given the widespread appearance of all the "omni" terms in both the formal and popular theological discourse of Joseph Smith's day, it is not surprising that he knew and used them on occasion to describe Deity. In an early account of his initial visionary experience, he wrote that God is "an omnipotant and omnipreasant power a being who makith Laws and decreeeth and bindeth all things in their bounds."[41] Elsewhere, Joseph Smith called God "the first Being—supreme intillegence; supreme power; supreme glory . . . comprehending

---

38. Quoted in Oliver D. Crisp, *Divinity and Humanity: The Incarnation Reconsidered* (Cambridge: Cambridge University Press, 2007), 133n. A related idea about physicality not limiting omnipresence is Calvin's teaching, later dubbed *extra calvinisticum*, that the eternal Son continued all his preincarnate divine functions, such as sustaining and filling the universe, during the period when he took on human nature as Jesus of Nazareth in first-century Palestine.

39. *JSP*, D12:499. Currently, the LDS *Bible Dictionary* entry for "God" describes God as "omnipresent," adding the parenthetical clarification "through his Spirit." *Bible Dictionary*, s.v. "God."

40. *Journal of Discourses*, 10:319.

41. *JSP*, H1:12. An early composition regarded as inspired but not canonized addressed God thus: "Omnipotence Omnipotence o may I see thee." *JSP*, R2:509.

all things, seeing all things: the invisible and eter[n]al godhead."[42] Some years later, despite Smith's deepening appreciation of God's corporeality and the new cosmology (theory of the universe) he was beginning to articulate, Smith still spoke of the Almighty as "eternal, omnipotent, omnicient, and omnipresent."[43] The practical importance of such affirmations for exercising faith in God and living a life of discipleship was such that the divine attributes were discussed at length in "Lectures on Faith." The lectures proclaim that "in order that any rational and intelligent being may exercise faith in God . . . a *correct* idea of his character, perfections and attributes" is necessary (D&C-1835, 36). That "correct" idea begins with the understanding that God is "the only supreme governor, and independent being, in whom all fulness and perfection dwells; who is omnipotent, omnipresent, and omniscient; without beginning of days or end of life; and that in him every good gift, and every good principle dwells" (D&C-1835, 12). The lectures then summarize the scriptural witness as teaching: "First, That he was God before the world was created, and the same God that he was, after it was created. Secondly, That he is merciful, and gracious, slow to anger, abundant in goodness, and that he was so from everlasting, and will be to everlasting. Thirdly, That he changes not, neither is there variableness with him; but that he is . . . the same yesterday to-day and forever. . . . Fourthly, That he is a God of truth and cannot lie. Fifthly, That he is no respecter of persons. . . . Sixthly, That he is love" (D&C-1835, 38–39).[44]

Although in the 1840s Joseph Smith advanced a new metaphysics of God and the cosmos that philosophically would seem to require modification of how the divine perfections are conceptualized, the lectures' declarations were not repudiated as antithetical to these developments. Indeed, in the church's institutional literature in the twenty-first century, the same basic points made in the lectures are reiterated. The current LDS *Guide to the Scriptures* succinctly affirms the three principal "omnis," linking them both to the Bible and LDS scripture: "God the Father is the supreme ruler of the universe. He is all powerful (Gen 18:14; Alma 26:35; D&C 19:1–3), all knowing (Matt 6:8; 2 Nephi 2:24), and everywhere present through His Spirit (Ps 139:7–12; D&C 88:7–13, 41)."[45] The

42. "Grammar and Alphabet of the Egyptian Language, circa July–circa November 1835," *JSP*, R4:121, 351.

43. *JSP*, J2:117.

44. Affirming these divine attributes was considered essential because without them the believer could fear that God might not be able to fulfill his promises, "but seeing he is God over all, from everlasting to everlasting, the creator and upholder of all things, no such fear can exist in the minds of those who put their trust in him, so that in this respect their faith can be without wavering" (D&C-1835, 39).

45. *Guide to the Scriptures*, s.v. "God, Godhead." The *Guide* has separate entries for

church's current college-level *Doctrines of the Gospel Student Manual* includes these affirmations: "God is infinite, eternal, and unchangeable (see Mormon 9:9; D&C 20:12, 17; 109:77). God is just, true, and righteous in all things (see Rev 15:3; Ps 89:14; Ether 3:12). God is perfect in His love and mercy (see Ps 103:17–18; 2 Nephi 9:8, 53; Exod 34:6–7; 1 Chr 16:34). God is the source of light and law (see D&C 88:12–13). God is the Supreme Being in the universe. God the Father is greater than all (see Eph 4:6; John 10:29)."[46] The paradoxical affirmation of these characteristics in light of Smith's distinctive cosmology is best understood by noting the pastoral and doxological context of their presentation.

Spirit and Matter

Where the Latter-day Saint account of God and his attributes and perfections diverges most noticeably from the constructions of classical Christian theism is in the realm of metaphysics. In addition to collapsing the ontological difference between divinity and humanity, Mormonism also puts "spirit" and "matter" on a single continuum. In the nonphilosophical language of his rural upbringing, Joseph Smith taught: "There is no such thing as immaterial matter. All spirit is matter, but it is more fine or pure" (D&C 131:7). Premodern debates over whether everything in the universe is composed of matter or is divided between two metaphysically distinct realities—matter *and* spirit—has a long and storied history. In general, prior to the decisive argument of René Descartes in favor of the latter view, "it was believed that the soul was indeed material, but of a vastly different *kind* of material . . . very much more refined." The ancients believed that "the soul was made up of substance. It may be refined, but it is still substance."[47] By the end of the eighteenth century, on the eve of the birth of Mormonism, a materialist metaphysics in one form or another was again seen by many scientifically inclined individuals as preferable to spirit-matter dualism. Thus, it is not surprising that Joseph Smith and the first Latter-day Saints, who shared the popular faith of the day in the fundamental compatibility of science and religion, expounded their own distinctive version of metaphysical materialism. To view spirit and matter as part of a single continuum of existence seemed eminently rational to the Latter-day Saints. Positing the materiality of God, angels, and spirits made them more perceptible and seemingly more real.

"Omnipotent," "Omnipresent," and "Omniscient," and the church's earlier *Topical Guide* to the scriptures listed dozens of passages under the headings "God, Omniscience of," "God, Perfection of," and "God, Power of."

46. *Doctrines of the Gospel Student Manual* (2010), 6.

47. Bart D. Ehrman, *Heaven and Hell: A History of the Afterlife* (New York: Simon & Schuster, 2020), 58–59.

"To talk of *immaterial* existences," wrote Thomas Jefferson in language that might have been voiced by Joseph Smith, "is to talk of *nothings*. To say that the human soul, angels, god, are immaterial, is to say they are *nothings*, or that there is no god, no angels, no soul. I cannot reason otherwise."[48] For Jefferson and Mormon thinkers such as early LDS apostle Orson Pratt, who wrote an influential essay entitled "Absurdities of Immaterialism," metaphysical dualism was heretical.[49] "At what age of the Christian church this heresy of *immaterialism*, this masked atheism, crept in, I do not know. But a heresy it certainly is," opined Jefferson. "Jesus taught nothing of it. He told us that 'God is a spirit' [John 4:24], but he has not defined what a spirit is, nor said that it is not *matter*. And the antient fathers generally, if not universally, held it to be matter."[50] Latter-day Saints concurred, so much so that in 1845, when the excerpts quoted above from Jefferson's recently published letter were reprinted in the church's periodical, it elicited this tongue-in-cheek editorial query, "Will the editor [of the Jefferson correspondence] . . . inform us whether Thomas Jefferson was a Mormon or not?"[51] As for John 4:24, because the Mormon doctrine that God has a glorified body of divinized flesh prevents an understanding that God is *only* spirit, Latter-day Saints read the passage to mean that God *has* a spirit, not that spirit defines the metaphysical totality of his existence.[52]

God, Time, and Progression

Undergirding and suffusing Latter-day Saint theology is yet another metaphysical chasm crossing—the modification of the traditional theistic distinction between "eternity" and "time." For Latter-day Saints, there is no such thing as a metaphysically distinct, timeless, God-only realm known as "eternity."[53]

48. Lester J. Cappon, ed., *The Adams-Jefferson Letters: The Complete Correspondence between Thomas Jefferson and Abigail and John Adams* (Chapel Hill: University of North Carolina Press, 1959), 2:568.

49. Orson Pratt, *Absurdities of Immaterialism; or, a Reply to T. W. P. Taylder's Pamphlet, Entitled: "The Materialism of the Mormons or Latter-day Saints, Examined and Exposed"* (Liverpool, 1849).

50. Cappon, *The Adams-Jefferson Letters*, 2:568.

51. *Times and Seasons*, July 1845, 970.

52. In his "New Translation" of the Bible, Joseph Smith emended John 4:23–24 to read that "true worshippers shall worship the Father in spirit and in truth: for the Father seeketh such to worship him. *For unto such hath God promised his spirit*, [instead of 'God is a spirit'] and they who worship him must worship him in spirit and in truth." *NTOB*, 450 (emphasis added).

53. For a classical articulation of this distinction, see Augustine's ruminations in *Confes-*

Everything, including God, participates in time in some way. "Eternity" and "eternal" are understood to refer to an unbegun and never-ending succession of temporal moments rather than to timelessness. This parallels how the Hebrew and Greek words behind "eternal" or "eternity" are used in the Bible. *Olam* and *'ad*, the Hebrew language's closest terms to "eternal" or "eternity," appear hundreds of times in the Old Testament and are typically translated as "ever," "everlasting," or "evermore." The Greek *aionios* similarly denotes everlastingness or existence without beginning or end. However, as later Christian theologians attending to Greek philosophical categories used the term, "eternal" came to refer less to God's longevity and more to his being wholly other, beyond time and space. Eternity was thought to describe ontology, not temporality.[54]

Given the Mormon rejection of divine timelessness, what are the implications for a Latter-day Saint theology of God? First, the LDS affirmation of God's temporality does not mean that Mormons believe that God as God is constrained by time or that his infinitude is diminished thereby. This should be clear from the previous discussion of his "omni" attributes. Still, the idea that the eternal God exists within time, that he has a history, a biography, so to speak, especially as Latter-day Saints so dramatically conceive it by positing his immemorial progression to Godhood, is incongruous with the assumptions of traditional Christian theism. Nonetheless, Mormonism embraces, even celebrates, the idea that all beings are capable of ongoing, everlasting growth and development. In Latter-day Saint doctrine, where God is viewed as partaking of the universe's materiality and mutability and sharing a familial, ontological link to humanity, the heavenly Father himself becomes the paradigm and paragon of eternal progress. Although Parent and progeny find themselves at vastly different points in their progression along the shared ontological continuum, it is imagined, as has been noted, that the Father was once as his children now are

---

sions 11.11–41 (Ruden trans. [New York: Modern Library, 2017], 355–83). See also Augustine's *The City of God against the Pagans* 11.4–8 (Dyson trans. [Cambridge: Cambridge University Press, 1998]), 452–59.

54. An exhaustive study of "time" and "timeless" eternity in late antiquity is Simon Goldhill, *The Christian Invention of Time: Temporality and the Literature of Late Antiquity* (Cambridge: Cambridge University Press, 2022). See also Ilaria Ramelli and David Konstan, *Terms for Eternity: Aionios and Aidios in Classical and Christian Texts* (Piscataway, NJ: Georgias, 2011). In recent decades, some theologians have argued that God is involved in a degree of temporality. A range of views on the matter can be sampled in Gregory E. Ganssle, ed., *God and Time: Four Views* (Downers Grove, IL: IVP, 2001). In longer studies, Paul Helm, *Eternal God: A Study of God without Time*, 2nd ed. (Oxford: Oxford University Press, 2010), defends the atemporality of God, while R. T. Mullins, *The End of the Timeless God* (Oxford: Oxford University Press, 2016), critiques it.

and that by mastering the eternal, spiritual laws of the universe, he "progressed" to Godhood. Given President Gordon Hinckley's comment that the details of how this occurred are not known, the doctrine is simply affirmed without elaboration, often in the succinct words of a couplet attributed to earlier church president Lorenzo Snow: "As man now is, God once was; as God now is, man may be[come]."[55] Particularly the latter phrase epitomizes the LDS concept of "eternal progression," a doctrine discussed at length in chapter 12.

If God is unfathomably perfect, beyond every superlative characterization imaginable, how can he be said to progress? Lacking definitive doctrinal pronouncements on the matter, Latter-day Saint answers are speculative and varied. Not long after the death of Joseph Smith, two of his apostles voiced contrasting perspectives. Orson Pratt emphasized the traditional scriptural texts proclaiming divine omniscience, while Brigham Young was captivated by the implications of Smith's doctrine of eternal progression. "Brother Orson Pratt, has in theory, bounded the capacity of God," declared Young. "According to his theory, God can progress no further in knowledge and power; but the God that I serve is progressing eternally."[56] Young's contemporary, apostle Wilford Woodruff, concurred: "God himself is increasing and progressing in knowledge, power, and dominion, and will do so, worlds without end."[57] Given Young's position as president of the church, his views were influential, but they were expressed in rudimentary form. Subsequently, such thinking received fuller development in the early twentieth-century writings of apostle John Widtsoe and others.

For Widtsoe, the idea of eternal progress meant that God "must have been engaged from the beginning, and must now be engaged in progressive development, and, infinite as God is, he must have been less powerful in the past than he is today."[58] Though Widtsoe considered God's omniscience and omnipotence limited in some sense and capable of further development, Widtsoe was quick to add that God "is infinite in all matters pertaining to us and transcends wholly our understanding in his power and wisdom." In short, as finite beings, we can "know no greater God than the omniscient, omnipotent Father."[59] God knows all things necessary and has all power necessary to

---

55. *Teachings: Lorenzo Snow*, 83. Although no patristic writer discussed the Father becoming divine, some fourth-century critics of the creed of Nicaea did argue, as will be seen later, that the Son "became" divine and had not always been so.

56. *Journal of Discourses*, 11:286.

57. *Journal of Discourses*, 6:120

58. John A. Widtsoe, *Rational Theology: As Taught by the Church of Jesus Christ of Latter-day Saints* (Salt Lake City: General Priesthood Committee, 1915), 23.

59. Widtsoe, *Rational Theology*, 63.

govern our universe and save his creations. He is redemptively sovereign and omniscient. This is how Widtsoe and others like him interpreted such passages as 2 Nephi 9:20—"O how great the holiness of our God! For he knoweth all things, and there is not anything save he knows it." In an ironic parallel to accommodationist hermeneutics, Latter-day Saints who advocate that God is progressing in knowledge and power do not interpret literally or univocally scriptural texts that proclaim divine omniscience. Instead, their philosophical presuppositions prompt them to regard the statements as designed to accommodate finite, human comprehension; God's actual reality is something else. For them, the logic of a material, changing universe of which God is a part demands that nothing, not even God, can be static. He, and all else, is either progressing or retrogressing. And since the latter is untenable for the believer, God must, it is inferred, be progressing in knowledge and power.[60] Still, the exalted, even inscrutable, nature of God's progression does not belie the human perception of divine omniscience and omnipotence.

On the other hand, a different line of analysis with regard to God's continuing progression can be drawn from Joseph Smith's teaching. This perspective focuses on Smith's statement that when Christ consummates the redemption of the earth and its inhabitants, it "will add to [the Father's] glory" and the Father "will take a Higher exaltation."[61] Here the argument is that God progresses not in knowledge but in glory by saving ever more of his creations, particularly those created in his image. "For behold, this is my work and my glory to bring to pass the immortality and eternal life of man" (Moses 1:39). "*In this,*" emphasized twentieth-century apostle and later church president Joseph Fielding Smith, "*is his progression.*"[62] The more worlds God creates, populates, and saves, the greater his glory. This is the only change or "progression" that God experiences according to advocates of this position. His character and attributes, his omniscience and omnipotence, are unchangingly and infinitely perfect and have been so ever since he reached Godhood. An influential twentieth-century commentary on the Doctrine and Covenants included this statement: "[God] is continually progressing in his works, expanding his dominions, creating worlds to be peopled by his children, and thus he is progressing, but in knowledge ... and other like virtues, he dwells in perfection."[63]

---

60. Stephen Webb summarized his take on this Mormon view in this way: "Matter is motion, and becoming closer to the divine is its goal. The whole universe is involved in a game of catch-up with God, who is matter's leading edge and guiding spirit." Webb, *Mormon Christianity*, 109.

61. *JSP,* D14:338.

62. *Doctrines of Salvation,* 1:7.

63. *DCC,* 199.

This understanding of God's progression explicitly rejects the idea that God progresses in knowledge. As Orson Pratt saw it, for God there is an "end of all progression in knowledge, because there [is] nothing more to be learned. The Father and the Son do not progress in knowledge, because they already know all things past, present, and to come."[64] A century later, church leader Neal Maxwell elaborated: "The omniscience of God in the minds of some well-meaning Latter-day Saints has been qualified by the concept of 'eternal progression.' Some have wrongly assumed God's progress is related to His acquisition of additional knowledge." Yet this is not so, explained Maxwell. "God derives His great and continuing joy and glory by increasing and advancing His creations, and not from new intellectual experiences. There is a vast difference, therefore, between an omniscient God and the false notion that God is on some sort of post-doctoral fellowship, still searching for additional key truths and vital data."[65] Then, in reasoning common to Christian defenders of divine omniscience, Maxwell concluded, "Were the latter so, God might, at any moment, discover some new truth not previously known to Him that would restructure, diminish, or undercut certain truths previously known by Him. Prophecy would be mere prediction. Planning assumptions pertaining to our redemption would need to be revised. Fortunately for us, however, His plan of salvation is constantly underway—not constantly under revision."[66]

The idea that God is perfect in knowledge and other divine attributes yet progressing by way of the creative and redemptive endeavors that add to his glory is the view that is promoted in the church's institutional literature today. As an example, in the church's *Doctrines of the Gospel Teacher Manual*, it is suggested that instructors specifically "ask the students" if God is progressing in attributes, knowledge, or power. In each case, the answer to be secured is no. At the same time, teachers are encouraged to affirm that "God does progress." To be clear, both schools of LDS thought regarding the nature of God's "progression"

64. *Seer,* August 1853, 117.

65. Neal A. Maxwell, *All These Things Shall Give Thee Experience* (Salt Lake City: Bookcraft, 1979), 14–15, and reproduced in *Book of Mormon Student Manual* (2009), 358–59. In declaring for absolute omniscience, Maxwell does not, however, make the conventionally concomitant argument that God exists outside time and space. Instead, with the acknowledgment that "we do not understand how," Maxwell simply affirms, based on such passages as D&C 38:2—God "knoweth all things, for all things are present before mine eyes"—that "past, present, and future are before God *simultaneously.*" Neal A. Maxwell, "A More Determined Discipleship," *Ensign,* February 1979, 69.

66. Maxwell, *All These Things,* 359. Joseph Fielding Smith stated simply, if there were truths God did not know, they would be *"greater than he, and this cannot be." Doctrines of Salvation,* 1:7.

affirm the "omnis"—one does so absolutely, the other relatively. And despite their differing perspectives, both proclaim the complete trustworthiness of the Almighty: "The scriptures are explicit that God [is omnipotent and omniscient] and that we can trust him, [but] they have not been explicit about what that means philosophically or theologically."[67] Latter-day Saint thinkers who maintain that God continues to increase in transcendent knowledge and power find congenial the theories of open theism and process theology (affinities detailed in chapter 2), grounded as they are in the same philosophical "finitism" (God exists within, not outside, the universe and time) that Mormonism embraces. Latter-day Saints who advocate such perspectives do not consider them a spiritual liability. Unconditional faith and devotion do not require an unconditioned God, only a Being whose purposes cannot be overcome by finite limitations.

Divine Simplicity and Divine Impassibility

As noted in the introduction, the accessible character of institutional LDS theology means that it rarely engages the technical aspects of classical theism or does so in standard philosophical language.[68] Still, Mormonism's notably nonphilosophical orientation does not entail automatic disagreement with all theistic propositions. In one sense, this is even true of the doctrine of "divine simplicity," which in its basic propositions seems far from Latter-day Saint theology. Formally speaking, divine simplicity is about God's/divine essence's lack of composition. That is, God is one, indivisible, not made up of parts. The Father, Son, and Holy Spirit are not simply third parts of God; each of the Three is identical with the entirety of the one God. These are ideas to which Mormon theology is clearly opposed. Yet simplicity can also be understood as rooting all the divine attributes in the divine essence. As Aquinas wrote, "In God, power, essence, will, intellect, wisdom, and justice are all identical. Nothing therefore can be in God's power which could not be in his just will or his wise intellect."[69] This is closer to Mormon thought. Although analytically and didactically useful, "the distinctions between

---

67. *Encyclopedia of Mormonism*, 4 vols. (New York: Macmillan, 1992), s.v. "foreknowledge of God."

68. Some philosophically trained Mormons, however, have engaged these issues in traditional theological fashion. See Sterling M. McMurrin in *Philosophical Foundations of Mormon Theology* (Salt Lake City: University of Utah Press, 1959) and *Theological Foundations of the Mormon Religion* (Salt Lake City: University of Utah Press, 1965). A subsequent, equally sophisticated, exploration in greater depth is Blake T. Ostler, *Exploring Mormon Thought: The Attributes of God* (Sandy, UT: Kofford Books, 2001).

69. Aquinas, *Summa Theologiae* 1a.25.5.

the attributes result from the creature's incapacity to comprehend infinite being in a non-discursive way. . . . Creatures must conceive of God serially and cumulatively, by enumeration and division of what is in itself one. And so to say 'God is good, wise, and loving' is not to add anything to the statement 'God is' but simply to speak of God in the only way available to temporal, finite creatures."[70] Latter-day Saints may not, in the fashion of divine-simplicity argumentation, pointedly state that in terms of God's interior life there is no distinction, say, between "justice" and "mercy." They would, however, be sympathetic to the idea that the qualities so named, however they are best understood, are intrinsic to the divine nature in a way that eludes full human comprehension.

Another aspect of classical theism that is of special interest in relationship to Mormon theology is the doctrine of divine impassibility. The word "impassibility" (*apatheia*) technically refers to an absence of feeling or emotion and an incapability of suffering. The classical attraction to impassibility as an attribute of God lay in its reinforcement of God's unchanging nature, his immutability. If God could be affected in some way by his creations, if he could be moved or persuaded by a creature's suffering or pleas, then that would imply the Creator's previous condition was imperfect. It would also imply that God as a "necessary" (uncaused, self-existent) being was in some way dependent on or influenced by "contingent" (caused, created) being, a metaphysical impossibility. Thus, God in his inner being had to be thought of as "impassive"—passionless, entirely impervious to emotion, suffering, or pain. Such philosophical reasoning, however, has always presented something of a theological problem because of the Bible's numerous depictions of God's emotions. A common solution has been to classify such anthropomorphic language as a divine accommodation to the weakness of human comprehension.[71] A variation on this theme was expressed by early church father Origen, who wrote, "We speak, indeed, of the 'wrath' of God. We do not, however, assert that it indicates any 'passion' on His part, but that it is something which is assumed in order to discipline by stern means those sinners who have committed many and grievous sins."[72]

---

70. Webster, "Attributes, Divine," 48. A probing discussion of divine simplicity is Paul R. Hinlicky, *Divine Simplicity: Christ the Crisis of Metaphysics* (Grand Rapids: Baker Academic, 2016).

71. "Such modes of expression," wrote Calvin, "do not so much express what kind of a being God is, as accommodate the knowledge of him to our feebleness." Calvin, *Institutes* 1.13.1. See also the chapter entitled "Divine Accommodation," in Paul Helm, *John Calvin's Ideas* (New York: Oxford University Press, 2004), 184–208.

72. Origen, *Against Celsus* 4.72, in *ANF*, 4:529.

Understood as uncontrolled emotion, passion is not becoming of Deity, but passion as a positive emotional force is. "The Father himself and God of all," added Origen, "is long-suffering, merciful and pitiful. Has he not then in a sense passions? The Father himself is not impassible. He has the passion of love."[73] In attempting to cling to a notion of impassibility, medieval theologians such as Anselm and Aquinas distinguished between humans experiencing the merciful *effects* of God's perfect nature and God himself *feeling* mercy. "Is God merciful?" asked Aquinas in his *Summa*. Yes, it is appropriate to "attribute mercy to God, but in its effect, not as a sentiment or feeling." Although it "belongs to [God] to drive away the misery of another," in God's inner being he "does not *feel* sad about another's misery."[74] A different tack was taken by early church father John Chrysostom, who wrote paradoxically of God's "impassible yet fervent" love. For Chrysostom, "impassibility means not that God . . . surveys existence with Epicurean impassivity from the shelter of a metaphysical insulation, but that His will is determined from within instead of being swayed from without." Thus, his love is born not of passionate and changing impulses, but is a consistent, unchanging act of will.[75]

In its strictest formulation, divine impassibility fell on hard times in the twentieth century, particularly in the aftermath of two world wars.[76] Many Christians had come to believe that the horrors of the first half of the century demanded a God who is not the remote and static deity of classical theism but who is dynamically engaged with his creatures and sympathetic to their suffering.[77] This would require a passible God, one who can "be touched with the feeling of our infirmities" (Heb. 4:15). The expectation in today's "more

---

73. Origen, *Homilies on Ezekiel* 6.6, as quoted in William C. Placher and Derek R. Nelson, *A History of Christian Theology*, 2nd ed. (Louisville: Westminster John Knox, 2013), 51.

74. Brian Davies and Brian Leftow, eds., *Thomas Aquinas, "Summa Theologiae": Questions on God* (New York: Cambridge University Press, 2006), 255 (emphasis added).

75. See Christopher A. Hall, *Learning Theology with the Church Fathers* (Downers Grove, IL: InterVarsity Press, 2002), 184–85.

76. Richard Bauckham, "'Only the Suffering God Can Help': Divine Possibility in Modern Theology," *Themelios* 9 (April 1984): 6–12. Although Thomas Weinandy goes on to support the traditional view, in the first chapter of his *Does God Suffer?* (Edinburgh: T&T Clark, 2000), he provides a succinct overview of the arguments for a passible God. A range of views is explored in Robert J. Matz and A. Chadwick Thornhill, eds., *Divine Impassibility: Four Views of God's Emotions and Suffering* (Downers Grove, IL: IVP Academic, 2019).

77. See Ronald Goetz, "The Suffering God: The Rise of a New Orthodoxy," *Christian Century*, April 1986, 385–89. Goetz writes, "The age-old dogma that God is impassible and immutable, incapable of suffering, is for many no longer tenable. The ancient theopaschite heresy that God suffers has, in fact, become the new orthodoxy" (385).

relational or participative view of God" is that "it would be an imperfection not to know affectively what creaturely experiences are like."[78] For God to truly love humanity, he must be vulnerable to human pain and suffering. True love entails being able to suffer in solidarity with the beloved. Although the idea of divine passibility in one form or another has been around since the early centuries, its renewed emphasis in the twentieth century included, somewhat ironically, philosophical support. Philosopher Grace Jantzen, for instance, saw an absolutely, immutably perfect God as less worthy of worship. "Would not a being who had a choice in the matter and consistently chose the good be more worthy of worship than a righteous robot who was necessarily good?"[79] Moreover, watershed work by philosophers Alfred North Whitehead and Charles Hartshorne critiqued classical theism and, among other revisions, argued for divine openness to creaturely influence.[80] As just one example of this reasoning, if God were completely impassible, so that nothing could act upon or influence him, how could petitionary prayer affect him in any meaningful way?

In the realm of Christian theology per se, divine passibility was urged by Dietrich Bonhoeffer, the German pastor-theologian who was imprisoned and ultimately executed for his opposition to the Nazi regime during World War II, and especially in the writings of later German theologian Jürgen Moltmann. Bonhoeffer, reflecting theologically on his experiences, wrote famously to a friend in 1944 that "only the suffering God can help." On another occasion, he stressed that "suffering and God is not a contradiction but rather a necessary unity; for me the idea that God himself is suffering has always been one of the most convincing teachings of Christianity."[81] Bonhoeffer had come to the firm conviction that God suffered in solidarity with suffering humanity. Moltmann wrote the highly influential *Crucified God*, in which he argued that impassibility, if true, would be a deficiency in Deity. "For a God who is incapable of suffering is a being who cannot be involved" and who "cannot love either." This

78. Keith Ward, "Cosmos and Kenosis," in *The Work of Love: Creation as Kenosis*, ed. John Polkinghorne (Grand Rapids: Eerdmans, 2001), 157.

79. Grace Jantzen, "On Worshipping an Embodied God," *Canadian Journal of Philosophy* 8 (September 1978): 515.

80. Accessible introductions to the thought of Whitehead and Hartshorne include C. Robert Mesle, *Process-Relational Philosophy: An Introduction to Alfred North Whitehead* (West Conschocken, PA: Templeton, 2008), and Charles Hartshorne, *The Divine Relativity of God* (New Haven: Yale University Press, 1948).

81. The first quote is from Bonhoeffer to Eberhard Bethge, July 16, 1944, in *Dietrich Bonhoeffer Works*, vol. 8, *Letters and Papers from Prison*, ed. John W. de Gruchy (Minneapolis: Fortress, 2010), 479. The second quote is from Bonhoeffer to the Leibholz family, May 21, 1942, *Letters and Papers from Prison*, 479n41.

is a truth captured in the popular aphorism "love is what we've been through together." An impassible God, Moltmann added poignantly, "cannot weep, for he has no tears."[82] Yet such divine passibility does not entail human-like mood swings. It is God's will and choice, born of divine wisdom and compassion, to suffer with humanity. The issue is not whether God is completely feeling-less, but whether or not those feelings are rational or irrational, voluntary or involuntary. What is really at stake is God's constancy and reliability.[83]

Latter-day Saint theology is very much in line with the idea of a "suffering God." Mormonism's belief that God is the Father, not just the Creator, of human souls leads naturally to an assumption of deep paternal compassion. Arguably the most powerful LDS expression of divine passibility appears in a revelation Joseph Smith received that describes an interaction between God and the biblical Enoch. In the account, God shows Enoch successive moments in human history, including the flood. At one point, when describing the future waywardness of humanity, God actually weeps. Enoch is stunned and asks, "How is it that thou canst weep, seeing thou art holy, and from all eternity to all eternity?" The Lord replies, "Behold these thy brethren; they are the workmanship of mine own hands, and I gave unto them . . . commandment, that they should love one another, and that they should choose me, their Father; but behold, they are without affection, and they hate their own blood" (Moses 7:29–33).[84] Not surprisingly, Mormon notions of divine passibility resonate with Martin Luther's "theology of the cross" and its assertion that the Father suffered with and for the Son as the Son suffered the physical

---

82. Jürgen Moltmann, *The Crucified God: The Cross of Christ as the Foundation and Criticism of Christian Theology* (New York: Harper & Row, 1974), 222. Upholding a traditional doctrine of impassibility are Weinandy, *Does God Suffer?*, and William C. Placher, *Narratives of a Vulnerable God: Christ, Suffering, and Scripture* (Louisville: Westminster John Knox, 1994).

83. Paul L. Gavrilyuk, *The Suffering of the Impassible God: The Dialectics of Patristic Thought* (Oxford: Oxford University Press, 2004), argues that in reality patristic notions of impassibility always made room for a kind of divine passibility. Furthermore, in the context of the times, Stoic *apatheia* did not mean complete absence of emotion. The Stoic "wise man" (*sophos*) experienced "good emotions" (*eupatheiai*) such as joy or caution but had overcome irrational passions and immature reactions. Troels Engberg-Pedersen, *Paul and the Stoics* (Louisville: Westminster John Knox, 2000), 70–73.

84. Popular twenty-first-century LDS writers Terryl and Fiona Givens produced a book-length essay based on the assumption of a possible God tellingly entitled *The God Who Weeps: How Mormonism Makes Sense of Life* (Salt Lake City: Deseret Book, 2012). Previously, Mormon philosopher David Paulsen explored the broader Christian turn to the idea of a suffering God and its harmonies with Latter-day Saint beliefs in "Are Christians Mormon? Reassessing Joseph Smith's Theology in His Bicentennial," *BYU Studies Quarterly* 45 (2006): 52–62.

pain of the crucifixion. From one perspective, the majesty of God is found in his suffering even more than his glory. As eloquent as any Lutheran or Molt-mannian description of God suffering in solidarity with his beloved Son on the cross, Latter-day Saint apostle Melvin Ballard penned this description: "In that hour I think I can see our dear Father, behind the veil looking upon these dying struggles until even he could not endure it any longer . . . so he bowed his head, and hid in some part of his universe, his great heart almost breaking for the love that he had for his Son."[85]

The Trinity

Almost from the beginning, Christianity seemed to present a challenge to the monotheism of its Jewish matrix. How could there be only one God if Jesus was also worshiped as God? This simple question was anything but simple to answer. Indeed, it took years to formulate a response deemed satisfactory by a majority of early Christianity's theologian-bishops. The fourth century was pivotal in this process and has been characterized as the century of the "Trin-itarian Controversy."[86] Even then, the eventual consensus that God is three "persons" in one "being" or "substance" produced more assent than under-standing. In spite of countless attempts across subsequent centuries to explain the mystery of the Three-in-One God, even the most brilliant theologians have had to conclude that in the end the doctrine of the Trinity is indeed a divine mystery, something that is beyond full comprehension. Contemporary Catholic theologian Paul Molnar remarked, "No one can explain *how* God can be One Being, Three Persons. One can only acknowledge the mystery in faith."[87] Protestant theologian Robert Jenson concurred, calling the doctrine of the Trinity "Christianity's big, difficult thing."[88] And the difficulty cannot

---

85. Melvin Ballard, "His Great Heart Almost Breaking," in Bryant S. Hinckley, *Sermons and Missionary Services of Melvin Joseph Ballard* (Salt Lake City: Deseret Book, 1949), 151–55.

86. This story is thoroughly told in R. P. C. Hanson, *The Search for the Christian Doc-trine of God: The Arian Controversy, 318–381* (Edinburgh: T&T Clark, 1988). Subsequent scholarly refinements can be found in Lewis Ayres, *Nicaea and Its Legacy: An Approach to Fourth-Century Trinitarian Theology* (New York: Oxford University Press, 2004), and Khaled Anatolios, *Retrieving Nicaea: The Development and Meaning of Trinitarian Doctrine* (Grand Rapids: Baker Academic, 2011). See also Gilles Emery and Matthew Levering, eds., *The Oxford Handbook of the Trinity* (Oxford: Oxford University Press, 2011).

87. Paul D. Molnar, "Response to Thomas H. McCall," in *Two Views on the Doctrine of the Trinity*, ed. Jason S. Sexton (Grand Rapids: Zondervan, 2014), 146.

88. Robert W. Jenson, *Theology in Outline: Can These Bones Live?* (New York: Oxford University Press, 2016), 41. Of the doctrine of the Trinity, historian Cyril Richardson

be resolved by simply claiming that a favorite theory is "biblical" while others are not. All Trinitarian interpretations draw on scripture, but these readings are always influenced by theological tradition.[89]

Little wonder, then, that theological discussion of how best to understand the relationship of Father, Son, and Holy Spirit has generated controversy. In addition to the earlier Trinitarian controversy of the patristic era, this has been particularly true since 1500. Notable challenges began to arise along the fringes of the Reformation as some Reformers carried the Protestant principle of *sola scriptura* to its logical conclusion, pointing out that the term "trinity" nowhere appears in the Bible, nor do the philosophical and nonbiblical concepts of "essence" and "nature" embedded in the creedal pronouncements of the fourth and fifth centuries. "The antitrinitarian critique of the unbiblical nature of the Trinity was couched in its desires to complete the Reformation."[90] Especially through the influence of various Italian reformers, these ideas became dominant in Polish Protestantism and were widely debated elsewhere in Europe in the later sixteenth century.[91] Often, anti-Trinitarianism led to a form of Unitarianism as the more logical and scriptural doctrine. Prominent sixteenth-century anti-Trinitarian Unitarians included Michael Servetus (burned to death for his beliefs) and Fausto Sozzini/Faustus Socinus (whence "Socinianism," a type of Unitarianism).[92] More sustained criticism was mounted in seventeenth-

---

quipped, "It has been observed that by denying it one may be in danger of losing one's soul, while by trying to understand it one may be in danger of losing one's wits." Richardson, "The Enigma of the Trinity," in *A Companion to the Study of St. Augustine*, ed. Roy W. Battenhouse (New York: Oxford University Press, 1955), 235.

89. As one scholar has noted, the practice of labeling a concept "biblical" often ends up being "a way of identifying interpretations of Christian Scripture with which we agree, and those which diverge are [classed as] 'unbiblical'" and pushed to the margins. Kent Eilers, review of *A Human-Shaped God: Theology of an Embodied God*, by Charles Halton, *Didaktikos 2021 Fall Books Preview*, 34.

90. Paul C. H. Lim, *Mystery Unveiled: The Crisis of the Trinity in Early Modern England* (New York: Oxford University Press, 2012), 11.

91. See Benjamin R. Merkle, *Defending the Trinity in the Reformed Palatinate: The Elohistae* (New York: Oxford University Press, 2016), 25–38. Merkle points out that "the reasoning process by which Calvin dismissed the Trinitarian significance of some of" the biblical texts traditionally used to support the doctrine of the Trinity "was easily aped, or just more radically applied, by the anti-Trinitarians, who largely credited the Reformed church for having taught them how to read the Bible." And "though there are exceptions, anti-Trinitarianism, when it surfaced, almost always surfaced within a Reformed church" (38).

92. Servetus first advanced his anti-Trinitarianism in *De Trinitatis Erroribus* (1531), with a fuller expression in *Christianismi Restitutio* (1553). Socinus's theology and influence are discussed throughout Lim, *Mystery Unveiled*. See also Robert Dan and Antal Pirnat, eds.,

century England by the likes of John Milton, John Biddle, and John Locke, and the eighteenth century witnessed a full-scale assault on Trinitarianism from within the ranks of the French and English Enlightenment.[93]

By the nineteenth century, even leading mainstream theologians demurred from the doctrine. Friedrich Schleiermacher relegated discussion of the Trinity to the conclusion of his two-volume opus *Christian Doctrine*, and the later "liberal" theologians of the nineteenth century considered discussion of the Trinity benignly irrelevant. Furthermore, critics of the doctrine never tired of pointing out the disconnect between Trinitarian language and the language of the Bible. Only in the twentieth century, beginning with the daring proposal of Karl Barth in *Christian Dogmatics* that theology should *start* with the doctrine of the Trinity, did a resurgence of interest in the Trinity manifest itself. A generation later, in the 1960s, major Catholic theologian Karl Rahner contributed significantly to the century's Trinitarian revival. Rahner commenced his influential volume *The Trinity* by bemoaning earlier attitudes (such as Immanuel Kant's) that the doctrine served no practical purpose, that "should the doctrine of the Trinity have to be dropped as false, the major part of religious literature could well remain virtually unchanged."[94] The renaissance of interest in Trinitarianism stimulated by Barth, Rahner, and others flourished in the closing quarter of the twentieth century and has continued unabated into the twenty-first century.[95]

The Church of Jesus Christ of Latter-day Saints was birthed during the nineteenth-century nadir of Trinitarianism in America and the high tide of the biblicism that fueled Trinitarianism's decline. Anti-Trinitarianism could

---

Antitrinitarianism in the Second Half of the 16th Century (Leiden: Brill, 1982). For Anabaptist anti-Trinitarianism, see George H. Williams, *The Radical Reformation* (Philadelphia: Westminster, 1962).

93. Anti-Trinitarianism in this period is helpfully overviewed in Ulrich L. Lehner, "The Trinity in the Early Modern Era (c. 1550–1770)," in Emery and Levering, *The Oxford Handbook of the Trinity*, 240–53. For England, see Lim, *Mystery Unveiled*, and Hans Hillerbrand, "The Decline and Fall of the True Christian Church: The English Deist View," *Zeitschrift für Religions- und Geistesgeschichte* 60 (2008): 97–110. Maurice F. Wiles, *Archetypal Heresy: Arianism through the Centuries* (Oxford: Oxford University Press, 1996), provides helpful contextualization. For eighteenth-century America, see Conrad Wright, *The Beginnings of Unitarianism in America* (Boston: Beacon, 1955). For Britain, see Matthew Kadane, "Anti-Trinitarianism and the Republican Tradition in Enlightenment Britain," *Republics of Letters: A Journal for the Study of Knowledge, Politics, and the Arts* 2 (December 2010): 38–54.

94. Karl Rahner, *The Trinity*, trans. Joseph Donceel (London: Continuum, 1970), 10–11.

95. Reliable entrées into the scholarship of the Trinitarian revival and Trinitarianism in general include Emery and Levering, *The Oxford Handbook of the Trinity*, and Peter C. Phan, ed., *The Cambridge Companion to the Trinity* (Cambridge: Cambridge University Press, 2011).

be found among a variety of religious groups, ranging from highbrow New England Unitarians to populist Christian primitivists (seekers after the first, "primitive," church). Some argued that God was (spiritually) corporeal and therefore physically separate from Christ and the Holy Spirit. Hiram Mattison, a Methodist minister concerned with such developments, provided examples: "[William] Kinkade has a chapter of fifteen pages to show that God has a body like man. [Jabez] Chadwick says he is 'prepared to defend' this sentiment; and Elder G. Fancher says, 'God has a body, eyes, ears, hands, feet, &c., just as we have.'" In other words, "most of them believe there are two bodies in Heaven, namely, the body of God, and the body of Christ—that God is literally seated on a throne, and that Christ sits at his right hand."[96] Joseph Smith had his own visionary reasons for making similar declarations: "Any person that has seen the heavens opened knows that [there are] three personages in the heavens."[97] Smith found support for what he concluded from his visions, among other places, in a prima facie reading of Christ's prayer in John 17, which seemed to compel a figurative understanding of divine oneness. Jesus prayed to the Father that his disciples "may be one, as we are," that they "may be one; as thou, Father, art in me, and I in thee, that they also may be one in us" (vv. 11, 21).[98] For Smith, this text revealed that Trinitarian unity was metaphorical, not metaphysical. Otherwise, continued Smith satirically, if all the disciples "are to be crammed into 1 God," he would be "a wonderful big God—he would be a Giant." Instead, argued Smith, the meaning of John 17 could best be grasped by replacing the word "one" with "agreed": "I am agreed with the Fa[the]r & the Fa[the]r is agreed with me & we are agreed as one."[99] Whatever may be the best reading of John 17, Joseph Smith's doctrine that both the Father and the

96. Hiram Mattison, *A Scriptural Defence of the Doctrine of the Trinity, Or A Check to Modern Arianism, as Taught by Unitarians, Hicksites, New Lights, Universalists and Mormons; and Especially by a Sect Calling Themselves "Christians"* (New York, 1846), 44.

97. *JSP*, D12:386.

98. A detailed theological study of John 17 from a broader Christian perspective is Marianus Pale Hera, *Christology and Discipleship in John 17* (Tübingen: Mohr Siebeck, 2013). Although Smith's interpretation has been common among non-Trinitarians, the early counter by Gregory of Nyssa has also been typical: "Since we are all by [spiritual] participation conjoined with Christ's unique body, we become one single body, viz. His." Cited in J. N. D. Kelly, *Early Christian Doctrines*, 5th ed. (New York: Harper & Row, 1978), 404.

99. *JSP*, D15:271. Latter-day Saints also find in Acts 4:32 and Moses 7:18 parallels for interpreting the oneness discussed in John 17 as agreement or concord among believers. The Book of Mormon discusses the divine oneness in terms of unified witness: "And thus will the Father bear record of me, and the Holy Ghost will bear record unto [you] of the Father and me; for the Father, and I, and the Holy Ghost are one" (3 Nephi 11:36).

Son are physically embodied made inconceivable any Trinitarian notion that the two shared the same numerically identical substance.

Latter-day Saints, of course, are not the only Christians who have discussed the oneness of God in volitional terms. As far back as the third century, Origen identified agreement of will as a crucial aspect of divine oneness. In his *Commentary on John*, Origen explained that the Son's perfect cooperation with the will of the Father made it such that "the will of the Son has become indistinguishable from the will of the Father, and there are no longer two wills but one. It was because of this one will that the Son said, 'I and the Father are one.'" In *Against Celsus*, Origen affirmed that while Christians "worship only one God, the Father and the Son . . . they are two distinct existences [hypostases], but one in mental unity, agreement, and identity of will."[100] In the lengthy fourth-century controversy over the Trinity, the middle decades saw the momentum shift temporarily to those who opposed Nicene assumptions about God. In 341, for instance, the Council of Antioch interpreted Jesus's command to baptize in the name of the Father, Son, and Holy Spirit as not only "indicating the distinct existences and order among the three," but also as defining their oneness as "that of 'agreement' rather than substance."[101]

Although the Mormon doctrine of divine corporeality prevents belief in the substantial unity of the Trinity, Latter-day Saints are as committed to proclaiming the oneness of the Father, Son, and Holy Ghost as they are to declaring their distinctness. In an influential address from early in the twenty-first century, apostle Jeffrey Holland explained, "We believe these three divine persons constituting a single Godhead [Trinity] are united in purpose, in manner, in testimony, in mission. We believe Them to be filled with the same godly sense of mercy and love, justice and grace, patience, forgiveness, and redemption. I think it is accurate to say we believe They are one in every significant and eternal aspect imaginable *except* believing Them to be three persons combined in one substance."[102] In the LDS view, only in material constitution are the Father, Son, and Holy Ghost distinguishable. This leads them to agree with philosopher John Stuart Mill, who argued that "if a plurality [of divine persons] be supposed" and there is "so complete a concert of action and unity

100. Origen, *Commentary on John* 13.228 and *Against Celsus* 8.12, as quoted in Christopher A. Beeley, *The Unity of Christ: Continuity and Conflict in Patristic Tradition* (New Haven: Yale University Press, 2012), 25, 27.

101. Khaled Anatolios, "Sacraments in the Fourth Century," in *OHST*, 145.

102. Jeffrey R. Holland, "The Only True God and Jesus Christ Whom He Hath Sent," *Ensign*, November 2007, 40.

of will among them, [then] the difference is for most purposes immaterial between such a theory and that of the absolute unity of the Godhead."[103]

In the long historical debate over the nature of the Trinity, the danger has always been present that too strong an emphasis on the oneness of God could lapse into a position ruled out of bounds in the early third century known as Monarchianism or modalism. At that time, certain strict Christian monotheists so stressed the singularity of God as "monad" (an indivisible unit of being) that they apparently taught that Son and Holy Spirit were merely God the Father by other names. Tertullian, the prolific Carthaginian lawyer-theologian, devoted an entire tract to combating one such individual named Praxeas, and Hippolytus of Rome attacked another known as Noetus.[104] Praxeas and Noetus reportedly taught that the Father himself as "Son" entered the womb of Mary and became Jesus. Such a notion prompted critics to claim the Monarchians "crucified the Father." As a result, this version of Unitarianism was mocked as *Patripassianism* ("Father-suffers"-ism). In the Greek East, Monarchianism was typically designated "Sabellianism," after a "heretic" named Sabellius who near the time of the controversies with Praxeas and Noetus was excommunicated by Pope Callistus for teaching something similar. The term "modalist" has also seemed an appropriate epithet for these extreme monotheists because of their notion that Father, Son, and Holy Ghost are merely names for the successive "modes" or phases through which the one God is thought to interact with the world. From a modalist perspective, God functioned as Father when he created the world, as Son when he became incarnate to redeem it, and now as Holy Spirit, who superintends and sanctifies the Christian community.[105] Although such views were repudiated by early Christian leaders, modalist thinking in various forms cast a long shadow in the centuries that followed and regularly had to be challenged. Some in the fourth century who opposed the Nicene Creed's use of *homoousios* (same/identical substance) to describe

---

103. John Stuart Mill, *Three Essays on Religion: Nature, the Utility of Religion, and Theism* (London, 1874), 133, as quoted in B. H. Roberts, *The Mormon Doctrine of Deity* (Salt Lake City: Deseret News, 1903), 138.

104. See Ernest Evans, ed. and trans., *Tertullian's Treatise against Praxeas* (London: SPCK, 1948), and Hippolytus, *Against Noetus*, in *The Cambridge Edition of Early Christian Writings*, vol. 1, *God*, ed. and trans. Andrew Radde-Gallwitz (Cambridge: Cambridge University Press, 2017), 58–70.

105. For more on patristic modalism, see Franz Dunzl, *A Brief History of the Doctrine of the Trinity in the Early Church* (London: T&T Clark, 2007), and James L. Papandrea, *Novatian of Rome and the Culmination of Pre-Nicene Orthodoxy*, Princeton Theological Monograph Series (Eugene, OR: Pickwick, 2011).

the relationship between the Father and the Son did so on the grounds that it seemed to promote belief in a Sabellian "Sonfather" (*huiopatōr*).[106]

As with the early opponents of Nicaea, Mormons, too, sometimes mistake Trinitarianism for Sabellianism or modalism. Unaware of the philosophical subtleties of the doctrine, it has seemed to some Latter-day Saints that the only rational way people could account for the divine Three-in-One is through some form of modalism. From the fourth century onward, however, Trinitarians have been as anxious as any to affirm distinctions within the Trinity. Key here was the early linguistic wrestle with the terms *hypostasis* and *persona*, both of which could be rendered as "person."[107] The Latin term *persona*, which had been used in the West since Tertullian first described the Trinity as three *personae* in one *substantia*, was difficult to translate acceptably into Greek. *Prosōpon*, the common choice, tended to connote outward appearance. It was the usual Greek word for "face" or "countenance" and could also refer to the mask an actor wore to identify the role he was playing at the moment. Because of *prosōpon*'s connotations of appearance and superficiality rather than essence and because of its potential to (mis)communicate modalist ideas of the Trinity, the Greek fathers rarely used the word. Instead, "hypostasis" became their preferred equivalent to the Latin *persona*, and they described the Trinity as consisting of three "hypostases."

On the other hand, a literal interpretation of *hypostasis* (*hypo*—"under," *stasis*—"standing, state") could be translated into Latin as *substantia*. Talk of three hypostases, therefore, could strike Latin ears as veering dangerously close to implying three Gods (tritheism) or divine substances.[108] However, the linguistic logjam was influentially broken in the late fourth century by three Greek fathers scholars label the "Cappadocians" (from a region in Turkey)—Basil of Caesarea, Gregory of Nazianzus, and Gregory of Nyssa. These theologians explicated *hypostasis* as "distinct individuality" or "individual existence" and favored another Greek term for substance or being—*ousia*. This enabled the

---

106. Stuart G. Hall, *Doctrine and Practice in the Early Church*, 2nd ed. (London: SPCK, 2005), 79; and Peter Heather, *Christendom: The Triumph of a Religion, AD 300–1300* (New York: Knopf, 2023), 32–35.

107. See Lucian Turcescu, *Gregory of Nyssa and the Concept of Divine Persons* (New York: Oxford University Press, 2005), and Johannes Zachhuber, "Individuality and the Theological Debate about 'Hypostasis,'" in *Individuality in Later Antiquity*, ed. Alexis Torrance and Johannes Zachhuber (London: Routledge, 2014), 91–110.

108. In classical Greek, *hypostasis* carried multiple meanings and could refer to anything from sediment at the bottom of a pond to the undergirding subject matter of a speech to the foundation that supports something from beneath. Figuratively, *hypostasis* could thus refer to one's "foundation" or ground of hope or confidence, as it is used in a few instances in the New Testament. The KJV does translate it as "person" once in Heb. 1:3.

Cappadocians to account for the divine three-ness by arguing that God was three hypostases while still being a single *ousia*. Gregory of Nazianzus expressed the relationship in these words: "So we adore the Father and the Son and the Holy Spirit, dividing their individualities (hypostases) but uniting their godhead (divinity); and we neither blend the three into one thing, lest we be sick with Sabellius's disease, nor do we divide them into three alien and unrelated things, lest we share Arius's madness."[109] The subtlety of the Cappadocians' formulation of three hypostases in one *ousia* was considered an acceptable equivalent in the Latin West to the confession that God was three *personae* in one *substantia*.[110] By the end of the fourth century, many church fathers in the Greek East and in the Latin West realized they shared a deep commitment to proclaim both God's three-ness and his oneness.

Without attempting to track Trinitarianism in the intervening centuries, our focus shifts now to the recent past. Here Trinitarian discourse may be plotted along a range of opinion from the quasi modalism of Karl Barth with his emphasis on God's three "modes of being" rather than three "persons" to the quasi tritheism of the "social Trinitarians" who envision the Trinity as a "community" of three separate acting agents/"subjects" and three distinct centers of consciousness. Each approach merits brief consideration. Early on, Irenaeus developed a solution about how to reconcile God's oneness and three-ness that in general concept has appealed to Barth and other twentieth-century Trinitarian theologians. Irenaeus distinguished God in his singular, intrinsic being from God in his historically unfolding and self-disclosing interactions with the world. These distinctions have come to be labeled, respectively, the "immanent (internal) Trinity" and the "economic (external) Trinity."[111] The immanent Trinity

---

109. Gregory of Nazianzus, *Orations* 20.5, as quoted in Brian Daley, *Gregory of Nazianzus* (London: Routledge, 2006), 100.

110. Still, there was ambiguity. To the query "three what?" Augustine could only write that "the formula three persons has been coined, not in order to give a complete explanation by means of it, but in order that we might not be obliged to remain silent." Stephen McKenna, trans., *Saint Augustine, "The Trinity"* (Washington, DC: Catholic University of America Press, 1963), 187–88.

111. Here "immanent" and "economic" have specialized theological meanings not obvious in everyday English. "Immanent," from the Latin *immanere*, literally means "to dwell in" or indwell. Thus, the "immanent Trinity" refers to the three divine distinctions (hypostases or "persons") intrinsically indwelling the single, eternal, transcendent Deity. "Economic" preserves the older sense of the Greek *oikonomia*, a composite term that literally referred to the *nomos* ("laws," arrangements, plans) by which an *oikos* or house(hold) was ordered. Theologically, "economy" designates God's grand scheme or plan of cosmic salvation and the ordered process by which, in bringing it about, he discloses himself to the created world.

maintains a three-ness in God's intrinsic, inner being as Father, Son, and Holy Spirit that diverges from the unacceptable modalist notion that the three-ness is merely a figurative conception highlighting the one God's successive roles as creator (Father), redeemer (Son), and sanctifier (Spirit). As for the economic Trinity, Barth emphasized that it corresponds precisely to the inner or "immanent" nature of the Trinity. That is, God's involvement with salvation history is a "repetition" or "reiteration" in time of what God is in his inner being.[112] Or, in the words of Karl Rahner's famous axiom: "The 'economic' Trinity is the 'immanent' Trinity and the 'immanent' Trinity is the 'economic' Trinity."[113] The effort here is to preserve the divine three-ness in the very intrinsic essence of God. Father, Son, and Holy Spirit are three distinct hypostases/persons/modes of being within the eternal and immanent triunity that jointly act to bring about the economy of salvation.

Latter-day Saint theology, of course, with its doctrine of the Trinity as three separate beings, has no need for the finely tuned immanent/economic distinction. Moreover, Mormons would agree with the assessment of Roman Catholic scholar Catherine LaCugna that Western theology has tended to "ignore God's revelation in the economy of salvation, preferring to engage in speculative reflection on the [immanent] divine nature itself." In LaCugna's view, "Our knowledge of the eternal being of God should in principle be coextensive with what we have learned from revelation in the divine economy of salvation" because "we have no access to the immanent life of God that goes beyond what has been revealed." LaCugna considers as "pointless and potentially misleading" the distinction between God's "inner and outer aspects" and calls for a return to "the biblical and pre-Nicene pattern of thought."[114] This is an orientation that parallels Latter-day Saint sensibilities.

More satisfactory to Mormon thought than the immanent/economic model of the Trinity is the twentieth-century Trinitarian approach known as "social" or "relational" Trinitarianism. In his 1942–1943 Croall Lectures, pioneering social Trinitarian Leonard Hodgson echoed anti-Trinitarians from earlier centuries and boldly asserted that Barthian Trinitarianism was "in flat contradiction to the biblical evidence." A proper Trinitarianism, Hodgson believed, acknowledges three "distinct Person[s] in the full sense of that word,"

---

112. Alan Torrance, "The Trinity," in *The Cambridge Companion to Karl Barth*, ed. John Webster (Cambridge: Cambridge University Press, 2000), 80–81.

113. Karl Rahner, *The Trinity* (Tunbridge Wells, UK: Burns & Oates, 1970), 22.

114. Catherine LaCugna, *God for Us: The Trinity and Christian Life*, quoted in Alister E. McGrath, *Christian Theology* (Chichester, UK: Wiley-Blackwell, 2011), 259–60.

each of whom "is a He, [not] an it." The Father, Son, and Holy Spirit are three "intelligent, purposive centers of consciousness."[115] Classical Trinitarian opponents of social Trinitarianism insist that "persons" not be understood in a modern, psychological sense lest it be popularly (mis)construed as a synonym for individuals and inadvertently foster tritheism.[116] However "persons" is best understood and whatever label it attracts, talk of the divine persons as three distinct centers of love, will, and knowledge, each of which is a separate personal acting "subject" mutually aware of, and existing in harmony with, the other two, comes very close to Mormon Trinitarianism. For this reason, some independent Latter-day Saint thinkers have endeavored to stay in conversation with Trinitarianism and venture a claim to Mormonism's Trinitarian bona fides by identifying parallels with social/relational Trinitarianism. It should be noted that while no opposition to this move to find common ground with social or relational Trinitarianism has been voiced by LDS church leaders, it is also not a position they have publicly endorsed or that is promoted in the church's institutional literature.[117]

If relational Trinitarianism transgresses conventional boundaries, Mormonism's separate-being Trinitarianism certainly does. And though Latter-day Saint theology shares many of the basic impulses of social Trinitarianism, the latter's undergirding metaphysics is too traditional to allow the conclusion that between social Trinitarianism and Mormonism there is more than a family resemblance. Relational Trinitarianism may describe the Trinity as very much *like* a community, but it falls short of considering it an actual community of three distinct divine beings. In the end, Mormon Trinitarianism is unique. And it is tritheistic. Although deep commitment to divine oneness causes Latter-day Saints to eschew the label "tritheists," technically the appellation

115. Leonard Hodgson, *The Doctrine of the Trinity* (New York: Scribner's Sons, 1944), 39. An accessible introduction to the issues at stake in social Trinitarianism is Cornelius Plantinga Jr., "The Threeness/Oneness Problem of the Trinity," *Calvin Theological Journal* 23 (April 1988): 37–53. See also the chapter on the Trinity in Richard Swinburne, *The Christian God* (New York: Oxford University Press, 1994), 170–91.

116. This aversion goes back at least to the late fourth century when in *Not Three Gods*, Gregory of Nyssa rejected the idea that the three divine hypostases are "filled with individual psychological content." Lewis Ayres, "On Not Three People: The Fundamental Themes of Gregory of Nyssa's Trinitarian Theology as Seen in *To Ablabius: On Not Three Gods*," *Modern Theology* 18 (2002): 470.

117. Most prominent and persistent in this effort is philosopher-theologian David L. Paulsen. See, for instance, the piece he coauthored with Brett McDonald, "Joseph Smith and the Trinity: An Analysis and Defense of the Social Model of the Godhead," *Faith and Philosophy* 25 (January 2008): 47–74.

is accurate since Mormon theology clothes the three distinct divine centers of intellect, love, and will with corporeality—the Father and the Son with glorified bodies of flesh and bone, the Paraclete with spirit corporeality. No matter how emphatically Latter-day Saints emphasize the unity of the Three, they still unapologetically confess, to the dismay of classical Trinitarians, that the divine persons are three Gods. As Joseph Smith expressed it near the end of his life, "I have always declared God to be a distinct personage, Jesus Christ a separate and distinct personage from God the Father, and that the Holy Ghost was a distinct personage and a Spirit: and these three constitute three distinct personages and three Gods."[118] To a local clergyman who expounded his traditional Trinitarian views, Smith remarked, "We don't agree with you. We believe in three Gods. There are three personages in Heaven—all equal in power and glory, but they are not one God."[119]

In reality, speaking of the Father and Son as "Gods" in the plural was not unheard of prior to the Trinitarian controversy of the fourth century as a reflection of the common view that the Son, though divine, was subordinate to the Father. Before Nicaea, "most Christians, even bishops, were in some vague sense subordinationists—that is, they believed that Christ was divine but not quite in the same way that God the Father was divine."[120] As such, "there seemed to be no way around the fact that this theology made it sound as though there is a first and a second God—in other words, two Gods."[121] Second-century apologist Justin Martyr, for instance, regarded the Son as *heteros theos* ("another"/"other" God) distinct from the Father "numerically, I mean, not in will."[122] For Justin, "the Son is not an impersonal power, but another God next to the Father of all, begotten by Him as a distinct person." Justin "thinks that in defending the *heteros theos* doctrine he does nothing more than repeat what the Scriptures say. So he reads Psalms 110:1; Psalms 45:7–8; Proverbs 8:22–31; Genesis 1:26; Genesis 3:22; etc. as irrefutable Scriptural evidence for the existence of another God next to the Father of all."[123] With Justin's reasoning in particular and with

---

118. *Teachings: Joseph Smith*, 41–42; cf. *JSP*, D15:268.

119. *Times and Seasons*, September 1842, 926.

120. Robert L. Wilken, "Why a Creed?" *Christian History and Biography*, Winter 2005, 15. Geza Vermes is more emphatic: "Every single mouthpiece of Christian tradition from Paul and John to Origen firmly held that the Father was in some way above the Son." Vermes, *Christian Beginnings: From Nazareth to Nicaea* (New Haven: Yale University Press, 2013), 241.

121. Ronald E. Heine, *Classical Christian Doctrine* (Grand Rapids: Baker Academic, 2013), 44.

122. Justin Martyr, *Dialogue with Trypho* 56, in *ANF*, 1:223.

123. Demetrius C. Trakatellis, *The Pre-existence of Christ in the Writings of Justin Martyr:*

the general early Christian sense of the Son and Spirit being subordinate to the Father, Latter-day Saints are in agreement.[124]

Although Mormons do not shy away from affirming that the Father, Son, and Holy Spirit are separate divine beings, they also stress, in the words of First Presidency member George Cannon, that "we worship them as one God, not three Gods. . . . We do not separate them in our thoughts and in our feelings."[125] Joseph Fielding Smith elaborated: "It is perfectly true, as recorded in the [Scriptures] that to us there is but one God. Correctly interpreted, God in this sense means Godhead [the term Latter-day Saints commonly use for the Trinity], for it is composed of Father, Son, and Holy Spirit . . . to us, the inhabitants of this world, they constitute the only God, or Godhead . . . unto whom we are subject."[126] Another way some Latter-day Saint leaders affirmed the divine oneness is by arguing that "God" is best understood as a reference to the divine nature itself rather than to the particular Person who participates in it. A being "is called God, not because of his [physical] substance," ventured Orson Pratt, "but because of the qualities which dwell in the substance."[127] B. H. Roberts, in a section of his *Mormon Doctrine of Deity* titled "Of God Being One in a Generic Sense," developed this line of analysis that "God," like "Godhead" in common Christian use, names the set of perfect properties, attributes, and powers that constitutes the divine nature. Roberts further argued

---

An Exegetical Study with Reference to the Humiliation and Exaltation Christology (Missoula, MT: Scholars Press for Harvard University, 1976), 180, 52.

124. Detailed discussion of the LDS perspective on the nature of the Son of God and his relationship to the Father appears in chapter 3.

125. Jerreld L. Newquist, ed., *Gospel Truth: Discourses and Writings of President George Q. Cannon*, 2 vols. (Salt Lake City: Deseret Book, 1974), 1:205.

126. Joseph Fielding Smith, *Answers to Gospel Questions*, 5 vols. (Salt Lake City: Deseret Book, 1957–1966), 2:142. The use of "Godhead" as a synonym for the Trinity is rare elsewhere, Pentecostals being a notable exception. The first definition of "godhead" in the *Oxford English Dictionary* is "The character or quality of being God or a god; divine nature or essence; deity." *OED*, s.v. "godhead." As typically used in Christian discourse, "godhead" refers to properties, not persons, to God-ness or divinity rather than three persons who have that quality. "Godhead" appears only three times in the King James Bible, where it translates *theios, theiotēs*, and *theotēs*, respectively, terms that elsewhere are rendered "divinity," "deity," or "divine nature." This meaning is clear, for instance, in Rom. 1:20: "For the invisible things of him from the creation of the world are clearly seen . . . even his eternal power and Godhead."

127. *Seer*, February 1853, 24. Pratt likened this to the nature of truth: "Truth is not a plurality of truths because it dwells in a plurality of persons, but it is one truth, indivisible, though it dwells in millions of persons" (24).

that the sharing of the divine nature is what qualifies the corporeally distinct Father, Son, and Holy Spirit to be considered one God.[128]

Too great a focus on the divine nature over the divine persons, however, can be doxologically disturbing to Latter-day Saints. In response to Orson Pratt's ideas, Brigham Young remarked: "I worship not the Atributes but that God who holds and dispenses [them]."[129] Still, if one considers that the ancient Greek term *homoousios*, which factored so prominently in the Trinitarian debates of the early centuries, can be translated "shared essence" or "same nature" as well as the usual "identical substance," the similarity with the LDS concept of the corporeally distinct Father, Son, and Holy Spirit sharing a generic divinity is apparent. Nonetheless, it is precisely this application of Aristotle's notion of "universals" and "particulars"—Divinity is the universal; Father, Son, and Holy Spirit are the particular instantiations of it—that Gregory of Nyssa endeavored to combat in his treatise *On Not Three Gods*. At the tract's outset, an unknown interlocutor named Ablabius offers the tritheistic analogy that "Peter, James, and John, being in one humanity, are called three men." So, should not the Father, Son, and Holy Spirit, who share a common divinity, likewise be considered three Gods? While the logic of such reasoning works for Latter-day Saints, the Nyssen negates it in his response to Ablabius by invoking church dogma: "In reference to the divine nature," he writes, "the argument of doctrine rejects the multitude of Gods and counting the hypostases does not admit a plural meaning." From that starting point, the Nyssen spends the rest of his tract attempting to explain why the case with the Trinity is different and why Father, Son, and Holy Spirit are "not three Gods."[130]

Although Latter-day Saints do speak of three Gods—God the Father, God the Son, and God the Holy Ghost—they do not consider their view of a separate-being Trinity to be polytheistic. Twentieth-century apostle Boyd Packer emphasized that acceptance of the Latter-day Saint understanding of the Trinity "does not mean accepting the multiple gods of mythology nor the polytheism of the pagans, which was so roundly condemned by Isaiah and the other

---

128. B. H. Roberts, *The Mormon Doctrine of Deity* (Salt Lake City: Deseret News, 1903), 162–66.

129. Quoted in Gary James Bergera, *Conflict in the Quorum: Orson Pratt, Brigham Young, Joseph Smith* (Salt Lake City: Signature Books, 2002), 139.

130. Gregory of Nyssa, "Concerning We Should Think of Saying That There Are Not Three Gods to *Ablabius*," in *The Trinitarian Controversy*, ed. and trans. William G. Rusch (Philadelphia: Fortress, 1980), 149–50. For theological analysis of the Nyssen's tract, see Cornelius Plantinga Jr., "Gregory of Nyssa and the Social Analogy of the Trinity," *Thomist: A Speculative Quarterly Review* 50 (July 1986): 325–52, and Ayres, "On Not Three People," 445–74.

prophets."[131] Mormons share the early Christian critique of pagan polytheism whose gods "were vulnerable to all too human passions."[132] Even in the earliest pentateuchal sources, "anthropomorphism took on a sophisticated form. . . . The gods of ancient Mesopotamia . . . remain 'crudely' anthropomorphic, while YHWH's anthropomorphic nature" retains its divine otherness and "rejects the perceived crudeness" of "the gods of the rest of the ancient New East."[133] So it is with Mormonism. The Trinity may consist of three separate though intimately united Gods, but Latter-day Saint doctrine intends nothing less than to proclaim a plurality of perfection in a plurality of transcendent, divine Deities.

Another way in which Latter-day Saints have endeavored to resolve the three-ness/oneness conundrum is through a concept they call "the divine investiture of authority." In 1916, the church issued one of the most important theological documents in its history—"The Father and the Son: A Doctrinal Exposition by the First Presidency and the Twelve." This eight-page document was published both in pamphlet form and in the church's principal periodical, the *Improvement Era*.[134] The exposition was intended to finally put "an end to controversy" that had cropped up intermittently during the previous seventy years over the precise identity of the three persons of the Trinity, as well as the nature of their oneness.[135] The controversy reflected Mormon recognition of the same ambiguity in the scriptural statements about Father, Son, and Holy Ghost that other Christians have noticed, as well as differing views among LDS Church leaders.[136] The purpose of "The Father and the Son" was to (1) clarify passages in which the Son is "designated" as the Father, and (2) explain the type of unity that exists among the three distinct personages of the Godhead. The document begins by acknowledging that both the Bible and LDS scripture employ the term "Father" with "plainly different meanings."[137] Before proceeding to discuss the "divine investiture of authority," the document reviews two figurative senses in which Christ may be considered the Father—as creator ("all things were made by him; and without

131. Boyd K. Packer, "The Pattern of Our Parentage," *Ensign*, November 1984, 66.

132. Henry Chadwick, *The Church in Ancient Society: From Galilee to Gregory the Great* (New York: Oxford University Press, 2001), 164.

133. Knafl, *Forming God*, 9.

134. "The Father and the Son," 934–42. The essay was drafted by apostle James Talmage, revised by the full Council of the Twelve and First Presidency, and issued in final form on June 30, 1916 (942).

135. The statement that the document was intended to put an end to the controversy is from *Improvement Era*, August 1916, 952.

136. Aspects of the controversy are summarized in Thomas G. Alexander, *Mormonism in Transition: A History of the Latter-day Saints, 1890–1930* (Urbana: University of Illinois Press, 1986), 289–326.

137. "The Father and the Son," 934.

him was not any thing made that was made"—John 1:3) and as "Father" of the spiritually begotten ("as many as received him, to them gave he power to become the sons of God, even to them that believe on his name"—John 1:12).[138]

The "divine investiture of authority" is the doctrine that the Father "place[s] His name upon the Son," investing him with full authority to act in his name and in his stead such that "His words and acts were and are those of the Father."[139] Thus, the Son, though a separate divine being, can speak in first person as the Father. The "divine investiture of authority" might be considered Mormonism's answer to modalism. Because Latter-day Saints are unequivocal in their insistence that the Three are separate divinities, they can never regard the Son as merely the Father acting in the role or mode of the Son. Yet, as has been noted, there is no lack of scriptural passages that talk about the Son in ways that make him seem identical to the Father. The Mormon way around this is to interpret such passages in terms of authorized representation. This interpretation should not be understood as demoting the Son to the status of heavenly messenger or authorized angel, even though he is subordinate to the Father in the sense that the Father presides over him. The Son is considered divine in every way the Father is and therefore fully able to function "as Father." Yet, he is understood to do so under the Father's direction. Thus, Latter-day Saint separate-being Trinitarianism makes room for a Trinity in which the Son and Holy Spirit are fully and equally divine with the Father, one with him in every way possible for separate beings, yet without collapsing into Unitarianism or even claiming, as some theologians have, that each of the Three is simultaneously and identically involved in all divine actions.[140]

In the end, for a variety of reasons, Mormonism's separate-being Trinitarianism is not likely to rise to the top of today's revitalized Trinitarian proposals. To summarize, several Latter-day Saint positions stand out as particularly radical: (1) The Father, Son, and Holy Spirit are not simply three distinct, divine hypostases but separate, embodied divine beings. (2) Divine nature and human nature are on the same ontological continuum; the vast difference

---

138. This latter notion is even more pointedly stated in LDS scripture. As an example: "And now, because of the covenant which ye have made ye shall be called the children of Christ, his sons, and his daughters; for behold, this day he hath spiritually begotten you; for ye say that your hearts are changed through faith on his name; therefore, ye are born of him and have become his sons and his daughters" (Mosiah 5:7). Additional passages are quoted in "The Father and the Son," 936–39.

139. "The Father and the Son," 940.

140. Adonis Vidu, *The Same God Who Works All Things: Inseparable Operations in Trinitarian Theology* (Grand Rapids: Eerdmans, 2021).

between them is not understood in the classical sense as one of kind, but of degree. (3) Given #2, since more than one human being can possess human nature, more than one divine being can possess or share divinity; each of the three is not the whole of the divine nature, although each is wholly divine. (4) Also given #2 and Mormonism's rejection of a timeless eternity, "eternal progression" becomes a theoretical possibility. Consequently, although from a finite perspective the Trinity has "always" been God, in an absolute sense, the personages of the Trinity have not eternally been divine. These four propositions and corollary concepts represent a significant departure from both classical Trinitarianism and Christian metaphysics, pushing Mormon Trinitarianism beyond the pale of philosophically inflected theism into historically unacceptable tritheism. That said, it should be recognized that all efforts to formulate Trinitarian doctrine, however it is constructed, are inevitably rooted in the theological presuppositions of the formulators. That Latter-day Saint Trinitarianism is similarly influenced merely presents a difference in outcome (albeit dramatic) rather than method.

Ironically, the traditional challenge of adequately accounting for the "three-ness" of God is such that in truth many of the arguments and biblical verses classical Trinitarians use to support the tri-personality of the Trinity are the same ones deployed by Latter-day Saints to support their tritheistic, separate-being Trinitarianism. A prime example is Genesis 1:26—"And God said, Let *us* make man in our image, after *our* likeness." "I ask you," queried Tertullian, "how it is that one only single [person] speaks in the plural . . . when he ought to have said, Let me make man after my image and likeness." And in Genesis 3:22—"the man is become as one of *us*"—was God "deceptive or joking in speaking in the plural while one and alone and singular"?[141] From Tertullian onward, and especially as popularized in the Middle Ages by Peter Lombard's influential textbook *Sentences*, Genesis 1:26 has been a key passage quoted to indicate the plurality of persons in the one divine Trinity.[142] Latter-day Saints, from Joseph Smith's day to the present, have likewise noticed the same plurality in the passage but interpreted it as a plurality of personages or beings, not persons. Joseph Smith's revision of Genesis 1:26 makes it explicit that the passage refers to the Father and the Son: "And I, God, said unto mine Only Begotten,

---

141. Evans, *Tertullian's Treatise against Praxeas*, 145.

142. For Lombard on this point, see Philipp W. Rosemann, *Peter Lombard* (New York: Oxford University Press, 2004), 74. See also Giulio Silano, trans., *Peter Lombard, The Sentences, Book 2: On Creation* (Toronto: Pontifical Institute of Mediaeval Studies, 2008), 68–69. The medieval popularity of using Gen. 1:26 to defend Trinitarianism is discussed in Merkle, *Defending the Trinity*, 3–24.

which was with me from the beginning, Let us make man in our image, after our likeness" (Moses 2:26). This is also clear in the creation account in the Book of Abraham: "And the Gods took counsel among themselves and said: Let us go down and form man in our image, after our likeness" (Abraham 4:26).[143] Still, despite Mormonism's insistence that the three divine Persons are separate and distinct beings, at the heart of Latter-day Saint theology is the common Christian proclamation of their oneness. "The Father, Son, and Holy Ghost are one God in a sense far greater than merely being one in purpose," wrote apostle Bruce McConkie. "They have the same character, perfections, and attributes. They think the same thoughts, speak the same words, perform the same acts. . . . They possess the same power, have the same mind, know the same truths, live in the same light and glory. To know one is to know the other; to see one is to see the other; to hear the voice of one is to hear the voice of the other. Their unity is perfect."[144]

143. In light of his belief in a plurality of divine beings, Joseph Smith preferred to interpret *elohim*, which grammatically is a plural noun, as "Gods." Smith once remarked that he thought *elohim* "ought to be in the plural all the way thro[ugh]" the Bible. *JSP*, D15:271. The passage in Abraham may also be referring to unidentified divine subordinates similar to the Hebrew notion of a primordial divine council (e.g., Ps. 82). Joseph Smith wrote of "the counc[i]l of the eternal God of all other Gods before this world was." *JSP*, D6:370; cf. D&C 121:32.

144. Bruce R. McConkie, *The Promised Messiah: The First Coming of Christ* (Salt Lake City: Deseret Book, 1978), 5, 9. This quote has been reproduced in several church manuals in the 2000s.

GOD

Creation, Providence, and Theodicy

Whereas the last chapter explored the "nature" of God, this chapter examines his "work." First to be considered is God's initial or originating work of creation. Then, the doctrine of providence, God's work of maintaining and providing for his creation, is discussed. In turn, this leads to a detailed exploration of key related issues such as the relationship between divine sovereignty and human freedom, the relationship between divine omnipotence and human agency, and the problem of evil.

CREATION

The Christian doctrine of creation addresses such perennial human inquiries as "How did the universe come to be?" "What is our place and purpose in it?" Answers are found starting with the opening lines of the Bible—"In the beginning God created the heaven and the earth" (Gen. 1:1). Rather than describe existence as the random, chance result of a unique convergence of cosmic forces, God is considered the "First Cause" or creator of the universe. Moreover, in contrast to ancient philosophies that portrayed matter as deficient, if not evil, and creation as the work of an inferior, if not evil, deity, the biblical witness is that "everything created by God is good, and nothing is to be rejected" (1 Tim. 4:4 NRSV). To the Old Testament accounts, Christian theology adds that God created through his only begotten Son—"All things were made by him; and without him was not any thing made that was made" (John 1:3). Furthermore, God had a loving purpose in creating, even if he knew that for a time his goodly creation would be spoiled by the effects of creaturely disobedience. His plan was that in the "fulness of times he might gather together in one all things in Christ, both which are in heaven, and which are on earth; even in him" (Eph. 1:10). Indeed, one of the most important implications of the Christian view of a good material creation is that it proclaims the redemption *of,* not redemption *from,* the created realm. This positive and purposive view of creation requires the corollary doctrine of providence as a kind of "continuing creation" in which God providentially guides his creation to its ultimate goal.

As it developed, another aspect of the Christian doctrine of creation and one that eventually gained prominence was *creatio ex nihilo* (creation out of nothing). Ex-nihilo creation is rooted in the philosophical idea that there are only two orders of existence—God and all else, Creator and created—and before there was an "all else," there was only God. Thus, God had to create out of nothing, since nothing else existed prior to creation. This was not, however, the earliest understanding. The consensus among Jewish and Christian scholars today is that both from a historical and a syntactical standpoint, *creatio ex nihilo* is not in view in the opening verses of Genesis. Commenting on Genesis 1:1, the *New Oxford Annotated Bible* states that scholars disagree on whether the verse should be read as "an independent sentence summarizing what follows" or "as a temporal phrase describing what things were like when God started," but "in either case, the text does not describe creation out of nothing."[1] The *Jewish Study Bible* concurs: Genesis 1:1 "describes things just before the process of creation began. To modern people, the opposite of the created order is 'nothing,' that is, a vacuum. To the ancients, the opposite of the created order was something . . . we can best term 'chaos.'"[2] The divine fashioning of the cosmos from "chaos" is how creation was generally understood in the ancient world and may have been the common view of Jews and Christians until the second century.[3] As succinctly stated in the apocryphal/

---

1. *New Oxford Annotated Bible,* 4th ed. (New York: Oxford University Press, 2010), 11. See also *The Interpreter's Bible* (Nashville: Abingdon, 1978), 1, and *The New Jerome Biblical Commentary* (Englewood Cliffs, NJ: Prentice Hall, 1990), 10–11. Gordon Wenham suggests that of four different ways in which the syntactical relationship between verse 1 and verses 2 and 3 may be construed, all but one "presuppose the existence of chaotic preexistent matter before the work of creation began." *Genesis 1–15,* Word Biblical Commentary (Dallas: Word, 1987), 11.

2. Adele Berlin and Marc Zvi Brettler, eds., *The Jewish Study Bible,* 2nd ed. (New York: Oxford University Press, 2014), 11.

3. Exactly when the notion of *creatio ex nihilo* became commonplace is a matter of scholarly debate. Arguing that the doctrine did not become widely accepted among Christians until the latter part of the second century is Gerhard May, *Creatio Ex Nihilo: The Doctrine of "Creation out of Nothing" in Early Christian Thought,* trans. A. S. Worrall (London: T&T Clark, 2004), and Frances Young, "'Creatio Ex Nihilo': A Context for the Emergence of the Christian Doctrine of Creation," *Scottish Journal of Theology* 44 (May 1991): 139–52. In his Anchor Bible commentary on the Wisdom of Solomon (New York: Doubleday, 1979),

deuterocanonical Wisdom of Solomon, God's "all-powerful hand . . . created the world out of formless matter" (Wis. 11:17). This perspective is reflected in modern English translations such as the NRSV, NABRE, and NJPS. The latter, for instance, translates the initial lines of Genesis as: "When God began to create heaven and earth—the earth being unformed and void, with darkness over the surface of the deep . . . God said, 'Let there be light'" (Gen. 1:1-3). In this rendering, what constitutes creation is God beginning to bring forth an ordered universe from primeval "chaos," the "'formless void' of primordial matter, the 'great deep' or 'abyss.'"[4]

The Mormon doctrine of creation harks back to this earlier Hebraic view. Joseph Smith's Hebrew teacher in the mid-1830s, Joshua Seixas, son of the renowned New York Jewish leader Gershom Mendes Seixas, may well have introduced Smith to this venerable, if by the nineteenth century uncommon, Jewish cosmogony (theory of the origin of the cosmos) and interpretation of Genesis. However he came to his view, Smith argued in an address at the church's 1844 general conference that the opening words of Genesis 1:1— *bere'shit bara Elohim* ("in the beginning God created")—did not require the corollary "out of nothing." Smith considered such an inference neither logically nor etymologically necessary. Instead, he offered his reading that the word *bara*, typically rendered "create," implied that "God Himself had materials to org[anize] the world out of chaos which is Element."[5] Smith acknowledged that the Christian theologians of the day generally "account it blasphemy to contradict the idea" of creation ex nihilo.[6] Yet, not only linguistics but meta-

---

David Winston argues that "the first explicit formulation" of "the concept of creation *ex nihilo* . . . appeared in the second-century Christian literature" (39-40). Challenge to these studies, along with arguments for the earlier appearance of a doctrine of *creatio ex nihilo*, is found in John C. O'Neill, "How Early Is the Doctrine of *Creatio Ex Nihilo*?" *Journal of Theological Studies* 53 (October 2002): 449-65, and Paul Copan and William Lane Craig, *Creation out of Nothing: A Biblical, Philosophical, and Scientific Exploration* (Grand Rapids: Baker Academic, 2004).

4. *OED*, s.v "chaos."

5. *JSP*, D14:321. In his study of Hebrew, Joseph Smith apparently used Josiah M. Gibbs, *A Manual Hebrew and English Lexicon Including the Biblical Chaldee. Designed Particularly for Beginners*, 2nd ed. (New Haven, 1832). *JSP*, J1:107-8. Gibbs defined *bara* as "to form, make, create" (36). The later *Peake's Commentary on the Bible* (London: Nelson, 1962) contends that "it is a mistake to suggest . . . that the Hebrew word *bara* ('made') implies creation *ex nihilo*" (179). Cf. Wenham, *Genesis 1-15*, 14. Still, some scholars find the fact that the verb *bara* is only ever used in the Bible with God as its subject at least opens the door to creation ex nihilo.

6. *JSP*, D14:331.

physics compelled him to do so. Though no fan of Greek philosophy, Joseph Smith ironically and perhaps unwittingly echoed ideas from Plato's cosmogony in *Timaeus*.[7] Like Plato, Smith believed that matter had always existed, that it was coeternal with God: "Element had an existence from the time [God] had," Smith declared, and it "never can have an ending."[8] Revelation put it simply: "The elements are eternal" (D&C 93:33). Since there are cosmic, elemental realities that are "not created or made, neither indeed can be" (D&C 93:29), creation, in Mormon thought, cannot be ex nihilo.

As Smith developed his cosmogony, it diverged, however, from the ancient Hebrew conception of chaos. Primeval element for the Mormon prophet was neither darkness nor watery abyss but "unorganized," eternal matter from which the earth and all other created entities were formed. In a statement that seemed to endorse the recently discovered "law of the conservation of matter (or mass)," Smith remarked, "The pure principles of element are principles that never can be destroyed. They may be organized, and reorganized, but not destroyed."[9] Thus, indestructible matter could change form and be reconfigured countless times. On one occasion, Smith taught that the earth "has been organized o[u]t of portions of other Globes that [have] ben disorganized."[10] Smith's apostolic associate Orson Pratt elaborated: "How many thousands of millions of times the elements of our globe have been organized and disorganized . . . or how widely the particles have been diffused through boundless space . . . is unknown." But they are "in a condition to come together." This should not conjure up images of countlessly disassembling and reassembling Lego blocks since the disorganized elements are "in a state of particles, instead of aggregate masses."[11]

The Book of Abraham describes the "morn of creation" thus: "And there stood one among them [the heavenly council] that was like unto God, and he

---

7. For a discussion of *Timaeus* and Plato's cosmogony, see Louis Markos, *From Plato to Christ: How Platonic Thought Shaped the Christian Faith* (Downers Grove, IL: IVP, 2021), 101–8. Some early church fathers such as Justin Martyr and Origen also gave voice to the idea that God created the cosmos from preexistent matter.

8. *JSP*, D14:331. Two of Smith's apostles, the brothers Parley and Orson Pratt, wrote extensively on this idea. See, for instance, Parley P. Pratt, *The Millennium, and Other Poems: To Which Is Annexed, a Treatise on the Regeneration and Eternal Duration of Matter* (New York, 1840), and Orson Pratt, *Great First Cause, or the Self-Moving Forces of the Universe* (Liverpool, 1851).

9. *JSP*, D14:331.

10. *JSP*, D7:492. Another notetaker recorded Smith's teachings thus: "this earth was organized or formed out of other planets which were broke up and remodelled and made into the one on which we live." *JSP*, D7:494.

11. Orson Pratt, "Formation of the Earth," *Seer*, April 1854, 249.

said unto those who were with him: We will go down, for there is space there, and we will *take of these materials*, and we will make an earth whereon [the previously created souls of human beings] may dwell. . . . And then the Lord said: Let us go down. And they went down at the beginning, and they, that is the Gods, *organized and formed* the heavens and the earth" (Abraham 3:24; 4:1 [emphasis added]). As Brigham Young remarked, "All this vast creation was produced from element in its unorganized state."[12] In the early twentieth century, the church's First Presidency and Council of Twelve Apostles stated officially: "The Creator is an Organizer. God created the earth as an organized sphere; but He certainly did not create, in the sense of bringing into primal existence the ultimate elements of the materials of which the earth consists, for 'the elements are eternal.'"[13]

Because Latter-day Saints view matter as eternal, they consider creation as matter's ongoing "reorganization," not as a single creative act that brought everything into existence. In the prefatory revelation to Joseph Smith's "New Translation" of the Bible, God tells Moses, "Worlds without number have I created . . . and by the Son I created them. . . . But only an account of this Earth, and the inhabitants thereof, give I unto you. For behold, there are many worlds that have passed away . . . and there are many that now stand and innumerable are they unto man. . . . And as one earth shall pass away, and the Heavens thereof, even so shall another come; and there is no end to my works" (Moses 1:33, 35, 38). With this background information, Smith then emended Genesis 1:1–2 to read, "And it came to pass that the Lord spake unto Moses, saying: Behold, I reveal unto you concerning *this* heaven and *this* earth . . . yea, in the beginning I created the heaven and the earth *upon which thou standest*" (Moses 2:1 [emphasis added]). In the LDS view, God's creative work has been repeated over and over again for aeons. There have been countless enactments of Genesis 1, so to speak, throughout the universe, or even the creation of multiple universes.[14] This earth and its inhabitants constitute merely a single chapter in the everlasting story of creation as a manifestation of divine love

---

12. *Journal of Discourses*, 7:285.

13. "The Father and the Son," 934–42. The notion of the Creator as "organizer" of pre-existing matter continues to be familiar to Latter-day Saints today as part of their sacred temple liturgy.

14. Reflecting on the expansiveness of God's creative activities "from everlasting," one of Joseph Smith's associates opined that God's creative activity "has been going on in this system, (not this world) almost *two thousand five hundred and fifty-five millions of years* [2.555 billion years]." W. W. Phelps to William Smith, December 25, 1844, in *Times and Seasons*, January 1844 [1845], 756.

and God's redemptive purposes. Among the numberless worlds that God has created, Latter-day Saints believe he populated some and that "the inhabitants thereof are begotten sons and daughters unto God" (D&C 76:24). Latter-day Saints also believe that God's reason for doing so is the same reason he created human beings for this earth: "Behold, this is my work and my glory—to bring to pass the immortality and eternal life of man" (Moses 1:39).

PROVIDENCE

In simplest terms, the doctrine of providence proclaims God's "provide-nce" for the universe he created. It promises he will sustain it and guide it to its destiny. "Providence" is derived from the Latin *providentia*, which translates the Greek *pronoia*. Both words literally mean "foresight" or "forethought," or, in this case, "provision," which connotes both providing for something or someone and doing so through foresight. This etymology captures well the theological notion that an omnipotent God sustains and directs the universe through his omniscient foreknowledge. Because God's loving providence for his creation has as its ultimate objective the redemptive transformation of creatures and cosmos alike, the doctrine of providence has important soteriological (salvation-related) and eschatological (End-related) ramifications. The *Catechism of the Catholic Church* declares that "Creation has its own goodness and proper perfection, but it did not spring forth complete from the hands of the Creator. The universe was created 'in a state of journeying' (*in statu viae*) toward an ultimate perfection yet to be attained, to which God has destined it. We call 'divine providence' the dispositions by which God guides his creation toward this perfection." As a result, God "is master of history, governing hearts and events in keeping with his will." In "every moment, [God] upholds and sustains [his creatures] in being, enables them to act and brings them to their final end."[15] All Christian traditions, including the Church of Jesus Christ of Latter-day Saints, maintain some version of a doctrine of providence. Eastern Orthodoxy, for instance, affirms that "all things are governed by God's providence" and that "God does provide entirely for all things. For from the smallest to the greatest, he knows them all, and every individual which he has made he particularly takes care of."[16]

---

15. *CCC* 302, 269, 301.

16. The first statement is from Cyril Lucar, patriarch of Constantinople, and the second from Peter Mogila, metropolitan of Kiev, as quoted in *Creeds & Confessions*, 1:552, 576. For reflections on the topic of providence, largely from an evangelical perspective, see Oliver D. Crisp and Fred Sanders, eds., *Divine Action and Providence: Explorations in Constructive*

Regardless of the particular Christian tradition, explication of the doctrine of providence draws on a rich array of biblical texts. God's sovereignty over, and solicitude for, the created realm, both natural and human, is boldly proclaimed.[17] Over the years, some theologians have promulgated a very strong doctrine of providence grounded in a very literal reading of pertinent biblical passages. Prominent among such theologians is John Calvin. A glimpse of his treatment of providence can be gained by noting these relevant chapter and section headings in his masterwork, *Institutes of the Christian Religion*: "God by His Power Nourishes and Maintains the World Created by Him, and Rules Its Several Parts by His Providence" (1.16.heading); "There Is No Such Thing as Fortune or Chance" (1.16.2); "God's Providence Governs All" (1.16.3); "God's Providence Also Directs the Individual" (1.16.5); "The True Causes of Events Are Hidden to Us" (1.16.9); and "God Firmly Executes His Plan" (1.17.14). The extent of God's control of the created realm is unbounded in Calvin's mind: all "power, action, or motion in creatures," he writes, is "governed by God's secret plan in such a way that *nothing happens except what is knowingly and willingly decreed by him*" (1.16.3 [emphasis added]). In some ways, Martin Luther was hardly less emphatic than Calvin in his view of God's providence, and he phrased it in personal terms in his *Small Catechism*: "God has given me and still preserves my body and soul.... In addition, God daily and abundantly provides ... all the necessities and nourishment for this body and life. God protects me against all danger, and shields and preserves me from all evil.... For all of this I owe it to God to thank and praise, serve and obey him."[18]

It is noteworthy how closely declarations in LDS scripture parallel the sentiment, if not the wording, of other Christian statements about providence. A Book of Mormon prophet proclaimed, "I say unto you, my brethren, that if you should render all the thanks and praise which your whole soul has power to possess, to that God who has created you ... and is preserving you from day to day, by lending you breath, that ye may live and move and do according to your own will,

---

Dogmatics (Grand Rapids: Zondervan, 2019). See also Dennis W. Jowers, ed., *Four Views on Divine Providence* (Grand Rapids: Zondervan, 2011).

17. To provide only a few examples, the Levites in Nehemiah's day praised God in these words: "Thou, even thou, art LORD alone; thou hast made heaven, the heaven of heavens, with all their host, the earth, and all things that are therein, the seas, and all that is therein, and thou preservest them all" (Neh. 9:6). The psalmist declared, "The LORD is good to all: and his tender mercies are over all his works" (Ps. 145:9). Similar pronouncements are made in the New Testament: "In him all things consist ['hold together,' NRSV]" (Col. 1:17), and God "worketh all things after the counsel of his own will" (Eph. 1:11).

18. *Small Catechism*, in *Book of Concord*, 354–55.

and even supporting you from one moment to another—I say, if ye should serve him with all your whole souls yet ye would be unprofitable servants" (Mosiah 2:20–21). As for God having and fulfilling a providential plan for human history, multiple verses attest to it: "The Lord knoweth all things from the beginning; wherefore, he prepareth a way to accomplish all his works among the children of men; for behold, he hath all power unto the fulfilling of all his words" (1 Nephi 9:6); "For the eternal purposes of the Lord shall roll on, until all his promises shall be fulfilled" (Mormon 8:22); and, reiterating the words of Isaiah, "For the Lord of Hosts hath purposed, and who shall disannul? And his hand is stretched out, and who shall turn it back?" (2 Nephi 24:27). In short, as stated in the Doctrine and Covenants, "His purposes fail not, neither are there any who can stay his hand" (D&C 76:3). In the face of menacing, even life-threatening, opposition, Joseph Smith was reassured that his persecutors' "bounds are set, they cannot pass. Thy days are known, and thy years shall not be numbered less" (D&C 122:9).

Like Job, who at the end of his dramatic experiences said to the Lord,

> "I know that you can do all things,
> and that no purpose of yours can be thwarted" (Job 42:2 NRSV),

Joseph Smith received a similar lesson in divine providence early in his ministry. After allowing the first part of the Book of Mormon manuscript to be borrowed and eventually lost, he learned to his relief that God had a backup plan for just such an event. By way of chastisement, though, Smith received a revelation containing one of the most forceful affirmations of divine providence in LDS scripture: "The works, and the designs, and the purposes of God cannot be frustrated, neither can they come to naught. For God doth not walk in crooked paths, neither doth he turn to the right hand nor to the left, neither doth he vary from that which he hath said, therefore his paths are straight, and his course is one eternal round. Remember, remember that it is not the work of God that is frustrated, but the work of men" (D&C 3:1–3). Reflection on this passage in an apostolically authored commentary on the Doctrine and Covenants provides a view of providence that is consistent with what is confessed in most Christian traditions: God "preserves and governs all His creatures, and directs their actions, so that the ultimate results will serve the ends He has in view. The universe and all that it contains is sustained by His power. . . . He overrules the affairs of nations. . . . The Lord turns the acts of men and nations to his purposes although they may design to overthrow his work and establish their own."[19]

19. *DCC*, 18.

As part of an American generation that grew up immersed in the Bible, it is hardly surprising that the first Latter-day Saints exhibited profound faith in divine providence.[20] An editorial in an early church periodical expresses views that might have come from any Christian: "The great Jehovah contemplated the whole of the events connected with the earth . . . before it rolled into existence. . . . He was acquainted with the situation of all nations and with their destiny; He ordered all things according to the counsel of His own will [glossing Eph. 1:11]."[21] Brigham Young's convictions would also have had broad resonance in Christendom: "The mysterious and invisible hand (so called) of Providence is manifested in all the works of God," not only in "how this Providence governs and controls the nations of the earth," but also in the way it "marks out the destinies of individual man."[22] Indeed, Joseph Smith and his people saw the hand of the Almighty even in seemingly mundane matters. "I purchased a Press & Types," reported Oliver Cowdery, one of the prophet's closest associates then on assignment for the fledgling church. "When they will arrive here is uncertain to us, as that depends upon the providences of our Heavenly Father."[23] With regard to a relocation move under contemplation, Joseph Smith wrote in his journal, "we finally came to the resolution to emigrate on or before the 15th of May next, if kind providence smiles upon us and openes the way before us."[24] Such expressions suggest a desire to not ungratefully overlook God's involvement in the details of their lives. Revelation taught the Saints that aside from the disobedient, the kind of people who "offend God" and incur his displeasure are "those who confess not his hand in all things" (D&C 59:21). Years later, Joseph F. Smith, Joseph Smith's nephew and then president of the church, acknowledged that "the hand of the Lord may not be visible to all. There may be many who cannot discern the workings of God's will in the progress and development of this great latter-day work. But," he added, "there are those who see in every hour and in every moment of the existence of the Church, from its beginning until now, the overruling, almighty hand of [God]."[25]

---

20. A pioneering study of the "moods and beliefs of the ordinary American people" in the biblically saturated "pre–Civil War generation, roughly 1830 to 1860" concluded that "no theme was more pervasive or philosophically more fundamental than the providential view. . . . The common people saw God ordering the cosmos and, directly or indirectly, all that was in it." Lewis O. Saum, *The Popular Mood of Pre–Civil War America* (Westport, CT: Greenwood, 1980), xi, xix, 3.

21. *Times and Seasons*, April 1842, 760.

22. *Journal of Discourses*, 1:336.

23. Cowdery to Ambrose Palmer, October 30, 1833, as quoted in *JSP*, D3:492.

24. *JSP*, J1:197.

25. *Gospel Doctrine*, 64.

Although the term "providence" and its cognates continued in common use among Latter-day Saints well into the twentieth century, the second half of that century witnessed a gradual decline in such usage to the point that it is rare to hear or see the term today. This, however, does not mean Latter-day Saints have changed their views or have less faith in divine providence. Rather, their speech patterns reflect the broader Anglophone shifts in language style and vocabulary over the past century that have come to favor less elevated and specialized vocabulary. Contemporary English-speaking Mormons often talk of God providing "blessings" or "protection," and they regularly acknowledge "the hand of the Lord" in their lives. Faith in God's superintendence of human history and church affairs, as well as individual lives, continues unabated among Latter-day Saints. In 2017, one of the church's apostles, Ronald Rasband, delivered a major address entitled "By Divine Design." "I know," he declared, "that the Lord will move us on that seeming chessboard to do His work. What may appear to be a random chance is, in fact, overseen by a loving Father in Heaven, who [alluding to providential favorite Matt. 10:29–30] can number the hairs of every head. Not even a sparrow falls to the ground without our Father's notice. The Lord is in the small details of our lives, and those incidents and opportunities are to prepare us to . . . build the kingdom of God on earth. Remember, as the Lord said to Abraham, 'I know the end from the beginning; therefore my hand shall be over thee' [Abraham 2:8]."[26] Latter-day Saints do not believe, however, that to accomplish his purposes God overrides human agency. Rasband made sure to qualify his chessboard analogy with these words: "Our lives are like a chessboard, and the Lord moves us from one place to another—*if we are responsive to spiritual promptings*."[27]

The Appeal of a Doctrine of Providence

One might ask, "Why do Christians affirm a doctrine of providence?" The short answer is because it gives meaning and purpose to life, and because it provides strength and reassurance in times of trial. As Calvin expressed it in his *Institutes*, "In times of adversity believers comfort themselves with

26. Ronald A. Rasband, "By Divine Design," *Ensign*, November 2017, 56. A decade earlier, Henry Eyring, counselor in the First Presidency, advised the Saints to nightly "pray and ponder, asking the question . . . Did I see [God's] hand in my life or the lives of my children?" The practice, he averred, would not only help the Saints "see the hand of God more clearly" but also "come to love Him and, through the power of the Atonement, become more like Him." Henry B. Eyring, "O, Remember, Remember," *Ensign*, November 2007, 69.

27. Rasband, "By Divine Design," 55 (emphasis added).

the solace that they suffer nothing except by God's ordinance and command, for they are under his hand."[28] In fact, "without certainty about God's providence life would be unbearable."[29] One of the most well-known appreciations of providence comes from the pen of the eighteenth-century poet William Cowper and ended up as the beloved hymn "God Moves in a Mysterious Way His Wonders to Perform." Cowper wrote, "Ye fearful saints, fresh courage take; The clouds ye so much dread, are big with mercy and shall break, in blessings on your head. Judge not the Lord by feeble sense, but trust Him for His grace; behind a frowning providence, He hides a smiling face. His purposes will ripen fast, unfolding every hour; the bud may have a bitter taste, but sweet will be the flow'r."[30] The hymn soon became a staple in Anglican and Protestant hymnbooks and has been included in LDS hymnals since the 1840s. For many Christians, the primary appeal of providentialism is the reassurance that "all things work together for good to them that love God" (Rom. 8:28).

This is especially true in times of difficulty. During a particularly intense period of persecution, Joseph Smith received a revelation reassuring his followers that God "giveth this promise unto you, with an immutable covenant that they shall be fulfilled; and all things wherewith you have been afflicted shall work together for your good, and to my name's glory" (D&C 98:3). A Book of Mormon prophet-father assured his son that God "shall consecrate thine afflictions for thy gain" (2 Nephi 2:2). When antagonists sought to expel the Mormons from their settlements in western Missouri (which the Saints called "Zion"), Joseph Smith wrote, "How far they will be suffered to execute their threats we know not, but we trust in the Lord, and leave the event with him to govern in his own wise providence."[31] Several years later, after suffering months of wintertime imprisonment and separation from his family, Smith received his own personal revelation: "If thou art called to pass through tribulation; if thou art in perils among false brethren . . . if thou art in perils by land or by sea . . . if the very jaws of hell shall gape open the mouth wide after thee, know thou, my son, that all these things shall give thee experience, and shall be for thy good . . . therefore, fear not what man can do, for God shall be with you forever and ever" (D&C 122:5–7, 9).

28. Calvin, *Institutes* 1.16.3.

29. Calvin, *Institutes* 1.17.10.

30. First published in John Henry Newton's *Twenty-six Letters on Religious Subjects; to which are added Hymns* (London, 1774).

31. JSP, D3:358.

Clearly, Latter-day Saints, like a great many other Christians, believe that God governs and sustains the universe he created and that this includes having a "plan" and *telos* ("end," "purpose") for humankind that make life meaningful and eschatologically beneficial. As Cowper expressed it, the common faith of the faithful is that even the clouds of adversity that believers might dread are "big with mercy and shall break, in blessings on [their] head[s]." Still, this general belief in divine providence invites closer inspection and raises a number of questions of theological interest. First is the overarching question of the relationship between God's sovereign providence and human freedom. If God is in charge and will always have his way, what does this say about human agency and autonomy? What role does God's "foreknowledge" play in all this? And how is the providence of a loving God to be squared with the existence of evil in the world? These are the questions to which we now turn.

Divine Sovereignty and Human Freedom

The saying in Matthew 10:29 quoted by LDS apostle Ronald Rasband and many other Christians over the years, that God notices even a sparrow's fall to the ground, deserves a second look. Consciously or subconsciously, the various English translations of this passage gesture toward one of the most profound questions pertaining to divine providence—how can everything happen according to God's will and humans still have genuine freedom? The final Greek phrase in Matthew 10:29 about the falling of a sparrow—*aneu tou patros hymon*—translates literally as "without [or 'apart from'] your Father." Many translations, though, add verbiage to clarify what they feel is implied. The RSV and NKJV, for instance, add "will," so that the phrase reads "without/apart from your Father's *will*." The Christian Standard Bible and the Good News Translation add "your Father's *consent*," and the International Standard Version and God's Word Translation read "your Father's *permission*." Other translations, however, see the implied meaning differently, rendering the phrase "unperceived by your Father" (NRSV-Anglicised); "without your Father knowing it" (New Century Version, NLT); or "without your Father knowing about it already" (Common English Bible). The difference is significant. The former set of additions give voice to a very strong notion of providential control. That even the falling of a single sparrow to the ground could represent the specific will of God, or at least that he consciously consents to, or permits, it, constitutes a very comprehensive or pervasive view of providence, something occasionally called "meticulous providence." The other textual endings signal divine omniscience and concern, but the occurrences may or may not reflect God's explicit will. Which view is correct? How much control does God exert, and how much freedom or contingency is compatible with that sovereignty?

The Bible does not settle the matter in favor of either divine sovereignty or human freedom exclusively. The two are maintained in healthy tension. Without so much as a nod to apparent contradiction, the New Testament and especially the Old Testament proclaim both divine providential control of events *and* human agency and responsibility. One has only to think of the many accounts where God is specifically mentioned as the disposer of events alongside numerous exhortations to righteousness with their promised consequences, positive or negative, depending on people's choices. At one end of the providential continuum, God is in complete control of the minutest matters (such as a sparrow falling to the ground) and is the real cause of seemingly random events—"The lot is cast into the lap; but the whole disposing thereof is of the LORD" (Prov. 16:33). God also governs on the grandest of scales, such as Isaiah's claim that the Lord used Cyrus, the Persian ruler, to restore the Jews to their homeland (45:1), or the even more extravagant Pauline claim that in the end "all Israel shall be saved" (Rom. 11:26). Juxtaposed to these bold declarations of divine sovereignty is the dramatic delineation in Deuteronomy of promised blessings or cursings dependent on whether or not one chooses to "hearken" to the Lord (Deut. 28–30). Or reference might be made to the array of exhortations in the Sermon on the Mount (Matt. 5–7), including the invitation, "Be ye therefore perfect, even as your Father which is in heaven is perfect" (5:48), that implies human agency and response-ability.

The reality and nature of human freedom are a matter that has been discussed and debated for millennia in both theological and philosophical circles.[32] As famed Renaissance scholar Desiderius Erasmus noted, "Among the many difficulties encountered in Holy Scripture—and there are many of them—none presents a more perplexed labyrinth than the problem of the freedom of the will."[33] One important aspect of this nettlesome theological question is how anthropology affects soteriology. Agreement is widespread that in the beginning God gave Adam and Eve complete freedom, but debate

---

32. The literature on the topic of human freedom is vast. A reliable overview of the many related issues is Robert Kane, ed., *The Oxford Handbook of Free Will*, 2nd ed. (New York: Oxford University Press, 2011). For particular focus on the topic as it relates to the theological proposition of divine sovereignty, see William Hasker's contribution, "Divine Knowledge and Human Freedom," 39–54. See also Alexander S. Jensen, *Divine Providence and Human Agency: Trinity, Creation, and Freedom* (London: Routledge, 2016), 67–114.

33. Desiderius Erasmus and Martin Luther, *Discourse on Free Will*, trans. and ed. Ernst F. Winter (London: Bloomsbury Academic, 2013), 11.

occurs over the degree to which their "fall" affected human agency with respect to salvation. Opposite ends of the contested continuum are iconically (and polemically) represented by the fifth-century clash between Augustine of Hippo and several opponents whom history has lumped together as "Pelagians," eponymously named after Pelagius, an ascetic living in Rome who popularized, though he did not originate, the ideas that troubled Augustine.[34] Augustine held that fallen humanity was so far enmeshed in evil that humans could not *not* sin (*non posse non peccare*). Technically they still retained free choice after the fall, but the will that drove their choices was so enslaved to sin that genuine freedom to choose between alternatives was a practical impossibility. Pelagius, on the other hand, as with many ascetics before him who promoted living in imitation of Christ's life, maintained that the will was not so debilitated by the fall that humans could not make a genuine choice of good over evil. Indeed, the original gift of freedom was still strong enough that they could choose God and follow Jesus.

This important salvific dimension of the sovereignty-freedom debate, as well as related matters, is taken up in detail in chapter 5 on anthropology and chapter 6 on soteriology. Here our concern is more general. How much genuine freedom do humans exercise in everyday affairs? The answer "humans are completely free" is the position philosophers designate as *libertarianism*. Libertarians (not to be confused with a political party) view human beings as self-determining agents who in theory are free from external causal constraints and are able independently to decide and act on any previously undetermined possibility. They are free to choose between all possible, competing options. At the opposite end of the spectrum is the notion of *determinism*. Those taking positions toward the determinist end of the continuum argue in one way or another that freedom is an illusion, a mirage, and that human "choice," if not entirely determined by God, is determined by any number of factors such as the unconscious mind, biological dispositions, or even the "selfish gene" of human survival. Some Christian theologians come close to an almost absolute determinism. Martin Luther spoke for determinists before and after him when he proclaimed, God "does all things by [his] own immutable, eternal, and infallible will. Here is a thunderbolt by which free choice is completely pros-

---

34. Recent scholarship regards as polemical distortion much that has been said over the centuries about the "arch-heretic" Pelagius and "Pelagianism." Everything from the novelty of Pelagius's teachings to how accurately they were represented by Augustine and others to whether there was anything resembling a cohesive school or movement that could appropriately by labeled "Pelagianism" has come under challenging scrutiny. See Ali Bonner, *The Myth of Pelagianism* (Oxford: Oxford University Press, 2018).

trated and shattered."[35] Many of the earliest church fathers fought against such hard determinism that existed in contemporary pagan philosophies claiming life to be completely controlled by "fate." In his later controversy over these issues, Augustine taught a similar but Christianized version of such strong determinism. In time, other theologians after him favored a "softer" form of determinism that scholars call *compatibilism.*

As the term "compatibilism" suggests, this is the view that actions may be technically free and yet causally determined at some level. From a theological perspective, this means that God's external (and eternal) control of human affairs does not cancel free choice. It does, however, acknowledge that chief among the factors that in some way shape the will and its consequent choices is God's sovereign plan for human history and individual human lives.[36] By a compatibilist understanding, Catholic doctrine holds that although God is the "Lord of human history as well as of salvation history, in the divine arrangement itself, the rightful autonomy of the creature, and particularly of man, is not withdrawn, but is rather reestablished in its own dignity and strengthened in it."[37] Similar faith in a "both/and" rather than an "either/or" relationship between sovereignty and freedom is expressed in other traditions as well. "For Orthodox Christians, divine freedom supports human freedom, and human freedom is called to cooperate with divine freedom. The divine will and the human will are not incompatible . . . together with God we can do good and creative things. So we do not have to choose either . . . divine sovereignty or human independence; Orthodox Christians affirm both."[38] Yet, how is this seemingly illogical position possible?

One of the oldest and best-known explanations of theological compatibilism is the distinction between "primary" and "secondary" causation. Here

---

35. Martin Luther, "The Bondage of the Will," in *The Annotated Luther*, vol. 2, *Word and Faith*, ed. Kirsi I. Stjerna (Minneapolis: Fortress, 2015), 170.

36. Anthony Flew, "Compatibilism, Free Will, and God," *Philosophy* 48 (1973): 231–32. To cite a common illustration, Calvinist compatibilism argues that "the elect are not elect because they freely come to Christ, *they freely come because they are elect.*" Jerry L. Walls, "The Free Will Defense, Calvinism, Wesley, and the Goodness of God," *Christian Scholars' Review* 13 (1984): 24 (emphasis added).

37. *Gaudium et Spes* (one of the Apostolic Constitutions promulgated at the Second Vatican Council in the 1960s), 4.41, in Denzinger 4341.

38. Nonna Verna Harrison, "The Human Person as Image and Likeness of God," in *The Cambridge Companion to Orthodox Christian Theology*, ed. Mary B. Cunningham and Elizabeth Theokritoff (Cambridge: Cambridge University Press, 2008), 82. An accessible look at Orthodoxy in general is Eve Tibbs, *A Basic Guide to Eastern Orthodox Theology: Introducing Beliefs and Practices* (Grand Rapids: Baker Academic, 2021).

are several examples: "God is the sovereign master of his plan. But to carry it out he also makes use of his creatures' co-operation," states the *Catechism of the Catholic Church*. "God grants his creatures not only their existence, but also the dignity of acting on their own, of being causes and principles for each other, and thus of co-operating in the accomplishment of his plan." In short, "God is the first cause who operates in and through secondary causes." Although humans as secondary causes are "often unconscious collaborators with God's will, they can also enter deliberately into the divine plan by their actions."[39] A similar position was expressed in the Westminster Confession (1647), the influential doctrinal statement of the Calvinist or Reformed wing of the Protestant Reformation. According to the Confession, the fact that God has predetermined all that will invariably come to pass does not mean that "violence [is] offered to the will of the creatures, nor is the liberty or contingency of second causes taken away, but rather established." This is so because "God, the first cause," by his "providence," orders things "to fall out according to the nature of second causes, either necessarily, freely, or contingently."[40]

Behind deliberate human choices is a "concurring" divine purpose and objective. "A man's heart deviseth his way: but the LORD directeth his steps" (Prov. 16:9). This is the common assumption in numerous biblical episodes, from Joseph being sold into Egypt to Cyrus's decision to send Jews back to their homeland. The reality of voluntary human choice alongside God's concurring providence is classically depicted in Philippians 2:12–13, where Paul urges his audience to exercise their agency and "work out your own salvation with fear and trembling," but adds that "it is God which worketh in you both to will and to do of his good pleasure." German philosopher Friedrich Schelling wrote, "That Judas became a betrayer of Christ, neither he nor any other creature could change, and nevertheless he betrayed Christ not under compulsion but willingly and with complete freedom."[41] In LDS scripture, such unconscious collaboration with divine ends even extends to Satan, who facilitated the fall by tempting Adam and Eve, "for he knew not the mind of God" (Moses 4:6). To apply Aristotle's categorizations of causality, God is

---

39. CCC 306–8.

40. WC 3.1; 5.2.

41. Schelling, *Philosophical Investigations*, 51, as quoted in Guy Elgat, *Being Guilty: Freedom, Responsibility, and Conscience in German Philosophy from Kant to Heidegger* (New York: Oxford University Press, 2022), 80. See also James M. McLachlan, "All's Well That Ends Well: Evil, Eschatology, and Love in F. W. J. Schelling and David L. Paulsen," in *Mormonism at the Crossroads of Philosophy and Theology: Essays in Honor of David L. Paulsen*, ed. Jacob T. Baker (Sandy, UT: Kofford Books, 2012), 337.

"final cause" (which brings about the ultimate ends of divine purpose) and may also be considered the "efficient cause" (the driving force, so to speak, of the action), but humans are the "instrumental" (intermediary) cause of many occurrences.[42]

MORMON DOCTRINE OF DIVINE SOVEREIGNTY AND HUMAN AGENCY

So, where do Latter-day Saints come down on the relationship between divine providence and human freedom? Mormonism has one of the most robust theologies of human agency of any Christian tradition. As apostle John Widtsoe noted, among Latter-day Saints, "perhaps no other gospel principle is more dearly cherished than the rights of free agency."[43] James Talmage wrote, "In all His dealings with man, [God] has left the mortal creature free to choose and to act, with no semblance of compulsion or restraint, beyond the influences of paternal counsel and loving direction."[44] Latter-day Saint commitment to the concept of a God who honors human agency is perhaps most dramatically stated by apostle Dallin Oaks: "God does not intervene to forestall the consequences of some persons' choices in order to protect the well-being of other persons—even when they kill, injure, or oppress one another—for this would destroy His plan for our eternal progress. He will bless us to endure the consequences of others' choices, but He will not prevent those choices."[45]

Such perspectives help explain the account mentioned in the previous chapter of God's weeping over creaturely disobedience. God does not, and perhaps cannot (because inconsistent with his character in the LDS view), control the free choices of his children. Thus, he laments to Enoch that "these thy brethren; they are the workmanship of mine own hands, and . . . gave I unto man his agency" (Moses 7:32). Yet, the gift was abused: "Among all the workmanship of mine hands there has not been so great wickedness as among thy brethren." To be sure, says God, "I can stretch forth mine hands and hold all the creations which I have made." Yet, because God honors the agency he has given humanity, and because humans have so completely mis-

---

42. Technically, "instrumental" is not one of Aristotle's famous "four causes," but the term works here to make the point of human involvement in conjunction with grand, undergirding causes.

43. John A. Widtsoe, *Evidences and Reconciliations: Aids to Faith in a Modern Day*, vol. 3 (Salt Lake City: Bookcraft, 1951), 125.

44. James E. Talmage, *The Articles of Faith: A Series of Lectures on the Principal Doctrines of the Church of Jesus Christ of Latter-day Saints* (Salt Lake City: Deseret News, 1899), 54.

45. Dallin H. Oaks, "Love and Law," *Ensign*, November 2009, 27–28.

used it, "Satan shall be their father, and misery shall be their doom." In such circumstances, asks God, "should not the heavens weep, seeing these shall suffer?" (Moses 7:36–37). Latter-day Saint commitment to human agency is so strong that many inside as well as outside the church might consider the Mormon position to be unmitigated libertarianism. Yet, because this strong emphasis on free will is coupled with a persistent belief in God's sovereign and providential governance of human history, it would be more accurate to consider LDS doctrine a form of compatibilism, albeit one much closer to pure libertarianism than to hard determinism. Joseph F. Smith put it this way: God always "effect[s] his purposes and execute[s] his will, in consonance with the laws of free agency which he has conferred upon man."[46]

For Mormonism, agency is integral to the very existence of intelligent beings. If they are not "independent" at some fundamental level, "there is no existence," proclaims LDS scripture. "Behold, here is the agency of man" (D&C 93:31–32). The Book of Mormon heading for 2 Nephi 2 reads: *Freedom of Choice (Agency) Is Essential to Existence and Progression.*[47] Although LDS scripture speaks of God "giving" humans their agency (e.g., Moses 7:32; D&C 101:78; 2 Nephi 2:16), there is also a tradition in Latter-day Saint thought that views freedom as a metaphysical given. Because Mormons believe that in some sense the intelligent core of human beings is uncreated and coeternal with God (see chapter 5), so is its inherent self-determining freedom to act. Like the eternal laws that God did not create and does not violate in exercising his divine sovereignty, God will not and cannot deprive intelligent beings of their agency. Brigham Young declared, "The volition of the creature is free; this is a law of their existence and the Lord cannot violate his own law; were he to do that, he would cease to be God. . . . This is a law which has always existed from all eternity, and will continue to exist throughout all the eternities to come. Every intelligent being must have the power of choice."[48] Whether human souls came to possess agency as a divine gift or it was part of their eternal makeup, the Father's supreme love for them causes him to foster that agency in ways that enable and maximize his children's eternal progress toward becoming like him.

This is strikingly apparent in the Mormon account of the genesis of human beings. Latter-day Saints believe that all human souls (God's "spirit children,"

---

46. *Gospel Doctrine*, 74.

47. These headings are not canonical, but they are church-endorsed study aids. Chapter headings in LDS scripture are italicized.

48. *Journal of Discourses*, 11:272.

as they prefer to call them), not just the Son, had a pre-earth existence or "pre-existence." They also believe that agency and choice were a part of that preexistence and were to be preserved in the physical creation. Indeed, part of God's rationale for populating the earth with his spirit children was to "prove them" and "see if they will do all things whatsoever the Lord their God shall command them" (Abraham 3:25). Without genuine freedom, there could be no real "probation" or test. Joseph Smith taught that God "has constituted mankind moral agents and given them power to choose good or evil."[49] LDS scripture depicts the Father as presenting to his preexistent spirit children his plan for their ultimate salvation and glorification, a plan that would require a redeemer. Although it was the Father's will that his beloved Son play that crucial role, he did not force it upon him and even allowed Lucifer or Satan (in LDS theology, also one of God's preexistent sons) to propose an alternative, saying, "Behold, here am I, send me . . . and I will redeem all mankind, that one soul shall not be lost, and surely I will do it; wherefore give me thine honor" (Moses 4:1). In this act, "Satan rebelled against [God] and sought to destroy the agency of man." For that reason, and because he sought divine power and glory, "[God] caused that he should be cast down; And he became Satan, yea, even the devil, the father of all lies" (Moses 4:3–4). God's intention in the great pre-earth council was to respect his children's agency and allow them to choose either his plan of earthly agency, risky as that might be (though it also entailed sending his Son as redeemer), or Satan's alternative of mandatory compliance with himself as enforcer.[50] Joseph Smith taught that although the majority "voluntarily subscribed" to the Father's plan "in their heavenly [preexistent] estate," others sided with Satan in his rebellion—"at that day, many followed after him" (Abraham 3:28)—and were cast down with Lucifer.[51] This is the Latter-day Saint interpretation of the "war in heaven" discussed in Revelation 12. Glossing the statement in Revelation 12:4 that the dragon (Satan) "drew the third part of the stars of heaven, and did cast them to the earth," LDS scripture declares that "a third part of the hosts of heaven [God's spirit children] turned he [Lucifer]

49. *Times and Seasons,* December 1839, 29.

50. This recalls the hypothetical depiction by William James of God's declaration on creation morn: "I am going to make a world not certain to be saved, a world the perfection of which shall be conditional merely, the condition being that each several agent does its own 'level best.' I offer you the chance of taking part in such a world. Its safety, you see, is unwarranted. It is a real adventure, with real danger, yet it may win through. . . . Will you trust yourself and trust the other agents enough to face the risk?" James, *Pragmatism: A New Name for Some Old Ways of Thinking* (New York: Longmans, Green and Co., 1907), 290–91.

51. *Teachings: Joseph Smith,* 213.

away from me because of their agency; And they were thrust down, and thus came the devil and his angels" (D&C 29:36–37). John Widtsoe pictured the pre-earth council in a way that highlights the importance of agency: "As each intelligent spirit possessed a free and untrammeled will which [had to] be respected, God called together the spirits in question, and presented the plan for their approval. . . . The great question [to be decided] was with respect to man's free agency."[52] A similar assessment of the significance of God respecting human agency was later made by famed literary figure and Christian thinker C. S. Lewis, who wrote, "In creating beings with free will, omnipotence from the outset submits to the possibility of defeat." For God to be "capable of being resisted by its own handiwork is the most astonishing and unimaginable of all the feats we attribute to the Deity."[53]

Consistent with such views, Joseph Smith felt the need to revise some of the key passages in the Bible that on the surface seemed to depict God directly controlling human choice. The classic example is the ancient pharaoh who refused to let Israel leave Egypt. Ten times in Exodus, in the course of as many chapters, it is stated that God "hardened" Pharaoh's heart. In each case, Smith emended the passage to read that Pharaoh hardened his own heart.[54] Smith also similarly changed the wording in several other Old Testament passages where God is identified as the direct cause of someone's hard-heartedness (e.g., Exod. 14:17; Deut. 2:30; Josh. 11:20; Isa. 63:17).[55] These emendations may simply reflect a desire to square such statements with the greater quantity of biblical passages that attribute hard-heartedness to human agency. It may also manifest Smith's desire to stress the secondary, human cause of unfortunate or evil outcomes. Whatever the motivation, at the very least it demonstrates quite clearly the Mormon aversion to viewing God as the cause of wickedness or unbelief.

Nor are Latter-day Saints the only Christians who think this way. Illustrative is commentary on John 12:40—"He hath blinded their eyes, and hardened their heart; that they should not see with their eyes, nor understand

---

52. John A. Widtsoe, *Rational Theology: As Taught by the Church of Jesus Christ of Latter-day Saints* (Salt Lake City: General Priesthood Committee, 1915), 33. See also 33–37.

53. C. S. Lewis, *The Problem of Pain* (New York: Simon & Schuster, 1966), 113–14.

54. Exod. 4:21; 7:3, 13; 9:12; 10:1, 20, 27; 11:10; 14:4, 8 (*NTOB*, 687, 691, 693). In eight other instances in these chapters, the text specifies that Pharaoh was the acting agent who hardened his heart, or the hardening is phrased in the subjectively indefinite passive voice—his heart "was hardened" (e.g., Exod. 8:15, 19, 32).

55. *NTOB*, 695, 709, 711, 829. Smith was less consistent in revising the few New Testament passages, such as John 12:40 or the oft-cited Rom. 9:18—"whom he will he hardeneth"—that also depict God as the primary cause of human choice.

with their heart." The passage quotes Isaiah 6:10 but modifies it from either the Septuagint or Masoretic versions to make God the agent in blinding eyes and hardening hearts.[56] The *Orthodox Study Bible* contends that "according to St. John Chrysostom, Isaiah's prophecy does not mean God causes spiritual blindness in people who would otherwise have been faithful. This is a figure of speech common to Scripture revealing God as giving people up to their own devices (as in Rom 1:24, 26). What is meant by *He has blinded* is that God has permitted their self-chosen blindness."[57] This is the same explanation Latter-day Saints give for similar verses in Romans 9. "These passages do not mean," explains the church's college-level New Testament study guide, "that God caused Pharaoh or other people to be wicked. Such an interpretation would contradict truths taught elsewhere in the scriptures." Rather, "Paul's point was that even though Pharaoh fought against God, this did not frustrate the Lord's work of delivering Israel. Ultimately, Israel's deliverance in spite of Pharaoh's stubbornness served to reveal the Lord's power. . . . Similarly, God did not *cause* Israel to reject [his word], but He *permitted* it . . . so that He could 'make known the riches of his glory . . . not of the Jews only, but also of the Gentiles.'"[58] Such explanations illustrate a form of compatibilist thinking whereby God, although not the instrumental cause of human history, may still be seen as its "final cause." James Talmage captured something of this sensibility in his essay "The Will of God: Though Opposed, Yet Eventually Supreme."[59] Like other compatibilist traditions, Mormonism has not chosen to resolve the paradoxes such positions entail. Instead, Latter-day Saints consistently and concomitantly make equally pointed affirmations of both the untrammeled nature of human agency *and* God's providential control of human history.

When considering the relationship between divine sovereignty and human freedom, two explanatory strategies that became prominent in the twentieth century—process theology and openness theology—bear resemblance to some aspects of Mormon doctrine and invite consideration. As a form of "naturalistic theism," process theology rejects the idea that God is a metaphysically sovereign being who may intervene decisively and determinatively at will in the natural order or in human affairs. Rather, process theologians understand

---

56. This would be a likely candidate for emendation by Joseph Smith. That he did not do so reflects his limited emendations of such texts in the New Testament, as mentioned in the previous note.

57. *OSB*, 1450.

58. *NT Student Manual* (2018), 353.

59. James E. Talmage, *The Vitality of Mormonism: Brief Essays on Distinctive Doctrines of the Church of Jesus Christ of Latter-day Saints* (Boston: Gorham, 1919), 314–17.

God as possessing only *persuasive* power to lure human beings and other creatures toward goodness and truth.[60] As one proponent explains, "God does not refrain from controlling the creatures simply because it is better for God to use persuasion, but because it is necessarily the case that God cannot completely control the creatures."[61] That human beings possess freedom and self-determination is not a contingent fact, but a metaphysical reality, a "necessity" in philosophical terms. Such thinking is in harmony with basic Mormon sensibilities about the eternality of agency and about a God who beckons to his children through persuasion and patience without controlling interference. For both process and Latter-day Saint theologies, God "must work with the universe in ways consistent with the uncreated metaphysical principles that govern it."[62] The difference is that in process thought, God *cannot* intervene. In the more scripturally based LDS thought, God is viewed as the loving Father who can and does on occasion selectively intervene in human affairs. As far as divine foreknowledge is concerned, process theism limits it dramatically with its radically libertarian view of human freedom. Since God does not control human actions even indirectly, he cannot know the future before it happens. This, as we shall see, is also a step beyond the Latter-day Saint view.[63]

In some ways, openness theology is closer to Latter-day Saint thinking than process theology. Open theists argue that in order for God to enter into genuine relationships with human beings, it must be possible for humans to respond freely to God's word and love. This can only happen, they argue, if God chooses to limit himself because of that love. Centuries ago, Aquinas argued that God's activity could be limited only by logical necessity and his own nature. God, for example, cannot round the square or torture children for amusement. Open theism extends divine limitation to include God's inability because of his loving nature to create free beings whose future is determined.

60. See Charles Hartshorne, *Omnipotence and Other Theological Mistakes* (Albany: State University of New York Press, 1984), 126–31.

61. David Griffin, *God, Power, Evil: A Process Theodicy* (Philadelphia: Westminster, 1976), 276. See also Griffin, "Process Theology and the Christian Good News: A Response to Classical Free Will Theism," in *Searching for an Adequate God: A Dialogue between Process and Free Will Theists*, ed. John B. Cobb Jr. and Clark H. Pinnock (Grand Rapids: Eerdmans, 2000), 1–38.

62. Brian D. Birch, "Mormonism and the Challenge of an Adequate Theodicy: A Response to David Paulsen et al.," *Element: The Journal of the Society for Mormon Philosophy and Theology* 6 (Spring 2015): 66.

63. See David Ray Griffin and James McLachlan, "A Dialogue on Process Theology," in *Mormonism in Dialogue with Contemporary Christian Theologies*, ed. Donald W. Musser and David L. Paulsen (Macon, GA: Mercer University Press, 2007), 161–210.

God chose to limit himself in certain respects to bring about a more desirable creation wherein humans could flourish and respond freely to God's love. In this way, open theists share with process theologians and Latter-day Saints an emphasis on the essentiality of human agency and divine persuasion. The idea of a completely determined world in which creatures are mere automatons (essentially the world Latter-day Saints believe Lucifer was proposing in the precreation heavenly council) is thought to be contrary to the nature of God.

What are the ramifications of such views for Christian worship? How does the interplay between divine sovereignty and human freedom impact the concept of petitionary prayer, for instance? A prominent advocate of open theism comments that "a key aspect" of the divine "project is that God has decided to make some of his actions contingent upon our requests and actions. God elicits our free collaboration in his plans for the achievement of his goals. Hence, God can be influenced by what we do, and God truly responds to what we do—God is 'open' to creation. God genuinely interacts and enters into dynamic give-and-take relationships with us. In order to bring this about, God has chosen to exercise a general rather than a meticulous form of providence."[64] That said, it must also be acknowledged that some believe it is possible to maintain both a strong sense of the absolute sovereignty of God *and* a potent belief in the efficacy of petitionary prayer. In his *Summa Theologiae*, Aquinas points out that "in proving the usefulness of prayer we must not" on the one hand deterministically "attribute necessity to human actions subject to divine providence, nor," on the other hand, "imply that the decree of divine providence is changeable."[65] Aquinas's solution is to argue that God has decreed that certain outcomes will be the effect of petitionary prayer. Thus, prayer does not change the decree of God whether one's sick child will be cured, but rather acts as a *secondary cause* of the child's restoration to health if it is divinely decreed. The purpose of prayer is not to change God's unchangeable will but to align oneself with that will in order to instrumentally aid in effecting the outcomes that God has decreed will follow from such human actions.

---

64. John Sanders, "God, Evil, and Relational Risk," in *The Problem of Evil: Selected Readings*, ed. Michael L. Peterson, 2nd ed. (Notre Dame: University of Notre Dame Press, 2016), 327–28. Openness theology has been criticized for limiting the omnipotence of God, but in Sanders's view, the criticism goes both ways: "If God cannot create personal agents who may act independently of the divine will, then God is limited. If it is impossible for God to make himself contingent on the decisions of creatures, then God is limited. Consequently, both sides of the sovereignty debate employ the concept of divine limitation, whether they admit it or not." Sanders, *The God Who Risks: A Theology of Providence* (Downers Grove, IL: InterVarsity Press, 1998), 225–26.

65. Aquinas, *Summa Theologiae* 2a2ae.83.2.

Omniscience, Foreknowledge, and Freedom

Proclaiming both divine providence and human freedom has always raised questions about the nature and extent of God's foreknowledge. For the determinist, there is no problem. God foresees all because he wills all, and his will is unfailingly carried out. As Calvin expressed it, God "foresees the things which are to happen simply because he has *decreed* that they are so to happen."[66] For the libertarian, there is also no problem. With a libertarian conception of freedom, complete free will and omniscient foreknowledge are logically incompatible. God only knows all that can be known. Where free agency is in full effect, the future is such that it cannot be known. Christians who hold this view, however, do not see it as detracting from God's divine attributes. To not know the impossible no more degrades Deity's omniscience than not being able to make a round square compromises his omnipotence. "God reacts to contingencies, even adjusting his plans, if necessary, to take into account the decisions of his free creatures. God is endlessly resourceful and wise in working toward the fulfillment of his ultimate goals. However, God's plan is not a detailed script or blueprint, but a broad intention that allows for a variety of options regarding precisely how his goals may be reached."[67]

Wherever one's theology of divine foreknowledge fits on the spectrum from total omniscience to qualified omniscience, the question is still asked philosophically, "Does not divine foreknowledge (to any degree) effectively predetermine the outcome of human choices?" The majority position within Christianity has been that it does not. At one point in the *City of God*, Augustine argues against the rejection of divine foreknowledge propounded by Cicero, concluding, "Neither let us fear that what we do by free will is not done by free will because He whose foreknowledge cannot fail foreknew that we would do it."[68] A millennium and a half later, the First Vatican Council's Dogmatic Constitution *Dei Filius* pointedly affirmed divine omniscience—all things "are open and laid bare to [God's] eyes [Heb. 4:13]"—and reiterated the compatibilist view that such foreknowledge included "those things that will be done by the free action of creatures."[69] Catholic theologians between Augustine and Vatican I generally took the same position. Anselm of Canterbury, for instance, early in the twelfth century, wrote an influential treatise

---

66. Calvin, *Institutes* 3.23.6 (emphasis added). Cf. 3.23.7 and 3.21.5.
67. Sanders, "God, Evil, and Relational Risk," 328.
68. Augustine, *City of God* 5.9.
69. Denzinger 3003.

entitled *De concordia* in which he endeavored to harmonize human freedom with God's foreknowledge. Some Protestants have done the same. In the view of Jacob Arminius, "freedom and determinism are strictly incompatible, but foreknowledge, which neither equates with nor entails necessity, indeed is consistent with genuine freedom."[70]

Similar views have been repeatedly expressed in LDS circles. Typical is James Talmage's comment that it is an "absurd conclusion that the mere knowledge of coming events must act as a determinative influence in bringing about those occurrences. God's knowledge of spiritual and of human nature enables Him to conclude with certainty as to the actions of any of His children under given conditions; yet such knowledge has surely no determining influence upon the creature."[71] On another occasion, Talmage wrote, "The omniscience of God does not operate to make of men automatons; nor does it warrant the superstition of fatalism. The chief purpose of earth life, as a stage in the course of the soul's progression, would be nullified if man's agency was after all but a pretense, and he a creature of circumstance compelled to do as he does."[72] Although Latter-day Saints hold differing views about the nature of God's knowledge, "there is accord on two fundamental issues: (1) God's foreknowledge does not causally determine human choices, and (2) this knowledge, like God's power, is maximally efficacious. No event occurs that he has not anticipated or has not taken into account in his planning."[73]

Figuring out *how* God's foreknowledge can be exhaustive and yet not determinative has challenged theologians and philosophers alike.[74] One proposal that has had lasting currency for some is the idea of God's "middle knowledge," a concept attributed to a group of late sixteenth- and early seventeenth-century Jesuits associated with Luis de Molina and Francisco Suárez. "Molinism," as it

70. Keith D. Stanglin and Thomas H. McCall, *Jacob Arminius: Theologian of Grace* (New York: Oxford University Press, 2012), 65. Some philosophers dispute the compatibility of divine foreknowledge and genuine freedom: "If God knows that a person is going to perform [an act], then it is impossible that the person fail to perform it—so one does not have a free choice whether or not to perform it." William Hasker, "The Openness of God: A Philosophical Perspective," in *The Openness of God: A Biblical Challenge to the Traditional Understanding of God*, ed. Clark H. Pinnock et al. (Downers Grove, IL: InterVarsity Press, 1994), 147.

71. Talmage, *Articles of Faith*, 197. Talmage's remarks are reprinted in *Pearl of Great Price Student Manual* (2017), 7.

72. Talmage, *Vitality of Mormonism*, 318.

73. *Encyclopedia of Mormonism*, 4 vols. (New York: Macmillan, 1992), s.v. "omnipotent God; omnipresence of God; omniscience of God."

74. See, for instance, the varying viewpoints expressed in Paul Helm et al., *Perspectives on the Doctrine of God: Four Views* (Nashville: B&H Academic, 2008).

has often been called, maintains that between God's necessary, natural knowledge of all that *could* be and his voluntary, free knowledge of all that *will* be due to the exercise of his will, there is a "middle knowledge" of all that *would* be under any given set of circumstances.[75] A leading modern proponent of middle knowledge offers this commentary on the idea: "While it is impossible in the composed sense, given God's foreknowledge, for anything to happen differently from the way it will, this sense is irrelevant to contingency and freedom. In the relevant, divided sense we are as perfectly free in our decisions and actions as if God's foreknowledge did not exist. Middle knowledge, therefore, supplies not only the basis for divine foreknowledge, but also the means for reconciling that foreknowledge with creaturely freedom and contingency."[76] In other words, God exerts his providential control by arranging creaturely life in accordance with his will in such a way that he knows what his children would freely choose to do in those particular circumstances. Philosopher William James offered a version of middle knowledge by way of an analogy from the game of chess. Because God knows all the possible "moves," he can react to human choice such that the outcome remains determined. Life is filled with contingencies, but "no matter how much of it might zigzag [God] could surely bring it home at last."[77]

DIVINE FOREKNOWLEDGE, SOVEREIGNTY, AND PROPHECY

Openness theology, process theology, and middle knowledge have yet to meet Mormonism institutionally, and the Church of Jesus Christ of Latter-day Saints has no definitive position on either the precise nature of God's knowledge or his sovereignty. For the most part, publications by its general authority leaders have been content to affirm that God's foreknowledge does not conflict with human agency rather than venture an explanation, especially one that is philosophically framed, as to how this could be true.[78] In part, this is because scripture and

75. John D. Laing, *Middle Knowledge: Human Freedom in Divine Sovereignty* (Grand Rapids: Kregel, 2018), xx–xxi.

76. William Lane Craig, "Middle Knowledge: A Calvinist-Arminian Rapprochement?" in *The Grace of God and the Will of Man*, ed. Clark H. Pinnock (Grand Rapids: Zondervan, 1989), 152. See also David Basinger, "Middle Knowledge and Classical Christian Thought," *Religious Studies* 22 (1986): 407–22, and Thomas Flint, "Two Accounts of Providence," in *Divine & Human Action: Essays in Metaphysics of Theism*, ed. Thomas V. Morris (Ithaca, NY: Cornell University Press, 1988), 147–81.

77. William James, "The Dilemma of Determinism," in *The Will to Believe and Other Essays in Popular Philosophy*, ed. William James (London: Longmans, Green, 1897), 182.

78. Apart from general authorities and institutional literature, some LDS thinkers in the "unsponsored sector" have found versions of openness, process, or middle-knowledge

church-leader teachings offer a range of views on the matter. Some general authorities such as B. H. Roberts have embraced a concept of omniscience and divine sovereignty similar to openness theology in which God knows all that *can* be known as it pertains to free human choices, which he never contravenes.[79] Others see God as having a highly scripted, providentially meticulous plan for the future. Neal Maxwell, for instance, suggested that "it was necessary for God to know how the economic difficulties and crop failures of the Joseph Smith Sr. family in New England would move this special family to the Cumorah [New York] vicinity where the Book of Mormon plates were buried. God's plans could scarcely have unfolded if—willy-nilly—the Smiths had been born Manchurians and if, meanwhile, the plates had been buried in Belgium!"[80]

Differing perspectives on the degree of meticulousness in God's providence also affect one's view of predictive prophecy. Is the future fully planned in advance by God and, therefore, perfectly predictable? Or is it less absolute because it is responsive to future contingencies and variability? Scriptural prophecies seem to fit both scenarios. The former view can be illustrated with several passages from LDS scripture. On one occasion, a Book of Mormon prophet makes a very specific pronouncement that "four hundred years pass not away save the sword of justice falleth upon this people" (Helaman 13:5). In another circumstance detailed in Doctrine and Covenants 10 and Words of Mormon 1:3–7, fourteen hundred years before Joseph Smith lost the first portion of the Book of Mormon manuscript, God made provision for that exact occurrence. Without explaining why, he commanded Mormon to include in his compilation a second account of the period covered in what would become the lost manuscript pages for Joseph Smith to use as a replacement.[81] On the

---

reasoning to be fruitful. See, for instance, Blake T. Ostler, *Exploring Mormon Thought: The Attributes of God* (Sandy, UT: Kofford Books, 2001), 137–86, 295–330.

79. "All the knowledge that is, all that exists, God knows," wrote Roberts. "All that shall be, he *will* know. The universe is not so much 'a being' as a 'becoming,' an unfolding. Much more is yet to be. *God will know it as it 'becomes'*; or as it unfolds." B. H. Roberts, *The Truth, the Way, the Life*, ed. John W. Welch (Provo, UT: BYU Studies, 1994), 416–18. As evidence of varying views among Latter-day Saint leaders, the particular apostles assigned to read Roberts's volume in manuscript form took exception to his qualification of divine omniscience (418n). Roberts's manuscript was unpublished at the time of his death in 1933, but it was finally edited and published in the 1990s.

80. Neal A. Maxwell, "A More Determined Discipleship," *Ensign*, February 1979, 71.

81. Of this inclusion, Mormon wrote, "I do this for a wise purpose; for thus it whispereth me, according to the workings of the Spirit of the Lord which is in me. And now, I do not know all things; but the Lord knoweth all things which are to come; wherefore, he worketh in me to do according to his will" (Words of Mormon 1:7).

other hand, some prophecies have been understood contingently. A dramatic example pertains to the timing of Christ's second coming. Many Christians, including many Latter-day Saints, assume that God has planned the exact time of Christ's return, that the second advent is scheduled on God's celestial calendar, so to speak. Yet, LDS Church president Spencer Kimball taught a more open understanding: "The time of Christ's return is affected by our conduct. . . . The Lord's timetable is directed a good deal by us. We speed up the clock or we slow down the hands . . . by our activities or by our procrastinations."[82]

That prophecy is also affected by divine accommodation to human agency is illustrated in the LDS doctrine of revocation: "I, the Lord, command and revoke, as it seemeth me good" (D&C 54:4). This reality is well illustrated in various revelations given to Joseph Smith. On several occasions, an earlier revelation commands or predicts a certain action and a subsequent revelation revokes it "in consequence of the stiffneckedness of my people" (D&C 54:6) or the opposition of outsiders. An example of the latter is the revocation of a prophecy about building a temple in the Mormon Zion in Missouri. Early on, revelation announced that the temple would "be reared in this generation. For verily this generation shall not all pass away until an house shall be built unto the Lord" (D&C 84:4–5). After years of attempting to fulfill the commandment and ultimately being driven from the state, revelation temporarily rescinded the directive: "Verily, verily, I say unto you, that when I give a commandment to any of the sons of men to do a work unto my name, and those sons of men go with all their might and with all they have to perform that work, and cease not their diligence, and their enemies come upon them and hinder them from performing that work, behold, it behooveth me to require that work no more at the hands of those sons of men, but to accept of their offerings. . . . Therefore, for this cause have I accepted the offerings of those whom I commanded to build up a city and a house unto my name, in Jackson county, Missouri, and were hindered by their enemies, saith the Lord your God" (D&C 124:49, 51). Apostle Bruce McConkie found in the doctrine of revocation a suitable explanation for why some prophecies are not fulfilled as originally predicted: "It is perfectly clear that the New Jerusalem, crowned by the Holy Temple . . . was destined to be built within the promised generation. The fact is that neither the city nor the temple yet graces Missouri's soil, and the generation is long

---

82. *The Teachings of Spencer W. Kimball*, ed. Edward L. Kimball (Salt Lake City: Deseret Book, 1982), 441–42.

since gone by. Why so? This is the foreshadowed case in which the Lord said he commanded and then revoked."[83]

Parallel perspectives on prophecy have also been voiced by other Christians. Thomas Aquinas devoted several questions in his *Summa Theologiae* to the nature of prophecy. One of the issues he considered was whether some (or all) prophecies deal with future contingencies.[84] Aquinas discussed several passages that have become foundational in this discussion. In Jeremiah 18, the prophet observes a potter who reworks a lump of clay when the original piece did not turn out as he had hoped. The Lord then tells Jeremiah that this is how he adjusts his prophecies in light of human agency. When "I shall speak concerning a nation, and concerning a kingdom, to pluck up, and to pull down, and to destroy it; if that nation, against whom I have pronounced, turn from their evil, I will repent of the evil that I thought to do unto them" (Jer. 18:7-8). Conversely, when "I shall speak concerning a nation, and concerning a kingdom, to build and to plant it; if it do evil in my sight, that it obey not my voice, then I will repent of the good, wherewith I said I would benefit them" (Jer. 18:9-10).[85] A prime example of this is the account in Jonah 3 of the people in the ancient city Nineveh. Jonah prophesied, "Yet forty days, and Nineveh shall be overthrown" (Jon. 3:4). But the people repented in sackcloth, and God relented and did not destroy them. Even Calvin interpreted such texts in a way that accommodated human agency. The prophecies were not absolute predictions of the future but were spoken to motivate people. "Jonah's prophecy," wrote Calvin, "was made so [Nineveh] might not fall." Similarly, when Isaiah told the sick king Hezekiah, "Thus saith the LORD . . . thou shalt die, and not live," Hezekiah, weeping "sore," pled with the Lord to rescind the prophecy. As a result, God sent Isaiah back with a revised word: "I have heard thy prayer, I have seen thy tears: behold, I will add unto thy days fifteen years" (Isa. 38:1-5). Referencing both the story of Nineveh and Hezekiah, Calvin asked, "Who now does not see that it pleased the Lord by such threats to

83. Bruce R. McConkie, *A New Witness for the Articles of Faith* (Salt Lake City: Deseret Book, 1985), 597-604. Revocation may entail postponement or divine repositioning as much as cancellation. What is not at risk in the Mormon view is the ultimate realization of God's providential designs for humankind. Adds McConkie, "Though the city and the temple were not built within the appointed generation, and though the early saints were excused from that labor yet the ultimate triumph of the cause of Zion remains unchanged" (604).

84. Aquinas, *Summa Theologiae* 2a2ae.171.1-6; see particularly 171.3 and 171.6.

85. In both passages the KJV renders *nacham* as "repent." In modern translations, the term is translated "change my mind" (NRSV) or "relent" (NASB, NIV).

arouse to repentance those whom he was terrifying, that they might escape the judgment they deserved for their sins?"[86]

Providence and the Problem of Evil

In the final section of this chapter, we consider one of the most perplexing of all theological conundrums (B. H. Roberts called it "the world's great mystery")[87]—how to account for evil and suffering in the world given what Christians typically claim about the goodness of God's creation and providence. Proposed solutions are often labeled "theodicies" (from *theos*-God + *dike*-justice) because they seek to "justify" the ways of God in light of what takes place on earth. Or to phrase differently the question theodicies seek to answer, how can God be considered just (and loving) when there is so much suffering and evil in the world? David Hume famously pointed out that "Epicurus's old questions are still unanswered. Is (God) willing to prevent evil, but not able? Then he is impotent. Is he able, but not willing? Then he is malevolent. Is he both able and willing? Whence, then, is evil?"[88] Theodicy is the search for an ethically comprehensible God. This tireless quest for a satisfactory explanation has resulted in a plethora of distinctions, categories, and explanations, only a few of which can be explored here.[89]

Theodicies often begin by defining evil, which in one sense is a matter of perspective. An explanation popular among the early Christian fathers was that evil is basically privation of the good (*privatio boni*). Evil has no positive existence; the word "evil" is merely used to describe the loss or lack of something good. Since all that God created is good, the deterioration or deprivation of that good is the result of the "evil" misuse of human agency. This line of reasoning was especially important to Augustine in his challenge to the dualist cosmology of Manichaeism, the popular Persian religion that spread throughout the Roman Empire beginning in the mid-third century. By Augustine's time, Manichaeism was already a formidable rival to Christianity,

86. Calvin, *Institutes* 1.17.14.

87. Roberts, *The Truth, the Way, the Life*, 332.

88. David Hume, *Dialogue concerning Natural Religion* (1779; reprint, New York: Harper & Row, 1948), part 10, 66.

89. For a sampling of the vast literature on this topic, see Peter T. Geach, *Providence and Evil* (Cambridge: Cambridge University Press, 1977), and Jacques Maritain, *God and the Permission of Evil*, trans. Joseph W. Evans (Milwaukee: Bruce Publishing, 1966). Noteworthy for being both profound and accessible is D. A. Carson, *How Long, O Lord: Reflections on Suffering and Evil*, 2nd ed. (Grand Rapids: Baker Academic, 2006).

and Augustine himself joined its ranks prior to his conversion to Christianity. Manichaeans maintained that both good and evil were primordial realities in perpetual conflict. In his treatise against the Manichaeans, Augustine argued that evil is neither eternal nor a creation of God, but solely the product of the abuse of the divine gift of free will.[90]

The patristic desire to cordon off God from culpability for evil and suffering has reverberated through Christian history to the present day. Reflecting centuries of tradition, the current *Catechism of the Catholic Church* states unequivocally that "God is in no way, directly or indirectly, the cause of moral evil."[91] Protestant churches large and small have made similar declarations. The Westminster Confession proclaims simply that human sinfulness "proceedeth only from the creature, and not from God; who, being most holy and righteous, neither is nor can be the author or approver of sin."[92] Even the little-known Waldensian ("Reformed Churches of Piedmont [Italy]") Confession of 1655 avers that God "governs and rules all by his providence, ordaining and appointing whatsoever happens in this world, without being the author or cause of any evil committed by the creatures, so that the guilt thereof neither can nor ought to be in any way imputed unto him."[93] Aquinas, building on his distinction between primary and secondary causes, argued that "evil and defects occur in things ruled by divine providence as a result of the establishment of secondary causes in which there can be deficiency." Because there is no deficiency in God, "it is evident that bad actions, according as they are defective, are not from God but from defective proximate [secondary] causes."[94] Calvin, whose meticulous providence faces the greatest challenge in terms of theodicy, also sought to exculpate God by placing responsibility on the earthly instruments of his will: "God so uses the works of the ungodly, and so bends their minds to carry out His judgments, that He remains pure

---

90. Augustine's *Against the Epistle of Manichaeus Called Fundamental*, in *NPNF*, 1/4:129–50. Examples of earlier works in which the privation theory is expressed include Origen, *On First Principles*; Athanasius, *On the Incarnation* and *Against the Gentiles*; and Gregory of Nyssa, *Great Catechism*. See John Hick, *Evil and the God of Love*, rev. ed. (San Francisco: Harper & Row, 1977), 38–53.

91. *CCC* 311.

92. *WC* 5.5.

93. *Creeds & Confessions*, 1:776.

94. Aquinas, *Summa contra Gentiles* III.1.71.13. David Griffin finds the "deficient secondary causes" argument itself deficient in exonerating God because "the so-called secondary causes are themselves creatures which are created ex nihilo. Any 'defects' in them are there because God willed them." Griffin, *God, Power, and Evil*, 81.

from every stain."[95] Latter-day Saints join with the rest of Christendom in the theological affirmation that evil cannot come from God: "To hold that these abominations accord with the Divine will," wrote James Talmage, "is to make God responsible for them, and therefore the author of sin. The very thought is blasphemous."[96]

Exculpation, however, is not explanation. God may not be the source of evil, but why does he permit it? A common move historically has been to emphasize the good that God can providentially bring out of evil and suffering. A long line of theologians has echoed Augustine's argument that because God "is supremely good, [he] would never allow any evil whatsoever to exist in his works if he were not so all-powerful and good as to cause good to emerge from evil itself."[97] As Aquinas wrote, "God allows evils to happen in order to bring a greater good therefrom: hence it is written (Rom 5:20), 'Where sin abounded, grace did much more abound.'"[98] Nor has this been the unique perspective of Western Christianity. One of the most influential historic statements of Eastern Orthodox belief is the confession promulgated by the Synod of Jerusalem in 1672. "We believe," it declared, "that all things that are, whether visible or invisible, are governed by the providence of God; but although God foreknows evils and permits them, yet in that they are evils, he is neither their contriver nor their author. But when they have come about, they may be overruled by the Supreme Goodness for something beneficial, not indeed as being their author but as engrafting on them something for the better."[99]

Some Christians, including Latter-day Saints, have emphasized the role of the devil or Satan in instigating and sustaining evil and suffering. This is not quite a Manichaean view because Satan is understood to be both a creature and under God's ultimate control. Still, a cosmic contest is under way, nonetheless. From Augustine's *City of God* to the latest twenty-first-century book on "spiritual warfare," the theme of conflict and contest has been highlighted.

95. Calvin, *Institutes* 1.18. For those who reject Calvin's meticulous providence, this argument can seem like sophistry. From a modern legal standpoint, in Calvin's construal, God would be considered an "accessory before the fact" or an "accomplice," and if current procedures were followed, would be criminally liable to the same extent as the actual perpetrator. Arminius went so far as to say that meticulous providence and God's manipulating all actions of the ungodly actually make him the "only sinner." Stanglin and McCall, *Jacob Arminius*, 145.

96. Talmage, *Vitality of Mormonism*, 316.

97. Augustine, *Enchiridion: On Faith, Hope, and Love* 3.11.

98. Aquinas, *Summa Theologiae* 3a.1.3.

99. *Creeds & Confessions*, 1:617–18.

Although created by God, the devil and his "angels" or "demons" were once good angels who fell and were "cast out in the earth" (Rev. 12:9) for rebellion. The Catholic Church teaches that "Satan was at first a good angel, made by God: 'The devil and the other demons were indeed created naturally good by God, but they became evil by their own doing.' . . . This 'fall' consists in the free choice of these created spirits, who radically and irrevocably rejected God and his reign."[100] What this view does theologically is maintain the goodness of God's creation while accounting for the genesis of evil through these angels' misuse of the good gift of free choice. In this way, evil is believed to have existed prior to the creation of Adam and Eve. As previously discussed, similarities are noticeable with the LDS account of the "war in heaven" and the consequent ejection of Satan and followers.[101] Latter-day Saints regard their fall as part of God's foreordained plan. Apostle Dallin Oaks explains: "So it is that the evil one, who opposed and sought to destroy the Father's plan, actually facilitated it, because it is opposition that enables choice, and it is the opportunity of making the right choices that leads to the growth that is the purpose of the Father's plan."[102]

Closely related to Oaks's latter point is the theodicy known as "soul-making" (a phrase borrowed from poet John Keats), which in its original iteration may be traced to Irenaeus and refers to the necessity of evil and suffering for the building of character in human beings. Humans were created with the potential for moral and spiritual growth, and for that to occur they need to experience both good and evil. Among the most prominent twentieth-century exponents of a soul-making or character-building theodicy is British philosopher John Hick. Hick argued that rather than expecting the world to be a hedonistic paradise, "its value is to be judged, not primarily by the quantity of pleasure and pain occurring in it at any particular moment, but by its fitness for its primary purpose, the purpose of soul-making."[103] This fitness for soul

---

100. *CCC* 391–92. Many Protestants agree with this interpretation. See, for instance, article 12 of the widely embraced 1561 Belgic Confession. *Creeds & Confessions*, 2:412.

101. LDS usage almost never refers to Satan's followers as "demons" but as his "angels" (e.g., D&C 29:28, 36–37; 2 Nephi 9:8–9, 16). One of few references to demons, though —Helaman 13:37—explicitly links them to the devil's angels. Moreover, in LDS theology, whether demons or the devil's angels, they are not regarded as a separate type of created being (as they are for many Christians), but as God's own rebellious spirit children.

102. Dallin H. Oaks, "Opposition in All Things," *Ensign*, May 2016, 115. Elsewhere in the speech Oaks states that "to be tested, we must have the agency to choose between alternatives. To provide alternatives on which to exercise our agency, we must have opposition" (114).

103. Hick, *Evil and the God of Love*, 259.

making includes "a world which contains real contingencies, real dangers, real problems and tasks and real possibilities of failure and tragedy as well as of triumph and success."[104]

The emphasis in soul-making theodicies on genuine human freedom and the necessarily interrelated nature of good and evil resonates with Mormon doctrine, as it does with Pentecostalism.[105] From the beginning, LDS apostles and prophets have extolled the "uses of adversity" (Shakespeare) and the potentially strengthening effect of life's trials. They remind the Saints that a covenant relationship with God is not to be seen as insurance against suffering but as a resource for coping with it. The gold of godliness is often refined in the crucible of adversity. LDS scripture teaches that at times divine blessings come only "after much tribulation" (D&C 58:4). Profound comments about the usefulness of life's countervailing forces are also found in the Book of Mormon. Lehi, the Book of Mormon father whose descendants account for most of the peoples discussed in the book, taught that "it must needs be, that there is an opposition in all things. If not so . . . righteousness could not be brought to pass, neither wickedness, neither holiness nor misery, neither good nor bad. Wherefore, all things must needs be a compound in one" (2 Nephi 2:11). To fully grasp why something is labeled "good" requires some understanding of what is *not* good. Lehi continues: "If ye shall say there is no sin, ye shall also say there is no righteousness" (2 Nephi 2:13). Moreover, "to bring about [God's] eternal purposes in the end of man, after he had created our first parents . . . it must needs be that there was an opposition; even the forbidden fruit in opposition to the tree of life; the one being sweet and the other bitter. Wherefore, the Lord God gave unto man that he should act for himself. Wherefore, man could not act for himself save it should be that he was enticed by the one or the other" (2 Nephi 2:15–16). In sum, without evil and suffering in the world, humankind would be in a state of "having no joy, for they knew no misery; doing no good, for they knew no sin" (2 Nephi 2:23).[106]

Not surprisingly, this strong statement on the necessity, not merely the contingency, of evil and suffering in the world is read by Latter-day Saints to

---

104. Hick, *Evil and the God of Love*, 375.

105. See Frank D. Macchia, *Tongues of Fire: A Systematic Theology of the Christian Faith* (Eugene, OR: Cascade, 2023), 122–44.

106. This teaching is reiterated in several other of Joseph Smith's revelations. For example: "It must needs be that the devil should tempt the children of men, or they could not be agents unto themselves; for if they never should have bitter they could not know the sweet" (D&C 29:39); and people must "taste the bitter, that they may know to prize the good" (Moses 6:55).

reinforce their belief that such contraries are intrinsic to the very warp and woof of eternal existence. Twentieth-century Mormon philosopher Sterling McMurrin remarked that "a conception of things, events, and experience, in terms of an opposition elemental to the very structure of reality [is] of course entirely consonant in Mormon thought with the concept that the world in its most fundamental and ultimate constituents is uncreated, underived, and characterized by dynamic process."[107] B. H. Roberts called good and evil the eternal "antinomies of the universe" and argued that "evil is as eternal as good; as eternal as space or duration or matter or force. God did not create any of these things, nor is He responsible for them. He found Himself, so to speak, co-eternal with these other eternal things, and so works out His creative designs in harmony with those existences."[108]

Over the years, more than just Latter-day Saints have seen value in locating evil outside the realm of God's creative endeavor, preferring a God in conflict with evil over a God implicated in it. Some have reasoned that if God is not the origin of evil, and evil exists, then it follows that evil has its origin apart from God's creative power. John Stuart Mill opined that "the author of the cosmos worked under limitations . . . obliged to adapt himself to conditions independent of his will."[109] Such LDS-like perspectives became more popular in the twentieth century as their value to theodicies was increasingly recognized. Anglican canon William Vanstone, for instance, wrote an influential pastoral volume in which he spoke of the "precariousness of divine creativity" that requires a loving God to work within the limitations of the world he chose to create. Like the artist who chooses to work on a canvas of a certain size, this "imposes a discipline upon his creativity."[110] From the perspective of philosopher Susan Neiman, for God, like a loving parent, to be "well-meaning but bounded . . . does less violence to our intuitions than do other options. It may be hard to acknowledge God's limits, but it's less frightening than denying his goodwill."[111] More than an option, process theologians, as we have seen, consider divine boundedness a moral imperative: "If God could have

107. Sterling M. McMurrin, *The Theological Foundations of the Mormon Religion* (Salt Lake City: University of Utah Press, 1965), 98.

108. Roberts, *The Truth, the Way, and the Life*, 332, 337–38.

109. John Stuart Mill, *Three Essays on Religion* (London, 1875), 177.

110. William H. Vanstone, *Love's Endeavour, Love's Expense: The Response of Being to the Love of God* (London: Darton, Longman and Todd, 1977), 63–64. Edgar S. Brightman took a similar position earlier in the century in his *Problem of God* (New York: Abingdon, 1930).

111. Susan Neiman, *Evil in Modern Thought: An Alternative History of Philosophy* (Princeton: Princeton University Press, 2002), 20. Neiman's comments come in the context of

stopped the Holocaust and failed to do so in order to honor the freedom of the Nazis, we would find God's judgment highly questionable."[112] The force of such reasoning led one prominent open theist to abandon the openness idea of divine self-limitation and agree with process theologians that "a loving God [simply] would not allow genuine evil that is preventable." He reasoned that because "God's preeminent attribute is uncontrolling love," he "cannot create controllable creatures."[113]

The problem with an all-controlling God is that "a God truly in control who apparently does nothing about Auschwitz or Darfur, Katrina or Myanmar or Chinese earthquakes, is not exactly a God whose character one would readily trust." Despite their best efforts to provide satisfying explanations, most "philosophers and theologians who dare to take up the topic of providence at all very often end up, by one path or another, upholding what amounts to a 'best of all possible worlds' defense."[114] This argument was famously popularized by Gottfried Leibniz in his 1710 *Theodicy*. In one sense, the argument is merely a more sophisticated way of expressing the age-old retreat into invoking the ultimate inscrutability of God's intentions and actions. Leibniz, who is credited with coining the term "theodicy," spends most of his lengthy book constructing an argument that God, by logical necessity, would have had to create the best of all possible worlds. We may only partially comprehend how that is so, but it is a necessity given his knowledge, power, and character. Since we live in the world that God did in fact create, all things considered, it must be the best. "It should even be concluded that there must have been great or rather invincible reasons which prompted the divine Wisdom to the permission of evil that surprises us, from the mere fact that this permission has occurred: for nothing can come from God that is not altogether consistent with goodness, justice and holiness."[115] As for the content of "best of all possible worlds" theodicies, they end up stressing "some mixture of the supreme desirability

describing French philosopher Pierre Bayle's notion that given how things are in the world, Manichaeism appears the more reasonable theodicy.

112. John B. Cobb Jr., *The Process Perspective: Frequently Asked Questions about Process Theology* (Atlanta: Chalice, 2003), 82.

113. Thomas Jay Oord, *The Uncontrolling Love of God: An Open and Relational Account of Providence* (Downers Grove, IL: IVP Academic, 2015), 68, 146–48.

114. Marguerite Shuster, "The Hidden Hand of God," in *Christian Philosophy of Religion: Essays in Honor of Stephen T. Davis*, ed. C. P. Ruloff (Notre Dame: University of Notre Dame Press, 2015), 319.

115. Gottfried Leibniz, *Theodicy: Essays in the Goodness of God, the Freedom of Man, and the Origin of Evil*, trans. E. M. Huggard (La Salle, IL: Open Court, 1985), 93–94. Voltaire famously satirizes this reasoning in *Candide*, which was written in the aftermath of the 1755

but also hazards of human freedom; the need for a stable natural order that necessarily operates according to uniform laws, without taking account of human suffering; and the relentless mutual obstructiveness of finite wills and finite things leads to the beautiful but troubled world we actually see."[116]

Although Mormonism rejects the idea that God is the source of evil, it retains faith in God's ultimate control over evil. Thus, many of the traditional questions remain. Living with this ambiguity and taking refuge in their own version of the "best possible world" argument have not seemed to trouble Latter-day Saints. Lacking any special revelation on the topic, the Church of Jesus Christ of Latter-day Saints has gone about the pastoral business of helping church members cope with evil and suffering rather than attempting to explain them. In current church literature, although there is very little effort to account for the gratuitous evils of human history or devastating natural disasters, calls for prayerful compassion and humanitarian assistance are frequent. Gone are the early days when epidemics, natural catastrophes, and even personal disasters were often interpreted as the chastising hand of divine judgment.[117] Although just such interpretations populate the pages of both the Bible and LDS scripture, the earlier tendency to extrapolate and apply such conclusions to contemporary natural catastrophes or physical disasters has virtually disappeared.[118]

Lisbon earthquake, a catastrophe of such magnitude that it made *Theodicy* and the optimism it typified an easy target for Voltaire's sardonic wit.

116. Shuster, "The Hidden Hand of God," 319.

117. As an example, in 1837, Mormon convert Mary Fielding reported to her sister Mercy that "a Mr. [Wycom] Clarke, a Miller who has been a great opposer of our Church," was returning home from Sunday worship at his church when "about one minuit after they passed the [LDS] House of the Lord their Horses took fright and started off the side of the hill, overthrew the Carrage and hurt Mr C and one child considerably but Mrs. C so seriously as to prove fatal. . . . Not quite a year since Bro J[oseph] S[mith] told Mr. C that the curse of God would be upon him for his conduct towards him and the Church. . . . [Clarke] has been a trouble in th[is] place but has prospered in buisness so much as to say he never prospered better and told a person some time ago that he was ready for another of Joseph Smiths Curses. I feel inclind to think he will never be heard to utter such words again. May the Lord forgive and save him and all others who raise their hand against the Lords anointed for I see more clearly than ever that this is no trifling sin in the sight of God." Mary Fielding to Mercy Fielding Thompson, circa September 1, 1837, in *Women's Voices: An Untold History of the Latter-day Saints, 1830–1900*, ed. Kenneth W. Godfrey, Audrey M. Godfrey, and Jill Mulvay Derr (Salt Lake City: Deseret Book, 1982), 66.

118. Certainly, by the later twentieth century, it was common to nuance the etiology of suffering. In 1955, then apostle Spencer Kimball delivered an influential address entitled "Tragedy or Destiny" (later reprinted in a book by the same title), in which he offered a

Still, the instrumental value of contending with quotidian evil and suffering—"opposition in all things"—continues to be considered essential to spiritual growth and development. As explained by apostle Jeffrey Holland, "God's premortal children could not become like him and enjoy his breadth of blessings unless they obtained both a physical body and temporal experience in an arena where both good and evil were present." When presented in the preexistence with the Father's plan for earth life, "we wanted the chance to become like [God], to face suffering and overcome it, to endure sorrow and still live rejoicingly, to confront good and evil and be strong enough to choose the good."[119] Apostle Howard Hunter similarly declared, "We came to mortal life to encounter resistance. It was part of the plan for our eternal progress. Without temptation, sickness, pain, and sorrow, there could be no goodness, virtue, appreciation for well-being, or joy."[120] In the Mormon version of the soul-making theodicy, "we cannot develop without stress nor be perfected without suffering."[121] Thus it is that Latter-day Saints, like other Christians, strive to see the "smiling face" of a heavenly Father behind a sometimes "frowning providence."

number of reasons for the existence of suffering, only one of which is "God causes it." Spencer W. Kimball, "Tragedy or Destiny," in *Speeches of the Year* (Provo, UT: BYU Press, 1955), 2.

119. Jeffrey R. Holland, *Christ and the New Covenant: The Messianic Message of the Book of Mormon* (Salt Lake City: Deseret Book, 1997), 200, 204.

120. Howard W. Hunter, *Conference Report*, April 1980, 34.

121. The quote is from twentieth-century LDS philosopher Truman G. Madsen in his essay "Evil and Suffering," in *Eternal Man* (Salt Lake City: Deseret Book, 1976), 57 (53–61). For philosophically influenced studies of this topic, see David L. Paulsen and Blake T. Ostler, "Sin, Suffering, and Soul-Making: Joseph Smith and the Problem of Evil," in *Revelation, Reason, and Faith: Essays in Honor of Truman G. Madsen*, ed. Donald W. Parry, Daniel C. Peterson, and Stephen D. Ricks (Provo, UT: Foundation for Ancient Research and Mormon Studies, 2002), 237–84, and James M. McLachlan, "The Problem of Evil in Mormon Thought," in *The Oxford Handbook of Mormonism*, ed. Terryl L. Givens and Philip L. Barlow (New York: Oxford University Press, 2015), 276–91.

3

Christ

His "Person" and Nature

In 2012, Roman Catholic scholar Stephen Webb wrote an op-ed piece entitled "Mormonism Obsessed with Christ" for the Christian magazine *First Things*. His aim was not only to share his evolving view of Mormonism but also to communicate his perception that everything the Church of Jesus Christ of Latter-day Saints "teaches is meant to awaken, encourage, and expand faith in" Jesus Christ.[1] To some, Webb's observation may come as a surprise, but to Mormons, it has always seemed true. From the beginning, Latter-day Saints have worshiped Christ, recommitting themselves to discipleship in a weekly communion service where the set prayers consecrating the eucharistic elements urge them to "always remember him" (D&C 20:77, 79). Founding prophet Joseph Smith exulted in "the condesention of the Father" in providing through Christ "a sacrifice for his creatures, a plan of redemption, a power of atonement, a scheme of salvation, having as its great objects, to bring men back into the presence of the King of heaven, crown them in the celestial glory, and make them heirs with his Son."[2] Indeed, when asked on one occasion "what are the fundamental principles of your religion," Smith replied in words that echo the Apostles' Creed: "The fundamental principles of our religion [are] the testimony of the apostles and prophets concerning Jesus Christ, 'that he died, was buried, and rose again the third day, and ascended up into heaven'; and all other things are only appendages to these, which pertain to our religion."[3] Later, the very first book authored by a prophet-president of the church was

1. Stephen H. Webb, "Mormonism Obsessed with Christ," *First Things*, February 2012, 21.
2. *JSP*, D3:414.
3. *Elders' Journal*, July 1838, 44. This quotation has been repeated frequently in LDS circles over the years. For example, during the second decade of the twenty-first century, four of the church's Twelve Apostles quoted it in their general conference remarks. See https://www.lds-general-conference.org/.

The Mediation and Atonement of Our Lord and Savior Jesus Christ, by John Taylor.[4] A Christocentric focus is also plainly manifest in LDS scripture. Notably, the title page of the Book of Mormon specifies that one of the volume's primary purposes is "the convincing of the Jew and Gentile that Jesus is the Christ," and since 1982, the book has carried the subtitle "Another Testament of Jesus Christ." The contents of the Book of Mormon exhibit a decided emphasis on Christ, including a multichapter account of a postresurrection visit of Jesus to the Americas.

Still, the church's in-house "obsession with Christ" has not always been apparent to the broader public. This reality was one factor that contributed to a renewed effort by church leaders beginning in the final quarter of the twentieth century to place more explicit and public emphasis on Latter-day Saint devotion to Jesus Christ. As a result of this intensified focus, church general conference addresses, magazine articles, lesson manual coverage, even visual arts and music all display a greater degree of attention than ever before to the person and work of Jesus Christ. One need only cursorily consult the church's website (churchofjesuschrist.org) to notice this emphasis. Renewed Latter-day Saint focus on Christ was epitomized in the declaration of church president Russell Nelson in August 2018 that "the Lord has impressed upon my mind the importance of the name He has revealed for His Church, even The Church of Jesus Christ of Latter-day Saints."[5] Nelson later elaborated, "For much of the world, the Lord's Church is presently disguised as the 'Mormon Church.' But we as members of the Lord's Church know who stands at its head: Jesus Christ Himself. Unfortunately, many who hear the term Mormon may think that we worship Mormon. Not so! . . . we are not Mormon's disciples. We are the Lord's disciples."[6] For decades, the church's logo, the full name of the church, sought to communicate its focus on Christ by highlighting "Jesus Christ" in noticeably larger letters. In 2020, the church took the additional step of topping the logo text with a visual image—a small representation of Bertel Thorvaldsen's marble statue the *Christus.* All these efforts and emphases recall a Book of Mormon verse that, not surprisingly, has been much quoted in recent decades: "We talk of Christ, we rejoice in Christ, we preach of Christ, we prophesy of Christ, and we write according to our prophecies, that our

4. John Taylor, *An Examination . . . of the Mediation and Atonement of Our Lord and Savior Jesus Christ* (Salt Lake City: Deseret News, 1882).

5. Russell M. Nelson, "The Name of the Church," The Church of Jesus Christ of Latter-day Saints, August 2018, https://newsroom.churchofjesuschrist.org/article/name-of-the-church.

6. Russell M. Nelson, "The Correct Name of the Church," *Ensign,* November 2018, 88.

children may know to what source they may look for a remission of their sins" (2 Nephi 25:26). How Latter-day Saints understand the "person" or nature of this Christ of whom they preach and in whom they are said to rejoice is the subject of this chapter.[7]

CHRIST'S PREEXISTENCE

Theological discussion of the "person of Christ" explores a range of topics, from Christ's preexistent glory to his earthly incarnation and eventual resurrection, ascension, and exaltation in glory. These stages are sometimes referred to as the "states" or "estates" of Christ. We begin by considering his preexistent state. For most Christians, the preexistent Son and the divine in Jesus of Nazareth are one and the same. Moreover, to proclaim the Son's preexistence is to proclaim his divinity. It is to say that the Son is "eternal" and "uncreated" like the Father, equal to him, indeed that he is, in the famous though then controversial phrase from the Nicene Creed, "*homoousios*" ("consubstantial," "of the same essence/substance") with the Father.[8] That the Son of God had such a precreation existence commensurate with the Father's has been the dominant Christian view since the fourth century. Yet before widespread consensus was reached, the 300s witnessed decades of hairsplitting theological debate about the precise nature of the Son's relationship to the Father. The controversy was triggered by an otherwise obscure presbyter (priest) in Alexandria named Arius, who sought to protect the incomparable transcendence of the Father by teaching that Christ was *not* eternal but created and that therefore there was a "time" (in timeless eternity) when the Son "was not."[9] Arius's particular ideas were anathematized at the Council of Nicaea in 325, but others had similar and more sophisticated ways to distinguish the Son from the Father, and the debate would persist for another half century.

But what of the pre-Nicene years? How soon did Jesus's followers recognize his divinity and begin to worship him alongside the Father? Did they

---

7. Scholars use "Christology" as an umbrella term for the theological study of the "person" and "work" of Jesus Christ. His "person"—who he was, the nature of his existence—is the subject of this chapter. His redemptive "work" is the Christological focus of the next chapter.

8. *Creeds & Confessions*, 1:159; cf. 156.

9. For Arius and the impact of his ideas, see Rowan Williams, *Arius: Heresy and Tradition*, rev. ed. (Grand Rapids: Eerdmans, 2002). For a thorough discussion of Christ's preexistent state, see Douglas McCready, *He Came Down from Heaven: The Preexistence of Christ and the Christian Faith* (Downers Grove, IL: InterVarsity Press, 2005).

consider him equal to the Father or, though divine, subordinate in some way? Such questions have been entertained for centuries, but scholarly study of Christ devotion began in earnest in the late nineteenth century with the rise of the "history of religions school" and gained momentum with the publication of Wilhelm Bousset's milestone 1913 *Kyrios Christos*.[10] Some scholars have claimed that "it is impossible to get behind [Christian] tradition to a 'dogmatically pure' notion of New Testament Christology."[11] Most, however, agree that by the time the Gospel of John received its final form, typically dated to the late first century, belief that the risen Lord was divine prior to creation was clearly present in some, perhaps most, sectors of early Christianity.[12] Referring to Christ as "the Word," John's "prologue" famously declares: "In the beginning was the Word, and the Word was with God, and the Word was God" (John 1:1). Subsequently, the Gospel of John offers several accounts of Jesus applying to himself the divine name, "I Am," a translation verbally related to the Hebrew *YHWH*, the answer God supplied to Moses when Moses asked what God's name was (Exod. 3:13–15). When antagonists baited Jesus by asking if he claimed to be greater than Abraham, Jesus replied, "Before Abraham was, I am" (John 8:58).[13] Such statements, as well as the "I have come" sayings in

10. Wilhelm Bousset, *Kyrios Christos: A History of the Belief in Christ from the Beginnings of Christianity to Irenaeus*, trans. J. E. Steely (Nashville: Abingdon, 1970). The depth of twenty-first-century scholarship on the topic is epitomized by two works that draw on decades of research: Larry Hurtado, *Ancient Jewish Monotheism and Early Christian Jesus-Devotion: The Context and Character of Christological Faith* (Waco, TX: Baylor University Press, 2017), and Richard Bauckham, *Jesus and the God of Israel: God Crucified and Other Studies on the New Testament's Christology of Divine Identity* (Grand Rapids: Eerdmans, 2008). Useful for providing first-century context and a summary of the current state of the question is Matthew V. Novenson, ed., *Monotheism and Christology in Greco-Roman Antiquity* (Leiden: Brill, 2020).

11. Oliver Crisp, "Incarnation," in *Oxford Handbook of Systematic Theology*, ed. John Webster, Kathryn Tanner, Iain Torrance (New York: Oxford University Press, 2007), 163. An accessible overview of the issues at stake is Bart D. Ehrman, Michael F. Bird, and Robert B. Stewart, *When Did Jesus Become God? A Christological Debate* (Louisville: Westminster John Knox, 2022). See also James D. G. Dunn, *Christology in the Making: A New Testament Inquiry into the Origins of the Doctrine of the Incarnation*, 2nd ed. (Grand Rapids: Eerdmans, 1996).

12. So argued in Hurtado, *Ancient Jewish Monotheism*, 483–506, but see also Simon J. Gathercole, *The Preexistent Son: Recovering the Christologies of Matthew, Mark, and Luke* (Grand Rapids: Eerdmans, 2006).

13. Richard Bauckham, *The Testimony of the Beloved Disciple: Narrative, History, and Theology in the Gospel of John* (Grand Rapids: Baker Academic, 2007), 243–47, reviews the arguments for understanding the "I Am" statements as declarations of Christ's divinity. David B. Capes, *Old Testament Yahweh Texts in Paul's Christology* (Tübingen: J. C. B. Mohr,

John (and elsewhere), imply preexistence. So does Jesus's prayer of petition, "O Father, glorify thou me with thine own self with the glory which I had with thee before the world was" (John 17:5).

Latter-day Saint scripture is at least as forthright as the Gospel of John in proclaiming the divine character of the preexistent Son. In several places in the Book of Mormon, Christ is referred to as "the eternal God" (e.g., Book of Mormon title page; 2 Nephi 26:12). Elsewhere in the book, a heavenly messenger prophesies that "the time cometh, and is not far distant, that with power, the Lord Omnipotent who reigneth, who was, and is from all eternity to all eternity shall come down from heaven among the children of men, and shall dwell in a tabernacle of clay . . . and he shall be called Jesus Christ, the Son of God, the Father of heaven and earth, the Creator of all things from the beginning; and his mother shall be called Mary" (Mosiah 3:5, 8; cf. 7:27, 28). Later, a Book of Mormon prophet adds, "I would that ye should understand that God himself shall come down among the children of men, and shall redeem his people; and because he dwelleth in flesh, he shall be called the Son of God" (Mosiah 8:5). Moreover, Latter-day Saint affirmation of Jesus Christ's preexistent divinity was plainly reiterated as part of an official declaration issued by the church's First Presidency and Quorum of Twelve Apostles in 2000 titled "The Living Christ."[14]

Yet, Latter-day Saint embrace of Christ's preexistent divinity differs from standard views in several important ways. First, Mormons do not see the Son as sharing the Father's substance. As discussed in the first chapter, Mormonism's separate-being Trinitarianism considers the Son numerically distinct from the Father rather than distinct hypostatically from the Father within the one triune God. The Son is a separate divine being who, recalling the LDS view of eternity as endless time, was begotten at some point in eternity. Second, Latter-day Saints do not believe the Son was created divine. Rather, they believe he was procreated with the potential to *become* divine, a potential they believe he cultivated to the fullest. From "then on" in the preexistence he was God the Son, not merely a son of God. In time, under the Father's direction, he was the Creator of worlds. Each of these key differences warrants further consideration.

The Greek word *logos* can be defined in a variety of ways. It is used to refer to "reason" or "rationality," as well as to its outward expression as "word" or

---

1992), demonstrates at length that the apostle Paul also "identified Jesus with Yahweh in a substantive way" (185).

14. "The Living Christ: The Testimony of the Apostles" (Salt Lake City: The Church of Jesus Christ of Latter-day Saints, 2000), 1.

"speech." Over the centuries, Greek philosophers articulated a vision of *the* Logos as the rational order that structures the cosmos and, therefore, is an intrinsic part of the Supreme Being. Indeed, the Logos was often described as divine Reason itself. When God chose to create the physical universe his Logos/Reason had conceived, he simply externalized the Logos in a way that is affirmed but not explained to perform the work of creation. Some early Christians, as evidenced by the Johannine writings, identified the Logos-Creator with Christ, calling him "the Word," and developed a "Logos Christology." Discussion of the Logos, however, is almost nonexistent in LDS discourse, although this is not surprising given Mormonism's limited engagement with Greek philosophy and its separate-being Trinitarianism. Even reference to Christ as "the Word" is uncommon in Mormon parlance. Joseph Smith actually revised John 1:1 to read: "In the beginning was the gospel preached through the Son. *And the gospel was the word*, and the word was *with* the Son, and the Son was with God, and the Son was of God."[15] For Smith, the propriety of associating Christ with the Word revolved around his saving message, not his metaphysics. A revelation glossed John thus: "Therefore, in the beginning the Word was, for he was the Word, even the messenger of salvation" (D&C 93:8). Even the well-read church leader B. H. Roberts seemed to be unaware of a metaphysical reading of John 1: "There can be no question but direct reference is here made to the Lord Jesus Christ, as being the 'Word.' . . . Why [he is] called the 'Word' I do not know, unless it is that by a 'word' we make an expression; and since Jesus Christ was to be the expression of God, the revelation of God to the children of men, he was for that reason called the 'Word.'"[16] The closest Mormonism comes to the classical conception of the Logos is a single passage in the book of Moses that discusses how the Father created the universe through the agency of his Son: "And by the word of my power, have I created them, which is mine Only Begotten Son" (Moses 1:32).[17]

15. *NTOB*, 442 (emphasis added).

16. B. H. Roberts, *The Mormon Doctrine of Deity* (Salt Lake City: Deseret News, 1903), 189.

17. Apostle James Talmage considered it fitting to call Christ "the Word" or "the word of my power" because Christ was "the executive through whom the . . . [creative] word of the Father was put into effect." Talmage, *Jesus the Christ*, 33. Ever since its publication in 1915, the 800-page *Jesus the Christ* has served as a semiofficial LDS portrayal of the life, person, and work of Jesus Christ. At the time of its publication, the church's First Presidency announced that "this important work has been prepared by appointment and is to be published by the Church," adding, "We desire that the work . . . be read and studied by the Latter-day Saints." *Improvement Era*, September 1915, 1011. As an outgrowth of that original endorsement, the church still keeps *Jesus the Christ* in print in many languages.

If lack of familiarity with Greek philosophy undergirds a distinctive LDS reading of John 1, an even greater reason why a Logos Christology never developed in Mormonism is its singular account of the Son as united with the Father yet still a separate divine being (see chapter 1). The Son participates in divinity as an individual, not as one metaphysically linked to the Father. As such, the Son has his own independent rationality and divine power to act, albeit in complete harmony with the Father's mind and will. Instead of being the Father's eternal Logos, Latter-day Saints believe the Son was begotten, as were all other spirit children of God, prior to the physical creation of the universe, but they emphasize that he was literally the first to be "born." This is how they interpret such passages as Romans 8:29—"the firstborn among many brethren"—or Colossians 1:15—"the firstborn of every creature."[18] Beyond this literal interpretation of *prōtotokos* (firstborn), Christ's primogeniture is also thought to be implied in the declaration that he is "the beginning *(archē)* of the creation of God" (Rev. 3:14). In addition to construing "firstborn" as a reference to spirit birth sequence, Latter-day Saints also regard the Son as "first" in terms of preexistent status. LDS scripture states: "These two facts do exist, that [where] there are two spirits, one being more intelligent than the other; there shall be another more intelligent than they, [and the Son is] more intelligent than they all" (Abraham 3:19). Although through the shared experience of spirit birth, the Son may be considered humanity's "Elder Brother," in the glory and divinity he ultimately attained in the preexistence, he was vastly superior to all other souls.[19]

Still, Latter-day Saints do not believe the Son was begotten fully divine. He was not eternally the second person of the Trinity; he *became* the second person. Consonant with the Mormon doctrine of "eternal progression," even this greatest of all begotten souls had to "develop" toward divinity in the preexistence.[20] Spirit birth is believed to have embryonically conferred upon all God's spirit progeny, including the Firstborn, divine attributes that could be developed in the preexistence and beyond.[21] Yet, if each soul in the preexistence had the opportunity to progress and become like the heavenly Father, only the Firstborn "by obedience, by righteousness, through faith, over long

18. The LDS interpretation of "firstborn" is officially set forth in "The Father and the Son," 934–42.

19. "The Father and the Son," 941–42.

20. On divine "progression," see "God, Time, and Progression" in chapter 1 and the discussion of humankind's potential to follow a similar path in chapter 12.

21. Mormon doctrine does not specify which divine attributes were embryonically bestowed upon God's spirit children, but this is generally discussed in terms of moral capacity.

ages and eons . . . advanced and progressed until he became like unto God in power, in might, in dominion, and in intelligence."[22] Why was this so? As the literal firstborn, did he simply have a dramatically longer period in which to progress? Was it because God endowed him at spirit birth with a unique set of divine traits or with additional or enhanced divine potentialities that enabled him to achieve what no other did or even could do? LDS scripture and church authorities are silent on the matter. How was it recognized that the preexistent Son had become divine? Did he gradually develop his intrinsic but embryonic divine traits to the point where his love was perfect, his knowledge omniscient, and his powers omnipotent? Or, at some point did the Father "confer" divinity upon him as a reward for his incomparable preexistent fidelity? Again, given the paucity of scriptural details, LDS or otherwise, about the preexistence, authoritative answers have not been forthcoming. McConkie's statements seem to emphasize personal development; other Latter-day Saint leaders have ventured the idea of conferral. James Talmage, for instance, believed that at the appropriate point in the Son's preexistent progress, he was "invested with the powers and rank of Godship."[23] However it occurred, church leaders have been unequivocal in proclaiming Christ's preexistent divinity.[24]

All of this, of course, falls outside the pale of traditional Christian theism in several key ways. For example, classical theism holds that a thing is either wholly, eternally divine or it is not divine at all and never can be. A related postulate is that divinity is immutable (unchanging), which makes the idea of "progressing" or "developing" into godhood impossible. The traditional view has been that only God is divine and the Only Begotten has always fully shared that divinity as the eternally or ever-begotten Son. In the timeless realm of eternity, the Son's "begetting" refers not to a single "birth" event/moment but to an ever-present, beginning-less relationship between "Father" and "Son." Before classical theism was fully worked out, though, matters were not so sharply defined. "Everyone understood that the Logos or Wisdom of God was divine. It was not clear, however, exactly what that term 'divine' meant. For example, it might denote a quality of which there can be degrees, and on

22. Bruce R. McConkie, "The Seven Christs," *Ensign*, November 1982, 32.
23. Talmage, *Jesus the Christ*, 10. Another twentieth-century church authority remarked that the Father "elevated" the Son to the "position" of "the Godhead . . . by divine investiture." *Conference Report*, October 1956, 46.
24. A typical expression is Bruce McConkie's statement that the Son's progress "ranked him as a God, as the Lord Omnipotent, while yet in his pre-existent state. As such he became, under the Father, the Creator of this earth and of worlds without number." McConkie, *Mormon Doctrine*, 121.

such an understanding it would be consistent to say that the Logos is divine and yet not God in the same sense, to the same degree, as the Father."[25] Justin Martyr was one who read the biblical texts in this way to proclaim the Son's divinity but also to emphasize "that the Son is not God the way the Father is."[26] The problem in early Christological reflection was that calling Jesus "divine" did "not yet answer the question 'Divine in what sense?' Christians, of course, divided and subdivided over that question for centuries."[27]

For the most part, "the ante-Nicene church was 'subordinationist' and did not believe in the full co-equality and co-eternity of Father, Son and Holy Spirit."[28] Ironically, Arius "was in many respects a profoundly conservative theologian" who "was a more faithful representative of many of the most venerable schools of Trinitarian thought than were the champions of the Nicene settlement." From this perspective, Arius "was seeking to preserve . . . the 'subordinationist' metaphysics that in his part of the Christian world had served for generations."[29] Accordingly, he declared that the Father "rules" over the Son "as his God," and that the Son "in some degree worships the Greater."[30] In this sense, Christ's reference to the Father as "my God" (John 20:17) was not to be understood merely as the expression of the human Jesus.

It is important to point out that for early Christians, to view Christ as subordinate to the Father was not a derogatory characterization. It may have seemed implicit in the filial position the Son bears with respect to his Father. Origen stressed that to describe the Father "as greater than the Son does not refer to any difference of divinity, power, wisdom, or truth [but] to the Father's unique role and character within the Trinity."[31] Latter-day Saints share a similar view of the Son's subordination. Explained early Mormon apostle Parley Pratt, "The difference between Jesus Christ and his Father is this: one is subor-

---

25. Richard A. Norris Jr., ed., *The Christological Controversy* (Philadelphia: Fortress, 1980), 17.

26. Quoted in Demetrius C. Trakatellis, *The Pre-existence of Christ in the Writings of Justin Martyr* (Missoula, MT: Scholars Press for Harvard University, 1976), 52.

27. Luke Timothy Johnson, "How Jesus Became God," *Commonweal*, February 6, 2015.

28. Geza Vermes, *Christian Beginnings: From Nazareth to Nicaea* (New Haven: Yale University Press, 2013), 241.

29. David Bentley Hart, *You Are Gods: On Nature and Supernature* (Notre Dame: University of Notre Dame Press, 2022), 91.

30. The first statement is from Arius to Alexander of Alexandria, as quoted in William G. Rusch, ed. and trans., *The Trinitarian Controversy* (Philadelphia: Fortress, 1980), 32. The second excerpt from Arius is quoted in R. P. C. Hanson, *The Search for the Christian Doctrine of God: The Arian Controversy, 318–381* (Edinburgh: T&T Clark, 1988), 15.

31. Quoted in Christopher A. Beeley, *The Unity of Christ: Continuity and Conflict in Patristic Tradition* (New Haven: Yale University Press, 2012), 26.

dinate to the other, does nothing of himself, independently of the Father, but does all things in the name and by the authority of the Father." Furthermore, Pratt sounds an Origenian note when he writes that the Son "differs in nothing from his Father, except" that the Father does "preside over him, and over all his dominions, for ever and ever."[32] Drawing an analogy from their ecclesiastical organization, Latter-day Saints have sometimes described the Trinity as a "presidency" (a typical LDS term for a governing council composed of a president and two "counselors"). John Taylor, on one occasion, referred to the Son as "one of the Presidency in the heavens," a "Counselor," so to speak, to his Father "President."[33] The Son's subordination to the Father is also implicit in Joseph Smith's vision of the heavenly afterlife in which some enjoy the "presence of the Son but not of the Father" (D&C 76:75, 77).

Several additional clarifications regarding Latter-day Saint views of the Son's preexistence are in order. The first addresses the statement in the church's official declaration, the "Living Christ," that Jesus Christ "was the Great Jehovah of the Old Testament, the Messiah of the New."[34] Reference to Jesus as the "Jehovah of the Old Testament," though certainly not unheard of in Christian circles, takes a somewhat different form in Mormonism that requires explanation. "Jehovah," the Anglicized version of the Hebrew *YHWH*, occurs more than six thousand times in the Old Testament. The KJV and most versions of the Bible almost universally render it as "LORD" in small caps as a respectful replacement for *YHWH*/Jehovah, the proper name of Israel's God (Exod. 6:3; Ps. 83:18). Latter-day Saints also regard "Jehovah" as a "name-title" for the God of the Old Testament, whom they consider to be the preexistent Christ (more on this shortly). *Elohim*, on the other hand, usually translated "God" and considered by Hebraists a generic noun for Deity, appears more than two thousand times in the Bible. Given their separate-being Trinitarianism, however, Latter-day Saints consider "Elohim" to be the *Father's* "name-title" rather than an alternate designation for the God of the Old Testament, *YHWH*/Jehovah, whom they regard as the Son.[35]

Such distinctive LDS usages took decades to develop. Early on, although Latter-day Saints distinguished the Father and the Son as separate beings, they sometimes used the terms "God" and "LORD," or even "Elohim" and "Jehovah," interchangeably or in combination to apply to either the Father or the Son.

---

32. Pratt, *Key to Theology*, 32, 31.
33. Taylor, *Mediation and Atonement*, 136.
34. "The Living Christ," 1.
35. "The Father and the Son," 934–42.

Joseph Smith, for instance, once commenced a written prayer, "O, thou . . . Jehovah, God; thou Eloheem that sitteth . . . enthroned in heaven." On another occasion, he urged a colleague to trust "in the arm of Jehovah the Eloheem who sits enthroned in the heavens."[36] Both instances appear to reflect the textual combination "*YWHW Elohim*" ("LORD God") that appears more than five hundred times in the Bible. In a lengthy prayer, later canonized, that was used to consecrate the Latter-day Saints' "House of the Lord" in Kirtland, Ohio, in 1836, God the Father is addressed alternatingly as "Holy Father," "Jehovah," and "Lord" (e.g., D&C 109:29, 33, 34, 42, 43, 47). The Father is also referred to as Jehovah in several early Mormon hymns. In reference to Jesus's baptism, one proclaims: "Jehovah saw his darling Son, And was well pleas'd in what he'd done, And own'd him from the skies. . . . This is my Son, Jehovah cries."[37] But "Jehovah" could also be applied to Christ. Joseph Smith heard "the Voice of Jehovah, saying, I am the first and the last. I am he who liveth. I am he who was slain. I am your Advocate with the Father" (D&C 110:3–4).

By the twentieth century, largely as a reflection of nomenclature employed in LDS temple liturgy, church linguistic conventions tended to limit referential use of "Jehovah" to the Son and "Elohim" to the Father. The temple liturgy also reinforced a theological perception held by Latter-day Saints and some early Christians that the Father almost always deals with earth's inhabitants through the Son. The standard Mormon view is set forth by James Talmage: "A general consideration of scriptural evidence leads to the conclusion that God the Eternal Father has manifested Himself to earthly prophets or revelators on very few occasions, and then principally to attest the divine authority of His Son, Jesus Christ."[38] So often in the past century has LDS discourse made the point that Jehovah-Christ is the God of the Old Testament and that the Father himself almost never appeared or spoke to anyone on earth, that members of the Church of Jesus Christ of Latter-day Saints today who are unfamiliar with the Hebrew text of the Old Testament are surprised to learn of the many passages in which *elohim* speaks directly to prophets. One way LDS Hebrew scholars resolve the dilemma is by pointing out that linguistically *elohim* functions similarly to *adam*—primarily as a generic term rather than a proper noun.

36. *JSP*, J2:117, 88.

37. *A Collection of Sacred Hymns for the Church of the Latter Day Saints* (Kirtland, OH, 1835), #56.

38. Talmage, *Jesus the Christ*, 39. See also "The Father and the Son," 939–40. LDS apostle Joseph Fielding Smith expressed a similar view: "The Father has never dealt with man directly and personally since the fall, and he has never appeared except to introduce and bear record of the Son." *Doctrines of Salvation*, 1:27.

Just as nearly all the hundreds of appearances of *adam* in the biblical text are translated "man" or "human being" and only rarely "Adam," so the numerous references to *elohim* almost always refer to the category "God" rather than to what Latter-day Saints take to be the Father's personal "name-title."

Thus, in their own distinctive fashion, Mormons end up in much the same place as many early Christian fathers who for philosophical reasons taught that the transcendent Father does not trifle with "accommodationist" appearances to human beings. Justin Martyr voices this view in his *Dialogue with Trypho*. He argues that "there exists and is mentioned in Scripture another God and Lord under the [Father]-Creator of all things, who . . . proclaims to man whatever the Creator of the world—above whom there is no other God—wishes to reveal to them." For Justin, this supreme God "whom we call Creator of all and Father" has "never been seen by any man, and with whom no man has ever conversed."[39] Thus, because this other "God and Lord" was the Son/Logos, "the OT theophanies . . . in effect become Christophanies."[40] Similar views have been expressed off and on over the centuries in both the Christian East and West. Eastern Orthodox consider Old Testament theophanies to be "actual appearances of the pre-incarnate Son."[41] In early modern England, the famous Protestant hymn writer and minister Isaac Watts composed an extended essay revealingly titled "A Survey of the Visible Appearances of Christ as God, before His Incarnation." Watts's hope was that it might be "confessed almost universally in the British islands, that our blessed Saviour had a real existence long before he appeared in flesh and blood."[42] A century later, Harriet Beecher Stowe noted that from her observations the identification of Jesus with Jehovah

---

39. Justin Martyr, *Dialogue with Trypho* 56.4,1, in *St. Justin Martyr—Dialogue with Trypho*, trans. Thomas B. Falls, rev. Thomas P. Halton (Washington, DC: Catholic University of America Press, 2003), 83–84.

40. Gerald O'Collins, *Christology: A Biblical, Historical, and Systematic Study of Jesus Christ* (Oxford: Oxford University Press, 1995), 171. Justin's extensive depiction of Christ as Jehovah, the God of the Old Testament, is detailed in Trakatellis, *Pre-existence of Christ in Justin Martyr*, 53–92. Eusebius of Caesarea concurs: "So, let this be our proof in brief that the divine Word pre-existed and appeared to some, if not to all, men." Roy Deferrari, trans., *Eusebius Pamphili: Ecclesiastical History, Books 1–5* (Washington, DC: Catholic University of America Press, 1953), 42. Eusebius develops this argument at length in *Theophania, or Divine Manifestation of Our Lord and Saviour Jesus Christ*, trans. and ed. Samuel Lee (Cambridge, 1843).

41. "Theophanies of Christ," in *OSB*, 1242.

42. The essay appeared in Isaac Watts, *The Glory of Christ as God-Man Display'd in Three Discourses* (London, 1746), 1–82. The quotation is from p. 1. Several excerpts from Watts's essay were cited approvingly in the LDS *Times and Seasons*, April 1844, 502–3.

of the Old Testament was "the approved sentiment of sound theologians" in America.[43] That the numerous Old Testament theophanies were really Christophanies is a view with which LDS theology is obviously in full agreement.

Before turning to the incarnation, a final observation about Latter-day Saint teachings regarding the preexistent Son may be helpful. Mormons believe that all souls are spiritually corporeal in human form and resemble in appearance the future human bodies they will inhabit. "The spirit of man is in the form of man," declared the First Presidency and Twelve Apostles, "and the spirits of all creatures are in the likeness of their bodies."[44] Tertullian maintained a similar view in his treatise *On the Soul*. "The soul," he contends, "is a corporeal substance" whose form is "none other than the human form; indeed, none other than the shape of that body which each individual soul animates and moves about." This includes "eyes and ears" and "all the other members of the body."[45] Because Tertullian does not advance a doctrine of the preexistence of souls, he does not explicitly claim that the preexistent Word had a human shape, but he does affirm the Word's visible corporeality and, like Justin and Eusebius of Caesarea, cites the Word's many preincarnation appearances to Old Testament prophets.[46] With specific regard to any resemblance of the Son's preexistent spirit to his future physical body, Mormon doctrine is unambiguous. The preexistent Son of God "looked like" the future Jesus Christ. This is explicitly stated in the Book of Mormon, where the Son explains his Christophany to a prophet to whom he is appearing: "Behold, I am Jesus Christ . . . this body, which ye now behold, is the body of my spirit . . . and even as I appear unto thee to be in the spirit will I appear unto my people in the flesh" (Ether 3:14, 16).

INCARNATION

If the Gospel of John affirms the preexistent divinity of Christ, it also proclaims that divinity's "incarnation" (fleshly embodiment) when it declares that the divine Word "was *made flesh*, and dwelt among us" (John 1:14). For most Christians, exactly how invisible, immaterial, incorporeal, uncreated Being could

43. Harriet Beecher Stowe, *Footsteps of the Master*, as quoted in Thomas E. Jenkins, *The Character of God: Recovering the Lost Literary Power of American Protestantism* (New York: Oxford University Press, 1997), 72. Jenkins adds, "Stowe declared that all appearances of Jehovah in the Old Testament were really 'preappearances' of Christ" (72).

44. "The Father and the Son," 940.

45. Tertullian, *On the Soul* 9, in *ANF*, 3:188–89.

46. For the Word's substantive corporeality, see Tertullian, *Against Praxeas* 7, in *ANF*, 3:602; for the Son/Logos's Old Testament appearances, see *Against Praxeas* 14–16, in *ANF*, 3:609–12.

unite with visible, material, corporeal, created human flesh is a divine "mystery," something known only to God and either unrevealed or unrevealable to finite humanity. Origen wrote that "of all the marvellous and magnificent things about [Christ], this altogether surpasses the astonishment of the human intellect . . . that [the] very Word of the Father . . . in whom were created all things visible and invisible, can be believed to have . . . entered into the womb of a woman, to be born an infant and to utter cries like the wailing of infants."[47] Not surprisingly, Christians, including Latter-day Saints, sometimes refer to the incarnation as the "condescension" of God.[48] Latter-day Saints speak of the incarnation as occurring in the "meridian of time"—the high noon of human history. In this they concur with Karl Barth, who wrote that because Christ lived for all other humans as their representative before God, his life is at once "the center, beginning, and end of all the times of all the lifetimes of all men."[49]

Christ's living as human for all other humans points to the core reason offered in Christian theology for the incarnation—fallen humanity stands in need of redemption, and only by God becoming human can that be brought about. The undergirding idea, expressed as early as the second century by Irenaeus, is that because a fully human Adam, composed of soul *and* body, "fell" and brought fatal and fateful consequences to humanity, an embodied, fully human "second Adam" was needed to redeem humanity, body and soul, and bring them back to their pristine, prelapsarian (before the fall) condition. The popular patristic axiom was "that which is not assumed [taken on] is not healed."[50] The potential healing of generic human nature is made possible

47. Origen, *On First Principles* 2.6.2, in *Origen, On First Principles*, trans and ed. John Behr (Oxford: Oxford University Press, 2017), 2:205. The *New Catholic Encyclopedia*, 2nd ed. (Detroit: Gale, 2003), 7:373, describes the incarnation as "the mystery of the Second Person of the Blessed Trinity's becoming man, the mystery of Jesus Christ's being God and man, the mystery of His being the God-Man." Just how complex philosophical probing of the "mystery" of the incarnation can become is illustrated in Richard Cross, *The Metaphysics of the Incarnation: Thomas Aquinas to Duns Scotus* (New York: Oxford University Press, 2002).

48. A typical theological expression is Thomas F. Torrance's statement that the Son "has condescended to reveal Himself to us with creaturely existence and contingency, and has assumed our humanity to meet us as man to man." Torrance, *Theological Science* (Oxford: Oxford University Press, 1970), 46. More popularly, see K. Scott Oliphint, *God with Us: Divine Condescension and the Attributes of God* (Wheaton, IL: Crossway, 2012). The phrase "condescension of God" appears in the Book of Mormon at 1 Nephi 11:16, 26.

49. Barth, *Church Dogmatics* III/2:440, as quoted in Robert D. Dawson, *The Resurrection in Karl Barth* (Farnham, UK: Ashgate, 2007), 67.

50. While this was said in one form or another by a number of church fathers, it is commonly associated with a statement made in Gregory of Nazianzus's *First Letter to Cledonius*

by its intimate association in Jesus with the Son's incarnated divinity. Here, the logic is rooted in the philosophical distinction between "universals" and "particulars." Universals are the features or characteristics shared by countless concrete particulars. In other words, "human nature," "humankind," or "humanity" names such a universal, while "Sarah" and "Sam" name concrete particulars of that universal. As the Christian tradition came to be articulated in such a philosophical framework, "the important thing about Christ therefore was not that the Word had become *a* [particular] man but that the Word had assumed [universal] *humanity* in order to save it."[51] Just as the fall of Adam was the fall of all humankind, so Christ, the second Adam, took on universal human nature to reverse the effects of the universal fall. Athanasius of Alexandria explained it thus: "For the solidarity of mankind is such that, by virtue of the Word's indwelling in a single human body, the corruption which goes with death has lost its power over all. . . . Through this union of the immortal Son of God with our human nature, all men were clothed with incorruption in the promise of the resurrection."[52]

Latter-day Saint Christology is in full agreement with the redemptive purpose of the incarnation, although Mormonism's distinctive metaphysics obviates the need to base it in a "that which is not assumed cannot be healed" rationale. LDS teaching highlights a slightly different dimension of Christ's redemption by emphasizing that the incarnation enabled Christ to empathize with humanity's infirmities not just spiritually but physically as well. Hebrews 2 proclaims that Christ fully took on human nature—"in all things it behooved him to be made like unto his brethren" (Heb. 2:17)—and because "he himself hath suffered being tempted ['tested,' NRSV, NABRE], he is able to succour them that are tempted" (Heb. 2:18). Hebrews 4:15 adds, "For we have not an high priest which cannot be touched with the feeling of our infirmities; but was in all points tempted like as we are, yet without sin." Reflecting on these passages, John Taylor explained that "It was absolutely necessary that [Christ] should . . . be subjected to the buffetings of Satan the same as we are, and pass through all the trials incident to humanity, and thereby comprehend the weakness and the true character of human nature, with all its faults and foibles, that we might have a faithful High Priest that

---

the *Presbyter* 5. It is rendered as "the unassumed is the unhealed" in Lionel Wickham, trans., *On God and Christ: The Five Theological Orations and Two Letters to Cledonius* (Crestwood, NY: St. Vladimir's Seminary Press, 2002), 158.

51. Maurice F. Wiles, *The Christian Fathers* (New York: Oxford University Press, 1982), 73.

52. *The Incarnation of the Word of God, Being the Treatise of St. Athanasius*, trans. Religious of CSMV (London: Centenary, 1944), 35.

would know how to deliver those that are tempted."[53] Apostle Erastus Snow added that Christ was "touched with the feelings of all our infirmities . . . in order that he might be filled with compassion, not to justify our sins, but to have mercy and compassion upon our infirmities."[54] Because he experienced the full range of human temptation and trial, Christ is able to be empathetic, even sympathetic, to all sinners. Indeed, the Greek term rendered in the KJV as "touched with the feeling" of our infirmities is *sympatheō*. Charles Hodge, the famed nineteenth-century champion of Reformed orthodoxy, made the same point about Christ being peccable (technically capable of sinning): "If from the constitution of his person it was impossible for Christ to sin, then his temptation was unreal and without effect, and He cannot sympathize with his people."[55] But he was peccable and suffered "temptations of every kind," though without succumbing, "that his bowels may be filled with mercy . . . that he may know *according to the flesh* how to succor his people according to their infirmities" (Alma 7:11–12 [emphasis added]).

Beyond this, Mormon doctrine adds several unique reasons for the incarnation. One is the LDS belief that the Son of God "needed" to acquire and eventually, in the resurrection, divinize a physical body like his Father's. Though the preexistent Christ was God the Son, the Creator of the universe, he lacked the divine *physical* body that was an aspect of his Father's divinity (see chapter 1). Though hypothetically the Father may simply have created such a body for the Son, Mormon doctrine teaches that God ordained the same path of bodily acquisition and perfection for the Son that he did for all his spirit children, namely, incarnation, resurrection, and glorification. Another LDS distinctive is the conception of earth life as a spiritual "probation" or proving

53. *Journal of Discourses*, 7:198–99.

54. *Journal of Discourses*, 7:358.

55. Charles Hodge, *Systematic Theology*, 2:457, quoted in Oliver Crisp, *God Incarnate: Explorations in Christology* (London: T&T Clark, 2009), 123. Jerome Van Kuiken, *Christ's Humanity in Current and Ancient Controversy: Fallen or Not?* (London: Bloomsbury T&T Clark, 2017), explores theological reflection on the meaning of Paul's statement that God sent "his own Son in the likeness of sinful flesh, and for [to deal with] sin" (Rom. 8:3). Van Kuiken compares patristic reflection with the Christological debate of the last two centuries over whether or not Christ assumed a "fallen" human nature, complete with a liability to sin and evil tendencies. In particular, Van Kuiken analyzes the writings of Karl Barth, Thomas F. Torrance, and Thomas Weinandy, who support the idea, and the views of Phillip Hughes and Scottish theologians Hugh Mackintosh and Donald Macleod, who reject it. Without attempting to settle the debate, Van Kuiken's recourse to the early fathers leads him to conclude that they kept in balance a belief in Christ's "prelapsarian sinlessness" with a commitment to "his salvific solidarity with our postlapsarian state" (162).

ground to see if God's children "will do all things whatsoever the Lord their God shall command them" (Abraham 3:24). Although chief among God's spirit children, the Son, despite his preexistent divinity, had to be "tested" and "proven" just like his spirit brothers and sisters in a human environment rife with sin and in a body subject to the mortal consequences of the fall. Mormon theology expresses no doubt that Christ would prove himself, but it also emphasizes that his earthly probation was no sham. This echoes patristic Christologies such as those associated with the region near the Syrian city of Antioch and labeled "Antiochene" that view Christ as "the forerunner, whose triumphant finishing of the course is the assurance that others will be able to complete it victoriously also."[56] Nonetheless, because of Christ's sinless perfection, it has been clear to all Christians, including Latter-day Saints, that Jesus of Nazareth was more than an ordinary man. What he experienced and accomplished during his earthly sojourn seemed at times to be the work of a god, but how and in what way(s) could he be both human and divine? This was the question that lay at the heart of formative Christological reflection for centuries.

Two Natures—Divinity and Humanity

Answers to this great Christological conundrum range along a spectrum of views. At either end are the heretical positions commonly labeled Ebionism and docetism. Ebionism refers to the doctrine of a cluster of second-century, reportedly Jewish Christian groups known as "Ebionites" (from *ebyon*: "poor men"). Ebionites supposedly taught that Jesus was merely a man who, although extremely righteous, was like all other men in his nature. Only at Jesus's resurrection (or perhaps at his baptism) did God elevate him to be his Son.[57] Docetism, from the Greek *dokein*, meaning "to seem" or "to appear," stressed Christ's divinity to the point of excluding his humanity, claiming that he only *appeared* to be human. Docetic views were rooted in the philosophical assumption that divinity and matter are utterly incompatible.[58] Between

---

56. Wiles, *The Christian Fathers*, 73.

57. The Ebionites are discussed by Hippolytus in his *Refutation of All Heresies* 22, in *ANF*, 5:114.

58. The views of Marcion of Sinope and Christian Gnostics in the second century are oft-cited examples of docetism. "Jesus, who brought to spirits imprisoned in matter a message of redemption and freedom, was thought by most Gnostic sects not to have had a real body, or to have experienced real human need or suffering." Brian E. Daley, "Christ and Christologies," in *Oxford Handbook of Early Christian Studies*, ed. Susan Ashbrook Harvey

the polar opposites of Ebionism and docetism are views that do not dismiss either Christ's humanity or his divinity but wrestle with how to balance the two. Particularly from the later fourth century to the middle of the fifth century, the relationship between Christ's humanity and his divinity was hotly debated. Scholars often refer to this as the "Christological controversy."[59] All sides avoided the extremes of Ebionism and docetism and embraced both Christ's divinity and his humanity, but some leaned in an Ebionite direction, intent on not letting his divinity eclipse his humanity, while others wanted to be sure that his divinity was firmly "in the driver's seat," so to speak. Consideration of the Christological controversy may appropriately begin by examining the thought of Apollinarius (also spelled Apollinaris) of Laodicea, from the earliest phase of the debate.

Apollinarius taught that the mind or intellect of Jesus, his "rational soul," was none other than the divine Son/Logos itself, the indwelling second person of the Trinity. Jesus of Nazareth was the temple in which the Son of God dwelt, the human clothing in which the Word of God lived out a human life.[60] Some have dubbed Apollinarianism "space-suit Christology." Just as an astronaut dons "an elaborate space suit which enables him to live and act in a new, unfamiliar environment, so the *Logos* put on a body which enabled him to [live] as a human being among human beings."[61] The idea that the divine Word ensouled Jesus was an old one by the time Apollinarius promoted it. It had been previously voiced by many, ranging from Paul of Samosata to Lucian of Antioch and Eusebius of Caesarea. Yet by Apollinarius's time, the Christolog-

---

and David G. Hunter (New York: Oxford University Press, 2008), 890. Docetic views may have been a problem already in the New Testament. First John 4:3 warns the faithful that any one that "confesseth not that Jesus Christ is come in the flesh is not of God."

59. The Council of Chalcedon in 451 is often seen as the terminus of this controversy, but in reality it lingered on for several centuries, extending to the third Council of Constantinople in 680 and even beyond to the not-unrelated "iconoclastic controversy" of the 700s. On the controversy, see Philip Jenkins, *A Storm of Images: Iconoclasm and Religious Reformation in the Byzantine World* (Waco, TX: Baylor University Press, 2023).

60. Apollinaris, "Fragments," in Norris, *The Christological Controversy*, 107–11. See also Beeley, *The Unity of Christ*, 176–78. Although Apollinarius sometimes assumed a two-part anthropology (soul and fleshly body), he generally maintained a tripartite anthropology of mind or rational soul, animating soul, and body. Either way, his crucial and consistent point was that the indwelling Son/Logos supplied Christ's controlling *nous* (mind or intellect).

61. Hanson, *Search for the Christian Doctrine of God*, 448. A similar, though less dramatic, analogy is the New Testament teaching that the human body is the "tabernacle"/tent (*skēnōma*) of the spirit, as when Paul calls his "tabernacle" his "earthly house" (2 Cor. 5:1) or Peter writes, "Knowing that shortly I must put off this my tabernacle" (2 Pet. 1:14).

ical consensus was moving in a different direction. In the spirit of the patristic aphorism that that which is not assumed is not healed, conceptual momentum favored the idea that what the Son/Logos inhabited was a total human being, complete with its own separate human mind/soul and its own distinct will.

Scholars sometimes distinguish the two views by calling the Apollinarian perspective a "Logos-flesh" Christology (Logos + fleshly body = Jesus Christ) in contrast to the ultimately dominant "Logos-human" Christology (Logos + rational *human* soul + fleshly body = Jesus Christ). For Apollinarius, however, a Logos-human Christology seemed incongruous. Such a "joint tenancy" would mean that "either the Logos would simply dominate the human soul and thus destroy the freedom by which it was human, or the human soul would be an independent center of initiative and Jesus would be, in effect, schizophrenic."[62] Instead, countered Apollinarius, "Christ is one, moved only by a divine will."[63] Here Latter-day Saint Christology resembles Apollinarianism in at least this respect: all begotten souls, including the Son's, are believed to provide the intellect and rational soul for the physical bodies they come to inhabit. In this sense, other than the crucial difference that the Son was vastly superior to all other souls (having reached godhood), Mormon doctrine does not make a distinction between the preexistent souls sent to inhabit human bodies and the preexistent Logos/Son that came to inhabit the body in Mary's womb.

Although Apollinarius's Logos-flesh Christology fell out of favor, the questions he raised about the psychological unity of Christ persisted. A generation later the influential bishop-theologian Cyril of Alexandria would take up these questions and endeavor to fashion an acceptably orthodox answer. "What hung in the balance" in this Christological controversy was whether Jesus Christ "should be regarded as having a single 'I' or in fact two 'I's."[64] Did he have multiple person-alities? Ultimately, the church fathers, influenced by Cyril, decided that a correct Christological understanding recognized two natures in Jesus, one divine and one human, but not two *persons* or two "I"s. As they tended to phrase it, there were not "two Sons." The Council of Chalcedon in 451 declared itself "opposed to those who attempt to tear apart the mystery . . . into a duality of sons." Instead, the Chalcedonian Definition of Faith confessed "one and the same Christ, Son, Lord, Only-begotten, acknowledged in two natures." The Council proclaimed that in addition to being "truly God,"

---

62. Norris, *The Christological Controversy*, 22.
63. Apollinaris, "Fragments," 110.
64. Charles M. Stang, "The Two 'I's of Christ: Revisiting the Christological Controversy," *Anglican Theological Review* 94 (Summer 2012): 533.

Christ was also "truly [hu]man, of a rational soul [contrary to Apollinarius] and a body," but they denied the presence of two acting subjects, two psychological centers of consciousness and activity, in their one Lord.[65]

How Christ could be understood to have two minds—the Son/Logos and an ordinary human intellect—and yet be a single acting subject is due primarily to the theological work of Cyril.[66] Cyril proposed that in the mystery of the incarnation a union of the Logos and human rational soul occurred that was so intimate it resulted in a single hypostatic "I." Yet, this miraculous union did not erase the distinctive properties of Christ's divinity or humanity. In attempting to explain how such an intimate yet property-preserving union could have taken place, Cyril invoked the earlier notion of *communicatio idiomatum* (an exchange/sharing of properties). By this metaphysical miracle, the single hypostasis/person of Jesus Christ was simultaneously passible (capable of suffering) in his humanity and impassible in his divinity. Cyril made clear that this "hypostatic union" was strong enough that all actions and utterances in the Gospels, those that seemed to demonstrate Christ's divine nature as well as those that made him seem quite human, were to be attributed to a single acting subject, a composite hypostasis/person, the Son-Jesus. Both Jesus's human and the Son's divine characteristics are, in philosophical language, "predicated of the whole," and Jesus Christ only "exists in the singleness of a commingled incarnate nature."[67] In this way, the indwelling divine Son/Logos was able to fully participate in Jesus's salvific suffering without violating his divine impassibility. In the words of one of Cyril's favorite Christological sayings, the Son "suffered impassibly (*apathos epathen*)."[68] This paradoxical mystery, sometimes called "theopaschitism" or "theopaschism" (God suffers [in the flesh]), has also been aptly captured in the phrase "the possibility of the impassible God."[69]

---

65. *Creeds & Confessions*, 1:179, 181.

66. Cyril's influential Christology is comprehensively discussed in John A. McGuckin, *St. Cyril of Alexandria: The Christological Controversy—Its History, Theology, and Texts* (Leiden: Brill, 1994).

67. The quotes are from Apollinarius, as cited in *The Case against Diodore and Theodore: Texts and Contexts*, ed. and trans. John Behr (New York: Oxford University Press, 2011), 10. Cyril would have resisted the use of "commingled" (*mixis*) since it could imply an unacceptable hybridity, but he shared Apollinarius's "resolute determination to avoid any suggestion of duality in the one Lord Jesus Christ" (9–10).

68. John McGuckin, "St. Cyril of Alexandria's Miaphysite Christology and Chalcedonian Dyophysitism," *Ortodoksia* 53 (2013): 40.

69. Paul L. Gavrilyuk, *The Suffering of the Impassible God: The Dialectics of Patristic Thought* (Oxford: Oxford University Press, 2004), 160. Cyril and Gregory of Nazianzus are

Through the concept of the hypostatic union, Cyril's theopaschism attributes the passion to the whole person of Christ.

Cyril's theopaschism, however, seemed blasphemous to his opponents, who restricted the passion to Jesus's human body alone while the divine, impassible Son "looked on," ontologically uninvolved, in a sort of out-of-body, in-body experience. But to Cyril's followers this seemed like splitting Christ in two. "If the life of Christ was a saving life and the death of Christ was a saving death, then the subject of every aspect of that life and death cannot have been other than the divine Word himself."[70] To be sure, the common commitment to divine impassibility compelled clarification that the Word experienced the crucifixion hypostatically linked to the human Jesus rather than in his divine essence alone, but the incarnate Son was still the sole acting subject of all Christ's earthly experiences.[71] Thus, Paul could in truth say of Christ's enemies, "they . . . crucified the Lord of Glory" (1 Cor. 2:8). Interpretation of this passage has been important in Christological reflection over the years. Augustine, for instance, affirmed that "the Lord of glory was crucified, because even God is rightly said to have been crucified, not after the power of the divinity, but after the weakness of the flesh."[72] And the Fifth Ecumenical Council (in Constantinople in 553) anathematized any who would not confess that he who "was crucified in his human flesh is truly God and the Lord of glory and one of the members of the Holy Trinity."[73]

The same willingness to declare Divinity's involvement in Christ's passion is plainly manifest in Mormonism, where a single-nature ontology obviates any need for the concept of a hypostatic union. LDS scripture records Christ's own description of the crucifixion in these words: "Which suffering caused myself, even *God*, the greatest of all, to tremble because of pain, and to bleed at every pore, and to suffer both body and spirit" (D&C 19:17 [emphasis added]). A Book of Mormon prophet foresaw that "the God of Abraham, and of Isaac, and the God of Jacob yieldeth himself . . . as a man, into the hands of wicked men, to be lifted

---

credited with coining the phrase God's "impassible passion." Christopher A. Beeley, "Christ and Human Flourishing in Patristic Theology," *Pro Ecclesia* 25 (May 2016): 133.

70. Wiles, *The Christian Fathers*, 66.

71. "As much as we might be attracted to the notion that God gains experiential knowledge of human misery in the passion and crucifixion," writes Charles Stang, "if that experiential knowledge does not penetrate to the divine nature, then we might be forgiven if we ask what God has in fact learned." "The Two 'I's of Christ," 543.

72. Augustine, *On the Trinity* 1.28.

73. *Creeds & Confessions*, 1:209. Thomas Aquinas reiterated this centuries later in *Summa Theologiae* 3a.46.12.

up . . . and to be crucified," adding in a parallel to 1 Corinthians 2:8, and "they crucify the God of Israel" (1 Nephi 19:10, 13). An influential early LDS doctrinal handbook adds that it was the Lord of Glory, the creator of the world, "this controller of the destinies of the human family, who, in his last moments, cried out in the agony of his soul, 'My God, my God, why hast thou forsaken me?'"[74]

Cyril's deft deployment of the concept of *communicatio idiomatum* and his articulation of the hypostatic union paved the way for the Council of Chalcedon to aver that "at no point was the difference between the [divine and human] natures taken away through the union, but rather the property of both natures is preserved and comes together into a single person and a single subsistent being; he is not parted or divided into two persons, but is one and the same only-begotten Son, God, Word, Lord Jesus Christ."[75] What the Council ruled against, however, and what Cyril had been combating was a line of Christological analysis typically labeled "Antiochene" (for its association with the ancient Syrian city of Antioch) and most prominently represented by Theodore of Mopsuestia, Nestorius of Constantinople, and Theodoret of Cyrrhus. Rather than proposing a hypostatic "union," the Antiochenes favored a "conjunction" (*synaphea*) of the two natures, one that allowed the Antiochenes to assiduously cordon off the impassibility of Christ's divine nature. Carefully parsing the life of Jesus Christ as detailed in the Gospels, they attributed all words and deeds that demonstrated passibility solely to his human nature and those that seemed supernatural to his divine nature. Theodore of Mopsuestia, for instance, contended that when Christ died, the "assumed man" was dying, but when Christ healed the sick, it was the assuming God who did the healing. "Divinity and humanity in Christ are for Theodore, not merely logical subjects to which different things can be attributed. Rather, divinity and humanity are discrete agents, separate ontological existences."[76]

The Antiochene perspective was thought to offer a double benefit. On the one hand, it ensured that Christ could be seen as "truly human" in every way, undergoing the full range of authentic human experiences. On the other hand, it did so without implicating the indwelling Word in any nondivine activity, even indirectly through the instrumentality of the body. Such a sharp distinction has led some scholars to characterize Antiochene Christology as more

---

74. *Compendium of Doctrines*, 79.

75. *Creeds & Confessions*, 1:181.

76. Aaron Riches, *Ecce Homo: On the Divine Unity of Christ* (Grand Rapids: Eerdmans, 2016), 28.

disjunctive than conjunctive.[77] It appeared so to Cyril, and eventually to the Council at Chalcedon, who anathematized such views as a "division" of natures. That, along with the concomitant depiction of Christ's divine and human natures as a two-person partnership rather than a single, united person/hypostasis, became the "heresy" known as Nestorianism. Although the Antiochene desire to preserve "the character proper to each of the two natures" was perfectly orthodox, their overemphasis on the matter led to the *un*orthodox position of envisioning a separate acting subject/person or "I" for each of the two natures. Nestorianism's "two-Son" Christology failed to make sufficient allowance for involving the incarnate *God* in Christ's redemptive human experiences.

For their part, the Antiochenes had cause to be concerned that Cyril's single-subject/single "I" Christology was so ontologically dense that it could spill over into heretical Monophysitism (one-nature-ism). It did so in the noted case of Eutyches, the Constantinopolitan archimandrite (monastery head) who was condemned for teaching that the union of the two natures was so profound that the incarnation actually resulted in a new, third nature, a *tertium quid* (third something), a hybrid of the divine and human natures. Eutyches declared "that our Lord was of two natures before the union, but after the union one nature," hence Monophysitism. In so teaching, Eutyches claimed to be "follow[ing] the doctrine of the blessed Cyril."[78] Given the extremely fine distinctions at work in the Christological controversy, Eutyches might be forgiven for missing the razor-thin difference between acceptable Cyrillian "Mia-physitism" and his own unacceptable "Mono-physitism" (*mia* and *mono* can both be translated "one" and, together with *physis* [nature], can mean "one nature"). Rooted in the idea of the hypostatic union, however, Cyril's version of "one-nature-ism" (Miaphysitism) did not go as far as Monophysite hybridity. Complicating matters even further was the fact that *hypostasis* was sometimes understood synonymously with *physis* (nature), thus facilitating a Monophysite, single-nature Christology rather than just a single-subject/person Christology of the kind we have been discussing. Ultimately, the Chalcedonian Definition of Faith attempted to steer a middle position, avoiding both the Monophysite conflation of natures and the Antiochene/Nestorian mere juxtaposition of natures. Thus, the Definition proclaimed the single Christ in

77. Justo L. González, *A Concise History of Christian Doctrine* (Nashville: Abingdon, 2005), 116.

78. Henry Bettenson and Chris Maunder, eds., *Documents of the Christian Church*, 4th ed. (Oxford: Oxford University Press, 2011), 51.

two natures "which undergo no confusion" yet "no division [or] separation," thereby setting the framework within which so-called orthodox Christology would subsequently be elaborated.[79]

In recent times, Chalcedonian Christology has faced a number of challenges. Prominent among them is logical coherence. For instance, "it is hard to conceive of a single individual possessing two actualized natures of distinctive quality—as, for example, in a pet that is both fully canine and fully feline at the same time." Another seemingly irresolvable paradox asks how Christ could in his single person concurrently be both omniscient and limited in knowledge. "Technically speaking, to be both consciously omniscient and non-omniscient is a contradiction—one cannot both know something and not know it at the same time." Moreover, if the incarnate Christ had a "dual consciousness—a fully divine awareness and a fully human awareness—this would seem to split the unity of his person, given that mind and consciousness are better seen as constituents of personhood rather than of nature."[80] Even laying aside such conceptual criticisms, the theological wrangling that continued for several centuries after Chalcedon has led some modern observers to consider the Council's Definition of Faith a problematic compromise at best. Still, others applaud it for distilling decades of debate into an inspired baseline confession that sets the parameters of "orthodox" Christology and properly leaves explanation to the realm of divine mystery that finite humans can never adequately comprehend.

LDS Christology

Although embracing neither Eutychean Monophysitism nor Cyrillian Miaphysitism, Mormon theology definitely fits on the single-subject end of the Christological continuum. Still, trying to place it on the standard Christological spectrum evokes the proverbial challenge of comparing apples and oranges. This is so primarily because Mormonism does not make the same sharp, ontological distinction between an uncreated, divine nature and a created, human nature that Christianity traditionally makes. As discussed in chapter 1, there is only a single nature shared by God and his human children, although they are at vastly different points along that single ontological continuum. A typical, if early, expression of Mormonism's version of Monophysitism comes from

---

79. *Creeds & Confessions*, 1:181.
80. Richard J. Plantinga, Thomas R. Thompson, and Matthew D. Lundberg, *An Introduction to Christian Theology* (Cambridge: Cambridge University Press, 2010), 246–48.

apostle Parley Pratt. He acknowledges the standard Christological premise that "God and man [are] two distinct species" or natures but finds it at odds with what he considers the great truth revealed through Joseph Smith: "Gods, angels and men, are all of one species, one race, one great family."[81] Such ontological monism takes the Chalcedonian confession that Christ is "consubstantial with us" to a new level. In B. H. Roberts's view, it was particularly problematic to talk "about the humanity of Jesus being separate from the divinity of Jesus" because "He Himself made no such distinctions."[82] From the perspective of LDS Monophysitism, the proper distinction to be made is between the ascended Christ, who is "a specimen of Divine, eternal Humanity . . . with attributes perfected," and "his [earthly] brethren who . . . although children of the same royal Parent in the heavens . . . are not perfected in their attributes."[83]

While the qualitative difference between God and his spirit children either in their preexistent or earth-life states is so dramatic as to be beyond human comprehension, the difference is still seen in Latter-day Saint ontology as one of degree, not of kind. For Mormonism, this avoids the classical conundrum of how best to describe the relationship between Christ's two supposedly ontologically distinct natures. It also precludes the need to imagine that Christ's "human" nature, in the sense of a separate "human" mind or will, only began when he was born on earth. Christ's "human" mind and will, like the minds and wills of all God's children, are the same mind and will that animated his preexistent soul and that accompanied his entrance into a physical body at birth. Latter-day Saint thought has never seriously considered the possibility of Christ possessing two distinct minds or wills as the ultimately orthodox "dyotheletism" ("two-wills-ism") would have it.[84] All rational, volitional, and

---

81. Pratt, *Key to Theology*, 31–33.

82. Roberts, *Course in Theology*, 3:188. The theological foreignness to Latter-day Saints of a two-natures Christology has led some to misread the subtlety of the Chalcedonian formulation of Christ as "one person in two natures" as an expression of *tertium quid* Monophysitism: "I have heard sectarian priests undertake to tell the character of the Son of God," complained Brigham Young, "and they make him half of one species and half of another, and I could not avoid thinking at once of the mule." *Journal of Discourses*, 4:217. Yet Eutychean notions of a Christological "mule" actually were ruled out of bounds at Chalcedon.

83. Pratt, *Key to Theology*, 31–32.

84. If will is an integral part of one's nature, then the confession of two natures logically entails two wills (dyotheletism). Yet, the strong emphasis on a single acting subject could support monotheletism (one-will-ism). Which best characterized the incarnate Son of God was still being debated in the 600s. The Ekthesis, an imperial confession of faith from early in the century, illustrates how monotheletism could be argued while still acknowledging two natures: the human will in Jesus "never made any movement deriving from its own

moral impulses for Christ were, as they are for each of God's spirit children, intrinsic to, and exercised by, his now-embodied preexistent soul/spirit. Rather than a "Logos-human" Christology, then, in which separate divine and human wills coexist and cooperate within the single, incarnate Christ, Mormonism's version of a single-subject Christology resembles the ancient "Logos-flesh" conception. For Latter-day Saints, this, along with Mormonism's rejection of impassibility and immutability as essential features of divinity, has eliminated the need for the careful ontological parsing of the divine and the human in the life of Christ that characterized much Christological thinking in earlier years. Thus, for example, Christ's famous passion exclamations "let this cup pass from me" and "why hast thou forsaken me" do not pose for Latter-day Saints the same interpretive challenge they have for many Christian theologians. Latter-day Saints interpret New Testament passages in which the text differentiates Christ's will from the Father's as proof that the Father and Son are two, separate, volitional *beings*, not as evidence of an internal divine-human distinction within Christ.

Beyond such metaphysical matters, Mormonism does acknowledge a certain dual quality to the incarnate Christ's nature. While proclaiming that Christ and humanity share the same ontological core, LDS teaching affirms that in a fallen world all humans, including the incarnate Christ, experience diverging internal impulses and attributes characterized by such contrasting labels as "human" versus "divine" or "spiritual" versus "carnal" (lit., of the flesh). In this descriptive, nonontological sense, LDS Church president David McKay referred to the "dual nature of man" and taught that "each of us has two contrasting natures."[85] Latter-day Saints believe that although Christ lived a sinless life, he entered fully into the fallen human experience and was peccable as are all others. Erastus Snow explained, "[Christ] came from the Father to sojourn in the flesh among men, to take upon him the infirmities of the flesh and the weaknesses of human nature . . . exposing himself to all the physical ills that prey upon the human system, and to all the powers of darkness that prey upon the intellectual faculties of man, exposing himself to the temptations of the hosts of hell. He had to combat all these contending powers . . . and to resist every other evil [that] flesh is heir to." For Snow, this is what Paul was referring

---

nature separately and of its own impulse in opposition to the will of God the Word, which was hypostatically united to it." Quoted in Cyril Hovorun, *Eastern Christianity in Its Texts* (London: T&T Clark, 2022), 561. Ultimately, however, dyotheletism won the day. The long and intricate Christological conversation that followed Chalcedon for the next several centuries is helpfully detailed in Hovorun, *Eastern Christianity*, 521–79.

85. *Teachings: David O. McKay*, 11–18.

to when he spoke of "God sending his own Son in the likeness of sinful flesh, and for sin, condemned sin in the flesh" (Rom. 8:3).[86]

Early church fathers and recent biblical commentators alike have understood *homoiōma* (likeness) in Romans 8:3 as intending to communicate "identity such that the Son did not merely resemble human flesh but participated fully in sinful flesh." Possessing fallen, "sinful (peccable) flesh," Christ was susceptible to temptation, genuinely "affected by the power of sin, although he did not himself sin." Thus, the passage in Romans "denotes the full identity of the Son with sinful humanity, though he never sinned."[87] Latter-day Saints concur. They acknowledge that sin is endemic to the fallen human condition, but they do not believe it is hardwired into humanity as "original sin" (see chapter 5). Infants are born innocent, and the *theoretical* possibility of sinlessness exists. Thus, for Latter-day Saints, there is no reason to distinguish between humankind's fallen "sinful flesh" and Christ's immaculate flesh. There is only one kind of flesh—innocent, guilt-free flesh—that all, including the Son, receive at birth. Still, in a fallen world, the countervailing forces of sin that shape the developing human being are so ubiquitous and intense that none but Christ has ever lived a sinless life. The Latter-day Saint position is that Christ entered the same fallen world and was exposed to the same temptations and trials as any other human being. Yet, unlike other humans, he was able to maintain his birth innocence and purity throughout life.[88] Emphasized Howard Hunter, "It is important to remember that Jesus was capable of sinning, that he could have succumbed . . . but that he remained true." He "was perfect and sinless, not because he had to be, but rather because he clearly and determinedly wanted to be."[89]

---

86. *Journal of Discourses*, 7:354–55.

87. Thomas R. Schreiner, *Romans*, 2nd ed., Baker Exegetical Commentary on the New Testament (Grand Rapids: Baker Academic, 2018), 398–99. Schreiner cites a number of church fathers and modern biblical commentators to support his claims, although a minority view has been that Christ's flesh was not fallen and that it only resembled or was "in *the likeness of* sinful flesh." See also note 55 above.

88. A doctrine of original sin compels Calvin (*Institutes* 2.13.4) and later Reformed dogmaticians, however, to deny that the Son took on fallen flesh with its inherent culpability for Adam's sin, since this would have disqualified Christ from vicariously atoning for humankind's sins if he himself was subject to the penalties of original sin. Noted in Douglas J. Moo, *The Letter to the Romans*, 2nd ed., New International Commentary on the New Testament (Grand Rapids: Eerdmans, 2018), 502.

89. Howard W. Hunter, *Ensign*, November 1976, 19. Reproduced in *NT Student Manual* (2018), 476.

Christ's Earth Life: Kenosis and *Prokopē*

Christians have long wondered what life was like for the perfect Jesus. How did being both human and divine affect his day-to-day experiences? If theologians have labored tirelessly to determine which nature was dominant at different points in his life, lay Christians have also imaginatively explored the topic through novels, plays, and films that range from the reverential to the controversial. Notable examples include *Jesus Christ, Superstar*; *The Last Temptation of Christ*; and, more recently, the *Chosen* series. Undergirding all such efforts is a nagging question, the answer to which Scripture provides only occasional and ambiguous hints—how could Jesus of Nazareth really have been divine and not have that reality overwhelm or compromise his humanity? One working hypothesis is a theory known as "kenoticism." Kenoticism is derived from Philippians 2:6–8, where the verb *kenoō* (to empty) is used to depict the way in which the divine, preexistent Son "in the form of God" took on "the form of a servant" as a human being by "emptying" himself of his divinity during his life on earth. Although kenoticism constitutes a minority report in Christian theology, it has been around in one form or another since the days of Irenaeus, who remarked that one aspect of the incarnation was that the divine Logos in Jesus "became quiescent so that [Jesus] could be tempted and be dishonored and be crucified and die."[90]

Carefully defined theologically, kenoticism refers to "views of the incarnation which state that the Word somehow empties himself of—or abstains from the use of all the powers of—one or more of his divine attributes, either functionally or ontologically."[91] Ontological kenoticism holds that during his earthly sojourn Christ simply did not possess (because he voluntarily relinquished) certain divine properties, generally the metaphysically maximal ones such as omniscience and omnipotence. By this account, he could not have wielded the supreme divine powers even if he had desired to do so. Functional kenoticism, on the other hand, posits that the divine traits were always pres-

---

90. Irenaeus, *Against Heresies* 3.19.3.

91. Oliver D. Crisp, *Divinity and Humanity: The Incarnation Reconsidered* (Cambridge: Cambridge University Press, 2007), 122. Recent discussions of kenoticism from a variety of viewpoints and time periods include David Brown, *Divine Humanity: Kenosis and the Construction of a Christian Theology* (Waco, TX: Baylor University Press, 2011); Paul T. Nimmo and Keith L. Johnson, eds., *Kenosis: The Self-Emptying of Christ in Scripture and Tradition* (Grand Rapids: Eerdmans, 2022); and Bruce Lindley McCormack, *The Humility of the Eternal Son: Reformed Kenoticism and the Repair of Chalcedon* (New York: Cambridge University Press, 2021).

ent with Jesus Christ but inaccessible until gradually unlocked by the Father. Thus, kenotically oriented Christologies vary somewhat in how and to what degree they see the Son relinquishing access to his divine attributes in the incarnation. Did he "turn them over" to the Father or merely "turn them off" during his earthly sojourn? And which powers were involved? To be sure, for classical theists, any form of kenoticism is unacceptable because withholding the exercise of divine attributes involves change in the divine nature, something the doctrine of divine immutability does not allow. The Chalcedonian position is that the incarnate Word's divinity was not changed or altered in any way by the hypostatic union. Kenotic theories, in contrast, imply that the Son's "actual ontological entering into the human condition [entailed] some real change in divinity itself."[92]

Rejecting as it does the idea of divine immutability, LDS thought is conceptually compatible with kenoticism. However, because Latter-day Saints use the KJV, where *kenoō* is translated rather unclearly as "made [himself] of no reputation," they have rarely invoked Philippians 2 to discuss the incarnation, and they do not use the term "kenosis." They do, however, maintain a version of the Son's incarnational "emptying," which they call "veiling." Explained James Talmage, "Over His mind had fallen the veil of forgetfulness common to all who are born to earth, by which the remembrance of primeval existence is shut off."[93] Joseph Fielding Smith corrected a church member who wondered if from the outset the veil was "thinner" for Christ or if he was allowed "more knowledge about his pre-existence as an infant and youth than any other mortal." Smith's answer was: "The Savior was like any other child in the matter of knowledge of his pre-existence."[94] On another occasion, Smith added, "Without a doubt, Jesus came into the world subject to the same condition as was required of each of us—he forgot everything, and he had to grow from grace to grace. His forgetting, or having his former knowledge taken away, would be requisite just as it is in the case of each of us, to complete the present temporal existence."[95] As a result, his divine omniscience was suspended. "When Jesus

---

92. See Brown, *Divine Humanity*, 1–2.

93. Talmage, *Jesus the Christ*, 111. Similar language, albeit with somewhat different meanings, has been used occasionally in Christian history. The fifth-century *Tome of Leo*, for instance, paraphrases Phil. 2:6–8 in these words: "The Lord of the universe veiled his measureless majesty and took on a servant's form." *Creeds & Confessions*, 1:116.

94. Joseph Fielding Smith, *Answers to Gospel Questions*, 5 vols. (Salt Lake City: Deseret Book, 1957–1966), 5:165.

95. *Doctrines of Salvation*, 1:33. The statement that Christ grew "from grace to grace" is from D&C 93:13.

lay in the manger, a helpless infant," remarked church president Lorenzo Snow, "He knew not that He was the Son of God, and that formerly He created the earth. When the edict of Herod was issued, He knew nothing of it."[96]

When considering the veil over the preexistence as an LDS form of kenosis, further questions arise. Should Christ's veiling be understood to include an onto-logical dimension whereby his preexistent divine powers were relinquished and not in his possession during his earthly sojourn, or functionally, in which case he continued to possess his divine powers but access to them was withheld at least initially? The Church of Jesus Christ of Latter-day Saints has no official position on the matter, largely because detailed Christological questions have rarely been a point of doctrinal focus. As with other Christian groups, proclaiming Christ and him crucified has been the primary concern. That said, individual Latter-day Saint leaders over the years have weighed in on a variety of matters relevant to a Christological understanding of the nature of Christ's earth life. Orson Pratt, for instance, seems to give voice to ontological kenoticism: "All that great and mighty power he possessed, and the great and superior wisdom that was in his bosom . . . vanished from him as he entered into the infant tabernacle."[97] B. H. Roberts, on the other hand, acknowledged the veil but described Christ's incar-nate experience in part as "the awakening of the Son of God in his earth-life to the consciousness of the really great powers he possessed."[98]

Where both Pratt's and Roberts's views agree, as do all LDS versions of kenoticism, is that from birth onward Christ grew in knowledge and power toward divinity again. In Pratt's view, Christ "was obliged to begin down at the lowest principles of knowledge, and ascend upward by degrees, receiving grace for grace, truth for truth, knowledge for knowledge, until he was filled with all the fulness of the Father, and was capable of ruling, governing, and controlling all things."[99] Roberts remarked, Jesus "knew not at first whence He came, nor the dignity of His station in heaven. It was only by degrees that He felt the Spirit working within Him and gradually unfolding the sub-lime idea that He was peculiarly and pre-eminently the Son of God in very deed."[100] Lorenzo Snow offered: "He grew up to manhood, and during His progress it was revealed unto Him who He was, and for what purpose He was in the world. The glory and power He possessed before He came into the

96. *Teachings: Lorenzo Snow*, 279.
97. *Journal of Discourses*, 1:56.
98. Roberts, *Course in Theology*, 3:132–33.
99. *Journal of Discourses*, 1:56.
100. Roberts, *Course in Theology*, 3:132–33.

world was made known unto Him."[101] In Snow's and Roberts's views, Christ's advancement was a process of overcoming his veil-induced "amnesia" and regaining full consciousness of his divine identity and resident divine attributes and powers.[102]

What primarily may be in view in an LDS concept of kenosis is the restriction of preexistent knowledge rather than the removal of characteristics cultivated in the preexistence. Latter-day Saints sometimes express the idea that one's preexistent progress has an impact on one's earth life even if that influence is difficult to discern because explicit knowledge of the preexistence is veiled. Bruce McConkie ventured that Christ's kenosis was limited in that his earthly growth and development "came to him quickly and easily because he was building . . . upon the foundations laid in preexistence. He brought with him from that eternal world the talents and capacities, the inclinations to conform and obey, and the ability to recognize truth that he had there acquired." Because the preexistence repertoire of characteristics and abilities from which the young Jesus was drawing was nothing less than his pre-earth godhood, McConkie could claim that "Jesus, when yet a child had spiritual talents that no other man in a hundred lifetimes could obtain."[103] From this perspective, what happened in the incarnation might be considered more a concealment than a complete ontological emptying of Christ's divinity. Such a view is similar to functionally kenotic Christologies that claim that Christ's "core divine attributes still remain, or else are initially latent but gradually come to consciousness."[104]

In some ways, deciding whether LDS kenoticism is more ontological or functional is to make a distinction without a significant difference. Both kenotic models contend that Christ was not born as fully divine as he was fully human, and in this key divergence with Chalcedonian Christology kenoticism coincides with Latter-day Saint thinking. Another important point of convergence with Mormon Christology is that both models of kenosis envision Christ eventually re(gaining) his full divinity, whether in life or in the resurrection, through the gracious assistance of the Holy Spirit. "Jesus performed his miracles, it seems, not by virtue of his own divine power," which had been

---

101. *Teachings: Lorenzo Snow*, 279.

102. This is somewhat akin to Plato's position in his *Meno* and elsewhere that when the human soul learns, it is merely recalling what it knew in the preterrestrial state, a sort of *anamnēsis* or recollection of prior knowledge.

103. Bruce R. McConkie, *The Mortal Messiah: From Bethlehem to Calvary*, 4 vols. (Salt Lake City: Deseret Book, 1979–1981), 1:369.

104. Brown, *Divine Humanity*, 21.

surrendered or suspended, "but by his dependence upon the Spirit, like other miracle-working biblical persons." Jesus lived perfectly "in the power and energies of the Spirit." Indeed, "one key Christological feature that is easily downplayed by a two-natures model is the role of Jesus as Messiah. This is, after all, his principal role and title—Jesus the Christ, Jesus the Messiah, which means that he is the special one anointed and empowered by God's Spirit."[105]

Latter-day Saints also ascribe Jesus's extraordinary deeds in the flesh and earthly progress toward divinity to the assistance of the Holy Spirit rather than to an indwelling, fully divine Son/Logos or to an intrinsic preexistent divine power that was active in him. Erastus Snow cited John 3:34—"God giveth not the Spirit by measure unto him"—and remarked that the Spirit "is measured out to you and me in the providence of the Lord, but for him" the Spirit was "an inexhaustible source of strength to draw from" that enabled him to "perform great and marvelous things."[106] In Joseph Smith's "New Translation" of the Bible, he amplified John 3:34 to read: "God giveth him not the Spirit by measure, for [the Spirit] dwelleth in him, even the fullness."[107] Apostle Orson Whitney explained, "By constantly growing in grace and godliness, living from day to day by every word that proceeded forth from the mouth of God, [Christ] gradually became entitled to the steadily increasing possession of the Holy Spirit, till finally 'it pleased the Father that in Him should all fullness dwell' [Col. 1:19]."[108] Bruce McConkie commented that in Christ's "study and in the learning process, he was guided from on high in a way that none other has ever been. Being without sin—being clean and pure and spotless—he was entitled to the constant companionship of the Holy Spirit."[109] At times in LDS discourse, a full and constant presence of the Holy Spirit in Christ's earthly life is envisioned as coming so rapidly to Jesus that the effects of initial kenosis are seen to be very short-lived. Joseph Smith reportedly remarked that Jesus, while "still a boy," had "all the intelligence necessary to enable Him to rule and govern the kingdom of the Jews, and could reason with the wisest and most profound doctors of law and divinity, and make their theories and practice to appear like folly compared with the wisdom He possessed."[110] Smith modified

---

105. Plantinga et al., *Introduction to Christian Theology*, 253.

106. *Journal of Discourses*, 21:25–26.

107. *NTOB*, 449. This may be echoing Col. 1:19 or 2:9.

108. Orson F. Whitney, "The Gospel of Jesus Christ," in *Scrap Book of Mormon Literature*, ed. Ben E. Rich (Chicago, 1911), 2:500.

109. McConkie, *Mortal Messiah*, 1:369.

110. *Teachings: Joseph Smith*, 53. Smith's comment was reported to an LDS Church historian a decade after it was made. Cyrus Wheelock to George A. Smith, December 29, 1854, JS

Luke 2:46—"after three days they found him in the temple, sitting in the midst of the doctors, both hearing them, and asking them questions"—to emphasize that the doctors "were hearing *him*, and asking *him* questions."[111]

Joseph Smith's comments may point to another, and unusual, line of LDS thought that has the potential to mitigate the impact of kenosis—Mormonism's understanding of Christ's paternity. The church's First Presidency in the early twentieth century declared, "Elohim is literally the Father of the spirit of Jesus Christ *and also* the body in which Jesus Christ performed His mission in the flesh."[112] Latter-day Saint Christology acknowledges the sanctifying, transfiguring involvement of the Holy Ghost with Mary in Christ's conception, but it does not ascribe Jesus's paternity to the Spirit. The Book of Mormon glosses the statement in Matthew 1:20—"that which is conceived in her is of the Holy Ghost"—to read that Mary would be "overshadowed and conceive *by the power of* the Holy Ghost" (Alma 7:10 [emphasis added]). Brigham Young stated the doctrine plainly: Jesus "was begotten in the flesh by . . . our Father in Heaven," adding, "Now remember from this time forth, and forever, that Jesus Christ was not begotten by the Holy Ghost."[113] Since Latter-day Saints believe all human souls were spiritually begotten of the Father in the preexistence, affirming that the Father was the earthly sire of Jesus is how Mormons interpret "only begotten" (*monogenēs*). They add three crucial, clarifying words to the Son's title—Christ is the "Only Begotten *in the flesh.*" Church president Ezra Taft Benson called this Christ's "honored title—The Only Begotten Son of God in the flesh."[114]

Exactly how the Father sired Jesus is not explained. Benson declared simply, "The [earthly] paternity of Jesus Christ is one of the mysteries of godliness. It may only be comprehended by the spiritually minded."[115] Logically, one

---

History Documents, ca. 1839–1860, Church History Library, The Church of Jesus Christ of Latter-day Saints. Seventh-Day Adventist leader Ellen G. White made a similar statement in *God's Amazing Grace*, 281.

111. *NTOB*, 372 (emphasis added).

112. "The Father and the Son," 935 (emphasis added). The same affirmation had been made previously by the First Presidency in 1909 in "Origin of Man," *Improvement Era*, November 13, 1909, 75–81, and was reiterated by a subsequent First Presidency in *Improvement Era*, September 28, 1925, 1090.

113. *Journal of Discourses*, 1:51.

114. Ezra Taft Benson, "Jesus Christ: Our Savior and Redeemer," *Ensign*, November 1983, 6. In the twenty-first century, church president Gordon Hinckley was also fond of using this expression. See, for example, Hinckley, "We Look to Christ," *Ensign*, May 2002, 90.

115. Ezra Taft Benson, "Five Marks of the Divinity of Jesus Christ," in Benson, *Come unto Christ* (Salt Lake City: Deseret Book, 1983), 2; reprinted in *Ensign*, December 2001, 8.

might assume that conception under such circumstances bequeathed to Jesus advantages unknown to the rest of humanity. Yet neither the details nor the consequences of Jesus's unique earthly paternity are spelled out in Latter-day Saint thought. The previously quoted First Presidency simply states, "Let it not be forgotten, however, that He is essentially greater than any and all others, by reason ... of His unique status in the flesh as the offspring of a mortal mother and of an immortal, or resurrected and glorified, Father."[116] This reality may be in view when the Book of Mormon declares, but does not explain, that Christ "shall suffer temptations, and pain of body, hunger, thirst, and fatigue, *even more than man can suffer*, except it be unto death" (Mosiah 3:7 [emphasis added]). And James Talmage elaborated only slightly when he wrote: "The Child Jesus was to inherit the physical, mental, and spiritual traits, tendencies, and powers that characterized His parents—one immortal and glorified— God; the other human—woman."[117] Yet beyond power over death, Talmage does not attempt to identify the particular "traits, tendencies, and powers" Jesus received from his Father. J. Reuben Clark Jr., a member of the church's First Presidency some years later, wrote, "[This] Divine Conception I do not understand. But I know it existed and I take it on faith."[118]

Aside from the important point that Scripture is silent on the topic, there may be a pastoral advantage for not making too much of Christ's unique paternity and acknowledging that although Jesus received certain divine traits and tendencies from his Father at birth, these were embryonic endowments to be developed rather than fully formed divinity. This, along with a qualified kenotic view of Christ's entrance into this world, tends to keep the earthly playing field level, so to speak, between Jesus and his spirit brothers and sisters and makes him more relatable. Regarding the value of a doctrine of kenosis, one evangelical scholar remarked:

> What can we possibly learn about how to live a life of obedience to God, of dependence upon God, and of cooperation with God from a God-man who switches on his divine powerpack whenever he needs to negotiate a difficult situation? To truly serve as an example to us, Jesus has to be like us, seeking to do the will of his Father in heaven and relying moment by moment on the leading and empowering of the Holy Spirit. But how can God possibly be tempted, even if he somehow joins humanity to himself,

---

116. "The Father and the Son," 942.
117. Talmage, *Jesus the Christ*, 81.
118. J. Reuben Clark, *Behold the Lamb of God* (Salt Lake City: Deseret Book, 1962), 97.

if he retains his divine powers? Kenotic Christology helps here as well, for in positing a Jesus who could not simply "turn on" his divinity like a lamp to banish sin, this theology upholds a truly useful example for us of a man who did not yield, ever, to sin.[119]

In addition to affirming Christ's solidarity with humanity in the universal struggle to resist sin, a kenotic model of Christology reminds us that "His boyhood was actual boyhood, His development was as necessary and as real as that of all children." Luke 2:52 declares that Christ "increased [*proekopten*] in wisdom . . . and in favour [*charis*/grace] with God." Through such *prokopē* (in the same lexical family as *proekopten* and meaning "progress" or "advancement"), and not by a "divine powerpack," "there came to Him expansion of mind, development of faculties, and progression in power and understanding."[120] Apostle Jeffrey Holland pointedly declared that "Christ's final triumph and ultimate assumption of godly powers on the right hand of his Father came *not* because he had a divine parent (although that was essential to the victory over death) and *not* because he was given heavenly authority from the beginning (although that was essential to his divine power) but ultimately because he was, in his own mortal probation, perfectly obedient, perfectly submissive, perfectly loyal to the principle that the spiritual in his life must rule over the physical. That was at the heart of his triumph." Such an understanding of the nature of Christ's earthly *prokopē* makes it "a lesson for every accountable man, woman, and child who ever lives."[121] Centuries earlier, Theodore of Mopsuestia wrote of Christ's "necessity to achieve virtue on our behalf by his own will," thereby "becoming a path to that goal for us."[122] Hebrews 2:10 calls Christ "the *archēgos* ('leader,' or 'pioneer'; KJV—'captain') of [our] salvation." As the lead climber, so to speak, he showed a followable way back to God's presence. A popular LDS hymn depicts Christ as *archēgos*: "He marked the path and

119. John G. Stackhouse Jr., "Jesus Christ," in *Oxford Handbook of Evangelical Theology*, ed. Gerald McDermott (New York: Oxford University Press, 2010), 151.

120. Talmage, *Jesus the Christ*, 111–12.

121. Jeffery R. Holland, *Christ and the New Covenant: The Messianic Message of the Book of Mormon* (Salt Lake City: Deseret Book, 1997), 193. The perspective that believers can draw inspiration from the fact that Jesus had to pursue the same path to glory they do is widespread in Mormon thought. See, for instance, *Doctrines of the Gospel Teacher Manual*, 10; *Life and Teachings of Jesus & His Apostles Course Manual* (1979), 25; and Bruce R. McConkie, "The Child, the Boy, the Man Few People Knew," *New Era*, December 1980, 6–7.

122. Theodore of Mopsuestia, *On the Incarnation*, as quoted in *Documents in Early Christian Thought*, ed. Maurice Wiles and Mark Santer (Cambridge: Cambridge University Press, 1975), 60, 61.

led the way, And every point defines; To light and life and endless day Where God's full presence shines."[123]

In what Bruce McConkie called the best "account known" of Christ's earthly *prokopē*, his "mortal progression and achievements,"[124] Doctrine and Covenants 93 records: "And I, John, bear record that he received a fulness of the glory of the Father; and he received all power, both in heaven and on earth. . . . And I, John, saw that he received not of the fulness at the first, but received grace for grace; And he received not of the fulness at the first, but continued from grace to grace, until he received a fulness" (D&C 93:16–17, 12–13).[125] The fact that the earthly Christ needed to progress from grace to grace to receive (or regain) the fullness of divinity, rather than simply being fully divine from birth and wielding his divinity at will, makes him the followable *archēgos* of human salvation. From a kenotic beginning, Christ experienced grace-aided *prokopē* until he received the fullness. The same possibility is open to all. Doctrine and Covenants 93 proclaims the possibility that the faithful "may come unto the Father in my name and in due time receive of his fulness. For if you keep my commandments you shall receive of his fulness and be glorified in me as I am in the Father: therefore, I say unto you, you shall receive grace for grace" (D&C 93:19–20). In Joseph Smith's vision of heaven, he sees the faithful "church of the firstborn" (Heb. 12:23) who "dwell in [God's] presence . . . having received of his fullness and of his grace. And he makes them equal in power, and in might, and in dominion" (D&C 76:94–95). Such a prospect led church president Joseph F. Smith to emphasize the followability of Christ's *prokopē* to the fullness: "If Jesus, the Son of God, and the Father of the heavens and the earth in which we dwell, received not a fulness at the first, but increased in faith, knowledge, understanding and grace until he received a fulness, is it not possible for all men who are born of women to receive little by little, line upon line, precept upon precept, until they shall receive a fulness, as he has received a fulness, and be exalted with him in the presence of the Father?"[126]

123. "How Great the Wisdom and the Love," *Hymns*, #195.

124. Bruce R. McConkie, *Promised Messiah: The First Coming of Christ* (Salt Lake City: Deseret Book, 1978), 548.

125. Colossians 2:9 affirms that "in him dwelleth all the fulness of the Godhead [*theotēs*, 'divine nature,' 'divinity'] bodily." It is possible from a functionally kenotic point of view to argue that the fullness of divinity was resident in Jesus but dormant until gradually awakened as he "continued from grace to grace" during his life.

126. *Gospel Doctrine*, 83. For similar expressions, see "Lectures on Faith" (D&C-1835, 54), and *Teachings: Wilford Woodruff*, 60. In keeping with its doctrine of eternal progression, LDS theology projects this possibility far into the future afterlife and then only for the most

The question might be asked, *when* did Jesus receive or regain this fullness? LDS teaching generally holds that it was "after He had finished His work on the Earth" and was enthroned at the right hand of the Father.[127] B. H. Roberts's comments are typical: "Not until after his resurrection" was he "able to come to his disciples and say: 'All power is given unto me in heaven and in earth' [Matt. 28:18]," because only then did he receive "all the plenary power of the Godhead."[128] Joseph Fielding Smith added a uniquely Mormon perspective: "Although [Christ in the preexistence] was a God, even the Son of God, with power and authority to create this earth and other earths, yet there were some things lacking which he did not receive until after his resurrection. In other words, he had not received the fulness until he got a resurrected body."[129] Bruce McConkie wrote that only after Christ "was resurrected in glorious immortality," only "in that perfected state" did he have "the same eternal perfection possessed by his Father."[130] An alternative though minor strand of LDS thought focuses on Doctrine and Covenants 93:15–17. In verse 15, John witnesses the descent of the Spirit following Christ's baptism. In verses 16–17, he bears record of Christ's reception of the fullness. This textual proximity prompted Orson Pratt to claim that the juxtaposition was intentional and "informs us of the period when this fullness was granted."[131] Bruce McConkie, on the other hand, felt there was a temporal separation between the two accounts and that in witnessing to Christ's reception of the fullness, John was "*looking forward to that day when Jesus would be raised in glorious immortality* to receive that [divinity]—and more—which was his before the world was."[132]

For many Christians, however, the question of when Christ received the fullness is irrelevant. Chalcedonian Christology claims he always possessed it, even if the exact interplay between his fully divine and fully human natures is unknown. A doctrine of kenosis that entails Christ's *prokopē* to full divinity is

---

faithful who persist in their grace-aided *prokopē* long after the next life has begun. See chapter 12 for a full discussion of the matter.

127. *DCC*, 592.

128. The first part of the quote is from B. H. Roberts, "Immortality of Man," *Improvement Era*, April 1907, 417–18. The latter portion is from Roberts, "Answer Given . . . Discourse Delivered in Salt Lake Tabernacle July 10, 1921," *Latter-day Saints' Millennial Star*, August 25, 1921, 534.

129. *Doctrines of Salvation*, 1:33.

130. Bruce R. McConkie, *Doctrinal New Testament Commentary*, vol. 3, *Colossians to Revelation* (Salt Lake City: Bookcraft, 1973), 158. See also McConkie, *A New Witness for the Articles of Faith*, 73.

131. *Seer*, August 1853, 120.

132. McConkie, *Mortal Messiah*, 1:430 (emphasis added).

unacceptable. Early on, Athanasius chided those who supported the concept that Christ became God "by improvement of conduct."[133] Indeed, if Christ "received what he possessed as a reward for his choices," argued Athanasius, if he "obtained it as a result of his virtue and *prokopē*, then he might reasonably be called 'Son' and 'God' [but] he is not 'true [*essentially*] God' [the Nicene phrase was that Christ was 'true God from true God']."[134] Similarly, Eusebius of Emesa challenged the claim that Philippians 2:9—"God also hath highly exalted him"—implied that the Son was exalted as a "reward for his obedience." Bristled Eusebius, Christ was "not somebody who was promoted to being God because of his behavior."[135] Characterizations of Christ's divinity as matters of "reward" and "promotion" are, of course, polemical distortions. Positively viewed, Christ's perfect life could provide an inspiring example to his followers. Explains one scholar, "The difference between [Christ's] sonship and that of the saints was quantitative rather than qualitative, for by their own perfect obedience they could eventually attain to a participation in the same sonship."[136] This ultimate possibility was not considered "a demotion of the Son, but a promotion of believers to full and equal status as Sons—that is, *huioi* [sons], understood to mean *theoi* [gods]."[137] Even someone like Marcellus of Ancyra, who rejected such an extreme characterization of Christians' salvation and maintained a strong distinction between the fully divine Word and Christ's human nature, could argue that the Word worked redemptively to "prepare" human nature "to become not only incorruptible and immortal, but even enthroned in the heavens with God."[138]

---

133. Athanasius, *Orations against the Arians* 3.24, in *NPNF*, 1/4:407.

134. Athanasius, *Orations against the Arians* 1.37, as rendered in Hanson, *Search for the Christian Doctrine of God*, 428–29. In a longer passage, Athanasius argued that scriptural statements about Christ's exaltation and *prokopē* apply to his human body, not to his indwelling divinity.

135. Quoted in Hanson, *Search for the Christian Doctrine of God*, 390.

136. Jaroslav Pelikan, *Development of Christian Doctrine: Some Historical Prolegomena* (New Haven: Yale University Press, 1969), 116.

137. Robert C. Gregg and Dennis E. Groh, "The Centrality of Soteriology in Early Arianism," *Anglican Theological Review* 59, no. 3 (1977): 275, 272. Gregg and Groh developed their argument at length in *Early Arianism: A View of Salvation* (Philadelphia: Fortress, 1981).

138. Quoted in Sara Parvis, "'Like Some Crown of Victory': The Soteriology of Marcellus of Ancyra," in *Salvation according to the Fathers of the Church*, Proceedings of the Sixth International Patristic Conference, ed. D. Vincent Twomey and Dirk Krausmuller (Dublin: Four Courts Press, 2010), 68.

RESURRECTION AND GLORIFICATION

A final matter to consider is Christ's own enthronement with God. It begins, of course, with his resurrection. Mormonism's metaphysical materialism and its literalist scriptural hermeneutics ensure that Jesus's resurrected body is understood to consist of glorified, celestial, everlasting flesh—*his* flesh. Although rarely sharing Mormonism's metaphysical and hermeneutical presuppositions, an affirmation of the fleshly reality of Christ's eternal body in heaven has been the dominant view throughout Christian history. This was first clearly proclaimed by second-century Christian "apologists" in their battle against Gnosticism. Irenaeus emphasized that Christ ascended in the flesh, and in such an ascension, Irenaeus saw the redemption of the entire material world. Later, Augustine also affirmed Christ's ascension in the flesh, and Chalcedon proclaimed that Christ *is,* not that he *was,* truly human. The idea that Christ, like the rest of us, retains his fleshly humanity forever is also enshrined in many Reformation documents, perhaps most succinctly in the Church of England's Thirty-Nine Articles of Religion: "Christ did truly rise again from death, and took again his body, with flesh, bones, and all things appertaining to the perfection of man's nature; wherewith he ascended into heaven, and there sitteth until he return to judge all men at the last day."[139] Acknowledging that Christ ascended in the flesh (albeit resurrected flesh) and that a physical body was not some necessary evil to be shed as soon as Christ accomplished his earthly mission underlines the point that his divine nature "is not contrary to his or our creaturely particularity."[140]

Although the dominant Christian view is that Christ was resurrected and ascended into heaven with a glorified body of flesh and bones (Luke 24:39), some have suggested that he will retain it only until the final transformation of the heavens and the earth. Marcellus of Ancyra, for instance, offered the opinion that Christ would keep his body only long enough to fulfill Zechariah's prophecy (as Marcellus read it) that in the end times the Jews would look upon him whom they pierced (Zech. 12:10).[141] Less prevalent are Christian traditions that prominently perpetuate the ancient philosophical antipathy to matter and envision the resurrection, including Jesus's, to be a process by which humans

---

139. Article 4, "On the Resurrection of Christ," in *Creeds & Confessions,* 2:528. See also Heidelberg Catechism, Questions 46–48, in *Creeds & Confessions* 2:437–38; and Formula of Concord, Article VIII, "Concerning the Person of Christ," in *Book of Concord,* 511–12.

140. Douglas B. Farrow, *Ascension Theology* (London: T&T Clark, 2011), 44.

141. Quoted in Hanson, *Search for the Christian Doctrine of God,* 228. See also the LDS gloss on Zech. 12:10 in D&C 45:51–53.

receive heavenly bodies composed of spirit. Athanasius and Gregory of Nyssa are typical of this point of view. They imagined the transformation of Christ's human nature in his resurrection to be so thorough that it precluded fleshly corporeality, no matter how glorified. As Gregory expressed it, "The flesh [does not] still exist in its own properties after the ascent into heaven." In fact, going beyond Origenist belief in a spiritual resurrection body, Gregory voiced the unusual opinion that after Christ's ascension, he was "purified of all form that can be contemplated visually." Gregory's thoroughgoing Platonism compelled such a position because, in his view, "the divine lies beyond every bodily conception." From this standpoint, "Christ's flesh is not so much spiritualized into a heavenly body as it transcends bodily limitations altogether by becoming God."[142] Most Christian theologians, however, have taught that "Christ will remain fully human as well as fully divine beyond the last judgment, into eternity. He is forever human as well as divine. . . . There is nothing temporary about the assumption of human flesh by the Word."[143]

LDS theology, as previously mentioned, is in full agreement with the position that Christ retains his resurrected, glorified, divinized body of flesh forever. Especially important to Latter-day Saints is what this common Christian belief does for the Mormon doctrine of God the Father (see chapter 1). In short, it provides Latter-day Saints with support for the plausibility of the Father also having a divinized, glorified body of flesh and bone. B. H. Roberts boldly asked,

> Will that resurrected, immortal, glorified [Christ] ever be distilled into some bodiless, formless essence [à la Gregory of Nyssa's view]? Will He become an impersonal, incorporeal, immaterial God, without body, without parts, without passions? . . . [No,] He has a body, tangible, immortal, indestructible, and will so remain embodied throughout the countless ages of eternity . . . *so, too, the Father* must be a man of immortal tabernacle, glorified and exalted: for as the Son is so also is the Father, a personage of tabernacle, of flesh and of bone as tangible as man's, as tangible as Christ's most glorious, resurrected body.[144]

---

142. *Antirrheticus*, as quoted in Beeley, *The Unity of Christ*, 215. Brian Daley reads Gregory to mean that "although Christ's humanity eternally remains, its fleshly characteristics and psychological and moral limitations are, for all practical purposes, abrogated by his ascent into glory." Brian E. Daley, "'Heavenly Man' and 'Eternal Christ': Apollinarius and Gregory of Nyssa on the Personal Identity of the Savior," *Journal of Early Christian Studies* 10 (Winter 2002): 474.

143. Crisp, *Divinity and Humanity*, 133.

144. Roberts, *Course in Theology*, 3:180 (emphasis added). Roberts further remarked,

Finally, a word should be said about the exaltation and "session" (seating) of the resurrected, glorified Son at the right hand of the Father. Historically, the session of Christ has signified completion of his redemptive work (Heb. 1:3), reception of supreme authority over the universe (Eph. 1:20–21; 1 Pet. 3:22), and authorization to pour out the Spirit on the fledgling Christian fold (Acts 2:33). With all these ideas Latter-day Saint theology is in agreement. Parley Pratt wrote that Christ "ascended up on high, and took his seat upon the right hand of God his Father, and he then shed forth the gift of the Holy Ghost, and bestowed gifts upon men."[145] Christ's ascension and glorification also signify for Latter-day Saints the *telos* of human destiny. "For our conversation is in heaven; from whence also we look for the Saviour, the Lord Jesus Christ: Who shall change our vile body, that it may be fashioned like unto his glorious body" (Phil. 3:20–21). From his seat at the right hand of God, the divine Christ exercises his mediatorial and priestly functions. From that seat, the Glorious Personage is expected one day to return to earth, at which time every knee shall bow and every tongue confess that Jesus Christ is Lord (Phil. 2:10–11). From the preexistent, divine Son of God to the Son of Man fully exposed to the fallen human condition to the resurrected, glorified, and exalted God the Son at the right hand of the Father, such is the "Person" of Jesus Christ in Latter-day Saint Christology.

"so long as [Christ's] spirit remains in His immortal body of flesh and bones, glorified and everlasting, [keeping] His place by the side of the Father, so long will the doctrine that God is an exalted man hold its place against the idle sophistries of the learned world" (3:188). Favorable consideration is given to the idea of an embodied God with glorified flesh in Stephen H. Webb, *Jesus Christ, Eternal God: Heavenly Flesh and the Metaphysics of Matter* (New York: Oxford University Press, 2012).

145. *Journal of Discourses*, 3:178.

4

CHRIST

His Atoning "Work"

C. S. Lewis expressed a profound truth when he wrote, "We are told that Christ was killed for us, that His death has washed out our sins, and that by dying He disabled death itself. That is the formula. That is Christianity. That is what has to be believed. Any theories we build up as to how Christ's death did all this are, in my view, quite secondary."[1] As suggested by Lewis, the transcendent reality of Christ's redemptive work is far more significant than any attempt to explain it. Nonetheless, the redemption is so central to the meaning of Christianity that it has been inevitable for disciples of Christ across the centuries to seek to comprehend the gracious miracle by which they are delivered from the lasting effects of sin and death. It has been common in some Christian circles to attempt to sketch the breadth of Christ's redemptive work by dividing it into three categories—Christ as "revealer" of God, the one who exemplified God and taught God's profound and saving truths; Christ as "reconciler" with God, the one who makes possible sinful humanity's reconciliation with God; and Christ as "ruler," the one who providentially rules over God's creation in general and the church in particular. This triad of Christ's roles—revealer, reconciler, ruler—is sometimes encapsulated as "prophet, priest, and king," a formulation commonly associated with John Calvin and popularized by its inclusion in the beloved Christian hymn "I Know That My Redeemer Lives."[2] Latter-day Saints, too, affirm these realms of Christ's redemptive work. His

---

1. C. S. Lewis, *Mere Christianity* (New York: HarperOne, 1952), 55–56.

2. Samuel Medley, an eighteenth-century English Baptist minister, wrote "I Know That My Redeemer Lives." John Calvin did not invent the "prophet, priest, and king" trio of terms. It was used occasionally in antiquity, but it did "not really become a topic of Christian dogmatics until the *Institutes* of John Calvin, whence it came into the doctrinal works of various denominations." Jaroslav Pelikan, *The Christian Tradition: A History of the Development of Doctrine*, vol. 2, *The Spirit of Eastern Christendom (600–1700)* (Chicago: University of Chicago Press, 1971), 293. Another alternative to "revealer, reconciler, ruler" is Eastern

roles as "prophet" and "king" are discussed elsewhere in the book. This chapter focuses on Christ's "priestly" role as the one who reconciles God and humankind through what Christians have come to call the "atonement."

The word "atonement" is thought to have first entered the English language in the early 1500s and may have been coined by Bible translator William Tyndale.[3] The word appears only once in the KJV New Testament, when translators chose to use it to render the Greek *katallagē* in Romans 5:11—"we also joy in God through our Lord Jesus Christ, by whom we have now received the atonement (*katallagē*)." In the few other instances in which *katallagē* and its derivatives appear in the New Testament, they are rendered as some form of the word "reconciliation."[4] That, of course, is also the basic meaning of "atonement" when the term is broken into its component parts—"at-one-ment." The definitions for "atonement" listed in the *Oxford English Dictionary* include "the condition of being at one with others; restoration of friendly relations between persons who have been at variance; reconciliation," as well as "the action of setting at one"; "propitiation of an offended or injured person"; "making satisfaction"; "appeasement"; and "expiation." These latter definitions of "atonement" point to the Old Testament, where the term is repeatedly used in the context of Israel's sacrificial system of ritual expiation and propitiation. There, the term typically translates the Hebrew verb *kipper* or *kaphar* (both from the *k-p-r* root), which literally means to "cover (over)" and is the word used to describe both what was understood to be the expiatory, sin-covering intent of Israelite sacrifices and offerings and their propitiatory, reconciling results. When Tyndale (and his successors who worked on the KJV) chose to render *kipper/kaphar* as "make atonement," the new term absorbed *kpr*'s double connotation and described both expiation (the act of atoning) and reconciliation (the achievement of atonement).[5] Thus, in English "atonement" came to refer both to the state of being reconciled and

---

Orthodoxy's "lawgiver, judge, king." The various triads are discussed in Millard J. Erickson, *Christian Theology*, 3rd ed. (Grand Rapids: Baker Academic, 2013), 697–703.

3. *OED*, s.v. "atonement."

4. For example, 2 Cor. 5:18–20: "And all things are of God, who hath reconciled (*katallaxantos*) us to himself by Jesus Christ, and hath given to us the ministry of reconciliation (*katallagēs*); To wit, that God was in Christ, reconciling (*katallassōn*) the world unto himself, not imputing their trespasses unto them; and hath committed unto us the word of reconciliation (*katallagēs*). Now then we are ambassadors for Christ, as though God did beseech you by us: we pray you in Christ's stead, be ye reconciled (*katallagēte*) to God."

5. The related Hebrew word *kapporeth* designated the covering or lid on the ark of the covenant, where the high priest annually sprinkled the blood of the sacrificial animal as a rite of community expiation. This term is paraphrastically translated in the KJV and elsewhere as "mercy seat." The Latin Vulgate *propitiatorium*, however, gets more to the

to the process by which such reconciliation is achieved. Just as sacrifice was the means of reconciling the Israelite covenant community to their God and to each other, New Testament writers reasoned that the same reconciliation or atonement was accomplished for Christians through a supreme, once-for-all sacrifice in the death of Jesus Christ, the "Lamb of God."[6]

The Church of Jesus Christ of Latter-day Saints incorporates these biblical terms and connotations regarding the atonement at various points in its doctrine. Furthermore, the biblical link between ritual sacrifice and Christ's atonement is pervasive in LDS scripture as well, beginning with the account of a fallen-but-repentant Adam and Eve, who offer sacrifice. When an angel visits the pair and asks, "Why dost thou offer sacrifices unto the Lord? . . . Adam said unto him: I know not, save the Lord commanded me. And then the angel spake, saying: This thing is a similitude of the sacrifice of the Only Begotten of the Father, which is full of grace and truth . . . that as thou hast fallen thou mayest be redeemed, and all mankind, even as many as will" (Moses 5:5–9). The Book of Mormon depicts the transplanted Israelites who populate its pages as observing the "law of Moses," but doing so with the understanding (in their enlightened moments) that "the whole meaning of the law" pointed to "that great and last sacrifice; and that great and last sacrifice will be the Son of God" (Alma 34:14). At times, the people had to be reminded "that salvation doth not come by the law alone; and were it not for the atonement, which God himself shall make for the sins and iniquities of his people, that they must unavoidably perish, notwithstanding the law of Moses" (Mosiah 13:28). Properly instructed, Book of Mormon peoples are described as knowing Christ and having "worshiped the Father in his name," firm in the "hope of his glory many hundred years before his coming" (Jacob 4:4–5). Eventually, when the resurrected Christ appears to the people of the Book of Mormon, he testifies: "I have come unto the world to . . . save the world from sin . . . for behold, by me redemption cometh, and in me is the law of Moses fulfilled." Therefore, "ye shall offer up unto me no more the shedding of blood; yea, your sacrifices and your burnt offerings shall be done away" (3 Nephi 9:21, 17, 19).[7]

---

linguistic point, as do such modern translations as "atonement cover" (NIV) or "seat of reconciliation" (Jubilee Bible 2000).

6. Linguistically related terms in the New Testament that point to Christ's atoning sacrifice include *hilasmos* (e.g., 1 John 2:2—Christ "is the propitiation for our sins"); *hilastērion* (e.g., Rom. 3:25—God "set forth [Christ] to be a propitiation . . . in his blood"); *hilaskomai* (e.g., Heb. 2:17—Christ was able "to make reconciliation ['a sacrifice of atonement' (NRSV)] for the sins of the people").

7. Apostle Russell Nelson summarized the links Latter-day Saints see between Torah-

Although New Testament authors and subsequent Christian theologians considered the analogy with sacrificial atonement to be helpful in understanding Christ's redemptive work, they also realized that it failed to capture the full significance of Christ's ministry, death, and resurrection. The atonement terms were amplified and supplemented by legal metaphors such as *justification* (acquittal) and commercial or transactional metaphors such as *redemption* (ransom). A law court demands *satisfaction* for crime, so a penalty must be paid, sometimes even death. Additional metaphorical attempts to convey the grandeur of Christ's role in effecting human salvation (itself a metaphor) include *victory* over death and the devil and *unia mystica* (mystical union) with Christ both in his sufferings and in his triumph over sin and death. Each of these and other images were applied to Jesus Christ in the New Testament and led in subsequent centuries to richly variegated understandings of his redemptive work.[8]

Theories of the Atonement—History and Types

A historical overview of Christian theories of the atonement provides necessary background and context for a consideration of Mormon reflection on the topic.[9] In the earliest Christian centuries, though Christ's redemption was widely discussed by church fathers, a doctrine of the atonement did not generate contention on the scale of the Trinitarian or Christological controversies and received no creedal formulation. Theologian Robert Jenson noted that even today, "it is a remarkable fact about Christian theology that there is no such thing as an official or even generally accepted doctrine of the atonement. . . . [One] can be a perfectly respectable Christian while rejecting any existing theoretical expla-

---

prescribed sacrificial ritual and the atonement: "The Atonement of Christ fulfilled these prototypes of the Old Testament. He was the firstborn Lamb of God, without blemish. His sacrifice occurred by the shedding of blood. . . . And His was a vicarious sacrifice for others." Russell M. Nelson, "The Atonement," *Ensign*, November 1996, 35.

8. For elaboration on what is discussed in this paragraph, see Martin Hengel, *The Atonement: The Origins of the Doctrine in the New Testament* (Philadelphia: Fortress, 1981), and James D. G. Dunn, *The Theology of Paul the Apostle* (Grand Rapids: Eerdmans, 1998).

9. Reliable introductions to atonement theory can be found in most theological handbooks and encyclopedias, as well as in Oliver D. Crisp, *Approaching the Atonement: Introducing the Reconciling Work of Christ* (Downers Grove, IL: IVP Academic, 2017); William Lane Craig, *Atonement and the Death of Christ: An Exegetical, Historical, and Philosophical Exploration* (Waco, TX: Baylor University Press, 2020); Derek Tidball, David Hilborn, and Justin Thacker, eds., *The Atonement Debate* (Grand Rapids: Zondervan, 2008); and James Beilby and Paul R. Eddy, eds., *The Nature of the Atonement: Four Views* (Downers Grove, IL: InterVarsity Press, 2006).

nation for precisely how that works."[10] Patristic discussion of Christ as "Savior" revolved around three thematic foci—Jesus's life and teachings, his sufferings and death, and his resurrection and exaltation.[11] Some early Christians emphasized divine revelation as the key to reconciliation with God. Jesus's teachings and example were believed to impart saving knowledge, enlightenment, and a proper understanding of God's will. If acted on in the "imitation of Christ," something of a mystical union would result and a consequent "exchange" or transfer of divine attributes would take place. Discussion of Christ's passion, the second thematic focus, highlighted Christ's sacrificial expiation for sin, the root idea of atonement just discussed. The early church fathers, however, paid the greatest attention to the third aspect of Christ's work—his resurrection and exaltation—and saw in it Christ's "victory" over death and the devil.

Only by Christ's "ransom" payment of his death could fallen humans be liberated from the devil and the forces of evil that held them captive: Christ "gave himself for our sins, that he might deliver us from this present evil world" (Gal. 1:4). Origen reasoned thus: "If then we have been bought at a price, as Paul also confirms, undoubtedly we were bought from someone whose slaves we were. . . . Now it was the devil who was holding us, to whom we had been dragged off by our sins. Therefore, he demanded the blood of Christ as the price for us."[12] The devil, however, was caught in a tragic miscalculation. Gregory of Nyssa is credited with popularizing the infamous analogy of the baited fishhook: the divine Word "was hidden under the veil of our [human] nature, that as is done by greedy fish, the hook of the Deity might be gulped down along with the bait of the flesh, and thus life [was] introduced into the house of death," routing the devil and Hades.[13] Despite a certain crudity to this

---

10. Robert W. Jenson, *Theology in Outline: Can These Bones Live?* (New York: Oxford University Press, 2016), 78.

11. See Jaroslav Pelikan, *The Christian Tradition: A History of the Development of Doctrine*, vol. 1, *The Emergence of the Catholic Tradition (100–600)* (Chicago: University of Chicago Press, 1971), 141–55.

12. Origen, *Commentary on Romans* 2.13.29, in *Origen, Commentary on the Epistle to the Romans: Books 1–5*, trans. Thomas P. Scheck (Washington, DC: Catholic University of America Press, 2001), 161.

13. Gregory of Nyssa, *Great Catechism* 22–24, as quoted in H. E. W. Turner, *The Patristic Doctrine of Redemption: A Study of the Development of Doctrine during the First Five Centuries* (London: Mowbray, 1952), 57. Even in the Nyssen's day, however, some resisted his analogy. His friend Gregory of Nazianzus rejected the idea of a ransom being paid to the devil. Ransom had to be paid, but not to "that robber." Humans are enslaved to the power of sin; these are the bonds that have to be broken. *Orations* 45.22, as quoted in J. N. D. Kelly, *Early Christian Doctrines*, 5th ed. (New York: Harper & Row, 1978), 383.

Christus Victor theory, it "remained the customary and orthodox statement of the doctrine of the atonement for nearly a thousand years."[14]

Other, less common themes in patristic atonement discourse loomed in the background and would become more important in subsequent centuries. Notable among these was the argument that became known as the "moral influence" or "moral exemplar" theory. On this account, Christ's atonement is understood as an exquisite display of divine love that should rouse humanity to repentance in grateful response.[15] Other fathers expounded the legal and commercial metaphors in the New Testament to argue that sin offended God and divine justice demanded a penalty be paid. Gregory the Great, the influential pope-theologian of the late sixth century, combined these inchoate ideas of moral influence and propitiation. In his view, Christ's suffering "both rebuked the sin of man by [inspiring] righteousness, and moderated the wrath of the Judge by undergoing death."[16] Pope Gregory's dual explanation illustrates what theologians call the "subjective" and "objective" dimensions of the atonement. Objective models are God-focused, explicating the principles of justice that must be satisfied before God's abundantly forgiving love can be put into reconciling effect. Objective theories stress that the atonement was, and could only be, a divinely initiated act that delivered helpless humanity from its inextricable predicament of sin and rebellion. Subjective theories, such as the moral influence theory, focus on the human response. The logic is that, overwhelmed by the divine love manifest on the cross, humans turn their hearts to God and seek relationship with him who is ever ready to forgive and embrace. In subjective theories, the problem the atonement solves lies with human attitudinal and behavioral impediments that must be removed before reconciliation can be achieved. In objective theories, it is something more transcendent—the wrath of God must be appeased, justice must be satisfied, or ransom must be paid.

Objective and subjective discussion of the atonement reached a high-water mark early in the second millennium in the work of Anselm of Canterbury and Peter Abelard, respectively. Subjective, moral-influence ideas received

---

14. Laurence W. Grensted, *A Short History of the Doctrine of the Atonement* (Manchester: University Press, 1920), 56. Versions of the doctrine emphasizing power over the demonic resurfaced in the twentieth century in the "Word of Faith" and "Emerging Church" movements, as well as in some feminist theologies.

15. For a recent discussion of this theory, see Meghan D. Page and Allison K. Thornton, "Have We No Shame? A Moral Exemplar Account of Atonement," *Faith and Philosophy* 38 (October 2021): 409–30.

16. Gregory, *Morals on the Book of Job* 9.61, in *Library of the Fathers of the Holy Catholic Church*, ed. J. H. Parker (London, 1844), 541.

their fullest expression in Abelard's writings in the late eleventh century. For Abelard, the atonement was principally about love. Though he does not deny its objective character, he maintains that the real power of the atonement lies in its display of "such grace" that Christ is able to "draw our minds away from the will to sin and incline them to the fullest love of Himself."[17] Abelard found certain aspects of the objective, satisfaction theory repugnant: "How cruel and wicked it seems that anyone should demand the blood of an innocent person as the price for anything . . . still less that God should consider the death of his Son so agreeable that by it he should be reconciled to the whole world!"[18] Yet Abelard's ideas were criticized for not adequately establishing the objective character of Christ's sacrifice. Bernard of Clairvaux wrote that Abelard seemed to believe that "Christ lived and died for no other purpose than that he might teach men how to live by his words and example and point them by his passion and death to what limits their love should go." His death on the cross, reasoned Bernard, was more than just a grand gesture; it had to meet a real need.[19] Bernard's criticisms, however, were overstated. Neither Abelard nor most subjectivists have argued that the atonement is reducible to its inspirational, exemplary value. The atonement can arouse an answering love in humanity and still be an objective act.[20] Some discern this in moral exemplar theories. The "change of attitude towards God in human persons" when stimulated by Christ's sacrifice "*is* a wiping out of sin. Sin cannot be some kind of independent entity, but is always the orientation and acts of sinners. If the death of Christ has the power to enable the response of worship and trust in God in those who see it, then it is the means of expiating sin and creating fresh life."[21]

17. Abelard, *Exposition of the Epistle to the Romans* 4, as quoted in F. W. Dillistone, *The Christian Understanding of Atonement* (London: SCM, 1984), 327.

18. Abelard, *Exposition of the Epistle to the Romans* 2, in *A Scholastic Miscellany: Anselm to Ockham*, ed. Eugene R. Fairweather (Philadelphia: Westminster, 1956), 283.

19. The quote is from Alister McGrath, "The Moral Theory of the Atonement: An Historical and Theological Critique," *Scottish Journal of Theology* 38 (1985): 205–20.

20. For Abelard's views, see Richard Weingart, *The Logic of Divine Love: A Critical Analysis of the Soteriology of Peter Abelard* (Oxford: Clarendon, 1970); and, on Abelard's views versus those of Bernard of Clairvaux, see Jonathan Beeke, "'Cur Deus Homo?' A Closer Look at the Atonement Theories of Peter Abelard and Bernard of Clairvaux," *Puritan Reformed Journal* 1, no. 2 (2009): 43–56.

21. Paul S. Fiddes, "Salvation," in *Oxford Handbook of Systematic Theology*, ed. John Webster, Kathryn Tanner, and Iain Torrance (New York: Oxford University Press, 2007), 184. For an extended discussion of this perspective, see Fiddes, *Past Event and Present Salvation: The Christian Idea of Atonement* (London: Darton, Longman and Todd, 1989).

The principal medieval exponent of an objective theory of the atonement was Anselm of Canterbury. His 1098 *Cur Deus Homo* (Why God Became Man) has been called "epoch-making" and "a virtuoso performance with few rivals in the history of Christian thought, Eastern or Western."[22] Anselm did not invent the idea of objective "satisfaction," but he gave it its most rigorous formulation to that point in history.[23] Naturally, his theory reflected his times. In an era when much of Europe was ruled by feudal lords and European history was shaped by lordly efforts to maintain their honor and prestige, Anselm conceived of the divine Lord in similar terms. The Benedictine monk explained that when humans fail to subject themselves to the will of God, they dishonor him, and God's injured honor requires satisfaction. "Nothing is less tolerable in the order of things," wrote Anselm in *Cur Deus Homo*, "than for the creature to take away the honor due to the Creator and not repay what he takes away." Like a feudal lord, Anselm's God was a governor, a ruler who needed to maintain justice and order in his kingdom. He could not arbitrarily forgive, even if he were so disposed. To remit sin without consequence would disrupt the moral "order of things." It would be "unseemly," "unfitting," and contrary to "God's nature" to allow law to be broken and himself dishonored with impunity. No, a penalty must be paid. God "leaves nothing disordered in his Kingdom. . . . Even the slightest incongruity is impossible in God."[24]

In the centuries after Anselm, satisfaction theories took on a more legalist character, and notions of "penal satisfaction" and "substitutionary atonement" received their fullest expression in the Reformation and its aftermath. Both Lutheran and Calvinist scholastics tended to emphasize that the payment of penalties is logically prior to the divine manifestation of mercy. Key to the penal theory is the idea that retribution is the primary function of justice and that it must be "mathematically" equivalent to the punishment due for each and every sin. In the late seventeenth century, Calvinist scholastic Francis Turretin, building on Calvin's legal understanding of the atonement, described satisfaction in terms of the payment of a debt owed to the divine Creditor: "If

---

22. John K. Mozley, *The Doctrine of the Atonement* (London: Duckworth & Co., 1915), 125, and Pelikan, *Christian Tradition*, 1:107.

23. At the turn of the third century, Tertullian first made extensive use of the Roman legal term *satisfactio* in his seminal discussion *On Penitence*. William P. Le Saint, ed. and trans., *Tertullian: Treatises on Penance—On Penitence and On Purity*, Ancient Christian Writers (New York: Newman, 1959), passim, 155–56. A generation later Cyprian applied it to the atonement. Gustav Aulén, *Christus Victor: An Historical Study of the Three Maine Typs* [*sic*] *of the Idea of the Atonement* (London: SPCK, 1931), 97–99.

24. *Cur Deus Homo* 1.12–13, 20, in Fairweather, *A Scholastic Miscellany*, 120–22, 136.

there be such an attribute as justice belonging to God, then sin must have its due, which is punishment." However, because Turretin also saw sin as a criminal offense, and not simply a civil obligation like debt, he wrestled with the justice of the transfer of penalty to a substitute sufferer. In the end, he decided that while an inferior judge could not transfer the penalty from the guilty criminal to a substitute, the Supreme Judge could "through his infinite wisdom and unspeakable mercy . . . relax somewhat the extreme rigor of punishment by admitting a substitute and letting the sinner go free."[25]

Another approach to the atonement, known as the "governmental" theory, was elaborated by the Dutch humanist Hugo Grotius in the early seventeenth century. In *De Satisfactione* (1617), Grotius responded to criticism by Faustus Socinus of the Reformed embrace of penal substitution. Socinus had argued that as with any creditor God could choose not to exercise his right to be recompensed and simply forgive the sinner-debtor. Lawyer and jurist Grotius replied that God, in accordance with private law, could certainly do that as *dominus* (sovereign). As a "public ruler" (*rector*), however, he was obliged to maintain public justice so that the moral government of the universe was upheld. The dilemma was solved by God choosing to operate under both forms of law. "Publicly" he chose to punish Christ; "privately" he chose to forgive the penitent. For many, the attraction of Grotius's solution was that both justice and mercy seemed to receive their due. Grotius's doctrine averted the need to justify how the suffering and death of one man, even a God-man, could mathematically satisfy the total sum of human sins and evil. Grotius's governmental theory has been characterized as "penal nonsubstitution," in contrast to the Reformed "penal substitution" theory.[26]

Governmental ideas of the atonement took hold among seventeenth-century Dutch Remonstrants (opponents of Dutch Calvinism; Grotius himself was one), Methodists in the eighteenth century, and the theological heirs of Jonathan Edwards in late eighteenth- and early nineteenth-century America.[27] Even some

25. Francis Turretin, *The Atonement of Jesus Christ*, trans. James R. Wilson (Eugene, OR: Wipf & Stock, 1978), 20.

26. See the discussion of Grotian theory in Oliver Crisp, "Penal Non-Substitution," *Journal of Theological Studies*, n.s., 59 (April 2008): 140–68, and Sarah Mortimer, "Human and Divine Justice in the Works of Grotius and the Socinians," in *The Intellectual Consequences of Religious Heterodoxy, 1600–1750*, ed. Sarah Mortimer and John Robertson (Leiden: Brill, 2012), 75–94. A succinct summary of Grotius's position is Gert van den Brink, "Hugo Grotius," in *T&T Clark Companion to Atonement*, ed. Adam J. Johnson (London: Bloomsbury, 2017), 523–25.

27. For the American scene, see Douglas A. Sweeney and Allen C. Guelzo, eds., *The New*

nineteenth-century American Baptists were persuaded. In an 1822 sermon, William B. Johnson, the first president of the Southern Baptist Convention, proclaimed that the cross represented "the strongest expression of [God's] abhorrence against sin and irrefragable evidence of his immaculate holiness." However, it was not to be regarded as "the payment of the sinner's debt on the principles of pecuniary or commercial justice, but [as] a satisfaction to moral justice, to open the way for the [legally] consistent exercise of mercy."[28] Penal substitutionary views of the atonement also encountered challenge in the nineteenth and twentieth centuries from religious liberals who championed a version of the moral influence theory. Such developments notwithstanding, penal substitutionary perspectives on the atonement continue to be common in the twenty-first century among certain sectors of Christianity, especially evangelicals.[29]

In the twenty-first century, it is widely recognized that no one theory can adequately explicate the atonement. Atonement theories today tend to be viewed as complementary rather than competitive, helping illuminate different facets of the incomparably brilliant diamond of divine salvation in Christ. Scripture offers "a collection of different images for atonement, none of them developed into a worked-out theory of how the death of Jesus is salvific, but each offering a helpful metaphor."[30] The theological approach that seeks to deploy all these images and metaphors has been dubbed the "kaleidoscopic" theory.[31] To be sure, "proponents of any of the theories [may] seek to demonstrate that their preferred doctrine best interprets the collected biblical data . . . but even a successful argument of this form would be rather different from claiming a clear biblical teaching. As with the developed doctrines of Trinity or Christology, Scripture does not offer us a worked-out theology of the Atonement."[32] Remarks another theologian, "Theories of atonement are, after all, conceptual

England Theology from Jonathan Edwards to Edwards Amasa Park (Grand Rapids: Baker Academic, 2006), and Oliver Crisp, "The Moral Government of God: Jonathan Edwards and Joseph Bellamy on the Atonement," in *After Jonathan Edwards: The Course of the New England Theology*, ed. Oliver D. Crisp and Douglas A. Sweeney (New York: Oxford University Press, 2012), 78–90.

28. As quoted in Michael A. G. Haykin, "Great Admirers of the Transatlantic Divinity: Some Chapters in the Story of Baptist Edwardseanism," in Crisp and Sweeney, *After Jonathan Edwards*, 204–5.

29. For recent assessments, see Johnson, *T&T Clark Companion to Atonement*, and Tidball et al., *The Atonement Debate*.

30. Stephan R. Holmes, "Penal Substitution," in Johnson, *T&T Clark Companion to Atonement*, 305.

31. Joel B. Green, "Kaleidoscopic View," in Beilby and Eddy, *Nature of the Atonement*, 157–85.

32. Holmes, "Penal Substitution," 305.

tools with which we try to grasp a mystery in the divine-human relationship. The Christian church has never made a single theory definitive for the meaning of the atonement, and has rather relied upon a series of metaphors [sacrifice, redemption, ransom, justification] for understanding the work of Christ."[33]

LATTER-DAY SAINT PERSPECTIVES ON SUBJECTIVE/OBJECTIVE MODELS OF ATONEMENT

Latter-day Saints have always cherished and promulgated a doctrine of the atonement, and they have done so by using a variety of metaphors and terms, just as occurs in the New Testament and Christian theology generally. More recently among the Saints, the designation "the atonement of Jesus Christ" (see note 138 below) has come to identify all that is involved in and results from the redemptive work of Christ. More than just the incomparable expiatory sacrifice that forgives sin, the atonement is viewed as the basis for making available to the responsive all the spiritual gifts and graces that unite them to the Son and reconcile them to the Father. It is an enabling power that sanctifies as well as justifies and exalts as well as redeems. In short, the atonement is thought to encompass every salvifically beneficial thing that Christ said or did from birth to ascension and beyond. What is more, it is seen as the hub to which all doctrinal, liturgical, and ecclesiastical spokes of the wheel of God's kingdom on earth are securely attached and from which they draw strength and meaning. Not surprisingly, reference to the atonement has increased among Latter-day Saints in recent decades as it has broadened into a helpful umbrella term for the full range of benefits and blessings made possible by Jesus Christ and as the church has intensified its emphasis on teaching about and inviting all to "come unto" the Savior of the world. A review of the number of times "atonement" has been mentioned by church leaders at general conferences illustrates this trend. Between 1850 and 1980 the term was used fewer than a hundred times each decade. In the 1980s, that number doubled to 208 and nearly doubled again to 393 in the 1990s. "Atonement" was used 583 times in the first decade of the new century, and in the 2010s, the number increased to 826. To put the last figure in perspective, the total number of uses from 1850 to 1980 was 850. Thus, church members in the second decade of the twenty-first century heard "atonement" as much in general conference as it had been mentioned in that setting during the 130 years prior to 1980.[34]

33. Fiddes, "Salvation," 180–81. See also Colin E. Gunton, *The Actuality of Atonement: A Study of Metaphor, Rationality, and the Christian Tradition* (Edinburgh: T&T Clark, 1988).

34. See LDS General Conference Corpus, https://www.lds-general-conference.org.

When focusing on Christ's atoning sacrifice per se, Latter-day Saint tradition exhibits similarities with the theories discussed in the previous section. Although less common as a theological explanation, moral-exemplarist ideas do show up pastorally in subjective, "I-stand-all-amazed" rhetoric deployed to motivate Latter-day Saint appreciation for, and appropriation of, the blessings of Christ's atonement.[35] Such hortatory expressions even appear occasionally in LDS scripture, as for instance in the Joseph Smith revelation encouraging the Saints with these words: "Behold the wounds which pierced my side, and also the prints of the nails in my hands and feet; [and] be faithful, keep my commandments and ye shall inherit the kingdom of heaven" (D&C 6:37). For the most part, Latter-day Saint discussion of the atonement parallels, although it does not exactly replicate, the satisfaction and penal substitutionary theories. It shares with these theories a conviction about the importance of justice being upheld and the necessity of punishment for sin and evil. Sin is defined as "transgression of the law" (1 John 3:4), and justice is understood to require punishment for broken laws. The Book of Mormon declares: "The law inflicteth the punishment; if not so, the works of justice would be destroyed, and God would cease to be God" (Alma 42:22). Therefore, Christ "offere[d] himself a sacrifice for sin, to answer the ends of the law" (2 Nephi 2:7) and "to appease the demands of justice" (Alma 42:15). "Hence," explained church president John Taylor, "the law of atonement had to be met as well as all other laws, for God could not be God without fulfilling it."[36]

The language of the law court is clearly in evidence here, as it is in most penal substitution/satisfaction theories of the atonement. "Under a reign of law," wrote B. H. Roberts, "God may not pardon men for their individual sins by arbitrary act of sovereign will." He cannot "set aside the claims of justice unsatisfied" because "the non-infliction of the penalty due to sin" would undermine the divine "attribute of Justice, which even the attribute of Mercy may not displace." Roberts then quoted a pithy rhetorical exchange from the Book of Mormon: "What, do ye suppose that mercy can rob justice? I say unto you, Nay; not one whit. If so, God would cease to be God" (Alma 42:25). So, con-

---

35. Latter-day Saints early on embraced, and for more than a century have regularly sung, the 1898 hymn composed by prolific gospel song writer Charles Gabriel that begins: "I stand all amazed at the love Jesus offers me, Confused at the grace that so fully he proffers me." The LDS Church first included the piece in its 1909 *Deseret Sunday School Songs* under the title "Oh, It is Wonderful" (#254). Today it appears as "I Stand All Amazed," *Hymns*, #193.

36. John Taylor, *An Examination . . . of the Mediation and Atonement of Our Lord and Savior Jesus Christ* (Salt Lake City: Deseret News, 1882), 168–69.

cludes Roberts, "God must act in harmony with his own attributes."[37] Roberts might have said, as other Latter-day Saint leaders have, that God must act in harmony with "eternal law." As we have seen in earlier chapters, Mormons historically have held such a strong view of eternal law that it is described as uncreated and independent of Deity, something within which even God himself is constrained to operate. Yet, if eternal law consists of transcendent, governing principles, like Platonic archetypes or Ideal forms that stand behind and shape all divine law, eternal law is always understood to be mediated to the created realm by God. God's attributes and actions are the perfect embodiment and outworking of eternal law, so that in this case, the eternal principle of justice and God's justice are identical. God is not just, as measured by some external, sovereign standard; God is the personification of justice, he is justice itself. In this way, Latter-day Saints affirm both the sovereignty of eternal law *and* the sovereignty of God. They are one and the same, and God may rightly be considered Lord over all.

One ramification of the Mormon doctrine that eternal law stands behind or is coexistent with God's law is that it mutes a sense of atonement as propitiation. Latter-day Saints almost never characterize the atonement as a matter of appeasing or placating an angry God who is personally provoked because the law he created is being disregarded. The violation of justice inherent in human transgression may be thought to elicit righteous indignation from the Father because it fractures the moral order of the universe and harms his children, but Latter-day Saints do not believe it prompts personal pique or irritation on his part. Able exponents of penal substitution theory such as the influential evangelical J. I. Packer may have sophisticated theological reasons for saying that Christ's sacrifice "quenches divine anger against sinners," but at the popular level such characterizations often get reduced to distorted and morally unworthy caricatures of the Father.[38] "Accordingly, the drama of Jesus's death becomes a manifestation of God's anger—with God as the distant Fa-

37. Roberts, *Course in Theology*, 4:102. Volume 4 was devoted entirely to "special and extended study [of] this theme of themes," the atonement of Jesus Christ. In so doing, Roberts produced a milestone publication on the topic. Later, in his *The Truth, the Way, the Life*, Roberts devoted six succinct chapters (40–45) to the atonement.

38. The quotation is from Packer, "Anger," in *New Dictionary of Biblical Theology* (Westmont, IL: InterVarsity Press, 2000), 382. See Packer's fuller discussion in "What Did the Cross Achieve? The Logic of Penal Substitution," *Tyndale Bulletin* 25 (1974): 3–46. In defense of God's "wrath" in the calculus of atonement, see Eric T. Yang and Stephen T. Davis, "Atonement and the Wrath of God," in *Locating Atonement: Explorations in Constructive Dogmatics*, ed. Oliver D. Crisp and Fred Sanders (Grand Rapids: Zondervan, 2015), 154–67.

ther who punishes his own son in order to appease his own indignation." Not surprisingly, one young Sunday school boy was heard to remark, "Jesus I like, but the Father seems pretty mean."[39] This is not the place to engage, let alone attempt to resolve, the extensive debate over penal substitution theory.[40] What does need to be made clear here is that although Latter-day Saint atonement doctrine constitutes a form of penal substitution theory, notions of divine appeasement, placation, and propitiation, no matter how sophisticatedly or elegantly expressed, are virtually nonexistent. This is so because in the LDS view "stern justice" rather than a stern Father is what needs to be satisfied.

Such a position reflects Latter-day Saint perceptions of God as both just and a supremely compassionate Father. The Book of Mormon stresses that the "demands of justice" must be met but still calls God's design to redeem his children through the atonement of his beloved Son "the plan of mercy." God's redemptive plan strikes the ideal balance between justice and mercy, making it possible "to appease the demands of justice, that God might be a perfect, just God, and a merciful God also" (Alma 42:15). Portraits of a merciful and benevolent Father, of course, are not unique to Mormonism. Since the days of combating the Marcionite heresy in the second century, Christian theologians have criticized the caricature of the Father as an indignant, petulant potentate. They cite the multiple biblical passages that affirm, in the words of the psalmist, that "the LORD is gracious, and full of compassion; slow to anger, and of great mercy" (Ps. 145:8). Verses that do depict God's anger or wrath are harmonized with paeans to his passionate love. What is unsatisfactory is any dichotomization that pits an angry, offended Father against a loving, self-giving Son. Otherwise, quips one theologian, "Perhaps we should alter John 3:16 to say that God so *hated* the world that Jesus had to come to assuage that wrath, so that whoever believes may be saved!" Because the famous passage actually says that God *so loved* the world that he sent his only begotten Son, "rather

---

39. Joel B. Green and Mark D. Baker, *Recovering the Scandal of the Cross* (Downers Grove, IL: InterVarsity Press, 2000), 30. See also Joel B. Green, "Must We Imagine the Atonement in Penal Substitutionary Terms? Questions, Caveats, and a Plea," in Tidball et al., *The Atonement Debate*, 153–71.

40. Useful overviews of penal substitutionary theory include Oliver D. Crisp, *Approaching the Atonement: The Reconciling Work of Christ* (Downers Grove, IL: InterVarsity Press, 2020), 96–113, and Holmes, "Penal Substitution," 295–314. Rather than a penal substitutionary view of the atonement, Crisp prefers to see Christ as representatively making "reparation" for fallen humanity. See his *Participation and Atonement: An Analytic and Constructive Account* (Grand Rapids: Baker Academic, 2022). Offering support for penal substitution is Thomas R. Schreiner, "Penal Substitution View," followed by critical responses, in Belby and Eddy, *The Nature of the Atonement*, 67–116. See also Tidball et al., *The Atonement Debate*.

than say that the Son satisfied the Father's wrath, one should say that the Son satisfied the Father's love."[41]

This is not to suggest that there is no place for a notion of divine anger. It is to say that the transcendent nature of God's "wrath" cannot be compared with the fallen, petty, pedestrian character of anger with which human beings are all too familiar. The divine balance between righteous indignation and abundant love is sometimes expressed in the old adage "God hates sin but loves the sinner." Combining the sentiments means that "God hates sin out of a holy love—for our sakes" because he "knows what sin does to us."[42] God is like the anxious, loving father in Jesus's parable yearning for the return of his prodigal son. In this case, the heavenly Father has sent his beloved Son to retrieve us prodigals from subsisting on the husks of sin and bring us back into the Father's loving, joyful embrace. Moreover, the Father is believed to have suffered in deep solidarity with his Son on the cross. Apostle Melvin Ballard used the Akedah ("binding" of Isaac) in Genesis 22 to illustrate the pathos implicit in John 3:16. "I think as I read the story of Abraham's sacrifice of his son Isaac," remarked Ballard, "that our Father is trying to tell us what it cost him to give his Son as a gift to the world [but] in his case the hand was not stayed . . . and the life's blood of his Beloved Son went out. His Father looked on with great grief and agony over his Beloved Son."[43]

Latter-day Saint emphasis on the Father's love, with its concomitant aversion to characterizing the atonement as appeasing an offended sovereign, also has some resonance with the debate over whether "expiation" or "propitiation" is the better translation of the *hilasmos* word group in the New Testament (e.g., Rom. 3:25; 1 John 2:2; 4:10). "The concepts of expiation and propitiation refer to sacrifices that have different purposes," explains one scholar. "Expiation refers to a sacrifice that wipes away or covers from sight that which offends. The object of expiation is nonpersonal. Propitiation refers to a sacrifice which turns away the wrath of a person. The object of propitiation is an offended moral agent. N. T. Wright captures the difference well: 'You propitiate a person who is angry; you expiate a sin, crime, or stain on your character.'"[44] According to

---

41. Frank D. Macchia, *Jesus the Spirit Baptizer: Christology in Light of Pentecost* (Grand Rapids: Eerdmans, 2018), 278–79.

42. Macchia, *Jesus the Spirit Baptizer*, 275. LDS apostle Dallin Oaks expressed this even more pointedly: "God's love is so perfect" that "God's anger and His wrath are not a contradiction of His love but an evidence of His love. . . . If anyone thinks that godly or parental love for an individual grants the loved one license to disobey the law, he or she does not understand either love or law." Dallin H. Oaks, "Love and Law," *Ensign*, November 2009, 27–28.

43. Melvin Ballard, "The Sacramental Covenant," *Improvement Era*, October 1919, 1029–31.

44. Graham A. Cole, "Expiation/Propitiation," in Johnson, *T&T Clark Companion to Atonement*, 489.

these definitions, it should be clear that Mormon doctrine favors "expiation."[45] However, because the KJV translates *hilasmos/hilastērion* as "propitiation" (rather than "expiation," as in the RSV), the term does appear occasionally in LDS discourse. When it is used, however, it is shorn of its connotation of placating an incensed deity.[46] As one church leader explained,

> I know that it is written by John and Paul that Christ was offered as a propitiation for our sins. I take it, if we had the original text, we would learn that it was not in the sense of appeasing the anger of God that he became a propitiatory gift. That the Lord may have been, and has been, grieved and sometimes angry with his stubborn people, I grant you, but I have never felt that God had to be "bought off," if you will allow the expression, through the death of his Son, from visiting upon us [deserved] punishment.[47]

That Latter-day Saints have a different understanding of what is being propitiated/appeased in the atonement, and that they never use the phrase "penal substitution" when talking about the atonement should not obscure the fact that their doctrine has typically been articulated within the same legal/judicial and pecuniary/transactional interpretive frameworks that one encounters in penal substitution models of the atonement. A prime example of this is their use of the debtor-creditor analogy, long common to such approaches to the atonement. The analogy has been known in Mormonism from the earliest days and received renewed attention among Latter-day Saints in the final quarter of the twentieth century through the influence of apostle Boyd Packer.[48] The church leader presented his version of the analogy as a parable in which the creditor demanding justice and the debtor pleading for mercy are at a stand-

45. See, for example, Russell M. Nelson, "The Atonement," *Ensign*, November 1996, 34.

46. Rather, Bruce McConkie explained the *hilasmos* passages in 1 John in this way: "Our Lord's atoning sacrifice brought the provisions of the law of propitiation into full force. That is, he appeased the demands of divine justice and effected a reconciliation between God and man." McConkie, *Doctrinal New Testament Commentary*, vol. 3, *Colossians to Revelation* (Salt Lake City: Bookcraft, 1973), 376.

47. Joseph E. Robinson, *Conference Report*, April 1918, 46. Current LDS literature is interested in repudiating the "angry God" assumption that underlies traditional use of "propitiation." One church manual contrasts Christ's sacrifice with Old Testament ritual in this way: "Instead of the sinners (us) offering a sacrifice to appease the One offended, propitiation was offered by the One who was sinned against. God the Father offered the reconciliation offering—His Son—as an atoning sacrifice for the remission of all our sins." *NT Student Manual* (2018), 339.

48. The debtor-creditor analogy first appeared in Mormon literature in the 1840s. See "The Blood of Christ," *Millennial Star*, May 1845, 200.

off until the debtor's friend offers to pay, telling the creditor, "You demanded justice. Though he cannot pay you, I will do so. You will have been justly dealt with and can ask no more. It would not be just." The creditor agrees and is paid in full by the mediator. As Packer summarized the parable, the creditor "had been justly dealt with. No contract had been broken. The debtor, in turn, had been extended mercy. Both laws stood fulfilled. Because there was a mediator, justice had claimed its full share, and mercy was fully satisfied."[49]

The corollary emphasis in Latter-day Saint theology, as it often is in strict penal substitution theory, is to extol the mathematical comprehensiveness of the atonement, to stress that Christ suffered the penalty due for each and every sin or broken law ever committed by any human being. Apostle Neal Maxwell put it this way: "The cumulative weight of all mortal sins—past, present, and future—pressed upon that perfect, sinless, and sensitive Soul," constituting "the awful arithmetic of the Atonement."[50] Added Jeffrey Holland, "It is 'a matter of surpassing wonder' that the voluntary and merciful sacrifice of a single being could satisfy the infinite and eternal demands of justice, atone for every human transgression and misdeed, and thereby sweep all humankind into the encompassing arms of His merciful embrace. But so it is."[51] Not specifically addressed in Latter-day Saint theology is the distinction debated by seventeenth-century English divines John Owen and Richard Baxter as to whether atoning for every human transgression is best understood as discharging "the exact sin debt in a commercial fashion" sin by sin, so to speak (Owen), or whether "the satisfaction made by Christ was an *equivalent value* for all sins" collectively (Baxter).[52] This is another way of differentiating between a Reformation view of atonement as substitutionary "punishment" for sin and Anselm of Canterbury's theory of "satisfaction" or compensation for sin. In whatever way Christ's atonement solves the salvific predicament of

49. Packer first presented the parable in general conference in 1977 (see *Ensign*, May 1977, 54–56). It was reproduced in Packer, *Truths Most Worth Knowing: An Apostle's Witness* (Salt Lake City: Deseret Book, 2015), 123–26. Another substitutionary parable that has been popular among Latter-day Saints is the old folktale about the poor, frail schoolboy who steals another's lunch and is about to be punished for it when another, bigger boy steps up and takes the requisite beating on the hapless boy's behalf. *He Took My Lickin' for Me: A Classic Folk Tale* (Salt Lake City: Deseret Book, 2003). Although insufficient as an adequate theological account of the atonement, the parable's depiction of substitutionary satisfaction as self-giving love keeps it in circulation.

50. Neal A. Maxwell, "Willing to Submit," *Ensign*, May 1985, 73.

51. Jeffrey R. Holland, "The Atonement of Jesus Christ," *Ensign*, March 2008, 38.

52. David L. Allen, *The Extent of the Atonement: A Historical and Critical Review* (Nashville: B&H Academic, 2016), 200.

sinful humanity, Latter-day Saints are regularly reminded of the redemptive magnificence of the atonement in the words of a favorite nineteenth-century hymn: "How great, how glorious, how complete, Redemption's grand design, Where justice, love, and mercy meet In harmony divine!"[53]

THE "INFINITE" NATURE OF THE ATONEMENT

In *Cur Deus Homo*, Anselm takes up the question of how Christ's death "outweighs the number and magnitude of all sins," any one of which is a supreme act of dishonoring Deity and demands something supremely valuable in recompense. In classic medieval reasoning, Anselm argues that Christ's life "is an incomparably greater good than [all] those sins are evil." Then Anselm asks, "And do you not think that so great a good . . . can avail to pay what is due for the sins of the whole world? Yes! it has even infinite value."[54] Although Anselm himself never used the phrase "infinite atonement," numerous theologians after him have restated his position by declaring that dishonoring an infinite being requires infinite satisfaction and that only the life of the Sinless One is of such "infinite value" that it could have made adequate reparatory satisfaction. Thomas Aquinas accented Anselm's point by declaring that "a sole drop" of Christ's precious blood "would suffice to save the whole world."[55] Anselm also reasoned that satisfaction could only be procured by someone who paradoxically was both a finite human being and an infinite God. A proper substitute for human sin needed to share humanity's nature: "It is necessary that the sinner himself, or one of the same race, should be the person who makes satisfaction." Yet only a "God-man," one who is both "perfect God and perfect man," could make such a satisfaction for all humankind. Anselm summarized the paradox thus: "None but true God" is capable of making satisfaction for sin, "and none but true man owes it."[56]

Over the years, Latter-day Saints have expounded what "The Living Christ," a formal pronouncement made in 2000 by the First Presidency and Twelve Apostles, calls the "infinite virtue" of the atonement.[57] They have done this in

53. "How Great the Wisdom and the Love," *Hymns*, #195.

54. The first quotation is from *Cur Deus Homo* 2.14, in *Anselm: Basic Writings*, ed. Thomas Williams (Indianapolis: Hackett, 2007), 307; Anselm's question and his foil Boso's answer are from the same chapter but as rendered in *St. Anselm: Basic Writings*, trans. S. N. Deane, 2nd ed. (La Salle, IL: Open Court, 1962), 277.

55. Quoted in Jean-Pierre Torrell, *Saint Thomas Aquinas*, vol. 1, *The Person and His Work*, rev. ed. (Washington, DC: Catholic University of America Press, 2005), 134.

56. *Cur Deus Homo* 2.7-8, in Fairweather, *A Scholastic Miscellany*, 151-52.

57. "The Living Christ," 2.

a variety of ways, including the Anselm-like use of "infinite" to refer to that which is not finite or mortal. Nineteenth-century apostle Orson Pratt declared, "Inasmuch as the sin was against an infinite being—a transgression of a law issued by an infinite being—the atonement must be an infinite atonement."[58] Oliver Cowdery wrote that Christ's redemptive mission was "such as none other could fill . . . it required an infinite atonement" for "man is mortal!"[59] The Book of Mormon states, "There is not any man that can sacrifice his own blood which will atone for the sins of another." Therefore, it cannot "be a human sacrifice; but it must be an infinite and eternal sacrifice" (Alma 34:10, 9). As Anselm averred, only such a being as the incarnate Son of God is ontologically capable of offering the requisite sacrifice. Joseph Fielding Smith explained, "It had to be made by an infinite being, someone not subject to death and yet someone who had the power to die and who also had power over death."[60] Only Jesus Christ could accomplish the atonement. "Only He had the power to overcome physical death. From His mortal mother, Mary, He inherited the ability to die. From God, His immortal Father, He inherited the power to live forever or to lay down His life and to take it up again."[61] In this sense of "infinite" as in-finite, it is Christ's status as an Anselmian "God-man" with the ability to transcend death that makes the atonement infinite.

Especially today, Mormons also use "infinite" in the dictionary sense of "without limit" or "unbounded" as applied to time, space, or character. Apostle Russell Nelson's summary of the ways in which the atonement is unlimited is illustrative: "His Atonement is infinite—without an end. It was also infinite in that all humankind would be saved from never-ending death. It was infinite in terms of His immense suffering. It was infinite in time, putting an end to the preceding prototype of animal sacrifice. It was infinite in scope—it was to be done once for all. And the mercy of the Atonement extends not only to an infinite number of people, but also to an infinite number of worlds created by Him." In short, it is "infinite beyond any human scale of measurement or mortal comprehension."[62] Nelson's comment about the atonement extending to an infinite number of people highlights the LDS conviction that the atonement, in one sense, is universal. Apostle Todd Christofferson quoted 1 John 2:2—"he

---

58. *Journal of Discourses*, 7:251.

59. Quoted in *JSP*, H1:51.

60. *Improvement Era*, June 1967, 119. The Book of Mormon adds, "Save it should be an infinite atonement this corruption could not put on incorruption" (2 Nephi 9:7).

61. "The Atonement of Jesus Christ," *Doctrinal Mastery Core Document* (Salt Lake City: The Church of Jesus Christ of Latter-day Saints, 2018), 12.

62. Nelson, "Atonement," 35.

is the propitiation for our sins: and not for ours only, but also for the sins of the whole world"—to emphasize that "the infinite reach of the Atonement of Jesus Christ" includes all who have ever lived.[63] This is consistent with the Book of Mormon teaching that Christ "cometh into the world that he may save all men if they will hearken unto his voice; for behold, he suffereth the pains of all men, yea, the pains of every living creature, both men, women, and children, who belong to the family of Adam" (2 Nephi 9:21). As apostle Patrick Kearon emphasized, Christ makes "it possible for every last one of His Father's children to receive the end goal of . . . eternal life. . . . None is excluded from this divine potential. If you are prone to worry that you will never measure up, or that the loving reach of Christ's infinite Atonement mercifully covers everyone else but not you, then you misunderstand. *Infinite* means infinite. *Infinite* covers you and those you love." To be sure, as discussed in chapter 6, although "God is in relentless pursuit of you . . . there [are] things we need to do, commandments to keep, aspects of our natures to change . . . but with His grace, those are within our reach, not beyond our grasp." When Jesus died on the cross, "the veil of the temple was rent in twain . . . symbolising that access back to the presence of the Father had been ripped wide open—to all who will turn to Him, trust Him, cast their burdens on Him, and take His yoke upon them in a covenant bond."[64]

Like many Christians, Latter-day Saints also believe that the atonement is infinite and universal in scope in that it redeems not just humankind but all creation. Wrote Parley Pratt early in the church's history, "the object of a Saviour to bleed and die as a sacrifice and atonement for sin, was not only to redeem man in a moral sense, from his lost and fallen state, but it was also to restore the physical world from all the effects of the fall; to purify the elements; and to present the earth in spotless purity before the throne of God, clothed in celestial glory, as a fit inheritance for the ransomed throng who are destined to inherit it in eternity."[65] Brigham Young declared that "by the shedding of [Christ's] blood he has redeemed men, women, children, beasts, birds, fish, [and] the earth itself."[66] More distinctively, Mormons posit that among the vast

---

63. D. Todd Christofferson, "The Redemption of the Dead and the Testimony of Jesus," *Ensign*, November 2000, 10.

64. Patrick Kearon, "God's Intent Is to Bring You Home," *Liahona*, May 2024, 87–89.

65. Parley P. Pratt, *The Millennium, and Other Poems: To Which Is Annexed, a Treatise on the Regeneration and Eternal Duration of Matter* (New York: W. Molineux, 1840), 124–25.

66. *Journal of Discourses*, 2:317. See also John A. Widtsoe, *Rational Theology: As Taught by the Church of Jesus Christ of Latter-day Saints* (Salt Lake City: General Priesthood Committee, 1915), 155–56.

creations of God's universe are other inhabited worlds in need of redemption.[67] In a poetic version of Joseph Smith's "Vision" of the afterlife (D&C 76), the following lines refer to Christ:

> By him, of him, and through him, the worlds were all made,
> Even all that career in the heavens so broad,
> Whose inhabitants, too, from the first to the last,
> Are *sav'd by the very same Saviour of ours.*[68]

This quatrain led Bruce McConkie to conclude, "The atonement of Christ, being literally and truly infinite, applies to an infinite number of earths."[69] Although never endorsed as official LDS doctrine, the idea that Christ's atoning sacrifice on this planet extends redemptively to all other inhabited worlds has been expressed from time to time since the 1950s when McConkie first brought the idea back into circulation among the Latter-day Saints.[70]

More mainstream in Mormon thought when considering the infinite atonement is linking the logic of infinite coverage to removal of the universal, negative effects of the fall. Church president Ezra Taft Benson remarked, "No one adequately and properly knows why he needs Christ until he understands and accepts the doctrine of the fall and its effect upon all mankind."[71] Moreover, "the transgression of Adam being infinite in its consequences, those consequences cannot be averted, except through an infinite atonement."[72] The infinite negative consequences of the fall are that all human beings became subject to both physical death and "spiritual death," the latter term being used to identify the spiritual alienation or estrangement from God resulting from sin. Since Latter-day Saints believe that Adam brought these consequences upon his posterity without their participation, Christ's atonement is likewise understood to remove the consequences without their participation, uncon-

---

67. For Christian reflection on the possibility of extraterrestrial life, see Andrew Davison, *Astrobiology and Christian Doctrine: Exploring the Implications of Life in the Universe* (Cambridge: Cambridge University Press, 2023).

68. *Times and Seasons*, February 1843, 83 (emphasis added).

69. McConkie, *Mormon Doctrine*, 62.

70. By including the previously little-known poetic quatrain in his widely read *Mormon Doctrine*, McConkie helped popularize the idea among Latter-day Saints beginning in the second half of the twentieth century. For twenty-first-century examples, see *Doctrines of the Gospel Student Manual* (2010), 25, and Keith McMullin, "Jesus, the Very Thought of Thee," *Ensign*, May 2004, 33–35.

71. Ezra Taft Benson, "The Book of Mormon and the Doctrine and Covenants," *Ensign*, May 1987, 85.

72. *Compendium of Doctrines*, 9.

ditionally. Explains Jeffrey Holland: "Some gifts coming from the Atonement are universal, infinite, and unconditional. These include His ransom for Adam's original transgression so that no member of the human family is held responsible for that sin."[73]

With regard to physical death, this means that "as in Adam all die, even so in Christ shall all be made alive" (1 Cor. 15:22). As succinctly stated in the LDS *Guide to the Scriptures*, "Because of the Atonement, all people will rise from the dead with immortal bodies."[74] "This [physical] salvation being universal," remarked Parley Pratt, "I am a universalist in this respect," and "this salvation being without works, or without any conditions except the atonement of Jesus Christ, I am in this respect a believer in free grace alone . . . for precisely what is lost in Adam's transgression without our agency, is restored by Jesus Christ without our agency."[75] As for the "spiritual death" brought on by the fall, the Doctrine and Covenants states: "God having redeemed man from the fall, men became again, in their infant state [as they had been in the preexistence], innocent before God" (D&C 93:38). "There is one thing," elaborated Pratt's brother Orson, contra Augustine, "which the atonement does for us, immediately upon our entrance into this mortal life; it sets us free from the first spiritual death. . . . As in Adam all died spiritually, even so in Christ all, in their infancy, are made alive spiritually. . . . This redemption from the spiritual death upon all mankind in their infant state, [also] is brought about without any conditions on the part of the creature; it is wrought out by the free grace of Christ alone, without works."[76]

Although Latter-day Saints acknowledge that as soon as children "begin to grow up, sin conceiveth in their hearts" (Moses 6:55), they believe that little children are accounted as sinless before God and covered by the grace of the atonement during their early years. Apostle Dallin Oaks explained, "We understand from our doctrine that before the age of accountability [eight years

---

73. Holland, "Atonement of Jesus Christ," 35. The LDS Church's Second Article of Faith affirms: "We believe that men will be punished for their own sins, and not for Adam's transgression."

74. *Guide to the Scriptures*, s.v. "atone, atonement."

75. Parley Pratt, "Regeneration and Eternal Duration of Matter," 125–26.

76. Orson Pratt, "The Fall and Atonement," *Millennial Star*, September 1866, 609–10. The Book of Mormon describes another sense in which the atonement redeems humanity from spiritual death: It "bring[s] to pass the resurrection of the dead, that thereby men may be brought into the presence of the Lord," thus "redeem[ing] all mankind from the first death—that spiritual death." Of course, that redemption is only temporary for purposes of the final judgment since "whosoever repente[d] not is hewn down and cast [out] and there cometh upon them again a spiritual death, yea, a second death, for they are cut off again as to things pertaining to righteousness." Helaman 14:15–18.

old] a child is 'not capable of committing sin' (Moroni 8:8). During that time, children can commit mistakes, even very serious and damaging ones that must be corrected, but their acts are not accounted as sins."[77] This unconditional gift of legal innocence extends from birth "until they begin to become accountable before [God]" (D&C 29:47) at age eight.[78] During this "grace period," "the blood of Christ atoneth for their sins" (Mosiah 3:16) and "little children are whole, for ... the curse of Adam is taken from them in [Christ], that it hath no power over them" (Moroni 8:8). Such gracious immunity from accountability for transgression, however, ceases at age eight, after which the atonement no longer shields individuals unconditionally from the consequences of their sins.[79] From that point forward, "none shall be found blameless before God, except ... through repentance and faith on the name of the Lord God Omnipotent" (Mosiah 3:21). Elaborated Parley Pratt, "Here ends universalism; here ends calvinism; here ends salvation without works—here is introduced the necessity of a salvation from actual sin,—from individual transgression, from which no man can be redeemed short of the blood of Jesus Christ applied to each individual transgressor; and which can only be applied on the conditions of faith, repentance, and obedience to the gospel."[80] Thus, a Book of Mormon prophet urged all to "come and be baptized unto repentance, that ye may be washed from your sins, that

---

77. Dallin H. Oaks, "Sins and Mistakes," *Ensign*, October 1996, 65.

78. Some Christians have interpreted Rom. 4:15—"where no law is, there is no transgression"—and Rom. 5:13—"sin is not imputed when there is no law"—in a similar fashion. Origen, for instance, wrote that the law in question is "natural law" and that it does not pertain until "a certain age when a person begins to be capable of reason and able to discriminate right from wrong and justice from injustice." Once that point is reached, "there is an internal law which prohibits; the faculty of reason points out what ought not be done." Origen cites the example of a young boy striking a parent and remarks: "Because natural law does not yet exist in him . . . he is not aware that he has committed an impious crime in this action." Thus, "sin is dead in him, for through the absence of natural law which does not yet exist in him, sin cannot be reckoned to him." Origen, *Commentary on the Epistles to the Romans* 5.1.24–26, in *Origen: Commentary on the Epistle to the Romans, Books 1–5*, trans. Thomas P. Scheck (Washington, DC: Catholic University of America Press, 2001), 317–18.

79. Excepted are those who for reason of disability or other special circumstance live in a condition "where there is no law given." In that case, "there is no punishment; and where there is no punishment there is no condemnation; and where there is no condemnation the mercies of the Holy One of Israel have claim upon them, because of the atonement. . . . For the atonement satisfieth the demands of his justice upon all those who have not the law given to them" (2 Nephi 9:25–26; see also Mosiah 3:11). Alexander Campbell thought the passage in 2 Nephi was an example of Mormon "Calvinism." Alexander Campbell, *Delusions: An Analysis of the Book of Mormon* (Boston, 1832), 14.

80. Parley Pratt, "Regeneration and Eternal Duration of Matter," 127.

ye may have faith on the Lamb of God, who taketh away the sins of the world, who is mighty to save and to cleanse from all unrighteousness" (Alma 7:14).

THE "LIMITED" NATURE OF THE ATONEMENT

The LDS distinction between conditional and unconditional benefits of the atonement points to the long-standing Christian debate over the "extent" of the atonement.[81] In the twelfth century, Peter Lombard influentially parsed the extent of the atonement in this way: Christ died "for all with regard to the sufficiency of the price, but only for the elect with regard to its efficacy."[82] Few Christian theologians have taken exception to the first clause in this "sufficiency-efficacy" distinction. Christ's redemption is universal in that it provides all with the *opportunity* to be saved. However, what is stated in Lombard's concluding clause regarding the extent of the *application* of the atonement is another matter. In part, the debate touches on the degree to which humans are thought to play a role in receiving the benefits of the atonement. As discussed in detail in chapter 6, for a long line of Christian theologians from Augustine to Luther, Calvin, and beyond, the atonement is made efficacious solely by God creating and sustaining saving faith in those he (s)elected for salvation before the world was created. For others, including the Latter-day Saints, the universal offer of the gospel entails the genuine possibility of salvation for all who hear it, but the choice to respond positively is theirs. Redemptive grace beckons and sustains, but it can be rejected; it is not irresistible. Biblical texts that proclaim the universality of God's saving intent in the gospel call stand in tension with Augustinian-Calvinist versions of predestination that assume the atonement is applicable only to the elect. The former position implies a universal atonement; the latter a limited one.

Belief in the *potentially* universal extent of the atonement, what some call "hypothetical universalism," is strengthened in some Protestant circles by interpretation of God's covenant of salvation not as a predestinarian *pactum salutis* (covenant of redemption), in which God unilaterally promises and ensures salvation to the elect, but as the conditional *pactum evangelicum* (evangelical covenant), which promises salvation upon certain conditions.[83] Notions of a more reciprocal or bilateral covenant through which the benefits of the atonement

---

81. Useful, though with a definite point of view, is Allen, *Extent of the Atonement*.

82. Peter Lombard, *Sentences* 3.20.5, in *On the Incarnation of the Word*, trans. Giulio Silano (Toronto: Pontifical Institute of Mediaeval Studies, 2008), 86.

83. For a detailed study of one who incorporated this approach in his theology of the work of Christ, see Michael J. Lynch, *John Davenant's Hypothetical Universalism: A Defense of Catholic and Reformed Orthodoxy* (New York: Oxford University Press, 2021).

are appropriated were not confined to the Dutch Arminian opponents of Calvinism but can be found among theologians ranging from Huldrych Zwingli and William Tyndale to John Davenant and Richard Baxter.[84] In words with which Latter-day Saints would agree, Tyndale taught that all biblical promises of blessing made possible by the atonement "do include a covenant: that is, God bindeth himself to fulfil that mercy unto thee only if thou wilt endeavour thyself to keep his laws."[85] Similar sentiments are found in these passages of LDS scripture: "I, the Lord, am bound when ye do what I say; but when ye do not what I say, ye have no promise" (D&C 82:10), and "all who will have a blessing at my hands shall abide the law which was appointed for that blessing, and the conditions thereof" (D&C 132:5). Early American Puritan conceptions of the covenant have been depicted as God "voluntarily t[ying] His hands, willingly agree[ing] to a set of terms."[86] From this perspective, application of the saving benefits of the atonement is almost "a *quid pro quo*, an 'if I believe' necessitating a 'you have to save me.'" In short, the Puritan God "is bound by certain commitments; He is compelled to play the game of salvation according to ascertained rules."[87] Joseph Smith held a similar view: "There is a law, irrevocably decreed in heaven before the foundations of this world, upon which all blessings are predicated. And when we obtain any blessing from God, it is by obedience to that law upon which it is predicated" (D&C 130:20–21).

Mormonism's views of the covenant of salvation and the corresponding conditions by which the benefits of the atonement may be appropriated are presented from the standpoint of hypothetical universalism and are rooted in a high view of human agency. As stated in the Book of Mormon, people are "free to choose liberty and eternal life, through the great Mediator of all men, or to choose captivity and death, according to the captivity and power of the devil" (2 Nephi 2:27). Thus, "whosoever perisheth, perisheth unto himself; and whosoever doeth iniquity, doeth it unto himself; for behold, ye are free; ye are permitted to act for yourselves; for behold, God hath given unto you . . . that

---

84. A convenient overview is Richard L. Greaves, "The Origins and Early Development of English Covenant Thought," *Historian* 31 (November 1968): 21–35. See also David A. Weir, *The Origins of the Federal Theology in Sixteenth-Century Reformation Thought* (Oxford: Clarendon, 1990), and Allen, *The Extent of the Atonement*.

85. Quoted in Theodore Dwight Bozeman, *The Precisianist Strain: Disciplinary Religion and Antinomian Backlash in Puritanism to 1638* (Chapel Hill: University of North Carolina Press, 2004), 24.

86. Perry Miller, *The New England Mind: The Seventeenth Century* (Cambridge, MA: Harvard University Press, 1938), 376.

87. Perry Miller, "The Marrow of Puritan Divinity," in *Errand into the Wilderness* (Cambridge, MA: Harvard University Press, 1956), 71.

ye might choose life or death" (Helaman 14:30–31). As discussed at length in chapter 6, such views envision appropriation of the benefits of the atonement in a decidedly synergistic fashion, as a cooperation between the Creator and the created. In what may seem a distinction without a difference, Calvin, Beza, and others also affirmed the conditionality of the covenant, but they did so in an unconditional way.[88] That is, God unfailingly supplies to his elect the empowering grace necessary for them to actively fulfill the covenant's conditions of saving faith. "As he requires a condition of thee," declared Puritan divine Thomas Hooker, "so he worketh the condition in thee."[89] Unlike Mormon synergism, Calvinism sees appropriation of the atonement's benefits from beginning to end as a divine monergism (work by God alone) on behalf of the elect.

Such salvific monergism tends to go hand in hand with a "limited" view of the atonement. Those who hold this view, sometimes called the doctrine of "particular redemption," argue that for Christ to have suffered for the sins of the reprobate would have been both wasteful and redundant since the damned will bear their own punishment in eternity. Hypothetical universalists reply that the atonement must be "as far applicable as it is announceable."[90] In other words, there is little point in preaching the gospel to all the world if its promised blessings are not appropriable by all who hear. The atonement is like a healing medicine "ready to be administered or applied to any member of the human family," all of whom are potentially curable.[91] Because Latter-day Saints believe that evangelization continues in the "intermediate state" between death and the resurrection, the possibilities for hypothetical universalism are expanded.[92] Joseph Smith's vision of differing degrees of glory for the resurrected in the heavenly afterlife proclaims the "glad tidings" that Christ "saves all the works of his hands, except those sons of perdition who deny the Son after the Father has revealed him." Latter-day Saint theology views these damned souls, the "sons of perdition," as a very small group. "All the rest shall be brought forth [to some degree of heavenly glory] by the resurrection of the dead, through the triumph and the glory of the Lamb" (D&C 76:43, 39). Thus, Mormonism takes

---

88. See Peter A. Lillback, "The Continuing Conundrum: Calvin and the Conditionality of the Covenant," *Calvin Theological Journal* 29 (1994): 42–74.

89. Quoted in Baird Tipson, *Hartford Puritanism: Thomas Hooker, Samuel Stone, and Their Terrifying God* (New York: Oxford University Press, 2015), 331.

90. John Davenant, "Dissertation on the Death of Christ," as quoted in Allen, *Extent of the Atonement*, 178.

91. Moore, "Extent of the Atonement," 140. See Moore's fuller discussion: *English Hypothetical Universalism: John Preston and the Softening of Reformed Theology* (Grand Rapids: Eerdmans, 2007).

92. On LDS beliefs about the intermediate state, see chapter 12 on eschatology.

a very optimistic view of hypothetical universalism such that it comes close to embracing an actual universalism. This perspective led one Book of Mormon prophet to write, "I pray the Father in the name of Christ that many of us, if not all, may be saved in his kingdom at that great and last day" (2 Nephi 33:12).

On the other hand, Mormonism may also be said to espouse a doctrine of limited atonement. Virtually all Christian traditions acknowledge that the extent of the atonement's efficacy or applicability in fully reconciling human beings to their Maker is restricted to those who exercise saving faith, however that faith is understood to come about. In this sense, when Latter-day Saints focus on the conditional rather than unconditional benefits of Christ's atoning work, they may be said to advance a doctrine of limited atonement. As LDS scripture declares, Christ "shall come into the world to redeem his people; and he shall take upon him the transgressions of those who believe on his name; and these are they that shall have eternal life, and salvation cometh to none else. Therefore the wicked remain as though there had been no redemption made, except it be the loosing of the bands of death" (Alma 11:40–41). That the enjoyment of the conditional benefits of the atonement will be limited is implicit in Joseph Smith's statement that glosses John 17:6 to read that the "Son laid down his life for the salvation of all his Father gave him out of the world."[93] The harmonization of Mormonism's quasi universalism with its sense of particular redemption resides in its eschatological doctrine of graded degrees of salvation. An afterlife in the presence of God himself is limited to those only who fully appropriate the benefits of the atonement. Others who refuse the gospel call either in this life or in the intermediate state but who are not incorrigibly evil will experience a decidedly lesser degree of eternal salvation and then only following a requisite season of preresurrection purgation.[94]

Christ's Passion

Another key aspect of LDS atonement doctrine is its portrayal of Christ's suffering, his passion. In a revelation to Joseph Smith, Christ declares that his suffering caused him "to tremble because of pain, and to bleed at every pore, and to suffer in both body and spirit" (D&C 19:18). To be sure, across all Christian traditions, Christ's "passion" has been viewed as central to the atonement. Yet at times and among certain groups it has received special attention. Aquinas, for instance, emphasized that Christ's "suffering was all-embracing and

---

93. *JSP*, D14:157.
94. See chapter 12 for a full discussion of these matters.

his pain so great" that his passion "was not only sufficient but superabundant atonement for the sins of mankind."[95] This point was further developed by subsequent Roman Catholic theologians and led to an emphasis on the severity and interiority of Christ's sufferings. The words of nineteenth-century Catholic controversialist Henry Oxenham are illustrative: Christ's "mental sufferings . . . greatly exceeded the bodily pains of the Passion," and "He suffered in every part of His Sacred Humanity, in Body and Soul alike."[96] Nor was this just a Catholic view. Protestants, too, have posited a spiritual suffering of the soul so profound that, in the evocative words of James Ussher, seventeenth-century archbishop of the Church of Ireland, "if Adam and all his sonnes had suffered world without end in hell fire it had not beene answerable to this sacrifice." Indeed, Christ "received the sword of God up to the very hiltes in his soule."[97]

Mormon doctrine situates this horrific agony primarily in Christ's experience in the Garden of Gethsemane, where, according to Luke 22:44, "being in an agony he prayed more earnestly: and his sweat was as it were great drops of blood falling down to the ground."[98] Doctrine and Covenants glosses this passage in a literal fashion, making explicit that Christ's suffering in Gethsemane caused him "to bleed at every pore" (D&C 19:18).[99] Although never the predominant interpretation, other Christians have construed the Lukan passage similarly. For example, Irenaeus wrote that Christ "sweated great drops of blood," and a non-Mormon contemporary of Joseph Smith queried, "What merely human being ever suffered so as to sweat 'great drops of blood,' and yet lived? Christ had not yet felt the nails or the soldier's spear; and yet, such was his 'agony,' even before he was betrayed, that the blood gushed from every pore, 'falling down to the ground'!"[100] This was agony that went far beyond

95. Aquinas, *Summa Theologiae* 3a.48.2. Aquinas outlines how Christ "suffered maximum pain" in 3a.46.6.

96. Quoted in Grensted, *History of the Atonement*, 187, 185.

97. James Ussher, "Sermon on Hebrews 9:14" (1626), as quoted in Richard Snoddy, *The Soteriology of James Ussher: The Act and Object of Saving Faith* (New York: Oxford University Press, 2014), 47, 46.

98. Although advances in textual criticism in recent centuries have drawn attention to the less-than-universal attestation of Luke 22:43–44 in extant manuscripts, the debate over whether they were later interpolations has been inconclusive.

99. Anglican scholar Douglas Davies, for years an astute theological observer of Mormonism, has written on the special attention Latter-day Saints give to Christ's experience in the Garden of Gethsemane. See Davies's *Joseph Smith, Jesus, and Satanic Opposition: Atonement, Evil, and the Mormon Vision* (Farnham, UK: Ashgate, 2010), 136–51, and passim; and Davies, *Introduction to Mormonism* (Cambridge: Cambridge University Press, 2003), 148–56.

100. Irenaeus, *Against Heresies* 3.22.2, in *ANF*, 1:454; see also 4.35.3 (*ANF*, 1:514). The

fear of the impending future or even the pain of crucifixion, which other men had experienced. As Calvin remarked, how "shameful" it would "have been (as I have observed) to be so excruciated by the fear of an ordinary death as to sweat drops of blood, and not even be revived by the presence of angels? What? Does not that . . . show that Christ [in Gethsemane] had a fiercer and more arduous struggle than with ordinary death?"[101]

Latter-day Saints agree. Writes James Talmage, "He struggled and groaned under a burden such as no other being who has lived on earth might even conceive as possible. It was not physical pain, nor mental anguish alone, that caused Him to suffer such torture as to produce an extrusion of blood from every pore but a spiritual agony of soul such as only God was capable of experiencing."[102] There is a similarity here with Eastern Orthodoxy. Sergei Bulgakov wrote of Christ's "spiritual suffering" in Gethsemane and his "corporeal suffering" on Calvary.[103] And Vladimir Lossky noted, "The true Passion begins on Holy Thursday" in Gethsemane.[104] More than many others, though, Latter-day Saints account for Christ's intense spiritual suffering in Gethsemane by explaining that "in some manner, actual and terribly real though to man incomprehensible, the Savior took upon Himself the burden of the sins of mankind from Adam to the end of the world."[105] In words from the Book of Mormon, "Blood cometh from every pore, so great shall be his anguish for the wickedness and the abominations of his people" (Mosiah 3:7).

For Latter-day Saints, as for Lossky, the passion begins in Gethsemane and culminates on the cross. This perspective was first adumbrated in the 1880s by John Taylor in his *Mediation and Atonement.* There he acknowledged that in Gethsemane Christ bore "the weight, the responsibility, and the burden of the sins of all men" to the degree that "blood oozed from His pores." But, Taylor added, that weight and burden continued with Christ on the cross, where "He bowed beneath the accumulated load and cried out in anguish, 'My God, my God, why hast thou forsaken me!'"[106] The idea that Gethsemane and

---

quote from Smith's contemporary is Hiram Mattison, *A Scriptural Defence of the Doctrine of the Trinity* (New York, 1846), 131.

101. Calvin, *Institutes* 2.16.12.

102. Talmage, *Jesus the Christ,* 613.

103. Sergius Bulgakov, *The Orthodox Church,* trans. Lydia Kesich (Crestwood, NY: St. Vladimir's Seminary Press, 1988), 106.

104. Vladimir Lossky, *Orthodox Theology: An Introduction* (Crestwood, NY: St. Vladimir's Seminary Press, 1978), 117.

105. Talmage, *Jesus the Christ,* 613. Talmage's point was expressed thus in the church's *Life and Teachings of Jesus & His Apostles Course Manual* (1979): Christ experienced "a suffering so intense that it covered the punishment due for the sins of all men" (92).

106. Taylor, *Mediation and Atonement,* 150–51.

Golgotha were dual venues for Christ's expiatory passion was given a novel expansion in the early twentieth century by James Talmage, who suggested that the sin-expiating "agony of Gethsemane" had "recurred" on the cross.[107] This distinctive notion lay fallow for a half century until Bruce McConkie began reiterating it in several of his books.[108] In his last public sermon, McConkie declared that while Christ "was hanging on the cross . . . all the infinite agonies and merciless pains of Gethsemane *recurred*. And, finally, when the atoning agonies had taken their toll—when the victory had been won, when the Son of God had fulfilled the will of his Father in all things—then he said, 'It is finished' (John 19:30), and he voluntarily gave up the ghost."[109] Current church general authorities and church publications, however, simply proclaim that Christ's expiatory suffering continued on the cross without explicitly affirming a "recurrence" of all the pains of Gethsemane. As one publication explains, "In Gethsemane [Christ] submitted to the will of the Father and *began* to take upon Himself the sins of all people. . . . The Savior *continued* to suffer for our sins when He allowed Himself to be crucified—'lifted up upon the cross and slain for the sins of the world' (1 Nephi 11:33)."[110]

Mormon hymnody, however, does not emphasize this dual-venues perspective. Most of the thirty or so hymns sung in conjunction with the weekly celebration of the Lord's Supper focus on Calvary (see chapter 10). Only two hymns mention or allude to Gethsemane.[111] Disproportionate attention to

107. Talmage, *Jesus the Christ*, 661.

108. For example, in Gethsemane, wrote McConkie, Christ suffered "both body and spirit in a way which is totally beyond mortal comprehension. *Then again on the cross*—in addition to all the physical pain of that horrifying ordeal—he felt the spiritual agonies of the sins of others." Bruce R. McConkie, *The Mortal Messiah: From Bethlehem to Calvary*, 4 vols. (Salt Lake City: Deseret Book, 1979–1981), 4:224 (emphasis added). See also his *Millennial Messiah: The Second Coming of the Son of Man* (Salt Lake City: Deseret Book, 1982), 88, and *A New Witness for the Articles of Faith* (Salt Lake City: Deseret Book, 1985), 264, 289.

109. McConkie, "The Purifying Power of Gethsemane," *Ensign*, May 1985, 10 (emphasis added).

110. *True to the Faith*, 17 (emphasis added). This is reiterated, in almost the same words, in the *Gospel Topics* article "Atonement of Jesus Christ" on the church's website; *Preach My Gospel: A Guide to Sharing the Gospel of Jesus Christ*, 2nd ed. (Salt Lake City: The Church of Jesus Christ of Latter-day Saints, 2023), 31, 36, 55; and *Gospel Fundamentals* (Salt Lake City: The Church of Jesus Christ of Latter-day Saints, 2002), 57.

111. One is "Reverently and Meekly Now," *Hymns*, #185: "Think of me, thou ransomed one; Think what I for thee have done. With my blood that dripped like rain, Sweat in agony of pain, With my body on the tree I have ransomed even thee." The other exception is an alternate version of an Isaac Watts hymn—"He Died! The Great Redeemer Died," *Hymns*, #192: "Come, Saints, and drop a tear or two; For him who groaned beneath your load; He shed a thousand drops for you, A thousand drops of precious blood."

Calvary, of course, is due to the Last Supper's symbolic focus on Christ's crucified body and shed blood. It also reflects the considerable attention given to the expiatory significance of the cross not only in the Bible but also in LDS scripture. Multiple times in the Book of Mormon the phrase "slain for the sins of the world" is used as a succinct summary of the atonement.[112] Revelations in the Doctrine and Covenants declare that "Jesus was crucified by sinful men for the sins of the world" (D&C 21:9) and proclaim that "redemption [has] been wrought through the sacrifice of the Son of God upon the cross" (D&C 138:35).[113] It is hardly surprising, then, that Latter-day Saint leaders, particularly in the church's earlier years, echoed the testimony of scripture in emphasizing the importance of the cross. In the entire *Journal of Discourses* (the twenty-six-volume collection of nineteenth-century church leader sermons), there is only one instance in which a general authority explicitly mentioned that Christ's suffering in Gethsemane resulted from him there taking on the sins of the world.[114] Typical of the standard emphasis on the cross are First Presidency counselor Heber Kimball's testimony that Christ surrendered his life "that his blood might be shed upon the cross, that our sins might be forgiven," and Orson Pratt's reference to "the great atonement that was wrought out on Mount Calvary."[115] This pattern continued into the twentieth century.[116] In 1914, for instance, First Presidency counselor Charles Penrose testified that Christ "died on the cross by way of atonement for the sins of the world."[117] And church president Heber Grant concluded his 1936 conference address with this affirmation: "I close my remarks by bearing my testimony to the world that I know, as I know that I live, that God lives, that Jesus Christ is his Son, the Redeemer of the world, who came to the earth with a divinely appointed mission to die on the cross for the sins of mankind."[118]

Yet, particularly in the second half of the twentieth century, some of the church's general authorities began to feel that Gethsemane had been under

112. See, for instance, 3 Nephi 11:14; 1 Nephi 11:33; and Alma 30:26.

113. See also D&C 46:13; 45:4; and 76:69.

114. See *Journal of Discourses*, 24:34.

115. *Journal of Discourses*, 6:122; 14:327.

116. Latter-day Saint commentary in general conferences about the meaning and significance of the cross is reviewed in John Hilton III, Emily K. Hyde, and McKenna Grace Trussel, "The Teachings of Church Leaders regarding the Crucifixion of Jesus Christ: 1852–2018," *BYU Studies Quarterly* 59 (2020): 49–80.

117. Charles W. Penrose, *Conference Report*, October 1914, 36. See also *Conference Report*, April 1917, 20.

118. Heber J. Grant, *Conference Report*, April 1936, 50.

appreciated.[119] Building on the earlier theological work of B. H. Roberts and James Talmage, who emphasized the significance of Gethsemane, long-time apostle Joseph Fielding Smith in a 1947 general conference address remarked, "We get into the habit of thinking, I suppose, that [Christ's] great suffering was when he was nailed to the cross by his hands and his feet and was left there to suffer until he died. As excruciating as that pain was, that was not the greatest suffering that he had to undergo." It was in Gethsemane that "he carried on his back the burden of the sins of the whole world . . . and so great was his suffering before he ever went to the cross, we are informed, that blood oozed from the pores of his body, and he prayed to his Father that the cup might pass if it were possible."[120] After Smith's address, it became more common for church leaders teaching about the atonement to make it a point to at least mention Gethsemane alongside Golgotha.[121] This, of course, did not preclude continued reference to the cross. Thomas Monson, for instance, who would later become church president, as a young apostle in the 1960s proclaimed that Jesus Christ "is our Redeemer; he is our Mediator with the Father. He it was who died on the cross to atone for our sins."[122]

Joseph Fielding Smith's concern to emphasize Gethsemane was given even sharper expression in the extensive and influential writings of his son-in-law, Bruce McConkie. In his *Doctrinal New Testament Commentary*, published in the late 1960s and early 1970s, McConkie asked: "Where and under what circumstances was the atoning sacrifice of the Son of God made? Was it on the Cross of Calvary or in the Garden of Gethsemane?" "On the Cross" is the typical Christian answer, "but in reality the pain and suffering, the triumph and

---

119. For a history of discussion of Gethsemane in general conference addresses, see John Hilton III and Joshua P. Barringer, "The Use of *Gethsemane* by Church Leaders, 1859–2018," *BYU Studies Quarterly* 58, no. 4 (2019): 49–76.

120. Joseph Fielding Smith, *Conference Report*, October 1947, 147–48. Similar comments are found in *Doctrines of Salvation*, 1:130.

121. A year after Smith's address, Marion Romney testified: "I believe that in Gethsemane and on the cross Jesus suffered for the sins of all men." *Conference Report*, April 1948, 77. Several years later as an apostle, Romney described the contrast between Christ's passion in the garden and on the cross in this way: "He suffered greatly on the cross, of course, but other men had died by crucifixion; in fact, a man hung on either side of him as he died on the cross. But no man, nor set of men, nor all men put together, ever suffered what the Redeemer suffered in the Garden." *Conference Report*, October 1953, 35. Other general authorities during this period who made it a point to mention both atonement venues include Joseph Wirthlin, *Conference Report*, October 1952, 108, and Milton Hunter, *Conference Report*, April 1960, 116.

122. Thomas S. Monson, *Conference Report*, April 1966, 63.

grandeur, of the atonement took place primarily in Gethsemane. It was there Jesus took upon himself the sins of the world on conditions of repentance. It was there he suffered beyond human power to endure. It was there he sweat great drops of blood from every pore. It was there his anguish was so great he fain would have let the bitter cup pass."[123] Yet, by the time McConkie was writing his six-volume *Messiah* series a decade later (and after his father-in-law had passed away), he chose to give more balanced attention to Gethsemane and Calvary. McConkie titled a section of one of his chapters "Atonement Completed on the Cross." In it he wrote: "That which began in Gethsemane was finished on the cross and crowned in the resurrection." Indeed, the believer who "contemplates the atonement wrought in the garden and on the cross . . . marvels at what God has done for him."[124] McConkie's expression anticipated the contemporary effort to not let Gethsemane eclipse Golgotha. In the words of Jeffrey Holland: "The utter loneliness and excruciating pain of the Atonement begun in Gethsemane reached its zenith when . . . Christ cried from the cross, 'Eli, Eli, lama sabachthani? that is to say, My God, my God, why hast thou forsaken me?'"[125]

Additional LDS Distinctives

As previously noted, Latter-day Saint discourse in recent years has tended to use the phrase "the atonement of Jesus Christ" broadly to refer to all aspects of Christ's redemptive work, not just to what he accomplished in his sacrificial suffering, death, and resurrection. His entire incarnate life is seen as redemptive in that he physically experienced and coped with all the vicissitudes of life, not just temptation to sin. John Taylor explained that Christ had to take on a physical

---

123. Bruce R. McConkie, *Doctrinal New Testament Commentary*, vol. 1, *The Gospels* (Salt Lake City: Bookcraft, 1965), 774.

124. McConkie, *The Mortal Messiah*, 4:224, 230. Still, McConkie placed greatest emphasis on Gethsemane: "As he came out of the Garden . . . the victory had been won. There remained yet the shame and the pain of his arrest, his trials, and his cross. But all these were overshadowed by the agonies and sufferings in Gethsemane. It was on the cross that he 'suffered death in the flesh,' even as many have suffered agonizing deaths, but it was in Gethsemane that 'he suffered the pain of all men, that all men might repent and come unto him' (D&C 18:11)." McConkie, *The Mortal Messiah*, 4:127–28.

125. Holland, "Atonement of Jesus Christ," 37. Church general authority Tad Callister asked, "What then is the Atonement of Jesus Christ? In one sense, it is a series of divine events that commenced in the Garden of Gethsemane, continued on the cross, and culminated with the Savior's Resurrection from the tomb." Tad R. Callister, "The Atonement of Jesus Christ," *Ensign*, May 2019, 85.

body "to comprehend the weaknesses and strength, the perfections and imperfections of poor fallen human nature." In so doing, he "had to grapple with the
hypocrisy, corruption, [and] weakness" of humankind. As a result, "He knows
how to estimate and put a proper value upon human nature, for he having been
placed in the same position as we are, knows how to bear with our weaknesses
and infirmities, and can fully comprehend the depth, power, and strength of the
afflictions and trials that men have to cope with in this world, and thus under-
standingly and by experience, he can bear with" us.[126] To be sure, this is not a
perspective unique to Latter-day Saints. The Arminian Confession of 1621, for
instance, affirmed that Christ was "truly subject to the same infirmities, passions,
labors, afflictions, straits, pains, griefs, shames, [and] reproaches" that ordinary
human beings experience "for the very purpose that being in all things made
like to his brothers (yet without sin) he might be a merciful and faithful high
priest."[127] Increasingly in the past several decades, however, in emphasizing the
power of Christ's atonement to heal more than just spiritual infirmities, Latter-
day Saint leaders have grounded their broadened atonement discourse in a Book
of Mormon passage that echoes and elaborates verbiage in Hebrews: "And he shall
go forth, suffering pains and afflictions and temptations of every kind; and this
that the word might be fulfilled which saith he will take upon him the pains and
the sicknesses of his people . . . and he will take upon him their infirmities, that
his bowels may be filled with mercy . . . that he may know according to the flesh
how to succor his people according to their infirmities" (Alma 7:11–12).[128]

What this passage has come to mean among Latter-day Saints is well illustrated by remarks from Dallin Oaks: "Most scriptural accounts of the Atonement concern the Savior's breaking the bands of death and suffering for our
sins. In [this] sermon recorded in the Book of Mormon, Alma taught these
fundamentals. But he also provided our clearest scriptural assurances that the
Savior also experienced the pains and sicknesses and infirmities of His people."
Referring to "this part" of Christ's atonement, Oaks quoted fellow apostle Boyd
Packer to say that Christ suffered "an accumulation of all of the guilt, the grief
and sorrow, the pain and humiliation, all of the mental, emotional, and physical
torments known to man—He experienced them all." Then referencing the remark by First Presidency counselor James Faust, that Christ "suffered anything

126. *Journal of Discourses*, 1:148.
127. *The Confession or Declaration of the Remonstrant Pastors*, 8.4, in *The Arminian Confession of 1621*, trans. and ed. Mark A. Ellis (Eugene, OR: Pickwick, 2005), 70.
128. Although rarely discussed by church leaders prior to the final quarter of the twenti-
eth century, this passage has become a pastoral commonplace in recent decades. See https://
www.lds-general-conference.org/.

and everything that we could ever feel or experience," Oaks concluded: "He therefore knows our struggles, our heartaches, our temptations, and our suffering, for He willingly experienced them all as an essential part of His Atonement. And because of this, His Atonement empowers Him to succor us—to give us the strength to bear it all."[129] "Think of it!" declared apostle Howard Hunter, Christ not only took upon him "the sins and temptations of every human soul who will repent, but all of our sickness and grief and pain of every kind. . . . He suffered them all. He did this to perfect his mercy and his ability to lift us above every earthly trial."[130] Remarked Neal Maxwell, "Nothing is beyond His redeeming reach or His encircling empathy."[131] Such views led general authority Merrill Bateman to characterize Christ's atonement as "intimate as well as infinite . . . intimate in that the Savior felt each person's pains, sufferings, and sicknesses." Fellow church leader Tad Callister ventured that the atonement helps people overcome "the common ailments of life such as depression, rejection and loneliness. . . . [Christ] suffered the consequence not only of every sin and weakness, but also of every disease, every rejection, every disappointment and every ailment of every soul who has ever lived."[132]

As can be seen, recent decades have witnessed an expanded appreciation among Latter-day Saints of the manifold blessings that the atoning work of Jesus Christ makes possible in addition to the forgiveness of sins. In 2012, apostle David Bednar noted that most Latter-day Saints "clearly understand that the Atonement is for sinners." He went on, "I am not so sure, however, that we know and understand that the Atonement is also for saints—for good men and women who are obedient, worthy, and conscientious and who are striving to become better and serve more faithfully."[133] Drawing on the gracious power and love of the Savior Jesus Christ to assist and fortify disciples in all aspects of their earthly pilgrimage has become an ever more pronounced theme in LDS discourse. Not surprisingly, the twenty-first century has seen a spate of popular books published on the atonement with titles like *The Atonement: Fulfilling God's Great Plan of Happiness*; *The Infinite Atonement*; *The Continuous Atonement*; and *The Gift of the Atonement*.[134] In such writings and

129. Dallin H. Oaks, "Strengthened by the Atonement of Jesus Christ," *Ensign*, November 2015, 61–62.

130. Howard W. Hunter, "He Is Risen," *Ensign*, May 1988, 16–17.

131. Neal A. Maxwell, "Overcome . . . Even as I Also Overcame," *Ensign*, May 1987, 72.

132. Merrill J. Bateman, "The Power to Heal from Within," *Ensign*, May 1995, 14, and Callister, *Church News*, March 29, 2015, 11, 13.

133. David A. Bednar, "The Atonement and the Journey of Mortality," *Ensign*, April 2012, 42.

134. Tad R. Callister, *The Infinite Atonement* (Salt Lake City: Deseret Book, 2000); Earl C.

elsewhere the "power" of Christ's atoning work is held up as the solution to a great variety of human infirmities. A church lesson manual urged students to ask themselves how the atonement of Jesus Christ has "transformed your weaknesses into strengths," and in 2015, the church's magazine, *Ensign*, solicited and printed responses from young adults in an article entitled "I Felt the Power of the Atonement of Jesus Christ When . . ."[135]

The same year, retired general authority Bruce Hafen, long attentive in his ministry to the topic of Christ's atoning work, noted the surge of interest in the Savior's atonement: "We Latter-day Saints have been teaching and testifying much more about the Atonement of Jesus Christ." He expressed satisfaction that so many Latter-day Saints today "speak not only of their having found forgiveness" through Jesus Christ but also of having found through Christ's atonement "strength and comfort" to meet "their most personal needs." Hafen characterized this expanded appreciation of Christ's work as "a veritable groundswell among Church members."[136] At the same time, he warned against a certain downside to this popular groundswell. He identified several exaggerated claims he had encountered at the folk level, such as crediting the atonement for helping a child find lost glasses or overcoming the devastation of a tsunami and urged that ordinary Latter-day Saints need to be better "anchored" in "doctrinal foundations."[137] Concern about overminting the conceptual coin of the atonement was also expressed at the church's April 2015 general conference by First Presidency counselor Dieter Uchtdorf, who urged church members not to let the Christ's atonement "become commonplace in our teaching, in our conversation, or in our hearts. It is sacred and holy."[138] Two years later, in the April 2017 general conference, Russell Nelson, president of the Quorum of Twelve Apostles, offered an even more pointed corrective: "It is doctrinally incomplete to speak of the Lord's atoning sacrifice by shortcut phrases, such as 'the Atonement' or 'the enabling power of the Atonement' or 'applying the Atonement' or 'being strengthened by the Atonement.' These expressions present a real risk of misdirecting faith by treating the *event* as if

Tingey, *The Atonement: Fulfilling God's Great Plan of Happiness* (Salt Lake City: Deseret Book, 2010); Brad Wilcox, *The Continuous Atonement* (Salt Lake City: Deseret Book, 2009); *The Gift of the Atonement* (Salt Lake City: Deseret Book, 2002). The latter volume featured dozens of shorter "Favorite Writings on the Atonement."

135. *Book of Mormon Student Manual* (2009), 381, and *Ensign*, September 2015, 14.

136. Bruce C. Hafen and Marie K. Hafen, *The Contrite Spirit: How the Temple Helps Us Apply Christ's Atonement* (Salt Lake City: Deseret Book, 2015), 4–5.

137. Hafen and Hafen, *The Contrite Spirit*, 6–15.

138. Dieter F. Uchtdorf, "The Gift of Grace," *Ensign*, May 2015, 107.

it had living existence and capabilities independent of our Heavenly Father and His Son, Jesus Christ." In reality, "there is no amorphous entity called 'the Atonement' upon which we may call for succor, healing, forgiveness, or power. Jesus Christ is the source." In short, "the Savior's atoning sacrifice—the central act of all human history—is best understood and appreciated when we expressly and clearly connect it to Him."[139]

Conclusion

This chapter has endeavored to make clear that Latter-day Saint understandings of the work of Christ echo main currents of other Christian theologies but do so with certain distinctive variations on those themes. The perception that Mormons have only recently "discovered" Christ and his atonement is far from correct, but it is true that LDS appreciation for Christ's work has become more vocal and visible in the past few decades. Today few friendly observers (or members) of the Church of Jesus Christ of Latter-day Saints doubt the extent of the enthusiastic Latter-day Saint affirmation of, and appreciation for, the atonement of Jesus Christ. Since the 1970s, much has happened to deepen this perception. What is clear is that the church's institutional emphasis of recent decades has provided the general church membership with a depth and breadth of analysis of the "work of Christ" not previously experienced.

139. Russell M. Nelson, "Drawing the Power of Jesus Christ into Our Lives," *Ensign*, May 2017, 40.

5

ANTHROPOLOGY

Humanity as "Royalty Deposed"

Having explored in previous chapters the nature and work of God (theology) and the nature and work of Jesus Christ (Christology), we turn now to a consideration of the nature of humankind (anthropology), a study as old as human existence itself. Since the dawn of time, *Homo sapiens* has sought to understand its nature, its composition and capabilities. Inevitably, whether in casual reflection or in systematic analysis, the investigation has returned a mixed verdict. Blaise Pascal expressed this as colorfully as anyone: "What sort of freak then is man! How novel, how monstruous, how chaotic, how paradoxical, how prodigious! Judge of all things, feeble earth-worm, repository of truth, sink of doubt and error, glory and refuse of the universe. . . . Man's greatness and wretchedness are so evident that the true religion must necessarily teach us that there is in man some great principle of greatness and some great principle of wretchedness!"[1] From the perspective of theological anthropology, that greatness is rooted in humanity's creation by God and the wretchedness is the result of what theologians call "the fall." Around these two foci, so central to Christian thought, is organized this chapter's exploration of humanity as "deposed royalty."[2]

THE HUMAN CONSTITUTION

Whether humankind is considered "royal" or "wretched" or some combination of both, a prior question is what constitutes a human being in the first place. The traditional answer, which has a long and venerable history in Christian theology, is that the human person consists of a physical body and

---

1. Blaise Pascal, *Penseés*, trans. A. J. Krailsheimer (London: Penguin Books, 1966), 64, 76.
2. The phrase is from Douglas Groothuis in "Deposed Royalty: Pascal's Anthropological Argument," *Journal of the Evangelical Theological Society* 41 (June 1998): 297–313.

a separate and separable immaterial soul. Most Christians accept this view unquestioningly as a basic biblical concept and a fundamental aspect of their self-understanding. Scholars label this a "dualist" or "dichotomist" anthropology. An alternate, minority view is "trichotomism," in which the human is believed to be made up of three distinct components—"soul," "spirit," and "body." In this formulation, the "rational soul" is the seat of intellectual perception and roughly corresponds to the mind. The spirit is the source of humanity's religious intuition and determines a person's spiritual characteristics. The existence of both dichotomist and trichotomist anthropologies reflects the ambiguity and inconsistency in how the underlying Hebrew and Greek terms translated as "soul," "spirit," and "body" are used in the Bible.[3] This lexical leeway is also manifest in LDS scripture. For instance, "soul" and "spirit" are sometimes used synonymously (e.g., Alma 40:7–14), but "soul" can also refer to the whole person (e.g., "the spirit and the body are the soul of man"—D&C 88:15). In general, when speaking of the constituent "parts" of the human being, Latter-day Saint discourse is dualist and prefers "spirit" over "soul" as the term to refer to humanity's inner life.

However Christians configure their anthropologies, it is important to recognize that traditional notions of the body "housing" a separate, ontologically distinct soul or spirit have been under siege from some quarters of biblical scholarship at least since the late nineteenth century and from various scientific disciplines since the 1600s. Before continuing to discuss the still-dominant body-soul dualism, it is worth pausing briefly to consider these challenges. We begin with the scientific objection. By the late twentieth century, the cumulative impact of developments in genetics and neuroscience had sufficiently permeated popular culture that literary gadfly Tom Wolfe could write his provocative essay titled "Sorry, but Your Soul Just Died."[4] The old dichotomy that distinctly associated mind or consciousness with an immaterial soul and brain with the physical body seemed to have broken down; all could now be accounted for in physical, biological terms.[5] Nobel laureate Francis Crick, one of the discoverers of DNA, claimed that the emotions and memories of human beings, their

---

3. The biblical data pertaining to the usage of "soul" and "spirit" is reviewed in detail in Wayne Grudem, *Systematic Theology: An Introduction to Biblical Doctrine*, 2nd ed. (Grand Rapids: Zondervan Academic, 2020), 600–611. Grudem's conclusion is that "although the arguments for trichotomy do have some force, none of them provides conclusive evidence that would overcome the wide testimony of Scripture showing that the terms *soul* and *spirit* are frequently interchangeable and are in many cases synonymous" (610).

4. Reprinted in Tom Wolfe, *Hooking Up* (New York: Picador, 2000), 89–109.

5. The history of this cognitive revolution and attempts to locate all that is human in

"identity and free will, are in fact no more than the behavior of a vast assembly of nerve cells and their associated molecules."[6] Brain imaging and neural research seem to have demonstrated that the physical brain and the body's neurons and synapses are capable of performing all the functions historically attributed to the intangible soul.[7] Moreover, since Darwin, many biologists have argued that the gradual evolution of hominids allows no certain historical point at which ensoulment can be detected and thus distinguish the "human race" from previous hominids or other primates. Even physics joined the assault, asking how the supposedly directive "energy" of a separate, nonphysical entity—the "soul"—could be transferred to a physical, human body.

Anthropological dualism also came under siege from biblical studies. From the nineteenth century onward, textual and historical analysis of the Old Testament has yielded a consensus verdict that ancient Israel conceived of the human being monistically (as one, in a singular fashion) as a body that God vitalized or brought to life, rather than a body into which he placed a soul. To be sure, the Hebrew language deploys different terms, such as *nephesh* (soul), *ruach* (spirit), or *leb* (heart), when describing human nature, but "a strict dualism, which feels that flesh and spirit, body and soul, are irreconcilable opposites, is completely unknown."[8] Thus, in the Genesis 2:7 depiction of Adam becoming "a living soul," *nephesh* "does not refer to a part of the human being, nor to the human's possession of a metaphysically separate entity distinguishable from the human body such as a 'soul' or 'spirit.' Indeed, this text provides no basis at all for imagining that . . . some part of the human being is 'spiritual' as opposed to 'earthy' (or material)."[9] If the Hebrew conception of the human being was that of an animated body, the Hellenistic notion, influential in early Christianity, was that of the incarnated soul.

---

the brain, including spirituality, is detailed in John L. Modern, *Neuromatic, or, A Particular History of Religion and the Brain* (Chicago: University of Chicago Press, 2021).

6. Francis Crick, *The Astonishing Hypothesis: The Scientific Search for the Soul* (New York: Simon & Schuster, 1994), 3.

7. See Elkhonon Goldberg, *The Executive Brain: Frontal Lobes and the Civilized Mind* (Oxford: Oxford University Press, 2001); Joseph LeDoux, *The Emotional Brain: The Mysterious Underpinnings of Emotional Life* (London: Weidenfeld & Nicolson, 1998); and Benjamin Lebet, Anthony Freeman, and Keith Sutherland, eds., *The Volitional Brain: Towards a Neuroscience of Free Will* (Thorverton, UK: Imprint Academic, 1999).

8. Walther Eichrodt, *Theology of the Old Testament*, trans. J. A. Baker, 2 vols. (Philadelphia: Westminster, 1961–1967), 2:147.

9. Joel B. Green, "Why the *Imago Dei* Should Not Be Identified with the Soul," in *The Ashgate Research Companion to Theological Anthropology*, ed. Joshua R. Farris and Charles Taliaferro (Burlington, VT: Ashgate, 2015), 184.

In some ways, Mormon doctrine straddles the two views. It sees the spirit as a distinct entity, separate and separable from the material body, as does Christian dualism, but it also views the spirit as composed of "matter," albeit more "fine or pure," and avers that ultimately "when our bodies are purified we shall see that it is all matter" (D&C 131:7–8). Thus, from the Latter-day Saint perspective, body-soul dualism and metaphysical monism are not mutually exclusive. Since all existence to one degree or another is material in nature, it can obviously take separate and distinct forms such as one's physical body and the more materially refined inner spirit or soul. Although a confirmed monist, twentieth-century theologian Rudolf Bultmann acknowledged that in 2 Corinthians 5:1–4, Paul "comes very close to Hellenistic-Gnostic dualism . . . in form of expression, by speaking of the *soma* [body] under the figure of 'tent-dwelling' and 'garment' . . . as a shell for the self (the 'inner nature,' *eso anthropos*)."[10] Others favor a more Hebraic anthropology known as "physicalism." Rather than viewing the human being dualistically as a body that clothes a distinct spirit or soul, physicalists see the human singularly as only a physical body that manifests the different characteristics or aspects traditionally labeled "soul" and "spirit."[11] Scientists and biblical scholars doubtless will continue to explore the human constitution, and their assessments may one day lead to a more widespread reconfiguration of Christian anthropology. For the moment, however, the persisting popularity of the belief that a separable human spirit or soul lives on after death in conscious, personal existence independent of the deceased body acts as a major deterrent to general Christian acceptance of a physicalist or monistic anthropology.

The Origin of Souls

If, then, the human body is inhabited by a distinct, identifiable entity known as a soul or spirit, where did it come from? Almost nothing is said in the Bible about the origin of souls, but by the end of the fourth century, three basic theories (all now bearing relatively modern titles) circulated among Christian

10. Rudolf Bultmann, *Theology of the New Testament*, trans. Kendrik Grobel (London: SCM, 1952), 201. See also Hans Dieter Betz, "The Concept of the 'Inner Human Being' (*eso anthropos*) in the Anthropology of Paul," *New Testament Studies* 46 (July 2000); 315–41.

11. See John W. Cooper, *Body, Soul, & Life Everlasting: Biblical Anthropology and the Monism-Dualism Debate*, 2nd ed. (Grand Rapids: Eerdmans, 2000); Joel B. Green and Stuart L. Palmer, eds., *In Search of the Soul: Four Views of the Mind-Body Problem* (Downers Grove, IL: InterVarsity, 2005); and Nancey Murphy, *Bodies and Souls, or Spirited Bodies* (Cambridge: Cambridge University Press, 2006).

thinkers. *Creationism* (not to be confused with the current name for a particular understanding of the origin of the earth) was the idea that in an ongoing
process of divine creation souls are tailor-made by God for each human em-
bryo and infused in the fetus at conception or sometime thereafter prior to
birth. *Traducianism* (from the Latin *traducere*, "to lead across, transmit") held
that the soul is transmitted biologically from generation to generation. God is
thought to have created only one soul—Adam's—and from that point forward,
soul is part of the biological inheritance parents pass on to their children. *Preexistentialism* was the concept that all souls were created simultaneously in the
beginning before the physical creation and kept "in storage" until implanted
in individual humans sometime between conception and birth. One modern
scholar has memorably dubbed these theories of the origin of the soul as,
respectively, "custom-made," "second-hand," and "ready-made."[12]

Of the three theories, Paula Fredriksen argues that in early Christianity
the preexistence of souls was "the one everyone would have preferred and
the one most natural to the Greek metaphysics that most of these theologies
presupposed."[13] The Greek metaphysics of an immortal soul presumes a preexistence of some kind. Additionally, the Hellenistic privileging of spirit over
matter made it reasonable to believe that the higher, spiritual/intellectual realm
would have been created before the lesser physical/material universe. Several
different versions of the theory of the preexistence of souls were in circulation
at the time, but because Origen's appropriation of the concept was eventually
anathematized, all became theologically suspect thereafter.[14] Origen's notion
of the preexistence was influenced by Platonic premises but diverged at points
from Platonic accounts, particularly of embodiment as the "fall" of souls.[15]
A prominent strand of Platonism (subtle variations had emerged since Plato,
such as the Middle Platonism and Neoplatonism of Origen's day) held that
embodiment was the unfortunate consequence of souls' wanton desire for

12. Lynne Rudder Baker, "Death and the Afterlife," in *The Oxford Handbook of Philosophy of Religion*, ed. William J. Wainwright (Oxford: Oxford University Press, 2005), 370.

13. Paula Fredriksen, "Beyond the Body/Soul Dichotomy: Augustine's Answer to Mani,
Plotinus, and Julian," in *Paul and the Legacies of Paul*, ed. William S. Babcock (Dallas:
Southern Methodist University Press, 1990), 245.

14. On the later censuring of aspects of Origen's theology, see Elizabeth A. Clark, *The
Origenist Controversy: The Cultural Construction of an Early Christian Debate* (Princeton:
Princeton University Press, 1992).

15. See Benjamin P. Blosser, *Become like the Angels: Origen's Doctrine of the Soul* (Washington, DC: Catholic University of America Press, 2012), especially chapter 6—"Preexistence
of Souls" (145–82).

materiality, something that was inappropriate for pure, spiritual being as the higher form of existence. As a result, souls, either voluntarily or out of necessity, became incarnate (and incarcerated) in human bodies. Origen, however, advanced a "softer" version of the "descent of souls," one that did not consider embodiment as punitive "entombment." His variation on the Platonic theme was that "the fall of the soul is not a 'fall into a body,' but rather a cooling of divine love, a Bride's spurning of her Bridegroom, on the part of a creature who is already [spiritually] embodied. The terrestrial body and the sensible cosmos in which it dwells are not a punitive prison, but rather works of a loving God, engineered so as to secure most effectively the salvation of the souls that dwell therein."[16]

Other contemporaneous theories of the preexistence also took a more positive tack on the genesis of souls, claiming that God created them good. It is not certain how widespread a doctrine of the preexistence of souls was or which church fathers espoused it, but it is mentioned by both Augustine and Jerome as one of several explanations for the origin of souls then in circulation.[17] Another theory, anathematized by those seeking to preserve the ontological uniqueness of God, was associated with Priscillianism—the idea that God created souls from his own substance.[18] Augustine was undecided about which theory of the soul's origin to embrace, but he was certain that Priscillian doctrine was wrong and that the soul must be distinguished ontologically from its Creator. The soul, wrote Augustine in his commentary *On Genesis*, "comes from God as a thing which he has made, not as being of the same nature as he is, whether as something he has begotten or in any way at all produced from himself."[19] As will be seen, what Augustine is opposing is actually very close

16. Blosser, *Become like the Angels*, 218; see all of chapter 7—"Descent of Souls" (183–219). Earlier readings of Origen's theory of the embodiment of preexistent souls tended to characterize it more negatively, but further analysis by text critics of surviving manuscripts of Origen's *On First Principles* has determined that the earlier critical text of the work contains non-Origenian interpolations that overstate the "fall of souls" and "bodily entrapment" motifs. The best version and translation of *On First Principles* to use now is John Behr, ed. and trans., *Origen: On First Principles*, 2 vols. (Oxford: Oxford University Press, 2017).

17. Augustine, Letter 166.12, in *NPNF*, 1/1:527, and Jerome, Letter 126.1, in *NPNF*, 2/6:252.

18. Augustine, *To Consentius: Against Lying* 8, in *NPNF*, 3:484. A Priscillian tractate refers to humans as the "*divinum genus.*" Henry Chadwick, *Priscillian of Avila* (Oxford: Clarendon, 1976), 67.

19. Augustine, *On the Literal Interpretation of Genesis* 7.2.3, ed. and trans. Edmund Hill, Works of Saint Augustine: A Translation for the 21st Century (Hyde Park, NY: New City, 2002), 325. In 415, Augustine also wrote a brief treatise *To Orosius in Refutation of the Priscillianists and Origenists*.

to the Latter-day Saint view. Although the idea of the preexistence of souls was eventually frowned upon, even anathematized at times, the doctrine in one form or another persisted along the popular periphery of Christian theology through the succeeding centuries. By the nineteenth century, noted American minister Edward Beecher could aver that "a large proportion of the human race, if not the majority, have always believed in some form of the doctrine of the preexistence of man."[20]

"MAN WAS ALSO IN THE BEGINNING WITH GOD"

Almost from its beginning, the Church of Jesus Christ of Latter-day Saints has proclaimed belief in the preexistence of humankind. As early as the 1830s, several Doctrine and Covenants revelations either imply or explicitly affirm a preexistence of souls/spirits.[21] Over time, the Latter-day Saint vision of the preexistence became decidedly more detailed and elaborate. Illustrative of this is Mormon reflection on the meaning of a phrase in Doctrine and Covenants 93:29 that states, echoing John 1:2—the Word "was in the beginning with God"—that "man was also in the beginning with God." Various interpretations of "the beginning" have been offered over the years and highlight different dimensions of Latter-day Saint belief about the preexistence.[22] In general, three different LDS readings emerged regarding how "man was also in the beginning with God." First, "beginning" was interpreted in a traditional Genesis fashion to refer to the physical creation of the universe. The phrase in question affirms that preexistent souls were already in existence and so were present on the morn of physical creation. Second, "beginning" can be read as referring to the prior spiritual creation of all things, including human souls/spirits (see chapter 2). A third reading of "beginning" sees it as a reference to the beginning-less beginning of eternity before any creation, spiritual or

20. Edward Beecher, *The Conflict of Ages; or, The Great Debate on the Moral Relations of God and Man* (Boston: Phillips, Sampson & Co., 1854), 218. Beecher's observation appears to be borne out in Terryl Givens, *When Souls Had Wings: Pre-Mortal Existence in Western Thought* (New York: Oxford University Press, 2009).

21. D&C 29:31–32, 36–37; 49:17; 93:23, 29. See also Moses 3:5–7.

22. This parallels early Christian debates with Neoplatonists about the meaning of *archē*, the Greek word for "beginning," "origin," or "source," and the term used in Septuagint (LXX) Gen. 1:1 to translate the Hebrew *re'shith*. See, for instance, Paul M. Blowers, *Drama of the Divine Economy: Creator and Creation in Early Christian Theology and Piety* (Oxford: Oxford University Press, 2012), 139–87, and Andrew Louth, ed., *Old Testament*, vol. 1, *Genesis 1–11*, Ancient Christian Commentary on Scripture (Downers Grove, IL: InterVarsity Press, 2001).

physical. As an example of the first view, Joseph Fielding Smith wrote that "the beginning was when the [heavenly] councils met and the decision was made to create this earth."[23] The second view is implied in an earlier verse in Doctrine and Covenants 93 where Christ says, "I was in the beginning with the Father, and am the Firstborn" (D&C 93:21) of his spirit children. A college-level Doctrine and Covenants study manual acknowledges both views 1 and 2: "The word *beginning* may refer to the time when we began as the spirit offspring of God or to the time when the earth began as a temporal sphere."[24]

The third reading of "man was in the beginning with God" requires more detailed discussion since the interpretation involves some speculative theology. What distinguishes it from the other two readings is that it engages the seemingly unrelated words in the rest of Doctrine and Covenants 93:29: "intelligence, or the light of truth, was not created or made, neither indeed can be." For most people, "intelligence" is an abstract concept. It could be so interpreted here, as it is elsewhere in Latter-day Saint scripture and discourse (e.g., D&C 130:18–19). Why, then, does this verse state the obvious about "intelligence" not being "created or made" as if it were a kind of substantive entity? One answer is that when read in conjunction with other statements made by Joseph Smith, Latter-day Saints have postulated that the "intelligence" here referred to may indeed have a material quality and that the verse may be suggesting the existence of uncreated "intelligent matter" that was "in the beginning with God." "The mind of man—the intelligent part—is co-equal with God Himself," declared Joseph Smith. "Intelligence is eternal & it is self-existing . . . there is no creation about it."[25] Doctrine and Covenants 93:29 and Smith's comments about the eternality of intelligence have been interpreted in one of two ways: (1) uncreated intelligence refers to generic, undifferentiated intelligent matter from which God in the spirit creation fashioned individual minds or intellects for his spirit children; or (2) intelligent matter has always existed in a differentiated state as distinct, self-conscious "intelligences." In this second reading, these primeval intelligences were the minds to which Smith was referring and constitute the core individual identities of eternal human "selves." Spirit creation merely clothed them with spirit bodies.[26] This second

23. Joseph Fielding Smith, *Church History and Modern Revelation*, 4 vols. (Salt Lake City: Council of the Twelve Apostles of the Church of Jesus Christ of Latter-day Saints, 1946–1949), 2:162.

24. *D&C Student Manual* (2001), 219.

25. *JSP*, D14:331, 339, 348.

26. For a full account of how Mormons have conceptualized uncreated "intelligence," see Kenneth W. Godfrey, "The History of Intelligence in Latter-day Saint Thought," in *The*

interpretation makes the extraordinary claim that not only is the Son coeternal with the Father (as John 1:1–2 is commonly understood to proclaim) but so are all individual intelligences. A crucial qualifier, though, is that because Latter-day Saints understand "eternity" and "eternal" as everlasting time rather than as a descriptor of God's unique ontology, in the Mormon schema, positing coeternality for essential human selves does not entail codivinity.

Further, it is important to reiterate that theologizing about the eternal nature of intelligence fits squarely in the category of what the church considers unresolved, speculative doctrine.[27] Neither of the two postulates mentioned above is discussed in LDS scripture or adjudicated by formal doctrinal pronouncement. A contributing factor to the interpretive ambiguity surrounding Doctrine and Covenants 93:29 and related texts is the interchangeable use of "soul," "spirit," and "intelligence" in early Mormon discourse. Joseph Smith used the three terms synonymously in a famous and influential 1844 general conference address later dubbed the "King Follett Sermon."[28] The same occurs in Abraham 3:18–23, the only place in scripture where the plural term "intelligences" appears (21, 22), and there "intelligences" are discussed interchangeably with "spirits" (18, 23) and "souls" (23).[29] In 1916, the First Presi-

---

Pearl of Great Price: Revelations from God, ed. H. Donl Peterson and Charles D. Tate (Provo, UT: BYU Religious Studies Center, 1989), 213–35.

27. Joseph Fielding Smith stated, "There has been some speculation and articles have been written attempting to explain just what these 'intelligences' are, or this 'intelligence' is, but it is futile for us to speculate upon it [in the absence of revelation]." Smith, *Church History and Modern Revelation*, 2:162. This warning is still being reproduced in current church instructional manuals. See, for example, *Doctrines of the Gospel Student Manual* (2010), 13; and *Pearl of Great Price Teacher Manual* (2017), 70, where a similarly worded statement from Smith is introduced thus: "*Caution:* . . . Inasmuch as questions arise concerning the nature and origin of 'intelligence,' it is imperative for the gospel teacher to consider the following statement by President Joseph Fielding Smith."

28. *JSP*, D14:311–40. Literary critic Harold Bloom called it "one of the truly remarkable sermons ever preached in America." Harold Bloom, *American Religion* (New York: Simon & Schuster, 1992), 95. For an introduction to the sermon, see Donald Q. Cannon, "The King Follett Discourse: Joseph Smith's Greatest Sermon in Historical Perspective," *BYU Studies* 18 (Winter 1978): 179–92.

29. Although little used in modern English, one of the definitions of "intelligence" in Webster's 1828 dictionary was: "A spiritual being; as a created intelligence. It is believed that the universe is peopled with innumerable superior intelligences." Similar nineteenth-century use of "intelligences" as a synonym for spirits or souls can be found in *Compendium of Doctrines*, 251, 182, 124, and John Jaques, *Catechism for Children: Exhibiting the Prominent Doctrines of the Church of Jesus Christ of Latter-day Saints* (Liverpool: F. D. Richards, 1854), 21.

dency offered their authoritative interpretation that in the Abraham passage "by 'intelligences' we are to understand personal 'spirits.'"[30] Still, rather than repudiate altogether use of "intelligences" as a reference to precreation, eternal human selves, the presidency's interpretation specifies how the term should be understood in Abraham 3. More broadly, what "must be carefully kept in mind" when "reading Latter-day Saint literature," explained apostle John Widtsoe, is "the twofold sense in which the terms *an intelligence* or *intelligences* are used—applied to [1] spiritual personages or [2] to pre-spiritual entities." Widtsoe referred to the second type as "the essence of man, his very self, his ego, that reaches back into the 'beginning' of things, into the dim eternities beyond the comprehension of mortal man."[31]

Positing a precreation *kosmos noētos*—a realm of bodiless, immortal intelligences or minds (*nooi*)—might have been palatable to Platonists, but it was unsatisfactory to some early twentieth-century LDS Church leaders. This discomfort was related to the increasing publicity the idea of eternal, individual intelligences was receiving in the church in the early years of the century.[32] Church general authority B. H. Roberts may have been the era's greatest champion of the idea.[33] It was also elegantly developed by several of Mormonism's first generation of professionally trained academics.[34] President Joseph F. Smith and his counselor Anthon H. Lund, however, explained to

30. "The Father and the Son," 934.

31. John A. Widtsoe, *Evidences and Reconciliations: Aids to Faith in a Modern Day*, vol. 3 (Salt Lake City: Bookcraft, 1951), 76–77. Joseph Fielding Smith distinguished eternal intelligence from "intelligences" in this manner: "The Lord declares that intelligence, something which we do not fully understand, was co-eternal with him and always existed . . . and therefore did not have to be created. However, intelligences spoken of in Abraham were created, for these are spirit children of God, begotten sons." Joseph Fielding Smith, *Answers to Gospel Questions*, 5 vols. (Salt Lake City: Deseret Book, 1957–1966), 3:125.

32. See Thomas G. Alexander, "The Reconstruction of Mormon Doctrine: From Joseph Smith to Progressive Theology," *Sunstone* 5 (July/August 1980): 30–31; Blake Ostler, "The Idea of Pre-Existence in the Development of Mormon Thought," *Dialogue: A Journal of Mormon Thought* 15 (Spring 1982): 59–78; and Godfrey, "History of Intelligence in Mormon Thought."

33. See Roberts, *Course of Theology*, 2:7–27, and B. H. Roberts, *The Truth, the Way, the Life*, ed. John W. Welch (Provo, UT: BYU Studies, 1994), chapter 26—"Man: Preexistence of Spirits, Eternal Existence of Intelligences" (247–57), and lxxxii–lxxxvi.

34. Examples include BYU professor Nels L. Nelson, who wrote *Scientific Aspects of Mormonism* (New York: Putnam's Sons, 1904), and William Henry Chamberlin, the first academic philosopher in Mormon history and devotee of personalist philosopher George H. Howison. Chamberlin wrote favorably of the eternity and ontological ultimacy of persons. See James M. McLachlan, "W. H. Chamberlin and the Quest for a Mormon Theology," *Dialogue: A Journal of Mormon Thought* 29 (Winter 1996): 151–67.

John Widtsoe, then a prominent Utah educator who was authoring a lesson manual for church use, that they wanted "all that pertained to intelligences before they became begotten spirits" removed because such ideas "would only be speculation."[35] Speculative doctrine, of course, may be seen as either true or false, but because it has not been dogmatically resolved one way or the other, church leaders did not want it included in church publications. Still, because the notion of eternal, pre-spirit-birth intelligences was never officially denounced, some Latter-day Saints, leader and lay alike, have continued to find the idea compelling.[36] At the same time, institutional wariness of speculative doctrine has also continued and has prevented open endorsement in current church publications of the idea that human beings were autonomous, self-conscious intelligences prior to spirit birth.

Freely acknowledged in the church's institutional literature, though, on the strength of the previously quoted First Presidency statement from the early twentieth century, is the use of "intelligences" to "refer to spirit children of God."[37] Mormon doctrine may be ambiguous about whether or not prior to spirit birth primeval intelligence-matter was differentiated as individual self-conscious, agency-exercising entities, but it unambiguously affirms that some essential, irreducible aspect of what constitutes humanity is eternal and uncreated. Concluded Joseph Fielding Smith, "Some of our writers have endeavored to explain what an intelligence is, but to do so is futile, for we have never been given any insight into this matter beyond what the Lord has fragmentarily revealed. We know, however, that there is something called intelligence which always existed. It is the real eter-

---

35. Lund, journal, December 11, 1914, as quoted in Ostler, "The Idea of Pre-Existence," 69. Similar requests were made of the prolific Roberts and for the same reason. As apostle Charles Penrose put it, he "preferred to label such notions as speculation." Penrose, diary, May 6, 1911, as quoted in Godfrey, "Charles W. Penrose: His Apostolic Contributions to LDS Church History and Doctrine, 1904–1925," in *Times of Transition*, ed. Thomas G. Alexander (Provo, UT: Smith Institute for Latter-day Saint History, 2003), 92.

36. Church president Spencer Kimball remarked in a 1977 address that "God has taken these intelligences, given to them spirit bodies, and given them instructions and training." Kimball, "Our Great Potential," *Ensign*, May 1977, 50. As recently as 2010, apostle Richard Scott made the passing comment that earth was the place where "intelligences tabernacled with spirits would receive a body." *Ensign*, May 2010, 75. Several mid-twentieth-century LDS philosophers also embraced and expounded the idea of intelligences as conscious, autonomous, eternal entities. See Sterling M. McMurrin, *The Philosophical Foundations of Mormon Theology* (Salt Lake City: University of Utah Press, 1959); McMurrin, *The Theological Foundations of the Mormon Religion* (Salt Lake City: University of Utah Press, 1965); and Truman G. Madsen, *Eternal Man* (Salt Lake City: Deseret Book, 1966).

37. See *Guide to the Scriptures*, s.v. "intelligence, intelligences."

nal part of man, which was not created nor made. This intelligence combined with the spirit constitutes a spiritual identity or individual."[38] In this combined sense, spirits are said to "have no beginning; they existed before, they shall have no end, they shall exist after, for they are . . . eternal" (Abraham 3:18).

"Spirit Birth"

When it comes to describing the preexistent creation of individual spirit beings, Latter-day Saint doctrine continues to be distinctive. Although Mormonism shares belief in a preexistent creation of souls with the strand of early Christian theology discussed previously, it does so on its own terms. The key difference is that Latter-day Saints believe God brought souls into existence by procreation rather than ex nihilo creation. In other words, human souls/spirits were "born," not "made." As such, they are understood to be literally the children of God. Latter-day Saints support their doctrine by a straightforward reading of such passages as Acts 17:29—Paul's declaration to the Athenians that "we are the offspring (*genos*) of God," Romans 8:16—"the Spirit itself beareth witness with our spirit, that we are the children of God," and Hebrews 12:9—God is "the Father of spirits." Authoritative Mormon sources do not explain *how* spirits were begotten, but over time "birth" and "procreation" (or derivatives) became the primary vocabulary for discussing the spirit creation. Although Latter-day Saints affirm that God the Father is male, neither sexless nor androgynous, it is important to note that when envisioning "spirit birth," Latter-day Saints are in fundamental agreement with sentiments expressed long ago by Hilary of Poitiers about the begetting of the Son. Hilary wrote that although God was willing to accommodate finite human understanding by using examples from human birth, believers should not take such analogies so far, or be so literal, as to include such reproductive details as "coition, conception, lapse of time, delivery."[39]

Early on, the inner logic of spirit procreation led to contemplation of the existence of the divine feminine, of a "heavenly Mother." Still sung by Latter-day Saints today are words first published in 1845: "I had learn'd to call thee father through thy spirit from on high, but until the key of knowledge was restor'd, I knew not why. In the heav'ns are parents single? No, the thought makes reason stare. Truth is reason—truth eternal tells me I've a mother there."[40] Besides the fact that this hymn is still included in the current LDS

---

38. Smith, *Answers to Gospel Questions*, 4:127.

39. Quoted in R. P. C. Hanson, *The Search for the Christian Doctrine of God: The Arian Controversy, 318–381* (Edinburgh: T&T Clark, 1988), 506.

40. "My Father in Heaven," *Times and Seasons*, November 15, 1845, 1039. The poem, written

hymnbook, the doctrine of a Mother in heaven has been affirmed by official pronouncements of the First Presidency on two separate occasions. In 1909, the First Presidency declared, "All men and women are in the similitude of the universal Father and Mother and are literally the sons and daughters of Deity . . . man, as a spirit, was begotten and born of heavenly parents and reared to maturity in the eternal mansions of the Father, prior to coming upon the earth in a temporal body."[41] Again in 1995, in a statement issued jointly by the First Presidency and the Council of the Twelve Apostles, it was reiterated that "all human beings—male and female—are created in the image of God. Each is a beloved spirit son or daughter of heavenly parents, and, as such, each has a divine nature and destiny."[42] Although the doctrine of a heavenly Mother has been consistently affirmed in LDS discourse, detailed discussion is restrained by the fact that nothing is known about her role in the process of spirit birth or about other aspects of her divine nature and activities.[43] In a general conference address in April 2022, apostle Dale Renlund spoke more extensively and positively about Mother in heaven than any previous apostle or prophet. He concluded his address, however, by reiterating counsel given thirty years earlier by church president Gordon Hinckley that, when praying, Latter-day Saints are to follow the pattern in the Lord's Prayer by addressing "Our Father which art in heaven" (Matt. 6:9) and not pray to heavenly Mother.[44]

The *Imago Dei*

The doctrine of divine parents procreating human spirits fosters an unusually strong and literal view of what being created in the image of God (*imago Dei*) means in LDS theology. This is especially true when it is remembered that despite vast, almost inconceivable, developmental differences, Latter-day Saints conceive

---

by Eliza R. Snow, was initially titled "Invocation, or the Eternal Father and Mother." Maureen Ursenbach Beecher, ed., *The Personal Writings of Eliza Roxcy Snow* (Salt Lake City: University of Utah Press, 1995), 109. It is included as "O My Father" in *Hymns*, #292. For a full discussion of this poem/hymn and its importance to Latter-day Saints, see Jill Mulvay Derr, "The Significance of 'O My Father' in the Personal Journey of Eliza R. Snow," *BYU Studies* 36 (1996–97): 84–126.

41. "Origin of Man: By the First Presidency of the Church," *Improvement Era*, November 13, 1909, 78, 80.

42. "The Family: A Proclamation to the World," *Ensign*, November 1995, 102.

43. A comprehensive discussion of LDS ideas about "Mother in Heaven" can be found in David L. Paulsen and Martin Pulido, "'A Mother There': A Survey of Historical Teachings," *BYU Studies* 50 (2011): 71–97. The church offers its own treatment of the topic in two brief essays—"Mother in Heaven" and "Heavenly Parents"—on its website: churchofjesuschrist.org.

44. Dale G. Renlund, "Your Divine Nature and Eternal Destiny," *Liahona*, May 2022, 70. See also Gordon B. Hinckley, "Daughters of God," *Ensign*, November 1991, 100.

of God and humanity as sharing a single ontological nature. Thus, Mormons believe (*pace* Augustine) that something of God's essence, an embryonic divine nature, was procreatively passed from Parents to spirit children in the preexistence. Latter-day Saints consider the divine characteristics conferred through spirit birth to be a "genetic inheritance" of sorts rather than the imprinting of the *imago Dei* on newly "made" creatures. For Mormons, the *imago Dei* is something deeply rooted in, and intrinsic to, the human soul, as a kind of divine DNA. Church president Lorenzo Snow taught that "there is the nature of deity in the composition of our spiritual organization; in our spiritual birth our Father transmitted to us the capabilities, powers and faculties which he himself possessed, as much so as the child on its mother's bosom possesses, although in an undeveloped state, the faculties, powers and susceptibilities of its parent."[45] That this doctrine continues to be affirmed among Latter-day Saints today is illustrated by remarks made at a 2017 church general conference by First Presidency counselor Dieter Uchtdorf: "Remember that you are of the royal house of the kingdom of God, [children] of Heavenly Parents, who reign throughout the universe. You have the spiritual DNA of God. You have unique gifts that originated in your spiritual creation and that were developed during the vast span of your premortal life."[46] Enthused another church leader in 2024: "[It is] stunning to think that the divine, spiritual DNA of Almighty God flows in each of us! Though still in their infancy, these seeds of godhood planted within us hold every attribute of godliness, which makes it possible for us to become like Him."[47]

Despite the conceptual difference in how souls are believed to have been generated, the particular moral, intellectual, and spiritual qualities that constitute the *imago Dei* bestowed by God are much the same in LDS and other Christian theologies. For many Christians, rationality or intelligence is at the center of those gifts; it is the essence of the human soul. Augustine gave voice to the common sentiment: "The image of the creator is to be found in the rational or intellectual soul of man." That soul "has been created according to the image of God in order that it may use reason and intellect in order to apprehend and behold God."[48] In addition to the rational soul's "understanding" (*intelligentia*) and "memory" (*memoria*), Augustine included "will" (*voluntas*) and sometimes

45. *Teachings: Lorenzo Snow*, 84 (also 84–86).

46. *Ensign*, November 2017, 17.

47. Brian K. Taylor, "Rise to Your Divine Identity, Purpose, and Destiny," BYU Speeches, March 19, 2024, https://speeches.byu.edu/talks/brian-k-taylor/rise-to-your-divine-identity-purpose-and-destiny/.

48. Augustine, *On the Trinity*, as quoted in Alister McGrath, *Creation* (Minneapolis: Fortress, 2005), 65.

"love" (*caritas*) among the gifts bestowed by the *imago Dei*. Associated with *voluntas* was the divine endowment of *libero arbitrio* ("free choice" or "free will"). Augustine's view echoed Origen, who had previously argued that it was "clearly defined in the teaching of the church that every rational soul is possessed of free will and volition."[49] With such descriptions of the soul's characteristics, Latter-day Saint theology is in full agreement. Whether viewed as intrinsic aspects of the soul's uncreated intelligence or divine bestowals at spirit birth, President Joseph F. Smith affirmed, "[Man] is made in the image of God himself, so that he can reason, reflect, pray, exercise faith."[50]

Given the familial relationship that Mormonism posits between God and his spirit children, Latter-day Saint theology also accords with the move in Christian theology in recent centuries, particularly during the twentieth century, to express the *imago Dei* in more relational terms. Rather than viewing it primarily as a set of natural endowments that constitutes humankind ontologically, no matter how impressive, prominent twentieth-century theologian Emil Brunner, for instance, chose to see the "formal" image of God as chiefly the freedom and capacity to respond to the abundant love of a God who desires fellowship with his creatures.[51] Brunner's view recalls the eloquent opening lines of Augustine's *Confessions*: "You made us for yourself, and our hearts are restless until they find their rest in you."[52] American theologian Robert Jenson considers the "heart of what is meant by the claim that human beings are made in the image of God" to be their capability of "being a kind of counterpart or conversation partner of God . . . creatures with whom God can have an active exchange, a back and forth, a *relationship*," as he did with Abraham and Moses.[53] These compelling characterizations of the possibility of humanity's relationship with God ring true in an even more profound way for Latter-day Saints who view humans as God's children, his family. It would be natural, literally, for family members to desire and delight in loving relationships. To be sure, Latter-day Saint theology, along with all other Christian theologies,

---

49. Origen, *First Principles*, Pref.5, in *ANF*, 4:240.

50. *Teachings: Joseph F. Smith*, 336.

51. Emil Brunner, *Man in Revolt: A Christian Anthropology*, trans. Olive Wyon (Cambridge: Lutterworth, 1957), 512–13.

52. Augustine, *Confessions* 1.1. A useful summary of Augustine's view of the *imago Dei* and how that view has been received, reformulated, or repudiated over the years is Richard Price, "The Image of God," in *Oxford Guide to the Historical Reception of Augustine*, ed. Karla Pollmann (New York: Oxford University Press, 2013), 1182–86.

53. Robert W. Jenson, *Theology in Outline: Can These Bones Live?* (New York: Oxford University Press, 2016), 69.

acknowledges that the actual human response to God's love falls far short, but through Christ the original image can be restored, or as Latter-day Saints might say, the divine DNA can be nurtured, and humans can become responsive, loving, and obedient to God, as they were created to be.

Without discounting the validity of centuries of rich theological reflection on the meaning of the *imago Dei*, theologians recognize that in one sense it "exceeds the meaning invested in it by the biblical authors and redactors."[54] In ancient Israel, interpretation of God's declaration "Let us make man in our image, after our likeness" (Gen. 1:26) was straightforward: *tselem* (image) and *demut* (likeness) denoted physical resemblance.[55] The influential Old Testament scholar Gerhard von Rad cautioned against interpretations that "proceed from an anthropology strange to the Old Testament and one-sidedly limit God's image to man's spiritual nature, relating it to man's 'dignity,' his 'personality' or 'ability for moral decision,' etc. The marvel of man's bodily appearance is not at all to be ex[cep]ted from the realm of God's image. This was the original notion, and we have no reason to suppose that it completely gave way in [later Israelite] reflection to a spiritualizing and intellectualizing tendency."[56] Given its doctrine of a corporeal, anthropomorphic God, Latter-day Saint theology includes physical resemblance as a fundamental feature of the *imago Dei*. Especially when exegeting the Genesis texts, similarity in appearance tends to be the first meaning Latter-day Saints derive. Joseph Smith emended Genesis 5:1 to make this interpretation explicit. To the sentence "In the day that God created man, in the likeness of God made he him," Smith added *"in the image of his own body."*[57] The point is also unambiguously made in the Book of Mormon when Jehovah shows a finger of his spiritual body to a prophet, "and

---

54. Anne M. Clifford, "Creation," in *Systematic Theology: Roman Catholic Perspectives*, ed. Francis Schüssler Fiorenza and John P. Galvin, 2nd ed. (Minneapolis: Fortress, 2011), 226–27.

55. This is the consensus view of Semitic philologists and Hebrew Bible scholars reaching back to Theodor Noldeke and Herman Gunkel at the turn of the twentieth century. See Claus Westermann, *Genesis 1–11: A Commentary*, trans. John J. Scullion (Minneapolis: Augsburg, 1984), and Stanley L. Jaki, *Genesis 1 through the Ages* (London: Thomas More, 1992).

56. Gerhard von Rad, *Genesis: A Commentary*, rev. and trans. John Marks, Old Testament Library (Philadelphia: Westminster, 1972), 58. Von Rad's claim is supported by examination of later rabbinic literature. Professor Alon Goshen Gottstein studied "all tannaitic and amoraic sources referring to [*tselem*]" and went so far as to argue that more than simply one aspect of the *imago Dei*, "following my stronger anthropomorphic reading of the rabbis, I suggest that the bodily meaning is the only meaning of *zelem* in rabbinic literature." Gottstein, "The Body of Image of God in Rabbinic Literature," *Harvard Theological Review* 87 (April 1994): 174 (171–95).

57. *NTOB*, 97, 608 (emphasis added). See also Moses 6:9.

it was as the finger of a man." Eventually, the Lord shows himself fully: "Seest thou that ye are created after mine own image?" he queries. "Yea, even all men were created in the beginning after mine own image. Behold, this body, which ye now behold, is the body of my spirit; and man have I created after the body of my spirit" (Ether 3:6, 15–16).[58]

This passage draws attention to another aspect of LDS belief about the preexistence—that the spirits God created for his children are corporeal in form. Hence the use of the phrase "spirit bodies" to describe them. This echoes early Christian theologians such as Tertullian and Origen, who also believed that souls are corporeal and material (in a refined sense). Tertullian was influenced by the materialism of Stoicism, which eschewed a difference between the material and the immaterial. Similar to how Joseph Smith contrasted refined spirit-matter with denser, visible matter, "Tertullian held to the Stoic opinion that everything real is in some sense material, and soul is a kind of invisible thinking gas."[59] Origen similarly maintained that "a bodiless soul, whether in the preexistent state or in the afterlife, could not subsist at all as an individual being. . . . Association with matter is simply a condition of creaturely existence." In Origen's view, "all rational creatures [*logikoi*], even in the preexistence, [were] embodied, although the constitution of this body [was] of a different nature than the present body." Preexistent bodies were "under the governance of the *pneuma* [spirit], rendering them entirely 'spiritual' or 'pneumatic.'" They were "subtle, luminous bod[ies] that serve[d] as a sort of 'corporeal envelope' for the soul."[60]

Tertullian also believed, as do Latter-day Saints, that "the soul conforms exactly to the shape of the body that it pervades, containing all the appendages, eyes, ears, mouth and the like, that distinguish the outer contours of the fleshly body."[61] Doctrine and Covenants expresses it this way: "that which is spiritual

58. Commenting on Heb. 1:3 in their 1909 proclamation, the First Presidency wrote: "If the Son of God be the express image (that is, likeness) of His Father's person, then His Father is in the form of man; for that was the form of the Son of God, not only during His mortal life, but before His mortal birth, and after His resurrection. It was in this form that the Father and the Son, as two personages, appeared to Joseph Smith." "Origin of Man," 77. See also B. H. Roberts, *The Mormon Doctrine of Deity* (Salt Lake City: Deseret News, 1903), 22, 26, 78, 85.

59. Henry Chadwick, *The Church in Ancient Society: From Galilee to Gregory the Great* (New York: Oxford University Press, 2001), 121.

60. Blosser, *Origen's Doctrine of the Soul*, 175–77.

61. Tertullian, *On the Soul* 9.7–8, as quoted in Carly Daniel-Hughes, *The Salvation of the Flesh in Tertullian of Carthage: Dressing for the Resurrection* (New York: Palgrave Macmillan, 2011), 67.

being in the likeness of that which is temporal; and that which is temporal in the likeness of that which is spiritual; the spirit of man in the likeness of his person, as also the spirit of the beast, and every other creature which God has created" (D&C 77:2). Furthermore, "this logic extends to sexual difference as well, which in Tertullian's view is not some accidental property of the flesh alone, thus discarded with the corruptible flesh at death, as a Platonist might conclude, but a distinction that pertains to soul and flesh alike."[62] Latter-day Saint theology concurs. The 1995 proclamation issued by the First Presidency and Twelve Apostles affirms that "gender [sexual distinction] is an essential characteristic of individual premortal, mortal, and eternal identity and purpose."[63]

More on Mormon Preexistentialism

In addition to its uncommon views on the creation and nature of human souls/ spirits, Mormon preexistentialism also stands apart in that it posits a lengthy preexistence in contrast to early Christian preexistentialists who typically located the creation of souls near the time of physical creation. Origen may have been the exception to this generalization in that his doctrine of the "progress" of preexistent intellects toward either imitation or rejection of God implied a preexistence of some duration. Still, few early Christians are known to have suggested anything like the extensive preexistent life of the soul envisioned in later Mormonism. The development of an LDS doctrine of preexistence began with Joseph Smith's textual insertion between what scholars today consider the two biblical accounts of creation—Genesis 1:1–2:4 and Genesis 2:5–25. Smith inserted: "I the Lord God created all things of which I have spoken spiritually before they were naturally upon the face of the Earth for I the Lord God had not caused it to rain upon the face of the earth & I the Lord God had created all the children of men & not yet a man to till the ground for in Heaven created I them."[64] This earliest LDS account of the spirit creation seems to associate

---

62. Daniel-Hughes, *The Salvation of the Flesh*, 67.

63. "The Family: A Proclamation to the World," 102. "The intended meaning of *gender* in the family proclamation is *biological sex at birth.*" *GH* 38.6.23.

64. *NTOB*, 88–89 (Moses 3:5). What is not clear is whether the placement of this textual amplification signals Smith's belief that Genesis contains two different creation accounts— a spiritual creation in chapter 1 and the physical creation in chapter 2—as some did in antiquity. Alternatively, it may be that he viewed the added text as simply a divine editorial insertion indicating that prior to the physical creation (depicted variously in both chapters), a spiritual creation not specifically mentioned in Genesis took place. In either case, what is clear is the affirmation of the preexistence of human beings. That point was reiterated later

it with the time of the physical creation, as early Christian sources had done, but this would change as Smith began expounding his views on eternity in the 1840s.[65] Subsequent Latter-day Saint reflection pictured the spiritual creation as taking place ages before the physical creation. Although no authoritative LDS source identifies when the begetting of souls took place, the assessment of Joseph Fielding Smith is typical: the spirit creation took place "untold ages before we were placed on this earth. . . . Man [was] not created in the spirit at the time of the creation of the earth, but long before."[66] As the notion of an aeons-long preexistence of spirits developed, Latter-day Saints began imagining what life would have been like during that period.[67] By the end of the nineteenth century, contemplation of the details and significance of the long preexistence of God's spirit children had produced a luxuriant growth of folk theology that today falls outside the realm of institutionally promulgated doctrine.[68]

If Latter-day Saint theology presents notable divergences from Christian preexistentialism, there are convergences as well. One is the perception that belief in the preexistence has the potential to provide a more satisfying theodicy.[69] Origen, for instance, was keenly interested in relieving God of culpability for the human predicament and taught that preexistent souls were endowed with freedom of choice and were personally responsible for their earthly circumstances.[70] Even Augustine, the eloquent exponent of God's absolute sovereignty, flirted with Origen's preexistentialism at one point in his earlier life for its potential to justify God's righteousness in the face of rampant evil and suffering in the world.[71] In Origen's view, "the Creator will [not] ap-

---

in another Smith expansion of Genesis: "I made the world, & men before they were in the flesh" (*NTOB*, 612 [Moses 6:51]).

65. For the early years, see Charles R. Harrell, "The Development of the Doctrine of Preexistence, 1830–1844," *BYU Studies* 28 (Spring 1988): 75–96.

66. *Doctrines of Salvation*, 1:76.

67. The earliest substantive LDS discussion of the preexistence was produced by Orson Pratt in 1853 and appeared serially in the *Seer*, February–September, 1853, 17–135.

68. An example is the imaginative portrayal of the preexistence in Nephi Anderson, *Added Upon* (Salt Lake City: Deseret News, 1898), one of the most popular early Mormon novels.

69. See the discussion of Christian theodicies in chapter 2.

70. For an extended discussion of Origen's theodicy, one that considers eschatology as well as anthropology, see Mark S. M. Scott, "Cosmic Theodicy: Origen's Treatment of the Problem of Evil," in *The Oxford Handbook of Origen*, ed. Ronald E. Heine and Karen Jo Torjesen (New York: Oxford University Press, 2022), 393–409.

71. Jesuit priest Robert J. O'Connell sparked a decades-long debate among Augustine scholars by making this claim in *St. Augustine's Early Theory of Man, A.D. 386–91* (Cam-

pear unjust, when, according to the antecedent causes [in the preexistence], he distributes to each one according to his merit; nor will the happiness or unhappiness of each one's birth, or whatever be the condition that falls to him, be deemed accidental." What were the "antecedent causes" Origen had in mind? Simply this: "Endowed with the faculty of free will, this freedom of will either incited each [soul] to progress by the imitation of God or drew him to defection through negligence. And this . . . is the cause of the diversity among rational creatures, drawing its origin not from the will or judgement of the Creator, but from the freedom of the individual will."[72] Origen applied this to the famous biblical case of God preferring Jacob over Esau. Although Paul felicitously attributes that preference to God's sovereign, electing choice (Rom. 9:10–15), Origen realized that some Bible readers see Jacob's preferential election as arbitrary and unjust. Origen's answer was that there is "no unrighteousness with God . . . if we suppose [Jacob] to be worthily beloved by God by the merits from a preceding life." Origen added that "this same sentiment should be observed in the case of all creatures" and the "justice of the Creator . . . will only be shown with real clarity, if each one . . . may be said to have the causes of diversity [in life circumstance] in himself, preceding his bodily birth."[73] Although Origen was later condemned as a heretic for a number of his views, the attractiveness of the idea of a preexistence in formulating an effective theodicy persisted. Centuries later, Edward Beecher, in his lengthy treatise *The Conflict of Ages* (1854), argued along similar lines that only a doctrine of preexistence could exonerate God from responsibility for human sin and censure for punishing the sinner.[74]

bridge, MA: Harvard University Press, 1968). Forty years later, the matter was still being discussed. See Ronnie J. Rombs, *Saint Augustine and the Fall of the Soul: Beyond O'Connell and His Critics* (Washington, DC: Catholic University of America Press, 2006). What is not contested is that later in his life Augustine moved away from his earlier affinity with preexistentialism when, consonant with the growing anti-Origenist sentiment in the fifth century, he explicitly repudiated Origen as a heretic.

72. Origen, *On First Principles* 2.9.6, in Behr, *Origen: On First Principles*, 2:247.

73. Origen, *On First Principles* 2.9.7, in Behr, *Origen: On First Principles*, 2:249. Such notions led Origen to articulate a distinctive version of what would later be called "original sin." As summarized by one scholar: "If human beings are sinful from birth, their wickedness is the legacy of their own misguided choices in the transcendental world, and has nothing to do with the disobedience of any first man." J. N. D. Kelly, *Early Christian Doctrines*, 5th ed. (New York: Harper & Row, 1978), 181.

74. One reviewer of Beecher's book quipped that the notion of preexistent sin made humans "old offenders, or old devils, when born." Jacob Blain, *A Review, Giving the Main Ideas in Dr. Edward Beecher's Conflict of Ages: and a Reply to Them* (Boston, 1858), 8.

Historically, Mormons have manifested strong belief in the idea that preexistent conduct impacts earth life socially, intellectually, and behaviorally. Along with Origen, Latter-day Saints have promoted the idea that in the free-will environment of the preexistence, some souls cultivated a greater responsiveness to God than others. This has been thought to account for varying inborn human tendencies toward good and evil. Some Mormons have suggested that in addition to the influence of genetics, people's personalities and even their innate talents are impacted by preexistent activity and development. Bruce McConkie believed that all human spirits "while yet in the Eternal Presence, developed aptitudes, talents, capacities, and abilities of every sort, kind, and degree." As prominent examples, McConkie opined that during the long preexistence "Mozart became a musician; Einstein centered his interest in mathematics; Michelangelo turned his attention to painting . . . Abraham and Moses and all of the prophets sought and obtained the talent for spirituality." McConkie added that when spirits leave the preexistence to become physically embodied, "we forget what went before because we are here being tested, but the capacities and abilities that then were ours are yet resident within us." And without being fully conscious of it, all human spirits "with their infinitely varied talents and personalities pick up the course of progression where they left it off when they left the heavenly realms."[75] Such an elaborate depiction of the preexistence and its impact on human life is less common in the twenty-first century. Latter-day Saints today are more cautious about extolling the explanatory power of the preexistence, particularly as theodicy, than they were in the past. Nonetheless, because their version of preexistentialism proclaims the even more compelling idea of literal kinship with God, the preexistence of human souls is still prominent in the pantheon of Mormon doctrines.[76]

THE FALL AND HUMAN NATURE

As we have seen, the consensus among Christians over the centuries has been that humanity's original creation was "good," that Adam and Eve were created in the very "image and likeness" of God. They were endowed with reason, choice, and the ability to live in loving relationship with God. Initially, Adam

---

75. Bruce R. McConkie, *The Mortal Messiah* (Salt Lake City: Deseret Book, 1979), 1:23, 25.

76. See lds-general-conference.org. A chapter or section on the preexistence is found in most church doctrinal manuals. See, for instance, "Our Premortal Life," in *Doctrines of the Gospel Student Manual* (2010), 13–15, and "Our Life in Heaven," in *Gospel Fundamentals* (Salt Lake City: The Church of Jesus Christ of Latter-day Saints, 2002), 5–8.

and Eve did so and "walked with God" in the garden of Eden, but as presented in the third chapter of Genesis, the pair partook of "forbidden fruit" and were expelled from the garden. In large part, because this simple, brief story is never mentioned again in the Old Testament nor by Jesus in the Gospels, interpretation of its significance has depended primarily on statements by the apostle Paul that in turn undergird subsequent Christian construction of "the fall" as a theological concept.[77] Although Paul himself never actually uses the noun *ptōsis* (a "fall") or the verb *piptō* (to "fall") to describe the primordial event(s) believed to have brought humanity to its present condition, he does introduce the idea that what occurred in the garden was "Adam's transgression" (*parabaseōs*) and that, because of it, "sin" (*hamartia*) and death "entered into the world" (Rom. 5:14, 12). As a result, humanity needed to be rescued from its "fallen" plight and restored to the purpose for which it was created. The "good news" Paul proclaimed was that Jesus Christ, as a "last [second] Adam" (1 Cor. 15:45), provided just such a remedy to the human predicament. Probing the implications and ramifications of this fall and redemption has been a central objective of Christian theology and is the subject of the remainder of this chapter and related chapters elsewhere in the volume.

At the outset, it should be noted that some Christians today do not believe in a historical Adam and Eve. They are influenced by scientific and biblical studies that call into question the Genesis account as actual history. Such studies claim that "the picture of the natural history of the human species in particular and the cosmos in general produced over the last two centuries by a convergence of data from geology, biology, paleontology, and genetics has strained the credibility of literal readings of the biblical creation stories past the breaking point."[78] However, even those who discount the story of Adam and Eve and their fall as historical realities often see them as *existentially* valid. Scholars typically define "myth" as a traditional story that represents deep truths about the world, nature, or human existence. In this way, some modern Christians view Adam's fall as a "mythic" paradigm that accounts for human sinfulness. Adam is the example, the prototype, of how all humans succumb to sin. Thus, one Catholic theologian has observed that "the single most important conclusion of Catholic biblical studies relative to original sin consists

77. A notion of a "fall" emerged in Second Temple Judaism prior to the birth of Christianity. See the detailed exegetical (and contextual) study of the relevant chapters in Genesis and their interpretation in antiquity is Mark S. Smith, *The Genesis of Good and Evil: The Fall(out) and Original Sin in the Bible* (Louisville: Westminster John Knox, 2019).

78. Ian A. McFarland, *In Adam's Fall: A Meditation on the Christian Doctrine of Original Sin* (Chichester, UK: Wiley-Blackwell, 2010), 143.

in breaking down the misinterpretations of the story of Adam and Eve and their 'fall' as a descriptive historical account, and breaking it open as an interpretation of ourselves."[79] Similarly, an Eastern Orthodox scholar remarked, "Mostly, it is the story of 'everyman'; it is a story that is true of each one of us: we have all turned away from God, we all inhabit the world of corruption and death."[80] Regardless of one's view of the historicity of the early chapters of Genesis, most Christians, including Latter-day Saints, agree that in some fashion Genesis narrates a profound truth about why we humans are the way we are and why we stand in need of redemption.[81]

Just as the nonbiblical phrase "the fall" became useful theological shorthand for the ramifications of events described in Genesis 3, so, too, did another related and widely used term not found in the Bible—"original sin." A historian of the doctrine noted the popular error of presuming that "the doctrine of original sin 'has always been there.' At its most extreme, this is the assumption that original sin is a universal belief. Less extreme is the more common view that original sin is 'in scripture.' To be sure, the story of Adam and Eve is in the Hebrew Bible, Paul refers to Adam's sin, and sin is a predominant theme in both testaments. But as scripture scholars and church historians insist, the idea of original sin is a post–New Testament development."[82] Although the idea is implicit in the writings of some earlier fathers, the term "original sin" (*peccatum originale*) appears to have been used for the first time by Augustine in the late fourth century. In other languages and earlier theologies, the concept is rendered as "hereditary sin," "birth sin," or "ancestral sin."[83] Augustine's

---

79. Roger Haight, "Sin and Grace," in *Systematic Theology: Roman Catholic Perspectives*, ed. Francis Schüssler Fiorenza and John P. Galvin, 2nd ed. (Minneapolis: Fortress, 2011), 389.

80. Andrew Louth, *Introducing Eastern Orthodox Theology* (Downers Grove, IL: IVP Academic, 2013), 72.

81. In recent years the historicity of Adam has become a problem even for conservative evangelicals. For a sampling of how they have engaged the question and its theological implications, see Hans Madueme and Michael Reeves, eds., *Adam, the Fall, and Original Sin: Theological, Biblical, and Scientific Perspectives* (Grand Rapids: Baker Academic, 2014); Ardel Canedy and Matthew Barrett, eds., *Four Views on the Historical Adam* (Grand Rapids: Zondervan, 2013); and C. John Collins, *Did Adam and Eve Really Exist? Who They Were and Why You Should Care* (Wheaton, IL: Crossway, 2011).

82. Tatha Wiley, *Original Sin: Origins, Developments, Contemporary Meanings* (New York: Paulist, 2002), 37.

83. In German, the traditional word for "original sin" is *Erbsünde* (used in the Augsburg Confession), meaning "hereditary sin." In article 9 of the Anglican/Episcopal Articles of Religion, "Birth-Sin" is used. For Orthodox use of "ancestral sin," see John Romanides, *The Ancestral Sin*, trans. George Gabriel (Ridgewood, NJ: Zephyr, 2002).

version was most fully developed in his extensive controversy over nature and grace with a varied group of opponents labeled "Pelagians" (after one of their number, Pelagius).[84] Although inchoate notions of original sin had been around for several centuries, Augustine's mature formulation of the doctrine has been called his "most original and nearly single-handed creation."[85]

As Augustine saw it, Adam's transgression had profound, pervasive, and, short of Christ's redemption, utterly irreparable effects on humankind. The death Paul speaks of that was passed on to all of Adam's posterity as a result of Adam's sin was not just physical death but moral and spiritual death as well. In addition to being condemned to return to the dust of the earth from whence they came, human beings' potential for relationship with God bestowed as the *imago Dei* was severely impaired. As a consequence of that relational rupture, the human will was greatly weakened and became enslaved to sin and evil. Thereafter, it was as if sinfulness was hardwired into fallen humanity. Human beings, in Augustine's famous formulation, became congenitally incapable of *not* sinning—*non posse non peccare* ("not able not to sin"). Thus, humanity at its core was a "lump of sin" (*massa peccati*) and therefore a "mass of perdition" (*massa perditionis*). Of such interpretations a modern scholar has observed, "It is one thing to claim that the first sin brought death into the world, however, and quite another to maintain that it renders all humankind congenitally sinful. Though not unprecedented in the early church, the claim that human beings inherit sinfulness as well as death from Adam was first fully developed by Augustine."[86]

Augustine also brought full-bodied development to earlier ideas about humankind's participation in and responsibility for Adam's sin, the other side of the conceptual coin of original sin. Expressed rudimentarily as early as the second century, some theologians such as Irenaeus viewed human beings as being "in" Adam *symbolically* because he represented the entire human race. Others, such as Tertullian, by way of the doctrine of traducianism, suggested that humankind was in Adam *seminally*. In the third century, Origen extrap-

84. A useful overview is Mathijs Lamberigts, "Pelagius and Pelagianism," in *Oxford Handbook of Early Christian Studies*, ed. Susan Ashbrook Harvey and David G. Hunter (New York: Oxford University Press, 2008), 258–79.

85. James J. O'Donnell, *Augustine: A New Biography* (San Francisco: HarperCollins, 2005), 296. Jaroslav Pelikan concurs, calling original sin "one of the most striking instances of the development of Christian doctrine." Pelikan, *Development of Christian Doctrine: Some Historical Prolegomena* (New Haven: Yale University Press, 1969), 73.

86. Ian McFarland, "The Fall and Sin," in *Oxford Handbook of Systematic Theology*, ed. John Webster, Kathryn Tanner, and Iain Torrance (New York: Oxford University Press, 2007), 142.

olated from Hebrews 7:9–10—"As I may so say, Levi also, who receiveth tithes, payed tithes in Abraham. For he was yet in the loins of his father, when Melchi-sedec met him." Origen argued that if Levi was "in the loins of Abraham, how much more were all men, those who are born and have been born in this world, in Adam's loins when he was still in paradise. And all men who were with him, or rather in him, were expelled from paradise when he was himself driven out from there; and . . . the transgression consequently passed through to them as well, who were dwelling in his loins."[87] Origen's words highlight this second aspect of the doctrine of original sin—not only did the fall bequeath to humans a sinful nature, it also made them jointly responsible for Adam's sin. Because Adam's transgression was their transgression symbolically if not genetically, God judged all human beings guilty of this original sin and held them accountable for it.

Significantly, it was the practice of infant baptism that solidified Augustine's ideas of original sin. If baptism is for a remission of sins, he argued, newborns, who have not lived long enough to commit personal sins, must have inherited some sin (and sinfulness) that needs to be washed away in the sacramental waters of baptism.[88] Augustine warned a fellow bishop that "the bond of guilt derived from Adam cannot be loosed in any other way than by the parents [or concerned others] presenting their children to receive the grace of Christ through baptism."[89] By reasoning in this manner, Augustine was following third-century theologians Origen and Cyprian. Cyprian, a North African bishop, taught that the infant "has not sinned, except in that, being born phys-ically according to Adam, he has contracted the contagion" of Adam's sins, and therefore "the sins remitted to him are not his own, but those of another."[90] In

---

87. Origen, *Commentary on the Epistles to the Romans* 5.1.14, in *Origen, Commentary on the Epistle to the Romans: Books 1–5*, trans. Thomas P. Scheck (Washington, DC: Catholic University of America Press, 2001), 310–11.

88. See Augustine, *The Punishment and Forgiveness of Sins and the Baptism of Little Ones* 1.23–25, 28, 63–64; 2.39–43; 3.7, 10–11, 18, in *Answer to the Pelagians, I*, trans. Roland J. Teske, Works of Saint Augustine: A Translation for the 21st Century (Hyde Park, NY: New City, 1997), 23:45–49, 106–9, 139–41. Later, Augustine debated the matter at length with Julian of Eclanum. See Teske, trans., *Answer to the Pelagians, II* (1998), 24:268–536, and Teske, trans., *Answer to the Pelagians, III* (1999), 25:56–725.

89. Letter 98, in *Saint Augustine Letters, Volume II (83–130)*, trans. Wilfrid Parsons (Washington, DC: Catholic University of America Press, 1953), 134.

90. Cyprian, *Epistle* 64.5, as quoted in Pelikan, *Development of Christian Doctrine*, 80. Pelikan adds: "A study of Cyprian suggests the conclusion that he developed his doctrine of original sin from the existing practice of the Church *a posteriori*, to make the diagnosis fit the cure" (87).

his *Commentary on Romans*, Origen refers to the Old Testament sin-offering for newborn babies and the Christian practice of infant baptism as proof that all humans "have the pollution of sin at birth and need to be cleansed from it."[91] Thus, the consequences of Adam's transgression and the responsibility for it were passed on to all humankind and needed to be absolved by baptism, as much for newborn infants as for adults.[92]

The general contours of what Augustine taught with regard to original sin and the fall became the dominant position in Western Christianity. However, "his extensively developed teaching is admittedly not always unambiguous," which is why later theologians sometimes "thoroughly disagreed on the essence of the doctrine [of original sin] in Augustine's work on the topic."[93] Particularly with regard to how original sin is viewed as a common human inheritance, "it needs to be said that there is no such thing as a universally accepted Christian doctrine of the transmission of original sin."[94] The fact of human sinfulness, however, is not contested. During the Reformation, Augustine's dire diagnosis of the consequences of the fall was emphatically reiterated, and in some ways amplified, by Reformers such as Martin Luther and John Calvin. Although most commonly associated with Calvin, the notion of the "total depravity" of fallen humanity and of humans' concomitant spiritual impotency was a standard theological trope during the Reformation. These ideas received one of their starkest formulations a century later in the influential Westminster Confession. In the sixth chapter, entitled "Of the Fall of Man, of Sin, and of the Punishment Thereof," Adam and Eve by their fall are described as "dead in sin, and wholly defiled in all the parts and faculties of soul and body." This they

---

91. See Origen, *Commentary on Romans* 5.9.11, in Scheck, *Origen, Commentary on the Epistle to the Romans*, 366–67. The summary quotation is from Scheck, *Origen and the History of Justification: The Legacy of Origen's Commentary on Romans* (Notre Dame: University of Notre Dame Press, 2008), 75.

92. By the mid-200s, the practice of infant baptism seems to have been fairly widespread, especially in Christian North Africa. See J. Patout Burns and Robin M. Jensen, *Christianity in Roman Africa: The Development of Its Practices and Beliefs* (Grand Rapids: Eerdmans, 2014). By the fifth century, even Augustine's Pelagian opponents, as well as most Eastern fathers, embraced the practice of infant baptism, but they did so because of the various spiritual benefits it provided, such as saving incorporation into the body of Christ, not because it remitted original sin.

93. Mathijs Lamberigts, "Original Sin," in Pollmann, *Oxford Guide to the Historical Reception of Augustine*, 1472–73.

94. Jenson, *Theology in Outline*, 77. While emphatic on the reality of original sin, Augustine was ambiguous on the process of its transmission. He toyed with traducianism but never formally embraced it or any other theory of transmission.

"conveyed to all their posterity" such that "we are utterly indisposed, disabled, and made opposite to all good, and wholly inclined to all evil."[95] Although these notions have remained prominent in both Catholic and Protestant Christianities,[96] they represent something of a divergence from the teachings of a number of early church fathers, as well as Latter-day Saints, regarding universal human culpability for Adam's sin and the complete spiritual paralysis that is said to result from the fall. Irenaeus, for instance, taught that rather than inheriting a sinful precondition, sinners have become such "through their own fault, since they [were] created free agents and exercised power over themselves."[97] Clement of Alexandria refused to believe that humans are born with the birth defect of congenital sinfulness. He interpreted Job's declaration "naked came I out of my mother's womb" to mean that Job came "out of the womb naked of evil and sin." And he inveighed against those who taught that such innocents were "under the curse of Adam."[98] Proceeding from a similar viewpoint, the Book of Mormon characterizes infant baptism as "solemn mockery before God" and declares that "he that supposeth that little children need baptism is in the gall of bitterness and in the bonds of iniquity" (Moroni 8:9, 14). The reason is that Christ "came into the world not to call the righteous but sinners to repentance . . . wherefore, little children are whole, for they are not capable of committing sin; wherefore the curse of Adam is taken from them in [Christ], that it hath no power over them" (Moroni 8:8).

As for human culpability for Adam's sin, Justin Martyr affirmed that "each man having sinned by his own fault" has "by [his] own fault . . . become worthy of punishment."[99] These words parallel Joseph Smith's declaration that "men will be punished for their own sins and not for Adam's transgression" (Articles of Faith 2). John Chrysostom asked a question that many have asked, including Latter-day Saints: "How does it follow that from Adam's disobedience someone else would become a sinner? For surely, if this were so, such a sinner

95. WC 6.1–4.

96. A variety of current Christian perspectives is explored in J. B. Stump and Chad Meister, eds., *Original Sin and the Fall: Five Views* (Downers Grove, IL: IVP Academic, 2020).

97. Irenaeus, *Against Heresies* 4.39.3–4, in *ANF*, 1:53.

98. Clement of Alexandria, *Stromata* 4.25.160, in *ANF*, 2:439, and *Stromata* 3.16.100, in *Library of Christian Classics*, vol. 2, *Alexandrian Christianity*, ed. John Ernest Leonard Oulton and Henry Chadwick (Philadelphia: Westminster, 1954), 87.

99. The first quotation is from Justin Martyr, *Dialogue with Trypho* 88, in *Writings of Saint Justin Martyr*, ed. and trans. Thomas B. Falls, Fathers of the Church (Washington, DC: Catholic University of America Press, 1948), 289. The second is from 2 *Apology* 14, in Falls, *Writings of Saint Justin Martyr*, 134.

would not deserve punishment, since his sins would not be his own fault."[100] This points to an early East-West, Greek-Latin divide in how to understand the phrase "for that all have sinned" in Romans 5:12—"Wherefore, as by one man sin entered into the world, and death by sin; and so death passed upon all men, for that all have sinned." Explains an Eastern Orthodox scholar, "In this passage there is a major issue of translation. The last four Greek words were translated in Latin as *in quo omnes peccaverunt* (in whom [i.e., in Adam] all men have sinned), and this translation was used in the West to justify the doctrine of guilt inherited from Adam and spread to his descendants. But such a meaning cannot be drawn from the original Greek." The *in quo* (in whom) of Latin is *eph' ho* in Greek and can be translated "because." Such a translation "renders Paul's thought to mean that death, which was 'the wages of sin' (Rm. 6:23) for Adam, is also the punishment applied to those who, like him, sin. It presupposes a cosmic significance for the sin of Adam but does not say that his descendants are 'guilty' as he was, unless they also sin as he sinned."[101] Latter-day Saint scripture concurs. In the book of Moses, after the fall, Adam is taught God's plan for redeeming humankind. God then speaks to Adam: "Behold I have forgiven thee thy transgression in the Garden of Eden. Hence came the saying abroad among the people, that the Son of God hath atoned for original guilt, wherein the sins of the parents cannot be answered upon the heads of the children, for they are whole from the foundation of the world" (Moses 6:53–54).

Although many early fathers shied away from considering the entirety of humankind culpable for Adam's sin, they had no hesitation in affirming that the fall had a universally corrupting effect on human nature. Cyril of Alexandria, for instance, argued that "our nature contracted the disease of sin because" of Adam. However, he clarified, "this was not because they sinned along with Adam, because they did not then exist, but because they had the same nature as Adam," a nature that had "acquired the weakness of corruption in Adam because of disobedience, and evil desires invaded it."[102] Here Cyril echoes the view of Gregory of Nyssa, who, influenced by Neoplatonism and coming close to a theory of original sin, held that "not Adam alone, but 'human nature' as embodied in Adam revolted against God." As a result, "human nature was alien-

100. Chrysostom, *Homilies on Romans*, Homily 10, in *Ancient Christian Commentary on the Scriptures: New Testament VI—Romans*, ed. Gerald Bray (Downers Grove, IL: Inter-Varsity Press, 1998), 148. Hereafter *ACC Romans*.

101. John Meyendorff, *Byzantine Theology: Historical Trends & Doctrinal Themes* (New York: Fordham University Press, 1974), 144.

102. Quoted in *ACC Romans*, 142.

ated from God" and thus all "the descendants of Adam are sinners in so far as they possess [that] nature which has been radically alienated from God."[103]

Augustinian views of human nature came to dominate Western Christianity and prevailed into the eighteenth century. Gradually new perspectives grounded in what scholars call Scottish "common sense realism" and the rationalism of the Enlightenment began to erode confidence in traditional notions of original sin. By the nineteenth century, concepts of the physical transmission of sin, of children being born sinful, and especially of humanity's inability to choose between good and evil were under assault. These Mormon-resonant ideas were most significantly propounded in the "New Haven theology," so called because it was articulated by a series of Yale theologians led by the influential Nathaniel W. Taylor, inaugural professor at Yale Divinity School. Taylor and his associates moved in very different social and intellectual circles than Joseph Smith, so it is not surprising that there is no evidence the Mormon prophet realized that many of his concerns with traditional Christian anthropology (in the West) were shared by some of the most prominent theologians of his day.[104]

Eastern Orthodox anthropology, on the other hand, had long been attuned to such perspectives. "Orthodox patristic, conciliar and liturgical formulations do not speak of the transmission of guilt from Adam," explains one Orthodox scholar. "They emphasise rather that, although the figure of Adam represents the beginning of human sin, anyone who sins does so of his or her own free choice, and assign no culpability for Adam's sin."[105] The similarity with the LDS second Article of Faith is striking. As for notions of inbred sinfulness, theological reflection "did not produce in the Orthodox East a doctrine of total depravity, which would run counter to [Orthodoxy's] conviction that human nature is at root good, even though distorted."[106] Added another Orthodox theologian, "Being according to the divine image is intrinsic to our nature. It gives us the capacity to become like God . . . to choose between good and evil, to live a life of virtue, to love God and neighbours . . . and to enjoy communion with God in heaven." Although we live "in a fallen condition . . . we still remain

103. Quoted in Ernest V. McClear, "The Fall of Man and Original Sin in the Theology of Gregory of Nyssa," *Theological Studies* 9 (1948): 198.

104. This important (if ultimately temporary) shift in anthropological thought is thoroughly explored in H. Shelton Smith, *Changing Conceptions of Original Sin* (New York: Scribner's Sons, 1955).

105. Peter Bouteneff, "Christ and Salvation," in *Cambridge Companion to Orthodox Christian Theology*, ed. Mary B. Cunningham and Elizabeth Theokritoff (Cambridge: Cambridge University Press, 2008), 105n.

106. Bouteneff, "Christ and Salvation," 94.

free, though it is more difficult to choose good."[107] Mormonism is closer to
Eastern Orthodox perspectives on the fall and its consequences than it is to
the anthropology articulated by Augustine, Luther, or Calvin.

Latter-day Saints and Orthodox also share a higher view of the postlapsarian
(after the fall) Adam than can be found in many other Christian theologies.
Orthodoxy envisions Adam more as the archetypal penitent than the archetypal sinner. Annually, on the Sunday before Christmas, he is commemorated
along with a host of others as "well-pleasing to God." And on Forgiveness
Sunday, the day before the commencement of Great Lent, worship texts focus
on Adam's lament at being expelled from Paradise and his turn back to God in
sorrow and repentance. "May He open to me the gates which I closed by my
transgression, and may He count me worthy to partake of the Tree of Life and
of the joy which was mine when I dwelt in you beforehand," is Adam's plaintive cry. In the twentieth century, the Russian monk known as St. Silouan the
Athonite (Simeon Ivanovich Antonov) wrote "Adam's Lament" and closed it
with these words: "Adam lost the earthly paradise and sought it weeping. But
the Lord through His love on the cross gave Adam another paradise, fairer than
the old—a paradise in heaven where shines the Light of the Holy Trinity."[108]

Even more positive (and elaborate) is the Mormon view of Adam and Eve
depicted in LDS scripture and the church's sacred temple liturgy. In its elevated estimation of Adam, Latter-day Saint scripture identifies Adam with
Michael "the Archangel" and even with Daniel's "Ancient of days," a title typically applied to Deity.[109] In the preexistence, Adam or Michael is understood
to have been sufficiently Godlike that he was called upon to assist the Son in
the creation of this earth.[110] He was also the faithful one chosen to father

107. Nonna Verna Harrison, "The Human Person as Image and Likeness of God," in Cunningham and Theokritoff, *The Cambridge Companion to Orthodox Christian Theology*, 80–81.

108. The information and quotations in this paragraph are from the section in Louth's
Eastern Orthodox Theology titled "Adam and Eve . . . and Repentance" (78–81).

109. D&C 27:11; 107:54; 116:1; 138:38. In the Bible, "Ancient of days" appears only in Dan.
7:9, 13, 22. Although "ancient of days" is a literal translation, some Bible translations choose
to render the underlying Hebrew words as "Ancient One."

110. "Our great prince, Michael, known in mortality as Adam, stands next to Christ in
the eternal plan of salvation and progression. In pre-existence Michael was the most intelligent, powerful, and mighty spirit son of God, who was destined to come to this earth,
excepting only the Firstborn, under whose direction and pursuant to whose counsel he
worked. . . . In the creation of the earth, Michael played a part second only to that of Christ."
McConkie, *Mormon Doctrine*, 2nd ed., 491. Reproduced in *OT Student Manual* (2003), 29.
See also *Pearl of Great Price Student Manual* (2017), 11, and *Doctrines of the Gospel Teacher
Manual* (2000), 19.

the human race. Joseph Smith's textual amplification of the early chapters of Genesis included in the book of Moses provides a Mormon counterpart, albeit much briefer, to the pseudepigraphical Life of Adam and Eve (also known as the Apocalypse of Moses) that presents stories of Adam and Eve's experiences after the fall. The book of Moses depicts a penitent Adam and Eve and a forgiving Father even more pointedly than in Eastern Orthodoxy. According to the book of Moses, after the expulsion from the garden, "Adam and Eve, his wife, called upon the name of the Lord, and they heard the voice of the Lord. . . . And he gave them commandments. . . . And Adam was obedient unto the commandments of the Lord" (Moses 5:4–5).[111] Subsequently "the Holy Ghost fell upon Adam . . . saying . . . that as thou hast fallen thou mayest be redeemed, and all mankind, even as many as will" (Moses 5:9). At some point, God fully instructs Adam in his "plan of salvation" made possible "through the blood of [his] Only Begotten" and tells a penitent Adam, "Behold I have forgiven thee thy transgression in the Garden of Eden" (Moses 6:62, 53).

Providing Adam and Eve with such a complete understanding of God's redemptive plan gives them a positive appreciation for their fall. In an expression foreshadowing the later Christian doctrine of the "fortunate fall" or *felix culpa,* Adam exclaims, "Blessed be the name of God, for because of my transgression my eyes are opened, and in this life I shall have joy, and again in the flesh I shall see God." Eve, too, was gladdened by the revelation and declares, "Were it not for our transgression we never should have . . . known good and evil, and the joy of our redemption, and the eternal life which God giveth unto all the obedient" (Moses 5:10–11). Buoyed by the understanding that their fall actually paved the way for the redemption, "Adam and Eve blessed the name of God, and they made all things known unto their sons and their daughters."[112] As the narrative continues, however, "Satan came among" Adam and Eve's sons and daughters and "commanded them, saying: Believe it not; and they believed it not. . . . And men began from that time forth to be carnal, sensual, and devilish." Still, a long-suffering Lord "called upon men by the Holy Ghost

111. Among the instructions Adam and Eve received was the commandment to "offer the firstlings of their flocks for an offering unto the Lord." This, they were told, was in "similitude of the sacrifice of the Only Begotten of the Father, which is full of grace and truth. Wherefore, thou shalt do all that thou doest in the name of the Son, and thou shalt repent and call upon God in the name of the Son forevermore" (Moses 5:5, 7–8).

112. "*O felix culpa*/O happy fault" is a refrain in the Easter Proclamation (Exsultet) sung during the Easter Vigil liturgy. The words surrounding it concord well with LDS belief: "O truly necessary sin of Adam, destroyed completely by the Death of Christ! O happy fault that earned for us so great, so glorious a Redeemer!" *The Roman Missal* (2011), 355.

everywhere and commanded them that they should repent and . . . be saved," warning that "as many as believed not and repented not, should be damned" (Moses 5:12–15). "And thus the Gospel began to be preached, from the beginning, being declared by holy angels sent forth from the presence of God, and by his own voice, and by the gift of the Holy Ghost" (Moses 5:58).[113]

As it turns out, Adam and Eve are left to "mourn" because the bulk of their posterity do "not hearken unto [God's] voice, nor believe on his Only Begotten Son" (Moses 5:27, 57). As "the works of darkness began to prevail among" Adam and Eve's descendants, God "cursed the earth with a sore curse, and was angry with the wicked, with all the sons of men whom he had made" (Moses 5:56). This, of course, set the stage for the biblical flood. Before that takes place, though, at the end of Adam's long life, he gathers together such of his numerous posterity as were willing to come and, "notwithstanding he was bowed down with age, being full of the Holy Ghost, predicted whatsoever should befall his posterity unto the latest generation" (D&C 107:56). On the same occasion, "the Lord appeared unto them, and they rose up and blessed Adam, and called him Michael, the prince, the archangel. And the Lord administered comfort to Adam, and said unto him: I have set thee to be at the head; a multitude of nations shall come of thee, and thou art a prince over them forever" (D&C 107:54–55).[114]

This extended Latter-day Saint portrait of Adam and Eve and the aftermath of their fall is, of course, strikingly different from most Christian theological reconstructions. Indeed, the term "fall" hardly fits the tenor of LDS theological

---

113. In an expansive version of *prisca theologia* (ancient theology), Latter-day Saint scripture consistently depicts the gospel as something that was taught from the beginning, not merely in limited fashion, nor just in types and shadows under the Mosaic dispensation, but fully, as it was during New Testament times. Although less common, this idea has been voiced by other Christians as well, classically so by Dante Alighieri in his *Divine Comedy*. On Dante's ascent through the heavenly spheres, in the sixth sphere Dante is surprised to find the Trojan hero Ripheus, who is mentioned in Virgil's *Aeneid*. The *Aeneid* describes Ripheus as "the most just among the Trojans" (2.426–27). Dante is told that because of Ripheus's uprightness, "God opened his eyes to our future redemption" and he became a "Christian in firm faith," figuratively baptized "more than a thousand years before baptizing began." Robert M. Durling, ed. and trans., *The Divine Comedy of Dante Alighieri*, vol. 3, *Paradiso* (New York: Oxford University Press, 2011), 405, 407 (Canto 20, lines 122–23, 104–5, 127).

114. LDS scripture even identifies northwest Missouri as "Adam-ondi-Ahman . . . or the land where Adam dwelt" and where on some future occasion "Adam shall come to visit his people" (D&C 117:8; 116:1). A hymn entitled "Adam-ondi-Ahman" was composed a mere five years into the church's history and has been included in church hymnals ever since. Currently, see *Hymns*, #49.

reflection on the event. Mormon valuing of the fall begins with a syllogism that has long been part of *felix culpa*/fortunate fall rhetoric: "By Adam came the fall of man. And because of the fall of man came Jesus Christ . . . and because of Jesus Christ came the redemption of man" (Mormon 9:12). In short, no fall, no need for redemption; no first Adam, no second Adam.[115] More distinctive to Mormonism is the view that partaking of the forbidden fruit, rather than being a sin of arrogant rebellion, was actually a necessary prerequisite to keeping the divine command to "multiply and replenish [fill] the earth." A popular Book of Mormon aphorism states, "Adam fell that men might be" (2 Nephi 2:25), and in the book of Moses, Eve declares, "Were it not for our transgression we never should have had seed" (Moses 5:11). An earlier church website introduced the fall to a general audience in this way: "You may know the story of Adam and Eve in the Garden of Eden, but did you know it was they who paved the way for the rest of us to come to earth? . . . If they hadn't eaten the forbidden fruit, they would have . . . never had children. Mankind never would have been born or the world populated."[116] Echoing the Book of Mormon aphorism is Joseph Smith's account of the preaching of Enoch: "Because that Adam fell, we are" (Moses 6:48). Early Christian theologians offered various speculations for why Adam and Eve had no children in the garden. Jerome suggested it was because they were ignorant of sexual intercourse. Augustine wondered if it was because they did not have time before they fell. LDS theology, however, takes it a step further by positing that the prelapsarian bodies of Adam and Eve were in some way physiologically incapable of sexual reproduction. Only as fallen, physically changed beings could Adam and Eve propagate the human race.[117]

Another positive LDS perspective is that far from being fatally debilitating, the fall is seen as generating the necessary preconditions for humanity's moral and spiritual growth. Remarked Brigham Young, "Some may regret that our first parents sinned. This is nonsense. . . . I will not blame Adam or Eve, why?

115. In the late nineteenth century, some Latter-day Saints, as other Christians at the time, used this logic to make evolutionary science appear to be anti-Christian. Evolution precluded a fall which in turn obviated the need for a redeemer. See, for example, B. H. Roberts, *The Gospel: An Exposition of Its First Principles*, rev. ed. (Salt Lake City: G. Q. Cannon & Sons, 1893), 314–17.

116. "God's Plan of Salvation," http://www.mormon.org/beliefs/plan-of-salvation.

117. *Why* Adam and Eve were unable to reproduce prior to the fall is not explained in LDS scripture or official pronouncements. A common view, however, is that their prelapsarian bodies were not vitalized by blood. The comments of heart surgeon–apostle Russell Nelson are typical: the fall "brought about the required changes in their bodies, including the circulation of blood and other modifications. They were now able to have children." Russell M. Nelson, "The Atonement," *Ensign*, November 1996, 33.

Because it was necessary that sin should enter into the world; no man could ever understand the principle of exaltation [the fullness of salvation] without its opposite; no one could ever receive an exaltation without being acquainted with its opposite."[118] In the words of a popular Book of Mormon verse, "it must needs be that there is an opposition in all things. If not so . . . righteousness could not be brought to pass" (2 Nephi 2:11). From this perspective, personal righteousness is loving God and doing good despite the tug of temptation toward sin and evil. Thus, true sanctity requires the existence of evil in opposition to the good. So does the actualization of agency and choice: "Wherefore, man could not act for himself save it should be that he was enticed by the one or the other" (2 Nephi 2:16). Jacob Blain, a Baptist contemporary of Brigham Young, expressed the thought succinctly: "To constitute *free agency* (a great object,) there must be *temptation*."[119] As discussed in chapter 2, such views have a long history in Christian theology. In combating the various religious and philosophical determinisms of their day, the Christian apologists of the second century deployed similar reasoning. To be truly good, argued Irenaeus in *Against Heresies*, "human beings must be free; the love of good has value only when a choice of the contrary evil has been rejected. . . . By experiencing the contrast between virtue and sin, human beings can come to appreciate, prefer, and preserve the good." And when they fail and make wrong choices, the suffering that follows serves as "an educational instrument."[120]

In Mormon thought, then, the fall was "not an obstruction to God's plan, and not a wrong turn in the course of humanity. . . . It was part of the Father's plan, being both foreknown to him and essential to the human family."[121] Cultivation of this perspective among Latter-day Saints is considered important enough that a church instructional manual provides these guidelines for how teachers should approach the topic of the fall: "The decision of Adam and Eve to eat the forbidden fruit was not a sin, as it is sometimes considered by other Christian churches. It was a transgression—an act that was formally prohibited but not inherently wrong. . . . Help class members appreciate that the fall of Adam and Eve enabled each of us to receive a body and come to earth to gain experience in choosing between good and evil."[122] As an LDS reference guide puts it, the fall "has a twofold direction—downward yet forward. In addition to introducing

---

118. *Journal of Discourses*, 10:312.

119. Blain, "A Review of Dr. Edward Beecher's *Conflict of the Ages*," 17.

120. J. Patout Burns, *Theological Anthropology* (Philadelphia: Fortress, 1981), 3. See the discussion of "soul-making" theodicies in chapter 2.

121. *Encyclopedia of Mormonism*, 4 vols. (New York: Macmillan, 1992), s.v. "fall of Adam."

122. *Preparing for Exaltation: Teacher's Manual* (1998), 13.

physical and spiritual death, it gave us the opportunity to be born on the earth and to learn and progress."[123] Given such positive perspectives on the fall, it is not surprising that LDS discourse over the years has stressed the nobility of Adam and Eve, sometimes even ascribing to them a divine status.[124] A mid-nineteenth-century poem eventually set to music and still included in the current LDS hymnbook reflects Mormon appreciation for the primal parents and celebrates Adam and Eve's predicted latter-day return to earth: "Sons of Michael, he approaches! Rise, the ancient father greet. Bow, ye thousands, low before him; minister before his feet. . . . Mother of our generations, glorious by great Michael's side, take thy children's adoration; endless with thy seed abide."[125]

Despite glowingly positive rhetoric about Adam and Eve, Mormon discourse does not shy away from acknowledging that in addition to making posterity possible and providing essential conditions for spiritual growth, the fall also introduced conditions that resulted in sin and death becoming the common human experience. With most other Christian traditions, Latter-day Saints affirm, in the words of the apostle Paul, that "by one man sin entered into the world, and death by sin; and so death passed upon all men" (Rom. 5:12). Mormons understand the death to which Paul referred to be both physical and spiritual in nature. Unlike the Pelagian circle of the fifth century who maintained that Adam was created mortal, Latter-day Saints side with the majority Christian view that Adam and Eve might have lived forever had they not sinned.[126] As with many Christian theologies over the centuries, Latter-day Saints see human mortality more as a plus than a punishment. First and foremost, like the exultation in the Catholic Easter Vigil liturgy, Mormons believe that physical death was an important reason for the incarnation. It enabled the Son to conquer death and bring about the potential of a transformative and

123. *True to the Faith*, 57.

124. Though repudiated today as an official doctrine of the Church of Jesus Christ of Latter-day Saints, laudatory reflection on Adam and Eve reached such heights in the mid-nineteenth century that Adam was spoken of as the "god" of this earth and the father of Jesus Christ. For a substantive discussion of this now-defunct "Adam-God" doctrine, see David John Buerger, "The Adam-God Doctrine," *Dialogue: A Journal of Mormon Thought* 15 (Spring 1982): 14–58. Rodney Turner, "The Position of Adam in Latter-day Saint Scripture and Theology" (master's thesis, Brigham Young University, 1953), places "Adam-God" doctrine in the broader sweep of LDS reflection on Adam.

125. "Sons of Michael, He Approaches," *Hymns*, #51.

126. "And now, behold, if Adam had not transgressed he would not have fallen, but he would have remained in the garden of Eden. And all things which were created must have remained in the same state in which they were after they were created; and they must have remained forever, and had no end" (2 Nephi 2:22).

divinizing bodily resurrection for humankind. In the positive characterization of the Book of Mormon: "death hath passed upon all men to fulfil the merciful plan of the great Creator" (2 Nephi 9:6). To be sure, the vicissitudes of earth life brought on by the fall make human beings "partakers of misery and woe" (Moses 6:48), Yet, Latter-day Saints, as other Christians who embrace a "soul-making" theodicy, regard such trials as potentially beneficial. They can be a refining fire in a crucible of adversity and occasions for receiving the enabling power of divine grace (see chapter 2).

The other type of death believed to be brought on by the fall is "spiritual death," or the alienating rupture in humanity's relationship with God. Latter-day Saints tend not to describe this as abjectly as Western Christians but are closer to Eastern Orthodoxy in their sensibilities. Mormons acknowledge that in humanity's fallen condition the *imago Dei* may dim and the love of God grow cold through sin. However, because Latter-day Saints view humanity's relationship with God as "genetic," the possibility of its restoration to loving mutuality is always on the horizon. Human "prodigals" may be estranged from their Father, but they are still "sons." As we have seen, the book of Moses depicts a postlapsarian world in which God does not close off communication. Instead, he lovingly and graciously continues to call on Adam's posterity to repent and proleptically receive salvation through the efficacy of his Only Begotten's future sacrifice: "I, the Lord God, gave unto Adam and unto his seed, that they should not die as to the temporal death, until I, the Lord God, should send forth angels to declare unto them repentance and redemption, through faith on the name of mine Only Begotten Son" (D&C 29:42). The Mormon estimation of humanity, even in its fallen condition, is among the most positive of all Christian anthropologies.

Yet despite a powerful vision of God's loving, persistent outreach, Mormonism unflinchingly acknowledges fallen humanity's proclivity to sin. Though Latter-day Saints reject original sin and total depravity, they can be just as emphatic as other Christians in affirming the reality of human sinfulness. A Book of Mormon prophet lamented, "O how foolish, and how vain, and how evil, and devilish, and how quick to do iniquity, and how slow to do good, are the children of men. Yea, how quick to hearken unto the words of the evil one, and to set their hearts upon the vain things of the world. . . . O how great is the nothingness of the children of men" (Helaman 12:4, 7). Brigham Young bluntly declared, "Mankind are revengeful, passionate, hateful, and devilish in their dispositions."[127] In short, the unregenerate "natural man is an enemy to

127. *Journal of Discourses*, 8:160.

God, and has been from the fall of Adam, and will be, forever and ever, unless he yields to the enticings of the Holy Spirit, and putteth off the natural man and becometh a saint through the atonement of Christ" (Mosiah 3:19). Even the spiritually reborn are depicted as continuing to struggle with the power and pervasiveness of sin. Echoing Paul's plaintive cry in Romans 7, a Book of Mormon prophet declared, "Oh, wretched man that I am! . . . my soul grieveth because of . . . the sins which do so easily beset me. And when I desire to rejoice, my heart groaneth because of my sins; nevertheless, I know in whom I have trusted. My God hath been my support. . . . O then . . . why should I yield to sin because of my flesh? . . . Awake, my soul! No longer droop in sin" (2 Nephi 4:17–19, 26–28). In this same spirit, apostle Spencer Kimball's widely distributed 1969 book *The Miracle of Forgiveness* has a chapter titled "None Righteous, No, Not One" with subheadings "All Are Sinners," "Church Members Need Repentance," and "Even Prophets Not Perfect."[128]

To be sure, Latter-day Saints believe that humankind is endowed with the same *posse non peccare* (power not to sin) as their primal parents, but Mormons acknowledge that life in a sinful world is such that humans inevitably succumb to temptation and choose poorly. The book of Moses glosses Psalm 51, commonly used to defend original sin, in this fashion: "Children are conceived in sin, even so when they begin to grow up, sin conceiveth in their hearts" (Moses 6:55). As one twentieth-century church leader explained, being "conceived in sin" means that children are born "in *the midst of* sin. They come into the world where sin is prevalent, and it will enter into their hearts."[129] Humanity's "carnal, sensual, and devilish" nature is described in the book of Moses not as congenital corruption inherited from Adam and Eve but as an acquired condition resulting from persistently choosing Satan, what philosophers would call an "accidental" rather than a "necessary" aspect of human nature. It might be said, contrary to Augustine, that sin is passed on by imitation, not propagation. Nonetheless, in words that come close to a declaration of inherited sin, Brigham Young dramatically depicted the hold that a sinful environment has on humanity. The "power of evil," he remarked, "is so prevalent upon the face of the whole earth. It was given to you by your father and mother; it was mingled with your conception in the womb, and it has ripened in your flesh, in your blood, and in your bones, so that it has become riveted in your very nature."[130]

128. Spencer W. Kimball, *The Miracle of Forgiveness* (Salt Lake City: Bookcraft, 1969), 31–37.
129. George Q. Morris, *Conference Report*, April 1958, 38 (emphasis added).
130. *Journal of Discourses*, 2:134.

At the same time, Latter-day Saint theology does not lose sight of innate human goodness, of a divine nature deep inside. Indeed, when Mormons focus on the positive aspects of humankind, they can wax eloquent, at times even making the Romantics' paeans to human potential pale in comparison. Human souls were procreated with embryonic characteristics of divinity and a birthright potential to become like their divine parents. Of course, that potential can be stifled through sin. As with any seeds, humankind's "seeds of divinity" must be nourished and cultivated in order to grow and flourish. This positive perspective often softens LDS anthropological discourse. The same Brigham Young who bemoaned human sinfulness could also examine it from a different angle of view. Should "we attribute all the mistakes or evils that we see in men to total depravity, and conclude that there is nothing good within them?" asked Young rhetorically. "Not by any means," he replied. "Do not attribute that wrong word or deed to total depravity. It is a weakness—it is a fault—it is a want of better judgment—it is the want of a correct understanding of things."[131] But it is not total depravity, and humans are not helpless in combating evil. Young could even go so far as to turn the phrase "natural man" on its head to make his point. "Paul says, in his Epistle to the Corinthians, 'But the natural man receiveth not the things of God,' but I say it is the unnatural 'man' that receiveth not the things of God.'" What he meant was that "spiritually we are the natural children of the Father of light and . . . the love of all good was incorporated in [our] nature. . . . It was never designed that [we] should naturally do and love evil." All humans start life as Adam and Eve did—naturally inclined toward God and good—but then experience their own fall: "So far as mankind yields to [evil] influences, they are so far removed from a natural to an unnatural state."[132]

Latter-day Saint anthropology might be summed up by modifying Martin Luther's famous assessment of humanity as *simul justus et peccator* (both

131. *Journal of Discourses*, 8:365.

132. *Journal of Discourses*, 9:305. A similar sentiment was expressed a century later by apostle Marion G. Romney: "I know the scriptures say that 'the natural man is an enemy to God' [Mosiah 3:19]. And so he is when he rejects the promptings of the Spirit and follows the lusts of the flesh. But he is not an enemy to God when he follows the promptings of the Spirit. I firmly believe that notwithstanding the fact that men, as an incident to mortality, are cast out from the presence of God and deprived of past memories, there still persists in the spirit of every human soul a residuum from his preexistent spiritual life which instinctively responds to the voice of the Spirit of Christ until and unless inhibited by the free agency of the individual. If I had time, I could cite many authorities on this point." Romney, *Conference Report*, April 1964, 123.

justified and a sinner) to read *simul divinitas et peccator* (simultaneously possessing both the seeds of divinity and sinful proclivities). Often the oscillation in Mormon emphasis on these two aspects of human nature has reflected the broader American culture. Thus, it is not surprising that candid expressions about human sinfulness were common in the early years of the Church of Jesus Christ of Latter-day Saints during the Second Great Awakening. Later in the 1800s and in the early 1900s, when perspectives labeled "liberal" theology or "modernism" shied away from proclaiming a doctrine of original sin, LDS discourse focused more on divine inheritance and potential for good. Then, in the mid-twentieth century, on the heels of Protestant neoorthodoxy's return to a pronounced emphasis on essential human sinfulness, Latter-day Saints rediscovered the Book of Mormon's strong affirmation of the sinfulness of the "natural man." The cup of human nature can be viewed as both partially full and partially empty. Whether one sees the divine potential in the cup or focuses on its equally manifest sinful emptiness, Latter-day Saints have consistently viewed the gospel and grace of Jesus Christ as the means to cultivating the good and conquering the evil in fallen human beings. Mormons may regard physical death as the inherited and inexorable consequence of Adam's transgression, but they do not view spiritual death as a permanent or insuperable condition. Repentance and reconciliation with God are readily available through the atonement of Jesus Christ and the divine grace it makes possible. How Latter-day Saints understand the operation of that reconciling grace in overcoming spiritual death or separation from God is the subject of the next chapter.

6

SOTERIOLOGY

Dimensions of Salvation

The April 2015 general conference of the Church of Jesus Christ of Latter-day Saints represented a milestone in the church's history. For the first time, a member of its governing First Presidency—Dieter Uchtdorf—delivered an address devoted entirely to the subject of grace.[1] To be sure, Latter-day Saints have always believed in grace. However, over the course of Mormon history the term was gradually overshadowed by other words and ideas believed to express it. Just as the underlying Hebrew and Greek terms for *grace* can also be translated "favor," "mercy," or "loving-kindness," Latter-day Saints came to use a variety of such words and expressions to describe God's munificence to humankind. The concepts of spiritual empowerment, divine assistance, and heaven-sent "blessings" have been particularly common. Beginning in the final quarter of the twentieth century, however, especially after "grace" was included in the church's new Bible dictionary (1979), use of the term itself became much more prominent.[2] Still, Uchtdorf's 2015 "The Gift of Grace" was pathbreaking in both substance and tone.[3] It clearly sought to dispel the idea that Mormonism teaches a doctrine of "works-righteousness." "Salvation," Uchtdorf began bluntly, "cannot be bought with the currency of obedience; it is purchased

1. Dieter F. Uchtdorf, "The Gift of Grace," *Ensign*, May 2015, 107–10.
2. *Bible Dictionary*, s.v. "grace." The total number of instances in which "grace" was mentioned in general conference addresses from 1900 to 1970 varied modestly from forty to over sixty per decade. This changed dramatically over the next fifty years. By the 2010s, the *annual* totals alone averaged around thirty references, making general-conference mention of "grace" approximately five times more common than in the past. https://www.lds-general-conference.org/, s.v. "grace."
3. Two decades earlier, church general authority Gene R. Cook discoursed substantively on grace in general conference (see his "Receiving Divine Assistance through the Grace of the Lord," *Ensign*, May 1993, 79–81), but Uchtdorf's prominent position and his particular interest in adjusting the rhetorical pendulum of the past made his address especially significant.

by the blood of the Son of God." Properly understood, obedience "comes as a natural outgrowth of our endless love and gratitude for the goodness of God." Uchtdorf used the Lukan account of Simon the Pharisee and the woman with the alabaster jar of ointment (Luke 7:36–50) to underline his point about grateful love: "Are we like Simon? Are we confident and comfortable in our good deeds, trusting in our own righteousness? . . . Or are we like this woman, who thought she was completely and hopelessly lost because of sin? . . . When we kneel to pray, is it to replay the greatest hits of our own righteousness, or is it to confess our faults, plead for God's mercy, and shed tears of gratitude for the amazing plan of redemption?" Simply put, "grace is a gift of God," and that gift "enabl[es] us to achieve things that otherwise would be far beyond our reach. It is by God's amazing grace that His children can overcome the undercurrents and quicksands of the deceiver [devil], rise above sin, and 'be perfect[ed] in Christ.'"[4]

The increased LDS emphasis on grace, including more frequent use of the term itself as epitomized by Uchtdorf's address, reflects a number of developments within Mormonism in the past several decades. These include the church's intensified focus on the life and work of Jesus Christ; the LDS re-encounter with the Book of Mormon and its Christocentric message, especially as urged by church president Ezra Taft Benson in the 1980s; and the church's interest in communicating to the world its Christian bona fides. Uchtdorf's 2015 address both reflects and reinforces these developments, providing fresh momentum to the growing popularity among Mormons of the language of grace. This trend has generated increased attention both inside and outside the church to the particulars of LDS thought about salvation more generally, prompting the question, "What *do* Mormons believe about key concepts in the contested arena of Christian soteriology (salvation doctrine) such as *election, justification,* or *sanctification*?" These are the topics addressed in this chapter.

What Is "Salvation"?

Few would dispute that the salvation of humankind is a central concern of all Christian traditions, but exactly what that salvation involves has been a matter of considerable debate for nearly two millennia. From the outset, the "good news" about what God has done for humanity in and through Jesus Christ has been considered so extensive and rich that biblical authors, as well as subsequent theologians, have struggled to articulate it. The apostle Paul,

4. Uchtdorf, "The Gift of Grace," 107–10.

whose writings are the fountainhead of most soteriological discourse, was compelled to employ a variety of images in his attempt to convey the grandeur and richness of the saving work of Christ. *Redemption, reconciliation, justification, birth, adoption, creation, citizenship, sealing, grafting,* even *salvation* itself were all metaphors from everyday life that Paul deployed in this endeavor. Only over time did these metaphors acquire precise theological definition and elaborate soteriological exposition.[5] Although salvation impacts the entire cosmos as well as single individuals, the material as well as the spiritual, this chapter narrows the discussion of salvation to its spiritual ramifications for humankind. Thus delimited, a broad theological definition of salvation satisfactory to most Christian traditions, including the Latter-day Saint faith, would be that salvation is the process by which God reconciles sinful humanity to himself, bringing human beings into loving and eternal relationship with the Trinity through the grace of Christ's redemptive sacrifice. Along the way, humans are delivered from sin, evil, and death, and ultimately are conformed to the divine image in which they were originally created. Salvation, then, in the fullest sense, is a multifaceted process that occurs in the past, present, and future. It is more than the single event or moment in time when one comes to faith in Jesus Christ that it is sometimes conceived to be in popular Christianity. Salvation is a series of gracious interventions that begins with God calling humanity to faith and discipleship in this life and ends with God glorifying them in his eternal presence in the afterlife.

Because soteriology is a complex field of study that overlaps and interconnects with most other branches of theology, to adequately assess it in all its richness requires more than a single chapter. Readers should begin with the earlier chapters on the "person" and "work" of Jesus Christ, "the author and finisher of our faith" (Heb. 12:2). Echoing the famous testimonial of Christ in Acts 4:12 that "neither is there salvation in any other," a Book of Mormon prophet proclaimed that "salvation was, and is, and is to come, in and through the atoning blood of Christ" (Mosiah 3:18). Also crucial to Latter-day Saint soteriology is the role of the sacraments, especially LDS temple rituals, as conduits of Christ's saving grace. Readers will find extended treatment of such

5. James D. G. Dunn, *The Theology of Paul the Apostle* (Grand Rapids: Eerdmans, 1998), 317–33, and Gordon D. Fee, "Paul and the Metaphors for Salvation: Some Reflections on Pauline Soteriology," in *Redemption: An Interdisciplinary Symposium on Christ as Redeemer,* ed. Stephen T. Davis, Daniel Kendall, and Gerald O'Collins (New York: Oxford University Press, 2004), 43–67. Differing soteriologies are presented in Rienk Lanooy, ed., *For Us and for Our Salvation: Seven Perspectives on Christian Soteriology* (Utrecht-Leiden: Insteruniversitair Instituut voor Missiologie en Oecumenica, 1994).

matters in the later chapters on the sacraments. And the final chapter on eschatology is essential reading as well. Latter-day Saints see the fullness of salvation, what they refer to as "exaltation" or "eternal life," as something experienced in the afterlife. "Exaltation" in the Mormon lexicon, like "glorification" in other Christian theologies, is the resurrection *telos* or end point of human flourishing made possible through Christ's atonement. As for the aspects of soteriology to be covered in the present chapter, a standard Protestant *ordo salutis* (order/ sequence of salvation) will serve as our analytical framework. Some Christians, such as those in the Wesleyan tradition, including Pentecostals, find the term *via salutis* more congenial because for them it more effectively connotes the ongoing nature of salvation as a lifelong, participatory journey bringing the Christian into conformity with Christ. Here we shall explore Christian and Mormon views on "election," "calling," "justification," and "sanctification," with special attention being given to the relationship between "grace" and "works." First, however, several framing matters need to be considered.

OVERARCHING ISSUES

Among the most persistent problems in Christian soteriology has been the challenge of determining the proper relationship between divine grace and human agency. The varying positions taken on this issue might be plotted along a continuum, with theological accounts that see God as the sole, exclusive agent in effecting human salvation located at one end of the continuum. Although this perspective was firmly in place by the fifth century, not until the nineteenth century was the term "monergism" (from the Greek for "single"/"sole" and "work") coined to identify it. As one moves down the continuum from a strictly monergistic position, varying degrees of human involvement in the process of salvation are discernible. Because such soteriologies envision some form of divine-human partnership in the process of salvation, they are classified as *synergistic* (from the Greek for "working together"). Synergistic soteriologies preserve a place for human agency as it co-operates with divine grace in bringing about salvation. Given the prevalence of theological reflection on the dialectic between divine sovereignty and human responsibility or between divine grace and human will in the process of salvation, this monergist-synergist continuum is one of the principal axes along which differing soteriologies may be plotted. The LDS position, which is decidedly synergistic, will be detailed in due course.

Another axis to be kept in mind is the individual-communal continuum. Toward one end of that continuum are soteriologies that emphasize the early church dictum *extra ecclesiam nulla salus* (outside the church there is no salvation).[6] Salvation both in this life and the next is linked to involvement with the church as the corporate "body of Christ." This is understood to be true both sacramentally and socially. Without the saving graces communicated through the church's sacraments, salvation in the fullest sense is not possible. Historically, this has been the position of liturgically oriented communions such as the Catholic, Orthodox, and LDS churches.[7] A slightly different communal emphasis in some traditions is that only "faith which worketh by love" (Gal. 5:6) counts for salvation, and love, it is emphasized, requires a community in order to be lived. Toward the other end of the spectrum are traditions that stress the intensely personal character of salvation. From the medieval mystic to the modern "born-again" believer cultivating a "personal relationship" with Christ, private religious experience tends to overshadow communal, and especially sacramental, participation. For some groups such as the Quakers, there is no sacramental mediation at all; grace and salvation are entirely internal and personal. The communal-individual continuum may also be characterized as contrasting external, church-channeled notions of grace with conceptions of grace as unmediated and internal.

While such classificatory continua are helpful analytically, it is problematic to plot a religious tradition along these axes as if its doctrine was fixed and unchanging. Over time, all Christian traditions, including Mormonism, have to some degree moved back and forth along these soteriological continua. In whatever way these shifts of emphasis are characterized, whether as the upward thrust of a spiral or the simple swing of a pendulum, they are clearly discernible in all traditions. Moreover, at any given point in time, a variety of viewpoints may be discerned among a tradition's adherents. No tradition is uniform or monolithic even in a particular historical moment, let alone over time. Thus, while Martin Luther might be classified as monergistic, his

6. Augustine, in *On Baptism* 4.7.24, is often cited as the source for this statement, but actually he is quoting Cyprian from a century and a half earlier. Cyprian, "Concerning the Baptism of Heretics," Epistle 72.21, in *ANF*, 5:384. Cyprian's Alexandrian contemporary Origen maintained the same view: "Let no one persuade himself, let no one deceive himself. Outside this house, that is, outside the Church, no one is saved." Origen, *Homilies on Joshua* 3.5, in *Origen: Homilies on Joshua*, trans. Barbara J. Bruce, Fathers of the Church (Washington, DC: Catholic University of America Press, 2002), 50.

7. Other Christian traditions also discern some link between church and salvation. Martin Luther, for instance, taught that "outside the Christian church there is no truth, no Christ, and no salvation." Quoted in Paul Althaus, *The Theology of Martin Luther* (Philadelphia: Fortress, 1966), 291. Additionally, it should be noted that today Catholic, Orthodox, and Mormon theologies are more muted in their claims of *extra ecclesiam nulla salus* than they once were. See chapter 7.

colleague Philip Melanchthon was less so. Yet both were architects of Lutheranism. Or consider the Church of England. From the beginning, disparate and competing soteriological interests were evident in England, ranging from a Reformed monergism embraced by some Puritans and post-Restoration Dissenters to earlier Laudian "high-churchmen" and later Latitudinarians who promoted an Arminian synergism.[8] "Ever since its emergence in the course of the sixteenth century," writes one historian, "the Church of England has represented a coalition of more or less disparate interests. Heterogeneity indeed is arguably of the 'Anglican' essence."[9] Examples of such in-house theological heterogeneity could be multiplied across traditions. In short, nuance and variety militate against sweeping generalizations and the use of hard-and-fast theological labels to describe any religious tradition, including Mormonism.

WHO GETS SAVED? DIVINE PLAN AND PURPOSES

One of the most beloved passages in the Bible is John 3:16: "For God so loved the world, that he gave his only begotten Son, that whosoever believeth in him should not perish, but have everlasting life." The prima facie reading of this and other New Testament passages such as 1 Timothy 2:4—"[God] will have all men to be saved, and to come unto the knowledge of the truth"—is that God desires to save all human beings.[10] This was the predominant view in the early centuries of Christianity. Hippolytus of Rome, for example, declared that Christ "seeks all, and desires to save all, wishing to make all the children of God."[11] Why, then, isn't everyone saved, asked John Chrysostom? Because they "would not. For grace, though it be grace, saves the willing, not those who will not have it, and turn away from it."[12] Augustine, however, played a major role in altering this soteriological landscape. Particularly in his later writings, he endeavored to argue that it was never God's intention to save all his creatures.

---

8. William Laud was the archbishop of Canterbury (principal leader of the Church of England) from 1633 until his death in 1645. Jacob Arminius and his supporters dissented from "five-point" Calvinism.

9. Nicholas Tyacke, "From Laudians to Latitudinarians: A Shifting Balance of Theological Forces," in *The Later Stuart Church, 1660–1714*, ed. Grant Tapsell (Manchester: Manchester University Press, 2012), 46.

10. Second Peter 3:9 adds: "The Lord is not slack concerning his promise, as some men count slackness; but is longsuffering to us-ward, not willing that any should perish, but that all should come to repentance."

11. Hippolytus, *On Christ and Antichrist* 3, in *ANF*, 5:205.

12. Chrysostom, *Homilies on Romans*, Homily 18, in *NPNF*, 1/11:483.

Augustine asserted that prior to creation God decreed that only *some* would be saved and chose who they would be. Hence the doctrines of *"predestination"* and "election" (from the Greek *eklektos* for "chosen" or "selected").[13] These ideas in Augustine's writings were further developed during the Reformation, especially by John Calvin.[14] Although not known for his predestinarian views, Martin Luther was compelled by his emphasis on the salvific sovereignty of God to sound like Calvin: "Since God has taken my salvation out of my hands into his, making it depend on his choice and not mine, and has promised to save me, not by my own work or exertion but by his grace and mercy, I am assured and certain."[15]

This predominantly Augustinian-Reformed version of election, however, has generated considerable criticism over the centuries, and disagreements tend to fall into two broad categories: (1) rejection of the salvifically circumscribed character of the doctrine; and (2) concern over its apparent dismissal of human freedom in the process of salvation. Regarding the first objection, critics have asked how a perfectly loving God could rightly choose to save only some of his creatures and allow the rest to suffer in eternal torment. This concern for fairness spills over into a second critique that asks how such a doctrine of election, when paired with monergism, could be reconciled with human freedom. Monergism seems to make of the elect little more than spiritual automatons. Some Catholic theologians have criticized the way in which Reformers (mis)construed the teachings of their beloved "doctor of the church," Saint Augustine, who, although a monergist in terms of initial conversion, was clearly a synergist with regard to how God thereafter continues to bring about

13. "While early Greek biblical commentators experienced little or no difficulty interpreting [1 Tim. 2:4], for Augustine and those who followed his later views on predestination, interpreting this verse became a Herculean task." Francis X. Gumerlock, "Fulgentius of Ruspe on the Saving Will of God," in *Grace for Grace: The Debates after Augustine and Pelagius*, ed. Alexander Y. Hwang, Brian J. Matz, and Augustine Casiday (Washington, DC: Catholic University of America Press, 2014), 155. See also Alexander Hwang, "Augustine's Interpretations of 1 Tim. 2:4," *Studia Patristica* 43 (2006): 137–42.

14. Calvin devoted chapters 21–24 in book 3 of *Institutes* to the doctrine of election. He also authored *Concerning the Eternal Predestination of God*, ed. and trans. J. K. S. Reid (1552; reprint, London: James Clarke, 1961). See also Martin Foord, "God Wills All People to Be Saved—or Does He? Calvin's Reading of 1 Timothy 2:4," in *Engaging with Calvin: Aspects of the Reformer's Legacy for Today*, ed. Mark D. Thompson (Nottingham: Apollos, 2009), 179–203.

15. Luther, "On the Bondage of the Will," in *Martin Luther's Basic Theological Writings*, ed. William R. Russell, 3rd ed. (Minneapolis: Fortress, 2012), 166. See also James E. McGoldrick, "Luther's Doctrine of Predestination," *Reformation & Revival* 8 (Winter 1999): 80–103.

the salvation of believers.[16] Criticism even arose *within* Reformed circles. One of the most influential critiques emanated from the Dutch Reformed minister Jacob Arminius, who challenged the claim that God wills only the salvation of a limited few and argued instead along the lines of hypothetical universalism that God elects anyone who with the help of his grace exercises free choice to believe and persevere in faith. Barely a decade after Arminius's death, however, the Dutch Reformed Church held a synod at Dordt that repudiated such ideas and produced a set of five canons (church laws) subsequently immortalized in English with the acronym TULIP—total depravity, unconditional election, limited atonement, irresistible grace, perseverance of the elect.[17]

The Canons of Dordt notwithstanding, "Arminianism" became widespread in the centuries that followed, so much so that it might be characterized as a "third force" in Protestant theology alongside Reformed and Lutheran thought. The mid-seventeenth-century theological writings of Simon Episcopius, a Dutch Remonstrant (opponent of the Dordt Canons), systematized Arminian theology and had wide influence on the European continent and beyond. In the seventeenth century, Reformed thinking within the Church of England was vigorously challenged by a growing number of Anglican divines such as Jeremy Taylor, Henry Hammond, and George Bull who enjoyed the patronage of successive Arminian-leaning archbishops William Laud, Gilbert Sheldon, and John Tillotson. By the end of the century, Arminian influence within the Church of England was prominent, if not dominant.[18] Not surpris-

---

16. Examples of how contemporary Catholic theologians and intellectuals have wrestled with the problem of predestination in light of the tradition's synergistic tendencies include Stephen A. Long, Roger W. Nutt, and Thomas Joseph White, *Thomism and Predestination: Principles and Disputations* (Washington, DC: Catholic University of America Press, 2017), and Matthew Levering, *Predestination: Biblical and Theological Paths* (Oxford: Oxford University Press, 2011).

17. Arminius and subsequent Arminians actually agreed with the first canon that stressed fallen human sinfulness. They did, however, take the opposite position on the other four canons.

18. "The second half of the seventeenth century saw many changes in English religious thought, but none more striking than the overthrow of Calvinism. . . . At the beginning of the century, it had dominated the religious life of England; by the end its power had been completely overthrown." Gerald R. Cragg, *From Puritanism to the Age of Reason: A Study of Changes in Religious Thought within the Church of England, 1660 to 1700* (Cambridge: Cambridge University Press, 1950), 13. Cragg's characterization is now considered an exaggeration, but even Stephen Hampton, *Anti-Arminians: The Anglican Reformed Tradition from Charles II to George I* (Oxford: Oxford University Press, 2008), acknowledges that the Reformed tradition, though far from eclipsed, was still at best only "a compelling and credible alternative to the majority view" (274).

ingly, in the eighteenth century, John Wesley was among those who articulated a version of Arminian soteriology.[19] His 1740 sermon on "free grace" was among his most pointed attacks on the implications of election and predestination. Calling the latter "a doctrine full of blasphemy," Wesley argued that it "has a manifest tendency to destroy holiness in general, for it wholly takes away those first motives to follow after it."[20] Wesley opposed an absolute monergism because he believed God cannot "force" belief "without destroying the nature which he had given [to humans]: For he made you free agents; having an inward power of self-determination, which is essential to your nature. And he deals with you as free agents from first to last. As such, you may shut or open your eyes, as you please."[21]

By the nineteenth century, especially in the United States during the Second Great Awakening and what has been called the "age of Methodism," the soteriological landscape had taken on a noticeably Arminian, synergistic character that reflected the democratic and libertarian cultural milieu of the new republic.[22] This is apparent even in the writings of Samuel Simon Schmucker, "the most prominent American Lutheran theologian of the early nineteenth century" and the "architect of 'American Lutheran' theology."[23] Schmucker

19. On Wesley's soteriology, see Thomas C. Oden, *John Wesley's Teachings*, vol. 2, *Christ and Salvation* (Grand Rapids: Zondervan, 2012). For "Wesleyan" soteriology more broadly, see William J. Abraham and James E. Kirby, *Oxford Handbook of Methodist Studies* (New York: Oxford University Press, 2009), 522–632.

20. John Wesley, "Free Grace" (Sermon 110), in *Works of John Wesley*, ed. Albert C. Outler (Nashville: Abingdon, 1986), 3:548, 554. See also Jerry L. Walls, "John Wesley on Predestination and Election," in Abraham and Kirby, *Oxford Handbook of Methodist Studies*, 618–23. Arminius, whose influence on Wesley was real but indirect, had written that the doctrine of predestination "hinders all zeal and careful regard for good works." Moreover, it "removes the salutary fear and trembling with which we are commanded to work out our own salvation [Phil. 2:12]." *A Declaration of the Sentiments of Jacobus Arminius*, section 2, in *Arminius and His Declaration of Sentiments: An Annotated Translation*, trans. W. Stephen Gunter (Waco, TX: Baylor University Press, 2012), 121.

21. "Signs of the Times" (Sermon 66), in Outler, *Works of John Wesley*, 2:531.

22. See Nathan Hatch, *The Democratization of American Christianity* (New Haven: Yale University Press, 1989), and Donald Meyer, "The Dissolution of Calvinism," in *Paths of American Thought*, ed. Arthur M. Schlesinger Jr. and Morton White (Boston: Houghton Mifflin, 1963), 71–85. For a modest corrective of the picture of Arminianism as the "American culture religion," see Douglas A. Sweeney, "Falling Away from the General Faith of the Reformation? The Contest over Calvinism in Nineteenth-Century America," in *John Calvin's American Legacy*, ed. Thomas J. Davis (New York: Oxford University Press, 2010), 111–46.

23. E. Brooks Holifield, *Theology in America: Christian Thought from the Age of the Puritans to the Civil War* (New Haven: Yale University Press, 2003), 397.

argued that "throughout the whole scriptures is man addressed as a free, a moral agent." Maintaining a conditional view of election, Schmucker added, "God from eternity decreed to distribute future happiness or misery according to the voluntary conduct of each individual." His conclusion was clear-cut and more in line with Melanchthon's thought than Luther's: "Though salvation is of grace, it is accepted or rejected by the voluntary faith or unbelief of every individual." To be sure, Schmucker affirmed with all Christians that the sole, meritorious cause of salvation was the redemptive work of Jesus Christ. Yet, although Christ's atoning sacrifice is a "naked gratuity . . . no gift ceases to be such because those to whom it is tendered choose to accept it."[24] Such is the theological matrix into which the Church of Jesus Christ of Latter-day Saints was born.

ELECTION IN MORMONISM

Latter-day Saint soteriology has much in common with the period's prevalent and marked emphasis on free will, synergism, and conditional election. In an 1841 sermon Joseph Smith offered his view that the "unconditional election of individuals to eternal life was not taught by the apostles." However, "God did elect or predestinate, that all those who would be saved, should be saved in Christ Jesus, and through obedience to the gospel."[25] According to the Book of Mormon, the Lord "sendeth an invitation unto all men, for the arms of mercy are extended towards them, and he saith: Repent, and I will receive you. Yea, he saith: Come unto me and ye shall partake of the fruit of the tree of life; yea, ye shall eat and drink of the bread and the waters of life freely" (Alma 5:33–34). In short, "all those who will obey his commandments are his elect."[26] While such statements *could* be read in a Calvinist fashion, Smith brings decidedly freewill assumptions to his discussion of the elect. In other words, believers qualify

24. S. S. Schmucker, *Elements of Popular Theology* (Andover, MA: Gould and Newman, 1834), 91, 99, 108, 107.

25. *JSP*, D8:152.

26. *JSP*, D1:217. Smith's statements echo how the elect are defined in the Doctrine and Covenants: "Mine elect hear my voice and harden not their hearts" (D&C 29:7); and "even so will I gather mine elect from the four quarters of the earth, even as many as will believe in me, and hearken unto my voice" (D&C 33:6). This view can also be found in "Article 7 —Predestination" in the influential 1610 *Short Confession of Faith*, a joint Anabaptist and proto-Baptist confession: "All those who now receive this grace of God in Christ (who came for the salvation of the world) with penitent and believing hearts and remain in him are and remain the elect whom God has ordained." *Creeds & Confessions*, 2:758.

themselves to be God's elect by the choices they freely make; their choices are not predetermined because God elected them before the foundation of the world. Such views led Joseph Smith to emend Acts 13:48, a passage commonly invoked by supporters of unconditional election and absolute predestination. Instead of "as many as were ordained to eternal life believed," Smith rephrased the verse to read: "as many as believed, were ordained to eternal life."[27] Further, the Book of Mormon spurned the double predestinarianism of the apostate Zoramites who prayed to God: "We believe that . . . thou hast elected us that we shall be saved, whilst all around us are elected to be cast by thy wrath down to hell" (Alma 31:16–17).

Latter-day Saint commitment to free agency makes any notion of "irresistible grace" seem coercive. From Augustine onward, monergists have attempted to overcome this criticism by arguing that God never coerces the will against its inclinations. Instead, he transforms those inclinations so that the elect choose God in accordance with their regenerated wills. Without such transforming grace, fallen human wills, although they technically retain the power of choice, can only choose evil. The "determinism of sovereign grace" is thus realized internally by the Spirit changing dispositions so that the graced will invariably chooses God. For Mormons, though, such an account of human freedom seems strained, even casuistical. LDS scripture proclaims simply: "ye are free to act for yourselves—to choose the way of everlasting death or the way of eternal life" (2 Nephi 10:23). Thus, "whosoever perisheth, perisheth unto himself; and whosoever doeth iniquity, doeth it unto himself; for behold, ye are free; ye are permitted to act for yourselves; for behold, God hath given unto you . . . that ye might choose life or death" (Helaman 14:30–31). Fittingly, the first hymn in the original hymnbook of the Church of Jesus Christ of Latter-day Saints was one borrowed from a Freewill Baptist:

> Know then that every soul is free,
> To choose his life and what he'll be;
> For this eternal truth is giv'n,
> That God will force no man to heav'n.
> He'll draw, persuade, direct him right;

---

27. *NTOB*, 473. A similar interpretation of the text was advanced earlier by reformer Martin Bucer (1491–1551). See Miriam Usher Chrisman, *Strasbourg and the Reform* (New Haven: Yale University Press, 1967), 85–88, and, more broadly, Brian Lugioyo, *Martin Bucer's Doctrine of Justification: Reformation Theology and Early Modern Irenicism* (New York: Oxford University Press, 2010).

Bless him with wisdom, love and light;
In nameless ways be good and kind,
But never force the human mind.[28]

So strong was the freewill animus against Augustinian-Reformed notions of unconditional election, irresistible grace, and the indefectibility of the elect that when such ideas were in view, early Latter-day Saints used the "elect" word group derisively. Indeed, the only place in the entire Book of Mormon where "elect" or its derivatives appear is in the previously referenced Alma 31 account of the Zoramites' apostate beliefs. However, when shorn of deterministic assumptions, Latter-day Saints use the "elect" word group positively. Their most common approach has been to follow the biblical use of "elect" and its derivatives to refer primarily to Israel as God's corporately chosen or elect people. Even Paul, who was intent on extending the blessings of saving grace to the gentiles, maintained that "as touching the election, [the people of Israel] are beloved for the fathers' sakes," and the day would come when "all Israel shall be saved" (Rom. 11:28, 26). Joseph Smith prefaced his previously cited criticism of unconditional election by outlining what he considered to be the correct doctrine of election. As reported in the local newspaper, he "read the 9th chap. in Romans, from which it was evident that the election there spoken of . . . had reference to the seed of Abraham."[29] This is also the perspective that appears in the detailed and much-reprinted discussion of election penned by two of Smith's trusted apostolic associates—Brigham Young and Willard Richards. In nine, double-column pages in the church's periodical, *Millennial Star*, the apostles argued in good Arminian fashion that: (1) election originally pertained to Israel and only later to gentile Christians by adoption; (2) both election and reprobation are inextricably connected to human choice; and (3) election is only maintained by obedience to God.[30] Although LDS discussion of election

28. *Sacred Hymns* (1835), "Hymn 1." The quoted portion consists of the first two stanzas of a seven-stanza hymn originally titled "Freedom of the Human Will" and published in an 1805 Freewill Baptist hymnal. See Hatch, *Democratization of American Christianity*, 43, 231–32. The hymn in shortened form can still be found in the current LDS hymnal. See *Hymns*, #240.

29. *JSP*, D8:151. Another account of Smith's sermon summarized his comments on Rom. 9 with the statement "all election that can be found in the scripture is according to the flesh and pertaining to the Preasthood." *JSP*, D8:153.

30. Brigham Young and Willard Richards, "Election & Reprobation," *Latter-Day Saints Millennial Star*, January 1841, 217–25. A later, equally substantive treatment of the topic is George Q. Cannon, "Foreordination and Predestination," in *Collected Discourses*, ed. Brian H. Stuy (Burbank, CA: BHS Publishing, 1988), 2:64–76.

or the elect is somewhat less common today because the church emphasizes the universality of its message and membership, the connection with Israel is still evident.[31] The LDS *Bible Dictionary* begins its treatment of election with these words: "A theological term primarily denoting God's choice of the house of Israel to be the covenant people with privileges and responsibilities, that they might become a means of blessing to the whole world."[32]

When Latter-day Saints do discuss the soteriological doctrine of election, however, it is almost always linked to freedom of choice and is thus understood to be conditional. With regard to the old debate as to which comes first—divine predestination or divine foreknowledge—Mormons weigh in on the side of God's foreknowledge as the prior determinant of a predestination based on foreseen faith.[33] Young and Richards interpreted Romans 8:28–29—"all things work together for good to them that love God, to them who are the called according to his purpose. For whom he did foreknow, he also did predestinate"—in this fashion: "For he foreknew that those, who loved him, would do his will and work righteousness." In other words, "the general principle of election [is] that God chose, elected, or ordained . . . on account of his foreknowledge of their obedience to his will and commandments."[34] In dealing with Romans 9:10–12, another predestinarian *locus classicus* that states that God chose Jacob over Esau before they were born, Young and Richards offered an interpretation consistent with LDS presuppositions about agency: God foresaw that Esau would sell his birthright to Jacob "of his own free will and choice, or acting upon that agency which God has delegated to all men." Rebekah may have been surprised that the traditional brotherly status was to be reversed when God told her that "the elder shall serve the younger" (Gen. 25:23), but, as Young and Richards read the passage, it illustrated that God's electing pur-

---

31. Indeed, under the influence of Russell Nelson, apostle and later church president, the first quarter of the twenty-first century witnessed a revival of language referring to the "gathering of Israel." This more recent usage, almost entirely shorn of literal or ethnic connotations, focuses on the idea that all who embrace the gospel of Christ, regardless of genetics or genealogy, are spiritually considered part of Israel.

32. *Bible Dictionary*, s.v. "election."

33. This was also the position taken in the first of the Five Articles in the Arminian Remonstrance of 1610. Before discussion of salvation became more individualistically oriented in the twentieth century, early Mormon discourse agreed with the article's clarification that "predestination does not seem to elect [individual] persons; it is rather a general rule of how God will proceed with believing/non-believing people." Quoted in Volker Drecoll, "Hugo Grotius," in Pollmann, *Oxford Guide to the Historical Reception of Augustine*, 1087.

34. Young and Richards, "Election & Reprobation," 219, 218.

poses reflected and respected his foreknowledge of Esau's free choice.[35] In the LDS view, divine foreordination is always dependent on, and follows, divine foreknowledge of how humans will freely exercise their agency.

The arguments of these Mormon apostles are not unique. Similar analyses have been advanced over the years by theologians who were wary of allowing God to be seen as either arbitrary in election or heedless of human freedom (see the discussion of human freedom and divine sovereignty in chapter 2). In combating the determinism of his day, Justin Martyr wrote in his *First Apology* that if human behavior was predestined to occur in a fixed manner, "no choice would be in our power at all." For if it is decreed "that this man is to be good and this other man evil, neither the former is praiseworthy, nor the latter blameworthy. Furthermore, if man does not have the free faculty to shun evil and to choose good, then, whatever his actions may be, he is not responsible for them."[36] Toward the end of his *Dialogue with Trypho*, Justin added, "I have already shown that they who were foreknown as future sinners, whether men or angels, do become so, not through God's fault, but each through his own fault."[37] Origen devoted a lengthy chapter in *On First Principles* to defending human self-determination and providing a freewill interpretation of biblical passages that some in his day read monergistically.[38] Similar regard for human

---

35. Young and Richards, "Election & Reprobation," 220–22. Young and Richards also quoted a passage from the Book of Mormon that talks about priests "being called and prepared from the foundation of the world according to the foreknowledge of God, on account of their exceeding faith and good works." The passage stresses that everyone has an equal opportunity to excel. "Left to choose good or evil," some harden their hearts and reject God, "while, if it had not been for this they might have had as great privilege as their brethren. Or, in fine, in the first place they were on the same standing with their brethren; thus this holy calling being prepared from the foundation of the world for such as would not harden their hearts" (Alma 13:3–5). Later, as the doctrine of preexistence came to exert significant influence on Mormon thought, this passage was read as referring to preexistent faith rather than earthly choices, and "first place" was understood not rhetorically but literally as a reference to the preexistent spirit world. As an example, later in the nineteenth century, apostle Franklin Richards and James Little reasoned thus: "Their calling and preparation from the foundation of the world were evidently based on their faith and good works, previous to their being called, and not on the possibilities of their future good conduct." *Compendium of Doctrines*, 139. For twentieth-century examples, see Talmage, *Jesus the Christ*, 28–29, and McConkie, *Mormon Doctrine*, 269–70.

36. Justin Martyr, *1 Apology* 43, in *Writings of Saint Justin Martyr*, ed. and trans. Thomas B. Falls, Fathers of the Church (Washington, DC: Catholic University of America Press, 1948), 79.

37. Justin Martyr, *Dialogue with Trypho* 140, in Falls, *Writings of Saint Justin Martyr*, 364.

38. Origen, *On First Principles* 3.1.1–24, in *Origen: On First Principles*, trans. and ed. John Behr (Oxford: Oxford University Press, 2017), 2:285–377.

freedom in the calculus of election has persisted in the Greek East to this day, as reflected in commentary found in the current *Orthodox Study Bible* (*OSB*). For instance, with regard to the much-cited Romans 8:29–30, the *OSB* warns, "'Predestined' must not be understood as overpowering man's free response, for man's free will is a gift from God." Although "God foreknows all things," he "does not predetermine all" (the same statement made by Joseph Smith). "God freely offers salvation to all, and man freely responds to it. All are 'called,' but all do not respond. . . . God compels no one." Instead, "based on His fore-knowledge, God assures, or predestines, that those who will choose to love and obey Him will be 'conformed to the image of His Son.'"[39] In like manner, the *OSB* assesses the Romans 9:13 statement "Jacob have I loved, but Esau have I hated" in this manner: "Both Jacob and Esau were called to salvation, for God loves all equally. But God foreknew how these two would freely respond to His call." The declaration "Esau have I hated" does "not mean God did not love Esau. Rather God foresaw the wickedness Esau would choose and hated it. Likewise, God foresaw Jacob's faith and obedience and knew Jacob would serve His purposes."[40]

As with Eastern Orthodoxy, Arminianism, and a variety of other theologies, the Mormon doctrine of election emphasizes God's foreknowledge of future, freely chosen faithfulness rather than the inscrutability of the divine, electing will. What is distinctive in Latter-day Saint thought is how the preexistence of human spirits factors into divine foreknowledge. Life in the preexistence for God's spirit children is thought to be similar to earthly existence in that loving obedience to a heavenly Father or willful neglect were both possible. "The Father of our spirits has a full knowledge of the nature and disposition of each of His children," wrote James Talmage, "a knowledge gained by observation and experience in the long ages of our primeval childhood, when we existed as un-embodied spirits, endowed with individuality and agency—a knowledge compared with which that gained by earthly parents through experience with their children in the flesh is infinitesimally small. [The Father] knows what each will do under given conditions, and sees the end from the beginning."[41] Thus, for Latter-day Saints, divine foreknowledge is grounded in past observation as

39. These quotations combine commentary from *OSB*, 1537, and St. Athanasius Academy of Orthodox Theology, *Orthodox Study Bible: New Testament and Psalms* (Nashville: Nelson, 1993), 358 (hereafter, *OSB-NT*).

40. *OSB-NT*, 359, 361, and *OSB* 1539. Others have given voice to similar perspectives. See pp. 195–96 above.

41. James E. Talmage, *The Vitality of Mormonism: Brief Essays on Distinctive Doctrines of the Church of Jesus Christ of Latter-day Saints* (Boston: Gorham, 1919), 317.

much as future prediction. It is how Mormons explain Jeremiah 1:5—"Before I formed thee in the belly, I knew thee; and before thou camest forth out of the womb I sanctified thee, and I ordained thee a prophet unto the nations."[42] In short, as the current LDS *Guide to the Scriptures* states, election is "based on premortal worthiness." Yet, the elect still must prove themselves on earth. "Even these chosen ones must be called and elected [again] in this life [because of their obedience] in order to gain salvation."[43]

CALLING

Another look at the previously cited Romans 8:30 is important here—"whom [God] did predestinate, them he also called: and whom he called, them he also justified: and whom he justified, them he also glorified." Some Christians have considered this passage paradigmatic, seeing in it the divine *ordo salutis*—predestination prompts calling, which leads to regeneration and justification, which eventuates in glorification. Having considered predestination, we turn now to the subject of "calling." In Christian theology, "calling" has reference to God bringing humanity generally, or the elect specifically, to an awareness of their sinful predicament and communicating to them the "good news" that through Jesus Christ deliverance is possible. Although Mormons today primarily use "call" and "calling" to discuss appointments to various positions of church service and ministry,[44] the traditional soteriological usage is nonetheless discernible in early LDS history. In the Book of Mormon, for

---

42. In Mormon doctrine, God's predeterminations for humanity, which Latter-day Saints prefer to call "foreordination" rather than "predestination," tend to focus on the roles his spirit children will play in salvation history, such as predetermining that Jeremiah would be a prophet.

43. *Guide to the Scriptures*, s.v. "election." This has long been recognized in Mormon teaching. Parley Pratt singled out Abraham as an example: "When he had been sufficiently proved according to the flesh, the Lord manifested to him the election before exercised towards him in the eternal world. He then renewed that election and covenant, and blessed him, and his seed after him." *Journal of Discourses*, 1:258–59. See also *Compendium of Doctrines*, 138–39.

44. Although most Christians understand "many are called, but few are chosen" (Matt. 22:14; cf. 20:16) soteriologically, LDS scripture sometimes applies this phrase to ministerial performance. See D&C 121:34–40; 95:5–6; and 105:33–37. First Presidency member James Faust referred to the common LDS use of "calling" to mean a ministerial appointment and interpreted the Matthean statements thus: "We are called when hands are laid upon our heads and we are given [church office], but we are not chosen until we have demonstrated to God our righteousness, our faithfulness, and our commitment." James E. Faust, "Called and Chosen," *Ensign*, November 2005, 55.

instance, a notable convert by the name of Amulek admits: "I was called many times and I would not hear; therefore I knew concerning these things, yet I would not know; therefore I went on rebelling against God, in the wickedness of my heart, even until the fourth day of this seventh month" (Alma 10:6).[45] And when Joseph Smith reiterated the urging in 2 Peter 1:10 to make one's "calling and election sure," he was discussing the need for the elect who had been called into the gospel fold to persevere through grace-aided godly living to eventually lay hold on eternal life.[46]

A necessary concomitant of calling, as the first step toward repentance and conversion, is "conviction." That is, in response to the proclamation of the gospel, individuals are convicted in the judicial court of their heart and mind as sinners alienated from God. For much of Western Christian history, prelates and preachers of every kind have painted the predicament of sinful and sinning humanity in stark and terrifying terms in order to humble sinners and bring them to a state of preparation to experience God's call effectually. Jonathan Edwards's iconic Great Awakening sermon "Sinners in the Hands of an Angry God" is but a later example of a homiletic tradition that dates to the thirteenth century. This "evangelism of fear" is discernible in both Protestant and Catholic history and has reflected as well as reinforced a distinctly Western "guilt culture." Characteristic of that culture have been a "hyper acute awareness of sin," an "obsession with hell," and an "almost morbid delight in original sin."[47] Preaching that incorporated such perspectives was designed to induce "humiliation" and "contrition" (which translates the Hebrew *dakkah*, meaning "crushed" [to powder]), or in other words "godly sorrow."[48]

---

45. Elsewhere, a Book of Mormon prophet reproves his people for having "gone astray, as sheep having no shepherd, notwithstanding a shepherd hath called after you and is still calling after you, but ye will not hearken unto his voice!" (Alma 5:37).

46. "Make your calling and election sure," Smith taught. "Go on from grace to grace untill you obtain a promise from God for yourselves that you shall have eternal life." *JSP*, D14:264. Based on other statements Joseph Smith made, LDS theological reflection over time generated a more elaborate interpretation of the meaning and results of making one's calling and election sure. For an extensive example of this, see Bruce R. McConkie, *Doctrinal New Testament Commentary*, vol. 3, *Colossians–Revelation* (Salt Lake City: Bookcraft, 1973), 325–50. It is worth noting, however, that making one's calling and election sure has not been mentioned in general conference since the early 1980s.

47. The quotes are from Jean Delumeau's *Catholicism between Luther and Voltaire*, trans. Jeremy Moiser (Philadelphia: Westminster, 1977), 126. See Delumeau's larger study *Sin and Fear: The Emergence of the Western Guilt Culture, 13th–18th Centuries*, trans. Eric Nicholson (New York: St. Martin's, 1990).

48. Webster's 1828 dictionary, s.v. "contrite," defines the word as "worn or bruised. Hence,

Mormon scriptural teaching about the need for a "broken heart and contrite spirit" is the LDS version of this "preparation" discourse, and it is readily observable in a Book of Mormon passage recounting the results of one particularly powerful proclamation of the gospel: "Now it came to pass that when king Benjamin had made an end of speaking . . . he cast his eyes round about on the multitude, and behold they had fallen to the earth, for the fear of the Lord had come upon them. And they had viewed themselves in their own carnal state, even less than the dust of the earth. And they all cried aloud with one voice, saying: O have mercy, and apply the atoning blood of Christ that we may receive forgiveness of our sins, and our hearts may be purified" (Mosiah 4:1-2). King Benjamin subsequently described this first step toward salvation as being "awakened" to a sense of one's "nothingness" before God and one's "worthless and fallen state" (Mosiah 4:5). Only such truly contrite individuals would be prepared to receive the full benefits of Christ's atonement: "Behold, he offereth himself a sacrifice for sin, to answer the ends of the law, unto all those who have a broken heart and a contrite spirit; and unto none else can the ends of the law be answered" (2 Nephi 2:7). In LDS penitential discourse, contrition and godly sorrow for sin constitute the necessary sacrifice sinners are to offer to the One who made the atoning sacrifice.[49]

The most detailed conversion account in the Book of Mormon, and one that clearly portrays both conviction of sin and effectual calling to faith, involves a prophet's wayward son named Alma, who had been persecuting the people of God. Following an event similar to Saul's experience on the road to Damascus, Alma recounts, "after wading through much tribulation, repenting nigh unto death, the Lord in mercy hath seen fit to snatch me out of an everlasting burning, and I am born of God. My soul hath been redeemed from the gall of bitterness and bonds of iniquity. I was in the darkest abyss; but now I behold the marvelous light of God. My soul was racked with eternal torment; but I am snatched, and my soul is pained no more" (Mosiah 27:27-29). Alma later describes the experience in more detail to his son Helaman: "I was racked with

---

broken-hearted for sin; deeply affected with grief and sorrow for having offended God." Article 12 of the 1530 Augsburg Confession defines contrition as "terrors that strike the conscience when sin is recognized." *Book of Concord*, 45.

49. Later in the Book of Mormon, when Christ appears to the people following his resurrection, he declares, "And ye shall offer up unto me no more the shedding of blood; yea, your sacrifices and your burnt offerings shall be done away. . . . And ye shall offer for a sacrifice unto me a broken heart and a contrite spirit. And whoso cometh unto me with a broken heart and a contrite spirit, him will I baptize with fire and with the Holy Ghost" (3 Nephi 9:19-20).

eternal torment, for my soul was harrowed up to the greatest degree and racked with all my sins . . . for which I was tormented with the pains of hell; yea, I saw that I had rebelled against my God. . . . And now, for three days and for three nights was I racked, even with the pains of a damned soul." At that point, in the midst of his torment, he recounts, "behold, I remembered also to have heard my father prophesy unto the people concerning the coming of one Jesus Christ, a Son of God, to atone for the sins of the world. . . . Now, as my mind caught hold upon this thought, I cried within my heart: O Jesus, thou Son of God, have mercy on me, who am in the gall of bitterness, and am encircled about by the everlasting chains of death." This was Alma's moment of coming to saving faith, of being "converted." "Behold, when I thought this, I could remember my pains no more; yea, I was harrowed up by the memory of my sins no more. And oh, what joy, and what marvelous light I did behold; yea, my soul was filled with joy as exceeding as was my pain!" (Alma 36:12–13, 16–20).

In these Book of Mormon accounts there is a clear sense of divinely induced conviction, humiliation, and godly sorrow. There is also pointed emphasis on gracious deliverance by the Lord—Alma was "snatched" from an "everlasting burning" in hell by the grace of God (a common trope in many Christian conversion accounts). To this extent, Alma's account might have been Martin Luther's. The difference is that Alma's account preserves a synergistic sense of human engagement, reflecting the implicit belief that the *imago Dei* was not fully erased by the fall. In contrast, monergists see fallen humanity as so completely captive to sin that human beings are utterly unable to participate in any active way in the process of coming to saving faith. Article 2 of the Lutheran Formula of Concord is unequivocal: "Before people are enlightened, converted, reborn, renewed, and drawn back to God by the Holy Spirit, they cannot in and of themselves, out of their own natural powers, begin, effect, or accomplish anything in spiritual matters for their own conversion or rebirth, any more than a stone or block of wood or piece of clay." Indeed, salvation from beginning to end has nothing to do with the exercise of "the human powers of the natural free will—neither totally, halfway, somewhat, nor in the slightest and smallest bit."[50] This initial grace that delivers the will from bondage to sin and restores enough of the *imago Dei* to enable the individual

---

50. *Book of Concord*, 548–49. Article 10 of the Anglican Communion's Articles of Religion expresses similar sentiments in these words: "The condition of man after the fall of *Adam* is such, that he cannot turn and prepare himself by his own natural strength and good works to faith and calling upon God: wherefore we have no power to do good works pleasant and acceptable to God, without the grace of God by Christ preventing [coming first to] us, that we may have a good will, and working with us when we have that good

to respond in faith to God's call is sometimes labeled *prevenient grace* (from the Latin *prevenire*, "to come before"). Christians who believe that fallen humans are congenitally incapable of initiating even the beginnings of a turn to God tend to discuss this prevenient or "special" grace primarily, if not exclusively, in terms of its restorative function.

Latter-day Saints, on the other hand, almost never use the term "prevenient grace," and with Catholics and Orthodox, they do not view the fall as having so completely erased the *imago Dei* in human beings that people are left without any ability to will what is pleasing to God, however weakly or infrequently (see chapter 5). Mormons do, however, acknowledge the priority and primacy of grace in making the gospel call efficacious. In so doing, they proclaim a more capacious understanding than many of what counts as God's prevenient grace. For Latter-day Saints, God's loving grace is perhaps most stunningly manifest even before earth life when God spiritually begot all souls in the preexistence, endowing each with the intrinsic potential and desire to become like him. Though with a different conception of how and when God creates souls, Karl Rahner similarly argued that God fashions souls with a "capacity" for grace that causes them implicitly to thirst for God and instinctively sense that they need God's grace for fulfillment.[51] Latter-day Saints believe that this God-inclining capacity was stifled but not fully extinguished by the fall. In the right circumstances, this primordial gift from God can stir a soul to seek him and desire to believe, which, with the further help of enabling grace, can lead to conversion and saving faith. In theological terms, this initial grace at spirit birth might be considered "sufficient" but not "efficacious" grace. It is activated and enabled by additional grace. Thus, salvation truly is a process of receiving "grace for grace" or "grace upon grace" (John 1:16; D&C 93:20).

A second kind of preceding grace in Mormon thought is the general moral illumination Latter-day Saints believe the Lord bestows on all people at physical birth. Mormons call it the "light of Christ," a phrase derived from the Johannine declaration that Christ "lighteth every man that cometh into the world" (John 1:9).[52] This grace, if not suppressed through actual sin, can also illumine and inspire initial steps toward God and good. A Doctrine and Cov-

---

will." *The Book of Common Prayer: The Texts of 1549, 1559, and 1662*, ed. Brian Cummings (Oxford: Oxford University Press, 2011), 676.

51. Karl Rahner, *Theological Investigations*, vol. 1, *God, Christ, Mary, and Grace*, trans. Cornelius Ernst (London: Darton, Longman & Todd, 1961), 310–15.

52. The LDS *Guide to the Scriptures* defines the light of Christ as the grace of "divine energy, power, or influence that proceeds from God through Christ and gives life and light to all things" (s.v. "light, light of Christ").

enants revelation combines the frank admission that "the whole world lieth in sin" with the declaration that "the Spirit giveth light to every man that cometh into the world," and eventually "every one that hearkeneth to the voice of the Spirit cometh unto God" (D&C 84:46–47). Centuries earlier, Chrysostom, in commenting on John 1:9, asked: If the Lord "enlightens every man who comes into the world, how is it that so many have remained unenlightened?" His answer, rooted in a synergistic soteriology, is one with which Mormons would fully agree: God does "as much as He is permitted to do. . . . But if some, deliberately closing the eyes of their minds, do not wish to receive the beams of this Light, darkness is theirs. . . . Grace has been poured forth upon all . . . and [God] calls all with equal honor. And they who do not wish to enjoy this gift ought rightly to attribute their blindness to themselves."[53]

LDS scripture also acknowledges a third type of prevenient grace that facilitates an effectual call. This is the kind that many Christians associate with the term. A Book of Mormon passage recounts: "The Lord did pour out his Spirit on all the face of the land to prepare the minds of the children of men, or to prepare their hearts to receive the word which should be taught among them . . . that they might not be hardened against the word, that they might not be unbelieving . . . but that they might receive the word with joy, and as a branch be grafted into the true vine" (Alma 16:16–17). While the *potential* for salvific responsiveness and the *capacity* for grace are present in all human beings, the Book of Mormon acknowledges the sobering reality that "the natural man is an enemy to God, and has been from the fall of Adam, and will be, forever and ever, unless he yields to the enticings of the Holy Spirit, and putteth off the natural man and becometh a saint through the atonement of Christ the Lord" (Mosiah 3:19). Yet, even in this stark assessment of fallen humanity, agency is preserved. The prevenient grace of the "enticings of the Holy Spirit" combines with the freely chosen acceptance of proffered grace implied in the verb "yields." Ezra Taft Benson interpreted in a similar fashion Revelation 3:20—"Behold, I stand at the door, and knock: if any man hear my voice, and open the door, I will come in to him, and will sup with him, and he with me." "Note," remarked Benson, "He does not say, 'I stand at the door and wait for you to knock.'" The Lord is taking the initiative, "calling, beckoning, asking that we simply open our hearts and let Him in."[54] Christians over the years

53. John Chrysostom, "Homily 8 (John 1:9–10)," in *Commentary on Saint John the Apostle and Evangelist: Homilies 1–47*, trans. T. A. Goggin, Fathers of the Church (Washington, DC: Catholic University of America Press, 1957), 81.

54. Ezra T. Benson, "A Mighty Change of Heart," *Ensign*, October 1989, 4.

have often cited Christ's declaration in John 6:44—"No man can come to me, except the Father which hath sent me draw him"—and his reiteration of the doctrine in John 6:65—"No man can come unto me, except it were given unto him of my Father"—to make a similar point. Recent Latter-day Saint teaching links these statements from John 6 with Mosiah 3:19. "To 'draw,'" explains a church instructional manual, "is to attract or to pull gently, as with 'the enticings of the Holy Spirit' [and] we cannot come to the Savior unless it is 'given' unto us by the Father. To have faith or repentance 'given' to us means receiving divine help to believe and follow Jesus."[55]

Yet another example of conversion-facilitating grace is the word of God itself. "Faith," wrote Paul, "cometh by hearing, and hearing by the word of God" (Rom. 10:17). The Book of Mormon elaborates: "When a man speaketh by the power of the Holy Ghost, the power of the Holy Ghost carrieth it unto the hearts of the children of men" (2 Nephi 33:1). For Latter-day Saints, the general conference talks of the church's apostles and prophets are a prime example of the grace of inspired preaching. This kind of grace-infused proclamation led Mormon to observe: "The preaching of the word had a great tendency to lead the people to do that which was just—yea, it had had more powerful effect upon the minds of the people than the sword, or anything else, which had happened unto them— therefore Alma thought it was expedient that they should try the virtue of the word of God" (Alma 31:5).[56] The Book of Mormon contains an account of two brothers who spent many years applying "the virtue of the word" in their evangelism and consequently had been instrumental in bringing thousands into the fold of God. When one of the brothers began to exult in their success, the other brother "rebuked him, saying: Ammon, I fear that thy joy doth carry thee away unto boasting." To this, Ammon replied, "I do not boast in my own strength, nor in my own wisdom. . . . Yea, I know that I am nothing . . . but I will boast of my God. . . . Behold, how many thousands of our brethren has he loosed from

---

55. *NT Student Manual* (2018), 222. However, to Joseph Smith and the earliest Mormons, the word "draw" in John 6:44 sounded too coercive. The underlying Greek term can mean to "drag off." Although Smith did not know Greek, he felt uncomfortable with the verse and revised it to include the human side of synergism: "No man can come unto me, except he doeth the will of my Father who hath sent me . . . and he who receiveth the testimony, and doeth the will of him who sent me, I will raise up in the resurrection of the just." *NTOB*, 457. Additionally, when the hymn "Know This That Every Soul Is Free" was first published in the LDS hymnbook, the editors replaced the word "draw" at the beginning of the second stanza with "call."

56. See the somewhat similar position of Luther and the Wittenberg Reformers elaborated in Robert A. Kolb, *Martin Luther and the Enduring Word of God: The Wittenberg School and Its Scripture-Centered Proclamation* (Grand Rapids: Baker Academic, 2016).

the pains of hell; and they are brought to sing redeeming love, and this because of the power of his word which is in us, therefore have we not great reason to rejoice? Yea, we have reason to praise him forever" (Alma 26:10–14).

In its various understandings of the priority of grace, Mormonism does not speak so much of grace as restoring the will's capacity to choose God but rather describes such divine gifts as stirring and enabling individuals to make the decision of faith Latter-day Saints believe God's children are graciously, constitutionally capable of making. For this reason, Mormons talk synergistically about actively *exercising* the gift of faith rather than merely passively *receiving* it, of synergistically *working with* grace in addition to being *worked upon* by grace. Still, they recognize that ultimately it is the grace made possible through the atonement of Jesus Christ that enables saving faith and that turns gospel preaching into an effectual, divine call. Alma preached to the people by the power of the Spirit, "and a mighty change was also wrought in their hearts, and they humbled themselves and put their trust in the true and living God" (Alma 5:13).[57] God effects the mighty change, but people must respond to his loving knock and open the door to their soul. Latter-day Saints believe that grace is never irresistible or coercive. It cooperates with, but does not co-opt, the human will. From the LDS standpoint, no matter how the divine call comes or in what manner divine grace is thought to be prevenient, whether through the not-totally-effaced primordial endowment of "divine DNA" or the universal bestowal of the "light of Christ" or a special, extraordinary, heart-softening outpouring of the Holy Spirit or through the inspired proclamation of the word, human agency is never violated. Echoing the hymn cited above, Mormons believe that in all God's various graces, he calls, persuades, directs aright, blesses with wisdom, love, and light, in nameless gracious ways is good and kind, but never forces the human mind.[58] To repeat, there is no doctrine

---

57. Essentially, this is the Arminian position. In the words of their 1621 confession, the divine call "is effected and executed by the preaching of the gospel, together with the power of the Spirit, and that certainly with a gracious and serious intention to save and so to bring to faith all those who are called, whether they really believe and are saved or not, and so obstinately refuse to believe and be saved." Confession 17.2, in *Arminian Confession of 1621*, trans. and ed. Mark A. Ellis (Eugene, OR: Pickwick, 2005), 106.

58. This perspective is captured in a few simple revisions that Joseph Smith made to 1 Cor. 1. Instead of describing the preaching of the cross as the "power of God" to "them which are called" (v. 24), Smith changed the final phrase to read "them who believe." And instead of declaring that "not many wise men after the flesh, not many mighty, not many noble, are called" (v. 26), Smith replaced "called" with "chosen." *NTOB*, 499. In LDS soteriology, all human beings may be called, but only some by belief will end up being the chosen or elect of God.

of irresistible grace in LDS thought. At the same time, however, Latter-day Saint doctrine freely acknowledges the pump-priming priority of grace and its role as indispensable enabler thereafter in the process of salvation (see the section "Grace and Works" below). Mormonism's broader view of grace and its emphasis on human participation in the process of salvation have never struck Latter-day Saints as demeaning to Deity nor antithetical to the fact that salvation is only in Christ.

JUSTIFICATION

The divine call, whether monergistically or synergistically effectual, leads to *justification*. Originally, justification was a legal metaphor that conveyed "the image of expunging a record of debt or criminal guilt."[59] In its Christian context, justification preserved the secular, judicial connotations of the term and evoked the image of humans receiving a "not guilty" verdict in the court of God's justice whereby their sins were forgiven and they were put right with God. The apostle Paul taught that this comes about through the "amnesty" of Christ's atoning grace "erasing the record that stood against us with its legal demands" (Col. 2:14 NRSV).[60] Later theologians labeled this view of justification "forensic," a word derived from the Latin *foro* (forum), or public marketplace, where judicial action often took place in the Roman Empire. Pardoning sin and setting one at rights with divine law and the divine Lawgiver is only one of the connotations that theologians have drawn from the New Testament use of the *dikaios* word group. Most commonly, *dikaios*-related terms are translated as "righteous" or "righteousness" rather than "just" or "justification."[61] In modern English, "righteousness" is a clearer and more obviously religious word. It implies a sanctity many Christians believe comes through participatory union with Christ and his righteousness. It also implies conformity to God's will. Particularly in the Gospel of Matthew, *dikaiosynē* (righteousness) is linked to obedience. Mary's husband Joseph is described as a *dikaos* ("righteous or just

---

59. Dunn, *The Theology of Paul the Apostle*, 328.

60. The eloquent phrase "amnesty of grace" is Sharon Ringe's translation of Elsa Tamez's book title *Contra Toda Condena*. See Elsa Tamez, *The Amnesty of Grace: Justification by Faith from a Latin American Perspective*, trans. Sharon Ringe (Nashville: Abingdon, 1993).

61. Alister McGrath discusses at some length the semantic range of this word group in *Iustitia Dei: A History of the Christian Doctrine of Justification*, 3rd ed. (Cambridge: Cambridge University Press, 2005), 6–21. Louis Martyn chooses to translate the Greek terms as "rectify" and "rectification" in his Anchor Bible commentary, *Galatians* (New York: Doubleday, 1997).

man"—Matt. 1:19) because he does what God commands. Jesus obediently is baptized to fulfill all *dikaiosynē* ("righteousness"—Matt. 3:15). Were it not inelegant, a neologism like "righteous-ification" might better convey what is involved in justification. The broad semantic range of *dikaios* and *dikaiosynē* has facilitated centuries of debate over whether justification is a single pardoning event that changes only how God views the believer or whether it is also transformative in that justifying grace enables an actual change in the nature of the believer. And, in the latter case, is the gradual righteous-ification of believers monergistic or synergistic?

Until the Reformation, most Western Christian theologians followed Augustine in affirming that justification entailed both a pardoning of sin *and* the divine infusion of a righteous disposition.[62] The latter was known as the "effective" aspect of justification, and it was understood to be a lifelong process in which the Holy Spirit, in synergistic collaboration with human effort, progressively purged pardoned Christians of their sinful inclinations and imparted a habit of inner holiness. In this view, such terms and metaphors as spiritual rebirth, *renovatio*, regeneration, and sanctification—whether understood somewhat synonymously and as occurring concomitantly with conversion or as distinct, possibly successive stages in the divine impartation of righteousness—all come under the umbrella of justification.[63] During the Reformation, however, Luther and the Wittenberg Reformers chose to narrow justification primarily to the forensic crediting or imputing of Christ's righteousness to sinners who come to faith.[64] God "hath made [Christ] to be sin for us, who knew no sin; that we might be made the righteousness of God in him" (2 Cor. 5:21).

62. The term "justification" was not commonly employed or emphasized by the earliest church fathers. "It has always been a puzzling fact," observed Krister Stendahl, "that Paul meant so relatively little for the thinking of the church during the first 350 years of its history. To be sure, he is honored and quoted, but, in the theological perspective of the West, it seems that Paul's great insight into justification by faith was forgotten." Krister Stendahl, *Paul among Jews and Greeks* (Philadelphia: Fortress, 1976), 83.

63. It has been noted that one could "search in vain to find in any theologian of the Middle Ages a deliberate distinction between justification and regeneration." Albrecht Ritschl, *Critical History of the Christian Doctrine of Justification and Reconciliation* (Edinburgh: Edmonston & Douglas, 1872), 90.

64. At the Regensburg Colloquy in 1541, Protestant reformers Philip Melanchthon and Martin Bucer and Catholic apologists Johannes Eck and Johann Gropper reached an agreement, subsequently accepted even by Martin Luther, that justification both imputed Christ's righteousness and graciously imparted a behavior-changing disposition toward godliness. The agreement, however, was soon seen on both sides as yielding too much to the opposition. See Peter Matheson, *Cardinal Contarini at Regensburg* (Oxford: Clarendon, 1972).

This *admirabile commercium* (wonderful exchange) makes believers righteous in God's eyes because in spiritual union with Christ they participate in Christ's righteousness. Christians are righteous because they are "in" Christ and share in *his* righteousness. Only in the resurrection will the justified be purged from sin and made truly holy. Until then, as Martin Luther expressed it in his famous dictum, Christians are *simul iustus et peccator* (simultaneously justified/ righteous and sinful). In other words, they are intrinsically sinful but extrinsically righteous through Christ's "alien" righteousness. This is how Luther understood Paul's statement that God "justifieth the ungodly" (Rom. 4:5). In the forensic sense, justification does not actually make the forgiven individual personally righteous any more than the pardoned criminal suddenly becomes an upstanding citizen. It simply suggests that the demands of justice have been met by Christ so that sinners are graciously acquitted of their transgressions in God's eyes. Additionally, Luther did envision a transformative process at work in the life of the sinner over time by the impact of the regularly proclaimed word of God.[65]

Rather than group all God's loving, salvific interventions on behalf of humanity under the label "justification," some Reformers, such as John Calvin, chose to distinguish righteousness-bestowing sanctification conceptually and sequentially from pardoning justification. Sanctification was viewed as the subsequent, progressive stage that followed the initial, instantaneous justifying pardon in the *ordo salutis*. Though distinct, the two concepts were viewed as a complementary pair likened to the sun's light and heat that cannot be separated in describing the full work of salvation. Two centuries later, John Wesley, who embraced the distinction, put it this way: "Proper Christian salvation" consists of "two grand branches, justification and sanctification. By justification we are saved from the guilt of sin and restored to the favour of God; by sanctification we are saved from the power and root of sin and restored to the image of God."[66] Latter-day Saints inherited this justification-sanctification distinction. It was expressed thus in their foundational Articles and Covenants: "We know that justification through the grace of our Lord and Savior Jesus Christ is just and true; and we know also, that sanctification through the grace of our Lord and Savior Jesus Christ is just and true, to all those who love and serve God [note the synergism] with all their mights, minds, and strength. But there is a possibility [note the Arminianism] that man may fall from grace and depart from

65. Kolb, *Martin Luther and the Enduring Word of God*, 174–208.
66. John Wesley, Sermon 85, "On Working Out Our Own Salvation" (1785), in Outler, *Works of John Wesley*, 3:203–4.

the living God; therefore let the church take heed and pray always, lest they fall into temptation" (D&C 20:30–33).[67] Several observations about this formative declaration are important. First, the affirmation of justification lacks the common accompanying phrase "by faith." Justification is merely proclaimed. It is neither explained nor does the statement take a position on controverted points, as is done with sanctification. In practice, Latter-day Saints over the course of their history have rarely used the term "justification," favoring instead the less technical and more descriptive "remission of sins" when considering justification's forensic dimension.[68] In contrast, sanctification in all its aspects has been a common concern in LDS discourse from the beginning.[69]

One of the few sustained LDS discussions of justification in the nineteenth century is an 1854 article by apostle Orson Pratt.[70] All Christians, he writes, "admit that the atonement of Christ is necessary to justification. The only dispute seems to be in regard to the conditions required of the creature by which he receives the justification purchased by the atonement." Pratt, like other Christians, was fully committed to justification by faith. The key is how he understands faith. With James, Pratt believes that "true faith," justifying faith, says, "I will shew thee my faith by my works" (James 2:18). "Real faith in the heart," declares Pratt, "is that which leads to obedience." Specifically, "the first effect of true faith is a sincere, true, and thorough repentance of all sins; the second effect is an immersion in water for the remission of sins; the third is the reception of the ordinance of the laying on of the hands for the baptism of the Holy Ghost." Alluding to Peter's response to the crowd's query on the Day of Pentecost (Acts 2:38), Pratt calls these "the first commandments in the Gospel." Summarizing, Pratt remarks, "A faith, then, that brings remission of sins or justification to the sinner, is that which is connected with repentance and baptism."[71] Does this

67. Not only does the latter sentence echo an Arminian perspective, but it is also the Roman Catholic position set forth in Canon 23 in the "Decree on Justification" at the Council of Trent: "If any one says that a man once justified cannot sin again and cannot lose grace . . . let him be anathema." Denzinger 1573.

68. An exception to this in recent decades is D. Todd Christofferson, "Justification and Sanctification," *Ensign*, June 2001, 18–25.

69. Explication and exhortation in the pervasive Mormon pursuit of holiness parallel much that is found in such hortatory milestones as William Law's *A Serious Call to a Devout and Holy Life* (1729), Jeremy Taylor's *The Rule and Exercises of Holy Living* (1650), and Thomas à Kempis's *The Imitation of Christ* (ca. 1420s).

70. "Faith," *Seer*, January 1854, 198–204. All quotes from Pratt in this paragraph and the next are taken from this article.

71. Many liturgically oriented, "high-church" Christians concur that baptism is the means or "instrumental cause" through which God justifies the believer. See chapter 9.

mean Latter-day Saints are opposed to justification by faith? "No," answers Pratt, for "faith is the starting point—the foundation and cause of our repentance and baptism which bring remission or justification; and being the cause which leads to those results, it is not improper to impute justification to faith."

Pratt also tackles Paul's repudiation of justification by "works." He understands Paul's reference to "works" in Romans the way many Christians have, not as obedience to the teachings of Jesus but as the works of the Mosaic law. Thus, "Paul could with propriety say that Abraham and others were not justified by works, that is, by such works of the law as circumcision, &c. which were given for a very different purpose than that of justification." Joseph Smith seems to have had the same idea in mind when, in his emendation of the Bible, he replaced "works" (and its cognates) in Romans 4:2, 4–6 with "the law of works" or Jewish religious law, what Jews call the halakah. As Paul observed in Romans 3, "a man is justified by faith without the deeds of the law" (Rom. 3:28), or as the NRSV renders it, "apart from works prescribed by the law." In his textual revision, Smith seems to have read Paul's use of justification in its broader sense that includes sanctification. This is clear when Smith modifies Romans 4:16—"therefore it is of faith, that it might be by grace"—to read: "Therefore ye are justified of faith *and* works, through grace."[72] The Mormon prophet had no intention of denying justification by faith, but for him genuine faith was manifest in works of Christian discipleship.

Part of Christian disagreement over the place of works in relation to justification is rooted in how works are perceived. The Orthodox, Catholics, Latter-day Saints, Anabaptists, and groups with roots in the Wesleyan-Holiness tradition view works as organically and inextricably linked to faith, as the essential "fruits" of a living faith. As such, works are simply part of the definition of faith itself, as if the term were really "faithworks" or "worksfulfillingfaith." The Anglican–Roman Catholic International Commission expressed it thus: "Faith is no merely private or interior disposition, but by its very nature is acted out. Good works necessarily spring from a living faith. They are truly good because, as the fruit of the Spirit, they are done in God, and in dependence on God's grace."[73] In a series of lectures on faith published with early editions of the Doctrine and Covenants, faith is described as a "principle of action," not as mere belief or trust.[74] Latter-day Saints teach justification by faith through a living, active faith.

---

72. Smith's emendations quoted in this paragraph are from *NTOB*, 483 (emphasis added).

73. Citation in Walter Kasper, *Harvesting the Fruits: Basic Aspects of Christian Faith in Ecumenical Dialogue* (London: Continuum, 2009), 41.

74. "Lecture First, On the doctrine of the church of the Latter Day Saints—Of Faith," D&C-1835, 5–7.

Latter-day Saints, of course, are not the only Christians who understand faith or read Romans in this fashion. Some have argued that this is actually what Paul intended. In the context of the reciprocity assumed in ancient gift-giving, Paul can be read to emphasize that the divine gift of faith expects obedience in return so as not to "subvert the moral order of the cosmos." To be sure, Christian obedience "arises in conjunction with faith" and in grateful response to that faith as a prior gift. Yet, while the gracious gift of saving faith "is entirely undeserved," it is "strongly obliging," compelling believers to live the new life in Christ that "they have been given." Obedience is not instrumental to salvation, "but it is integral to the gift itself, as God wills [believers to] express in practice their freedom from sin and slavery." In short, it is possible to read Paul as saying that "without this obedience, grace is ineffective and unfulfilled."[75] Two centuries after Paul, Origen consistently emphasized "the intimate connection of faith and good works as the two complementary conditions of salvation." And "Origen's discussions of justification assisted later Catholic theologians in demonstrating the equal necessity of faith and postbaptismal good works for justification."[76]

Eastern Orthodoxy has long maintained a similar view. A recent example is from the *OSB*: "Some have erroneously interpreted Paul, particularly in Romans 4, to be condemning all works. A careful reading of Romans, however, reveals Paul is not putting down works in general, but *dead works"*—either the halakic regulations and performances of the now-fulfilled law of Moses or preconversion "works of the flesh." Paul's real message is that "being forgiven comes by God's mercy through repentance, faith, and humility, not by works of the law." In an excursus entitled "Justification by Faith," the *OSB* sounds a note quite similar to the thoughts of Joseph Smith and Orson Pratt: "Justification by faith, though not the major New Testament doctrine for Orthodox as it is for Protestants, poses no problem. But justification by faith *alone* brings up an objection. It contradicts Scripture, which says, 'You see then that a man is justified by works, and not by faith only' (Jas 2:24). We are 'justified by faith apart from the deeds of the law,' but nowhere does the Bible say we are justified by faith 'alone.' On the contrary, 'faith by itself, if it does not have works, is dead' (Jas 2:17)."[77] An older Anglican Arminian tradition epitomized by George Bull's seventeenth-century *Harmonia Apostolica* stakes out a similar

75. John M. G. Barclay, *Paul and the Gift* (Grand Rapids: Eerdmans, 2015), 473, 518–19. See also Barclay's earlier *Obeying the Truth: A Study of Paul's Ethics in Galatians* (Edinburgh: T&T Clark, 1988).

76. Thomas P. Scheck, *Origen and the History of Justification: The Legacy of Origen's Commentary on Romans* (Notre Dame: University of Notre Dame Press, 2008), 11–12.

77. *OSB*, 1529.

position with which Latter-day Saints would also agree: Paul rejects "ritual works prescribed by the ceremonial law" and "moral works performed by the natural powers of man," but repentance and such "moral works" as are enabled by the grace of God do "efficaciously conduce to the justification of man and his eternal salvation, and so are absolutely necessary."[78]

The Latter-day Saint perception is that once individuals have been awakened to their spiritual predicament and see Christ as the only solution, it is inevitable that they feel a godly sorrow and, by grace-aided repentance, strive to turn away from the past. Further, it is natural that they desire to signify their repentance by symbolically burying the "old man" of sin in the waters of baptism and coming forth to a "newness of life" in Christ (Rom. 6:3–11). These responses are what makes faith in Jesus Christ faith and what generates the "wonderful exchange" of justification. They are not distinct good deeds that deserve or merit justification. There is no cause-and-effect relationship here. No human action in and of itself can "merit" justification; Christ is the sole meritorious cause of justification. In the words of the Book of Mormon, justification simply cannot occur "save it be through the merits, and mercy, and grace of the Holy Messiah" (2 Nephi 2:8). Though God enables cooperation with grace, humans still have to do the cooperating. This is hardly works righteousness. Believers who understand the nature of justification do not say to God, "Look at all the good works I have done. These certainly entitle me to have my sins forgiven. You owe me this." No comprehending Christian— Mormon, Orthodox, or otherwise—thinks of justification in this way.

JUSTIFICATION AS SANCTIFICATION

In the final decades of the twentieth century, scholars and clerics from the Lutheran World Federation and the Roman Catholic Church met repeatedly in a sustained effort to reconsider their centuries-old differences regarding justification. Eventually they issued the landmark *Joint Declaration on the Doctrine of Justification (JDDJ)*.[79] In it "a distinction but not a separation" is affirmed "between justification itself and the [sanctifying] renewal of one's way of life that necessarily follows from justification." In other words, those who are justified by faith are thereafter to continue to "live by faith" and "must constantly

---

78. Quoted in Hampton, *Anti-Arminians*, 58. See also Tyacke, "From Laudians to Latitudinarians," 46–67.

79. The Lutheran World Federation and the Roman Catholic Church, *Joint Declaration on the Doctrine of Justification* (Grand Rapids: Eerdmans, 1997).

hear God's promises anew, confess their sins (1 John 1:9), participate in Christ's body and blood, and be exhorted to live righteously in accord with the will of God. That is why the Apostle says to the justified: 'Work out your own salvation with fear and trembling.'" Initially in justification, "we are accepted by God and receive the Holy Spirit." Going forward, the Holy Spirit "renews our hearts while equipping and calling us to good works." Indeed, the apostle Paul speaks of "the obedience that comes from faith" (Rom 1:5 NIV). Thus, justified Christians are "active in love" and "cannot and should not remain without works" in their lives, though this gives them no cause to boast before God.[80] Such statements closely parallel the Latter-day Saint perspective. Moreover, all Christian theologies anticipate that in the end any who are received into God's presence will need to have been ontically purged of sinfulness and made holy or glorified. Hebrews enjoins, "Follow . . . holiness, without which no man shall see the Lord" (Heb. 12:14). As Revelation makes clear, those admitted to the eschatological "marriage supper of the Lamb" will be "arrayed in fine linen, clean and white: for the fine linen is the righteousness of saints" (Rev. 19:7–9).

Disagreement among Christians, however, arises as to when and how this spiritual renewal will take place. On one end of the spectrum are those who see no real transformation of fallen Christians into ontically righteous beings until they are admitted to heaven. For these Christian theologies, as it was for Luther, justification is primarily forensic, reflecting God's favorable view of redeemed humanity made possible by the *admirabile commercium* effected by Christ. Toward the other end of the continuum are Catholic, Orthodox, Mormon, and Wesleyan theologies that expect some degree of actual sin-cleansing purification and positive growth in holiness in the believer during earth life. As to how such sanctification occurs, Calvin writes that the Holy Spirit "dwells in us and by his power the lusts of our flesh are each day more and more mortified; we are indeed sanctified, that is, consecrated to the Lord in true purity of life, with our hearts formed to obedience to [divine] law."[81] Traditional Catholic theology perceived sanctification as a process that begins at baptism as the Spirit infuses into the believer through participation in God a strengthening *habitus*, typically understood as a lasting disposition, inclination, or propensity toward charity and godlikeness.[82] Sanctification is thus

---

80. *JDDJ*, pars. 12, 15, 25, 26 (pp. 14–15, 19).

81. Calvin, *Institutes* 3.14.9.

82. "The roots of *habitus* are found in Aristotle's notion of *hexis*, elaborated in his doctrine of virtue, meaning an acquired yet entrenched state of moral character that orients our feelings and desires in a situation, and thence our actions. The term was translated into Latin as *habitus* (past participle of the verb *habere*, to have or hold) in the thirteenth century

effected by a lifelong collaboration or synergism between Spirit and *habitus* that actually transforms human nature, conforming it ever more to the image of Christ (Rom. 8:29). Thus, the "graced movement of the elect toward God" is understood to be gradual and progressive.[83]

This long-term, progressively sanctifying dimension of justification is typically referred to in the East as "theosis" and by some in the West as "deification."[84] As Orthodox priest-theologian John McGuckin writes, "Orthodoxy uses the stark term *theosis* in order to connote just what a radical transfiguration of the old human nature has been brought about."[85] And the transformation happens gradually, progressively. "This concept of salvation as process is crucial. Unlike the later Protestant tradition, particularly the evangelical tradition, which tends to view salvation as a discrete, easily identifiable event . . . theosis (salvation) in Eastern Christianity is *process*."[86] Latter-day Saint doctrine, as will be seen, echoes this emphasis. Despite the ontic nature of theosis, or sanctifying justification, the transformation effected, even in the Orthodox view, is understood to be modest in comparison with its final culmination in glorification or deification (the Mormon view of theosis/deification is discussed at length in chapter 12). The Eastern understanding is that it "is a process that will lead to union with God in part in this life and in full in the life to come."[87] Moreover, human holiness, while regarded as intrinsic and ontic, is never viewed as entirely one's own possession in the sense that the individual has complete control over it, disposing it at will. One's righteousness is dependent on Christ just as the baby is connected to its mother by an umbilical cord. The baby's health is an internal, physiological reality, but it is entirely dependent on the mother, who is the constant and sole supplier of life-sustaining nourishment. Without the umbilical connection, the infant would soon die. Without union with Christ,

by Thomas Aquinas." Jens Beckert and Milan Zafirovski, eds., *International Encyclopedia of Economic Sociology* (Oxford: Routledge, 2006), s.v. "habitus."

83. Daria Spezzano, *The Glory of God's Grace: Deification according to St. Thomas Aquinas* (Naples, FL: Sapienta Press of Ave Maria University, 2015), 3.

84. "Deification" encompasses a variety of Christian understandings as to its nature and means of achievement. See Daniel Keating, "Typologies of Deification," *International Journal of Systematic Theology* 17 (2015): 267–83. Western appreciation for a doctrine of deification has increased noticeably in the past generation, particularly in the twenty-first century. See Paul Gavrilyuk, "The Retrieval of Deification: How a Once-Despised Archaism Became an Ecumenical Desideratum," *Modern Theology* 25 (October 2009): 647–59.

85. McGuckin, *Orthodox Church*, 154.

86. Bryn Geffert and Theofanis G. Stavrou, *Eastern Orthodox Christianity: The Essential Texts* (New Haven: Yale University Press, 2016), 133.

87. Geffert and Stavrou, *Eastern Orthodox Christianity*, 133.

there would be no saving righteousness in human beings, and they, too, per Athanasius, would eventually dis-integrate spiritually and physically.

During and after the two transatlantic "Great Awakenings" of the eighteenth and nineteenth centuries, respectively, some Christians spoke boldly of the regenerative power of conversion that occurred at revivals, describing it as a spiritual rebirth that brought genuine sanctity into the life of the convert. For Methodism and similar Protestant traditions, "regeneration was the subjective correlate of justification. It was the inner event that accompanied the divine pardon, the inward change from the love of sin to the love of God, the supernatural bestowing of a new heart."[88] Although Latter-day Saints have always been wary of revivals, there are echoes of such Methodist/pietist views in the Book of Mormon. The dramatic conversion accounts of Alma or King Benjamin's people recited earlier are prime examples. Benjamin responded to his people's experience in these words: "This day [Christ] hath spiritually begotten you; for ye say that your hearts are changed through faith on his name; therefore, ye are born of him and have become his sons and his daughters" (Mosiah 5:7).

Although some Book of Mormon accounts seem to imply an instantaneous, completely regenerative conversion at the outset of one's turn to the Lord, other passages make clear that spiritual rebirth is merely the beginning of the process of sanctification. Thus, although King Benjamin's converts proclaimed that the Spirit "has wrought a mighty change in us, or in our hearts, that we have no more disposition to do evil, but to do good continually" (Mosiah 5:2), the king still urged them to "be steadfast and immovable, always abounding in good works, that Christ, the Lord God Omnipotent, may seal you his, that you may be brought to heaven, that ye may have everlasting salvation and eternal life" (Mosiah 5:15). For Latter-day Saints, spiritual rebirth and reception of the sacraments of Christian initiation merely constitute the "gate" by which one enters the "strait and narrow path" (2 Nephi 31:17–18).[89] After that, the new Christian must synergistically "press forward with a steadfastness in Christ, having a perfect brightness of hope, and a love of God and of all men." Unless they thus "endure to the end, in following the example of the Son of the living God, [they] cannot be saved" (2 Nephi 31:20, 16). Full sanctification requires the initial sacraments of baptism and reception of the Holy Ghost along with subsequent, lifelong synergistic collaboration with the Holy Spirit.

The Latter-day Saint perspective on sanctification as gradual and progressive resembles the teachings of Pentecostals, Catholics, Orthodox, and oth-

88. Holifield, *Theology in America*, 269.
89. "Being born again comes by the Spirit of God through ordinances [sacraments]," declared Joseph Smith. *JSP*, D6:548.

ers for whom baptism admits catechumens into the body of Christ and the "state of grace" in which they can grow and progress for the rest of their lives. Augustine reasoned that if "a completely new condition were brought about in baptism, the Apostle would not say . . . *the interior human being is being renewed from day to day* (2 Cor 4:16). Certainly those who are still being renewed from day to day have not been wholly renewed" or regenerated.[90] Even for the Reformers, there was "an implicit distinction between the effectual infusion of regenerating grace [coincident with justification], which is instantaneous, and the gradual manifestation of it, understood as the actualization of gracious habits."[91] From this perspective, being born again is more about a first stage of regeneration than about immediate, total transformation. In his resistance to the revivalist tendencies of the day, Horace Bushnell, an influential nineteenth-century American theologian, argued emphatically in his *Discourses on Christian Nurture* (1847) that the most lasting conversions to Christ occurred gradually through gospel teaching and spiritual nurture.[92]

Such views came to dominate Mormon thinking in the twentieth century. To be sure, the importance of spiritual rebirth is forthrightly affirmed. Still quoted is Alma's declaration "that all mankind . . . must be born again; yea, born of God, changed from their carnal and fallen state, to a state of righteousness . . . and unless they do this, they can in nowise inherit the kingdom of God" (Mosiah 27:25-26). While this description and related phrases such as the "mighty change" (Mosiah 5:2; Alma 5:12) sound like the regeneration that some Christian theologies envision accompanying initial conversion, experience on the ground eventually led Latter-day Saints to acknowledge that these depictions could only truly apply to a sanctified state into which one enters progressively over a long period of time. Apostle Bruce McConkie clarified for his Mormon audience, "Being born again is a gradual thing. . . . As far as the generality of the members of the Church are concerned, we are born again by degrees."[93] President Ezra Taft Benson taught that "becoming Christlike is a

90. Augustine, *The Punishment and Forgiveness of Sins and the Baptism of Little Ones* 2.9, in *Answer to the Pelagians, I*, trans. Roland J. Teske, Works of Saint Augustine: A Translation for the 21st Century (Hyde Park, NY: New City, 1997), 86. Augustine repeatedly construed the "washing of regeneration" (Titus 3:5) as water baptism.

91. William K. B. Stoever, *"A Faire and Easie Way to Heaven": Covenant Theology and Antinomianism in Early Massachusetts* (Middleton, CT: Wesleyan University Press, 1978), 219.

92. Horace Bushnell, *Discourses on Christian Nurture* (Boston: Massachusetts Sabbath School Society, 1847). For a range of such sentiments across American theological history, see Holifield, *Theology in America*, 85-87, 150, 212, 218, 248-50, 454-56.

93. Bruce R. McConkie, "Jesus Christ and Him Crucified," in *1976 Brigham Young University Devotional Speeches of the Year* (Provo, UT: BYU Publications, 1977), 399.

lifetime pursuit and very often involves growth and change that is slow, almost imperceptible. The scriptures record remarkable accounts of men whose lives changed dramatically, in an instant, as it were. . . . But we must be cautious as we discuss these remarkable examples. Though they are real and powerful, they are the exception more than the rule." For the vast majority of the faithful, "day by day they move closer to the Lord, little realizing they are building a godlike life."[94] If in LDS scripture or past experience spiritual rebirth and the "mighty change" sometimes described a single, dramatic event, Latter-day Saint teaching today has moved decidedly toward characterizing such terms as primarily having reference to the gradual, almost imperceptible, process of spiritual development and sanctification that takes place synergistically throughout the faithful disciple's earthly pilgrimage.

Here the Latter-day Saint experience invites comparison with Holiness-Pentecostal debates as to whether sanctification is primarily "crisis" or "process." That is, does holiness come in a series of definite, datable, extraordinary events in the life of the believer, a series of dramatic "mighty change" moments in which the disposition to do evil is overcome? Or, is it a gradual, more subtle process of pursuing and experiencing incremental growth in holiness with the ongoing aid of the Holy Spirit? For those in the Holiness-Pentecostal movement who embrace the traditional milestone-moments view of sanctification, the question has been whether they all happen at once at conversion in conjunction with being born of water and spirit, as is the doctrine of Oneness Pentecostals and seems to parallel the dramatic conversion accounts in the Book of Mormon. Or, is there a second, subsequent work of sanctification—the "second blessing," "Christian perfection," or "baptism in the Spirit" that purifies the soul? Or, is there yet a third work of grace that separates out baptism with the Holy Ghost as a culminating work that dramatically empowers the believer to be a powerful instrument in the Lord's hand, equipped with the extraordinary gifts of the Spirit to perform a mighty ministry on his behalf? Some answer yes to all of the above and see sanctification as an ongoing process punctuated periodically by a series of extraordinary spiritual boosts.

What of LDS doctrine? On the one hand, its sacramental interpretation of John 3:5—"Except a man be born of water and of the Spirit"—views spiritual rebirth as a metaphor for receiving baptism and confirmation (see chapter 9). Yet, as we have seen, LDS discourse additionally deploys images of spiritual rebirth and "mighty change" to convey a sense of deepening, ongoing sanctification that truly turns the individual into a "new creature" in Christ (2 Cor. 5:17). The same duality of meaning is also apparent regarding "conversion." In LDS teaching,

94. Ezra Taft Benson, "A Mighty Change of Heart," *Ensign*, October 1989, 5.

the term often refers to becoming a member of Christ's church as a result of "receiving a witness" or "gaining a testimony" of the truthfulness of the good news about Jesus Christ and his earthly kingdom. "Conversion," though, in its fullest, deepest sense is another way of describing the process of sanctification. Testimony is an inaugural "gift from God," explains apostle David Bednar. "Conversion is an enlarging, a deepening, and a broadening of the undergirding base of testimony." It is a lifelong process of transformation and sanctification. "Line upon line and precept upon precept, gradually and almost imperceptibly our motives, our thoughts, our words, and our deeds become aligned with the will of God. Conversion unto the Lord requires both persistence and patience."[95] For Latter-day Saints, as for other Christians, this conceptual and experiential interplay between the initial and the ongoing, whether in terms of conversion and spiritual rebirth or the relationship between justification and sanctification, points to an entire life of growing in grace for those united to Christ. Some theologies depict this in monergistic terms; others see it synergistically.

Consider the Mormon doctrine of "endurance to the end." It is synergistic in contrast to the Augustinian-Calvinist conception of a monergistically realized "perseverance of the saints." LDS doctrine contemplates a life of grace-aided growth in holiness that brings ever fuller sanctification as believers follow their divine Exemplar, Jesus Christ, who they believe "continued from grace to grace, until he received a fullness" (D&C 93:13). A call for synergistic collaboration with the gift of divine grace is expressed in Paul's plea to the Corinthians: "As we work together with him, we urge you also not to accept the grace of God in vain" (2 Cor. 6:1 NRSV). In ways that resonate with Mormon doctrine, such exhortation to profit from God's gracious gift and experience a deepening conversion to Christ is captured well in John Wesley's notable sermon "The Almost Christian." For Wesley, the "almost Christian" was the Anglican (and one could insert Mormon here) who had an outward "form of godliness," doing "nothing which the gospel forbids," "frequent[ing] the house of God," and performing "all manner of good, to all men," but who has not truly experienced the gracious gifts of charity or pure love of God and trusting faith in Christ. For the outwardly conforming "almost" Christian (or Latter-day Saint), Wesley asked, "The great question of all, then, still remains. Is the love of God shed abroad in your heart? Can you cry out, 'My God and my

---

95. David A. Bednar, "Converted unto the Lord," *Ensign*, November 2012, 106–7; see also Bednar, "Ye Must Be Born Again," *Ensign*, May 2007, 19–22. First Presidency member Henry B. Eyring declared that conversion "will not be a single event or something that will last for just one season of life but will be a continuing process." Eyring, "Testimony and Conversion," *Ensign*, February 2015, 5.

All!' Do you desire nothing but him? . . . Is he your glory, your delight, your crown of rejoicing?"⁹⁶ And here we return to Alma's similar interrogatories about the deeper meaning of conversion and spiritual rebirth: "Now behold, I ask of you, my brethren of the church, have ye spiritually been born of God? Have ye received his image in your countenances? Have ye experienced this mighty change in your hearts . . . have [ye] felt to sing the song of redeeming love . . . I say unto you, if ye [have] not ye are not prepared to meet God" (Alma 5:14, 26, 28).

Mormon belief in such progressive, deepening sanctification is sufficiently robust that it has sometimes been characterized as "perfectionism" and bears similarities to other theologies that take seriously Jesus's injunction "be ye therefore perfect" (Matt. 5:48). Here one thinks again of Wesleyan Holiness doctrine and Pentecostal theologies of sanctification. The salvific journey moves from an initial outpouring of regenerating divine love to dramatic moments of "entire sanctification" and glory-filled "spirit baptism" to continued growth in grace until the final, full renewal in the image of Christ.⁹⁷ For Catholics, the Apostolic Constitution *Lumen Gentium* proclaims that "all Christians" are "called to the fullness of Christian life and to the perfection of charity," adding that "in order to reach this perfection the faithful should use the strength dealt out to them by Christ's gift so that . . . they may wholeheartedly devote themselves to the glory of God and to the service of their neighbor."⁹⁸ Pope John Paul II described the Christian life in words that might have been expressed at any LDS general conference: Christian discipleship is "the believer's personal journey in the footsteps of the Redeemer: it is an exercise of practical asceticism, of repentance for human weaknesses, of constant vigilance over one's own frailty." Through acts of love toward God and humankind, "the pilgrim progresses along the path of Christian perfection, striving to attain, with the support of God's grace, 'the state of the perfect man, to the measure of the full maturity of Christ' (Eph 4:13)."⁹⁹ John Wesley came to espouse what he variously called "Christian perfection," "entire sanctification," or "perfect love." When one has the "mind of Christ" (1 Cor. 2:16) and is motivated by the grace of *agapē* (Christlike love; translated as "charity"

96. Albert C. Outler and Richard P. Heitzenrater, eds., *John Wesley's Sermons: An Anthology* (Nashville: Abingdon, 1991), 61–68.

97. See Frank D. Macchia, *Tongues of Fire: A Systematic Theology of the Christian Faith* (Eugene, OR: Cascade, 2023), 286–318, and Dale M. Coulter, "Sanctification," in *The Routledge Handbook of Pentecostal Theology*, ed. Wolfgang Vondey (London: Routledge, 2020), 237–46.

98. Quoted in CCC 2013.

99. *Incarnationis Mysterium*, 8, in *Pope John Paul II: A Reader*, ed. Gerald O'Collins et al. (New York: Paulist, 2007), 242.

in the KJV), Wesley believed that entire sanctification, in the sense of being wholly devoted to God, was possible. Wesley taught that the very roots of the *disposition* to sin could be destroyed and replaced by "perfect love" of God and man. This, however, could not prevent a "thousand mistakes"—inadvertent sins or transgressions growing out of ignorance—endemic to human frailty even in the sanctified.[100]

Likewise, Latter-day Saints have never affirmed the possibility of sinless perfection in this life, but they are enjoined to "love and serve God with all their mights, minds, and strength" (D&C 20:31), and to "offer [their] whole souls as an offering unto him" (Omni 1:26). These statements parallel Wesleyan (and other Christian) conceptions of sanctification as involving complete surrender to God. The Book of Mormon describes people who sought such holiness in these words: "They did fast and pray oft, and did wax stronger and stronger in their humility, and firmer and firmer in the faith of Christ . . . even to the purifying and the sanctification of their hearts, which sanctification cometh because of their yielding their hearts unto God" (Helaman 3:35). Thus, an entreaty included in the final chapter of the Book of Mormon is consonant with perspectives on sanctification found in many Christian traditions: "Come unto Christ, and be perfected in him, and deny yourselves of all ungodliness; and if ye shall deny yourselves of all ungodliness, and love God with all your might, mind and strength, then is his grace sufficient for you, that by his grace ye may be perfect in Christ" (Moroni 10:32).

GRACE AND WORKS

What one scholar has called "the controversy of the centuries" is the matter of deciding the proper relationship between grace and works.[101] Because Mormonism has sometimes been characterized as overemphasizing works and underemphasizing grace, it is important in this final section of the chapter to

100. John Wesley, *A Plain Account of Christian Perfection* (1777; reprint, London: Methodist Publishing, 2007). A useful overview of Wesley's doctrine of Christian perfection is William J. Abraham, "Christian Perfection," in Abraham and Kirby, *Oxford Handbook of Methodist Studies*, 587–601. A more extensive treatment is John Leland Peters, *Christian Perfection and American Methodism* (1956; reprint, Grand Rapids: Francis Asbury, 1985).

101. The quote is from Owen Chadwick, "Introduction," in *John Cassian Conferences*, trans. Colm Luibheid (New York: Paulist, 1985), 27. A useful if selective overview of Western Christian debates about grace is Edward T. Oakes, *A Theology of Grace in Six Controversies* (Grand Rapids: Eerdmans, 2016). Particularly valuable for the early centuries is Rebecca Harden Weaver, *Divine Grace and Human Agency* (Macon, GA: Mercer University Press, 1996). For Orthodoxy, see Jaroslav Pelikan, *The Christian Tradition: A History of the Development of Doctrine*, vol. 2, *The Spirit of Eastern Christendom (600–1700)* (Chicago: University of Chicago Press, 1974), passim.

CHAPTER 6

explore in some detail LDS thought on their relationship in the experience of salvation. When Joseph Smith emended Romans 4:16 to read: "Therefore ye are justified of faith *and* works, through grace," he presented a succinct, single-sentence summary of the Mormon position. Justification in its full, sanctifying sense is understood to be the result of both faith *and* works. As explained earlier, the two are organically linked and both are considered possible only "through grace." In somewhat different words, Joseph Smith later wrote, "We believe that through the Atonement of Christ all mankind may be saved by obedience to the laws and ordinances of the Gospel" (Articles of Faith 3). This statement is sometimes viewed as a declaration that although Christ's atonement makes salvation possible, it must be actualized by obedience to gospel laws and ordinances. This accurately reflects one aspect of LDS soteriology, but it is also true that the sentence can be read to mean that while faith-full obedience is essential to salvation, such obedience is only possible *through* the grace bestowed by the atonement of Jesus Christ. Joseph Smith clearly believed that every salvifically efficacious good work, every growth in godliness, and all aspects of the functioning of the church ultimately were only possible through divine grace. In the preface to the Book of Mormon, he wrote: "To be obedient unto the commandments of God, I have, through his grace and mercy, accomplished that which he hath commanded me respecting this thing."[102] Similarly, in the church's Articles and Covenants, Joseph Smith attributed his foundational ministry "to the grace of our Lord and Savior Jesus Christ, to whom be all glory, both now and forever" (D&C 20:4). Nor was it uncommon in Smith's correspondence with church members to petition the Lord that they might enjoy and grow in grace.[103] The prophet expressed deep appreciation for the sanctifying and empowering grace of Jesus Christ, "who has opened a way whereby [all] may come unto him, even by the sacrifice of himself." Such was the Saints' rejoicing, he noted, that "our hearts melt within us for [Christ's] condescension."[104]

The essentiality of grace for the Christian life and personal sanctification was a conviction also forcefully expressed by Joseph Smith's successors. Brigham Young declared, "In and of ourselves we have no power to control our own minds and passions; but the grace of God is sufficient to give us perfect victory."[105] In fact, added Young, "The best man that ever lived on this

102. "Preface," Book of Mormon, iv.
103. See, for instance, *JSP*, D1:176; D1:273; D3:6; D3:77.
104. *JSP*, D3:364.
105. *Journal of Discourses*, 8:226. Similarly, an early revelation declared, "My grace is

earth" can only "save himself through the grace of God. . . . It requires all the atonement of Christ, the mercy of the Father . . . and the grace of the Lord Jesus Christ to be with us always, and then to do the very best we possibly can, to get rid of this sin within us" and enter "into the celestial kingdom."[106] Church president John Taylor was equally emphatic: "We derive every blessing we enjoy, whether of a temporal or of a spiritual nature from our heavenly Father; and without him we can do or perform no good work, for in him 'we live and move and have our being,' and from him, and through him we receive all blessings pertaining to this life, and we shall hereafter, if we possess eternal lives, inherit them and obtain them through the goodness, mercy and long-suffering of God our Eternal Father, through the merits and redemption of Jesus Christ our Savior."[107]

Despite a pronounced emphasis on the essentiality of grace, considerable attention historically has also been given in Latter-day Saint discourse to the human side of the synergism of salvation. In this Mormon doctrine has echoed the *via moderna* teaching of certain medieval Catholic scholastics that salvation requires both the primacy of grace and the human need to *facere quod in se est* (do what [the best that] is in oneself).[108] At times, though, encouragement to do one's best has overshadowed an emphasis on grace. This seems to have been the result of several factors. First, as has been the case with many Christian clerics and ascetics over the centuries, the need for pastoral and practical exhortation sometimes takes precedence over ensuring theological balance. Perhaps a more important factor in the LDS case is the stunning potency of the notion that human souls are God's literal children, endowed with "seeds" of divinity. One early revelation counseled the Saints to be "anxiously engaged in a good cause, and do many things of their own free will, and bring to pass much righteousness; for," affirmed the revelation, "the power is in them" (D&C 58:27–28). This elevated anthropology (see chapter 5) was

---

sufficient for you; you must walk uprightly before me and sin not" (D&C 18:31). A Book of Mormon passage, echoing 2 Cor. 12:9, made the point that human "weaknesses" can be overcome because God's "grace is sufficient for all men that humble themselves before me; for if they humble themselves before me, and have faith in me, then will I make weak things become strong unto them" (Ether 12:27).

106. *Journal of Discourses*, 11:301.

107. *Journal of Discourses*, 19:301.

108. The LDS parallel is illustrated in a 1920s church editorial that commented, drawing attention to Phil. 2:12–13: "Although it is man's duty to work out his own salvation, and we emphasize that work strongly . . . yet, 'it is God which worketh in you both to will and to do.'" To be sure, Paul "was an indefatigable worker, but he was always conscious of the secret of all success—that in the last instance it comes from God." *Improvement Era*, March 1925, 483.

reinforced by the practical demands of colonization and community building in the American West during the second half of the nineteenth century. The need to establish their new Israel imbued Latter-day Saint preaching with a pragmatic "can-do" quality. Not surprisingly, Mormonism's decidedly synergistic view of salvation has sometimes been perceived as "Pelagian" for its (over-) emphasis on human striving at the expense of grace.[109] A sociologist who did extensive fieldwork among the Mormons in the 1950s went so far as to remark that in his view "Mormonism has elaborated an American theology of self-deification through effort, an active transcendentalism of achievement."[110]

Not to be excluded as part of the explanation for Mormonism's occasional overemphasis of the human side of synergism is the influence of similar attitudes that were widespread in the nineteenth century.[111] It seemed inconceivable to many in the boundlessness of the new republic that human beings were left so powerless by the fall, so completely devoid of any control over mind and will, that they could neither take the first steps toward God nor pursue holiness without supernatural intervention. Epitomized by the "New Haven theology" discussed in the previous chapter, such perspectives were popularized by the legendary evangelist Charles Finney. One of Finney's sermons was provocatively titled "Sinners Bound to Change Their Own Hearts." His text was Ezekiel 18:31—"Cast away from you all your transgressions, whereby ye have transgressed; and make you a new heart and a new spirit: for why will ye die, O house of Israel?"[112] Conversion, wrote Finney, is not an entirely passive act

109. Deploying "Pelagian" as an epithet to discredit one's opponent is an age-old practice that has continued more or less unabated since the original "Pelagian controversy" in the fifth century. As just one example, in a notable late medieval dispute over the meritoriousness of human actions, Thomas Bradwardine and especially Gregory of Rimini attacked synergist theologians of the day such as Duns Scotus and William of Ockham as "*Pelagiani moderni*" and "super-Pelagians" for "attributing too much to our powers and too little to God's grace." Ulrich G. Leinsle, *Introduction to Scholastic Theology*, trans. Michael J. Miller (Washington, DC: Catholic University of America Press, 2010), 231. See also Gordon Leff, *Bradwardine and the Pelagians* (Cambridge: Cambridge University Press, 1957). This soteriological tension continued for the next two centuries and received heightened attention during the Reformation and its aftermath.

110. Thomas F. O'Dea, *The Mormons* (Chicago: University of Chicago Press, 1957), 154.

111. Religious historian William G. McLoughlin argues that by the mid-nineteenth century, such views were so pervasive that they had become "in fact the national religion of the United States." McLoughlin, *Modern Revivalism: Charles Grandison Finney to Billy Graham* (New York: Ronald, 1959), 65–66.

112. Charles G. Finney, "Sermon 1—Sinners Bound to Change Their Own Hearts," in Finney, *Sermons on Important Subjects* (New York: John S. Taylor, 1836), 3–42.

in which the sinner is left "waiting for God to make him a new heart." It also requires an act of the will and a conscious turning toward God on the part of the sinner. Conversion is a synergism: "It is strictly true the act is his own act, the turning [to God] is his own turning, while God by the truth has induced him to turn; still it is strictly true that he has turned and has done it himself. Thus," concluded Finney, "you see the sense in which it is the work of God, and also the sense in which it is the sinner's own work."[113] In Finney's more technical *Lectures on Systematic Theology*, he wrote that "regeneration does not express or imply the creation of any new faculties or attributes of nature, nor any change whatever in the constitution of the body or mind." Adding a perfectionist note, the sinner, declared Finney, possesses "all the faculties and natural attributes requisite to render perfect obedience to God."[114]

Similar views were expressed by other contemporaries of Joseph Smith such as Protestant luminaries Lyman Beecher, Nathaniel W. Taylor, and Daniel Whedon. In an 1816 sermon, Taylor declared, "Men are as complete moral agents, as able to perform their duty, *if* they would, as Adam was before his fall." He further expounded his position in a tract titled "Man, a Free Agent without the Aids of Divine Grace."[115] His strong emphasis on moral agency did not mean he denied the work of the Holy Spirit, but he considered it an "influence" only. The Spirit did not change the individual's heart; it only helped him change his own heart. "The sinner, under its operation, chooses and acts just as voluntarily, as when he yields in any case to the solicitations of a friend."[116] Methodists in this period also affirmed the potency of human agency. Prominent professor and theologian Daniel Whedon "looked to the natural capacities of human nature to perform what 'prevenient grace' or 'grace ability' had accomplished for earlier Methodists. So solicitous was he of human freedom that divine grace faded nearly away: 'Man does not thereby receive any new faculty. He is not even organically *made* to be a free agent; for he never ceased to be such.'"[117] Whether in the modified Calvinism of Nathaniel Taylor, the Methodism of Daniel Whedon, the Lutheranism of Samuel Schmucker,

---

113. Finney, "Sinners Bound to Change Their Own Hearts," 23, 22.

114. Charles G. Finney, "Lecture XXXIX—Regeneration," in Finney, *Lectures on Systematic Theology* (Oberlin, OH: James M. Fitch, 1846), 494.

115. Quoted in Mark A. Noll, *America's God: From Jonathan Edwards to Abraham Lincoln* (New York: Oxford University Press, 2005), 279, 523n26.

116. Quoted in George M. Marsden, *The Evangelical Mind and the New School Presbyterian Experience: A Case Study of Thought and Theology in Nineteenth Century America* (New Haven: Yale University Press, 1970), 51 (49–51).

117. Noll, *America's God*, 358.

or the Mormonism of Joseph Smith, a more positive anthropology and more prominent role for human agency in the synergism of salvation seemed neither offensive to God nor antithetical to the fact that salvation is only in Christ. As John Wesley had earlier remarked, "How is it more for the glory of God to save man irresistibly, than to save him as a free agent, by such grace as he may either concur with or resist?"[118]

Latter-day Saints have always considered it crucial to Christian discipleship to be able to respond proactively to the numerous biblical exhortations to love and serve God and one's "neighbor." In their eyes, they seek to "walk worthy of the Lord unto all pleasing, being fruitful in every good work" (Col. 1:10) for Christ "gave himself for us, that he might . . . purify unto himself a peculiar people, zealous of good works" (Titus 2:14). Like Wesley, Mormons do not view such efforts as detracting from Deity. In the words of an LDS apostle, "the doctrine of work does not rob [God] of any of His glory." Furthermore, just as in life generally, "there is no advancement without effort." So, too, "in the spiritual world, in the development of our spirits, there is no growth without effort. There is no salvation without work."[119] Apostle David McKay, the man who made these remarks, was a young apostle in 1909 when he delivered this message at a general conference of the church. He would later serve in the church's First Presidency and eventually as president for nearly twenty years. Throughout his long ministry, he consistently promoted a synergistic view of salvation. McKay restated his position in the 1930s and again (almost verbatim) as church president in the 1950s: "To work out one's salvation [Phil. 2:12] is not to sit idly by dreaming and yearning for God miraculously to thrust bounteous blessings into our laps. It is to perform daily, hourly, momentarily, if necessary, the immediate task or duty at hand, and to continue happily in such performance as the years come and go." McKay was aware that some might charge him with overemphasizing human endeavor:

> I am not unmindful of the scripture that declares: "by grace are ye saved through faith; and that not of yourselves: it is the gift of God" [Eph. 2:8–9]. That is absolutely true, for man in his taking upon himself mortality was impotent to save himself. . . . But the Lord, through his grace, appeared to man, gave him the gospel or eternal plan whereby he might rise. . . . He who

118. Wesley, "Predestination Calmly Considered," 50, in *John Wesley*, ed. Albert C. Outler (New York: Oxford University Press, 1964), 449.

119. David O. McKay, *Conference Report*, October 1909, 90.

would ascend the stairway leading upward to eternal life must tread it step by step from the base stone to the summit of its flight.[120]

In light of Mormonism's pointed emphasis on human responsibility in the synergism of salvation, it is important to reiterate that such efforts are not considered salvifically meritorious in and of themselves. As has been noted, only Christ's atoning sacrifice merits, earns, and makes salvation possible for humankind. Acts of human responsiveness to and cooperation with divine grace such as repentance, participation in the sacraments, and obedience to Christ's commands may be considered part of the "instrumental cause" of salvation, but Latter-day Saints never consider them the "meritorious cause." Thus, from the Mormon perspective, "St. Paul is right . . . when he says: 'By grace are ye saved through faith.' And yet St. James is right when he says, 'By works a man is justified, and not by faith only'; for it is through a union of the grace of God and the faithful obedience of man that he at last shall see salvation."[121] At the end of the second decade of the twenty-first century, apostle Dale Renlund explained the path to salvation in this way: Salvation is "neither earned by frenetically accruing 'good deed coupons' nor by helplessly waiting to see if we win the blessing lottery. No, the truth is much more nuanced but more appropriate for the relationship between a loving Heavenly Father and His potential heirs . . . blessings are never earned, but faith-inspired actions on our part, both initial and ongoing, are essential."[122] Works are integral to, but not the cause of, salvation. Thomas Aquinas's thought on the matter is in fundamental agreement with LDS theology. Salvation entails "both the absolute causal primacy of God—operatively and cooperatively working through the grace of the Holy Spirit—and the proper instrumental causality of the graced human subject, whose intellect and will informed by the theological virtues and gifts are actively engaged in full freedom in their movement toward the end of beatitude [eternal blessedness]."[123]

Early in the twentieth century, apostle Orson Whitney endeavored to strike the appropriate balance between grace and works with an analogy that would become popular among Latter-day Saints—the image of a pit and a ladder: "When Adam fell," Whitney explained, "it was as if the human race had fallen into a pit, from which they were powerless, by any act of their own, to emerge;

---

120. McKay, *Conference Report*, April 1938, 18. See also *Conference Report*, April 1957, 7–8. Joseph Smith left Paul's strong message in Eph. 2:8–9 unchanged in his Bible revision.
121. "Editor's Table," *Improvement Era*, December 1897, 131.
122. Renlund, "Abound with Blessings," *Ensign*, May 2019, 70.
123. Spezzano, *Glory of God's Grace*, 4–5.

having no means whereby to climb up and out, and not even knowing how to climb. But a Friend, all-wise and all-powerful, comes to the mouth of the pit, compassionate to its wretched inmates, and proposes to rescue them from their unhappy situation. He makes of his own life a ladder, lets it down into the pit, and says: 'Now climb!'" For Latter-day Saints, the ladder of divine grace is not an escalator, nor is otherwise hapless humanity monergistically *carried* up the ladder by Christ. Whitney cites the usual Mormon favorites—"faith without works is dead" (James 2:20) and "work out your own salvation" (Phil. 2:12)—but he adds: "we work it out through Jesus Christ, and not independently of Him. WE DO NOT SAVE OURSELVES. We but avail ourselves of the means of salvation provided by our Lord and Savior, the God who died that man might live."[124] In the twenty-first century, apostle Jeffrey Holland chose an image from the Gospel of John to emphasize Whitney's point that it is only "through Jesus Christ, and not independently of Him," that we work out our salvation. John 15:5 preserves this image from Jesus: "I am the vine, ye are the branches: He that abideth in me, and I in him, the same bringeth forth much fruit: for without me ye can do nothing." Commented Holland, "Jesus said, 'Without me ye can do nothing.' I testify that that is God's truth. Christ is everything to us. . . . For the fruit of the gospel to blossom and bless our lives, we must be firmly attached to Him. . . . He is the vine that is our true source of strength and the only source of eternal life. In Him we not only will endure but also will prevail and triumph in [His] holy cause."[125]

In reality, little is different here from the confessions of the major Christian faiths. The Catholic *Catechism*, for instance, states: "Christ's gift of salvation offers us the grace necessary to persevere in the pursuit of the virtues. Everyone should always ask for this grace of light and strength, frequent the sacraments, cooperate with the Holy Spirit, and follow his calls to love what is good and shun evil."[126] This synergistically cooperative pursuit of sanctity and

124. Orson F. Whitney, *Conference Report*, October 1927, 149. Whitney first introduced the analogy of the ladder in *Conference Report*, April 1908, 149. In the twenty-first century, another church leader attempted a different analogy, using a sky jump and parachute as his imagery: "When we sin, we are like the foolish man who jumped from the plane. No matter what we do on our own, only a crash-landing awaits us. We are subject to the law of justice, which, like the law of gravity, is exacting and unforgiving. We can be saved only because the Savior, through His Atonement, mercifully provides us with a spiritual parachute of sorts. If we have faith in Jesus Christ and repent (meaning we do our part and pull the rip cord), then the protective powers of the Savior are unleashed on our behalf and we can land spiritually unharmed." Tad R. Callister, "The Atonement of Jesus Christ," *Ensign*, May 2019, 85.
125. Jeffrey R. Holland, "Abide in Me," *Ensign*, May 2004, 32.
126. *CCC* 1810–1811.

eternal life "arises from the fact that God has freely chosen to associate man with the work of his grace . . . and then follows man's free acting through his collaboration, so that the merit of good works is to be attributed in the first place to the grace of God, then to the faithful. Man's merit, moreover, itself is due to God, for his good actions proceed in Christ, from the predispositions and assistance given by the Holy Spirit."[127] Not only do Latter-day Saints agree with such statements, but upon reflection they would likely even concur with Augustine's famous aphorism that, in a sense, on judgment day, "when God crowns our merits, he only crowns his own gifts."[128] Latter-day Saints likewise might be willing to include their name alongside Catholics in this *JDDJ* statement: "When Catholics affirm the 'meritorious' character of good works, they wish to say that, according to the biblical witness, a reward in heaven is promised to these works. Their intention is to emphasize the responsibility of persons for their actions, not to contest the character of those works as gifts, or far less to deny that justification always remains the unmerited gift of grace."[129] In these forms of synergism, good works are rewarded with eternal blessings because God promised they would be, not because of some inherent quality that enables the worker to enter heaven independent of God's graciousness. Regardless of the quality or quantity of good works, in and of themselves, they are never commensurate with the gift of eternal life in God's presence.

Medieval scholastic theology worked out a fine-grained distinction between the merit of an unbeliever's morally upright behavior that is "congruent" with God's goodness and the merit of good works performed by a Christian in cooperation with habitual grace. The latter graced works were considered "condign," or equal to and deserving of the promised divine reward. While such a meritology is not found in Mormonism, LDS scripture does make a distinction between good works in general and those performed with divinely assisted "real intent." It has long been recognized in many Christian traditions that motive and "heart-set" are what distinguish ordinary ethical behavior from salvifically efficacious good works. Because human motives are mixed, often self-serving in their quest for recognition or reward, they fall short. Only when one's actions are motivated by a grace-inspired love of God are they salvifically beneficial. The Book of Mormon declares that if a person "offereth

---

127. CCC 2008.

128. Augustine, Letter 194.5.19, in *Letters 156–210*, ed. and trans. Roland Teske, Works of St. Augustine (Hyde Park, NY: New City, 2004), 296. This statement is repeated in the Roman Missal—*Praefatio I de Sanctis*.

129. *JDDJ*, par. 38 (p. 25).

a gift, or prayeth unto God, except he shall do it with real intent it profiteth him nothing. For behold, it is not counted unto him for righteousness . . . for God receiveth none such." The text even goes so far as to state that a work performed without real intent "is counted evil unto a man," and that such persons are "counted evil before God" (Moroni 7:6–9). Although never explicitly stated as such, the presumption is that "real intent" is a graced disposition. As previously noted, following their conversion experience, King Benjamin's people credit "the Spirit of the Lord Omnipotent" as having "wrought a mighty change" in them, or in their hearts, that they had "no more disposition to do evil, but to do good continually" (Mosiah 5:2). Elsewhere in the Book of Mormon, in a passage that parallels Paul's declaration in 2 Corinthians 9:8, "God is able to make all grace abound toward you; that ye . . . may abound to every good work," Alma taught his followers that the theological or cardinal virtues—"faith, hope, and charity"—would enable them to "always abound in good works" (Alma 7:24). While the divine source of these virtues is implicit, Alma's gloss begins with the synergistic urging to "see that ye have" them.

Eastern Orthodoxy maintains a similarly synergistic position. The Reformation "raised the question for the Orthodox East: Why this new polarization of faith and works? It had been settled since the apostolic era that salvation was granted by the mercy of God to righteous men and women. Those baptized into Christ were called to believe in Him *and* do good works. An opposition of faith *versus* works was unprecedented in Orthodox thought."[130] Patristic scholar Patout Burns says the same of the major early commentaries on Romans, whether written in the Greek East or Latin West: "Both faith and works were taken as necessary for righteousness by all commentators."[131] In the Orthodox view, good works "are both good in themselves and done for a good purpose—the glory of God." They are also synergistically accomplished: "When we do living works, we rely on the strength and grace of God."[132] Moreover, we "nurture" our "love for Him through our works," and salvation "is impossible unless you acquire love for Him through your works."[133] In truth, most Protestants do not disagree with such views, as even Martin Luther makes clear in his *Treatise on Good Works*.[134] Later English Puritans "demanded theological concern for the human will. . . . Without denying the objective, purely gracious character

130. *OSB*, 1529.

131. J. Patout Burns Jr., *Romans: Interpreted by Early Christian Commentators* (Grand Rapids: Eerdmans, 2012), 62.

132. *OSB*, 1601.

133. *OSB*, 1676.

134. Martin Luther, *Treatise on Good Works*, trans. Scott H. Hendrix (1520; reprint, Minneapolis: Fortress, 2012).

of God's redemptive acts, they wished also to make a place for the willing, knowing, repenting, thanking, loving acts of the human person."[135] Relevant also is John Wesley's sermon "On Working Out Our Own Salvation," which is regarded as his "most complete and careful exposition of the mystery of divine-human interaction, his subtlest probing of the paradox of prevenient grace and human agency." In that sermon, Wesley taught that because "God works, therefore you *can* work; God works; therefore you *must* work." In other words, God's grace both enables us and obliges us to cooperate synergistically.[136]

To be sure, despite the prevalence of such perspectives among Christians, some conservative Protestant theologians consider any notion of a human role in the salvation process as an affront to God's salvific omnipotence and a detraction from his glory. The so-called partitive criticism of synergism is that it supposedly divides agency in, and "credit" for, righteous acts between God and believer and implies an equal partnership between two asymmetrical acting subjects. Yet, this is neither the dominant theological view nor the perspective from the pew of most Christians, including Latter-day Saints.[137] An interesting barometer for twentieth-century Mormon views on the relationship between divine grace and human effort is the mixed LDS reaction to the famous late nineteenth-century poem "Invictus," penned by British Anglican author and poet William Henley. Henley refused to be defeated by a crippling disease and composed these lines to express his inner resolve:

> Out of the night that covers me,
> Black as the Pit from pole to pole,
> I thank whatever Gods may be
> For my unconquerable soul.
> In the fell clutch of circumstance
> I have not winced nor cried aloud,
> Under the bludgeonings of chance

135. Sydney Ahlstrom, "Theology in America," in *The Shaping of American Religion*, ed. James Ward Smith and A. Leland Jamison (Princeton: Princeton University Press, 1961), 240.

136. John Wesley, "On Working Out Our Own Salvation," in Outler, *Works of John Wesley*, 3:199–209.

137. One study determined that "the most prevalent and popular assumption about heaven" in the United States in the late twentieth century was that it "is earned by the ethical and upright." Quoted in Gary Scott Smith, *Heaven in the American Imagination* (New York: Oxford University Press, 2011), 6. Despite a general soteriological conservatism among evangelical theologians, a survey taken in 2014 of more than 550 self-identified American evangelicals indicated that 56 percent held the synergistic belief that "people must contribute their own effort for personal salvation." "Evangelicals' Favorite Heresies," Christianitytoday .com, November 2014.

My head is bloody, but unbowed. . . .
It matters not how strait the gate,
How charged with punishment the scroll,
I am the master of my fate:
I am the captain of my soul.[138]

Given Mormonism's robust doctrine of free will and its strong encouragement toward independence and self-reliance in everyday life, many Latter-day Saints, including some church leaders, resonated with the poem, particularly the final two lines. A general authority in the 1930s, for instance, quoted the concluding quatrain and affirmed, "this is the condition of every man and woman in the world."[139] Another remarked that "such a philosophy, if universally adopted, would soon transform our world into God's paradise." But soteriologically, it was unsatisfactory. Orson Whitney, while admiring the poem's commitment to human drive and determination, composed a poetic response which in the context of Christ's redemption challenged Henley's final line—"I am the captain of my soul":

Art thou in truth? Then what of him
Who bought thee with his blood?
Who plunged into devouring seas
And snatched thee from the flood?
Who bore for all our fallen race
What none but him could bear.—
The God who died that man might live,
And endless glory share?
Of what avail thy vaunted strength,
Apart from his vast might?
Pray that his Light may pierce the gloom,
That thou mayest see aright.
Men are as bubbles on the wave,
As leaves upon the tree.
Thou, captain of thy soul, forsooth!
Who gave that place to thee?
Free will is thine—free agency,
To wield for right or wrong;

138. William Ernest Henley, *Poems* (London: D. Nutt, 1898), 119.
139. Samuel O. Bennion, *Conference Report*, April 1932, 17.

But thou must answer unto him
To whom all souls belong.
Bend to the dust that head "unbowed,"
Small part of Life's great whole!
And see in him, and him alone,
The Captain of thy soul.[140]

As compelling as Whitney's poem is, it received little attention in the years following its 1926 publication.[141] The poem's emphasis on Christ's primary role in the synergism of salvation—"of what avail thy vaunted strength, / Apart from his vast might?"—did not coincide with the pastoral emphasis on human striving still dominant in Mormonism in the first half of the twentieth century. In the second half of the century, however, particularly during its final decades when a conscious effort was under way, as previously noted, to highlight the enabling grace of Jesus Christ, Whitney's poem, rather than Henley's, was more serviceable.

What, then, in the Mormon estimation is the ideal characterization of the relationship between grace and works, between divine empowerment and human endeavor? Despite some variation in emphasis over the years, Latter-day Saint soteriology, particularly as it is being articulated in the twenty-first century, bears striking resemblance to the views of John Cassian, a monk who lived some sixteen hundred years ago in what is today southern France.[142] Cassian's perspective is aptly and eloquently summarized by prominent Christian historian Owen Chadwick: "The soul is always at the mercy of God. It is helpless without His help. Man is free to choose. You must exercise your moral judgment. You must try. You must discipline yourself. But still the soul is helpless without God. The grace of God must help you to begin, continue, and end. Purity of heart is a gift, not an achievement. Still, you must try." Where Augustine and those in his tradition interpreted the gospel message to be (for the predestined elect) "rest in me and *I* will do it," Cassian taught

140. Orson F. Whitney, "The Soul's Captain," *Improvement Era*, May 1926, 611.

141. Whitney's poem would not be quoted in a general conference address or cited in a Latter-day Saint periodical or church manual until the 1960s.

142. Eastern Orthodox find a similar resemblance to Cassian's views in their own soteriology: "The Orthodox position is expressed best by John Cassian—who is often regarded as 'semi-Pelagian' in the West." Rather than the polar extremes of Pelagius or Augustine, "the Fathers argued instead for 'synergy,' a mystery of God's grace being given with the cooperation of the human heart." Anthony Hughes, "Ancestral Sin versus Original Sin," *Journal of Psychology and Christianity* 23 (2004): 276n4.

that the voice of God was "rest in me, and I will help you, so that *we* shall do it together. . . . You have moral freedom. . . . You have to recognize that you are under a responsibility to choose the right. Yet you are still helpless without God's grace."[143] For some, Cassian took a step too far, one that Latter-day Saints sometimes take, in that he saw in scripture the rare instance, such as in the parable of the prodigal son, where "the first tiny initiative comes from the soul turning back because sick of husks, and then God comes with his saving grace." To Cassian's (and Mormonism's) critics this smacked of Pelagianism, and indeed centuries later Cassian and his followers were tarred with the label "semi-Pelagians."[144] Polemic distortion aside, however, "No one can doubt that Cassian was a deeply Christian moralist and never for an instant supposed that a soul could ascend any ladder, or fight any fight, without God pouring in His grace. . . . If Cassian's formula for reconciling freedom with grace may cause doubt to anyone who thinks hard on these matters, no one who reads him with attention and sympathy will fail to admire his endeavor to reconcile the maximum sense of moral freedom and moral responsibility with the maximum sense of dependence on God."[145]

A maximum sense of moral responsibility combined with a maximum sense of dependence on God seems to be the perspective that the Church of Jesus Christ of Latter-day Saints has periodically put forward and today is making a point to emphasize. As we conclude this chapter, then, we return to its beginning—to First Presidency counselor Dieter Uchtdorf's milestone address, "The Gift of Grace." In his sermon, Uchtdorf tackled a passage on grace in the Book of Mormon that in previous years had often been interpreted to stress the importance of human effort and good works: "It is by grace that we are saved, after all we can do" (2 Nephi 25:23). Yet, mused Uchtdorf, "I wonder if sometimes we misinterpret the phrase 'after all we can do.' We must understand that 'after' does not equal 'because.' We are not saved 'because' of all that we can do. Have any of us done all that we can do? Does God wait until we've expended every effort before He will intervene in our lives with His saving grace?" No, as Cassian taught, divine grace launches us, accompanies us, and consummates our efforts toward salvation. "We cannot earn our way into heaven . . . but all is not lost. The grace of God is our great and everlasting

---

143. Owen Chadwick, "Introduction," in *John Cassian Conferences*, trans. Colm Luibheid (New York: Paulist, 1985), 26–27 (emphasis added).

144. This label, though retroactively applied across Christian history, was not coined until the late sixteenth century in the heat of the Molinist-Jansenist controversy over the correct balance between moral endeavor and divine grace.

145. Chadwick, "Introduction," 27.

hope." Uchtdorf deftly paired his call for a maximum sense of dependence on God with a synergistic commitment to maximum human responsibility: "Trying to understand God's gift of grace with all our heart and mind gives us all the more reasons to love and obey our Heavenly Father with meekness and gratitude. As we walk the path of discipleship, [grace] refines us, it improves us, it helps us to become more like Him, and it leads us back to His presence."[146] Although a delicately balanced synergistic view of salvation has been articulated by other church leaders in the Latter-day Saint past, Uchtdorf's sermon epitomizes the current effort in the Church of Jesus Christ of Latter-day Saints to kindle deeper appreciation for saving grace and Christ's atonement without omitting the importance of Christian striving and discipleship in cooperation with that divine grace.[147]

146. Uchtdorf, "The Gift of Grace," 107–10.

147. Early in the church's intensified focus on grace in recent decades, Dallin Oaks similarly declared, "After all our obedience and good works, we cannot be saved from the effect of our sins without the grace extended by the Atonement of Jesus Christ." Oaks, "What Think Ye of Christ?" *Ensign*, November 1988, 67. Even a century before, though such comments were uncommon, they were not unknown. First Presidency counselor George Cannon observed regarding 1 Cor. 10:12—"let him that thinketh he standeth take heed lest he fall"—that "there is no one so strong that he can be sure he will get through. It is only by the grace of God that we can expect to be faithful and to receive salvation." Cannon, "Living Our Religion," May 26, 1889, in *Collected Discourses*, 1:277.

7

CHURCH

Images, Models, and "Marks"

For many Americans, "church" is either a religious building or a religious institution. In the New Testament, however, where the word translates the Greek *ekklēsia*, it refers to people. Linked to the verb *kaleō* (to call) and *ek* (out/out of), *ekklēsia* may be broadly defined as a "summoned assemblage of people." *Ekklēsia*, from which "ecclesiastical" and "ecclesiology" are derived, appears over a hundred times in the New Testament (although only three times in the Gospels and then only in Matthew). New Testament authors obviously found the image of a summoned people meaningful to depict disciples who profess faith in Christ and have been called out of the "world" to unite "in the apostles' doctrine and fellowship, and in breaking of bread, and in prayers" (Acts 2:42). In the New Testament, *ekklēsia* sometimes refers to the whole body of Christians and sometimes to specific congregations, such as "the church that was at Antioch" (Acts 13:1) or "the churches of Macedonia" (2 Cor. 8:1). As Christian theology developed over the years, "church" even came to include the entirety of God's people past, present, and future, on earth and in heaven, as a cosmic *communio sanctorum* ("communion of saints/holy ones"). On this point, the Orthodox proclamation is typical: "Those who are alive on earth" as well as "those who have finished their earthly course" and "those in future generations" are "all united together in one Church, in one and the same grace of God."[1] Finally, by way of introduction, the English word "church" is etymologically related to several earlier European terms, such as the German *Kirche*, which in turn derive from the Greek *kyriakos* ("the Lord's," from *kyrios*/"Lord") and so can refer either to the Lord's people or the Lord's house.[2]

---

1. McGuckin, *Orthodox Church*, 247.
2. Frederick William Danker, ed., *Greek-English Lexicon of the New Testament and Other Early Christian Literature*, 3rd ed. (Chicago: University of Chicago Press, 2000), s.v. "*ekklēsia*" (303-4); "*kyriakos, kyrios*" (576-79). Martin Luther, who wished to emphasize that

These definitions and connotations of *ekklēsia* are generally consistent with LDS understandings of "church." The temporal dimension, for instance, is reflected in the very name of the church—the Church of Jesus Christ of Latter-day Saints. Because the one church of Jesus Christ spans the ages, Latter-day Saints recognize they constitute only the "latter-day" portion of the "communion of saints." The dual application of "church" in the New Testament, its collective and congregational character, is echoed in the Book of Mormon where it is said that the believers "did assemble themselves together in different bodies, being called churches [but] notwithstanding there being many churches they were all one church, yea, even the church of God" (Mosiah 25:21–22; cf. 1 Cor. 1:2). An early revelation refers to "the church at Colesville [New York]" (D&C 26:1), and the founding Articles and Covenants directs that "all members removing from the church where they reside, if going to a church where they are not known, may take a letter certifying that they are regular members and in good standing" (D&C 20:84). In time, however, the terms "branch" or "ward" (following the nineteenth-century term for the geographical units into which some cities were divided for administrative and political purposes) became the common designations for local LDS congregations. This terminology is universal in the church today. Another variation is that in their own doctrinal discussions, Latter-day Saints almost never use "the church" in the singular to refer to the global collectivity of contemporary Christian churches and their members, as is typical in theological discourse (and this chapter). Instead, they use the plural "churches" or speak of "Christians" and "Christianity" around the world.

Identifying the meanings of *ekklēsia* and why that term is a fitting appellation for Christians and their congregations only scratches the ecclesiological surface. Scripture deploys an array of images to adequately evoke the richness of the nature, purpose, and destiny of Christ's church. The church is like a gemstone with many facets and features to be appreciated. One study has identified over ninety images in the New Testament used to depict the church. They range from minor images such as "seed" or "vine" to major images such as "people of God," "new creation," "fellowship in faith," and "body of Christ."[3] Other scripturally based images emphasized by theologians include "bride of Christ," "household of God," "temple" of God/Holy Spirit, "kingdom of God,"

---

the church was first and foremost God's *people*, preferred to render *ekklēsia* as *Gemeinde* (community, congregation, group of people).

3. Paul S. Minear, *Images of the Church in the New Testament* (Philadelphia: Westminster, 1960).

and even "mystery." Over the centuries, these images have served as the basis for a vast array of expository sermons and theological reflection on the nature of the church. While no Christian tradition rejects any of the biblical metaphors, different theologies have found certain images particularly meaningful for their self-characterization. Reformation theologians, for instance, plumbed the notion of the church as the "people of God." Liturgical communions have found special meaning in the "body of Christ." Pentecostals emphasize that the church is the "temple of the Holy Spirit." And Latter-day Saints find the "kingdom of God" especially relevant. At root, the images are straightforward and easy to understand, but their implications are manifold.

CHURCH AS KINGDOM OF GOD

Students of the New Testament familiar with Greek know that *basileia tou theou* can be translated as either the "kingdom of God" or "God's reign/rule." Many Christian traditions favor the latter rendering because it avoids connotations of a political kingdom, the kind Jesus's opponents assumed he intended to establish and even his followers had in mind at first.[4] When the Pharisees asked him "when the kingdom of God should come," Jesus replied, "The kingdom of God cometh not with observation: Neither shall they say, Lo here! or, lo there! for, behold, the kingdom of God is within you" (Luke 17:20–21). Jesus also famously told Pilate, "My kingdom is not of this world: . . . [it is] not from hence" (John 18:36). Many Christians consider the kingdom of God to be present spiritually whenever Jesus's followers allow him to "reign" in their lives. In a sense, Jesus was the personification of the kingdom of God, as he taught in word and deed what it means to let God reign in one's life. At the end of time, in the "new heavens and new earth," Christ's reign will also be tangible and cosmic. Theologians often characterize this dual nature of the kingdom as "already/not yet."[5] Latter-day Saints agree that there is an already/not yet dimension to the kingdom of God, but like the Catholic Church through much of its history, they interpret the present kingdom primarily in institutional terms as the church, not just as Christ reigning spiritually in the lives of his disciples. This interpretation prevails even when exegeting passages that seem to

4. During Christ's forty-day postresurrection ministry, his disciples "asked of him, saying, Lord, wilt thou at this time restore again the kingdom to Israel?" (Acts 1:6).

5. Passages in the New Testament that talk about God or Christ's reign are often translated in the present tense—"reigns"—but the underlying Greek is in the "aorist" tense, which is a distinctive past tense that indicates that something has already begun but is not yet finished or has not reached its point of culmination or completion.

be stressing the internal, spiritual character of the kingdom. For instance, the LDS Church's college-level study manual for the New Testament discusses the passage in Luke 17 cited above in this manner: "Many translations of the New Testament render the phrase 'the kingdom of God is within you' (Luke 17:21) as 'the kingdom of God is *among* you' because the pronoun *you* is plural in Greek. The Joseph Smith Translation changes this phrase to read, 'The kingdom of God *has already come unto* you.' . . . Both renderings of the phrase point to the truth that Jesus Christ had established the kingdom of God, which is His Church, on the earth at that time and would again establish it in our day."[6]

Revelations received by Joseph Smith often refer to the Church of Jesus Christ of Latter-day Saints as God's earthly kingdom. At the dedication of the first LDS meetinghouse, the Mormon prophet prayed, "Remember all thy church, O Lord, . . . that the kingdom, which thou hast set up without hands [echoing Dan. 2:34–35] may become a great mountain and fill the whole earth" (D&C 109:72).[7] Many revelations such as Doctrine and Covenants 45:1—"Hearken, O ye people of my church, to whom the kingdom has been given"—address the Saints as part of God's earthly kingdom.[8] Early church ministers were referred to as "the first laborers in this last kingdom" (D&C 88:74), and the presiding officers were "to preside in council and set in order all the affairs of this church and kingdom" (D&C 90:16; cf. 94:3). The LDS practice of using "church" and "kingdom" interchangeably continues to the present day.[9] Referring to the church as the kingdom of God was particularly prevalent during the latter half of the nineteenth century prior to Utah being granted statehood (1896). During this period, the Church of Jesus

---

6. *NT Student Manual* (2018), 175.

7. In Dan. 2:34–45, Daniel interprets Nebuchadnezzar's dream of a colossal statue that ultimately is pulverized by a divinely quarried stone that grows until it fills the whole earth. This, Daniel explains, refers to a future day in which the "God of heaven [will] set up a kingdom, which . . . shall break in pieces and consume all these kingdoms, and it shall stand for ever" (v. 44). Although this has seemed to many Christians as a prophecy of the "not yet" eschatological kingdom, Latter-day Saints have long read this account as a prediction of the latter-day restoration through Joseph Smith of the institutional church of Christ. For recent examples, see Gordon B. Hinckley, "The Stone Cut Out of the Mountain," *Ensign*, November 2007, 83–86, and Neil L. Andersen, *Ensign*, November 2016, 35.

8. See D&C 29:5; 35:27; 38:9, 15; 43:10; 50:35; 62:9; 64:4; 72:1; 78:18; 82:24; 84:76; 136:41.

9. As just one of many examples, early in the twenty-first century, apostle Russell Ballard remarked simply, "The Church is the kingdom of God on earth." *Ensign*, November 2005, 42. At the same general conference, apostle Jeffrey Holland expressed his conviction that the Church of Jesus Christ of Latter-day Saints "really is the church and kingdom of God on earth." *Ensign*, November 2005, 30.

Christ of Latter-day Saints, as the dominant institutional entity in the Utah Territory, involved itself in social, economic, and political affairs. In doing so, it resembled the theocratic kingdoms of ancient Israel, a point not lost on the Latter-day Saints. Early Mormonism's biblical restorationism was as strongly connected to the Old Testament as it was to the New Testament. Thus, visualizing the church as an Israel-like kingdom seemed both natural and appropriate to the Saints.

Latter-day Saints view the kingdom of God not only as the earthly, institutional church but also as the heavenly realm of the saved. The church's scriptural study aid, *Topical Guide to the Scriptures*, categorizes scriptural passages that mention the kingdom under two headings—"Kingdom of God, on Earth" and "Kingdom of God, in Heaven." Verses listed under the former heading almost always refer to the church. Passages included in the latter category typically reference either the heavenly kingdom of the saved or the heaven-like, thousand-year terrestrial reign known as the "millennium" that Mormons believe Christ will institute near the end of human history (see chapter 12). Both senses are apparent in a prayer included in the Doctrine and Covenants. In the first part of the prayer, the kingdom in view is the church: "Call upon the Lord, that his kingdom may go forth upon the earth, that the inhabitants thereof may receive it, and be prepared for the days to come, in the which the Son of Man shall come down in heaven, clothed in the brightness of his glory, to meet the kingdom of God which is set up on the earth." The prayer then clearly juxtaposes the two senses of God's *basileia*: "Wherefore, may the kingdom of God go forth, that the kingdom of heaven may come, that thou, O God, mayest be glorified in heaven so on earth" (D&C 65:5-6).

In the Bible, "kingdom of heaven" is found only in Matthew, and many interpreters view "heaven" in "kingdom of heaven" simply as a metonym for God. As a result, they see no distinction between the "kingdom of God" and the "kingdom of heaven." LDS scripture and discourse, however, rarely refer to the earthly, institutional kingdom or church as the "kingdom of heaven." They do, on the other hand, readily use "kingdom of God" to refer to the heavenly realm of the saved. The Book of Mormon declares, "Wherefore the final state of the souls of men is to dwell in the kingdom of God, or to be cast out because of that justice of which I have spoken" (1 Nephi 15:35). Moreover, the righteous are described as praying that one day they "may be received into the eternal kingdom of God, that [they] may praise him through grace divine" (2 Nephi 10:25).[10] Of

10. Instances in which "kingdom of God" is used to refer to God's kingdom in heaven are numerous: 2 Nephi 9:18, 23; 25:13; 28:8; 31:21; 33:12; Jacob 6:4; Alma 5:24; 7:21; 9:12; 29:17;

course, "kingdom of heaven" and "kingdom of my Father" are obvious names for God's heavenly *basileia* and are used as such.[11] If "kingdom of God" and "kingdom of heaven" are sometimes interchangeable when the eschatological "not yet" or heavenly kingdom is in view, the vast majority of references to the "already" kingdom of God in Mormon discourse refer to the church. So does the corollary phrase "build/building the kingdom of God," which is used to describe all kinds of church ministry and service. "Building the kingdom" not only means helping church members more fully open their hearts to God's sovereignty in their personal lives, but it also refers to doing whatever is necessary to strengthen the church as a communion and institution.

Latter-day Saints are not the only Christians who have talked about "building the kingdom." The expression was widespread in the eighteenth and nineteenth centuries, especially among Christians of pietist and evangelical persuasions.[12] But building the kingdom involved something more for these groups than it did for Mormons. It entailed a vision of social activism, of endeavoring to extend God's sovereignty and justice, his kingly rule and reign, beyond the church into the broader society. "For Pietists, all practical measures, in education as well as in social work, were essential and meaningful only as parts of their efforts in building the Kingdom of God."[13] The consecrated Christian was to carry the gospel into every walk of life, and in nineteenth-century America

---

34:36; 38:15; 39:9; 40:25–26; 41:4; 3 Nephi 11:33, 38; 12:20; 14:21; 27:19; 28:2–3, 8, 10, 40; 4 Nephi 1:17; Mormon 7:7; Ether 4:19; 15:34; Moroni 9:6; 10:21, 26. Passages in the D&C include 6:3, 13; 11:3; 12:3; 14:3; 20:29; 27:4 (reiterates Matt. 26:29).

11. Alma 5:25, 28, 50–51; 7:9, 14, 25; 9:25; 10:20; 11:37; Helaman 3:30; 5:32; D&C 6:37; 10:55; 15:6; 16:6; 18:15–16, 25, 44, 46; 33:10; 39:19; 58:2; 84:38, 58, 74; 101:65, 100; 106:3; 132:49. In rare cases, "kingdom of heaven" serves as a synonym for the earthly kingdom of God. For instance, Joseph Smith's journal contains this statement: "The virtue of the [above] Priesthood is to hold the keys of the kingdom of heaven, or the Church militant." *JSP*, J1:34.

12. The concept and expression were so pervasive in the nineteenth century that they are discussed in most studies of Christianity in that era. For the United States, see Timothy L. Smith's seminal *Revivalism & Social Reform in Mid-Nineteenth-Century America* (New York: Abingdon, 1957). Also useful is Donald W. Dayton, *Discovering an Evangelical Heritage* (Peabody, MA: Hendrickson, 1988). For an overview of pietist views on the matter, see Jonathan Strom and Hartmut Lehmann, "Early Modern Pietism," in *Oxford Handbook of Early Modern Theology, 1600–1800*, ed. Ulrich L. Lehner, Richard A. Muller, and A. G. Roeber (New York: Oxford University Press, 2016), 402–35.

13. Strom and Lehmann, "Early Modern Pietism," 424. Pietists "were convinced that the more time, energy, and compassion they invested in the building of God's kingdom, the sooner Christ would return." In short, "the lesson for all true children of God was clear: if they wanted to attain eternal salvation, they had to engage themselves in building this kingdom" (425, 408).

reborn believers banded together in a great variety of interdenominational associations and reform societies to do so. Scholars have labeled this network of groups intent on Christianizing the social and political fabric of the United States the "Benevolent Empire."[14]

Not everyone agreed with this vision, however. To some it seemed to arrogate to humanity a role reserved for God's grace alone. Human involvement with kingdom building detracted from God's glory and led to human pride. In a version of this objection, early Mormons decried "the perfect folly of all the pretended reformations of ancient and modern times when there were not inspired men at the head of them, both apostles and prophets, for without such the God of heaven never at any time produced a reformation."[15] In the satirical style of the day, one LDS publicist mocked: "God has done his work and we don't need any more prophets. We have bible societies, missionary societies, abolition of slavery societies, and temperance societies to convert the world and bring in the millennium."[16] As it turned out, the determined energy of those committed to reform and "social gospel" efforts to Christianize the political and socioeconomic world around them was no match for the corporate greed, aggressive industrialization, mass immigration, and consequent poverty of the later nineteenth century. Nor were these kingdom builders subsequently able to avert the bellicosity and brutality of nominally Christian nations that were on display in World War I or overcome the ethical disarray of its hedonistic aftermath. Not surprisingly, kingdom-building optimism waned, and among some, such as prominent theologian Karl Barth and his followers, it was declared bankrupt.

Others sought to retain the vision by placing less emphasis and expectation on human efforts. "We do not build the kingdom of God. Rather, we build up human community in light of the kingdom of God."[17] Such semantic hairsplitting, however, has seemed unnecessary to at least one prominent contemporary theologian. "Let's be quite clear," remarked N. T. Wright, "God builds God's kingdom. But God ordered his world in such a way that his own work within that world takes place not least through . . . human beings who reflect his image." As a result, "the objection about us trying to build God's kingdom

14. See Smith, *Revivalism & Social Reform in Mid-Nineteenth-Century America*, and Clifford S. Griffin, *Their Brothers' Keepers: Moral Stewardship in the United States, 1800–1865* (New Brunswick, NJ: Rutgers University Press, 1960).

15. *The Evening and the Morning Star*, May 1834, 153.

16. *Latter Day Saints' Messenger and Advocate*, April 1835, 97.

17. Erwin Fahlbusch et al., *Encyclopedia of Christianity*, 5 vols. (Grand Rapids: Eerdmans, 1998–2008), 4:829.

by our own efforts, though it seems humble and pious, can actually be a way of hiding from responsibility, of keeping one's head well down when the boss is looking for volunteers." The reality is that "if you want to benefit from Jesus's saving death, you must become part of his kingdom project . . . a salvation that is both *for* humans and, *through* saved humans, for the wider world. This is the solid basis for the mission of the church."[18] German theologian Jürgen Moltmann maintains a similar view in which the eschatological kingdom of God is brought about through a latter-day outpouring of the Holy Spirit working through the agency of God's people.[19] Orthodox scholar John McGuckin summarized the Eastern viewpoint eloquently: "Our lives and discipleship may be the child's building blocks of the Kingdom of God, but God, in his mercy, accepts and validates them as part of the architecture of his own glory."[20]

Whatever may be the best way to conceptualize and characterize the extension of God's kingdom into all walks of life, a Christian vision of social and humanitarian engagement continues to be central to the endeavor. This is also true for the Church of Jesus Christ of Latter-day Saints today. Long gone is its initial disparagement of such activity. Twenty-first-century Mormons are encouraged to engage in any good cause that fosters human flourishing. The church institutionally spends hundreds of millions of dollars every year in humanitarian and relief efforts and in partnering with other faiths and NGOs worldwide to meet a variety of social and economic needs.[21] Despite active participation in this modern version of the Benevolent Empire, for Latter-day Saints, the primary venues for building the kingdom of God continue to be the church and the home. In similar fashion, Pope John Paul II, in his 1981 Apostolic Exhortation *Familiaris Consortio*, spoke repeatedly of the family's role in "building up" the body of Christ and the kingdom of God. "Among the fundamental tasks of the Christian family," he wrote, "is its ecclesial task: the family is placed at the service of the building up of the Kingdom of God in history by participating in the life and mission of the Church." In words that any Latter-day Saint could endorse, John Paul II continued, "The Christian family

18. N. T. Wright, *Surprised by Hope: Rethinking Heaven, the Resurrection, and the Mission of the Church* (New York: HarperOne, 2008), 207, 204–5.

19. Jürgen Moltmann, *The Coming of God: Christian Eschatology*, trans. Margaret Kohl (Minneapolis: Fortress, 1996).

20. McGuckin, *Orthodox Church*, 149.

21. In 2023, the church spent $1.36 billion in over four thousand humanitarian projects in nearly two hundred countries and territories. See *Caring for Those in Need: 2023 Summary of the Church of Jesus Christ of Latter-day Saints*, https://www.churchofjesuschrist.org/serve /caring/annual-summary?lang=eng.

also builds up the Kingdom of God in history through . . . the love between husband and wife and between the members of the family—a love lived out in all its extraordinary richness of values and demands. . . . Therefore, love and life constitute the nucleus of the saving mission of the Christian family in the Church and for the Church."[22]

Although Latter-day Saints have been particularly drawn to the image of church as the kingdom of God, other important aspects of LDS ecclesiology invite detailed consideration. These may be profitably examined within the framework of the familiar Nicene-Constantinopolitan affirmation that the church is "one, holy, catholic, and apostolic."[23] Historically, Latter-day Saints have been leery of creeds, and none are recited in any of the church's liturgies. Still, properly "translated," these four creedal *notae ecclesiae* (marks of the church) are compatible in important ways with Mormon doctrine. In other cases, they provide an appropriate context for highlighting Latter-day Saint distinctives. As previously mentioned, in LDS discourse, when "the church" and its nature are considered, it is the Church of Jesus Christ of Latter-day Saints that is being discussed. In theological reflection elsewhere, "the church" typically refers to Christianity as a whole. As a result of this referential difference, the remainder of the chapter necessarily proceeds along two tracks: (1) an overview of Christian theological discourse on the "marks" of the church at large, and (2) consideration of how those marks apply to the Church of Jesus Christ of Latter-day Saints specifically.

Church Is One

The multitude of Christian communions in existence today make it obvious that the church is *not* one, either institutionally or theologically. Rival forms of Christianity were already in competition as early as the second century. At the end of the first millennium, long-standing differences between Western and Eastern Christianity finally led to a formal split. Five hundred years later, the Reformation splintered Western Christianity. And Protestantism has continued to divide into various sects and denominations. Christendom has had a long and sad history of internecine conflict, sometimes involving violence. Bloody battles between Catholics and Protestants not only took place in the years following the Reformation but have occurred as recently as the

---

22. *Familiaris Consortio*, 49, 50, at https://www.vatican.va/content/john-paul-ii/en/apost
_exhortations/documents/hf_jp-ii_exh_19811122_familiaris-consortio.html.

23. *Creeds & Confessions*, 163.

late twentieth century in Northern Ireland. Nor has Protestant-Catholic strife been confined to Europe. The United States, particularly in the nineteenth century, fared little better. Among themselves, Protestant communions have also proven combative. No, Christianity is not one.

The irony is that it appears not to have been one almost from the beginning. Biblical scholarship over the past century has provided an important corrective to the long-popular myth of a monolithic early Christianity. Pioneering twentieth-century German scholar Walter Bauer examined the evidence and concluded that instead of a single, universally accepted "orthodoxy" from which later "heresies" diverged, diversity actually was the order of the day from the beginning.[24] While Bauer's seminal work has not escaped criticism, Rowan Williams, British theologian and former archbishop of Canterbury, notes that the scholarly consensus today acknowledges "with Bauer, the insuperable problems in supposing there to have been from the beginning a single, clearly identifiable 'mainstream'" Christianity.[25] Counseled prominent Catholic theologian Hans Küng, "Only if we take the New Testament as a whole, with all its divergences and nuances, can we avoid the temptation to harmonize the conflicting ecclesiological statements of the New Testament . . . and produce schematization and uniformity."[26] In truth, there are many ways to understand the oneness of the church depending on the vantage point from which the topic is addressed. If, for instance, oneness is not understood as uniformity, then there is room for diversity within unity. As Williams points out, "normative" Christianity has always been "an interwoven plurality of perspectives on . . . how [the gospel] is being assimilated in diverse and distant communities, culturally and historically strange."[27] If the kaleidoscope of Christianity is one, the patterns within it are multitudinous.

Fundamentally, unity resides in there being "one Lord, one faith, one baptism" (Eph. 4:5). Catholics describe the "sacred mystery of the church's unity"

---

24. Walter Bauer, *Orthodoxy and Heresy in Earliest Christianity* (1934; reprint, Philadelphia: Fortress, 1971).

25. Rowan Williams, "Does It Make Sense to Speak of a Pre-Nicene Orthodoxy?" in *The Making of Orthodoxy: Essays in Honour of Henry Chadwick*, ed. Rowan Williams (Cambridge: Cambridge University Press, 1989), 18 (1–23). See also James D. G. Dunn, *Unity and Diversity in the New Testament: An Inquiry into the Character of Earliest Christianity* (London: SCM, 1977), and Helmut Koester, *Introduction to the New Testament*, vol. 2, *History and Literature of Early Christianity*, 2nd ed. (New York: de Gruyter, 2000).

26. Hans Küng, *The Church* (London: Burns & Oates, 1967), 40.

27. Williams, "Does It Make Sense to Speak of a Pre-Nicene Orthodoxy?," 18.

as located in the Trinity, where the Father is the "source" of unity, Christ is the "founder" of unity, and the Holy Spirit is the "soul" of unity.[28] Orthodox agree, and for this reason bishop-theologian Kallistos Ware called the church "the Icon of the Trinity."[29] Catholics consider that as the "soul of unity," it is the Holy Spirit "dwelling in those who believe and pervading and ruling over the entire Church, who brings about that wonderful communion of the faithful and joins them together so intimately in Christ that he is the principle of the Church's unity."[30] The church is indeed the "temple of the Holy Spirit." His presence provides the mystical solidarity of the body of Christ. In the words of Irenaeus, "Where the Church is, there is the Spirit of God; and where the Spirit of God is, there is the Church and all grace."[31] This perspective has been a rallying cry of Pentecostal churches for over a century.[32] Such mystical unity fosters rather than damages the rich diversity of the global Christian community. The apostle Paul says the church has "many members, yet but one body" (1 Cor. 12:20). Each "member" makes a distinct contribution through the Spirit, for "there are diversities of gifts, but the same Spirit" (1 Cor. 12:4). What brings unity to diversity is the one "head," Jesus Christ, and that "by one Spirit are we all baptized into one body" (1 Cor. 12:13). Many Christian traditions, including the Church of Jesus Christ of Latter-day Saints, find the idea of ecclesial oneness aptly expressed through this image of the church as the single "body of Christ."[33]

As previously noted, when Latter-day Saints talk of "the church," they are re-

---

28. CCC 813.

29. Timothy Ware, *The Orthodox Church* (Baltimore: Penguin Books, 1964), 247.

30. CCC 813.

31. Irenaeus, *Against Heresies* 3.24.1.

32. For early Pentecostalism, see Grant Wacker, *Heaven Below: Early Pentecostals and American Culture* (Cambridge, MA: Harvard University Press, 2001). Edith W. Blumhofer, *Restoring the Faith: The Assemblies of God, Pentecostalism, and American Culture* (Urbana: University of Illinois Press, 1993), treats the early history of the world's largest Pentecostal denomination (now numbering nearly ninety million worldwide). For an overview of Pentecostalism generally, see Allan H. Anderson, *An Introduction to Pentecostalism: Global Charismatic Christianity*, 2nd ed. (Cambridge; Cambridge University Press, 2014); for Pentecostal theology, see Stephen J. Land, *Pentecostal Spirituality: A Passion for the Kingdom* (Sheffield: Sheffield Academic Press, 1993); Wolfgang Vondey, *Pentecostal Theology: Living the Full Gospel* (London: Bloomsbury T&T Clark, 2017); Frank D. Macchia, *Tongues of Fire: A Systematic Theology of the Christian Faith* (Eugene, OR: Cascade, 2023); and Tony Richie, *Essentials of Pentecostal Theology: An Eternal and Unchanging Lord Powerfully Present &Active by the Holy Spirit* (Eugene, OR: Resource Publications, 2020).

33. For church as the "body of Christ," see also 1 Cor. 10:16; Rom. 12:4–5; Eph. 4:4; Col. 1:24; 3:15.

ferring to their own denomination, and their discussions of unity are internally focused. Given its worldwide membership today, the Church of Jesus Christ of Latter-day Saints not only acknowledges but celebrates the diversity of its global communion. "All Church members are united in the knowledge that they are children of a Heavenly Father," declares a church statement. "They know He loves each of His children equally. This knowledge builds a feeling of unity in every building and worship service around the world and ties all members of the Church together." Moreover, "Just as Paul in the New Testament taught that the Church is a body with each part adding beauty and purpose to the whole, so too does The Church of Jesus Christ of Latter-day Saints experience strength from its diversity."[34] In commenting further on Paul's analogy in 1 Corinthians 12, an LDS publication notes, "Each of us has unique talents, gifts, and abilities that make us crucial" to the functioning of the body of Christ. "That's true whether we're from Boston or Buenos Aires; whether we're old, young, single, married, widowed, divorced, from a part-member family, childless, or have a house full of kids. Whoever you are, wherever you are, you're a valuable member of the body of Christ."[35] Not surprisingly, a popular song written for Latter-day Saint youth, "The Body of Christ," picks up on this theme. Its first stanza reads,

> We are part of a family
> There's a role we all play
> Ev'ryone has a purpose
> All united in His name
> There is strength in our numbers
> With our hearts intertwined
> Moving forward together
> In the body of Christ.[36]

Apostle Todd Christofferson commented on the spiritual refinement that comes from being a diverse group united in the single body of Christ: "All of us are imperfect; we may offend and be offended. We often test one another with our personal idiosyncrasies. In the body of Christ, we have to go beyond

34. "Diversity and Unity in the Church of Jesus Christ of Latter-day Saints," The Church of Jesus Christ of Latter-Day Saints, https://www.churchofjesuschrist.org/study/manual /gospel-topics/diversity-and-unity?lang=eng.

35. David Dickson, "Strengthening 'the Body of Christ,'" *Ensign*, September 2019, 17, 14.

36. "The Body of Christ," The Church of Jesus Christ of Latter-Day Saints, https://www .churchofjesuschrist.org/study/manual/peace-in-christ-2018-youth-album/the-body-of -christ?lang=eng.

concepts and exalted words and have a real 'hands-on' experience as we learn to 'live together in love' [D&C 42:45]."[37] Thought to be helpful along that path is the old aphorism "in essentials unity, in non-essentials liberty, in all things charity."

To be sure, Paul's vision of oneness is aspirational, even within a single denomination or congregation. Paul knew that diversity was a reality among his converts. He also knew that the key to being "perfectly joined together in the same mind and in the same judgment" (1 Cor. 1:10) was to be "in the Lord" (Phil. 4:2). Early on it was recognized that an important means of being and remaining united "in the Lord" was through participation in the Eucharist, or Lord's Supper (see chapter 10). This insight developed into a full-blown communion ecclesiology. In recent decades, building on the pioneering work of twentieth-century theologians Yves Congar, Henri de Lubac, and Karl Barth, this vision of eucharistic communion (Gk. *koinōnia*) in Christ through the power of the Spirit has received renewed attention.[38] The Catholic *Catechism* expresses it thus: "The term 'communion of saints' has two closely linked meanings: 'communion in holy things (*sancta*)' and 'among holy persons (*sancti*).'" The celebrant of the Eucharist in Eastern liturgies elevates the sacramental elements and proclaims "*Sancta sanctis!* ('God's holy gifts for God's holy people'). . . . The faithful (*sancti*) are fed by Christ's holy body and blood (*sancta*) to grow in the communion of the Holy Spirit."[39]

Some Christian traditions have included in their consideration of the church's oneness a focus on an "invisible" dimension. This variation on the theme of the "communion of saints" is the idea that from across all churches in all lands an invisible or hidden fellowship of true believers exists. This hidden communion is not visibly discernible in or between ecclesial bodies, but it is known to God. Theologians have labeled this notion the doctrine of the "invisible church" or "hidden church." The "invisible church," the *real* church of Christ, is a spiritual, mystical fellowship that transcends institutions. Although similar characterizations date to the patristic era, this concept was emphasized in the Reformation. It enabled Protestants who had broken away from the Catholic Church to make the creedal affirmation that the true church of Christ is one, in that it stands above institutional affiliation. It is thought that the con-

---

37. D. Todd Christofferson, "Why the Church," *Ensign*, November 2015, 109.

38. For a historical overview, see Gabriel Flynn, "*Ressourcement* and Theologies of Communion," in *Oxford Handbook of Catholic Theology*, ed. Lewis Ayres and Medi Ann Volpe (Oxford: Oxford University Press, 2015), 683–700. See also Dennis M. Doyle, *Communion Ecclesiology: Vision and Versions* (Maryknoll, NY: Orbis Books, 2000).

39. CCC 948.

stituency of this invisible church will only be revealed on judgment day. From Augustine in the fifth century to Friedrich Schleiermacher in the nineteenth century to Wolfhart Pannenberg in the late twentieth century, theologians have stressed that only then, when Christ has winnowed out the pseudo-Christian chaff from the authentic Christian grain, or, to change the metaphor, when the tares have finally been separated from the wheat, will there be true unity within the body of Christ. Thus, whatever provisional unity the church can achieve now is but a foretaste of the eschatological unity that will be realized in the final consummation of history.

Not all Christian traditions speak of an "invisible church." For the Orthodox, "there is no separation between the visible and the invisible for the two make up a single and continuous reality." The First Vatican Council also disavowed any visible/invisible distinction. "No one should ever believe that the members of the Church are united with merely internal, hidden bonds and that, therefore, they constitute a hidden and completely invisible society." Instead, in addition to the "spiritual and invisible bonds by which the faithful through the Holy Spirit adhere to the supreme and invisible head of the Church, there should be corresponding external, visible bonds also in order that this spiritual and supernatural society [the so-called invisible church] might appear in external form and be conspicuously evident."[40] This is an ideal to which Latter-day Saints also aspire. Although they do not use the terms "visible church" and "invisible church," they do acknowledge a distinction between the nominal and the devout. The Book of Mormon notes: "There was peace [in the land], save it were the pride which began to enter into the church—not into the church of God, but into the hearts of the people who professed to belong to the church of God" (Helaman 3:33; cf. 4:11).

The closest LDS scripture comes to the notion of an invisible church is in a revelation received prior to the church's formal organization in 1830 and promising its forthcoming establishment: "And for this cause have I said: If this generation harden not their hearts, I will establish my church among them. Now I do not say this to destroy my church, but I say this to build up my church; Therefore, whosoever belongeth to my church need not fear" (D&C 10:52–56). Since there was no LDS Church at this time, "my church" may have referred, as it does in other Christian theologies, to an invisible, spiritual fellowship known only to God and consisting of people, regardless of their institutional affiliations, whose pri-

---

40. "Chapter 4: The Church Is a Visible Society," in "The First Draft of the Dogmatic Constitution of the Church," in *The Church Teaches: Documents of the Church in English Translation*, ed. John F. Clarkson et al. (St. Louis: Herder, 1955), 89.

vate beliefs and behaviors constituted them as part of the Lord's hidden church. Referring to those in faithful relationship with Christ as "my church" may have worked before the LDS "Church of Christ" was established, but soon thereafter the potential confusion of what would have amounted to a visible/invisible distinction led to the abandonment of any further use of "my church" terminology. This did not mean, however, that Mormons then or since have abandoned the notion that God has people of faith outside the Church of Jesus Christ of Latter-day Saints with and through whom he works as he will (see chapter 8).[41]

However the concept of an invisible/hidden church plays out within particular Christian traditions, achieving visible, external unity *between* Christian churches raises thorny issues for many ecclesial bodies. Would interdenominational oneness require ecclesial reunification or merely a loose federation of churches that practice liturgical and ministerial mutuality? How far does unity demand interchurch consistency in structure, doctrine, and liturgy? What are the limits of legitimate diversity within unity? Early on, Christian ecumenists may have dreamed of ecclesial reunification, but over the past century such a dream has encountered significant impediments. One of the most deep-rooted has been that some churches see themselves as the sole locus of legitimate ministerial and sacramental authority and the only place where a fullness of truth can be found. This is true of the Roman Catholic Church, many Orthodox churches, and the Church of Jesus Christ of Latter-day Saints. For such groups, the ultimate answer to the question of unity is for all Christians to become part of the one fully true and uniquely approved church of Christ—theirs.

In his 1928 encyclical *Mortalium Animos*, Pope Pius XI criticized ecumenists as "pan-Christians who turn their minds to uniting the churches" and arrange "conventions, meetings and addresses" hoping to achieve a Christian version of the League of Nations. "Who," he asked, "can conceive a Christian Federation, the members of which retain each his own opinions and private judgment, even in matters which concern the object of faith?" "No," he responded. "The union of Christians can only be promoted by promoting the return to the one true Church of Christ of those who are separated from it."[42] Since the Second Vatican Council, the point has been made more gently but no less unequivocally. *Lumen Gentium* declares that "the sole Church of Christ which in the Creed we profess to be one, holy, catholic, and apostolic . . . sub-

---

41. Passages that have been read in this way include 2 Nephi 29:10–12; Alma 29:6–8; D&C 29:7; 33:6.

42. *Mortalium Animos*, 9, 2, 10, https://www.vatican.va/content/pius-xi/en/encyclicals /documents/hf_p-xi_enc_19280106_mortalium-animos.html.

sists in the Catholic Church. . . . Nevertheless, many elements of sanctification and of truth are found outside its visible confines."[43] Vatican II's Decree on Ecumenism (*Unitatis Redintegratio*) adds that "it is through Christ's Catholic Church alone, which is the universal help toward salvation, that the fullness of the means of salvation can be obtained." That being the case, the Catholic Church is "the one Body of Christ into which all those [seeking Christian unity] should be fully incorporated who belong in any way to the people of God."[44] The Orthodox position is summarized by Bishop Kallistos Ware: "Orthodoxy, believing that the Church on earth has remained and must remain visibly one, naturally also believes itself to be that one visible Church." Ware recognizes that this is a bold claim but adds that "Orthodox believe that they are the true Church, not on account of any personal merit, but by the grace of God." To deny their claim to be "the one true Church" would make the Orthodox "guilty of an act of betrayal in the sight of heaven."[45]

Latter-day Saints take a similar tack. They are unequivocal in their declaration that the "one true church" of Christ is coterminous with the Church of Jesus Christ of Latter-day Saints, and it would feel to them like a betrayal to claim otherwise. Sounding much like Pope Pius XI, apostle Boyd Packer stated that the reason "we keep our distance from the ecumenical movements" is simply this: "the restored gospel is the means by which Christians must ultimately be united."[46] Collaborative unity with other churches is experienced, however, through Christian service. The LDS Church has published this statement: "While members of The Church of Jesus Christ of Latter-day Saints have no desire to compromise the distinctiveness of the restored Church of Jesus Christ, they wish to work together with other Christians—and people of all faiths—to recognize and remedy many of the moral and family issues faced by society. . . . There has never been more urgent need for unity in proclaiming the divinity and teachings of Jesus Christ."[47] Many Mormons testify of having established lasting friendships through such united efforts and through

43. *Lumen Gentium*, 8, and *CCC* 870.

44. *Unitatis Reintegratio*, 3.5, as quoted in *CCC* 816.

45. Ware, *Orthodox Church*, 250–51. In 2000, the Bishops Council of the Russian Orthodox Church issued a similar statement that "the Orthodox Church is the true Church of Christ established by our Lord and Saviour Himself." It alone "is the One, Holy, Catholic and Apostolic Church, the keeper and provider of the Holy Sacraments throughout the world." Quoted in Geoffrey Wainwright, "One Baptism, One Church?" in *OHST*, 479.

46. Boyd K. Packer, "The Only True Church," *Ensign*, November 1985, 82.

47. "Are 'Mormons' Christians?" The Church of Jesus Christ of Latter-day Saints, https://www.churchofjesuschrist.org/study/manual/gospel-topics-essays/christians?lang=eng.

respectful interfaith dialogue.[48] Joseph Smith himself remarked, "The inquiry is frequently made of me, 'Where in do you differ from other[s] in your religious views?'—In reality & essence we do not differ so far in our religio[us] views but that we could all drink into one principle of love" as the means to "weld together" the various Christian denominations.[49] Still, Smith hoped that ultimately "all the world [would] embrace" the restored fullness of the gospel. Then they would "see eye to eye & the blessings of God would Be poured out upon the people, which is my whole soul Amen."[50] In the end, as church president Harold Lee expressed it, the fullness of the gospel restored through Joseph Smith constitutes "the only basis of a united and universal church."[51]

For Latter-day Saints, Orthodox, and Catholics, then, while cooperation in holy endeavors and the cultivation of interfaith friendships and good will are important steps toward Christian unity, ultimately, the kind of ecumenism in which they are most invested might be called "conversion ecumenism" or "return ecumenism." To be sure, the attraction of the doctrine of a "one true church" is psychologically powerful. E. R. Dodds, noted early twentieth-century scholar of antiquity, explained the parallel appeal of early Christianity in this striking statement:

> [Its] very exclusiveness, its refusal to concede any value to alternative forms of worship, which nowadays is often felt to be a weakness, was in the circumstances of the time a source of strength. The religious tolerance which was the normal practice had resulted by accumulation in a bewildering mass of alternatives. There were too many cults, too many mysteries, too many philosophies of life to choose from: you could pile one religious insurance on another, yet not feel safe. Christianity [as also the idea of one true Church of Christ today] made a clean sweep. It lifted the burden of freedom from the shoulders of the individual: one choice, one irrevocable choice, and the road to salvation was clear.[52]

---

48. In one prominent example, church president David O. McKay cultivated close friendships with prominent leaders of other Salt Lake area churches. In one charming example, he and Arthur Moulton, the Episcopal bishop of Salt Lake, concluded their mutual seventy-eighth birthday celebration by each laying his hands on the other to pronounce a blessing upon him. Gregory Prince and Robert Wright, *David O. McKay and the Rise of Modern Mormonism* (Salt Lake City: University of Utah Press, 2005), 121.

49. *JSP*, D12:455.

50. *JSP*, D11:361–62.

51. *Ensign*, July 1973, 5.

52. E. R. Dodds, *Pagan and Christian in an Age of Anxiety: Some Aspects of Religious Experience from Marcus Aurelius to Constantine* (Cambridge: Cambridge University Press, 1965), 59.

Despite the attraction of such a perspective, many churches today agree that while full, visible Christian unity is elusive, especially if it entails merging into a single Christian fellowship, steps can be taken in that direction. At the beginning of the twenty-first century, the Faith and Order Commission of the World Council of Churches (WCC) distilled down to three key actions what it considers the path to achieving greater Christian unity and "mutual recognition." These are: (1) "persons recognizing one another individually as Christians"; (2) "churches recognizing one another as churches, that is, as authentic expressions of the One Church of Jesus Christ"; and (3) "churches recognizing the baptism of a person from one church who seeks entrance into another church."[53] Most Christian churches find the first recognition easy enough to make. Depending on how the second is interpreted, its affirmation, too, can be fairly widespread. The third can also be common, again depending on the meaning and significance attached to baptism. What is conspicuous in its absence from the list is mention of ministerial mutuality (the ecumenically fraught topics of ministry, authority, and governance are addressed in the next chapter). As for the Latter-day Saints, they have always freely embraced the first proposal, but to date their ecclesiology is less conducive to taking the second and third actions. The WCC emphasizes that "baptism is first into the one body of Christ, and second into a particular church or confession." Yet, for Latter-day Saints, perhaps even more than for Catholics or Orthodox, the two are one and the same when their own church is in view.

Before concluding consideration of oneness as the first of the *notae ecclesiae*, an additional distinctive of the LDS approach to ecclesial unity merits consideration. In the study Avery Cardinal Dulles made of the church, he notes that "the manufacturing of supplementary images [of the church] goes on wherever the faith is vital."[54] This has clearly been the case with the Church of Jesus Christ of Latter-day Saints. One such image—"Zion"—has provided Mormons with a distinctive vision of unity among the people of God. "Zion" appears over 150 times in the Old Testament as a reference to a hilltop in Jerusalem, more broadly to the city itself, and occasionally even to the land and people of Israel. In the New Testament, "Zion" only appears in a few quotations from the Old Testament and as a synonym for "the city of the living God, the heavenly Jerusalem" (Heb. 12:22). In Latter-day Saint scripture, however, Zion takes on an additional meaning, one that highlights the theme of unity. In a revealed expansion of Genesis 5, where Enoch, "the seventh from Adam"

---

53. *One Baptism: Towards Mutual Recognition*, Faith and Order Paper No. 210 (Geneva: World Council of Churches, 2011), 4.

54. Avery Dulles, *Models of the Church*, expanded ed. (New York: Image Books, 2002), 14.

(Jude 14), is mentioned, a detailed description of Enoch's ministry is provided. In this account, the result of Enoch's "preaching in righteousness unto the people of God" is that in time they "walked with God" and "the Lord called his people ZION, because they were of one heart and one mind, and dwelt in righteousness; and there was no poor among them" (Moses 7:18–19). Inspired by this description, Latter-day Saints have spent much of their history seeking to become a "Zion people" and create a "Zion society." It is still a cherished ideal. To give only two recent examples: In 2020, apostle Quentin Cook remarked that "the clarion call to members of The Church of Jesus Christ of Latter-day Saints is to strive to be a Zion people." And in 2021, apostle Gerrit Gong devoted an entire essay to the theme entitled "Bring Forth Zion."[55]

Because unity is rooted in relationships, a key early Mormon doctrine was "the gathering." In that era, the gathering meant physically moving to live together in a single location and attempting to build a Zion-like utopia. It happened first in western Missouri, then along the Mississippi River in Illinois, and finally in Utah. Today, in a global church, the "gathering" and the quest to re-create Zion are understood figuratively and play out in congregational settings all over the world. Through it all, the consistent conceptual thread has been the oft-quoted injunction "be one; and if ye are not one ye are not mine" (D&C 38:27). That oneness entails not just spiritual unity but concern for equal access to Earth's resources for all. "It is not given that one man should possess that which is above another, wherefore the world lieth in sin" (D&C 49:20). Therefore, "look to the poor and the needy, and administer to their relief that they shall not suffer" (D&C 38:35). All of this was to be achieved because at root "this is Zion—the pure in heart" (D&C 97:21).[56]

Church Is Holy

As it has turned out for all Christian traditions in a fallen world, including the Church of Jesus Christ of Latter-day Saints, cultivating and maintaining purity and holiness of heart among their adherents have been challenging endeavors.

55. Cook, *Liahona*, November 2020, 21; and Gong, *Liahona*, September 2021, 7–9.
56. The Book of Mormon describes a period in antiquity during which a New World Zion was created: "There was no contention in the land, because of the love of God which did dwell in the hearts of the people. . . . There were no robbers, nor murderers, neither were there Lamanites, nor any manner of -ites; but they were in one, the children of Christ, and heirs to the kingdom of God." And "surely there could not be a happier people among all the people who had been created by the hand of God" (4 Nephi 1:15–17).

Despite Paul's vision that if anyone "be in Christ, he is a new creature" and "old things are passed away" (2 Cor. 5:17), for some, old ways keep creeping back. The common experience of believers falling short and falling into sin has presented Christians with persistent questions about the extent of repentance and forgiveness. In the early church, rigorists like Tertullian proposed harsh consequences for serious sins. Some could only be forgiven once. To be a light to the world, the church had to maintain its purity.[57] Issues of purity within the Christian fellowship were subsequently brought to a head in significant controversies that followed two major Roman persecutions—one under Emperor Decius in 250–251, and another a half century later under the imperial Tetrarchy in the early 300s. In both cases, some Christians complied with the empire's anti-Christian demands. Others refused and were tortured, stripped of property, or killed. Christians who capitulated were labeled the "lapsed," and those who held fast to the faith and survived the persecution were honored as "confessors." As the church endeavored to carry on after each of these major persecutions, serious debates arose over the status of the lapsed. Should these betrayers, even if penitent, still be considered part of the church? If so, what penance should be required? Responses reflected a range of undergirding views, from insistence that the church must be a "pure body" to the idea that in the present world it would always be a "mixed body" of saints and sinners.[58]

Another perspective on holiness is rooted in the Hebrew language definition of holiness as being "set apart" or "consecrated" to God. By this view, the church's holiness consists not of nearly perfect people but of a community consecrated to the Lord. Their holiness is measured in terms of collective dedication to Deity and a distinctiveness grounded in Christ's declaration to his disciples: "ye are not of the world . . . I have chosen you out of the world" (John 15:19). Being called out of the world as a people apart, as already noted, is the essential Greek meaning of *ekklēsia*. Moreover, that call brings with it the promise of a cleansing by the One who gave himself for the *ekklēsia* "that he might sanctify and cleanse it with the washing of water by the word, that he might present it to himself a glorious church, not having spot, or wrinkle, or any such thing; but that it should be holy and without blemish" (Eph. 5:26–27).

---

57. See William P. Le Saint, ed. and trans., *Tertullian: Treatises on Penance—On Penitence and On Purity*, Ancient Christian Writers (New York: Newman, 1959). Le Saint acknowledges that Tertullian's exact views about penance and reconciliation are sometimes difficult to discern and subject to varying interpretations (5–6).

58. See detailed discussion of the lapsed in chapter 9 and penance in chapter 11.

Theologically speaking, the church's holiness is that of a pardoned people declared righteous in a forensic sense but still a "pilgrim people" on a journey toward an inner sanctity that will only be fully realized with postresurrection glorification. This is how Augustine (and many after him) explained the holiness of the church. It was not a matter of present moral purity. Neither those who succumbed to persecution nor those who did not had any greater claim to that. Only the eschatological church will be truly "holy and without blemish." To argue for more than limited purity in the present would be both premature and presumptuous. Still, the pursuit of holiness must be taken seriously as a divine commandment: "As he which hath called you is holy, so be ye holy in all manner of conversation; because it is written, Be ye holy; for I am holy" (1 Pet. 1:15–16; cf. Lev. 11:44–45); and "Follow . . . holiness, without which no man shall see the Lord" (Heb. 12:14).

The Church of Jesus Christ of Latter-day Saints is a Christian tradition that tends toward a "pure-body" ecclesiology yet acknowledges a "mixed-body" reality. Mormon doctrine parallels Augustinian realism and recognizes that complete purity and perfection will never be realized in this life. Nonetheless, in the spirit of the Petrine injunction just quoted and the words of the popular Philip Bliss hymn "More Holiness Give Me," Mormon sermons regularly encourage prayerful seeking after the gift of holiness. Holiness in LDS discourse is discussed in terms of righteousness and personal sanctity, as well as consecration to God. This sanctity is to be realized through the power of the Holy Spirit in divinely aided synergistic striving to live a Christlike life (see chapter 6). First Presidency counselor Henry Eyring emphasized that "holiness is made possible through the Atonement of Jesus Christ cleansing and perfecting us." Thus, the Lord declared, "I am able to make you holy" (D&C 60:7). Regarding the human side of the divine synergism, Eyring added that "we can be sanctified or become more holy when we exercise faith in Christ, demonstrate our obedience, repent, sacrifice for Him, receive sacred ordinances, and keep our covenants with Him." Therefore, "qualifying for the gift of holiness" requires human effort in cooperation with the Holy Spirit in "humility, meekness, and patience."[59]

This recognition that holiness is a divine gift from the Spirit to be synergistically sought through diligent responsiveness to divine leadings and the revealed will of God parallels Arminian soteriological sensibilities common to Holiness and Pentecostal churches and the earlier Wesleyan-Holiness quest for "Christian perfection."[60] Contemporary Pentecostal theologian Dale Coulter

---

59. Henry B. Eyring, "Holiness and the Plan of Happiness," *Ensign*, November 2019, 100–101.

60. For Wesley's views, see his *A Plain Account of Christian Perfection* (1777; reprint,

notes that "sanctification is not simply an internal work . . . it requires cooperation with God. The Pentecostal theology of sanctification continues the Wesleyan understanding of synergism as comprising mutual reciprocity between the divine and the human. . . . Synergism entails conscious choices to follow Christ in light of the divine initiative of the Spirit." Moreover, like Latter-day Saints, "Pentecostals retain a special place for 'covenant-making' practices that renew and reinforce one's vows to the Lord and to the community." Rather than simply venues for ecstatic release, "revivals, camp meetings, services of foot washing, and watch night services . . . were special times set apart for consecration and renewal of the covenant. To come down to the altar in a Pentecostal service means a movement to renew one's covenant with God, a new level of consecration as the person tarried before the Lord for his work of deliverance and union."[61] In the past, when members of the Church of the Nazarene, the largest denomination to emerge from the Wesleyan-Holiness movement, were asked what they believed about holiness, a common response, one with which a Latter-day Saint might agree, was to affirm belief in the Sermon on the Mount and the Holy Spirit's willingness to empower them to live it.[62]

In addition to the pursuit of inner holiness and sanctity, Latter-day Saints also maintain a Hebraic sense of holiness as the quality of being set apart from the world and consecrated to God. The Mormon ideal of "Zion" is contrasted with "Babylon" or the "world," and historically much homiletic energy has been

---

London: Methodist Publishing, 2007). Differences on sanctification between Wesley and influential early Methodist theologian John Fletcher are discussed in Laurence W. Wood, "Pentecostal Sanctification in John Wesley and Early Methodism," *Wesleyan Theological Journal* 34 (Spring 1999): 24–63. For the appropriation and modification of Wesley's thought in American Methodism, see John Leland Peters, *Christian Perfection and American Methodism* (1956; reprint, Grand Rapids: Francis Asbury, 1985). Wesleyan influence on the "holiness revivals" of the nineteenth century and the later formation of Holiness and Pentecostal churches is traced in Melvin E. Dieter, *The Holiness Revival of the Nineteenth Century*, 2nd ed. (Lanham, MD: Rowman & Littlefield, 1996); Donald W. Dayton, *Theological Roots of Pentecostalism* (Grand Rapids: Francis Asbury, 1987); and Vinson Synan, *The Holiness-Pentecostal Tradition: Charismatic Movements in the Twentieth Century*, 2nd ed. (Grand Rapids: Eerdmans, 1997).

61. Dale Coulter, "Sanctification," in *The Routledge Handbook of Pentecostal Theology*, ed. Wolfgang Vondey (London: Routledge, 2020), 244–45. See also Stanley M. Burgess and Gary B. McGee, eds., *Dictionary of Pentecostal and Charismatic Movements* (Grand Rapids: Zondervan, 1988), s.v. "Christian Perfection," esp. "The Human Factor" (174–75).

62. Timothy L. Smith, *Called unto Holiness: The Story of the Nazarenes*, 2 vols. (Kansas City, MO: Nazarene Publishing House, 1962–1983). For an illuminating comparison with early Mormonism, see Smith's "The Book of Mormon in a Biblical Culture," *Journal of Mormon History* 7 (1980): 3–21.

expended on motivating believers to "come out" of Babylon and "gather" to Zion, both literally (at first) and figuratively (at present). Although it has been many decades since the primary, almost sole, location of the Church of Jesus Christ of Latter-day Saints was in the Intermountain West, sung well into the twenty-first century, if only in a metaphorical sense, was the chorus of the popular Mormon hymn "Ye Elders of Israel"—"O Babylon, O Babylon, we bid thee farewell, we're going to the mountains of Ephraim to dwell."[63] For Latter-day Saints, the necessary balance between pure-body and mixed-body mentalities is also captured in the well-known axiom "be in the world but not of the world." Moreover, an important sense of the church's holiness resides in the realm of the tangible. Some places and things are thought to bear an intrinsic holiness, such as Latter-day Saint temples and temple-related attire (see chapter 11).[64] Inscribed at the entrance to Mormon temples are the words "Holiness to the Lord—The House of the Lord." President John Taylor urged the people to translate the sacrality of the temple into their own souls: "Let 'holiness to the Lord' be written in every heart" as well as "upon the bells of the horses" (Zech. 14:20).[65]

Such a pursuit of holiness in any Christian communion calls for regular repentance and reformation of character, and some churches, including the Church of Jesus Christ of Latter-day Saints, offer an assist to this with formal penitential practices and church discipline where needed (see chapter 11). The more a church tends toward a pure-body ecclesiology, the more aggressively it is likely to restrict membership to the truly converted in the first place and enact church discipline thereafter, including stringent measures such as limiting fellowship with other church members or even excommunication. A prime example of the former is the Puritan practice in early seventeenth-century New England of admitting as full, covenant members only "visible saints," those who could give a satisfactory relation of their experience of transformative grace.[66] When this resulted in diminishing numbers of full members later in the century, the ministers decided to allow those who had been baptized as

63. *Hymns*, #319.

64. Latter-day Saints share a sense of sacrality about the temple not only that is pervasive in the Old Testament but selectively manifest in the New Testament. See Eyal Regev, *The Temple in Early Christianity: Experiencing the Sacred* (New Haven: Yale University Press, 2019).

65. *Journal of Discourses*, 26:76.

66. The classic study is Edmund S. Morgan, *Visible Saints: The History of a Puritan Idea* (Ithaca, NY: Cornell University Press, 1963). See also Patricia Caldwell, *The Puritan Conversion Narrative: The Beginnings of American Expression* (New York: Cambridge University Press, 1983).

infants but had not yet "owned the covenant" to have their children baptized, a practice previously reserved for visible saints. The ministers, however, held out for a holy, pure-body church by still requiring a relation of saving faith in order to participate in the Lord's Supper.[67] Even that was changed in some churches in the later years of the seventeenth century and first decades of the eighteenth century as ministers came to see the Lord's Supper as a converting ordinance. For congregations intent on maintaining a pure and holy church, ecclesiastical discipline was also routinely practiced to help reform the sinner and deter others from sinning.[68]

No specifiable conversion experience is required for adult baptism into the Church of Jesus Christ of Latter-day Saints. What is necessary, though, is a profession of faith, repentance, and covenantal willingness to keep God's commandments. Subsequently, through a well-developed system of church discipline, the church does patrol the perimeters of holiness and assist in the process of repentance. By so doing, they are also able to "protect the [spiritual] integrity of the Church" as a fellowship committed to pure-body ideals.[69] The church's holiness and integrity are also believed to be maintained by dealing with "apostasy" (defection, lit., "standing away/apart from"). Apostasy can be difficult to pinpoint because intent can matter as much as content. In the LDS case, what constitutes apostasy is "persisting in teaching as Church doctrine what is not Church doctrine after being corrected by the [local church leaders]" and "repeatedly acting in clear and deliberate public opposition to the Church, its doctrine, its policies, or its leaders."[70] All forms of holiness-promoting discipline in the Church of Jesus Christ of Latter-day Saints are to be carried out in the spirit of the Book of Mormon directive that the disciplined are not to be "cast out" of the church's "places of worship." The instruction continues, "For unto such shall ye continue to minister; for ye know not but what they will return and repent, and come unto me with full purpose of

67. The membership compromise of the 1660s and beyond is detailed in Robert G. Pope, *The Half-Way Covenant: Church Membership in Puritan New England* (Princeton: Princeton University Press, 1969).

68. For examples of the perspectives summarized in this paragraph, with special attention to lay experience, see David D. Hall, *Worlds of Wonder, Days of Judgment: Popular Religious Belief in Early New England* (New York: Knopf, 1989), 117–65.

69. *GH* 32.2. Protecting the integrity of the church is explained as "restricting or withdrawing a person's Church membership [which] may be necessary if his or her conduct significantly harms the Church. The integrity of the Church is not protected by concealing or minimizing serious sins—but by addressing them." *GH* 32.2.3.

70. *GH* 32.6.3.2.

heart, and I shall heal them; and ye shall be the means of bringing salvation unto them" (3 Nephi 18:32).[71]

CHURCH IS CATHOLIC

Many Christian traditions other than Roman Catholicism incorporate the Nicene or Apostles' Creed in their liturgies. As a result, thousands of non-Catholic congregants weekly affirm that the church is "catholic." Here an etymological understanding of the term is helpful. "Catholic" is a loanword from the Latin loanword *catholicus* from the Greek *katholikos* meaning "whole," "general," or "entire."[72] Thus, scholars label the later New Testament epistles as Catholic Epistles because they are addressed to the entire church rather than to an individual church such as the one at Corinth or Ephesus. Looking at the historical development of the use of "catholic," Hans Küng has observed that in the second century, "catholic church," quite unpolemically, referred to "the increasingly apparent reality of a whole Church, within which the individual churches are bound up together, a general and all-embracing Church."[73] Over the years, additional meanings became attached to the term—"catholic" as orthodox, in contrast to the heretical offshoots; "catholic" as worldwide, geographically universal; "catholic" as the temporally continuous, uninterrupted historical existence of God's people; "catholic" as all-encompassing in terms of religious truth and all-encompassing with respect to the universality of the church's membership irrespective of ethnicity, gender, and social status. The gospel is for all and preached to all. In the fifth century, Vincent of Lérins defined orthodox Christian doctrine in terms of catholicity. It is, he wrote, that which "has been believed everywhere, always, and by all. This is truly and properly 'catholic,' as indicated by the force and etymology of the name itself, which comprises everything truly universal."[74] Still another dimension of catholicity is the concept that all the essential characteristics of the whole church exist in each local church. That is, although a local church is obviously not the whole church, it is still "wholly church." It is "catholic" in the sense that it incorporates all the essential constituent components.

The Church of Jesus Christ of Latter-day Saints applies each of these aspects of catholicity to itself. Like the Catholic and Orthodox churches, it considers

71. *GH* 32.15.
72. For obvious reasons, some non-Catholics have chosen not to transliterate *katholikē* but to translate it as "universal" or even interpret it simply as "Christian."
73. Küng, *The Church*, 384.
74. Vincent, *Commonitorium* 2.6, in *Vincent of Lerins*, trans. Rudolph E. Morris, Fathers of the Church (Washington, DC: Catholic University of America Press, 1949), 270.

itself to have the best claim to the *notae ecclesiae*. As such, it makes essentially the same proclamation as the Roman Catholic Church, which declares that the church "proclaims the fullness of the faith. She bears in herself and administers the totality of the means of salvation. She is sent out to all peoples. She speaks to all men. She encompasses all times."[75] Several additional observations are appropriate here. First, Latter-day Saints from the beginning have proclaimed the restoration of the "fullness" of the gospel, principally through the publication of the Book of Mormon. The book is said to contain "the fulness of the gospel of Jesus Christ to the Gentiles and to the Jews also" (D&C 20:8–9; cf. 42:12). Of Joseph Smith, revelation declares, "I have sent forth the fulness of my gospel by the hand of my servant Joseph; and in weakness have I blessed him" (D&C 35:17). Indeed, the catholicity of the Mormon claim to be the repository of the restored fullness of the gospel and the authority to administer its saving sacraments is at the very heart of the church's raison d'être (reason for being). Generations of Latter-day Saints have shared this good news about *the* good news with the vigor of its first witnesses, reflecting their catholic conviction that God "will have all men to be saved, and to come unto the knowledge of the truth" (1 Tim. 2:4).[76]

It should be clarified, however, that the intent of the phrase "fullness of the gospel" is to assert the LDS claim to a catholic understanding of Christ's redemptive mission and the plan of salvation, not to profess possession of all truth. As a member of the First Presidency, Dieter Uchtdorf reiterated the Mormon affirmation of fullness but offered an important clarification: "Yes, we do have the fulness of the everlasting gospel, but," he added, "that does not mean that we know everything. . . . The great miracle of the Restoration was not just that it corrected false ideas . . . but that it flung open the curtains of heaven and initiated a steady downpour of new light and knowledge that has continued to this day."[77] In the first year of Russell Nelson's ministry as prophet-president of the church (2018), he emphasized that the fullness of the gospel was not restored all at once through Joseph Smith. Rather, he said, "We're witnesses to a process of restoration. If you think the Church has been fully restored, you're just seeing the beginning. There is much more to come."[78]

75. CCC 868.

76. Of the numerous sermons, articles, and pamphlets from Mormonism's early years, a typical example by an "ordinary," otherwise unknown Latter-day Saint is Moses Martin, *A Treatise on the Fulness of the Everlasting Gospel* (New York, 1842).

77. Dieter F. Uchtdorf, "What Is Truth?" BYU, January 13, 2013, https://speeches.byu.edu /talks/dieter-f-uchtdorf/what-is-truth/.

78. Russell Nelson, "Latter-day Saint Prophet, Wife and Apostle Share Insights of Global

Several years later, Nelson added, "The Restoration is a process, not an event, and will continue until the Lord comes again."[79] Such expressions echo the church's eleventh Article of Faith: "We believe all that God has revealed, all that He does now reveal, and we believe that He will yet reveal many great and important things pertaining to the Kingdom of God."

The clear implications of an "ongoing Restoration" are that at no point do Latter-day Saints consider themselves to be in possession of all divine truth. Moreover, in addition to direct continuing revelation as a source of truth, Dieter Uchtdorf declared, "We continually seek truth from all good books and other wholesome sources."[80] Joseph Smith himself remarked that one of "the grand fundamental principles of Mormonism is to receive truth let it come from where it may." If a "Presbyterian" has "truth, embrace that." The same with a "Baptist, Methodist, &c." To "get all the good in the world" is to "come out a pure Mormon."[81] Here the LDS sense of catholicity parallels one of the meanings Cardinal Dulles attached to it for the Catholic Church. "I am of the opinion," he wrote, "that the Catholic Church in the name of 'catholicity,' must at all costs avoid falling into a sectarian mentality. Being 'catholic,' this Church must be open to all God's truth, no matter who utters it. As St. Paul teaches, it must accept whatever things are true, honorable, just, pure, lovely, gracious, and excellent (cf. Phil 4:8). Thus I find no conflict between being Catholic and being ecumenical."[82] Latter-day Saints, too, have been inspired by Paul's words, enshrining them in their concluding Article of Faith—"if there is anything virtuous, lovely, or of good report or praiseworthy, we seek after these things" (Articles of Faith 13).

The doctrine of the "communion of saints," that God has a people in and from all ages, is a form of temporal catholicity. The idea that the church is catholic in the sense that it has existed in every era is particularly strong in Mormonism. More than just a term for post-Easter Christianity, Latter-day

Ministry," news release, The Church of Jesus Christ of Latter-day Saints, October 30, 2018, https://newsroom.churchofjesuschrist.org/article/latter-day-saint-prophet-wife-apostle -share-insights-global-ministry. Nelson's remarks stimulated the introduction of new expressions into LDS discourse. Instead of simply referring to "the Restoration" with the implicit understanding that it denotes a past event, it has now become common to hear reference to "the ongoing Restoration" or "the continuing Restoration." See, for instance, https://www.lds-general-conference.org/.

79. *Liahona*, November 2021, 94.
80. Uchtdorf, "What Is Truth?"
81. *JSP*, D12:455, 493. Brigham Young agreed that all Christian traditions "have more or less truth." *Journal of Discourses*, 7:283.
82. Dulles, *Models of the Church*, 3.

Saints speak of "the church in all ages of the world" (D&C 107:8). Joseph Smith taught, "Some say the kingdom of God was not set up on earth untill the day of Pentecost. . . . But I say in the name of the Lord that the kingdom of God was set upon the earth from the days of Adam to the present time. Whenever there has been a righteous man on earth unto whom God revealed his word & gave power & authority to administer in his name . . . there is the kingdom of God."[83] Latter-day Saints also make the concomitant claim to the "antiquity of the Gospel." Not only did God preach "before the gospel unto Abraham" (Gal. 3:8), but even Adam and Eve were taught the good news. "And thus the Gospel began to be preached, from the beginning" (Moses 5:58). In a striking declaration of temporal catholicity, Joseph Smith stated that "The gospel has always been the same; the ordinances to fulfill its requirements, the same, and the officers to officiate, the same; and the *signs* and *fruits* resulting from the promises, the same."[84] Smith's counselor in the First Presidency, Sidney Rigdon, elaborated that "what seems to put the matter at rest as relates to the antiquity of the gospel proclamation is that the apostle Paul says that the gospel which he proclaimed . . . was devised before the foundation of the world, and that it was God's fixed purpose to save men in that way or by that plan and none other; so that if there was salvation at all among the ancients, it was because they had the gospel among them."[85] In short, the gospel has been made known "to the Saints of God in former, as well as in latter days, and is like its Author, the same in all ages, and changeth not."[86] No surprise, then, that from the earliest compendium of Latter-day Saint beliefs to B. H. Roberts's multivolume course of gospel study, the notion of the "antiquity of the gospel," sometimes even the phrase itself, was a common trope in Mormon literature.[87]

At the heart of proclaiming the temporal catholicity of the gospel is what might be termed the catholicity of Christ's atonement. President John Taylor emphasized that the atonement "applies not only to the living, but also to the dead, so that all men who have existed in all ages, who do exist now, or who

83. *JSP*, D11:357.

84. *Times and Seasons*, September 1842, 904.

85. *Messenger and Advocate*, May 1835, 119.

86. *Times and Seasons*, July 1839, 1.

87. Franklin D. Richards, "Antiquity and Unchangeableness of the Gospel," in *A Compendium of the Faith and Doctrines of the Church of Jesus Christ of Latter-day Saints* (Liverpool, 1857), 6–16, and B. H. Roberts, "Lesson XX—the Antiquity of the Gospel," in Roberts, *Course in Theology*, 2:100–106. See also Roberts's introduction to the *History of the Church of Jesus Christ of Latter-day Saints*, ed. B. H. Roberts, 2nd ed., 7 vols. (1951; Salt Lake City: Deseret Book, 1976), 1:xxv–xxxi.

will exist while the earth shall stand, may be placed upon the same footing, and that all men may have the privilege . . . of accepting the conditions of the great plan of redemption provided by the Father, through the Son, before the world was; and that the justice and mercy of God may be applied to every being . . . that ever has existed, that does now exist, or that ever will exist."[88] "Eternal" and "infinite" are adjectives that Latter-day Saints often apply to the atonement of Jesus Christ. Among the meanings that these adjectives can convey is temporal catholicity. No period of time and none of the earth's inhabitants fall outside the capacious reach of Christ's redemptive gifts (see chapter 4).

Church Is Apostolic

When Christians proclaim their agreement with the last of the four creedal *notae ecclesiae*—that the church is "apostolic"—they can mean a variety of things. They can be proclaiming that their tradition perpetuates the doctrine taught by the apostles, the basic "canon of truth" or "rule of faith" (*regula fidei*) from the early centuries of Christianity. The Reformers emphasized that what made a church "apostolic" was the proclamation of the Word. Others find "apostolicity" in living the same Christian life, both morally and liturgically, that the apostles inculcated. Still others claim that their church's polity, its ministerial structure and form of governance, is what the apostles put in place. Proclamations of structural apostolicity have been made by those who interpret New Testament ecclesial organization as congregational, as well as by traditions that are convinced it was "connectional," either presbyterial or episcopal. In sum, the affirmation of apostolicity is the claim of continuity in one way or another with the doctrine, practice, or polity the apostles are believed to have set in place during their lifetimes. Various Christian communions even make all three of these assertions of apostolicity.

Some link apostolicity to the notion of "apostolic succession," the claim that the apostles passed on by ordination their ministerial powers and prerogatives to successors. In turn, these successors did the same, and the process has continued uninterrupted from generation to generation to the present day. Consequently, the church's current ministry is believed to possess the identical rights and powers that Christ conferred on his original apostles. The Roman Catholic doctrine of apostolic succession, for instance, is that the apostles, specially endowed alongside Peter with the "keys of the kingdom," ordained

88. John Taylor, *An Examination . . . of the Mediation and Atonement of Our Lord and Savior Jesus Christ* (Salt Lake City: Deseret News, 1882), 181.

bishops (*episkopoi*) as their legitimate successors to continue the exercise of apostolic *episkopē* ("oversight," "supervision") over the whole church. From there, these rights and responsibilities have been passed on to the present "college" (council) of bishops through an unbroken chain of episcopal succession. Orthodox churches maintain a similar understanding but emphasize the equality and conciliarity of their bishops, with none being the head or "primate" (chief bishop, leader of first rank) over all the other bishops like the bishop of Rome, who alone exercises final *episkopē* for the whole church (see chapter 8). Other Christian groups, such as the Anglican Communion or Lutheran churches, claim apostolic succession by perpetuating an episcopal polity as the apostolic pattern but without professing an unbroken historical succession of bishops from the first century.

Although the Church of Jesus Christ of Latter-day Saints was not born until the 1800s, it proclaims an apostolic succession as literal as the Catholic or Orthodox churches. It does this by declaring that Joseph Smith received his ordination directly from Peter, James, and John, believed to have returned to earth as angelic beings to confer the apostleship. An early revelation referred to this occasion: "Peter, and James, and John, whom I have sent unto you, by whom I have ordained you and confirmed you to be apostles, and especial witnesses of my name, and bear the keys of your ministry and of the same things which I revealed unto them." Thus, unto Joseph Smith and his associates, the revelation declared, "I have committed the keys of my kingdom, and a dispensation of the gospel for the last times" (D&C 27:12–13; cf. 128:20). In the Mormon view, here is apostolic succession at its purest. By virtue of this conferral, Smith constituted a council of twelve men whom he designated "apostles" and conferred these keys on them as well. They, in turn, passed them on to successor apostles. Early twentieth-century apostle Melvin Ballard declared, "We proclaim that . . . Peter, James and John did come to the earth and laid their hands upon the heads of Joseph Smith and Oliver Cowdery, and bestowed upon them the holy apostleship with all of its rights and authority; and that every man who has been ordained an apostle in this Church, each and all of them, has received his authority in an unbroken chain back to those who held the keys from the Master himself."[89]

Apostolic succession is made even more pronounced in the Church of Jesus Christ of Latter-day Saints by use of the term "apostles" rather than "bishops" to refer to these modern successors of the first Twelve. This replicates Jesus's action when from among his disciples "he chose twelve, whom also he named

89. Melvin J. Ballard, *Conference Report*, April 1935, 22.

apostles" (Luke 6:13). The LDS Church continues the replication by having a Council ("Quorum," commonly used) of Twelve Apostles that numbers exactly twelve. This council serves as the church's chief governing body in conjunction with the church's president-"prophet" and his two "counselors," also apostles, who constitute the First Presidency (see chapter 8). Such an ecclesiastical arrangement reflects LDS interpretation of Paul's teaching that the "household of God" should be "built upon the foundation of the apostles and prophets" (Eph. 2:19–20). Mormons understand this less as a reference to ancient apostles and prophets and more as a call for the church to be led by living apostles and prophets. Latter-day Saints also find in Ephesians a rationale for the perpetuity of apostles as their chief episcopacy. Ephesians 4:11–14 indicates that Christ "gave some, apostles" (along with other ministers) "for the perfecting of the saints, for the work of the ministry, for the edifying of the body of Christ: till we all come in the unity of the faith . . . unto a perfect man, unto the measure of the stature of the fulness of Christ" and to ensure that the faithful are not "carried about with every wind of doctrine." Until these objectives are met in full, argue Latter-day Saints, apostles are still needed to exercise *episkopē* over the whole church.

In their quest for apostolicity, virtually all Christian churches seek to structure their church organization and government in line with what they take to be the New Testament pattern. The distance in time and culture dictates that for the most part the replication will be one of function more than specific office. This is also how best to understand the sixth Article of Faith of the Church of Jesus Christ of Latter-day Saints that proclaims: "We believe in the same organization that existed in the Primitive Church, namely, apostles, prophets, pastors, teachers, evangelists, and so forth."[90] The "and so forth" suggests that the statement is intended to establish a general rather than an exact link to New Testament polity, one that points toward ministerial function more than to a specific organizational roster. In other words, to speak of the "same organization" that existed in the primitive church is really to speak about an organization that carries out the same ministerial functions as the early church. Thereby the "sameness" of the modern and primitive churches is plausible, especially given the acknowledged variety and ambiguity of church structures and ministry in earliest Christianity.

This is apparent, for instance, when considering the role of "pastors." That both the sixth Article of Faith and Ephesians use "pastor" in a figurative or

---

90. The affirmation clearly echoes Eph. 4:11—"And [Christ] gave some, apostles; and some, prophets; and some, evangelists; and some, pastors and teachers."

functional sense rather than as a particular ecclesiastical position is clear from the fact that no office by that title is attested in either the New Testament, early Christianity, or the Church of Jesus Christ of Latter-day Saints.[91] Rather, "pastor" describes the function of various church ministers. "Pastor" translates *poimēn*, which in every instance other than Ephesians 4:11 is rendered "shepherd" in the KJV. Pastoring in the sense of "shepherding" (feeding, nourishing, caring for) God's flock gets to the heart of the Christian concept of ministry.[92] Three groups named in the New Testament seem to have functioned in some way as pastors—*episkopoi, presbyteroi,* and *diakonoi. Episkopoi,* as the meaning of the term in Greek indicates, are those who "look upon" or "watch over" Christ's flock as surrogate "good shepherds." The KJV translates *episkopoi* as "bishops" or "overseers." Another group of pastors are the *presbyteroi,* a term that generally designates advanced age. In many ancient civilizations, presiding authority was vested in those who by reason of age or experience were thought best qualified to govern. Although the common English translation of *presbyteroi* is "elders," to avoid too close a connection to age, the transliteration "presbyters" is also common in English-speaking churches.

Some scholars have argued that in the New Testament *episkopos* and *presbyteros* are interchangeable terms that identify the same presiding congregational minister but highlight different characteristics. That is, as "presbyter" the minister would be an experienced individual, a seasoned servant of the Lord, and as "bishop" he would oversee and minister to the congregation. Whatever the precise ministerial structure of New Testament churches, and it may have varied from place to place, by the beginning of the third century, *episkopos* and *presbyteros* clearly identify two *distinct* pastoral offices—bishop and presbyter/elder—in the ecclesiastical structure of the church.[93] For our

91. For a brief period in the mid-nineteenth century, the LDS Church in Britain did have such a position. See William G. Hartley, "LDS Pastors and Pastorates, 1852–1855," in *Mormons in Early Victorian Britain,* ed. Richard L. Jensen and Malcolm R. Thorp (Salt Lake City: University of Utah Press, 1989), 194–210.

92. Responding to one of Peter's replies to his query "Lovest thou me?" the resurrected Lord said, "Feed [*poimainō*] my sheep" (John 21:16). Later Peter passed on the same advice to the elders of the church: "Feed [*poimainō*] the flock of God which is among you" (1 Pet. 5:2).

93. Other scholars claim that the distinction was in place from the beginning. A paucity of unambiguous data means that the nature of the earliest ecclesiastical structure(s) in Christianity has been debated for centuries, and volumes have been written on the subject. For a more recent and careful reexamination of the evidence, see Alistair C. Stewart, *The Original Bishops: Office and Order in the First Christian Communities* (Grand Rapids: Baker Academic, 2014).

purposes, whether the terms identify a single office or two different ones, the important point is that what the New Testament emphasizes in either case is their pastoral duty to shepherd and "feed" the flock of God.[94] First and foremost, bishops and presbyters/elders are to be pastors. So are *diakonoi*. In its various verbal forms, the *diakonos* word group is almost always translated as "minister," "ministry," and "minister/unto," or "servant" and "serve." In a few instances, it is transliterated as "deacon(s)." The term's meanings are obvious synonyms for "pastor" and "pastoring" with their connotations of feeding and caring for the flock of God. As with *episkopoi* and *presbyteroi*, *diakonoi* may describe several different ministerial offices or none. In some cases, it may even refer to the mutual ministry, service, and concern to which the entire body of Christ is called as pastors to one another.

Along with perpetuating at the congregational level the key pastoral ministries of the early church in its own unique ecclesiastical configuration, the Church of Jesus Christ of Latter-day Saints maintains, as previously mentioned, an episcopal and pastoral ministry for the entire church through its "apostles" and "prophets." In addition to referring to the Twelve as *apostoloi* (from *apostellō*, "to send forth"), the New Testament also employs the term for other "apostles," ranging from evangelizing missionaries to individuals sent on official church errands (e.g., 2 Cor. 8:23; Phil. 2:25; Gal. 2:8). Initially, this more general use of "apostle" was known among Latter-day Saints.[95] John Taylor, a member of the original Council of Twelve Apostles, wrote to a friend in England two years after the council was created: "You ask what is the number of the apostles. There are twelve that are ordained to go to the nations, and there are many others, no definite number."[96] Here "apostle" is used in the Greek sense of "one who is sent forth" to preach the gospel as an "evangelist"

---

94. For example, in his farewell speech to the elders (*presbyteroi*) of the local churches in "Asia," Paul urges: "Take heed therefore unto yourselves, and to all the flock, over the which the Holy Ghost hath made you overseers [*episkopoi*], to feed [*poimainō*] the church of God" (Acts 20:28). Similarly, Peter declares, "The elders [*presbyteroi*] which are among you I exhort, who am also an elder [*presbyteros*]. . . . Feed [*poimainō*] the flock of God which is among you, taking the oversight [*episkopē*] thereof, not by constraint, but willingly" (1 Pet. 5:1–2).

95. The paragraph in the church's original Articles and Covenants listing the duties of an elder (D&C 20:38–44) begins with the words "an apostle is an elder." This connection is clear, for instance, in John Whitmer's elder's "license" dated June 9, 1830: "Given to John Whitmer signifying & proveing that he is an Apostle of Jesus Christ an Elder of this Church of Christ" (*JSP*, D1:144). Later, but before the first Quorum of Twelve Apostles was constituted, a group of elders were addressed thus: "As I said unto mine apostles, even so I say unto you, for you are mine apostles" (D&C 84:63).

96. *Latter Day Saints' Messenger and Advocate*, June 1837, 514.

(*euangelistēs*, "announcer of good news"). Over the next decade, however, as the Twelve assumed episcopal responsibilities for the whole church, the application of "apostle" began to be more restricted. Eventually, the term came to refer only to men ordained as "apostles" to participate in the church's hierarchy.[97] Today, the tens of thousands of missionaries sent forth annually by the Church of Jesus Christ of Latter-day Saints to evangelize the world are never referred to as "apostles." Nor are they called "evangelists," due in part to a rare, specialized use of the term in church nomenclature.[98] Yet, Mormon missionaries definitely proclaim the good news of Christ's redemptive life, death, and resurrection.[99]

A similar terminological narrowing occurred with the use of "prophet." In the New Testament, *prophētēs* generally describes a "proclaimer of the divine, inspired message."[100] When Paul wrote about *propheteia* (prophecy), as is particularly clear in 1 Corinthians 14, he seems to have had in mind the divine gift or *charism* of inspired utterance, of Spirit-guided expression. The sense of

97. In the history of the Church of Jesus Christ of Latter-day Saints, a few have been ordained "apostles" and functioned in the hierarchy without being members of the Quorum of the Twelve Apostles, but this has been rare, and they did not hold the keys of the kingdom along with the Twelve.

98. The first LDS Twelve were instructed that one of their duties was "in all large branches of the church, to ordain evangelical ministers, as they shall be designated unto them by revelation" (D&C 107:39). Joseph Smith later clarified, "An Evangelist is a patriarch" and wherever "the Church of Christ is established in the Earth there should be a Patriarch for the benefit of the posterity of the Saints, as it was with Jacob in giv[ing] his patriarchal bles[s]ing unto his Sons &c." *JSP*, D6:526. The office of blessing-pronouncing "patriarch" continues in the LDS Church today. Any worthy church member who so desires may receive a "patriarchal blessing." It is considered inspired, personalized life guidance for the recipient. See *GH* 18.17.

99. Female missionaries bear the title "sister"; male missionaries carry the title "elder." The use of "elder" reflects the name of the LDS priestly office held by male missionaries (see chapter 8). As currently used in reference to missionaries, the term "elder" is unrelated to the etymology or connotation of advanced years discussed above. Most male missionaries today are between eighteen and twenty-one years of age.

100. Gerhard Kittel and Gerhard Friedrich, eds., *Theological Dictionary of the New Testament*, 10 vols. (Grand Rapids: Eerdmans, 1977), 6:828. See also David Noel Freedman, ed., *The Anchor Bible Dictionary* (New York: Doubleday, 1992), 5:496, s.v. "early Christian prophecy." Examples of individuals in the New Testament who are either called "prophets" or who "prophesy" include John the Baptist (Luke 7:26); Agabus (Acts 11:27–28 and 21:10–14); Anna (Luke 2:36–38); the four daughters of Philip (Acts 21:9); Barnabas, Simeon, Lucius, Manaen, Saul at Antioch (Acts 13:1); and Judas Barsabbas and Silas (Acts 15:32). Indeed, Jesus was regarded by the people (and regarded himself) as a prophet (see Matt. 21:11; Luke 7:16; Mark 6:2–4).

prophecy as speaking under inspiration was also part of early Mormon doctrine. The church's ministers were directed to "speak as they are moved upon by the Holy Ghost" (D&C 68:2), and Joseph Smith explained to an eastern correspondent that "he no more professed to be a prophet than every man must, who professes to be a preacher of righteousness. . . . If a man professes to be a minister of Jesus, and has not the spirit of prophecy, he must be a false witness, for he is not in possession of that gift which qualifies him for his office."[101] Ministerial appointments were to be made by prophetic inspiration: "We believe that a man must be called of God, by prophecy, and by the laying on of hands by those who are in authority, to preach the Gospel and administer in the ordinances thereof" (Articles of Faith 5).[102] Moreover, the gathering in which the ordained ministry was to educate itself was known as the "school of the prophets" (D&C 88:127).[103] Today, these uses of "prophet" and "prophecy" have largely been eclipsed by popular reference to the president of the church as "the Prophet," and by inclusion of "prophets" in the title that officially designates the First Presidency and Quorum of the Twelve Apostles as "Prophets, Seers, and Revelators."[104] The generous use of "prophet" in Latter-day Saint nomenclature also reflects the fact that early Mormon primitivism drew on the Old Testament for models as readily as it did on the New Testament. In this case, the influential archetype was the prophet-leader Moses. Revelation directed Joseph Smith to "preside over the whole church, and to be like unto Moses . . . yea, to be a seer, a revelator . . . and a prophet, having all the gifts of God which he bestows upon the head of the church" (D&C 107:91–92).

In terms of apostolic polity, one additional ministry—that of "teacher"—is specifically mentioned in Paul's list in Ephesians and in the LDS Church's

---

101. *Times and Seasons*, May 1843, 200.

102. This Article of Faith reflects Paul's words to Timothy: "Neglect not the gift that is in thee, which was given thee by prophecy, with the laying on of the hands of the presbytery" (1 Tim. 4:14).

103. In using this designation, Latter-day Saints were simply following the older colonial practice of referring to ministers or preachers as "prophets" and the colleges, such as Harvard and Yale, where they received their education and training, as "schools of the prophets." See, for instance, Richard Warch, *School of the Prophets: Yale College, 1701–1741* (New Haven: Yale University Press, 1973).

104. Not long after constituting the first Quorum of the Twelve Apostles, Joseph Smith presented them to the church gathered in conference and asked that they also be acknowledged "as Prophets and Seers." *JSP*, J1:204. The practice of "sustaining" the apostles at church conferences continues to this day. From later in the nineteenth century, the language used has been standardized to read "Prophets, Seers, and Revelators." See *Journal of Discourses*, 19:114, 124; 21:47.

sixth Article of Faith. The most frequent use of *didaskalos* (teacher) in the New Testament is as a way of addressing Christ. In these instances, the KJV translators consistently chose to render *didaskalos* as "Master." Elsewhere, they use "teacher." With the change in the English language over the past four centuries, the sense of addressing Jesus as a teacher when calling him "Master" has been all but lost for the many Christians who use the King James Bible.[105] In addition to the ministerial list in Ephesians, Paul tells the Corinthians that "God hath set some in the church, first apostles, secondarily prophets, thirdly teachers" (1 Cor. 12:28). An active teaching ministry presumably is at the heart of the "Teacher's" church in any era. Latter-day Saints in every ministerial position in the church have received the invitation "teach ye diligently" (D&C 88:78). Those who have risen to the occasion understand well why Paul would put teachers in the third position behind only apostles and prophets. In the end, when considering ministerial apostolicity, what matters most is that the ministerial *functions* of the apostolic church are replicated. The names or titles, as well as the particular "job portfolio," of Christ's servants almost invariably change over the years, but the basic functions of the apostolic ministry can be preserved. In this sense, then, the First Presidency and Council of Twelve Apostles are able to "declare that The Church of Jesus Christ of Latter-day Saints, organized on April 6, 1830, is Christ's New Testament Church restored."[106]

Another way in which the LDS Church exhibits apostolicity as the "New Testament Church restored" is through its proclamation of spiritual giftedness. In this it shares with Pentecostal and charismatic churches a claim to what might be called "experiential apostolicity."[107] The seventh Article of Faith of the Church of Jesus Christ of Latter-day Saints affirms: "We believe in the gift

105. The older sense of "master" as "teacher" is preserved in the term "schoolmaster," although its use today with reference to a male schoolteacher has also become somewhat archaic.

106. First Presidency and Council of the Twelve Apostles, "The Restoration of the Fulness of the Gospel of Jesus Christ: A Bicentennial Proclamation to the World," *Ensign*, May 2020, 91–92.

107. This point is epitomized by the fact that a number of Pentecostal churches include "Apostolic" in their name, which in turn reflects the title of the early Pentecostal periodical the *Apostolic Faith*, which was associated with the foundational 1906 "Azusa Street revival" in Los Angeles, California. For an overview of the importance to Pentecostalism of the presence and gifts of the Holy Spirit, see Matthias Wenk, "Spiritual Gifts: Manifestations of the Kingdom of God," in Vondey, *The Routledge Handbook of Pentecostal Theology*, 301–10. For more in-depth discussions, see Max Turner, *The Holy Spirit and Spiritual Gifts: In the New Testament Church and Today*, rev. ed. (Grand Rapids: Baker Academic, 1997), and Craig S. Keener, *Gift & Giver: The Holy Spirit for Today* (Grand Rapids: Baker Academic, 2020).

of tongues, prophecy, revelation, visions, healing, interpretation of tongues, and so forth." Although historically most Christian groups have viewed these "extraordinary" gifts of the Spirit as confined to the apostolic age, early Latter-day Saints, like later Pentecostals and charismatics who rejected cessationism, believed they were essential aspects of authentic Christianity.[108] The Markan account of the Great Commission was considered paradigmatic: "Go ye into all the world, and preach the gospel to every creature . . . and these signs shall follow them that believe; In my name shall they cast out devils; they shall speak with new tongues; they shall take up serpents; and if they drink any deadly thing, it shall not hurt them; they shall lay hands on the sick, and they shall recover" (Mark 16:15–18). "I wish the reader never to pass this commission," declared early apostle Parley Pratt, "until he understands it, because, when once understood, he never need mistake the kingdom of God, but will at once discover those peculiarities, which were forever to distinguish it from all other kingdoms or religious systems on earth."[109] Here indeed were crucial *notae ecclesiae*.[110]

Not surprisingly, revelation renewed the Great Commission for Latter-day Saints: "Go ye into all the world, preach the gospel to every creature . . . and he that believeth shall be blest with signs following, even as it is written" (D&C 68:8–10). A subsequent revelation reiterated, "As I said unto mine apostles, I say unto you again," and then repeated almost verbatim the signs promised in Mark 16 (D&C 84:64–72). Nor was this latter-day restoration of miraculous gifts and graces to be any less dramatic than in the apostolic age:

108. When the bishop of Rome rejected the legitimacy of a second-century outbreak of prophecy among the followers of one Montanus, a disappointed Tertullian wrote, "He put to flight the Paraclete [Holy Spirit]." Tertullian, *Against Praxeas* 1. Thereafter, in the colorful but exaggerated words of historian Adolf von Harnack, the Spirit "was chased into a book," meaning the apostolic gifts of the Spirit were to be read about (in the Bible) rather than experienced in one's own life and time. Harnack, *Origin of the New Testament* (Berlin, 1914), 36. An exegetical and theological challenge to cessationism is Jon Mark Ruthven, *On the Cessation of the Charismata: The Protestant Polemic on Post-Biblical Miracles*, rev. ed. (Tulsa, OK: Word & Spirit Publishing, 2011). Challenging cessationism on historical terms is Stanley M. Burgess, ed., *Christian Peoples of the Spirit: A Documentary History of Pentecostal Spirituality from the Early Church to the Present* (New York: New York University Press, 2011).

109. Parley P. Pratt, *A Voice of Warning and Instruction to All People, Containing an Introduction to the Faith and Doctrine of the Church of the Latter-Day Saints, Commonly Called Mormons* (New York: W. Sandford, 1837), 100.

110. This is a perspective shared among Pentecostals. See Kimberly Ervin Alexander and John Christopher Thomas, "'And the Signs Are Following': Mark 16.9–20—a Journey into Pentecostal Hermeneutics," *Journal of Pentecostal Theology* 11, no. 2 (2003): 147–70.

"Whoso shall ask it in my name in faith, they shall cast out devils; they shall heal the sick; they shall cause the blind to receive their sight, and the deaf to hear, and the dumb to speak, and the lame to walk" (D&C 35:9).[111] A Book of Mormon prophet asked rhetorically, "if there were miracles wrought then, why has God ceased to be a God of miracles, and yet be an unchangeable Being?" (Mormon 9:19). Early Latter-day Saints would have heartily concurred with a characterization attributed to famed nineteenth-century preacher A. J. Gordon that Christendom "had framed the excuse that the age of miracles was past simply to camouflage its own impotence. If the age of miracles was past, it was due to the church's lack of faith."[112] The final Book of Mormon prophet similarly warned in his valedictory: "And now I speak unto all the ends of the earth—that if the day cometh that the power and gifts of God shall be done away among you, it shall be because of unbelief" (Moroni 10:24).

That early Mormonism spoke for a faith-filled, gifted Christianity was apparent to observers like nineteenth-century Quaker poet and journalist John Greenleaf Whittier, who observed a "Mormon conventicle" in Lowell, Massachusetts. "They contrast strongly the miraculous power of the gospel in the apostolic time with the present state of our nominal Christianity," reported Whittier.

They ask for signs of divine power; the faith . . . which opened the prison doors of the apostles, gave them power over the elements, which rebuked disease and death itself, and made visible to all the presence of the Living God. They ask for any declaration in the Scriptures that this miraculous power of faith was to be confined to the first confessors of Christianity. They speak a language of hope and promise to weak, weary hearts, tossed and troubled, who have wandered from sect to sect, seeking in vain for the primal manifestations of the divine power.[113]

A hymn composed in the 1830s and sung at the dedication of the Saints' sanctuary in Ohio joyously proclaimed, "The Spirit of God like a fire is burning; The latter-day glory begins to come forth; The visions and blessings of old are returning; The angels are coming to visit the earth. . . . We call in our solemn assemblies, in spirit . . . that we through our faith may begin to inherit

111. See also D&C 58:64; 63:9; 124:98–100.

112. Adoniram Judson Gordon, *The Ministry of Healing* (1882), as paraphrased by Paul G. Chappell, "Healing Movements," in Burgess and McGee, *Dictionary of Pentecostal and Charismatic Movements*, 362.

113. [John Greenleaf Whittier], *The Stranger in Lowell* (Boston: Waite, Pierce & Co., 1845), 28–29.

the visions, and blessings, and glories of God . . . We'll sing & we'll shout with the armies of heaven; Hosanna, hosanna to God and the Lamb!"[114]

Among such notable spiritual manifestations, in addition to the previously discussed gift of prophecy, the seventh Article of Faith proclaims the present reality of healings, tongues, and the interpretation of tongues. Healings are frequently attested by church members (see chapter 11), and decades before the birth of Pentecostalism, the gifts of tongues and interpretation of tongues were being experienced by Latter-day Saints.[115] Indeed, so commonly were the gifts of the Spirit experienced in the earliest years of the church that in places and at times Mormonism seemed to be a form of proto-Pentecostalism.[116] As just a single example among many, an early LDS convert recounted that at one of the church conferences he witnessed "the visible manifestations of the power of God as plain as could have been on the day of Pentecost," including "the healing of the sick, casting out devils, speaking in unknown tongues, discerning of spirits, and prophesying with mighty power."[117] At the same time, revelation warned the Saints to "require not miracles." There were, however, two exceptions "except I shall command you" and, echoing Mark 16, "except casting out devils, healing the sick, and against poisonous serpents, and against deadly poisons." Even then, the demonstration of these divine powers was designed to answer the "weary," seeking souls who had failed to encounter the apostolic charismata elsewhere: "And these things ye shall not do, except it be required of you by them who desire it, that the scriptures might be fulfilled; for ye shall do according to that which is written" (D&C 24:13–14).

The prevalence of extraordinary manifestations among early Mormons meant that both revelations and instruction in church periodicals were needed at times to provide assistance in discerning legitimate spiritual gifts from the counterfeit.[118] In the two centuries since its founding, the Church of Jesus Christ of Latter-day Saints has moderated much of its early Pentecostal, charis-

---

114. *A Collection of Sacred Hymns for the Church of the Latter Day Saints* (Kirtland, OH, 1835), #90.

115. Extensively documented in Mark L. Staker, *Hearken, O Ye People: The Historical Setting of Joseph Smith's Ohio Revelations* (Salt Lake City: Kofford Books, 2009), passim.

116. For a comparative look at charismatic experience and belief in Pentecostalism and Mormonism, see Alan J. Clark, *The Full Gospel in Zion: A History of Pentecostalism in Utah* (Salt Lake City: University of Utah Press, 2022), and J. Christopher Thomas, *A Pentecostal Reads the Book of Mormon: A Literary and Theological Introduction* (Cleveland, TN: CPT Press, 2016).

117. Quoted in *JSP*, D1:322.

118. See, for instance, *JSP*, D1:303–8, 281–83; D10:150–62; and D9:323–37.

matic character. Discussion of lay visions, dreams, and speaking in tongues has been reframed, and the gifts reinterpreted in ways that accommodate modern sensibilities.[119] Prophecy is reserved for the "prophets, seers, and revelators" who govern the church, and "today the gift of tongues is most often manifested in Spirit-enhanced learning" of the particular foreign language LDS missionaries need to know "in their mission[s]."[120] Still, if in some ways Mormonism has experienced what sociologists call the "routinization of charisma," Latter-day Saint beliefs and values to a notable degree have managed to avoid the desacralization characteristic of much of modern society. Spiritual gifts, especially healings, continue to be experienced, though in quieter, less dramatic fashion, and this perpetuation of "life in the Spirit," albeit more refined, enables Latter-day Saints to continue to affirm the church's "experiential apostolicity."[121]

Having explored the images, models, and "marks" of the church of Christ in this chapter, we turn in the next chapter to matters of ecclesiastical authority and ministry. We probe further what for some is the key authorizing concept of apostolic succession and the fundamental notion of priesthood. We examine church polities and the meaning of ecclesiastical "primacy." And we analyze the nature of authoritativeness in church teaching. Each of these investigations sheds important light not only on the Church of Jesus Christ of Latter-day Saints but on ecclesiological perspectives and values generally in the Christian world today.

---

119. This transformation, largely effected in the first decades of the twentieth century, is outlined in Thomas G. Alexander, *Mormonism in Transition: A History of the Latter-day Saints, 1890–1930* (Urbana: University of Illinois Press, 1986), 289–326.

120. *Preach My Gospel: A Guide to Sharing the Gospel of Jesus Christ*, 2nd ed. (Salt Lake City: The Church of Jesus Christ of Latter-day Saints, 2023), 143–44. The transition to this understanding of tongues is recounted in Matthew R. Davies, "The Tongues of the Saints: The Azusa Street Revival and the Changing Definition of Tongues," in *Joseph F. Smith: Reflections on the Man and His Times*, ed. Craig K. Manscill et al. (Provo, UT: BYU Religious Studies Center, 2013), 470–85.

121. The Pentecostal Assemblies of God have experienced a similar moderating trajectory over the past century. See Margaret M. Poloma and John C. Green, *The Assemblies of God: Godly Love and the Revitalization of American Pentecostalism* (New York: New York University Press, 2010).

8

CHURCH

Authority, Priesthood, and Ministry

In 1990, renowned Yale historian Jon Butler published an important and popular revisionist study of American religious history titled *Awash in a Sea of Faith*.[1] The title accurately conveys an image of the waves of religious fervor that washed over the American cultural landscape between the Revolution and the Civil War. With the disestablishment of religion in the final quarter of the eighteenth century that did away with governmental sponsorship (Massachusetts and Connecticut held on into the nineteenth century), denominations had to compete with each other for adherents. Having previously relied on the state for support, the old established colonial communions such as the Anglicans (subsequently, Episcopalians in the USA) and Congregationalists were often ill-equipped to participate in the religious "free market" that emerged in the early republic. Other denominations, however, especially the Methodists and newer "upstart" groups, quickly adapted to this environment. As a result, religion in the new republic "flourished in response to religious deregulation."[2] Historian Martin Marty quipped: "The evangelizers started a Soul Rush that soon outpaced the Gold Rush [and] was a textbook example of free enterprise in the marketplace of religion."[3] Many preachers rose to prominence on the insistence that they were guiding listeners back to the simple truths of the Bible. Contemporary theologian John Nevin concluded that "the principle 'No creed but the Bible'" was "the distinctive feature of American religion"

1. Jon Butler, *Awash in a Sea of Faith: Christianizing the American People* (Cambridge, MA: Harvard University Press, 1990).

2. Roger Finke and Laurence R. Iannaccone, "Supply-Side Explanations for Religious Change," *Annals of the American Academy of Political and Social Science* 52 (May 1993): 29. See also Roger Finke and Rodney Stark, "How the Upstart Sects Won America: 1776–1850," *Journal for the Scientific Study of Religion* 28 (March 1989): 27–44.

3. Martin E. Marty, *Pilgrims in Their Own Land: 500 Years in America* (Boston: Little, Brown, 1984), 169.

during this era.[4] Ironically, this *ad fontes* ("[back] to the sources") approach only amplified the cacophony of competing voices.[5]

The result, recounted one period Baptist historian, "was a civil war. . . . The mad spirit of the hour . . . pervaded the worshiping assembly and invaded the sacred precincts of the hearthstone and family altar. Every form of public worship became a subject of wrangling and debate."[6] "In the midst of this war of words and tumult of opinions," Joseph Smith later recalled, "I often said to myself: What is to be done? Who of all these parties are right; or, are they all wrong together? If any one of them be right, which is it, and how shall I know it?"[7] Richard McNemar, a Methodist-turned-Presbyterian-turned-Christian-turned-Shaker, spoke from experience when he penned these lines: "Ten thousand Reformers like so many moles; have plowed all the Bible and cut it [in] holes. And each has his church at the end of his trace; built up as he thinks of the subjects of grace."[8] What was needed in this highly charged and competitive environment was authoritative guidance from the Almighty himself. Only an individual or individuals divinely authorized to settle doctrinal disputes, a sort of supreme court of Christianity, could end the confusion. Methodist restorationer James O'Kelley observed that such a definitive resolution would require "a Prophet or Apostle."[9] According to Latter-day Saint history, and to Joseph Smith's considerable surprise, this is precisely what God did with and through him. If God had previously called humble fishermen, why could he not call a young farm boy to be his prophetic instrument?

Nearly two centuries earlier, Roger Williams, maverick Puritan and famed advocate of "soul liberty," also saw the need for new apostles, having decided that the Christian world had fallen into complete apostasy. The idea that drift and apostasy had occurred within Christianity at least from the era of its corrupting alliance with Constantine in the fourth century, if not earlier, was stock-in-trade of Protestant anti-Catholic polemics and had been since the

---

4. Quoted in Nathan Hatch, *The Democratization of American Christianity* (New Haven: Yale University Press, 1989), 81.

5. See Richard T. Hughes, ed., *The American Quest for the Primitive Church* (Urbana: University of Illinois Press, 1988).

6. John H. Spencer, *A History of Kentucky Baptists: From 1769 to 1885*, 2 vols. (Cincinnati: J. R. Baumes, 1885), 1:617.

7. *JSP*, H1:210. Later included in the Pearl of Great Price as Joseph Smith—History 1:10.

8. Richard McNemar, "The Moles' Little Pathways," quoted in Hatch, *Democratization of American Christianity*, 81.

9. Quoted in Gordon S. Wood, "Evangelical America and Early Mormonism," *New York History* 61 (October 1980): 378.

days of the Reformation. For Williams, though, the situation was beyond drift and digression. In his view, there had been "a totall Routing of the *Church* and *Ministry* of *Christ Jesus,* put to flight, and retired into the *Wildernesse of Deso-lation.*"[10] Robert Baillie, one of several Presbyterian ministers sent by Scotland to take part in England's Westminster Assembly in the 1640s, summarized Williams's claim: "There is no church, no sacraments, no pastors, no church-officers or ordinances in the world, nor has [there] been since a few years after the Apostles."[11] Two centuries later, this would become the standard Mormon position as well. Williams did, however, allow that there had always been an "invisible" church of the elect who worshiped God in spirit and truth. The problem was that there were no authentic "visible" churches, no legitimate ec-clesial bodies, in which to do so. Williams surveyed the "so-called churches" of England and New England and "could not find that God had authorized these or any other gatherings for worship that now claimed the name of church. They were all the product of wishful thinking, human inventions all, and to read God into them was only another example of human presumption."[12] As noted New England minister and Williams's opponent John Cotton reported, Williams believed "that the Apostasy of Antichrist [Rome] hath so far cor-rupted all, that there can be no recovery out of that Apostasy till Christ shall send forth new Apostles to plant Churches anew."[13]

Roger Williams's position that long ago apostasy from apostolic moorings "had completely extinguished the ministry established by Christ" would later be echoed by Joseph Smith.[14] In his first open letter to the American public, Smith declared, "By the foregoing testamonies . . . we may look at the Chris-tian world and see the apostacy there has been from the Apostolic platform, and who can look at this, and not exclaim in the language of Isaiah [24:5], the earth is defiled under the inhabitants thereof because they have transgressed the Laws; changed the ordinances and broken the everlasting covenant."[15] Only a fresh start, a divinely effected reinstatement of an authentic ministry and a reestablishment of Christ's visible church, could rectify the situation. "Apostasy

10. Roger Williams, *The Hireling Ministry None of Christs* (London, 1652), 2.

11. Quoted in Edmund S. Morgan, *Roger Williams: The Church and the State* (New York: Norton, 1987), 53.

12. Morgan, *Roger Williams*, 54.

13. John Cotton, *The Bloudy Tennent . . . whereunto is added a Reply to Mr. Williams Answer, to Mr. Cottons Letter* (London, 1647). *Reply* is appended to *Bloudy Tennent* with its own pagination. The quote is from p. 9.

14. The quote is from Morgan, *Roger Williams*, 45.

15. *JSP,* D2:352.

resolved by Restoration" became something of a Mormon conceptual mantra. In the LDS view, a complete apostasy required a total restoration under direct, divine guidance. This is why Latter-day Saints distinguish their reformation of Christianity from all other reformations by calling it a "restoration." In the Mormon idiom, "reformation" implies human initiative and execution, the kind of "wishful thinking" and "human presumption" that Williams disdained. "Restoration," on the other hand, connotes for Latter-day Saints divine initiative and direct, divine involvement, those crucial elements that Mormons believe (and Williams believed) are necessary to reestablish the church on its apostolic foundation. Divine authority received by ordination at the hands of Christ's original apostles and passed on in orderly succession thereafter is the heart of the daring claim of the Church of Jesus Christ of Latter-day Saints to be "the only true and living church upon the face of the whole earth" (D&C 1:30). The church's *General Handbook* states the key claim succinctly: "The Church of Jesus Christ of Latter-day Saints is the only organization on earth with priesthood authority."[16] First Presidency member Charles Penrose acknowledged that "there are many learned professors and teachers of theology . . . men blest of God with the gift of speech, and it is beautiful to hear [them]." Still, "there is one thing which they all lack—every sect, every denomination, every section or faction of Christendom is lacking the power of God to administer in His holy name *by authority*. This is a matter of the very greatest importance."[17]

William Hague was minister of the Providence, Rhode Island, Baptist church that claimed continuity with the one Roger Williams was briefly associated with two centuries earlier. In remarks on the occasion of the church's bicentennial in 1839, Hague opined that the idea of apostolic succession and Williams's concern with direct divine authority were the *sine qua non* (indispensable conditions) of authentic Christian churches. This view, "if *strictly followed out to its legitimate conclusion*," averred Hague, "would lead any one of us, either to become a seeker, and wait for a new apostleship [as Williams did], or else to unite with the church of Rome."[18] A similar conclusion about apostolic succession was drawn years later by a Catholic theologian in conversation with LDS apostle Orson Whitney. "You don't even know the strength of your own position," the Catholic cleric is reported to have remarked. "It is so strong that there is only one other position tenable in the whole Christian world, and that is the position of the Roman Catholic Church. The issue is between

---

16. *GH* 3.1.
17. Charles W. Penrose, *Conference Report*, October 1910, 59.
18. William Hague, *An Historical Discourse* (Providence, RI: B. Cranston & Co., 1839), 179.

Mormonism and Catholicism. If you are right, we are wrong. If we are right, you are wrong. And that's all there is to it. . . . It is either the perpetuation of the gospel from ancient times, or the restoration of the gospel in latter days."[19] Whitney's account was popular in LDS circles for its striking all-or-nothing perspective on the importance of ministerial authority. For Catholics and Mormons alike, as well as for Orthodox, whom Whitney's Catholic conversation partner did not mention, the essentiality of an authoritative, historically continuous, ordained ministry to govern Christ's church is paramount.

Confident in the belief that their church enjoyed unique, divine sponsorship, early Mormons tended to draw a sharp contrast between the recently restored "Church of Christ" (the original name of the church) and the apostate condition of establishment Christianity. This sometimes led to expressions that understandably were offensive to other Christians. Perhaps most well-known is Joseph Smith's reminiscence of what he learned from his initial encounter with Deity: "The Personage who addressed me said that all their creeds were an abomination in his sight." Moreover, the Messenger applied to the churches of the day words of criticism found in the New Testament, averring that the churches "teach for doctrines the commandments of men [cf. Matt. 15:9], having a form of godliness, but they deny the power thereof [2 Tim. 3:5]."[20] Equally jolting is the vision of the Book of Mormon prophet who sees in the centuries following the apostolic era a "great and abominable church" whose "founder" is "the devil" (1 Nephi 13:2–6). The vision depicts this "church" as perverting the "plain and precious" truths taught by the apostles, and "because of these things which are taken away out of the gospel of the Lamb, an exceedingly great many do stumble, yea, insomuch that Satan hath great power over them" (1 Nephi 13:26–29). Here and in the next chapter, 1 Nephi 14, as the vision continues, the great and abominable church is linked with "Babylon," the "mother of harlots," the "great whore," of Revelation 17. Especially in the context of centuries of Protestant anti-Catholic conditioning, when looking back at early Christian history, there seemed to be no candidate for this great and abominable church other than the Roman Catholic Church. What is noteworthy is that despite the LDS Church being born in an era of virulent

19. Orson F. Whitney, *Conference Report*, October 1924, 19–20. Whitney again recounted this conversation in *Conference Report*, April 1928, 60; and later, apostle Legrand Richards (1886–1983) included the account in his much-reprinted, mid-twentieth-century book *A Marvelous Work and a Wonder* (Salt Lake City: Deseret Book, 1950), 3–4. This line of reasoning in one form or another has been present in Mormonism from its early years. See, for example, *Times and Seasons*, February 1842, 694.

20. *JSP*, H1:214 (Joseph Smith—History, 1:19).

anti-Catholicism, early Mormons actually spent very little time criticizing the Catholic Church or Catholics in general in their effort to declare Christendom spiritually bankrupt.[21] Latter-day Saints were far more interested in assailing the "sectarian" Protestant churches around them.[22]

By the early twentieth century, however, Latter-day Saint perceptions of other Christian churches and Mormon characterizations of "the Great Apostasy" were beginning to soften.[23] Church leader B. H. Roberts, for instance, offered this interpretation of the discussion in 1 Nephi 13–14: "'The church of the devil' here alluded to, I understand to mean not any particular church among men, or any one sect of religion, but something larger than that—something that includes within its boundaries all evil wherever it may be found; as well in schools of philosophy as in Christian sects; as well in systems of ethics as in systems of religion—something that includes the whole empire of Satan."[24] Today, LDS Sunday school teachers are instructed to "emphasize that the great and abominable church is a symbol of apostasy in all its forms. It is a representation of all false doctrine, false worship, and irreligious attitudes. It does not represent any specific church in the world today."[25]

In the past century, much has been said by Latter-day Saint leaders to affirm that divine truth and authentic spiritual experience are found outside the confines of the Church of Jesus Christ of Latter-day Saints. Apostle Dallin Oaks

21. See Matthew J. Grow, "The Whore of Babylon and the Abomination of Abominations: Nineteenth-Century Catholic and Mormon Mutual Perceptions and Religious Identity," *Church History* 73 (March 2004): 139–67. For nineteenth-century context, see Jenny Franchot, *Roads to Rome: The Antebellum Protestant Encounter with Catholicism* (Berkeley: University of California Press, 1994).

22. How the boldness of the LDS proclamation could sometimes spill over into intemperate and hyperbolic rhetoric is illustrated in such nineteenth-century comments as these: "There is no more similarity between Christianity, as it now exists, with all its superstitions, corruptions, jargons, contentions, divisions, weakness, and imbecility, and this KINGDOM OF GOD, as spoken of in the Scriptures, than there is between light and darkness . . . or a taper [and] the glorious luminary of day." John Taylor, *The Government of God* (Liverpool: S. W. Richards, 1852), 92.

23. For a history of LDS attitudes toward "the Apostasy," see Miranda Wilcox and John D. Young, eds., *Standing Apart: Mormon Historical Consciousness and the Concept of Apostasy* (New York: Oxford University Press, 2014).

24. B. H. Roberts, *New Witnesses for God, II—The Book of Mormon* (Salt Lake City: Deseret News, 1909), 3:264n. Bruce McConkie later offered a similar interpretation in *Mormon Doctrine*, 2nd ed., 137–38, after complaints were registered that in the first edition of the book he perpetuated the old identification of the Catholic Church with the "great and abominable church."

25. *Book of Mormon Gospel Doctrine Teacher's Manual* (2003), 18.

offered this irenic qualifier to earlier rhetoric about other belief systems: "These descriptions . . . are surely undiplomatic, but I hasten to add that Latter-day Saints do not apply such criticism to the men and women who profess these beliefs."[26] The LDS dispute has been with traditions, not individuals. The same John Taylor who in other situations could excoriate institutional Christianity remarked, "There were men in those dark ages who could commune with God, and who, by the power of faith, could draw aside the curtain of eternity and gaze . . . upon the face of God, have the ministering of angels, and unfold the future destinies of the world. If those were dark ages, I pray God to give me a little darkness."[27] "We believe," stated Dallin Oaks, "that most religious leaders and followers are sincere believers who love God and understand and serve him to the best of their abilities. . . . We are indebted to the men and women who kept the light of faith and learning alive through the centuries to the present day. . . . We honor them as servants of God."[28] The *General Handbook* summarizes the church's current position: "Much that is inspiring, noble, and worthy of the highest respect is found in many other faiths."[29]

In the scholarly schema that categorizes attitudes toward other religions as either "exclusivist," "inclusivist," or "pluralist," Latter-day Saints today, like Catholics and many others, would be inclusivists. Exclusivism claims that there is one true religion, one correct path to salvation, and that all other religions are mistaken attempts at understanding God and achieving salvation. Inclusivism maintains that there is one religion that best understands God and the path to salvation but also holds that God is at work in other religions in an inferior or incomplete way. Pluralism claims that truth sufficient for salvation is found in many religions so that each provides an equally valid path to God and heaven. To be sure, Mormonism's strong "only true church" rhetoric and determined prose-lytizing would seem to place it squarely on the exclusivist end of the spectrum. In ways this is true, certainly in the past. Yet, as illustrated above and as discussed in the previous chapter, a degree of inclusivism has always flickered in the rhetorical background and has steadily become more prominent in the past century.

---

26. Dallin H. Oaks, "Apostasy and Restoration," *Ensign*, May 1995, 85.

27. *Journal of Discourses*, 16:197.

28. Oaks, "Apostasy and Restoration," 85.

29. GH 38.8.29. In the twenty-first century, a reporter for the *Washington Post* visited an LDS Church meeting in Nigeria. Afterward, the reporter interviewed a new member who told of his conversion. The newcomer recounted how "he jumped off a city bus and walked into the [LDS Church building]. . . . He immediately liked what he heard inside, especially that no one preached that people of other faiths were going to hell." Quoted in Quentin L. Cook, "Our Father's Plan—Big Enough for All His Children," *Ensign*, May 2009, 37.

Setting the tone in the early twentieth century for this more decided inclusivism in the Church of Jesus Christ of Latter-day Saints was the irenic ministry of apostle and later church president George Albert Smith. In a subsequently oft-cited account, Smith reported his respectful response to a minister who was annoyed that the LDS Church had sent missionaries to his already Christian country: "You have a misconception of the purpose of the Church," Smith stated. "First of all, we are asking all you fine people over here to keep all the glorious truths that you have acquired in your churches, that you have absorbed from your scriptures, keep all that . . . you have gained from every source. . . . Then let us sit down and share with you some of the things that have not yet come into your lives that have enriched our lives and made us happy."[30] Joseph Smith put it succinctly years before: "We do not ask any people to throw away any good they have got, we only ask them to come & get more."[31] Despite such inclusivist expressions, what has been consistently identified throughout LDS history as lacking outside the Church of Jesus Christ of Latter-day Saints is a fullness of gospel truth and plenary authority directly delegated from Deity to administer the Christian sacraments and function as the visible, "official" church of Christ. This is why from Joseph Smith onward, Latter-day Saints have earnestly endeavored to persuade fellow Christians to come and partake of the fullness they believe is uniquely available in the Church of Jesus Christ of Latter-day Saints.

Keys of the Kingdom

Any discussion of ministerial authority from God needs to consider the meaning of the "keys of the kingdom." The phrase comes from an account in Matthew of a verbal exchange between Jesus and Peter. To the interrogatory,

> Whom say ye that I am? . . . Peter answered and said, Thou art the Christ, the Son of the living God. And Jesus answered and said unto him, Blessed art thou, Simon Barjona: for flesh and blood hath not revealed it unto thee, but my Father which is in heaven. And I say also unto thee, That thou art Peter, and upon this rock I will build my church; and the gates of hell shall not prevail against it. And I will give unto thee the keys of the kingdom of heaven: and whatsoever thou shalt bind on earth shall be bound in heaven: and whatsoever thou shalt loose on earth shall be loosed in heaven. (Matt. 16:13–19)

30. George Albert Smith, *Sharing the Gospel with Others: Excerpts from the Sermons of President Smith* (Salt Lake City: Deseret New Press, 1948), 200.
31. *JSP*, D11:361.

Subsequently, in the context of a brief discussion on resolving intrachurch disputes, Jesus repeated to his apostles what he had previously said to Peter: "Verily I say unto you, Whatsoever ye shall bind on earth shall be bound in heaven: and whatsoever ye shall loose on earth shall be loosed in heaven" (Matt. 18:18). Later, when Jesus appeared to the apostles after his resurrection, he declared, in what many see as a related expression, "Whose soever sins ye remit, they are remitted unto them; and whose soever sins ye retain, they are retained" (John 20:23).

Considerable attention over the course of Christian history has been given to explicating these three passages of scripture. What is their meaning? Are they related? If so, how? And how do they elucidate what is meant by "keys of the kingdom"? Before exploring the obvious significance of these passages for Catholics and their parallel importance for Latter-day Saints, we consider Protestant perspectives. John Calvin, hoping to find a way through the interpretive thicket, suggested optimistically that if Christians could "agree among [themselves] on the word 'keys' and on the manner of binding, all contention will cease at once." He then proposed this solution: "Since heaven is opened to us by the doctrine of the gospel, the word 'keys' affords an appropriate metaphor. Now men are bound and loosed in no other way than when faith reconciles some to God, while . . . unbelief constrains others the more." Especially because in Matthew 16 the full expression is "keys of the kingdom of heaven," the keys are interpreted symbolically as a commission to preach the saving gospel that admits people into the church and ultimately into the kingdom of heaven. In sum, for Calvin, the keys refer "solely to the ministry of the word."[32] Huldrych Zwingli took the same interpretive tack: "Here then are the keys which Christ committed to the apostles, by which they unlocked the gates of Heaven—they preached the gospel."[33] The Reformers also challenged the monarchical role of the bishop of Rome's "Petrine office" by stressing that the powers conferred upon Peter were conferred upon all the apostles. To underline this point, Calvin cited Augustine to the effect that in making his declaration of faith in Christ, Peter was speaking for all the apostles. Jesus's question—"whom say *ye* that I am?"—was directed to all, and Peter replied on their behalf. "Being one, he said the former for all and received the latter [the keys] with all."[34]

The Reformers also saw something additional intended in Matthew 18 and John 20. Because Christ's promise in Matthew 18 that whatsoever the apostles

32. Calvin, *Institutes* 4.6.4.

33. Quoted in Clarence N. Heller, ed. and trans., *Latin Works of Huldreich Zwingli*, vol. 3 (Philadelphia: Heidelberg, 1929), 18.

34. Calvin, *Institutes* 4.6.4.

"shall bind on earth shall be bound in heaven: and whatsoever [they] shall loose on earth shall be loosed in heaven" was made in the context of guidance for how the church should deal with transgressors, Calvin considered the Matthew 18 referent to binding and loosing to be different from that in Matthew 16 (and John 20): "They differ in this respect," he wrote, Matthew 16 "relates specially to the preaching which the ministers of the word perform," whereas the binding and loosing mentioned in Matthew 18 "relates to the discipline of excommunication which has been committed to the Church."[35] The two actions, however, could be considered different dimensions of the same keys. Question 83 of the Heidelberg Catechism asks, "What is the office of the keys? The preaching of the holy gospel and Christian discipline. By these two means the kingdom of heaven is opened to believers and shut against unbelievers."[36] Martin Luther and his followers also interpreted Matthew 18 and John 20 as discussing the disciplinary exercise of the office of the keys. Luther considered this one of the marks of a true church. "God's people, or holy Christians," he taught, "are recognized by the office of the keys exercised publicly. That is, as Christ decrees in Matt. 18, if Christians sin, they should be reproved; and if they do not mend their ways, they should be bound in their sins and cast out."[37]

While there is some overlap with Protestant views, the Catholic doctrine of the keys and interpretation of the relevant scriptural passages are distinctive. The Catholic focus is on ecclesiastical government and *episkopē* (oversight). The *Catechism* explains: "The 'power of the keys' designates authority to govern the house of God, which is the Church. Jesus, the Good Shepherd, confirmed this mandate after his resurrection: 'Feed my sheep.'" Under that interpretive umbrella, the Catholic understanding of the keys draws in aspects touched on in all three of the scriptural passages: "The power to 'bind and loose' connotes the authority to absolve sins, to pronounce doctrinal judgements, and to make disciplinary decisions in the Church. Jesus entrusted this authority to the Church through the ministry of the apostles and in particular through the ministry of Peter, the only one to whom he specifically entrusted the keys of the kingdom."[38] Orthodox interpretation is similar: "The keys of the kingdom refers to a special authority that [was] given to both Peter and the other apostles after the Resurrection." It "includes all the teaching, sacramen-

---

35. Calvin, *Institutes* 4.11.1,2.
36. *Creeds & Confessions*, 2:446.
37. Martin Luther, *On the Councils and the Church* (1539), in *The Annotated Luther*, vol. 3, *Church and Sacraments*, ed. Paul W. Robinson (Minneapolis: Fortress, 2016), 426.
38. *CCC* 553.

tal, and administrative authority of the apostles [which] was in turn transmitted to the bishops of the Church." The Orthodox, however, offer an important qualifier with regard to Peter's relationship to the other apostles: "Peter was not a leader over the others, but among them. . . . Papal claims in later centuries must not be confused with the NT witness regarding Peter."[39]

How do Latter-day Saints understand the keys of the kingdom? With other Christian traditions, Mormonism holds that Christ bestowed the keys on the original Twelve collectively. In the LDS view, those keys were to be exercised by the apostles as a body. Because they were unable to perpetuate themselves as a council (or "college"), however, Latter-day Saints regard the keys as having been lost in the apostasy that followed. In the Mormon conception, the keys of the kingdom remained lost until they were restored to Joseph Smith by angelic conferral. At that point, revelation could again proclaim: "the keys of the kingdom of God are committed unto man on the earth" (D&C 65:2). This restoration of apostolic authority has always been at the heart of the Mormon evangel. On one occasion in the 1970s, church president Spencer Kimball and several apostles visited the Copenhagen Cathedral. Its nave is lined with individual marble statues of Christ's twelve apostles (Paul replaces Judas Iscariot), and the world-famous *Christus* stands in a niche above the altar. During Kimball's visit he and his entourage paused to admire the statue of Peter holding a large set of keys in one hand. Kimball remarked to the caretaker, "We are *living* apostles of the Lord Jesus Christ. . . . We hold the real keys, as Peter did, and we use them every day."[40]

Beyond conferring crucial ministerial authority, Latter-day Saint understandings of what the keys authorize are similar to how Catholics, Orthodox, and others understand the three relevant passages in the Gospels. Echoing John 20, Joseph Smith was told: "I have conferred upon you the keys and power of the priesthood . . . and whosesoever sins you remit on earth shall be remitted eternally in the heavens; and whosesoever sins you retain on earth shall be retained in heaven" (D&C 132:45–46). Reflecting the Matthean passages, revelation instructed that all ministerial actions and ordinances are performed "in the power of the [restored] priesthood, by the revelation of Jesus Christ, wherein it is granted that whatsoever you bind on earth shall be bound in heaven, and whatsoever you loose on earth shall be loosed in Heaven" (D&C 128:8). Joseph Smith explained, "in one sense of the word, the keys of the kingdom" refer to "the sealing and binding power" by which

---

39. *OSB*, 1300.
40. Reported by Rex D. Pinegar, "The Living Prophet," *Ensign*, November 1976, 69.

the performance of sacraments is divinely recognized both on earth and in heaven.[41] Remarked church president Russell Nelson, "Without priesthood keys, the Church could serve only as a significant teaching and humanitarian organization but not much more. . . . Priesthood keys distinguish The Church of Jesus Christ of Latter-day Saints from any other organization on earth. Many other organizations *can* and *do* make . . . life better here in mortality. But no other organization *can* and *will* influence . . . life after death" in this eternally efficacious manner. From an LDS perspective, this "sealing power" of the keys "is *supernal* evidence of how much God loves *all* of His children everywhere and wants *each* of them to choose to return home to Him." Rejoiced President Nelson, "The power of these priesthood keys is infinite and breathtaking."[42]

Over time, in addition to viewing keys as the symbol of divine empowerment, LDS discourse placed emphasis on keys as the right of the church's presiding authorities at all levels of leadership, from the congregational to the general, to exercise *episkopē* over the use of that authority within their respective jurisdictions. This particular meaning of keys is the one that is predominant in the church's *General Handbook* as it serves to set in place functional boundaries and ministerial lines of responsibility. The point of this use of "keys" is to clarify that although individual ministers receive certain powers by ordination, the exercise of those powers is to occur under the guidance and with the approval of the episcopal key-holder. The *General Handbook* explains: "Priesthood keys are the authority to direct the use of the priesthood on behalf of God's children. The use of all priesthood authority in the Church is directed by those who hold priesthood keys."[43] This is true even at the highest levels of church governance: "Each Apostle holds all the keys of the kingdom [but] exercises those keys under the direction of the President of the Church."[44]

PRIMACY, POPES, AND PROPHETS

Although the term "primacy" is not typically used in Latter-day Saint discourse, the word's meaning as being first in rank or authority is applicable to the hierarchical structure of the Church of Jesus Christ of Latter-day Saints. Orthodox, Anglican, Lutheran, and other Christian communions also have governing

41. *JSP*, D11:64. Cf. D&C 128:14.
42. Russell M. Nelson, "Rejoice in the Gift of Priesthood Keys," *Liahona*, May 2024, 121; see also his "Keys of the Priesthood," *Ensign*, October 2005, 40–44.
43. *GH* 3.4.1.
44. *GH* 5.1.1.1.

"primates" in their ecclesiastical organizations, but here our primary, though not exclusive, comparative focus will be on the Roman Catholic Church. Both the LDS and Catholic Churches have a history of ecclesial leadership that has varied along a spectrum of governance style ranging from the pope or prophet functioning alone as primate to the collegial exercise of primacy that includes the bishops or apostles and in which the pope or prophet is the *primus inter pares* (first among equals). Consider the Catholic experience. Prior to the Council of Chalcedon in 451, the bishop of Rome was influential but not definitively recognized as supreme pastor to whom all Christians owed obedient loyalty.[45] Even after Chalcedon, it would not be until reforms under Gregory I in 600 that such a status was firmly in place. From that point onward, the historical arc was toward an ever-greater concentration of power in the hands of the pope.[46] By the 1200s, under Innocent III, the Roman "vicar of Christ" exercised supreme power not only spiritually but also in the secular realm. Audacious as were early Mormon aspirations to establish a society in which spiritual concerns prevailed in all aspects of life—social, economic, and political—they never quite matched the medieval vision of the "perfect [complete] society" in which the pontiff exercised a true "fullness of power (*potestas plenitude*)." The 1570 *Regnans in Excelsis* of Pope Pius V that excommunicated and attempted to depose Queen Elizabeth declared that God appointed the pope as the one and only "prince over all nations and kingdoms, to root up, pull down, waste, destroy, plant and build, so that he might preserve his faithful people. . . . In fulfillment of this office . . . we declare [Elizabeth] to be deprived of her pretended claim to the aforesaid kingdom and of all lordship, dignity and privilege whatsoever."[47] Even in their most expansive vision of bringing the broader society under the "government of God," prophets Joseph Smith and Brigham Young never claimed such power.

The absolute power of the medieval pope, however, did not go unchallenged. The pontiff's monarchical authority was called into question most sig-

---

45. "Rome was distinguished among the local churches from an early date as the place of martyrdom of the princes of the apostles, Peter and Paul. A more specific focus just on Peter, and the idea that the bishop of Rome—the pope—stands among the bishops who succeed the apostles as the successor of Peter, is a later idea that developed only in the Christian West." Paul McPartlan, "The Church," in *Oxford Handbook of Catholic Theology*, ed. Lewis Ayres and Medi Ann Volpe (Oxford: Oxford University Press, 2019), 202.

46. A reliable historical overview is Eamon Duffy, *Saints and Sinners: A History of the Popes* (New Haven: Yale University Press, 2001). See also Peter Heather, *Christendom: The Triumph of a Religion, AD 300–1300* (New York: Knopf, 2023).

47. *Regnans in Excelsis* in *The European Reformations Sourcebook*, ed. Carter Lindberg, 2nd ed. (Chichester, UK: Wiley-Blackwell, 2014), 221.

nificantly in the 1300s and early 1400s by the "conciliarist" movement swirling around the Great Schism (1378–1417), a time when for several decades there were two, then three, rival popes. Conciliarist bishops among the episcopate argued that supreme power should reside in the college/council of bishops and that the college even had the authority to depose a pope. At the Council of Constance (1414–1418), the question of the relative authority of the pope and the episcopal college was extensively debated. Theologians, canon lawyers, and bishops all weighed in. The same early church fathers—Cyprian, Augustine, and Aquinas—were called on for support by both sides of the debate. In ways, it was a dress rehearsal for the Reformation a century later. Ultimately, the Council ruled in favor of the pope's unique authority and primacy.[48] Still, the subtleties and intricacies of the arguments for a greater role for the episcopacy would be aired again, and by the time of the Second Vatican Council in the 1960s, they would be quite influential. It has been observed that of all the issues addressed at Vatican II, nothing "turned out to be more contentious and more central to the council's agenda than the relationship of the bishops, or episcopal hierarchy, to the papacy."[49]

In the end, the Second Vatican Council was able to agree on the Dogmatic Constitution *Lumen Gentium*. The third chapter—"The Hierarchical Structure of the Church and in Particular the Episcopate"—addressed the contested issues. It did so first by affirming with Vatican I the "sacred primacy of the Roman Pontiff and of his infallible Magisterium [teaching office]." The document then dealt with the episcopate. The "council teaches that bishops by divine institution have succeeded to the place of the apostles, as shepherds of the Church, and he who hears them hears Christ, and he who rejects them rejects Christ." In addition to the bishops' liturgical and pastoral duties, episcopal consecration "confers the office of teaching and of governing." However, it is emphasized that these functions "can be exercised only in hierarchical communion with the [pope] and the members of the college." In other words, "the college or body of bishops has no authority unless it is understood together with the Roman pontiff, the successor of Peter as its head." *Lumen Gentium* acknowledged that just as "St. Peter and the other apostles constitute one apostolic college, so in a similar way the Roman

---

48. Engagingly detailed in Jaroslav Pelikan, *The Christian Tradition: A History of the Development of Doctrine*, vol. 4, *Reformation of Church and Dogma (1300–1700)* (Chicago: University of Chicago Press, 1984), 69–126.

49. John W. O'Malley, *What Happened at Vatican II* (Cambridge, MA: Harvard University Press, 2008), 7.

pontiff, the successor of Peter, and the bishops, the successors of the apostles, are joined together." Still the Dogmatic Constitution insisted that "the pope's power of primacy over all, both pastors and faithful, remains whole and intact. In virtue of his office, that is, as vicar of Christ and pastor of the whole Church, the Roman pontiff has full, supreme, and universal power over the Church. And he is always free to exercise this power." The college of bishops, too, have "supreme and full power over the universal Church, provided we understand this body [acts] together with its head, the Roman pontiff, and never without this head."[50]

Despite affirming episcopal powers and the pope's subsequent creation of a Synod of Bishops to assist him in his deliberations, a heightened collaborative role between papacy and episcopacy did not immediately materialize in the decades following Vatican II. "Collegiality," notes one scholar, "ended up an abstract teaching without point of entry into the social reality of the church. It ended up an ideal, no match for the deeply entrenched system" of papal supremacy.[51] In contrast, Orthodoxy has long rejected the idea of universal primacy for one bishop in favor of collegiality or "synodality." Orthodoxy views "all bishops, from the pope and the patriarchs down to the least of bishops [as] equal."[52] To be sure, the presiding bishops or patriarchs of the four ancient churches—Constantinople, Alexandria, Antioch, and Jerusalem—are accorded an honorific primacy of influence among other Orthodox churches, but they have no ecclesiastical jurisdiction over them. The other Orthodox churches, usually national or ethnic in character, are self-governing ("autocephalous"/autonomous), as indeed are the four principal patriarchates. It is only as a gathered body in ecumenical council that Orthodox bishops collectively exercise primacy. As a point of order, one will preside or moderate, but his "primacy" only exists in relation to the convened council. He has no jurisdiction over other Orthodox churches and exercises no primacy apart from his conciliar function. Roman Catholicism, too, accepts the equality of bishops with regard to sacramental administration, but not jurisdictionally. That Catholics consider the bishop of Rome alone among all the other bishops to have universal jurisdiction over the whole church is the nub of the ecclesial divide between Catholic and Orthodox churches. Despite ecumenical advances between the two bodies since the 1960s, Catholic unwillingness to

---

50. *Lumen Gentium*, 18, 20–22, in Denzinger 4142, 4144–4146.

51. O'Malley, *What Happened at Vatican II*, 311.

52. John Zizioulas, "Recent Discussions on Primacy in Orthodox Theology," in *Petrine Ministry: Catholics and Orthodox in Dialogue*, ed. Walter Kasper (New York: Paulist, 2006), 235.

yield the primacy of the Roman "Petrine office" and Orthodoxy's resistance to embracing it remains a major point of separation.[53]

On the face of it, ecclesiastical primacy is not a concern for most Protestant churches, especially those that do not espouse an episcopal form of church government. Still, there are other manifestations of hierarchy. The General Assembly in Presbyterian churches exercises a form of primacy as the court of last resort on a variety of church matters, including faith and order. The Southern Baptist Convention (SBC) is comprised of over fifty thousand independently governed congregations known as "cooperating churches." The 2000 Baptist Faith and Message is a confession of faith that exercises a form of doctrinal primacy among these independent churches, but they retain full power to chart their own course. The same holds true for the tens of thousands of nondenominational churches that make up a large part of Christendom today. Ceding primacy to an individual or group other than those regarded as chief shepherds in one's own church or denomination is difficult to envision. This constitutes one of the greatest obstacles to global Christian unification. Some churches involved in ecumenical dialogue do, however, see theoretical value in having a form of ecclesiastical primacy that could function both as a visible representation of Christian unity and a safeguard of apostolicity in a reunited, universal church. Methodists, and other denominations with an episcopal polity such as Anglicans and Lutherans, are said to be "prepared to receive a Petrine ministry exercised collegially within a [transdenominational] college of bishops as a final decision-making authority in the Church, at least insofar as essential matters of faith are concerned."[54] For such episcopal churches, the presumption is that their bishops would be part of a universal council of bishops that would exercise primacy over a reunited Christian church somewhat along the lines of the Orthodox conciliar model. Lutherans reportedly are even willing to entertain a Christian reunification that in addition to a universal episcopate would include "a special Petrine office" that could be exercised "by an individual bishop respected by all Christians."[55]

---

53. See A. Edward Siecienski, *The Papacy and the Orthodox: Sources and History of a Debate* (New York: Oxford University Press, 2017), and Kasper, *Petrine Ministry*. An earlier discussion exhibiting a range of Orthodox views is J. Meyendorff, *The Primacy of Peter in the Orthodox Church* (London: Faith Press, 1963).

54. International Commission for Dialogue between the Roman Catholic Church and the World Methodist Council, *Toward a Statement on the Church* (1986), and *The Grace Given You in Christ* (2006), as quoted in Walter Kasper, *Harvesting the Fruits: Basic Aspects of Christian Faith in Ecumenical Dialogue* (London: Continuum, 2009), 137.

55. International Lutheran–Roman Catholic Commission on Unity, *The Gospel and the Church—Malta Report* (1972), as quoted in Kasper, *Harvesting the Fruits*, 135.

Although some churches with an episcopal polity are tentatively disposed to work toward a mutually satisfactory form of universal primacy, a formally agreed-upon solution remains elusive.

Primacy in the Church of Jesus Christ of Latter-day Saints is similar though not identical to that in the Catholic Church. It can be exercised in three ways: by the prophet alone, by the prophet in conjunction with his appointed "counselors" (typically, two) as the First Presidency, and by the combined "college" of apostles sustained as "prophets, seers, and revelators" known as the Council of the First Presidency and Quorum of the Twelve Apostles. The prophet holds and controls the keys bestowed on Peter: "Under the Lord's direction, the [prophet-president] presides over the Church and is the only person on earth authorized to exercise all priesthood keys."[56] From the beginning, the prophet has been regarded as the church's primate. On the day the church was formally organized, revelation reminded its members that he was "inspired of the Holy Ghost to lay the foundation" of the church "and to build it up unto the most holy faith." Church members were instructed that "his word ye shall receive, as if from mine own mouth, in all patience and faith" (D&C 21:2, 6). Several months later, when confusion arose over an alleged revelation for the church from another individual, the word of the Lord was: "Verily, I say unto thee, no one shall be appointed to receive commandments and revelations in this church excepting [the prophet], for he receiveth them even as Moses. . . . For I have given him the keys of the mysteries, and the revelations which are sealed" (D&C 28:2, 7). Although these revelations had the founding prophet, Joseph Smith, in view, they have been applied to subsequent prophets as well. Profound regard for the living prophet continues unabated in the LDS Church today. "Of all mortal men," declared apostle Ezra Taft Benson, "we should keep our eyes most firmly fixed on the captain, the prophet, seer, and revelator, and president of The Church of Jesus Christ of Latter-day Saints. This is the man who stands closest to the fountain of living waters. . . . All men are entitled to inspiration, and various men are entitled to revelation for their particular assignment. But only one man stands as the Lord's spokesman to the Church and the world, and he is the president of the Church."[57]

The prophet-president, however, is also authorized to exercise his presidential episcopacy in consultation with his counselors as the First Presidency. Revelation declares that the counselors are "accounted as equal with [the prophet] in holding the keys of this last kingdom" (D&C 90:6) and with him "constitute

---

56. *GH* 5.1.1.1.
57. *New Era*, May 1975, 16.

a quorum and First Presidency to receive the oracles for the whole church" (D&C 124:126).[58] The First Presidency is considered "the highest council of the church of God" and the source of "a final decision upon controversies in spiritual matters" (D&C 107:80). The church's first prophet-presidents exercised primacy on their own in a number of instances but also began to work in concert with their counselors such that over the course of the nineteenth century, the scriptural vision of the role of the First Presidency was fully realized. By the twentieth century, Joseph F. Smith, upon acceding to the office of church president in 1901, could declare,

> I propose that my counselors and fellow presidents in the First Presidency shall share with me in the responsibility of every act which I shall perform in this capacity. I do not propose to take the reins in my own hands to do as I please; but I propose to do as my brethren and I agree upon, and as the Spirit of the Lord manifests to us. I have always held, and do hold, and trust I always shall hold, that it is wrong for one man to exercise all the authority and power of presidency in the Church of Jesus Christ of Latter-day Saints. I dare not assume such a responsibility, and I will not.[59]

A quarter-century later, the Council of the Twelve issued this clear and unequivocal statement: "The supreme governing power of the Church is vested in the President of the Church with his counselors . . . they in turn being chiefly supported by the Council of the Twelve. The First Presidency preside over all councils, all quorums, and all organizations of the Church. . . . The First Presidency are the living oracles of God and the supreme adjudicators and interpreters of the law of the Church."[60] The role of the First Presidency, however, has never prevented the prophet from acting alone and on his own initiative to receive and promulgate revelatory guidance for the church. As in the beginning, the prophet today "has authority to receive revelation and declare the will of God for the whole Church," even though he "presides over

---

58. Latter-day Saints consider Peter, James, and John to have been the "First Presidency" in the apostolic church (*GH* 5.1.1.1) and believe their keys were given to them "on the Mount when they were transfigured before [Christ]." *JSP*, D6:543–44.

59. *Conference Report*, October 1901, 82.

60. "Declarations of the Council of Twelve Relating to the First Presidency," December 9, 1926, in *Priesthood and Church Government in the Church of Jesus Christ of Latter-day Saints*, comp. John A. Widtsoe (Salt Lake City: Deseret Book, 1939), 255. This statement was reiterated in Joseph Fielding Smith, "The First Presidency and the Council of the Twelve," *Improvement Era*, November 1966, 978.

and directs all the affairs of the Church" in conjunction with his counselors as the First Presidency.[61]

The primacy of the prophet and First Presidency is a function of the keys each received when ordained as an apostle. In a statement that has been quoted over the years to reinforce this point, Brigham Young explained, "All the Priesthood, all the keys, all the gifts, all the endowments, and everything preparatory to entering into the presence of the Father and of the Son, are in, composed of, circumscribed by, or I might say incorporated within the circumference of, the Apostleship."[62] Consistent with this understanding, as has been mentioned, all apostles are considered "prophets, seers, and revelators." No additional keys or authority are conferred on the senior apostle when as such he assumes the presidency (or on his counselors when appointed to the First Presidency). As Spencer Kimball explained, each apostle at the time of his ordination is "given the precious, vital keys to hold in suspension pending a time when he might become the senior apostle and the President."[63] A noteworthy parallel in the Roman Catholic Church is the statement in the early Vatican II schema *De Ecclesia* that all bishops are "vicars of Christ" and have "inalienable authority by virtue of their [ordination]," not simply as a delegation of authority from the pope. Still, as with the LDS apostles functioning in harmony with the church president, such authority can only properly be exercised in communion with the papal vicar of Christ.[64]

While the third manifestation of primacy—the conciliar acts of all the apostle-prophets, seers, and revelators combined as the Council of the First Presidency and Quorum of the Twelve Apostles—has been in place from early in LDS history, the latter part of the twentieth century witnessed an increase in this mode of primatial exercise. A factor that gave impetus to this development is the typically advanced age of the senior apostle who has acceded to the presidency of the church.[65] In several instances, in the final few years of a president's administration, he has been largely incapacitated due to age-related considerations. In these situations, the counselors in the First Presidency, although canonically empowered "to preside in his stead" (D&C 102:11), have

61. *GH* 5.1.1.1.
62. *Journal of Discourses*, 1:134–35.
63. Spencer W. Kimball, *Conference Report*, April 1970, 118.
64. O'Malley, *What Happened at Vatican II*, 176–77.
65. Prophets and apostles serve until death, and there is no provision for resignation. Although it is possible for the bishop of Rome to resign, as in the 2013 case of Pope Benedict XVI (1927–2022), it is extremely rare and had not happened for six hundred years prior to Benedict's resignation.

acted in close consultation with their fellow key-holding apostles. Gordon Hinckley was a counselor in the First Presidency when this occurred in the early 1980s and again in the early 1990s.[66] When Hinckley reached seniority among the apostles and became president of the church in the mid-1990s, he chose to continue this pattern of heightened primatial collaboration between the First Presidency and the Twelve. As a prominent, public example of this, shortly after Hinckley's accession to the presidency, the Council of the First Presidency and Quorum of the Twelve Apostles issued a major, formal proclamation entitled "The Family."[67] Slightly different than the 1920s statement quoted above reserving primacy to the First Presidency "supported by the Council of the Twelve," a century later, the current *General Handbook* states that the Council of the First Presidency *and* Quorum of the Twelve Apostles" jointly exercising primacy "has authority to declare and interpret doctrine and establish policy for the Church."[68]

AUTHORITATIVE TEACHING—MAGISTERIUM

When the First Presidency and the Twelve act together to declare and interpret church doctrine, they are the functional equivalent of the Catholic magisterium. The term "magisterium," prominent in Catholicism but unknown in Mormonism, has multiple meanings. The Latin *magister*, from which "master" is derived, can refer both to someone in authority and, in older English, to a "teacher," particularly one whose teaching is authoritative, a master of the subject, so to speak. In Catholicism, the "magisterium" generally refers to the pope and the bishops in communion with the pope when acting in their teaching office. The term can also refer to the corpus of their authoritative teaching. The primary task of the magisterium is to guard the apostolic "deposit of faith" (cf. 1 Tim. 6:20; 2 Tim. 1:14) and "preserve God's people from deviations and defections and to guarantee them the objective possibility of professing the true faith without error."[69] Beyond the scriptural deposit of faith, additional apostolic teachings are believed to have been passed on verbally to the apostles' successors, the bishops. Whether these insights expand or merely explain the

---

66. Hinckley's account of his experience and close consultation with the Twelve is detailed in *Ensign*, November 1990, 50.

67. "The Family: A Proclamation to the World," *Ensign*, November 1995, 102.

68. *GH* 5.1.1.1 (emphasis added).

69. *CCC* 890. Vatican I taught that the magisterium exists to "reverently guard and faithfully explain the revelation or deposit of faith that was handed down through the apostles." *Pastor Aeternus*, 4, in Denzinger 3070.

written canon, they have been incorporated into the expositions of the faith of successor bishops (especially the bishops of Rome), have been included in the church's liturgies, and have influenced doctrinal development over the centuries. Collectively, they constitute the church's "tradition" and are to be guarded by the magisterium. "The task of authentically interpreting the Word of God, whether written [Scripture] or handed on [tradition], has been entrusted exclusively to the living teaching office of the Church."[70] This does not mean, however, that every expression of the episcopacy is considered binding "dogma."[71] There are gradations of authoritativeness in the magisterium's exercise of the teaching office, what Vatican II's Decree on Ecumenism called "a 'hierarchy' of truths."[72]

When referring to the magisterium as a body of teaching, Catholic theology distinguishes what it calls the "supreme" or "extraordinary" magisterium from the "ordinary" magisterium. The supreme/extraordinary magisterium, as the name implies, refers to the exceptional circumstances in which "solemn" definitions of dogma and judgments on matters of "faith and morals" are "infallibly" promulgated by the pope either alone or in conjunction with the college of bishops. As stated in the *Catechism*, "The Roman Pontiff, head of the college of bishops, enjoys . . . infallibility in virtue of his office, when, as supreme pastor and teacher of all the faithful . . . he proclaims by a definitive act a doctrine pertaining to faith or morals . . . for belief as being divinely revealed."[73] In this statement, the *Catechism* invokes the foundational Catholic definition of papal "infallibility" approved by the First Vatican Council in its Dogmatic Constitution *Pastor Aeternus*. Included there is the declaration that when the Roman pontiff "speaks *ex cathedra* ['from the chair' (of Peter)],

70. *Dei Verbum*, 2, 10, in Denzinger 4214.

71. Although etymologically "dogma" has a range of meanings such as "opinion," "belief," "doctrine," or "tenet" (see *OED*, s.v. "dogma"), dogma has come to refer to beliefs or doctrines that are authoritatively set forth. Catholic practice goes even further in asserting that "by dogma" is "meant a truth of revelation that has been formulated and infallibly proposed by the Catholic Church . . . as an accurate expression of the reality contained in revelation. . . . Catholic doctrine includes not only these dogmas but other truths and positions taught by the Church but not as revealed." *New Catholic Encyclopedia*, 2nd ed. (Detroit: Gale, 2003), 4:815.

72. *Unitatis Redintegratio*, 2, 11, in Denzinger 4192. "Over the past two centuries the Catholic Church has developed an increasingly complex language for delineating authoritative statements concerning Christian belief and action and increasingly complex modes of describing the relative authority of those statements." Lewis Ayres, "What Is Catholic Theology?" in Ayres and Volpe, *Oxford Handbook of Catholic Theology*, 14–15.

73. *CCC* 891.

that is, when, acting in the office of shepherd and teacher of all Christians, he defines, by virtue of his supreme apostolic authority, a doctrine concerning faith or morals to be held by the universal Church, [he] possesses through the divine assistance promised to him in blessed Peter the infallibility with which the Divine Redeemer willed his Church to be endowed in defining the doctrine concerning faith or morals; and that therefore such definitions of the Roman pontiff are therefore irreformable."[74]

Additionally, "the infallibility promised to the Church is also present in the body of bishops when, together with Peter's successor, they exercise the supreme Magisterium, above all in an Ecumenical Council."[75] The act of issuing infallible declarations is a manifestation of the magisterium's charge to guard the faith and the faithful. "The infallibility of the Magisterium of the Pastors extends to all the elements of doctrine, including moral doctrine, without which the saving truths of the faith cannot be preserved, expounded, or observed."[76] Even in such cases, to enjoy the full charism of infallibility, conciliar decrees and the pope's exercise of the Petrine ministry must signal an *intention* to solemnly define what is being promulgated as "divinely revealed" dogma. The decrees of the early ecumenical councils at Nicaea and Chalcedon are regarded as communicating such intention. In contrast, the "constitutions" and "decrees" of Vatican II, profoundly influential as they are, do not claim such intention of infallibility. So rare are infallible definitions of dogma that only a handful have been issued in the past thousand years, the most recent being pronouncements on the immaculate conception (1854) and the assumption of Mary (1950).[77]

"Divine assistance is also given to the successors of the apostles, teaching in communion with the successor of Peter, and, in a particular way, to the bishop of Rome, pastor of the whole Church, when, without arriving at an infallible definition and without pronouncing in a 'definitive manner,' they propose in the exercise of the *ordinary* Magisterium a teaching that leads to better understanding of Revelation in matters of faith and morals."[78] This is a carefully worded acknowledgment that not everything the pope or bishops teach is considered

74. *Pastor Aeternus* 4, in Denzinger 3074.

75. *CCC* 891.

76. *CCC* 2051, 2035.

77. Francis A. Sullivan, *Creative Fidelity: Weighing and Interpreting Documents of the Magisterium* (New York: Paulist, 1996), 86. See also Richard R. Gaillardetz, *By What Authority? A Primer on Scripture, the Magisterium, and the Sense of the Faithful* (Collegeville, MN: Liturgical Press, 1997).

78. *CCC* 892 (emphasis added).

infallible. This far more common exercise of the "ordinary magisterium" is still to be respected as normative for the church, but it is distinct from the "irreformable" *extraordinary* magisterium. In the exercise of ordinary magisterium, "the Roman Pontiff and the bishops, as authentic teachers, preach to the People of God the faith which is to be believed and applied in moral life" and Christian discipleship.[79] "To this ordinary teaching the faithful 'are to adhere with religious assent,' which, though distinct from the assent of faith [expected as one's response to the Word of God, including the infallible, extraordinary magisterium], is nonetheless an extension of it."[80] Regarding the exercise of the ordinary magisterium by bishops and the bishop of Rome, Catholics are counseled that they "can rest assured that these men do not seriously err in carrying out their ministry without demanding that in every instance they must be able to give an infallible and hence irrevocable definition. In insisting too much on the question of infallibility, one runs the risk of demeaning . . . the ordinary pastoral function of the magisterium."[81]

In the Church of Jesus Christ of Latter-day Saints, too, there are gradations of magisterial authoritativeness. At the highest level is the previously mentioned possibility of the prophet receiving and promulgating canonical revelation. This happened over a hundred times in Joseph Smith's ministry, resulting in the publication of the Book of Mormon and the revelations compiled in the Doctrine and Covenants. So abundant were these revelations that Joseph Smith found it necessary to remind his followers that there was a difference between his canonical, extraordinary magisterium and his ordinary, sermonic magisterium. "A Prophet is not always a Prophet," Smith told some visiting church members, "only when he is acting as such."[82] He reportedly complained that when, like Paul, who declared, "the rest speak I, not the Lord" (1 Cor. 7:12), "he ventured to give his private opinion on any subject of importance, his words were often . . . given out as the word of the Lord because they came from him."[83]

The distinction between ordinary and extraordinary magisterium can be a rather fine line in the Church of Jesus Christ of Latter-day Saints. An early revelation directed to Oliver Cowdery, Joseph Smith's colleague and "second

79. *CCC* 2050.
80. *CCC* 892.
81. *New Catholic Encyclopedia*, 13:781.
82. *JSP*, J2:256.
83. Quoted in Hyrum L. Andrus and Helen Mae Andrus, *They Knew the Prophet: Personal Accounts from over 100 People Who Knew Joseph Smith* (American Fork, UT: Covenant Communications, 2004), 140.

elder" in the church, instructed Cowdery that while only the prophet is "appointed to receive [canonical] commandments and revelations in this church," nonetheless "thou shalt be heard by the church in all things whatsoever thou shalt teach them by the Comforter, *concerning* the revelations and commandments which I have given." The invitation to Cowdery was the same as it is to the modern apostles—provide inspired instruction *about* scripture and canonical revelations, but do not claim to receive them yourself. Still, the door was wide open to participate in the ordinary magisterium: "If thou art led at any time by the Comforter to speak or teach . . . thou mayest do it. But thou shalt not write by way of commandment [canonical revelation], but by wisdom" (D&C 28:1–5). This depiction of inspired, Spirit-led teaching illustrates the weighty nature of the ordinary magisterium in the Church of Jesus Christ of Latter-day Saints today. It is only distinguished from the supreme magisterium by the fact that it is the prophet's sole prerogative to "write" canonical revelations. The inspired character of the church's ordinary magisterium and its authoritative proximity to the extraordinary magisterium are clear in the promise to Cowdery: "Thou shalt have revelations, but write them not by way of commandment" (D&C 28:8). Elsewhere the noncanonical revelations of the ordinary magisterium are even described as "scripture": "Whatsoever they shall speak when moved upon by the Holy Ghost shall be scripture" and the "voice of the Lord, and the power of God unto salvation" (D&C 63:4). Here a similarity with Pentecostalism is noteworthy. For Pentecostals, "words and even writings can be understood as inspired in some sense for a specific task or moment in time but are not understood to rise to the level of canonical Scripture."[84]

As with Catholicism's rare exercise of infallible supreme magisterium, additions to LDS scripture have been made in only a few instances since the ministry of Joseph Smith.[85] One of these was in 1978, when the prophet, Spencer Kimball, announced a revelation that "all worthy male members of the Church may be ordained to the priesthood without regard for race or color" (Official Declaration 2). "We do not accept the theory," declared Kimball shortly before

84. J. Christopher Thomas, *A Pentecostal Reads the Book of Mormon: A Literary and Theological Introduction* (Cleveland, TN: CPT Press, 2016), 385.

85. Subsequent to Joseph Smith's death, additional revelations and teachings from the founding prophet were added to LDS scripture, expanding the size of the Doctrine and Covenants in 1876, creating the Pearl of Great Price in 1880, and adding D&C 137 in 1976. An 1847 revelation to Brigham Young was also added to the Doctrine and Covenants in 1876, and a vision of the redemption of the dead that Joseph F. Smith experienced in 1918 was canonized (now D&C 138) in 1976.

receiving the revelation, "that the Old Testament constituted the total words of God's prophets; nor do we believe the New Testament to be the end of revelation. We testify that rather than an end of revelations of God, they continue to pour forth from God for the welfare and benefit of men." Kimball was anxious, however, that church members understand that the infrequency of canonization does not mean that the flow of revelation has dwindled. "The heavens are indeed open and . . . we testify to the world that revelation continues and that the vaults and files of the Church contain these revelations which come month to month and day to day."[86] Kimball did not specify whether such revelations come to the prophet alone or to all the "prophets, seers, and revelators" acting in concert. Nor did he identify these divine communications as either Cowdery-like revelations that are part of the inspired but "ordinary" magisterium or revelations waiting to be canonized as the equivalent of the LDS exercise of "supreme" magisterium. What Kimball's testimony was meant to affirm, though, is that "surely the Lord GOD will do nothing, but he revealeth his secret unto his servants the prophets" (Amos 3:7).

Whether considering the flood of canonical revelations received by Joseph Smith or Spencer Kimball's bold profession of regular uncanonized revelation, Latter-day Saints do not view such revelations as contradicting the fundamental principles of truth, the "deposit of faith," communicated by past prophets and apostles and preserved in the Bible. In Doctrine and Covenants 20, a brief delineation of the church's beliefs concludes with this declaration, glossing Revelation 22:18–19: "These things are true and according to the revelations of John, neither adding to, nor diminishing from the prophecy of his book, [or] the holy scriptures" (D&C 20:35). George Cannon, counselor in the First Presidency in the late nineteenth century, elaborated: "The rock upon which this Church is built and the foundation stone thereof is new revelation from God to men, and that revelation being of divine origin it must of necessity agree with the revelations which have already been given; hence, the doctrines taught by the Prophet Joseph Smith and the organization of the Church as he was directed to accomplish it was all in perfect harmony with the truths contained in this book (the Bible). It cannot be otherwise and be what it professes to be."[87] With that caveat, Kimball was intent on affirming "the constant flow of revealed communication" to the church's prophets. He concluded his remarks on the matter with a very personal expression: "I say, in the deepest of humility,

---

86. Kimball, "Revelation: The Word of the Lord to His Prophets," *Ensign*, May 1977, 76–78.

87. Jerreld L. Newquist, ed., *Gospel Truth: Discourses and Writings of President George Q. Cannon*, 2 vols. (Salt Lake City: Deseret Book, 1974), 1:313.

but also by the power and force of a burning testimony in my soul, that from the prophet of the Restoration [Joseph Smith] to the prophet of our own year, the communication line is unbroken, the authority is continuous, and light, brilliant and penetrating, continues to shine. The sound of the voice of the Lord is a continuous melody and a thunderous appeal. For nearly a century and a half there has been no interruption."[88]

THE "ROCK" OF REVELATION

Because revelation looms so large in both the LDS lexicon and lifestyle, it is hardly surprising that it has even influenced Mormon interpretation of Christ's declaration "Thou art Peter (*petros*), and upon this rock (*petra*) I will build my church" (Matt. 16:18). Catholics, of course, interpret "this *petra*" to be *Petros* himself.[89] Others have understood it as the faith Peter demonstrated or the content of his confession—that Jesus is the Christ—or even that Christ himself is the rock.[90] Although sympathetic to each of these ideas in other contexts, Latter-day Saints understand the antecedent of "this rock" to be the divine revelation—"flesh and blood hath not revealed it unto thee, but my Father which is in heaven"—by which Peter was able to make his faith-filled confession of Christ. It was the mechanism more than the content of the confession that caught Joseph Smith's attention. He asked rhetorically, "What rock" was Christ referring to when he spoke to Peter? He answered in one word: "Revelation."[91]

This is the standard Mormon reading of the Matthean passage, and the conviction that the "rock of revelation" is indispensable to the church's vitality and progress has been expressed numerous times in general conferences over the years. As just one example from the later twentieth century, Howard

88. Kimball, "Revelation: The Word of the Lord to His Prophets," 78.

89. "Jesus entrusted a unique mission to" Peter. "Because of the faith he confessed Peter will remain the unshakable rock of the Church. His mission will be to keep this faith from every lapse and to strengthen his brothers in it." *CCC* 552.

90. See, for instance, Manlio Simonetti, ed., *Ancient Christian Commentary on Scripture: New Testament; Matthew 14-28* (Downers Grove, IL: IVP Academic, 2002), 45. Luther interpreted the Lord's words thus: "On this rock, that is, on me, Christ, I will build all of my Christendom" (*Luther's Works*, 75 vols. [Philadelphia: Fortress; St. Louis: Concordia, 1955-], 41:314). For an exegetical study of the passage, see Chrys C. Caragounis, *Peter and the Rock* (New York: de Gruyter, 1990).

91. *JSP*, D11:360. Apart from this comment by Smith, LDS scripture deploys the image of the "rock" in more traditional ways, such as with reference to "the gospel" (D&C 33:12-13; D&C 11:15; 18:5; 3 Nephi 11:39).

Hunter posed the same rhetorical question and gave the same answer: "Upon what rock? Peter? Upon a man? No, not upon a man, upon the rock of revelation."[92] John Taylor glossed more of the Matthean passage, emphasizing that "whenever the church is built upon that rock and [has] the revelation of heaven for their guide, as Peter had, the gates of hell cannot prevail against it."[93] The LDS Church chose 2020 to mark the bicentennial anniversary of events that launched the "Restoration of the Fullness of the Gospel of Jesus Christ." On that occasion, the First Presidency and Council of the Twelve jointly issued a "solemn proclamation" that included this testimonial: "With reverence and gratitude, we as His Apostles invite all to know—as we do—that the heavens are open. We affirm that God is making known His will for His beloved sons and daughters." Because his children have yet to "come in the unity of the faith, and of the knowledge of the Son of God, unto a perfect man, unto the measure of the stature of the fulness of Christ" (Eph. 4:13), "we gladly declare that the promised Restoration goes forward through continuing revelation."[94]

While Latter-day Saints may be among the most emphatic in their affirmation of divine revelation, other Christian churches also share a belief in the ongoing guidance of the Holy Spirit. Eastern Orthodoxy, for instance, offers a vibrant vision of the dynamic, charismatic nature of its tradition. "Tradition," writes Orthodox theologian Georges Florovsky, is "the Spirit's unceasing revelation and preaching of good tidings . . . the eternal, continual voice of God."[95] Later Orthodox theologian John McGuckin, in a chapter-length discussion of the Orthodox sense of tradition, sees it as the dynamic movement of God in history and observes, "The Western systematic tradition would probably have entitled such a chapter as this the 'doctrine of revelation'; but while Orthodoxy recognizes a definitive 'change' from the apostolic period that saw the closing of the New Testament canon, onwards into the later eras of the church, it does not wish to create an over-elaborate barrier between those periods such that the inspiration of the Spirit of God in the apostolic period substantially ceased with the end of the apostolic age."[96]

Orthodox appreciation for ongoing divine guidance is matched if not exceeded by Pentecostalism and the later charismatic renewal movement of

92. Howard W. Hunter, *Conference Report*, October 1965, 112. For a sermonic paean to this principle, see Bruce McConkie, *Conference Report*, April 1981, 102–3.

93. *Times and Seasons*, February 1842, 693.

94. First Presidency and Council of the Twelve Apostles, "The Restoration of the Fulness of the Gospel of Jesus Christ: A Bicentennial Proclamation to the World," *Ensign*, May 2020, 91–92.

95. Georges Florovsky, quoted in McGuckin, *Orthodox Church*, 93–94.

96. McGuckin, *Orthodox Church*, 116.

the 1960s. "While there are some continental and national differences in the Charismatic Renewal as to origins, development, emphases, and style, the distinguishing characteristics of the movement are everywhere the same." Prominent among these "essential elements" is "the conviction that God speaks to his people, corporately and personally, as directly and as regularly as in the first Christian century."[97] Traditional Pentecostals concur. "While the Nicene-Constantinopolitan creed reminds believers that the Holy Spirit 'spoke through the prophets,' Pentecostals remind the church that the Spirit continues to speak through prophets and even directly to individual believers."[98] The Pentecostal proclamation is that the Spirit "directs the everyday life and witness of believers and the church as they are led into all truth."[99] In this they (and Latter-day Saints) are in agreement with the Orthodox view. "Orthodoxy does not subscribe [to] the notion of the end of the age of revelation," writes John McGuckin. Rather, the Orthodox position is that "the Spirit breathes in his church to this day, and his revelation continues in different modes, and at different levels . . . creating the vitality of the church."[100]

To be sure, Roman Catholicism also considers both its extraordinary and ordinary magisterium to be guided by the Holy Spirit "to illumine with the light of faith the new situations and problems which had not yet emerged in the past."[101] But Catholicism is more wary of applying the term "revelation" to that ongoing guidance than Orthodox, Pentecostals, or Latter-day Saints, lest it be confused with, or be considered on par with, the biblical revelation. Catholicism accepts "no further Revelation" of this kind. Still, "even if Revelation is already complete, it has not been made completely explicit; it remains for Christian faith gradually

97. Stanley M. Burgess and Gary B. McGee, eds., *Dictionary of Pentecostal and Charismatic Movements* (Grand Rapids: Zondervan, 1988), s.v. "charismatic movement." Charismatics are "found across the entire spectrum of Christianity, within all 150 traditional non-Pentecostal ecclesiastical confessions, families, and traditions . . . speaking in 8,000 languages, and [reaching] 95% of the world's total population." David Barrett and Todd Johnson, "Global Statistics," in *The New International Dictionary of Pentecostal and Charismatic Movements*, ed. Stanley M. Burgess and Eduard van der Maas (Grand Rapids: Zondervan, 2002), 284.

98. Andrew K. Gabriel, "Pneumatology," in *The Routledge Handbook of Pentecostal Theology*, ed. Wolfgang Vondey (London: Routledge, 2020), 208.

99. Stephen J. Land, *Pentecostal Spirituality: A Passion for the Kingdom* (Sheffield: Sheffield Academic Press, 1993), 100. See also R. Hollis Gause, *Living in the Spirit: The Way of Salvation*, rev. ed. (Cleveland, TN: CPT Press, 2009), and Andrew K. Gabriel, *Simply Spirit-Filled: Experiencing God in the Presence and Power of the Holy Spirit* (Nashville: Nelson, 2019).

100. McGuckin, *Orthodox Church*, 116. See entire chapter 2—"The Orthodox Sense of Tradition" (90–119).

101. "Apostolic Constitution *Fidei Depositum* on the Publication of the Catechism of the Catholic Church," 4, in *CCC*, prefatory material.

to grasp its full significance over the course of the centuries." Thus, Catholicism does acknowledge that the Holy Spirit, working through the magisterium and even through some "so-called 'private' revelations," can help the faithful "in a certain period of history . . . live more fully by" the apostolic deposit of faith. Catholicism, however, "cannot accept 'revelations' that claim to surpass or correct the Revelation of which Christ is the fulfillment."[102] Neither, for that matter, do most other Christians, including even the most inspiration friendly, such as Pentecostals and charismatics. That acknowledged, Catholicism and Orthodoxy place a high value on the inspiration of their "tradition." As stated, Orthodoxy does not wish to draw too sharp a distinction between the canonical revelation preserved in the New Testament and the vibrant, ongoing revelation manifest in the tradition. Here, too, is similarity with Mormonism, for although the Church of Jesus Christ of Latter-day Saints proclaims an "open canon" and populated it extensively during Joseph Smith's lifetime, since then it has primarily experienced a steady flow of noncanonical revelation to its prophets and apostles in conciliar deliberations, and has accumulated its own inspired "tradition" or magisterium through nearly two centuries of their regular teaching at general conferences, in church publications, and in other media.

For Latter-day Saints, how the church is built upon the "rock of revelation" also extends beyond the hierarchy to the laity through the church's cherished doctrine of "personal revelation." President Russell Nelson renewed the long-standing Latter-day Saint commitment to this principle by imploring church members to seek to "hear" the Lord and be guided through life's challenges and opportunities by the leadings and promptings of the Holy Spirit. "Do whatever it takes," he urged, "to increase your spiritual capacity to receive personal revelation."[103] Along with this plea, Latter-day Saints are reminded that private revelation is jurisdiction-specific. In most instances, the jurisdiction is one's own life. Inspired guidance is also believed to come in the context of ministry but never for individuals or situations outside one's ministerial jurisdiction. Thus, parents may receive revelation to guide their family and a ward bishop may receive divine guidance in counseling his congregation, but only prophets receive revelation for the whole church. Moreover, the legitimacy of personal revelation, whether for one's own benefit or to assist in one's jurisdictional episcopacy, is always contingent upon it being in doctrinal harmony with the magisterium of the prophets and apostles. To put a Mormon spin on the apostle Paul's directive to the Corinthians, such personal and ministerial revelations are to be

---

102. *CCC* 66, 67, 73.
103. Russell Nelson, "Hear Him," *Ensign*, May 2020, 90.

"subject to the prophets. For God is not the author of confusion, but of peace, as in all churches of the saints" (1 Cor. 14:32–33). Apostle Gary Stevenson offered Latter-day Saints an additional "word of caution" about individual revelation: "Sometimes we want to be led by the Spirit in all things. However, often the Lord wants us to use our God-given intelligence and act in ways that are consistent with our best understanding."[104] Thus qualified, personal revelation among the general membership is considered the lifeblood of the church and an important part of the way in which the church is built upon the rock of revelation.

In both the Church of Jesus Christ of Latter-day Saints and the Roman Catholic Church, a laity guided and empowered by the Holy Spirit also plays a part in determining the authoritativeness of magisterial teaching. *Lumen Gentium* reflects the heightened Catholic view of the role and responsibility of the laity that emerged during Vatican II. The document even extends to the laity a certain collective infallibility: "The entire body of the faithful, anointed as they are by the Holy One, cannot err in matters of belief. They manifest this special property by means of the whole peoples' supernatural discernment in matters of faith when 'from the Bishops down to the last of the lay faithful' they show universal agreement in matters of faith and morals. That discernment in matters of faith is aroused and sustained by the Spirit of truth."[105] This supernatural, Spirit-endowed gift of discernment enjoyed by the laity as a whole (cf. 1 John 2:20, 27) is sometimes referred to as the *consensus fidelium* or *sensus fidelium*. *Sensus Fidei*, a 2014 document issued by the Catholic International Theological Commission, explains that because of the anointing of the Holy Spirit, "the faithful have an instinct for the truth of the Gospel, which enables them to recognise and endorse authentic Christian doctrine and practice, and to reject what is false."[106]

A Mormon counterpart to this was explained by J. Reuben Clark Jr., longtime counselor in the First Presidency, in an address to LDS religious educators entitled "When Are the Writings and Sermons of Church Leaders Entitled to the Claim of Being Scripture?" Clark based his remarks on the Doctrine and Covenants passage about the LDS ordinary magisterium being considered non-canonical "scripture," when it is "moved upon by the Holy Ghost" (D&C 63:4). Clark explained that "even the President of the Church" in his ordinary magisterium "may not always be 'moved upon by the Holy Ghost,' when he addresses

---

104. Gary E. Stevenson, "Promptings of the Spirit," *Liahona*, November 2023, 45.

105. *Lumen Gentium*, 2, 12, in Denzinger 4130.

106. International Theological Commission, *Sensus Fidei in the Life of the Church*, 2, https://www.vatican.va/roman_curia/congregations/cfaith/cti_documents/rc_cti_20140610 _sensus-fidei_en.html.

the people." According to Clark, such rare occasions usually have been when the Prophet was discussing doctrine "of a highly speculative character." In such instances, the *consensus fidelium* of "subsequent Presidents of the Church and *the people themselves* have felt that in declaring the doctrine, the [prophet] was not 'moved upon by the Holy Ghost.'"[107] Added Bruce McConkie, "The truth or error" of any leader's utterance ultimately "will have to be judged by the standard works and the spirit of discernment and inspiration that is in those [leaders and laity alike] who actually enjoy the gift of the Holy Ghost."[108]

The *sensus fidelium* in the Church of Jesus Christ of Latter-day Saints is an aspect of the church's broader doctrine of "common consent." Within weeks of the organization of the church, Joseph Smith received a revelation that declared, "And all things shall be done by common consent in the church, by much prayer and faith" (D&C 26:2). Although the church is obviously not congregational in its polity and ministerial appointments are proposed by those exercising episcopacy rather than the body of the church, the founding Articles and Covenants made clear that "no person is to be ordained to any office in this church where there is a regularly organized branch of the same, without the vote of that church" (D&C 20:65). The same is true of church-wide appointments: "A commandment I give unto you that you should fill all these offices and approve of those names which I have mentioned, or else disapprove of them at my general conference" (D&C 124:144). Consistent with the profound Mormon respect for agency and choice, church members are not required to "rubber-stamp" proposals from the hierarchy. Joseph Smith himself on occasion was overruled by the membership of the church.[109] Even in so weighty a matter as the revelation Spencer Kimball received in 1978, its canonization required the *consensus fidelium*. At the church's first general conference following Kimball's reception of the revelation, his counselor in the First Presidency made the following motion: "Recognizing Spencer W.

---

107. J. Reuben Clark Jr., "When Are the Writings and Sermons of Church Leaders Entitled to the Claim of Being Scripture?" in *J. Reuben Clark: Selected Papers on Religion, Education, and Youth*, ed. David H. Yarn Jr. (Provo, UT: BYU Press, 1984), 102 (emphasis added). A rare example of this would be the "Adam-God" doctrine advanced by Brigham Young, which later prophets and Latter-day Saints generally have found unacceptable. See chapter 5, note 124.

108. McConkie, *Mormon Doctrine*, 547.

109. An instance of this was when he proposed to "release" Sidney Rigdon, his counselor in the First Presidency, for "not having received any material benefit from his labors or counsels" for several years, but the "Conference voted that elder Sidney Rigdon be permitted to retain his station as Counsellor." *Times and Seasons*, September 1843, 329–30.

Kimball as the prophet, seer, and revelator, and president of The Church of Jesus Christ of Latter-day Saints, it is proposed that we as a constituent assembly accept this revelation as the word and will of the Lord. All in favor please signify by raising your right hand. Any opposed by the same sign. The vote to sustain the foregoing motion was unanimous in the affirmative" (Official Declaration 2). In one sense, then, the Mormon magisterium and their primacy are ultimately subject to the *consensus fidelium*.[110]

Ministerial Priesthood

Respect for the church's rank and file is also manifest in that every willing and worthy male member may be ordained to the priesthood, not just the handful who have received formal theological and ministerial training. Both in this sense and because Mormon ministers are not financially remunerated, the Church of Jesus Christ of Latter-day Saints may be said to have a "lay priesthood." Before taking a closer look at priesthood in the LDS tradition, we step back to explore the history of the term. The *OED* defines "priesthood" variously as the "office or function of a priest; the condition or status of being a priest; the order of priest" and as "a body of priests; priests collectively."[111] In antiquity generally, and in the Hebrew Bible specifically, priests were religious officiators specially consecrated or set apart to serve as mediators between humanity and the gods. They did so in temples, holy sites where priests offered propitiatory and expiatory sacrifices on behalf of the people. Embedded in the Old Testament are varying accounts of those who served as priests and how they did so. Also apparent is an evolution in priestly arrangement, activity, and status from preexilic Israel to postexilic Judaism. In general, though, it is agreed that priestly service was hereditary and linked to the lineage of the tribe of Levi, particularly to the descendants of Moses's brother Aaron who served as "high priests." Although criticism of the priesthood and calls for its reform were not unknown in Israel's history (e.g., Ezra and Nehemiah), only later during the

---

110. Scholarly studies of ancient prophecy make the same point: "The prophetic performance has to be acknowledged by a community that ultimately decides whether or not it was to be appreciated as transmitting a divine word. The prophetic process of communication is not a one-way street from the deity through the prophet and eventual go-betweens to the recipients, but a form of social communication: the community keeps prophecy alive and ultimately makes it functional." Martti Nissinen, "Prophetic Intermediation in the Ancient Near East," in *The Oxford Handbook of the Prophets*, ed. Carolyn J. Sharp (New York: Oxford University Press, 2016), 5–6.

111. *OED*, s.v. "priesthood."

Maccabean period did the Qumran sects castigate the entire priestly class, supposed guardians of Jewish holiness, as corrupt to the point of illegitimacy.

Some of that same sentiment is present in the New Testament. There, the priestly establishment, and especially the high priest, is presented as blind to God's work in Christ and vigorously opposed to the Christian cause. Not surprisingly, the New Testament never uses the term "priesthood" or "priest" (*hiereus*) with reference to the ordained *Christian* ministry. The "priesthood" of Christ, however, is discussed in the book of Hebrews, where Christ is called our "high priest" and a "priest after the order of Melchizedek," but most Christians have understood these references metaphorically. The application of priestly terminology to Christ has seemed appropriate because of his atoning self-sacrifice and heavenly intercession with God to benefit humankind. First Timothy 2:5 declares that there is "one mediator between God and men, the man Christ Jesus," and Hebrews refers to him as the "mediator" of the "new covenant" (Heb. 12:24; 9:15; 8:6). The message of Hebrews seems to be that Christ's "priestly" sacrifice and offering are superior to the temple cult of ancient Israel,[112] which elsewhere in the New Testament is seen as fulfilled and superseded in Christ. Because of a conscious effort to dissociate itself from Israel's priest-centered form of worship, the New Testament speaks of "ministers" and "ministry" rather than "priests" and "priesthood" to describe those in the church whose vocation is to serve Christ and his people.

Along with Catholics, Orthodox, and some other Christian groups, Latter-day Saints, however, do use the term "priesthood" when discussing the ministry, but their use of the term is distinctive. For Mormons, priesthood is more than a metaphor for how Christian ministers intercede for the people. Priesthood is divine "authority" and "power" granted to God's people "on earth to help carry out [his] work."[113] As God's "power," priesthood has an objective reality and existence independent of the priests who receive it. Priesthood is both abstract—permission or authority to act in God's name—and concrete— an actual endowment of divine power that God graciously bestows on human ministers to enable them to accomplish their service. Joseph Smith taught that

---

112. "'Cult' means 'system of worship,' what people do in order to cultivate a Deity and win his/her favor. The 'Temple cult' is the sum total of what the priests and worshipers do there in order to attain and maintain God's favor. How and why this perfectly innocent and useful word became a pejorative designation for 'a small religious group, whose policies and way of life are seen as sinister and threatening by society at large,' I do not know." Shaye J. D. Cohen, *From the Maccabees to the Mishnah*, 3rd ed. (Louisville: Westminster John Knox, 2014), 56.

113. *GH* 3.0.

"the Priesthood is an everlasting principle & Existed with God from Eternity & will to Eternity, without beginning of days or end of years."[114] The Mormon conception of priesthood might be classified in terms of Aristotelian "universals" and "particulars." It is a "universal" in the sense of its independent, eternal existence, but a "particular" because it always resides in individual, "particular" priests. To emphasize the difference between priesthood as divine power and those who receive it, Latter-day Saint leaders in the later twentieth century began instructing church members to refer to men who had received the priesthood as "holders" or "bearers" of the priesthood, not simply as "the priesthood." The idea that priesthood is God's power held in trust by the bearer is captured in a much-quoted and later canonized letter written by Joseph Smith. "The rights of the priesthood," wrote Smith, "are inseparably connected with the powers of heaven, and the powers of heaven cannot be controlled nor handled only upon the principles of righteousness. They may be conferred upon us, it is true; but when we undertake to cover our sins . . . or to exercise control or dominion or compulsion upon the souls of the children of men, in any degree of unrighteousness, behold, the heavens withdraw themselves; the Spirit of the Lord is grieved; and when it is withdrawn, Amen to the priesthood or the authority of that man" (D&C 121:36–37).

As distinctive as are Mormon understandings of priesthood, something of a convergence with other Christian conceptions of the ordained ministry may be discernible. Consider, for instance, this definition presented in the World Council of Churches' ecumenical document *Baptism, Eucharist, and Ministry*: "The term 'ordained ministry' refers to persons who have received a charism [gift] and whom the church appoints for service by ordination through the invocation of the Spirit and the laying on of hands."[115] The empowering Spirit that is invoked in the ordination ceremony is something real and "tangible," something external that is bestowed on the minister, as the gift of "priesthood" is viewed in Mormon doctrine. Then, too, there is the Catholic understanding of ordination as a sacrament—the sacrament of holy orders. As Catholic sacraments both signify and convey extrinsic divine grace, it is again possible to see similarity with LDS notions of ordination. In the Middle Ages, ordination was described as conferring sacramental powers on the individual. Peter Lombard defined ordination as a seal "by which spiritual power and office are granted to the one ordained." Thomas Aquinas wrote that "power of this sort was given by Christ to his disciples in such a way" that it could "flow on through them

---

114. *JSP*, D6:543. See also D&C 84:17.
115. *BEM*, 7c.

to others."[116] The medieval conversation about priestly ordination conferring actual, divine power, as with the Mormon view of priesthood, is not merely metaphorical or figurative but substantial. Even Christians who view priesthood as something that can be exercised by all believers still acknowledge that the empowering endowment of the Spirit received upon becoming a Christian is what constitutes them as priests.

Because God's power is one, priesthood is technically one. Yet, in the Church of Jesus Christ of Latter-day Saints, God channels his gift of divine power and authority through *two* orders of priesthood, "one is the Melchizedek Priesthood, and the other is the Aaronic or a Levitical Priesthood" (D&C 107:6). The latter, or "lesser" order, is believed to be the same priesthood that Aaron's sons exercised in the era of the Old Testament, though the scope and application of its power are arranged differently today. Its rights are summarized as having "power in administering outward ordinances" (D&C 107:14, 20). The other branch of priesthood is the superior priesthood Mormons believe Christ possessed, that others can, too, and that Hebrews says is "after the order of Melchisedec" (Heb. 6:20; 7:17), the priest-king of Salem (Gen. 14:18).[117] Mormons thus understand the reference in Hebrews to be to an actual priesthood order that has always existed, not simply another way of saying that Christ is a priest "like" Melchizedek.[118] Revelation describes the power and prerogatives of this order to be that of holding "the keys of all the spiritual blessings of the church" and consequently to "administer in spiritual things" (D&C 107:18, 8). Each of these two orders of priesthood exercises God's power through a set of offices with distinct privileges and performances. Aaronic priesthood offices are "deacon," "teacher," "priest," and "bishop." Melchizedek priesthood offices are "elder," "high priest," "patriarch," "seventy," and "apostle."[119] The particular roles and responsibilities of the various offices, as well

116. Peter Lombard, *Sentences* 4.24.13; and Aquinas, *Summa contra Gentiles* 4.74.3, as quoted in Frederick Christian Bauerschmidt and James J. Buckley, *Catholic Theology: An Introduction* (Chichester, UK: Wiley-Blackwell, 2017), 293.

117. "Why [it] is called the Melchizedek Priesthood is because Melchizedek was such a great high priest. Before his day it was called the Holy Priesthood, after the Order of the Son of God. But out of respect or reverence to the name of the Supreme Being, to avoid the too frequent repetition of his name, they, the church, in ancient days, called that priesthood after Melchizedek, or the Melchizedek Priesthood" (D&C 107:2–4). Latter-day Saints have a rich lore about the life of Melchizedek, whom they regard as an actual historical figure that lived in the time of Abraham. See, for instance, *NTOB*, 17, and Alma 13:14–19.

118. Joseph Smith remarked that "all the Prophets had the Melchizedeck Priesthood." *JSP*, D7:494.

119. *GH* 8.1. In the Latter-day Saint view, "the office of Seventy in the Melchizedek Priesthood is referenced in both the Old and New Testaments (see Exod 24:1, 9–10; Num-

as how the holders of each office are organized in different-sized "quorums," needn't detain us here.[120] What does require brief clarification is the relationship between the offices and priesthood itself, as well as between priesthood and other aspects of the ordained ministry.

In Mormon theology, priesthood is prior to and undergirds the specific offices of its two orders. This perspective is preserved in Latter-day Saint ordination rites. First, priesthood, either the Melchizedek priesthood or the Aaronic priesthood, is "conferred." Then the individual is "ordained" to one of the aforementioned offices within the designated order.[121] The particular priesthood is conferred only once in a person's life. With each successive ordination to priesthood office, the underlying priesthood is not reconferred. In this, LDS practice resembles that of Christian traditions for which ordination to ministerial office is permanent and unrepeatable. What is distinctive about LDS priesthood practice is that today the offices of the Aaronic priesthood are primarily staffed by teenage boys. A worthy and willing boy has the opportunity to receive the Aaronic priesthood and be ordained to the office of deacon as early as the beginning of the year in which he turns twelve. The Aaronic priesthood is considered the "preparatory priesthood."[122] Offices in the Aaronic priesthood are held temporarily, generally for two years, and progressively from deacon to priest. Aaronic priesthood service functions as a kind of apprenticeship or novitiate for receiving the Melchizedek priesthood and ordination to its offices as adults.

Most of what priesthood holders do is administer the church's various sacraments or ordinances (discussed at length in the next several chapters). The primary responsibility of Aaronic priesthood holders, for instance, is to pre-

---

bers 11:16–17, 24–25; Luke 10:1, 17). Today, there are General Authority Seventies and Area Seventies. They act under the keys and direction of the Quorum of the Twelve Apostles. They assist the Twelve in building up and regulating the Church in all nations (see Doctrine and Covenants 107:34–35, 38)." *GH* 5.1.1.2.

120. A vast Mormon literature discusses the priesthood. Along with some initially specified rights and responsibilities, the functions of the various offices have evolved over the years. Much of the early development is discernible in the Doctrine and Covenants. An entrée into this rich and complex history can be gained by perusing such revelations as D&C 20, 84, 107, and 124. A detailed study is William G. Hartley, *My Fellow Servants: Essays on the History of the Priesthood* (Provo, UT: BYU Press, 2010).

121. *GH* 3.4.2.

122. "The Aaronic Priesthood is often called the preparatory priesthood," although it is not a canonical phrase. "Aaronic Priesthood," in *Doctrinal Mastery Core Document* (Salt Lake City: The Church of Jesus Christ of Latter-day Saints, 2018), 9. The same observation is made in *True to the Faith*, 4, and in *Principles of the Gospel* (Salt Lake City: The Church of Jesus Christ of Latter-day Saints, 2014), 10.

pare and officiate in the weekly sacrament of the Lord's Supper. In addition to performing various ordinances as a result of their priesthood ordination, men may be consecrated to perform other ministries in the church, what Latter-day Saints refer to as "callings." So may women. To avoid conceptual confusion, individuals are "set apart" to callings. "Ordain" and its derivatives are used only with reference to installment in priesthood offices. In either case, it is believed that God endows recipients with all the divine grace and gifts of the Holy Spirit necessary to perform their service. Callings are no less important or of lesser status than ordinations; it is not a laity-clergy distinction. Indeed, callings constitute some of the most significant ministries in the church. They perform nearly all the church's extensive pastoral and episcopal activities at the congregational, regional, and general levels. Only the apostles and the seventies under them exercise their episcopal and pastoral ministry by virtue of priesthood ordination (D&C 107:25, 34, 38). Thus, a high priest may be appointed to serve in the calling of stake president (pastoral leader over from five to ten congregations), but he is set apart to do so, not ordained to the position. A woman may be called to serve as the president of the local Relief Society (the church's women's organization), but she is set apart to do so, not ordained. In both cases, the extent and impact of their episcopal and pastoral ministries, not to mention the hours involved in their service, significantly exceed what a high priest or elder without a calling does in his priesthood office. Only when performing the designated ordinances pertaining to their office in the priesthood are men serving by virtue of the priesthood per se.

Aside from episcopal callings that entail presiding over particular groups in the church, there are numerous callings that serve pastoral or other ministerial functions at the congregational level. Here LDS practice resembles the ministry in other Christian churches where there are nonordained ministries for dealing with youth, education, Christian formation, worship, and so on. The list is extensive in many Christian churches. In the Church of Jesus Christ of Latter-day Saints, the number of callings in a congregation may reach between fifty and a hundred. Indeed, most adult church members who are willing have a calling. Such widespread involvement in ministry points to the common Christian understanding of church membership as a call to service, a service often characterized as "priestly."

PRIESTHOOD OF ALL CHRISTIANS

The slogan popular in some churches today—"Every Member a Minister"—is a modern version of the "priesthood of all believers" concept first forcefully articulated during the Protestant Reformation.[123] Famously associated with Martin Luther, this doctrine contends that all Christians by virtue of their conversion and baptismal incorporation in Christ share in his priestly mission and ministry. All are to be witnesses of Christ and proclaimers of his gospel. Ordained ministers merely exercise publicly the commission that all Christians receive. "We are all priests," wrote Luther in *The Babylonian Captivity of the Church*, "as many of us as are Christians."[124] Luther rejected the Catholic concept that holy orders confers on priests an "indelible [ontological] character" that imparts to them unique divine power and constitutes them a separate class apart from the laity.[125] In Luther's mind, such concepts and practices led to mischief. Ordination in the Catholic Church was hierarchically initiated, controlled, and perpetuated, and from Luther's perspective, it fostered a corrupt elitism in the body of Christ. The way it should be understood, argued Luther, is that "priests, as we call them," are simply "ministers chosen from among us," and their "priesthood is nothing but a ministry" that principally entails preaching the gospel. "Whoever does not preach the Word . . . is no priest at all."[126]

Other Reformers concurred, claiming that in theory all Christians have the right to preach and administer the sacraments. Practicality and orderliness, however, demanded that a select few should be appointed by the congregation to take the lead in these matters in public worship. Thus, most Protestant churches perpetuated an "ordained" ministry in the sense of ceremonially consecrating or setting apart fellow Christians to a particular service. They did not, however, regard this as elevating them to a higher, separate status or imparting unique and permanent powers not shared by other Christians. In this way, Protestants ended up with a concept of two ministries or priesthoods metaphorically—the ordained ministry/priesthood and the common priesthood of all baptized believers. In a remarkable development in the twentieth century during Vatican II, Catholic bishops (with the pope) arrived at a similar position, at least in terms of elaborating an inclusive vision for a "common" or "royal" priesthood of all the faithful.[127] This opened the door for subsequent ecumenical dialogues in

---

123. "The expression 'every member a minister' has gained wide popularity among the churches," many printing it "on their weekly bulletin." Indeed, from one perspective, "the laity should be considered the primary ministers of the church." Randy Pope, *The Intentional Church*, rev. ed. (Chicago: Moody Press, 2006), 131–32.

124. Luther, *Babylonian Captivity of the Church*, 116.

125. A useful overview of ordination rites in Christian history is Paul F. Bradshaw, *Rites of Ordination: Their History and Theology* (Collegeville, MN: Liturgical Press, 2013).

126. Luther, *Babylonian Captivity*, 116.

127. This is eloquently delineated in *Lumen Gentium*. See also the contemporaneously

which Catholics and Protestants agreed that "the royal priesthood of the whole people of God and a special ordained ministry are both important aspects of the church, and not to be seen as mutually exclusive alternatives."[128]

Protestants and Catholics alike find foundational support for their vision of a priestly laity in 1 Peter. Echoing Exodus 19:5–6, 1 Peter 2:9 proclaims: "Ye are a chosen generation, a royal priesthood, an holy nation, a peculiar people; that ye should shew forth the praises of him who hath called you out of darkness into his marvellous light." First Peter 2:5 states, "Ye also, as lively stones, are built up a spiritual house, an holy priesthood, to offer up spiritual sacrifices, acceptable to God by Jesus Christ." In these passages, 1 Peter addresses the whole church, the entire "summoned assembly" (*ekklēsia*) of male and female Christians, and provides a powerful set of images for what they should be and do. Little wonder that these verses are widely cited in Christian circles today when priesthood is discussed. The priesthood of Christ and the priesthood of his churchly body, the baptized, share in their respective ways a ministry of sacrifice and intercession. As Christ offered himself for all on the cross, Christians offer their all as "a living sacrifice" (Rom. 12:1) to God. As Christ intercedes before the Father in heaven, Christians intercede on earth for the church and the salvation of the world.[129]

Citing 1 Peter 2:9, the Lutheran–Roman Catholic Commission on Unity declared that "Catholics and Protestants are in agreement that all the baptized who believe in Christ share in the priesthood of Christ and are thus commissioned to 'proclaim [his] mighty acts.'. . . Hence no member lacks a part to play in the mission of the whole body."[130] The "goal" of "Christ's own ministry," summarizes a Methodist-Catholic dialogue, is "to reconcile all people to God and to each other and to bring them into a new community," the church. Christ's ministry "did not end with his life on earth, but by the power of the Spirit [it] continues now in and through his church." Indeed, "the whole people of God

---

composed and extensive Hans Küng, *The Church* (London: Burns & Oates, 1967), where in the final section the Catholic scholar discusses and affirms both "the priesthood of all believers" and the "ecclesiastical office as ministry."

128. *The Church: Towards a Common Vision* (Geneva: WCC Publications, 2013), 12.

129. In the Catholic Liturgy of the Hours or daily prayer of the church, "the royal priesthood of the baptized is exercised, and this sacrifice of praise is thus connected to the sacrifice of the Eucharist, both preparing for and flowing from the Mass." "Liturgy of the Hours," United States Conference of Catholic Bishops, https://www.usccb.org/prayer-and-worship/liturgy-of-the-hours.

130. *The Apostolicity of the Church: Study Document of the Lutheran–Roman Catholic Commission on Unity* (Minneapolis: Lutheran University Press, 2006), 124.

has been sent by Christ into the world to witness to the love of the Father in the power of the Holy Spirit."[131] As for the ordained ministry, those so commissioned "may appropriately be called 'priests' because they fulfill a particular priestly service by strengthening and building up the royal and prophetic priesthood of the faithful through word and sacraments, through their prayers of intercession, and through their pastoral guidance of the community."[132]

Especially in terms of their concept of "callings," Latter-day Saints have no quibble with a vision of the ministry of all the faithful, but for several reasons expressions such as the "priesthood of all believers" or the "common priesthood" have seemed foreign to them. Mormons have a long history of using the term "priesthood" with reference to men alone. Moreover, much of what has been said historically about the priesthood has focused on the idea of divine permission to function on God's behalf. Thus, reference to priesthood has typically conjured up images of authority more than of ministry. Yet, in their own idiom, where the terms "ministry" and "service" abound, Latter-day Saints have promoted from early in their history a vision of church-wide engagement in the work of the Lord similar to the concept of a "common priesthood." Had the Saints understood that the "priesthood" of all believers was really proclaiming the *ministry* of all believers, they might have affirmed it enthusiastically from the start. Indeed, few Christian churches have promoted such a vision more intensely or with greater success than the Church of Jesus Christ of Latter-day Saints. The call to minister to the spiritually and temporally needy, to be a witness for Christ, and to love and serve one's neighbor are not only regular themes in Mormon homilies, they are part and parcel of normal LDS Church life. With James, Latter-day Saints stress the importance of being "doers of the word, and not hearers only" (James 1:22). In addition to offering virtually every adult member a formal calling, willing adults, often together with an apprenticing youth, are assigned to be "ministering brothers" or "ministering sisters" to several individuals or families in the congregation. As such, church members can cultivate deep, caring friendships that enable them to effectively pastor one another. In short, every LDS member *is* to be a minister.[133] As for bearing witness of Christ to the world, despite an organized force of tens of thousands of young adult missionaries who carry the good

---

131. Kasper, *Harvesting the Fruits*, 102.

132. *BEM*, 20.

133. In 2019, the church formally launched a major effort to engage the laity to an even greater degree by characterizing all aspects of church life and ministry as "home-centered, church-supported." See Russell M. Nelson and Quentin L. Cook, *Ensign*, November 2018, 7–11.

news of the gospel to all parts of the globe, the church has long urged universal member involvement with its slogan "Every Member a Missionary."

While the Church of Jesus Christ of Latter-day Saints has a robust record of involving both women and men in lay Christian ministry, prophets and apostles in the twenty-first century have repeatedly and explicitly connected this to the concept of priesthood. By broadening the use of "priesthood," much as other Christians do, to refer to the priesthood or ministry of the whole people of God, church leaders have endeavored to assuage concerns over the fact that women presently are not part of the "ordained," ministerial priesthood. Recent editions of the church's *General Handbook* continue to define priesthood as "the authority and power of God," but do so without adding, as has traditionally been done, words like "delegated to *men* on earth to act in God's name." Instead, the *General Handbook* states that "God grants authority and power to His sons *and daughters* on earth to help carry out this work."[134] This important if subtle semantic move to include women in the "royal priesthood" of all the faithful has opened the door to labeling as "priesthood" the divine power and authority to do the Lord's work that LDS women have always received and wielded as recipients of temple ordinances and in their church callings.[135] Speaking to the women of the church, President Russell Nelson declared, "When you are set apart to serve in a calling . . . you are given priesthood authority to function in that calling."[136] Dallin Oaks acknowledged, "We are not accustomed to speaking of women having the authority of the priesthood in their Church callings, but what other authority can it be? When a woman— young or old—is set apart to preach the gospel as a full-time missionary, she is given priesthood authority to perform a priesthood function . . . when a woman is set apart to function as an officer or teacher in a Church organization," she "exercises priesthood authority in performing her [ministry]."[137]

By defining "priesthood" as God's power and authority shared with both women and men, apostles and prophets in recent decades have begun to reorient church members away from seeing priesthood as the province and possession of men alone. Church leaders distinguish the vast array of divine powers (priest-

---

134. *GH* 3.0 (emphasis added).

135. This reality is paralleled in Eastern Orthodoxy. Despite not being able to be part of the ordained priesthood, "Orthodox women still work for the glory of God and the spread of his kingdom, motivated by a deep belief in the royal priesthood of believers." Niki J. Tsironis, "Women in Orthodoxy," in *Encyclopedia of Eastern Orthodox Christianity*, ed. John A. McGuckin (Chichester, UK: Wiley-Blackwell, 2011), 641.

136. Russell M. Nelson, "Spiritual Treasures," *Ensign*, November 2019, 78.

137. Dallin H. Oaks, "The Keys and Authority of the Priesthood," *Ensign*, May 2014, 51.

hood) available to women (and men) ministering in what other Christians call "the priesthood of all believers" from the much smaller set of powers (priesthood) reserved only for the ordained (male) ministry in the discharge of their duties. Critically, President Nelson clarified that the remark "I'm sorry you don't have the priesthood in your home" was incorrect. In the past this had sometimes been offered as an expression of sympathy to a faithful Latter-day Saint woman not living with a priesthood holder. "You may not have [an ordained] priesthood bearer in your home," he told the women of the church, "but you have received and made sacred covenants with God," and "from those covenants flows an endowment of His priesthood power upon you." Nelson's latter comment has particular reference to what women experience in LDS temples, which Nelson characterized in this manner: "Those who are endowed in the house of the Lord receive a gift of God's priesthood power by virtue of their covenant, along with a gift of knowledge to know how to draw upon that power. The heavens are just as open to women who are endowed with God's power flowing from their priesthood covenants as they are to men who bear the priesthood."[138]

As reinforcement for this perspective, the future may yet find common among the Latter-day Saints a reading of 1 Peter 2 that recognizes that women are included in the passage's mention of a "royal priesthood" just as much as they are in its reference to a "chosen generation." Such a reading, incidentally, would parallel Jewish interpretation of God's declaration to ancient Israel, "ye shall be unto me a kingdom of priests" (Exod. 19:6). Jewish scholarship reads "priests" in this passage not in the halakic and ceremonial sense that involved only certain males of the tribe of Levi but rather as a metaphor for an entire nation of men *and* women who, *like* priests, devoted their lives to the service of God and fellow beings.[139] Joseph Smith glossed Exodus 19:6 when he told the women of the newly founded Relief Society in 1842 that "he was going to make of [their] Society a kingdom of priests."[140] "Most early Latter-day Saints understood this connection between

138. Nelson, "Spiritual Treasures," 79, 77. On temple ordinances in general, see chapter 11. See also the church's Gospel Topics Essay, "Joseph Smith's Teachings about Priesthood, Temple, and Women," at churchofjesuschrist.org.

139. See, for example, Tamara Cohn Eskenazi and Andrea L. Weiss, *The Torah: A Women's Commentary* (New York: CCAR Press, 2008), 413, and Martin I. Lockshin, ed. and trans., *Rashbam's Commentary on Exodus: An Annotated Translation* (Atlanta: Scholars Press, 1997), 202. For similar Christian readings, see Terence E. Fretheim, *Exodus: Interpretation; A Bible Commentary for Teaching and Preaching* (Louisville: Westminster John Knox, 1991), 212, and Carol Meyers, *Exodus* (New York: Cambridge University Press, 2005), 147.

140. Minutes, "Female Relief Society of Nauvoo," March 31, 1842, in *The First Fifty Years of Relief Society: Key Documents in Latter-day Saint Women's History*, ed. Jill Mulvay Derr et al. (Salt Lake City: Church Historian's Press, 2016), 43.

priesthood and women as a part of temple worship." Long-lived Bathsheba W. Smith, founding member of the Relief Society and recipient of temple ordinances from Joseph Smith, recalled in 1905, "[Joseph Smith] wanted to make us, as the women were in Paul's day, 'A kingdom of priestesses.' She then explained, 'We have that ceremony in our [temple] endowments as Joseph taught.'"[141] Subsequent interpretation of how temple ordinances establish women as "priestesses" situated its fulfillment in the afterlife. Joseph Fielding Smith taught, "It is within the privilege of the sisters of this Church to receive exaltation in the [heavenly] kingdom of God and [there] receive authority and power as queens and priestesses."[142] Current discussion of what temple ordinances confer on women, though, as illustrated by the remarks of President Nelson above, focuses on women's reception of "priesthood power" in the here and now.

In sum, the current conceptual and linguistic trajectory is clearly toward describing women's callings as a form of priesthood and emphasizing the priestly powers conferred on women in temple ceremonies.[143] This moves steadily in a direction where the language of a "common priesthood" or "priesthood of all the faithful" might be used and understood to include women without fear that such expressions were claiming for women participation in the "ordained priesthood" of the Melchizedek and Aaronic orders. Nor would such a broadened application of priesthood language diminish the importance of the ordained priesthood per se. The priesthood orders are not only critical to the organizational vitality of the church, but they are the indispensable conduits to its sacramental life. It is in the sacraments that Latter-day Saints and other Christians find spiritual nourishment and, for many traditions, saving grace. It is to a detailed consideration of this important dimension of Christian life and theology that we now turn in the chapters ahead.

141. *First Fifty Years of Relief Society*, 43n.

142. Joseph Fielding Smith, *Relief Society Magazine*, Jan. 1959, 5–6.

143. In addition to reviewing what has been said about "priesthood" in the general conferences prior to the 1980s and comparing it with church-leader discourses in the twenty-first century, one can also discern differences by comparing the content of two Deseret Book publications of general authority teachings forty years apart—Spencer W. Kimball et al., *Priesthood* (Salt Lake City: Deseret Book, 1981), and Dale G. Renlund and Ruth Lybbert Renlund, *The Melchizedek Priesthood: Understanding the Doctrine, Living the Principles* (Salt Lake City: Deseret Book, 2018).

9

Sacraments

Theory and Application

It is widely recognized that the term "sacraments," which is related to the Latin root *sacr* designating that which is "sacred" or "holy," refers to sacred ceremonies or religious rites characteristic of Christian churches. Less well known is that the term never actually appears in the New Testament with reference to such sacramental rituals as baptism or the Lord's Supper (Eucharist). Labeling these ceremonies as "sacraments" (*sacramenta*) is a later Christian development unattested in the Latin-speaking West prior to the end of the second century and uncommon before the fourth century. Christians who understand proper reception of the sacraments to include a personal commitment to discipleship sometimes point to the early Latin meaning of *sacramentum* as an "oath, solemn obligation, or sacred engagement" (originally, it was the preliminary oath of allegiance taken by enlisted Roman soldiers) to explain its application to the sacred rites of the church.[1] In the Greek-speaking East, *mysteria* (mysteries) became the umbrella term for these rituals. *Mysteria* refers to that which is secret or hidden, both in the sense of the unrevealed, as in God's private counsels, and that which is beyond normal understanding, as in a transcendent reality best perceived through analogies and symbols.[2] The precise history of how *mysteria* in the East and *sacramenta* in the West came

---

1. See G. E. Lampe, ed., *A Patristic Greek Lexicon* (Oxford: Clarendon, 1965), 891–93. The first church figure known to employ this usage was Tertullian around AD 200 in his short address *To the Martyrs*. At the beginning of the third chapter, he writes, "We were called to the service in the army of the living God in the very moment when we gave response to the words of the sacramental oath." Rudolph Arbesmann, Emily Joseph Daly, and Edward A. Quain, trans., *Tertullian: Disciplinary, Moral, and Ascetical Works*, Fathers of the Church (Washington, DC: Catholic University of America Press, 1959), 22.

2. See Frederick William Danker, ed., *A Greek-English Lexicon of the New Testament and Other Early Christian Literature*, 3rd ed. (Chicago: University of Chicago Press, 2000), s.v. "*mysterion*."

to be the terms of choice to designate sacred Christian rituals is uncertain. Yet, the terms are compatible and consistent with Paul's emphasis on the hiddenness (to the world) of God's saving work in Christ (Col. 1:27). Sacraments as mysteries remind us that Christian rites are richly symbolic, sacred manifestations of Christ's gift of redemption that is so infinitely profound that it eludes complete comprehension and remains a glorious secret only partially grasped by finite humans.

Latter-day Saints agree with the profundity of Christ's saving work and its mediation through the sacraments, but they almost never refer to these ceremonies as "mysteries" or even "sacraments." Instead, echoing a preference among "low-church" (less liturgical) Protestants, such as Baptists and Pentecostals, Mormons use the term "ordinances." In LDS scripture, as in the Bible, "ordinance" and "ordinances" broadly signify anything that is instituted or commanded by God. This includes, but is not restricted to, the sacraments.[3] Over time, however, Latter-day Saint use of "ordinance(s)" narrowed, and today it is used almost solely as a synonym for the sacraments. "An ordinance," explains the church's *General Handbook*, "is a sacred act" with "symbolic meaning that points individuals to Heavenly Father and Jesus Christ. . . . Each ordinance allows individuals to receive rich spiritual blessings."[4] In a rare Latter-day Saint discussion of sacraments per se, apostle Jeffrey Holland indicated that "a sacrament could be any one of a number of gestures or acts or ordinances that unite us with God and his limitless powers." The Lord's Supper "is the one [Latter-day Saints] have come to associate most traditionally with the word *sacrament*, [but] it is technically only one of many such moments when we formally take the hand of God and feel His divine power."[5]

Consistent with the symbolic nature of the sacraments, Augustine is credited with popularizing the idea that sacraments are "signs." That is, basic to a sacrament is a material likeness to the spiritual reality it represents. Additionally, Augustine, and especially later medieval Catholic theologians, argued that the sacraments are signs in a dual sense: they both draw attention to and convey divine grace. Peter Lombard's influential medieval theological text-

---

3. As an example of a nonsacramental usage, after early Mormon leader Sidney Gilbert was given several tasks to perform, the revelation concluded: "Behold, these are the first ordinances which you shall receive; and the residue shall be made known in a time to come, according to your labor in my vineyard" (D&C 53:6). See also D&C 77:14; 124:133–34.

4. *GH* 3.5.2. *Guide to the Scriptures*, s.v. "ordinances," defines the sacraments simply as "sacred rites and ceremonies . . . that have spiritual meaning."

5. Jeffrey R. Holland, *Of Souls, Symbols, and Sacraments* (Salt Lake City: Deseret Book, 2001), 27–28.

book, *Sentences,* put it succinctly: A sacrament is a sign of grace in that it both "bears its image and exists as its cause. Sacraments were instituted, therefore, for the sake, not only of signifying, but also of sanctifying."[6] It became formal Catholic doctrine that the sacraments "contain the grace which they signify, and bestow it on those who do not hinder it."[7] For this reason, some Catholic theologians recognize this duality by referring to the sacraments as "effective signs" or "sign-causes."[8] Participation in the sacraments is believed to be one of the primary ways in which Christ's saving grace and divine life flow to his disciples. As noted in the current Catholic *Catechism,* the sacraments "communicate" (convey) the "fruits of the Paschal Mystery." Indeed, it is in the sacraments that "divine blessing is fully manifested and communicated."[9] Many Protestants—Anglicans, Methodists, and Lutherans, for instance—concur. The definition in the Episcopal Church's Book of Common Prayer is illustrative: "The sacraments are outward and visible signs of inward and spiritual grace, given by Christ as sure and certain means by which we receive that grace."[10] That the sacraments are both signs of grace and means of grace is a perspective with which Mormonism is in clear agreement. LDS scripture affirms that "in the ordinances . . . the power of godliness is manifest" (D&C 84:20). Jeffrey Holland elaborated: the sacraments are occasions on which "we can unite symbolically with [God] and, in so doing, gain access to His power. . . . They allow us to feel the grace and grandeur of God's power. . . . At such moments we not only acknowledge His divinity, but we also quite literally take something of that divinity to ourselves. Such are the holy sacraments."[11]

While similar to other religious ceremonies and rites, the sacraments are also distinct. In the first place, they are believed to have been instituted by Jesus Christ. For some, this is understood literally. For others, it is approached more broadly in that any church rite whose purpose comports with, and can be seen as a continuation of, Christ's redemptive ministry, even if Christ did not

---

6. As quoted in Maxwell E. Johnson, *Sacraments and Worship: The Sources of Christian Theology* (Louisville: Westminster John Knox, 2012), 6.

7. Ludwig Ott, *Fundamentals of Catholic Dogma,* trans. Patrick Lynch, 6th ed. (St. Louis: Herder, 1964), 328.

8. Romanus Cessario, "The Sacraments of the Church," in *Vatican II: Renewal within Tradition,* ed. Matthew L. Lamb and Matthew Levering (New York: Oxford University Press, 2008), 139.

9. *CCC* 1076, 1082–1083.

10. *The Book of Common Prayer . . . according to the Use of the Episcopal Church* (New York: Church Publishing, 2007), 857.

11. Holland, *Of Souls, Symbols, and Sacraments,* 27–29.

personally command its practice, is considered a sacrament. By this capacious view, Catholics and Orthodox eventually came to number the sacraments at seven.[12] These include three sacraments of "initiation" or "illumination" (baptism, confirmation, and Eucharist), two sacraments of "healing" (penance and anointing of the sick), and two sacraments that focus on vocation and commitment (holy orders [ordination to the priesthood] and matrimony).[13] Most Protestants, on the other hand, acknowledge just two sacraments—baptism and the Lord's Supper—because these are the only ones they believe were explicitly commanded by the Lord. Additionally, the Anglican Communion admits five lesser "sacramental rites." The Church of Jesus Christ of Latter-day Saints acknowledges a variety of sacraments or ordinances but designates five as the essential "ordinances of salvation and exaltation." They are baptism, confirmation, ordination to the priesthood (for men), and two ordinances performed only in LDS temples—the "endowment" and marriage "sealing."[14] Somewhat like Anglicanism's "sacramental rites," additional LDS ordinances enable "God's children to receive His power, healing, comfort, and guidance." These include administering to the sick (similar to anointing of the sick) and naming and blessing children (similar to christening).[15]

A second feature that sets Christian sacraments apart from other religious ceremonies is that they are entrusted to the church to perform. In part, this means that they are generally performed in public. Hence, the eventual application to the sacraments of the term "liturgy" (Gk. *leitourgia*, lit. "public work"—from the roots *laos* [people], the source of the English term "laity," and *ergon* [work]). Moreover, in the New Testament, a *leitourgos* is translated "minister" and *leitourgia* is "service" or "ministry." Many early Christians came to believe that performance of the sacraments necessitated special ministerial ordination and ecclesiastical authorization, which is another way in which the sacraments are entrusted to the church. This, it will be remembered, is a matter

12. The number seven was not dogmatically fixed in the West until the Second Council of Lyon in 1274. See Denzinger 860. The East has never been as interested in specifying a set number of sacraments, and "many Orthodox theologians nowadays, without suggesting that any of the 'seven' should be abandoned, regard the limitation of the sacraments, or mysteries, to seven as an aspect of Western medieval theology that fits ill with the approach of Orthodox theology." Andrew Louth, *Introducing Eastern Orthodox Theology* (Downers Grove, IL: IVP Academic, 2013), 104.

13. This clustering of the sacraments into the three named categories, as well as their particular names, reflects current Catholic convention. See *CCC* 1210–1666.

14. *GH* 18.1.

15. *GH* 18.2. See also "Basic Doctrinal Principles," in *Teaching the Gospel in the Savior's Way* (Salt Lake City: The Church of Jesus Christ of Latter-day Saints, 2012), 15, and *True to the Faith*, 110–11.

of particular importance to the Latter-day Saints. The church's fifth Article of Faith states: "We believe that a man must be called of God, by prophecy, and by the laying on of hands by those who are in authority, to preach the Gospel and administer in the ordinances thereof." Added Joseph Smith, "All the ordinances . . . on the earth [are] of no use to the children of men unless they are . . . authorized of God; for nothing will save a man but a [legal] administrator; for none others will be acknowledged either by God or Angels."[16] From the beginning, emphasis on the restoration of divine priestly authority to administer the saving ordinances has been central to Mormonism's raison d'être (reason for being) and its evangelical proclamation to the world (see chapter 8).

Ex Opere Operato or Ex Opere Operantis?

Although nearly every aspect of sacramental theology has been debated over the centuries, a key issue that has received considerable attention is whether the sacraments are efficacious *ex opere operato* (from the work performed) or *ex opere operantis* (by the work of the worker). As fully developed in medieval theology, to be effective *ex opere operato*, a sacrament needs to meet certain criteria. It must be performed (1) by an ecclesiastically recognized officiant, (2) for the intent envisioned by the church, (3) in the correct manner, and (4) be received by a recipient who presents no behavioral or attitudinal "obstacle" to it. In such cases, the sacrament is considered valid and effective regardless of the level of spiritual comprehension, personal holiness, or religious commitment of the officiant/celebrant. *Ex opere operantis*, on the other hand, means that the efficacy of the sacrament *is* impacted by the inner disposition of the officiant or the recipient.[17]

Although a doctrine roughly equivalent to *ex opere operato* had been around for many years, it was most fully developed by Augustine in opposition to the Donatists of North Africa.[18] Donatism arose in the early 300s in the aftermath of an empire-wide persecution in which Christian clergy were required to turn over their sacred books to imperial officials or suffer the consequences. Clergy who refused were imprisoned and tortured. Numbers lost

---

16. *JSP*, D11:361.

17. Heiko Augustinus Oberman, "A Nominalistic Glossary," in *The Harvest of Medieval Theology: Gabriel Biel and Late Medieval Nominalism*, rev. ed. (Grand Rapids: Eerdmans, 1967), 467.

18. See W. H. C. Frend's pioneering work on the Donatists: *The Donatist Church: A Movement of Protest in Roman North Africa* (Oxford: Clarendon, 1971), and, more recently, Richard Miles, ed., *The Donatist Schism: Controversy and Contexts* (Liverpool: Liverpool University Press, 2016).

their property and even their lives. The Donatists were a group of Christians who thought that those who had succumbed to persecution and surrendered the sacred works were unworthy to participate in episcopal ordinations or administer the sacraments. The Donatists labeled the capitulators *traditores* (the Latin verb *tradere* means to "hand over" and is the source of the English word "traitors") and argued that a valid sacrament, especially the sacrament of baptism, could only be performed by clergy whose ordination lineage was uncontaminated by traditor participants. When fellow North African Christians disagreed and sided with Rome, which allowed penitent lapsed clergy to celebrate the sacraments, the Donatists broke fellowship and insisted that they alone constituted the true, read "pure," church of Christ.

By the early 400s, in the Donatist view, Catholic sacraments had been compromised for a century. Thus, as they saw it, no Catholic living at that time had received a legitimate baptism. Because the Donatists and Catholics were at a standoff in Roman Africa, the empire, by then Christianized, wanted the schism resolved in the name of political unity. In synodal councils and in written letters and treatises, the North African bishop Augustine disputed the Donatist claims over a period of years. He emphasized that the validity of a sacrament was inherent in its performance (*ex opere operato*) and was not dependent on the holiness of the performer (*ex opere operantis*). Citing baptism as an example, Augustine wrote that "the quality of the baptism is commensurate with the quality of the person [Christ] by whose power it is given, not with the quality of the person through whose ministry it is given." Thus, even "those whom Judas baptized, Christ baptized. Likewise, therefore, those whom the drunkard baptized . . . Christ baptized. This sacrament is so holy that it cannot even be polluted when a murderer administers it."[19] In Augustine's view, the Donatists crucially had failed to distinguish the divine Giver of grace from the earthly officiant. Any Christian baptism properly performed, even a Donatist baptism, as a baptism by Christ, carried the hoped-for consequences of the remission of sins and incorporation into the body of Christ.

From the fifth century, such an *ex opere operato* sacramentology has been dominant in Christianity. As Isidore of Seville remarked, the Spirit "in a hidden way brings about the aforesaid effect of the sacraments. Hence, although they may be dispensed through the Church of God by good or by bad ministers,

---

19. Augustine, *Tractates on the Gospel of John* 5.6.2; 5.18.4; 5.19.3, in *St. Augustine: Tractates on the Gospel of John, 1–10*, trans. John W. Rettig, Fathers of the Church (Washington, DC: Catholic University of America Press, 1988), 113, 126, 127. Augustine's sentiments are echoed in the current Catholic *Catechism*: "By his power [Christ] is present in the sacraments so that when anybody baptizes, it is really Christ himself who baptizes." *CCC* 1088.

nevertheless because the Holy Spirit mystically vivifies them . . . these gifts are neither enlarged by the merits of good ministers nor diminished by the bad."[20] The iniquity of an officiating priest was no more thought to nullify the efficacy of the sacrament administered than the immorality of a math teacher invalidates the principles of algebra he or she teaches to students.[21] Over time, however, a distinction was made between the validity of the sacrament administered and its spiritual *fruitfulness* in the life of the recipient. By the late medieval period, "an effect *ex opere operantis* [was] added to the basic effect *ex opere operato.*" Thus, it was thought that "a proper disposition on the part of the recipient [would] provide him with grace above and beyond the amount of grace received *ex opere operato.*"[22] Current Catholic teaching perpetuates this dual character of the sacraments. Explains a scholar of sacramental theology, the *ex opere operantis* principle "means that we cannot receive a sacrament with personal benefit without being actively engaged in the sacramental event through faith and interior conversion."[23] Adds another theologian, "the promised effects of sacramental grace can be better welcomed, diminished, or even blocked altogether depending upon the subjective dispositions of the recipient."[24]

Other Christian traditions also value the *ex opere operantis* position. Orthodox doctrine is that "the abundance of the harvest [of grace] depends on the receptivity and the will of the person receiving the sacrament."[25] The Church of England's Article of Religion on the sacraments states that "only as [we] worthily receive the same [do] they have a wholesome effect or operation."[26]

20. Quoted in Lewis Ayres and Thomas Humphries, "Augustine and the West to A.D. 650," in *OHST*, 167.

21. A 1208 profession of faith prescribed by Pope Innocent III for a Waldensian "heretic" returning to the Catholic faith affirmed that "even though these sacraments be administered by a sinful priest, as long as he is recognized by the Church," it is as acceptable as if it were "performed by the most just man. For the evil life of a bishop or priest has no harmful effect on either the baptism of an infant or the consecration of the Eucharist or other ecclesiastical duties performed for the faithful" because the administration occurs "in cooperation with the inestimable and invisible power of the Holy Spirit." Denzinger 793.

22. Oberman, *Harvest of Medieval Theology*, 135, 467.

23. Susan K. Wood, "The Liturgy and Sacraments," in *Blackwell Companion to Catholicism*, ed. James J. Buckley, Frederick C. Bauerschmidt, and Trent Pomplun (Chichester, UK: Wiley-Blackwell, 2010), 346.

24. Thomas Joseph White, "Sacraments and Philosophy," in *OHST*, 587–88.

25. The quote is from the renowned twentieth-century Greek dogmatician Panagiotis Trembelas, as quoted in Peter Galadza, "Twentieth-Century and Contemporary Orthodox Sacramental Theology," in *OHST*, 439.

26. Article 25, "Of the Sacraments," in *Articles of Religion of the Church of England.* The Westminster Confession of Faith (WC) also affirmed that participants must be "worthy receivers" to gain the sacraments' benefits. WC 28.3. Regarding the Lord's Supper, the WC

Mormonism, too, in its own way, embraces both an *ex opere operato* and an *ex opere operantis* understanding of the sacraments. LDS theology affirms the *ex opere operato* position in terms of the fundamental validity of ordinances properly performed by recognized "priesthood authority."[27] The personal rectitude of the officiant is not a factor in whether the church accepts the liturgical legitimacy or efficacy of the sacramental performance. As in other Christian traditions, if the sacrament is performed by a properly ordained and authorized minister using the proper words of institution and carried out in the correct form, the sacrament stands, regardless of the minister's depth of theological understanding or degree of sinfulness. Moreover, Latter-day Saints share Augustine's view that the real administrator of the sacraments is Christ. In a passage of LDS scripture referring to the sacrament of priestly ordination, the Lord declares, "Behold, I will lay my hand upon you by the hand of my servant Sidney" (D&C 36:2).

At the same time, Latter-day Saint theology is deeply committed to an *ex opere operantis* understanding of the sacraments with regard to the recipient. This is reinforced by emphasizing the covenantal character of the sacraments and stressing that any covenant "that [is] not made and entered into and sealed by the Holy Spirit of promise . . . [is] of no efficacy, virtue, or force" (D&C 132:7). Explained Joseph Fielding Smith, "The Holy Spirit of Promise . . . places the stamp of approval upon every ordinance . . . received through faithfulness. If a person violates a covenant, whether it be of baptism, ordination, marriage or anything else, the Spirit withdraws the stamp of approval, and the blessings will not be received. Every ordinance is sealed with a promise of [grace] based upon faithfulness."[28] Paul famously remarked that "he is not a Jew which is one outwardly; neither is that circumcision, which is outward in the flesh." A "real" Jew "is one inwardly" whose "circumcision is that of the heart" (Rom. 2:28–29). Latter-day Saints see in Paul's comments an *ex opere operantis* understanding of the fruitfulness of the sacraments. Notes an LDS instructional manual, a sacrament "has meaning only if it is [received] with sincerity and real intent."[29]

---

declared that "although ignorant and wicked men receive the outward elements in this sacrament, yet they receive not the thing signified thereby" (WC 29.8).

27. *GH* 18.0.

28. *Doctrines of Salvation*, 1:45. LDS theology, of course, makes provision for repentance whereby the individual can regain the Spirit's stamp of approval and the sacrament's attendant blessings.

29. *NT Student Manual* (2018), 338.

BAPTISM

Having discussed some of the overarching issues in sacramental theology, we turn our attention to an exploration of particular sacraments, beginning with baptism, the first of several "sacraments of initiation."[30] *Baptizō* and its derivatives appear more than ninety times in the New Testament.[31] The terms have a range of meanings in classical and New Testament Greek from "dip in, or under, water" to "wash," "plunge," or "immerse."[32] Baptism, therefore, is the sacrament in which water is liturgically applied in some fashion (immersion, pouring, or sprinkling) to the individual. Nearly all Christian theologies consider baptism a divine commandment, reflecting Christ's "Great Commission" to his apostles—"Go ye therefore, and teach all nations, baptizing them in the name of the Father, and of the Son, and of the Holy Ghost" (Matt. 28:19). The World Council of Churches' ecumenical "convergence document," *Baptism, Eucharist, and Ministry (BEM)*, expresses views that have been embraced by many Christian denominations. In it, baptism is described succinctly as that which "unites the one baptized with Christ and with his people." Baptism brings about "incorporation into Christ" and "entry into the New Covenant between God and God's people." Baptism is "the sign of new life through Jesus Christ."[33] That said, scripture deploys a variety of different images and metaphors to describe the significance and benefits of baptism. This has occasioned a certain amount of diversity in baptismal theory and practice over the years.[34] Most teachings about the purpose and effects of baptism can be

---

30. Latter-day Saints do not refer to baptism as a sacrament/ordinance of "initiation" or as an "initiatory" sacrament/ordinance because "initiatory" is used primarily to refer to ordinances performed in LDS temples (see chapter 11). Covering the history of each of the sacraments of initiation is Maxwell Johnson's *Rites of Christian Initiation: Their Evolution and Interpretation*, revised and expanded ed. (Collegeville, MN: Liturgical Press, 2007). For special attention to the teachings of the Catholic magisterium, see Liam G. Walsh, *The Sacraments of Initiation: Baptism, Confirmation, Eucharist* (London: Geoffrey Chapman, 1988).

31. Studies of biblical perspectives on baptism are myriad. A pioneering study that is still useful is George R. Beasley-Murray, *Baptism in the New Testament* (Grand Rapids: Eerdmans, 1962). From a Catholic perspective, see Isaac A. Morales, *The Bible and Baptism: The Fountain of Salvation* (Grand Rapids: Baker Academic, 2022). Succinct surveys of different denominational and historical positions can be found in various chapters of *OHST*, 52–122.

32. H. G. Liddell, *An Intermediate Greek-English Lexicon Founded upon the Seventh Edition of Liddell and Scott's Greek-English Lexicon* (1889; reprint, Oxford: Clarendon, 1972), s.v. "*baptizo*," and Danker, *Greek-English Lexicon of the New Testament*, s.v. "*baptizo*."

33. *BEM*, 1, 2, 6.

34. Although substantial convergences in baptismal theology and practice exist among

grouped under the three broad section headings that follow: (1) "Incorpo-ration into Christ and His Body, the Church," (2) "Forgiveness of Sins," and (3) "Spiritual Rebirth."

INCORPORATION INTO CHRIST AND HIS BODY, THE CHURCH

Baptism is a visual marker of boundary crossing and status transformation, a sign of having entered into the Christian community and covenantal relation-ship with Christ. In Paul's words, Christians are "all baptized into one body . . . the body of Christ, and [are its] members in particular" (1 Cor. 12:13, 27). The New Testament pattern, particularly noticeable in the book of Acts, is that those who come to faith are baptized soon thereafter and become constituent members of the *ekklēsia*.[35] That baptism is the means of incorporation into the church is also repeatedly affirmed in LDS scripture. The Book of Mormon calls baptism the indispensable "gate by which ye should enter" (2 Nephi 31:17) and records Christ as saying that "the people of my church" are "all those who shall believe and be baptized in my name" (3 Nephi 18:5; also 3 Nephi 26:21). An Acts-like pattern is also apparent: "And it came to pass that there were many that did be-lieve in their words; and as many as did believe were baptized . . . and they did establish a church among them" (Alma 19:35). Elsewhere it is reported "that the work of the Lord did prosper unto the baptizing and uniting to the church of God, many souls, yea, even tens of thousands" (Helaman 3:26). Joseph Smith was emphatic about the importance of baptism as the path to ecclesial incorporation: "God has made certain decreas which are fixed & unalterable . . . upon the same principle do I contend that Baptism is a sign, ordained of God for the believer in Christ to take upon himself in order to enter into the kingdom of God."[36]

Integration into the household of faith is closely related to incorporation into Christ himself. At the conclusion of the Last Supper, Jesus petitioned the

---

various Christian traditions, "not a single point remains uncontested by one group or an-other." Susan K. Wood, "Baptism," in *The Oxford Handbook of Ecumenical Studies*, ed. Geof-frey Wainwright and Paul McPartlan (New York: Oxford University Press, 2017), 241. For examples, see David F. Wright, ed., *Baptism: Three Views* (Downers Grove, IL: InterVarsity Press, 2009), and John H. Armstrong and Paul E. Engle, eds., *Understanding Four Views on Baptism* (Grand Rapids: Zondervan, 2007).

35. Examples in Acts include the multitude on the Day of Pentecost (2:37–41), the people of Samaria (8:12), the Ethiopian eunuch (8:35–38), Paul (9:17–18), Cornelius and his house-hold (10:47–48), Lydia (16:14–15), the Philippian jailor and his household (16:30–33), and Crispus, the synagogue leader and "many" Corinthians (18:8).

36. *JSP*, D9:292.

Father that believers "may be one in us" and "I in them" (John 17:21, 23, 26). This spiritual union between believers and Christ involves baptism. Twice in the New Testament (Gal. 3:27; Rom. 6:3), Paul speaks of being baptized "into" Christ (*eis Christon*). "In Greek and Jewish usage, prepositions of entrance ('to' or 'into') or location ('in') followed by 'the name of X' indicated not simply belonging but also relationship."[37] Thus, the KJV rendering of being baptized "into Christ" is helpfully amplified in some modern translations as "baptized into union with Christ Jesus" (Good News Translation) or "joined with Christ Jesus in baptism" (NLT). In Galatians 3:27, Paul added another image depicting this baptismal union when he declared: "For as many of you as have been baptized into Christ have put on Christ" ("clothed yourselves with Christ" in NRSV, NASB). Some baptismal rites reinforce this symbolism by clothing the newly baptized in a fresh, white garment. The imagery of putting on new clothes captures well not only the idea of having a new identity as a Christian but also of being totally enveloped by that relationship. Yet another New Testament image of the relationship resulting from baptism is marriage. Just as marriage entails a covenant or pledge of complete devotion to one's beloved such that "the two become one" (cf. Eph. 5:31), so the baptized as the "bride" of Christ enter into an intimate spiritual union with him, pledging themselves in love and obedience to the Bridegroom. First Peter 3:21 speaks of baptism as "the pledge of a clear conscience toward God" (NIV).[38] *BEM* summarizes the view of multiple Christian traditions: baptism is "a rite of commitment to the Lord" through "life-long growth into Christ." The baptized are to "live for the sake of Christ, of his Church and of the world."[39]

In addition to agreeing with such imagery and sentiments, Latter-day Saints gesture toward incorporation with their own turn of phrase—"take upon you the name of Christ" (e.g., 2 Nephi 31:13; 3 Nephi 27:5; D&C 18:21). The church's Articles and Covenants expects baptismal candidates to be "willing to take upon them the name of Jesus Christ, having a determination to serve him to the end" (D&C 20:37; cf. Moroni 6:3); and the Book of Mormon describes many who "were desirous to be baptized as a witness and a testimony that they were willing to serve God with all their hearts" (Mosiah 21:35; cf. 18:10). Such

---

37. Nicholas Perrin, "Sacraments and Sacramentality in the New Testament," in *OHST*, 58.

38. The notion of baptism as a pledge of fidelity is reinforced by how some render the lexically difficult *eperōtēma* in 1 Pet. 3:21 "to mean 'pledge' (i.e. in the sense of a contractual obligation)," which "implies that baptism, again consistent with its covenantal framework, betoken[s] the believer's public commitment to moral purity." Perrin, "Sacraments and Sacramentality in the New Testament," 64–65.

39. *BEM*, 1, 9.

is the loving and lifelong devotion required of those who seek to be united to the Bridegroom as his churchly bride. Joseph Fielding Smith elaborated: "In the waters of baptism we covenanted that we would . . . serve the Lord; that . . . with all our hearts we would prove to Him that we would . . . be obedient and humble, diligent in His service, [and] do all things with an eye single to the glory of God."[40]

FORGIVENESS OF SINS

Another widely acknowledged effect or benefit of baptism is the forgiveness of sins. Rituals of ablution and purification are nearly universal in the ancient Near East, so it is hardly surprising that the "washing away" of sin would be associated with baptism.[41] John the Baptist preached "the baptism of repentance for the remission of sins" (Mark 1:4; Luke 3:3). Baptism is understood to be a demonstration of repentance, a turning away from the "world" and toward the Lord. The phrases "baptism of repentance" (Mark 1:4; Luke 3:3; Acts 13:24; 19:4) and baptism "unto repentance" (Matt. 3:11) highlight the integral relationship between repentance and baptism. Peter invited his hearers on the Day of Pentecost, "Repent, and be baptized every one of you in the name of Jesus Christ for the remission of sins" (Acts 2:38). Latter-day Saints consider baptism to be "the culminating step, the capstone of our repentance."[42] The Matthean phrase baptism "unto repentance" appears repeatedly in the Book of Mormon. There, the word of the Lord is that "whosoever is baptized shall be baptized unto repentance . . . and him will I freely forgive. For it is I that taketh upon me the sins of the world" (Mosiah 26:22–23). Reminiscent of accounts in the Gospels of the effect of John the Baptist's ministry, the Book of Mormon records that many "came forth and did confess their sins and were baptized unto repentance" (Helaman 5:17).[43] Such a baptism brings forgiveness of sins.

Reiterating the scriptural link between baptism and the remission of sins, Christians from the fourth century onward have proclaimed, in the simple words of the Nicene-Constantinopolitan Creed of 381, "We confess one bap-

40. *Teachings: Joseph Fielding Smith*, 178.

41. Readers interested in scholarship on baptism's ancient parallels may profitably sample the essays in *Ablution, Initiation, and Baptism: Late Antiquity, Early Judaism, and Early Christianity*, ed. David Hellholm et al. (Berlin: de Gruyter, 2011).

42. D. Todd Christofferson, "Born Again," *Ensign*, May 2008, 78.

43. The phrase "baptized unto repentance" also appears at Alma 5:62; 6:2; 7:14; 8:10; 9:27; 48:19; 49:30; Helaman 3:24; 5:19; 3 Nephi 1:23; 7:26.

tism for the forgiving of sins [*in remissionem peccatorum*]."[44] During the Reformation, many Protestants continued to uphold this conviction. The influential Heidelberg Catechism, something of an effort to bridge Reformed and Lutheran divisions, asked, "How does holy Baptism remind and assure you that the one sacrifice of Christ on the cross avails for you? A[nswer] In this way: Christ has instituted this external washing with water and by it has promised that I am as certainly washed with his blood and Spirit from the uncleanness of my soul and from all my sins, as I am washed externally with water."[45] In modern times, *BEM* similarly affirmed that one of the results of baptism is "a washing away of sin," adding that the New Testament represents baptism as "an ablution which washes the body with pure water, a cleansing of the heart of all sin, and an act of justification (Heb 10:22; 1 Pet 3:21; Acts 22:16; 1 Cor 6:11). Thus, those baptized are pardoned, cleansed and sanctified by Christ."[46]

Some in the Reformed and Baptist traditions take exception to seeing baptism as "an act of justification." For them, baptism is separated from any direct connection to regeneration, justification, or adoption. They do, however, see the ordinance as a ratifying sign of, and public testimony to, such saving graces.[47] Their view is that baptism signals that saving grace *already has been* conveyed, not that justifying grace *is being* conveyed through the sacrament. John Calvin denied that baptism is the instrumental means of removing sin but called it "a sign of our forgiveness" already received in the prior moment when Christ entered the hearts of the elect and renewed them. It is "a token and proof of our cleansing." Thus, although for Calvin baptism is not how justifying pardon is received, it does "secure it," and that benefit is not insignificant in his estimation. Baptism, he wrote, "is like a sealed document to confirm to

44. *Creeds & Confessions*, 163.

45. Arthur C. Cochrane, ed., *Reformed Confessions of the Sixteenth Century*, rev. ed. (Louisville: Westminster John Knox, 2003), 317.

46. *BEM*, 2, 4. Similar statements can be found in the Catholic *Catechism*, Orthodox theologies, the Lutheran *Book of Concord*, the Anglican Articles of Religion, and the Westminster Confession, to name just a few.

47. Thomas J. Nettles, "Baptist View," in Armstrong and Engle, *Understanding Four Views on Baptism*, 25-41. Nettles goes so far as to say that "the person baptized has no scriptural warrant to believe that in baptism Christ's saving activity is initiated, augmented, or completed" (25). Conversely, an equally strong critique of what Jason Vickers calls the "theological reductionism" at stake in separating saving grace "from the sacramental life of the church," is Vickers, "To Know and to Love God Truly: The Healing Power of Conversion," in *Immersed in the Life of God: The Healing Resources of the Christian Faith; Essays in Honor of William J. Abraham*, ed. Paul L. Gavrilyuk, Douglas M. Koskela, and Jason E. Vickers (Grand Rapids: Eerdmans, 2008), 1-20.

us that all our sins are so abolished, remitted, and effaced that they can never come to his sight, be recalled, or charged against us." In fact, "the chief point of baptism" is that it is received "with this promise: 'He who believes and is baptized will be saved.'"[48] Even Paul's dramatic conversion on the road to Damascus needed to be accompanied by baptism to seal the remission of his sins. Christ told him to "go into the city" where Ananias, after ministering to him, urged, "Arise, and be baptized, and wash away thy sins" (Acts 22:16).[49]

A majority of Christians, however, including Latter-day Saints, agree with the Catholic *Catechism* that in some sense justification "is granted us through Baptism."[50] As the Council of Trent's "Decree on Justification" (1547) phrased it, justification "cannot take place without the waters of rebirth." Baptism is the "instrumental cause" of our justification "without which justification comes to no one."[51] For most, again including Latter-day Saints, being "saved" is not a separate, prior act in which God forgives the sinner he brings to faith. Baptism is the instrumental "sign-cause" through which Christ chooses to effect his gracious act of forgiveness.[52] Of course, as previously noted, no sacrament *au-*

48. Calvin, *Institutes* 4.15.

49. A variation of Calvin's position was later expounded by Alexander Campbell (1788–1866), who came out of a Reformed background and eventually founded the Disciples of Christ/Churches of Christ. "When any one believes with his heart the gospel [as in Paul's case]," wrote Campbell, "he is forgiven provisionally. But he is not forgiven 'formally,' or in fact, till he has been baptized." "A. Campbell to A. Broaddus," *Millennial Harbinger* 6 (1842): 150

50. CCC 2020. Much, of course, depends on how "justification" is defined, and, as illustrated in chapter 6, there is notable variation on this matter among Christian traditions.

51. "Decree on Justification," 4, 7, in *Creeds & Confessions*, 2:828, 830 (826–39). Alexander Campbell put a fine point on it. Justifying forgiveness of sins, he wrote, comes "through the very act and in the very instant" of baptism. Campbell, "Ancient Gospel—No. VII: Christian Immersion," *Christian Baptist*, July 1828, 269.

52. There are, however, two passages in LDS scripture that could be read as reflecting the Reformed view of forgiveness as a previously given grace independent of, and merely signaled by, baptism. In the Book of Mormon, men were ordained "that all such as should come unto them should be baptized with water, and this as a witness and a testimony before God, and unto the people, that they had repented and received a remission of their sins" (3 Nephi 7:23–26). Likewise, in the church's Articles and Covenants, those who "shall" be "received unto baptism" are they who "truly manifest by their works that they received the spirit of Christ unto the remission of their sins" (D&C 20:37). Verb tenses in both cases could be read in Reformed fashion, but they could also simply be indicating that baptism is the way in which believers receive a remission of their sins. Early Mormon leader and former Reformed Baptist Sidney Rigdon, when assisting Joseph Smith with editing his revelations, may have sought to prevent a Reformed reading of the D&C passage when he replaced "remission of their sins" with "conviction of their sins." *JSP*, R1:81.

tomatically confers benefits. Water baptism in and of itself does not remit sins; only the atoning blood of Jesus Christ does (Matt. 26:28). Moreover, it is the Holy Spirit that is the actual agent of baptismal purification. For this reason, invoking John the Baptist's promise that Christ would baptize "with the Holy Ghost, and with fire" (Matt. 3:11 / Luke 3:16), Joseph Smith taught that "The baptism of water without the baptism of fire and the Holy Ghost attending it is of no use." Both "are necessary."[53] Apostle Bruce McConkie explained why: "We become clean when we actually receive . . . the Holy Ghost. It is then that sin and dross and evil are burned out of our souls as though by fire."[54] And no matter how firmly Latter-day Saints and other Christians proclaim God's promise of forgiveness through baptism, they also acknowledge the possibility that recipients may place disqualifying "dispositions" in the way of receiving the promised grace. This may be part of what Mormon 9:29 intends: "See that ye are not baptized unworthily."

Spiritual Rebirth

Associated with the fresh start of the forgiveness of sins are the colorful images of baptism as rebirth and baptism as burying the old sinful self and rising to a new life in Christ. Both images suggest renewal and regeneration, a reorientation from sin to sanctity. In the Gospel of John, Jesus teaches Nicodemus, "Verily, verily, I say unto thee, Except a man be born again [or, *from above*]," that is, "Except a man be born of water and of the Spirit, he cannot enter into the kingdom of God" (John 3:3–5).[55] With adult converts in view, *BEM* expresses the common Christian doctrine that recipients "are given as part of their baptismal experience a new ethical orientation under the guidance of the Holy Spirit."[56] Paul used Christ's death and resurrection as a metaphor for the renewing effect of the grace of baptism. Just as "we are buried with him by

---

53. *JSP*, D14:350. The Book of Mormon prophet Nephi taught that after water baptism, "then shall ye receive the Holy Ghost; yea, then cometh the baptism of fire and of the Holy Ghost" (2 Nephi 31:13). Other passages that replicate the Baptist's wording include D&C 33:11; 19:31; Mormon 7:10; 2 Nephi 31:13; 3 Nephi 9:20; 19:13; Moses 6:64–66.

54. Bruce R. McConkie, *A New Witness for the Articles of Faith* (Salt Lake City: Deseret Book, 1985), 290.

55. Throughout Christian history, this passage has almost universally been understood to refer to baptism. That reading, however, has not gone unchallenged. Richard Bauckham summarizes several alternate interpretations in "Sacraments and the Gospel of John," in *OHST*, 85–89.

56. *BEM*, 4.

baptism into death," so "like as Christ was raised up from the dead . . . even so we also should walk in newness of life" (Rom. 6:4). Conceiving entrance into a new society as death and rebirth was a common initiation pattern in antiquity, but elsewhere "there is nothing as explicit and resounding as the passages in the New Testament" and virtually no evidence "that such groups enacted the death-rebirth symbolism through baptism."[57] In baptism, "our old man is crucified with him, that the body of sin might be destroyed" (Rom. 6:6). Thus "renewed in the spirit [attitude] of your mind . . . ye put on the new man, which after God is created in righteousness and true holiness" (Eph. 4:23–24). In short, "if any man be in Christ, he is a new creature ('creation' [NRSV, NIV, ESV]; 2 Cor. 5:17), and above all things is to "put on charity, which is the bond of perfectness" (Col. 3:14). Martin Luther summarized the "power" of baptism in this way: not only does it bring about a "full and complete justification," but it effects "the new creation, regeneration, and spiritual birth."[58] Latter-day Saint scripture also links regeneration with baptism: "The Spirit saith if ye are not born again ye cannot inherit the kingdom of heaven; therefore come and be baptized unto repentance" (Alma 7:14). And Joseph Smith taught that "being born again comes by the Spirit of God through ordinances."[59]

As with any birth, spiritual rebirth implies parentage and entrance into a family. Paul taught the Galatians that "as many of you as have been baptized" have become "the children of God by faith in Christ Jesus" (Gal. 3:27, 26). A loving Father "sent forth his Son" to redeem us, "that we might receive the adoption of sons" (Gal. 4:4–5).[60] While figurative, this change in identity is profound. "Because ye are sons, God hath sent forth the Spirit of his Son into

---

57. Walter Burkert, *Ancient Mystery Cults* (Cambridge, MA: Harvard University Press, 1987), 101. Burkert does concede, however, that in the more developed baptismal liturgies of the post–New Testament period, "There are some features" that "irresistibly remind one of pagan mystery initiations." These, he opines, "are probably not just parallels in the common context of initiation patterns but rather some direct borrowings that took place" (102).

58. Martin Luther, *The Babylonian Captivity of the Church*, in *The Annotated Luther*, vol. 3, *Church and Sacraments*, ed. Paul W. Robinson (Minneapolis: Fortress, 2016), 70.

59. *JSP*, D6:548.

60. "The Greek and Roman legal categories of adoption (Gk, *huiothesia*; Lat, *adoptio*) provided a ready model for the initiatory rites of groups whose participants were not members by birth. . . . This juridical process conferred full legal entitlements of kinship by birth, with its rights and privileges. Such rights were largely conferred upon males to assure continuity and inheritance within a familial dynasty, or to males and females to augment membership within a particular special interest group, for example, by conversion to a new religion." Luther H. Martin, "Initiation," in *The Oxford Handbook of Early Christian Ritual*, ed. Risto Uro et al. (New York: Oxford University Press, 2018), 335.

your hearts, crying, Abba, Father" (Gal. 4:6).[61] The prologue to the Gospel of John proclaims, "As many as received [the Word], to them gave he power to become the sons of God, even to them that believe on his name: which were born, not of blood . . . but of God" (John 1:12–13). This theme of spiritual adoption into the family of God is echoed in Latter-day Saint scripture. The hope is expressed that all should be "born again; yea, born of God, changed from their carnal and fallen state, to a state of righteousness, being redeemed of God, becoming his sons and daughters" (Mosiah 27:25–26). The voice of the Lord declared to Joseph Smith, "I [will] give unto as many as will receive me, power to become my sons" (D&C 39:3–4).[62] An official First Presidency statement from the early twentieth century reiterated "that by obedience to the gospel men may become sons of God, both as sons of Jesus Christ, and, through Him, as sons of His Father." The spiritual rebirth associated with baptism is how this takes place: "By the new birth—that of water and the Spirit—mankind may become children of Jesus Christ. . . . He having been made their Father through the second birth—the baptismal regeneration."[63]

Because Latter-day Saints today typically use the phrase "children of God" to indicate humanity's preexistent generation by their Father in heaven (see chapter 5), Mormon doctrine requires a distinction between the two meanings of "children of God." The LDS *Guide to the Scriptures* states, "The scriptures use these terms in two ways. In one sense, we are all literal spirit children of our Heavenly Father. In another sense, God's sons and daughters are those who have been born again through the Atonement of Christ."[64] A church manual notes, "While all people are spirit children of our Heavenly Father, those who make gospel covenants such as baptism . . . also become God's covenant children."[65] It is this distinction between "covenant children" of God and "spirit children" of God that provides the interpretive lens through which Latter-day Saints read scripture. Paul writes, "As many as are led by the Spirit of God, they

---

61. This new identity as sons and daughters of God subsumes and supersedes all old identities, whether ethnic, social, or sexual: "There is neither Jew nor Greek, there is neither bond nor free, there is neither male nor female: for ye are all one in Christ Jesus" (Gal. 3:28).

62. See also D&C 11:30; 25:1; 34:3; 35:2; 45:8; Moses 6:64–68; 3 Nephi 9:17.

63. "The Father and the Son," 937–39.

64. *Guide to the Scriptures*, s.v. "sons and daughters of God." Howard Hunter reasoned, "The fatherhood of God is universal in the sense that we are all his created children, but those who believe in Christ, who accept him as the Son of God and the Savior of the world, have the right to become true sons of God. This is a gift of God dependent upon faith in Christ." *Conference Report*, October 1968, 141.

65. *NT Student Manual* (2018), 348, 199.

are the sons of God . . . and if children, then . . . heirs of God, and joint-heirs with Christ" (Rom. 8:14, 17). Here Mormon doctrine compels the clarification that the blessings of heirship mentioned in Romans 8 "are enjoyed by God's covenant children, but not necessarily by all of His spirit children."[66] In the LDS view, becoming God's adopted covenant children and thus heirs of God is the primary purpose of life. Joseph F. Smith remarked, "The object of our earthly existence is that . . . we may become the sons and daughters of God, in the fullest sense of the word, being heirs of God and joint heirs with Jesus Christ."[67]

THE NECESSITY OF BAPTISM

Given the abundance of gifts and graces most Christians associate with baptism, it is not surprising that the words "essential" and "necessary" often appear in theological discussions of the relationship between baptism and salvation. In the Catholic *Catechism*'s discussion of baptism, one section is titled "The Necessity of Baptism" and opens with these statements: "The Lord himself affirms that Baptism is necessary for salvation" and "the Church does not know of any means other than Baptism that assures entry into eternal beatitude."[68] The Council of Trent's "Canons on the Sacrament of Baptism" (1547) put it even more bluntly: "If anyone says that baptism is optional, that is, not necessary for salvation, let him be anathema."[69] Some Protestants, too, have affirmed the essentiality of baptism. The Lutheran Augsburg Confession, for instance, proclaims simply, "It is necessary for salvation."[70] These affirmations are rooted in such passages as "he that believeth and is baptized shall be saved" (Mark 16:16) and "except a man be born of water and of the Spirit, he cannot enter into the kingdom of God" (John 3:5).[71] Christian traditions that consider baptism essential to salvation, of course, do not consider it the sole necessary component, but they do consider it indispensable.

Few Christian groups emphasize the necessity of baptism as emphatically as do the Latter-day Saints, a point that is repeatedly made in both Mormon scripture and sermons. LDS scripture contains multiple reiterations of Mark 16:16,

---

66. *NT Student Manual* (2018), 348.

67. *Gospel Doctrine*, 553.

68. *CCC* 1257.

69. Denzinger 1618.

70. "Article IX—concerning Baptism," in *Book of Concord*, 43.

71. Other passages, too, are sometimes cited to make the point. First Peter likens the temporal salvation of Noah's family on the ark to the spiritual salvation "whereunto even baptism doth also now save us" (1 Pet. 3:21).

sometimes verbatim (Mormon 9:23; D&C 68:9; 112:29), and sometimes adding that genuine "belief" includes repentance and a willingness to "endure to the end" in faith (Ether 4:18; D&C 18:22; 20:25). Reference to John 3:5 is pervasive in LDS discourse and scripture. The classic restatement of both Markan and Johannine language is the account of Christ's words to the people of the Book of Mormon: "This is my doctrine . . . whoso believeth in me, and is baptized, the same shall be saved; and they are they who shall inherit the kingdom of God. And whoso believeth not in me, and is not baptized, shall be damned. . . . And again I say unto you, ye must repent, and be baptized in my name, and become as a little child, or ye can in nowise inherit the kingdom of God" (3 Nephi 11:32–34, 38).[72] The church's Articles of Faith considers baptism fundamental: "We believe that the first principles and ordinances of the Gospel are: first, Faith in the Lord Jesus Christ; second, Repentance; third, Baptism by immersion for the remission of sins; fourth, Laying on of hands for the gift of the Holy Ghost" (Articles of Faith 4). With regard to these "principles and ordinances," Joseph Smith remarked, "There is no other way beneath the heavens whereby God hath ordained for man to come to him, to be saved, and enter into the kingdom of God . . . any other course is in vain."[73]

Baptism is considered so important by Latter-day Saints that they even see necessity in Jesus being baptized. All Christians agree that Jesus was sinless and, therefore, was not baptized for the forgiveness of sins. The explanation often given for his baptism is that he did so to set an example. Augustine's *Tractates on the Gospel of John* illustrates this line of reasoning: "In order to exhort us to receive His baptism, He received the baptism of His servant [John]." Augustine asked, "Why was it necessary for Christ to be baptized?" Augustine's answer was that Christ had come "to make himself the very way of humility . . . that an example of humility might be given to us by the Lord, for obtaining the saving power of baptism." Consequently, "his servants might know with what eagerness they ought to run to the Lord's baptism since he himself did not disdain to receive a servant's baptism."[74] Similar sentiments are expressed in the Book of Mormon where it is said that Christ, "notwithstanding he being holy, he showeth unto the children of men that, according to the flesh he humbleth himself before the Father, and witnesseth unto the Father that he would be obedient unto him in keeping his commandments" (2 Nephi 31:7). By

---

72. Other expressions of the necessity of baptism include 2 Nephi 9:23—"And [the Lord] commandeth all men that they must repent, and be baptized in his name, having perfect faith in the Holy One of Israel, or they cannot be saved in the kingdom of God."

73. *Times and Seasons*, April 15, 1842, 752.

74. Augustine, *Tractates on the Gospel of John* 5.5; 5.3.2; 5.5.2, in Rettig, *St. Augustine*, 111–12.

humbly being baptized, Christ showed "unto the children of men the straitness of the path, and the narrowness of the gate, by which they should enter, he having set the example before them" (2 Nephi 31:9). Augustine's remark about how Christ's baptism should prompt Christians to "run" to baptism is also echoed in the Book of Mormon: "Now, if the Lamb of God, he being holy, should have need to be baptized by water, to fulfil all righteousness, O then, how much more need have we, being unholy, to be baptized, yea, even by water!" (2 Nephi 31:5).

Yet, Latter-day Saints see something else occurring in Christ's baptism, something that more fully explains Jesus's response to a demurring John the Baptist: "Suffer it to be so now: for thus it becometh us to fulfil all righteousness" (Matt. 3:15). "Christ fulfilled all righteousness," explained Joseph Smith, "in becoming obedient to the law which [he] himself had given." In essence, Jesus said, "John, I must be baptized by you. Why[?] to answer my [own] decrees."[75] As B. H. Roberts remarked, "He who said that men must be baptized . . . would honor that law by obedience unto it. Thus we learn that God can not only give law, but he can obey law."[76] These ideas continue to circulate among Latter-day Saints today. A college-level instruction manual states that "like us, Jesus was subject to all of the terms and conditions of Heavenly Father's plan."[77] In the beloved, oft-sung LDS children's song "Baptism," the first two stanzas read: "Jesus came to John the Baptist, in Judea long ago, And was baptized by immersion in the River Jordan's flow. 'To fulfill the law,' said Jesus, When the Baptist questioned why, 'And to enter with my Father in the kingdom up on high.'"[78] Joseph Smith taught that because John the Baptist was at that time "the only legal administrator in the affairs of the Kingdom that was then on the Earth," Jesus "could not enter except by the administration of John."[79] In sum, Jesus's response to the Baptist was a "solemn declaration to John:—now let me be baptized: for no man can enter the kingdom without obeying this ordinance, for thus it becometh us to fulfil all righteousness." Part of John's "greatness" lay in the fact that it was his "privilege to Baptize [Christ] or induct him into his Kingdom."[80]

75. *JSP*, D11:373; D12:495.

76. B. H. Roberts, *The Mormon Doctrine of Deity* (Salt Lake City: Deseret News, 1903), 197–98.

77. *Jesus Christ and the Everlasting Gospel* (2016), 32.

78. *Children's Songbook of the Church of Jesus Christ of Latter-day Saints* (Salt Lake City: The Church of Jesus Christ of Latter-day Saints, 1989), 100–101.

79. *JSP*, D11:373; D8:83.

80. *JSP*, D11:31 (original italics and capitalizations removed); D11:373.

Other theologies maintain a different interpretation of what Jesus meant when he said his baptism was to "fulfill all righteousness." In part, this is because they do not view the baptisms John performed as salvifically efficacious "Christian" baptisms or necessarily even prototypes thereof.[81] Joseph Smith, however, believed that John "preached the same gospel & Baptism that Jesus & the Apostles preach[ed] after him."[82] This was consistent with Smith's version of *prisca theologia* (theology of the ancients), in which he claimed that the Christian gospel, as "eternal" gospel, had actually been revealed to Adam after the fall and to ancient prophets and certain of their followers throughout pre-Christian history (see chapter 7, the section "Church Is Catholic").[83] Joseph Smith taught that "whenever there has been a righteous man on earth unto whom God revealed his word & gave power & authority to administer in his name . . . there is the kingdom of God."[84] In Smith's view, this was particularly true with John the Baptist. The people in Jesus's day did not have to "wait for the days of Pentecost to find the kingdom of God, for John had it with him . . . he had his authority from God . . . and was called to preach the Gospel of the kingdom of God." Indeed, "the kingdom of God for a season seemed to be with John alone," and "our Savior submitted to that authority himself by being baptized by John."[85] Thus, Latter-day Saints understand John's ministry to be a part of, not apart from, the Christian mission. This belief is strikingly symbolized by the fact that in Mormonism's sacred historical narrative, it is a resurrected John the Baptist who appears to Joseph Smith to instruct him on

81. The first of the Council of Trent's "Canons on the Sacrament of Baptism" states, "If anyone says that the baptism of John had the same force as the baptism of Christ: let him be anathema." Denzinger 1614. This ruling built on tradition firmly in place since the time of Augustine, who in his *Tractates on John* distinguished at length the baptism of John from Christian baptism. Modern scholarship tends to concur. As Krister Stendahl expressed it, "There is little or no indication that Mt. is aware of Jesus' baptism as a prototype for the baptism practiced by the church." Stendahl, "Matthew," in *Peake's Commentary on the Bible*, ed. Matthew Black and H. H. Rowley, rev. ed. (London: Nelson, 1962), 773. See also Andrew B. McGowan, *Ancient Christian Worship: Early Church Practices in Social, Historical, and Theological Perspective* (Grand Rapids: Baker Academic, 2014), 139.

82. *JSP*, D11:361.

83. Examples in LDS scripture include Adam (Moses 6:51–68), Enoch (Moses 7:11), and Noah (Moses 8:23–24).

84. *JSP*, D11:357.

85. *JSP*, D11:358, 360. Joseph Smith, however, acknowledged that there "is a difference between the Kingdom of God & the fruits & blessings that flow from that Kingdom because there was more miracles gifts graces visions healings, tongues &c in the days of Jesus Christ & the Apostles & on the day of pentecost than under Johns Administration, [but] it does not prove by any means that John had not the Kingdom of God" (360).

baptism and confer upon him the authority to perform Christian baptisms in the newly restored church of Christ.

Another way in which Latter-day Saint theology uniquely stresses the essentiality of baptism is by its practice of proxy baptisms for the unevangelized deceased. Mormons believe baptism for the dead was practiced in antiquity and is alluded to in 1 Corinthians 15:29—"Else what shall they do which are baptized for the dead, if the dead rise not at all? why are they then baptized for the dead?" Biblical scholars vary in how they understand this puzzling passage, but they generally regard baptism for the dead as an illegitimate Christian institution. Latter-day Saints, however, consider it a satisfying part of the answer to the problem of the unevangelized, and they perform vicarious baptisms for the dead as a sacred ritual in their temples.[86] Christians who affirm the necessity of baptism have often faced the question from critics as to how a God of love could require baptism for admittance into his kingdom when most human beings have died or will die unbaptized. The Latter-day Saint answer is that before the End, everyone who has ever lived on earth and died without the opportunity to hear the gospel will have that chance in the intermediate state, as well as the opportunity to have a vicarious baptism performed on their behalf by someone living on earth.

Mode of Baptism

One prominent scholar of early Christian sacraments has observed that "to study the rites of Christian initiation in the early church is to encounter not one but several liturgical traditions in development, each with its own unique ritual patterns, structures, and theologies."[87] As far as the *mode* of baptism, however, the consensus is that during the earliest years of Christianity baptism was generally performed by immersion.[88] This reflects New Testament usage

---

86. For a full discussion of the problem of the unevangelized and the Mormon doctrine of the "redemption of the dead," see chapter 12.

87. Maxwell E. Johnson, "Christian Initiation," in *The Oxford Handbook of Early Christian Studies*, ed. Susan Ashbrook Harvey and David G. Hunter (New York: Oxford University Press, 2008), 693. Johnson adds, "What we often appeal to as *the* early Christian pattern for initiation is but the end result of a process of assimilation, adaptation, and change, wherein some of the distinctive and rich theologies and patterns of an earlier period either disappear or are subordinated to others" (702).

88. The most detailed study of early Christian baptism is Everett Ferguson's exhaustive *Baptism in the Early Church: History, Theology, and Liturgy in the First Five Centuries* (Grand

where *baptizō* implies immersion, as for instance when Paul speaks of believers being "buried" with Christ by baptism (Rom. 6:4; Col. 2:12).[89] Nonetheless, by the second century explicit provision was being made in some locations and under certain conditions for alternatives to baptism by immersion. According to the early Christian Didache ("The Teaching"), if the candidate could not be immersed in "living" (running) or still water, "cold" or "warm," then it was acceptable for the officiant to "pour water on the head."[90] Although baptism by immersion continued into the Middle Ages, for a variety of cultural and historical reasons such as the increasing prevalence of infant baptism, the acceptable alternatives of baptism by affusion (pouring water on the head) or aspersion (sprinkling) became dominant in the West. Still, in the early centuries, the most widely attested practice was baptism by immersion, typically a "trine" (triple) immersion reflecting Christ's command to baptize "in the name of the Father, and of the Son, and of the Holy Ghost" (Matt. 28:19) and possibly symbolizing his three days in the tomb.[91] Trine immersion for both infants and adults, except in cases of sickness or other extenuating circumstances, was

---

Rapids: Eerdmans, 2009). As might be expected for a subject so hotly contested over the centuries, even Ferguson's *magnum opus* has not settled all debates. An entire issue of the *Journal of Early Christian Studies* (20, no. 3 [Fall 2012]) was devoted to a probing roundtable discussion of Ferguson's work.

89. With regard to the mode of baptism, New Testament texts are suggestive but not unambiguous. "Certainty regarding the modality of early Christian baptismal practices on the basis of an equivocal New Testament witness is elusive," and "inferences based on philological grounds are dubious." Perrin, "Sacraments and Sacramentality in the New Testament," 58. Other scholars are less uncertain. Baptist theologian Bruce A. Ware remarks, "One cannot help but wonder how the church's grappling with the issue of baptism might have been altered had the translators of our earliest English Bibles actually translated *bapto* and *baptizo* instead of transliterating the term. If we had read in our English Bibles that Jesus was 'immersed' in the Jordan by John the Baptist . . . one cannot help wonder how differently the thinking of Christian people may have been." Ware, "Believers' Baptism View," in Wright, *Baptism*, 21n.

90. Didache 7, in *Apostolic Fathers*, ed. Michael W. Holmes, 2nd ed. (Grand Rapids: Baker Books, 1989), 153. The dating of the Didache is uncertain, but the work was likely composed no later than the early third century. "The other occasion when an exception to immersion was allowed was in cases of deathbed baptism. Cyprian, bishop of Carthage (248–258), defended pouring or sprinkling, which he designated 'divine abridgements,' when 'necessity compels and God bestows his mercy,' on the basis of instances of aspersion in the Old Testament." Everett Ferguson, "Sacraments in the Pre-Nicene Period," in *OHST*, 127.

91. Robin M. Jensen, *Living Water: Images, Symbols, and Settings of Early Christian Baptism* (Leiden: Brill, 2010), 136–42, and Paul F. Bradshaw, *Reconstructing Early Christian Worship* (London: SPCK, 2009), 79–80.

also dominant in the East from the beginning and continues to be standard practice in Orthodoxy today.[92]

During the Reformation, baptism was not a major point of contention between most Reformers and the Catholic Church. The Reformers did, however, understand some of the effects of baptism differently and voiced varying degrees of dissatisfaction with the traditional, extrascriptural symbols that had become part of the baptismal liturgy. Such liturgical enhancements included anointings, renunciations and exorcisms, consecration of the baptismal water, making the sign of the cross, clothing the newly baptized in a white garment, giving the newly baptized a candle or new name, and elaborate verbal accompaniment along the way. Different reforming groups retained or dropped these elements as they chose, but most perpetuated the long-accepted practice of triple baptism by affusion or aspersion. At first, this even included some Reformers known as "Anabaptists" (rebaptizers), whose primary concern was to insist on adult, believer baptism rather than a particular mode of baptism. Other Anabaptists, however, read the New Testament to imply that only immersion baptism was acceptable to God. As it happened, in the next century, this interpretation became general among English Baptists, who were in contact with Continental Anabaptists, as well as among American Baptists. Whether to baptize forward or backward in the water and whether it was to be done in the traditional trine fashion or by a single immersion continued to be debated among immersionist groups, with single immersion eventually coming to predominate in Anglo-American contexts.[93]

Nineteenth-century America witnessed the strongest campaign for the necessity of baptism by immersion. As noted before, the perennial reforming quest for the purity of apostolic practice experienced a widespread surge in this era. *Sola scriptura* was taken to a new level, and the slogan "no creed but the Bible" was used to trim many traditional practices. Not surprisingly, be-

---

92. Timothy Ware, *The Orthodox Church* (London: Penguin Books, 1964), 284. Eighteenth-century Orthodox polemical treatises, such as *Against the Latins* (1756), "excoriate[d] the neglect of full immersion in Western baptism," some churches going so far as "to receive as unbaptized those aspirants to Orthodoxy who were not baptized with three immersions" in Orthodox fashion. Brian A. Butcher, "Orthodox Sacramental Theology," in *OHST*, 342. This position softened somewhat in the twentieth century. See John H. Erickson, "The Reception of Non-Orthodox into the Orthodox Church: Contemporary Practice," *St. Vladimir's Theological Quarterly* 41 (1997): 1–17.

93. See, for example, the reasoning of Baptist Jacob Bower in "Baptist Conversion," in *Documentary History of Religion in America to 1877*, ed. Edwin S. Gaustad and Mark A. Noll, 3rd ed. (Grand Rapids: Eerdmans, 2003), 375–76.

cause the Bible gives no clear example of baptism by affusion or aspersion and implies immersive "burial" in the water, immersion was common among these Christian "primitivists." The iconic manifestation of such principles was in the Christian Church (Disciples of Christ), founded in the 1830s by restorationists Alexander Campbell and Barton Stone, which insisted on baptism by immersion. Landmark Baptists, a group that emerged in the mid-1800s, were also stringent advocates of baptism by immersion. Landmarkians determined "that baptism by immersion was essential to the validity of a church and that the only valid baptism came from an immersed believer acting under the authority of a local congregation, even if this meant that Baptist ministers should rebaptize anyone who had been immersed by unauthorized ministers."[94] Although some Baptists in the twenty-first century have moved to embrace infant baptism as an acceptable alternative, the Southern Baptist Convention (SBC), the largest Baptist denomination in the world, has not. In 2000, the SBC issued this statement on baptism in their normative Baptist Faith and Message: "Christian baptism is the immersion of a believer in water in the name of the Father, the Son, and the Holy Spirit. It is an act of obedience symbolizing the believer's faith in a crucified, buried, and risen Saviour."[95] This view is shared by many other Christians today who, as noted in *BEM*, see "the act of baptismal submersion or immersion [as] a vibrant sign of the Christian dying and rising to new life in Christ."[96]

Latter-day Saints agree with Baptists and others who insist on the indispensability of baptism by immersion. The Mormon mode of baptism is succinctly outlined in the church's foundational Articles and Covenants: "Baptism is to be administered in the following manner unto all those who repent—The person who is called of God and has authority from Jesus Christ to baptize, shall go down into the water with the person who has presented himself or herself for baptism, and shall say, calling him or her by name: Having been commissioned of Jesus Christ, I baptize you in the name of the Father, and of the Son, and of the Holy Ghost. Amen. Then shall he immerse him or her [gently backward] in the water, and come forth again out of the water" (D&C 20:72-74).[97] Joseph Fielding Smith was unambiguous about why the LDS Church performs only baptisms by immersion. "Baptism," he explained, "cannot be by any other

---

94. See E. Brooks Holifield, "Sacramental Theology in America: Seventeenth–Nineteenth Centuries," in *OHST*, 392.

95. Baptist Faith and Message (2000), 7.

96. *One Baptism: Toward Mutual Recognition*, Faith and Order Paper No. 210 (Geneva: WCC, 2011), 6.

97. This is a nearly verbatim repetition of Christ's instructions to the Book of Mormon people as recorded in 3 Nephi 11:23–28.

means than immersion of the entire body in water, for the following reasons: 1) It is in the similitude of the death, burial, and resurrection of Jesus Christ, and 2) Baptism is also a birth and is performed in the similitude of the birth of a child into this world."[98] Such imagery is to be exactingly fulfilled in the LDS practice of immersion baptism. The church's *General Handbook* states as policy that "if part of the person's body, hair, or clothing is not completely immersed," the officiating minister must repeat the ceremony.[99]

If for Latter-day Saints baptism by any means other than complete submersion is not a bona fide baptism, neither is a baptism performed by someone who is not properly authorized and ordained in the Church of Jesus Christ of Latter-day Saints. Here, the LDS position parallels Orthodoxy's "strict Cyprianic stress on the invalidity of sacraments outside the visible boundaries of the Orthodox Church."[100] When the LDS Church was only days old, several individuals who previously had been baptized by other Christian ministers sought affiliation in the new church without rebaptism. In response, the revelation Joseph Smith received explained that other baptisms were abrogated in God's new latter-day work:

> Behold, I say unto you that all old covenants have I caused to be done away in this thing; and this is a new and an everlasting covenant. . . . Wherefore, although a man should be baptized an hundred times it availeth him nothing, for you cannot enter in at the strait gate by the law of Moses, neither by your dead works. For it is because of your dead works that I have caused this last covenant and this church to be built up unto me, even as in days of old. Wherefore, enter ye in at the gate, as I have commanded. (D&C 22:1–4)[101]

Such audacity, of course, has not been limited to either the Latter-day Saints or the Orthodox. Before the rise of a sustained ecumenical movement in the past century, rejection of the validity of baptisms performed outside one's

98. *Doctrines of Salvation*, 2:323–24.

99. *GH* 18.7.6.

100. Galadza, "Twentieth-Century and Contemporary Orthodox Sacramental Theology," 437. In his influential *Pedalion* or "Rudder" (1800), the Athonite monk Nicodemus (1749–1809) wrote that the "baptism of the Latins . . . is not acceptable or recognizable" because Western clerics lacked "the grace of the Holy Spirit" attendant upon authorized ordination "with which Orthodox priests," as the only authentic clergy, "perform the mysteries." Butcher, "Orthodox Sacramental Theology," 342–43.

101. Later, Joseph Smith, invoking another biblical metaphor, commented that admitting the validity of other churches' baptisms was "like putting new wine into old bottles and putting old wine into new bottles . . . the bottles burst and the wine runs out." *JSP*, D8:289.

own communion was not uncommon. This began to change, however, in the early twentieth century and gained momentum in the aftermath of the Second Vatican Council in the 1960s.

Who Should Be Baptized?

The biggest theological problem surrounding the sacrament of baptism has not been who has the right to perform the ordinance or which particular liturgical practices should be followed, including the amount of water used in the baptism. Rather, the most contentious issue has been who should be baptized. Specifically, is infant baptism, whether by immersion as in the Eastern rite or by affusion or sprinkling in Western churches, legitimate?[102] As previously noted, although infant baptism is not explicitly attested in scripture, from the second century there is indirect evidence for its practice, and by the fourth century, it was prevalent. Was infant baptism, therefore, an acceptable alternative to adult baptism or a heretical deviation without scriptural warrant? In a classic example of the axiom that theological development follows liturgical practice (*lex orandi, lex credendi*), Augustine gave infant baptism lasting theological support by tightening its link to the increasingly dominant doctrine of original sin. The rationale was that because all people are born with a shared and fatal culpability for Adam's sin removable only through the grace of baptismal regeneration, even infants must be baptized or be damned.[103] Given the high rate of infant mortality in antiquity, Augustine's doctrine added urgency to the practice of pedobaptism (child baptism). Moreover, by the end of the fourth century, the Roman Empire had become nominally Christian. With far fewer adult converts being baptized and infant baptism serving to perpetuate the union between church and state, it is hardly surprising that pedobaptism became the norm for the next thousand years.

Pedobaptists then and now draw supportive scriptural inferences from: (1) New Testament statements about whole "households" (which presumably included children) being baptized (e.g., Acts 16:15; 1 Cor. 1:16); (2) Jesus's request

---

102. A prominent twentieth-century example of this controversy was the vigorous debate carried on between renowned German scholars Joachim Jeremias and Kurt Aland in the late 1950s and early 1960s over the extent of infant baptism in the early church. See Joachim Jeremias, *Infant Baptism in the First Four Centuries* (London: SCM, 1960); Kurt Aland, *Did the Early Church Baptize Infants?* (Philadelphia: Westminster, 1963); and Jeremias, *The Origins of Infant Baptism: A Further Reply to Kurt Aland* (Naperville, IL: Allenson, 1963).

103. Pier Franco Beatrice, *The Transmission of Sin: Augustine and His Sources* (New York: Oxford University Press, 2013). See especially his chapter "Infant Baptism and Original Sin" (77–91).

to let the little children come unto him because "of such is the kingdom of heaven" (Matt. 19:14; cf. Mark 10:14; Luke 18:16); (3) Peter's Pentecost declaration that the invitation to be baptized and receive the Holy Spirit is "unto you, and to your children" (Acts 2:38–39); and (4) because the Great Commission was to preach the gospel to "every" creature (Mark 16:15) and "all" nations (Matt. 28:19).[104] Historically, one of the most popular passages deployed in support of infant baptism has been Colossians 2:11–12—"in [Christ] also ye are circumcised with the circumcision made without hands, in putting off the body of the sins of the flesh by the circumcision of Christ: Buried with him in baptism, wherein also ye are risen with him through the faith of the operation of God." Defenders of pedobaptism interpret the "circumcision of Christ" as a reference to baptism.[105] Just as circumcision marked inclusion in God's covenant with Israel and was performed shortly after birth, so baptism is the sign of inclusion in the new covenant in Christ and should be performed on newborns. Although LDS theology disagrees with the circumcision-baptism connection, Mormon doctrine is similar to the Reformed idea of birthright inclusion in the covenant in that the children of parents who marry in an LDS temple are considered "born in the covenant" and "entitled to the Spirit of the Lord and all the blessings of the kingdom."[106]

Others have found this interpretation of Colossians to be more eisegetical than exegetical, noting that Paul is simply arguing that in Christ believers receive an inner, spiritual circumcision that excises the carnality of one's fleshly sinfulness just as physical circumcision removes the fleshly foreskin of the male body. "No longer, says St. Paul, is circumcision accomplished by the knife, but in Christ himself," taught John Chrysostom. For "the Spirit circumcises not a part but the whole person."[107] As Philip Melanchthon put it, "being cir-

---

104. In addition to Jeremias's work (noted above), thorough defenses of pedobaptism include Pierre-Charles Marcel, *The Biblical Doctrine of Infant Baptism: Sacrament of the Covenant of Grace*, trans. Philip Edgcumbe Hughes (London: James Clarke, 1959), and Geoffrey W. Bromiley, *Children of Promise: The Case for Baptizing Infants* (Grand Rapids: Eerdmans, 1979).

105. For a detailed discussion, see Martin Salter, "Does Baptism Replace Circumcision? An Examination of the Relationship between Circumcision and Baptism in Colossians 2:11–12," *Themelios* 35 (2010): 15–29.

106. Brigham Young, *Journal of Discourses*, 18:249. The difference is that in the LDS conception the covenant into which children are born is not the covenant of grace in general but the parents' marriage covenant whereby they become part of an eternal family unit. The formal definition is that "children who are born after their mother has been sealed to a husband in a temple are born in the covenant of that sealing." *GH* 27.4.

107. Quoted in Ferguson, *Baptism in the Early Church*, 560.

cumcised with the circumcision of Christ simply mean[s] true repentance."[108] Moreover, the reference to the "circumcision of Christ" being "made without hands" was considered "a 'type' of rebirth, not of baptism."[109] Joseph Smith was among those who disputed the circumcision-baptism analogy, and plainly stated his view that "circumcision is not Baptism. Baptism is for remission of sins [and] children have no sins."[110] In his "New Translation" of the Bible, Smith emended the Genesis 17 discussion of circumcision in such a way that it could no longer be interpretively construed to support infant baptism. In his view, circumcision of male infants at eight days of age (Gen. 17:12) was a typological symbol of the fact that children do not become accountable for their conduct, and therefore qualified for baptism, until "eight *years*" of age.[111]

Joseph Smith also took issue with how pedobaptists read 1 Corinthians 7:14— "For the unbelieving husband is sanctified by the wife, and the unbelieving wife is sanctified by the husband: else were your children unclean; but now are they holy." Notes one historian, "With the exception of the Scripture passage where Jesus blesses little children, no passage has been laid under a more laborious contribution to serve the cause of infant baptism than this one."[112] The common pedobaptist interpretation, especially among those in the Reformed tradition, is that the child of a Christian parent is derivatively and automatically part of the covenant of grace and thereby "holy" (like the parent) in the sense of being set apart from the world and consecrated to God. Because of this "federal holiness," the child is entitled to baptism as the sign and seal of inclusion in the covenant.[113] The frequent use of 1 Corinthians 7:14 to support infant baptism likely provides the context for Doctrine and Covenants 74 that Joseph Smith dictated pertaining to this passage before the church was a year old. The revelation imagines a first-century Corinthian scene in which the "unbelieving husband" is Jewish, not a Roman pagan, and "desirous that his children should be ... brought up in subjection to the law of Moses" (v. 3). As a result, the children "gave heed to the traditions of their fathers and believed not the Gospel of Christ wherein they became unholy"

108. "Notes on Paul's Letter to the Colossians," as quoted in *Reformation Commentary on Scripture—New Testament XI: Philippians, Colossians*, ed. Graham Tomlin (Downers Grove, IL: IVP Academic, 2013), 187–88.

109. Holifield, "Sacramental Theology in America," 384.

110. *JSP*, J3:56.

111. *NTOB*, 132 (emphasis added).

112. Paul K. Jewett, *Infant Baptism and the Covenant of Grace* (Grand Rapids: Eerdmans, 1978), 122.

113. In addition to Jewett, see Gregg Strawbridge, ed., *The Case for Covenantal Infant Baptism* (Phillipsburg, NJ: P&R, 2003).

(v. 4) because they found themselves outside the covenant of Christian grace. Aside from identifying the specific non-Christian group responsible for the children's covenantal uncleanness, the revelation to this point makes no exceptional claims. Next, however, it proceeds to its key concern—the "tradition" that "little children are unholy" (v. 6). Claiming it was "had among the Jews" (v. 6) at the time but evoking images of the later Christian doctrine of original sin, here was the false conception of newborns' status before God that required correction. "Little children," counters the revelation, "are holy being sanctified through the atonement of Jesus Christ" (v. 7) and thus do not need, and should not receive, baptism. Assumptions aside about the theological anthropology of Second Temple Judaism, the revelation, in its repudiation of a pedobaptist reading of 1 Corinthians 7:14, reiterates the core Latter-day Saint objection to infant baptism.

Battles over biblical interpretation are often driven by theological difference. It is so in this case. Of the undergirding reasons for rejecting infant baptism, two stand out: (1) the need for baptism to represent a conscious, personal choice and commitment, something infants cannot make; and (2) belief in the moral innocence of children that makes the posited damnation of unbaptized infants appalling. Latter-day Saint doctrine aligns with both views, and each invites further discussion. The first major challenge to infant baptism came during the Reformation from the Anabaptists because they believed that the only meaningful (and scriptural) baptism was one received by adults who could make the requisite profession of faith. Declarations of faith by godparents or other sponsors on behalf of the infant, as had long been common in Christianity, would not satisfy, and no claim on the corporate faith of the church was sufficient.[114] In the words of Anabaptist cofounder Conrad Grebel, "Basing ourselves on the aforesaid biblical texts," because infants cannot have faith, "we conclude . . . that baptism of children is a senseless, idolatrous abomination, contrary to all Scripture."[115] The Anabaptist break with the practice of infant baptism opened the way for others to join in its opposition. Eventually Anabaptism's heirs (e.g., Mennonites, Amish, Hutterites) were numerically dwarfed by the expansive growth of independent Baptist traditions that also championed adult, believers' baptism. The Latter-day Saint position, articulated early in the church's history and still in effect, is that "no one can be

114. For an overview of the Anabaptist position, see John D. Rempel, "Sacraments in the Radical Reformation," in *OHST*, 298–312. Detailed discussion is found in Rollin S. Armour, *Anabaptist Baptism: A Representative Study* (Scottdale, PA: Herald, 1966).

115. Grebel to Thomas Muntzer, as quoted in Carlos M. N. Eire, *Reformations: The Early Modern World, 1450–1650* (New Haven: Yale University Press, 2016), 258.

received into the church of Christ unless he has arrived unto the years of accountability before God and is capable of repentance" (D&C 20:71). As noted above, that point is reached at age eight in LDS thought.[116] In preparation, parents are urged to teach their children the gospel of Jesus Christ so that they can "be baptized for the remission of their sins when eight years old" (D&C 68:27). The twentieth century witnessed the explosion of Pentecostal and independent Christian churches, many of which also reject infant baptism for similar reasons. And in the realm of academic theology, believers' baptism garnered its most significant convert in the person of famed Swiss theologian Karl Barth.[117] Nonetheless, restricting baptism to those old enough to make their own profession of faith is still technically a minority phenomenon among the world's two-billion-plus Christians (the majority of whom are affiliated with Catholic or Orthodox churches), although it is a substantial minority.

As for recoil from the notion that unbaptized infants are damned, it was manifest in early Christianity and has been regularly voiced from the rise of Anabaptism to the present day. Among the early Greek fathers, the moral innocence of newborns was the common view. Notes one scholar, "Greek writers consistently espoused the sinlessness of infants."[118] Later, no less a proponent of infant baptism than John Calvin remarked, "Few realize how much injury the dogma that baptism is necessary for salvation, badly expounded, has entailed."[119] A prominent nineteenth-century American Lutheran theologian celebrated Reformed theologian Charles Hodge's "movement away from the 'horrors' of a [doctrine] that consigned many dying infants to damnation" to a view that "all who died in infancy were probably saved."[120] Christians in the Wesleyan tradition maintain that children are "covered by the atonement of Jesus Christ until they reach the age of accountability," and "most free-church Protestants such as Baptists and Pentecostals [also] believe that God regards infants and children as innocent in spite of original sin until they mature to the

---

116. Age eight is close to the traditional Catholic "canonical" age of seven at which children are believed to have reached the "age of discretion" and become accountable by virtue of being able to exercise enough reason to discern basic right from wrong. Canon 891, Code of Canon Law, https://www.vatican.va/archive/cod-iuris-canonici/eng/documents/cic_lib4-cann879-958_en.html.

117. Karl Barth, *Church Dogmatics* IV/4, *The Doctrine of Reconciliation*, ed. and trans. G. W. Bromiley (Edinburgh: T&T Clark, 1969).

118. Paul M. Blowers, "Original Sin," in *Encyclopedia of Early Christianity*, ed. Everett Ferguson (New York: Garland, 1990), 669.

119. Calvin, *Institutes* 4.15.20.

120. Holifield, *Theology in America*, 388.

age of accountability."[121] Thus, "the majority of evangelicals today assume that all who die before 'the age of accountability' automatically go to heaven."[122] Even the Catholic Church itself, in the wake of Vatican II, stepped away from an unmitigated affirmation of damnation for unbaptized infants: "As regards *children who have died without Baptism*, the Church can only entrust them to the mercy of God. . . . Indeed, the great mercy of God who desires that all men should be saved . . . allows us to hope that there is a way of salvation for children who have died without Baptism."[123]

Latter-day Saints share these sentiments. Joseph Smith declared, "The doctrin of Baptizing Children or sprinkling them or they must welter in Hell is a doctrin not true not supported in Holy writ & is not consistent with the character of God. . . . Having been redeemed by the Blood of the Lamb, they will [in the resurrection] enjoy a fulness of that light Glory & intelligence which is received in the celestial kingdom of God."[124] Joseph Smith saw in vision that "all children who die before they arrive at the years of accountability are saved in the celestial kingdom of heaven" (D&C 137:10). The innocence of infants is passionately proclaimed in the Book of Mormon: "Awful is the wickedness to suppose that God saveth one child because of baptism, and the other must perish because he hath no baptism." Were that the truth, God would be "a partial God" and "a respecter to persons; for how many little children have died without baptism!" Rather, "all little children are alive in Christ" because "the curse of Adam is taken from them in [him], that it hath no power over them," and "unto such baptism availeth nothing." Instead, baptism is for "those who are accountable and capable of committing sin." Infant baptism "denieth the mercies of Christ, and setteth at naught the atonement of him and the power of his redemption." In short, "it is solemn mockery before God" to "baptize little children" (Moroni 8:8–23). Part of Joseph Smith's resistance to infant baptism may have resulted from the fact that he and his wife Emma lost several children at birth. The prospect that unbaptized infants would be damned for eternity was reprehensible to them, and it was the focus of Smith's attack on infant baptism.

Despite the fact that a doctrine that damns innocent children has long provided a powerful polemical opportunity to denounce infant baptism, one

121. Roger E. Olson, *Mosaic of Christian Belief: Twenty Centuries of Unity & Diversity* (Downers Grove, IL: IVP Academic, 2002), 218. Unsurprisingly, Anabaptists hold similar beliefs. See Rempel, "Sacraments in the Radical Reformation," 308.

122. Gregory A. Boyd and Paul R. Eddy, *Across the Spectrum: Understanding Issues in Evangelical Theology*, 2nd ed. (Grand Rapids: Baker Academic, 2009), 306.

123. *CCC* 1261.

124. *JSP*, D9:291, 294.

advantage pedobaptism has provided to its practitioners is a way of linking children to the church community from infancy. Yet, churches who do not practice infant baptism have found their own ways to accomplish this. "Some churches have developed rites for welcoming and blessing children as an initial step towards membership."[125] The African Methodist Episcopal Church, for instance, holds such a ceremony. It begins with prayers of thanksgiving for the newborn and "continues with the giving of a name to the child (accompanied with the laying on of hands), the congregation's promise to nurture the child in the faith, and the entry of the child's name in the Roll of Preparatory Members."[126] The Church of Jesus Christ of Latter-day Saints also has an infant dedication ceremony or ordinance called "Naming and Blessing Children." This typically takes place within weeks of the infant's birth and usually is performed on a Sunday in front of the local congregation.[127] Public presentation of the child in this manner and its ceremonial dedication to a life of devotion to God parallel a key ecclesial objective of either infant or adult baptism—bringing the individual into the nurturing embrace of the church. As the Book of Mormon expresses it, "their names [are] taken, that they might be remembered and nourished by the good word of God, to keep them in the right way, to keep them continually watchful unto prayer, relying alone upon the merits of Christ, who [is] the author and the finisher of their faith" (Moroni 6:4).

Preparation/Requirements for Baptism

Spiritual nurture of the kind mentioned in Moroni is considered vital in the life journey of any disciple of Christ. Most Christian traditions offer such assistance to the newly baptized, and many provide it in preparation for baptism as well. On the other hand, it is also true that in Christianity's (and Mormonism's) beginnings, conversion and baptism were often spontaneous and immediate, leaving little time for sustained prebaptismal preparation.[128] Yet, "as soon as

125. *One Baptism*, 12. This is particularly popular in evangelical churches.

126. Karen B. Westerfield Tucker, "Sacraments and Life-Cycle Rituals," in *The Cambridge Companion to American Methodism*, ed. Jason E. Vickers (New York: Cambridge University Press, 2013), 140.

127. "Every member of the church of Christ having children is to bring them unto the elders before the church, who are to lay their hands upon them in the name of Jesus Christ and bless them in his name" (D&C 20:70). Current procedural guidelines for this rite can be found in *GH* 18.6.1–3.

128. This pattern, apparent in the book of Acts, is also demonstrable in early Mormonism. An Ohio newspaper reported the establishment of the LDS church in its region with

we find evidence of actual practice in organized communities," preparation for baptism becomes "a slower and more rigorous affair."[129] By the turn of the third century, Tertullian could argue that the conversions and baptisms described in Acts were exceptions merited only by special divine intervention. In his view, "according to the circumstances and disposition, and even age, of each individual, the delay of baptism is preferable" so that the candidate is properly prepared.[130] This period of instruction and preparation, later denominated the "catechumenate" (from Gk. *katecheō*, "to instruct, teach"), ranged from three weeks among Christians in Armenia to the three years called for in the *Apostolic Tradition*.[131] The nature of the catechumenate also varied by time and place. As the word "catechesis" implies, generally it included instruction (originally more ethical than doctrinal, but later attending adequately to the creeds), as well as appropriate ascetic disciplines such as fasting and prayer, a series of preparatory rites from exorcisms to anointings, and, of course, a profession of faith, along with renunciation of the devil and his evil domain. Prior to the baptismal ceremony, or as part of it, the catechumen was expected to affirm the faith by responding to a series of baptismal interrogatories and, later, by creedal recitation.[132]

Catechetical customs would ebb and flow over the years, diminishing significantly during the Middle Ages, but catechesis received new life in the Reformation. Thanks to contemporaneous developments in printing technology, production of inexpensive, printed catechisms became a viable possibility, and many Reformers seized this opportunity to inculcate their faith. Luther's Large and Small Catechisms are among the more famous examples. Catholics soon responded in kind. Still, because both groups practiced infant baptism, this was designed to facilitate a *post*baptismal catechumenate that could lead

---

only a little exaggeration: "Wherever Mormonism obtained a footing it spread like wild fire. Scores were awakened, converted, baptized and endowed with the holy spirit in a few hours at a single meeting." *Advocate*, April 13, 1833, p. 2, col. 5.

129. McGowan, *Ancient Christian Worship*, 146.

130. Tertullian, *On Baptism* 18, in *ANF*, 3:678.

131. The *Apostolic Tradition* is an early church order providing rules or guidelines for the functioning of the church. See Paul F. Bradshaw, Maxwell E. Johnson, and L. Edward Phillips, *Apostolic Tradition: A Commentary*, Hermeneia (Minneapolis: Fortress, 2002).

132. For an overview of the catechumenate in early Christianity, see Ottorino Pasquato, "Catechumenate-Discipleship," in *Encyclopedia of Ancient Christianity*, ed. Angelo di Beradino (Downers Grove, IL: InterVarsity Press, 2014), 457–71; Ferguson, *Baptism in the Early Church*, 776–816; Johnson, *Rites of Christian Initiation*, 185–98; and J. Patout Burns and Robin M. Jensen, *Christianity in Roman Africa: The Development of Its Practices and Beliefs* (Grand Rapids: Eerdmans, 2014), 168–69, 202–8.

to a mature profession of faith in either the sacrament of confirmation or something resembling it in Protestant confessions. Today, prebaptismal catechumenates are popular not only in churches teaching believers' baptism but also in pedobaptist traditions that now consider adult or mature baptism an acceptable alternative to infant baptism. Catholicism's post–Vatican II reinstitution of an adult catechumenate as part of its *Rite of Christian Initiation of Adults* (*RCIA*) both reflects and reinforces this trend.[133]

The Church of Jesus Christ of Latter-day Saints offers a robust program of pre- and postbaptismal catechesis for both youth and adults. Prebaptismal catechesis for LDS children is considered the primary responsibility of their parents. The church's *General Handbook* explains: "Parents have the vital responsibility to help their children . . . understand the doctrine of faith in Jesus Christ, repentance, baptism, and the gift of the Holy Ghost (see Doctrine and Covenants 68:25)."[134] Assisting parents in this task is the church's "Primary" organization that each Sunday carries out a program of graded gospel instruction and spiritual formation for children ages three through eleven. "At home, parents teach children the gospel. At church, Primary leaders and teachers support parents through lessons, music, and activities" and "help children prepare for baptism."[135] Prior to baptism, one of the local pastoral leadership team (known as the "bishopric") interviews the child to ensure that he or she "understands the purposes of baptism," as well as "the baptismal covenant and is committed to live by it."[136]

For adults who seek to be baptized and affiliate with the Church of Jesus Christ of Latter-day Saints, the prebaptismal catechumenate, so to speak, is more compact, lasting from several weeks to several months. The "catechists" are the church's numerous missionaries, mostly young adults, who rely on what is essentially a several-hundred-page catechetical handbook entitled *Preach My Gospel*. This handbook is designed to both guide them in their own spiritual preparation as catechists and detail the course of instruction and prebaptismal invitations to obey God's laws that catechumens (traditionally called "investigators" in LDS nomenclature; now simply, "friends") are to receive.[137]

---

133. International Commission on English in the Liturgy, *Rite of Christian Initiation of Adults* (Totowa, NJ: Catholic Book Publishing, 1988). The *RCIA* was instituted in 1972.

134. *GH* 2.1.3.

135. *GH* 12.1; 12.2.1.1. Congregational leaders are tasked with seeing that these things happen. *GH* 31.2.3.

136. *GH* 31.2.3.1.

137. *Preach My Gospel: A Guide to Sharing the Gospel of Jesus Christ*, 2nd ed. (Salt Lake City: The Church of Jesus Christ of Latter-day Saints, 2023).

Just prior to baptism, as with young children, adult baptismal candidates are interviewed to ensure that they understand the basics of Christian doctrine and are committed to live a Christian life.[138] Missionaries continue to shepherd their former catechumens for a time after they are baptized. In addition to the missionaries, special "ministering brothers" and "ministering sisters" are assigned to nurture spiritually and socially the newly baptized. Congregational leaders meet to "plan specific ways to teach and strengthen new members from the time of their baptism and confirmation until they receive the temple endowment."[139] All such interaction serves as a kind of postbaptismal "mystagogy" (progressive initiation into the Christian life). Most of it continues for at least one year after adults are baptized, as their new life in Christ seasons and they prepare themselves to receive the temple endowment.[140] Some aspects of this ministry will extend throughout their lives.

CONFIRMATION

With baptism thoroughly explored, it remains to closely examine what some Christians, including Latter-day Saints, consider to be baptism's sister sacrament—confirmation.[141] In earliest Christianity, there was no separate sacrament of confirmation, nor is Jesus on record as explicitly instituting one. The Bible does, however, describe the bestowal of the Holy Spirit in conjunction with baptism. Jesus himself received the Holy Spirit immediately after his baptism (Matt. 3:16; Mark 1:10; Luke 3:22), and many believe he paired the two in his famous statement about the need to be "born of water and of the Spirit" (John 3:5). On the Day of Pentecost, Peter promised those who were baptized

138. Baptismal candidates are asked if they believe in God and Christ; have repented of past sins; are willing to take upon them the name of Christ; are committed to obeying God's commandments, ranging from keeping the Sabbath day holy to living the law of chastity; and believe Christ has reconstituted his church on earth by, and continues to guide it through, living prophets. *GH* 31.2.3.2.

139. *GH* (2020) 7.5.1. "Joining the Church is both wonderful and challenging for many. It brings great blessings, but it also requires adjusting to new beliefs, new habits, and new relationships (see 1 Thessalonians 1:6). Each new member needs friendship, opportunities to serve, and spiritual nourishment." *GH* 23.2. Ministry to the newly baptized is discussed in *GH* 23.5.2.

140. *GH* 27.2.1.1. On the temple "endowment," see chapter 11.

141. Helpful historical and theological overviews of confirmation abound. For starters, see Walsh, *The Sacraments of Initiation*, 111–64; Johnson, *Rites of Christian Initiation*, passim; and Aidan Kavanagh, *Confirmation: Origins and Reform* (Collegeville, MN: Liturgical Press, 1988).

that they would "receive the gift of the Holy Ghost" (Acts 2:38). Christian theologians over the centuries have debated the meaning of these statements in John, Acts, and elsewhere. Are they meant to simply highlight the Spirit's regenerative work in the sacrament of baptism itself, or do they refer to an additional sacramental endowment of the Spirit subsequent to what the Spirit effects through water baptism? Christian traditions such as Mormonism that affirm the latter interpretation often cite passages in the book of Acts that link descent of the Holy Spirit with the imposition of the apostles' hands. For instance, after coming to faith through the teaching of the evangelist Philip, Samaritan believers were visited by Peter and John, who "laid they their hands on them, and they received the Holy Ghost. And when Simon [the sorcerer] saw that through laying on of the apostles' hands the Holy Ghost was given, he offered them money, saying, Give me also this power, that on whomsoever I lay hands, he may receive the Holy Ghost" (Acts 8:17–19).[142] The book of Hebrews also mentions "the doctrine of baptisms, and of laying on of hands" as foundational to "the doctrine of Christ" (Heb. 6:1–2).

In the earliest postapostolic period, sources such as the Didache and Justin Martyr's works make no mention of any rite accompanying water baptism in which the Holy Spirit is ceremonially conferred or sealed on the newly baptized. Toward the end of the second and beginning of the third centuries, however, Christian sources begin to attest the ritual conferral of the Holy Spirit, both by the imposition of hands and by the practice of anointing with *chrism/myron* (consecrated oil perfumed with balsam or myrrh). Tertullian, for instance, notes that in Carthage, as soon as the neophytes came out of the water, they were anointed with chrism, and "thereafter, a hand is laid on [them] by way of blessing, summoning and inviting the Holy Spirit." Tertullian had previously clarified that Christians do not "obtain the Holy Spirit in the water, but having been cleansed [of sin] in the water, we are being prepared . . . for the Holy Spirit."[143] Several decades later, Cyprian of Carthage wrote that following baptism hands are laid "upon the person baptized so that he may receive the Holy Spirit."[144] Anointing or "chrismation," as it was called in the East, was also part of the postbaptismal rite, but early sources do not specify whether it was part of a hand-laying conferral of the Holy Spirit or a separate gesture symbol-

---

142. Later in Ephesus, Paul encountered a group of believers, "and when Paul had laid his hands upon them, the Holy Ghost came on them" (Acts 19:6).

143. Tertullian, *On Baptism* 8.1; 6:1, in *Tertullian's Treatises*, trans. Alexander Souter (New York: Macmillan, 1919), 54–55.

144. *Letters* 74 (73).5.1, as quoted in Ferguson, *Baptism in the Early Church*, 354.

izing that conferral.[145] Although Cyprian "could acknowledge a distribution of the baptismal blessings among the several acts of the ceremony, he argued strenuously . . . against a separation of baptism from the imparting of the Holy Spirit by the laying on of hands. He wanted to keep all the acts together as one unified ceremony."[146] Yet, because the liturgical "bestowal of the indwelling of the Holy Spirit" was seen as something "separate from the baptismal activity of the Spirit," it provided the basis for the eventual separation of baptism and the special conferral of, or sealing with, the Holy Spirit by the imposition of hands with or without anointing.[147]

In Rome, whose rites in time became "*the* postbaptismal rites of Western Christianity," it was considered the bishop's prerogative to confer the Holy Spirit.[148] Yet, once the Roman Empire became largely Christianized and the number of people served in dioceses (ecclesiastical territories governed by bishops) expanded, the bishop was generally unavailable to perform this duty soon after baptisms took place. Instead, episcopal anointing and imposition of hands became a separate, schedulable rite, often associated with Easter, where many could receive it in a single setting. In this way, the bishop was able to personally attend to what in time would become the fully developed sacrament of confirmation. Urban-based bishops in the East were just as pressed as those in the West to visit all the churches in their dioceses, but in the East the desire to keep chrismation and baptism temporally united transcended concern about maintaining episcopal prerogative. As a result, local presbyters who were already performing baptisms and the other related anointings were authorized to perform the Spirit-conferring chrismation immediately after baptism. This

145. "Chrismation" and "chrism" are derived from the Greek *chrisma*, which means "anointing." *Chrisma* and its root, *chriō*, are used in the New Testament specifically in conjunction with a *divine* anointing, such as bestowal of the Holy Spirit. The words obviously relate to Jesus's title as "Christ," as the "Anointed One." In the East, "the postbaptismal chrismation was interpreted as a messianic anointing and a strengthening of the neophyte." Ferguson, *Baptism in the Early Church*, 480.

146. Ferguson, *Baptism in the Early Church*, 354. Long after the full emergence of the separate rite of confirmation, medieval theologians argued that "all the faithful ought to receive the Holy Spirit after baptism through the imposition of the hands of the bishop so that they may be found to be fully Christians." Boyd Taylor Coolman, "The Christo-Pneumatic-Ecclesial Character of Twelfth-Century Sacramental Theology," in *OHST*, 210.

147. Ferguson, "Sacraments in the Pre-Nicene Period," 128.

148. Johnson, *Rites of Christian Initiation*, 200. By the early 400s, although presbyters were administering the other baptism-related anointings, Pope Innocent I made it clear that it was the right of "the bishops alone [to] bestow the Spirit, the Paraclete." Letter to Bishop Decentius of Gubbio, March 19, 416, in Denzinger 215.

is still the practice in Orthodoxy today, where the basic understanding is that "Chrismation emulates the Spirit's descent at Christ's baptism."[149]

In the West, by the early fifth century, the words *confirmare* and *confirmatione* were being used with reference to the separate Spirit-imparting, episcopal anointing/hand laying. The Latin words seemed to connote the concluding, completing, or perfecting of baptism.[150] As the sacrament of confirmation continued to develop in the West, *confirmatione* took on additional meanings. From a Catholic standpoint today, "the theological tradition has given us two sets of reflections upon the purpose of the Sacrament of Confirmation. The first emphasizes Confirmation as the completion of Baptism by conferring upon the recipient an increase in the Gifts of the Holy Spirit. . . . The second emphasizes Confirmation as empowering people to bear public witness for the faith and to engage in spiritual combat" against forces of evil in the world.[151] This second purpose of confirmation, obviously, cannot be achieved in infancy. Consequently, confirmation gradually shifted over time to be a sacrament received during adolescence. After a period of maturation, the young Christian would be confirmed with the understanding that the sacrament "*deepens* the grace of baptism and *deputizes* the Christian at 'the perfect age' for bearing public witness to Christ."[152] The ceremonial imposition of hands and prayer that accompanied anointing the forehead with the sign of the cross were thought to symbolize the truth proclaimed in 2 Corinthians 1:21–22—"Now he which stablisheth us with you in Christ, and hath anointed us, is God; who hath also sealed us, and given the earnest of the Spirit in our hearts." The Vatican II Dogmatic Constitution on the Church *Lumen Gentium* summarizes current Catholic teaching on the subject: "By the sacrament of Confirmation [the faithful] are more perfectly bound to the Church and are endowed with the special strength of the Holy Spirit. Hence, they are, as true witnesses of Christ, more strictly obliged to spread and defend the faith by words and deed."[153]

Something parallel to confirmation became common in Reformation churches as well. Reformer Martin Bucer, for instance, outlined his influential vision of an "evangelical confirmation" in several documents written during

---

149. Butcher, "Orthodox Sacramental Theology," 334. See also the discussion of chrismation in Galadza, "Twentieth-Century and Contemporary Orthodox Sacramental Theology," 433–51.

150. Johnson, "Christian Initiation," 704.

151. Jacob W. Wood, *Do This in Remembrance of Me: An Introduction to the Sacraments* (Steubenville, OH: St. Paul Center, 2019), 38.

152. Chad C. Pecknold and Lucas Laborde, "Confirmation," in *OHST*, 498.

153. *Lumen Gentium*, 11, as quoted in *CCC* 1285.

the 1530s and 1540s. The basic elements included a revival of catechetical instruction, public examination of the candidate by local church representatives, and the capstone imposition of hands (without anointing, which seemed too "Catholic") to invoke the Holy Spirit.[154] Protestant parallels to confirmation recognized the value of adolescent Christians' personal ratification or renewal of baptismal promises made on their behalf in infancy by godparents or sponsors.[155] By the twentieth century, "attention to the *necessary* connection between baptism and confirmation [had] led almost all churches . . . to restore (or add), partially at least, those traditional postbaptismal rites that [had become] confirmation historically to the rites of baptism itself."[156] In sum, current Christian sentiment with regard to confirmation/chrismation is well summarized in *BEM*: "Christians differ in their understanding as to where the sign of the gift of the Spirit is to be found. Different actions have become associated with the giving of the Spirit. For some it is the water rite itself. For others, it is the anointing with chrism and/or the imposition of hands, which many churches call confirmation. For still others it is all three, as they see the Spirit operative throughout the rite. All agree that Christian baptism is in water and the Holy Spirit."[157]

From the beginning, Latter-day Saints have cited the Acts 8 account of the evangelization of Samaria not as an exception for how the Holy Ghost is conferred but as the divinely instituted pattern for its bestowal. In the Doctrine and Covenants, the official directive is: "On as many as ye shall baptize with water, ye shall lay your hands, and they shall receive the gift of the Holy Ghost" (D&C 39:23).[158] Elsewhere in LDS revelation, Sidney Rigdon, former ministerial associate of Alexander Campbell and convert to Mormonism, is commended for having previously preached faith, repentance, and baptism by immersion for the remission of sins. Yet, in the revelation's view, his followers

---

154. Amy Nelson Burnett, "Martin Bucer and the Anabaptist Context of Evangelical Confirmation," *Mennonite Quarterly Review* 68 (January 1994): 95–122. Bucer wrote, "We could re-establish . . . the old practice from which confirmation arose, when the bishops laid their hands on those who had been baptized and bestowed on them the Holy Spirit according to the example of the apostles in Samaria [Acts 8]" (110).

155. See the full array of Protestant denominational documents collected in Peter J. Jagger, *Christian Initiation, 1552–1969: Rites of Baptism and Confirmation Since the Reformation Period* (London: SPCK, 1970). See also Kavanagh, *Confirmation*, and Robert L. Browning and Roy A. Reed, *Models of Confirmation and Baptismal Affirmation* (Birmingham, AL: Religious Education Press, 1995).

156. Johnson, *Rites of Christian Initiation*, 448–49.

157. *BEM*, 14.

158. See also D&C 20:41; 33:15; 49:13–14; 52:10; 76:52.

"received not the Holy Ghost." As a Latter-day Saint minister, Rigdon was told, "I give unto thee a commandment, that thou shalt baptize by water, and they shall receive the Holy Ghost by the laying on of the hands, even as the apostles of old" (D&C 35:5–6). Over the years, Latter-day Saints have often pointed to their confirmation procedure as most closely replicating the apostolic actions of Peter and John. In this, they have not been alone. As previously discussed, the imposition of hands, in whatever way it has been interpreted and applied, has been part of Spirit-conferral liturgies from the early centuries. "Pointedly," notes the Catholic *Catechism*, "it is by the Apostles' imposition of hands that the Holy Spirit is given. . . . The Church has kept this sign of the all-powerful outpouring of the Holy Spirit in its sacramental epiclesis [invocation]."[159]

LDS doctrine, in common with other Christian traditions, understands confirmation as the rite that ceremonially confirms or completes a person's entrance into the church through baptism. Baptism and confirmation are seen as a unit, as two sides of the same coin of admission into Christ's church. In affirming such sacramental unity, Mormons concur with Cyprian and traditions such as Orthodoxy that view confirmation as "an organic part" of the sacrament of baptism, "performed as its fulfillment."[160] The Latter-day Saint position is that "baptism in water and in that fire which is 'holy spirit' is but one baptism."[161] This shared Orthodox-Mormon emphasis on the unity of the two sacraments is manifest in their parallel practice of performing confirmation/chrismation at the time of baptism, not months or years later, as is the majority practice among other Christian churches.[162] The perceived complementarity of baptism and confirmation prompted Joseph Smith to colorfully

---

159. *CCC* 699. In the early modern period, French Jesuit scholar Denis Petau, "following the older canonists, believed the imposition of hands (*impositio manuum*) to be the sole matter of the sacrament. Others, such as Bellarmine and van Est, following St. Thomas Aquinas, argued the anointing with the chrism oil (*chrismatio*) to be the only matter. Most other theologians believed both to constitute the matter of the sacrament." Trent Pomplun, "Catholic Sacramental Theology in the Baroque Age," in *Oxford Handbook of Early Modern Theology, 1600–1800*, ed. Ulrich L. Lehner, Richard A. Muller, and A. G. Roeber (New York: Oxford University Press, 2016), 140.

160. Sergey Trostyanskiy, "Chrismation," in *The Encyclopedia of Eastern Orthodox Christianity*, ed. John A. McGuckin (Chichester, UK: Wiley-Blackwell, 2011), 115.

161. *DCC*, 174.

162. A similar stance was taken by the "Six Principle Baptists," contemporaries of the early Latter-day Saints. An 1836 compendium of religious groups in the United States reported that "this appellation is given to those who hold the imposition of hands, subsequent to baptism, and generally on the admission of candidates into the church, as an indispensable prerequisite for church membership and communion." John Hayward, *The*

quip that one "might as well baptise a bag of sand as a man if not done in view of the getting of the Holy ghost.—baptism by water is but 1/2 a baptism—& is good for nothi[n]g with[out] the other, the Holy Gho[s]t."[163]

Latter-day Saint baptism and confirmation usually take place during a simple ceremony led by an ordained Mormon minister in which interested friends, family, and members of the local congregation participate.[164] The service consists of prayer, songs, and brief discussion of the meaning and significance of baptism, followed by the actual baptism. There is no set liturgy or order of worship in the prebaptismal portion of the service. Unordained church members may take part in any of it and, when invited to speak or pray, do so according to their own lights. There are, as previously discussed, specific procedures to be followed and set words to be used in the performance of the baptism itself. If the local Latter-day Saint "meetinghouse" (church building) is equipped with a baptismal font, the baptismal service usually takes place there, generally on a day other than Sunday, when the building is heavily utilized. Children are normally confirmed immediately after baptism in the final part of the service. Reflecting its primitivist roots, the Church of Jesus Christ of Latter-day Saints insists that the laying on of hands to confer the Holy Spirit should stand alone liturgically, without accompanying chrismation or other rites typically associated with it. Adults who seek baptism may also be confirmed as part of their baptismal service, but to help incorporate adult converts into the church family, ecclesiastical guidelines recommend that they be confirmed in front of the entire congregation the Sunday following their baptism. Children confirmed at the time of their baptism are formally welcomed into the church on the Sunday following their baptism. Such incorporative actions in the presence of the assembled church body parallel other Christian practices at the time of formal admission into the church.

A matter of some importance in Mormon theology is the distinctive LDS doctrine about what constitutes the "gift" (distinct from the "gifts") of the Spirit. Joseph Smith distinguished the "gift" of the Holy Ghost from the general, superintending influence of the Holy Ghost. "There is a difference," he taught, "between the Holy Ghost & the gift of the Holy Ghost. Cornelius [the Roman centurion who according to Acts 10 sought Peter's ministrations] received the Holy Ghost before he was Baptized which was the convincing power

---

Religious Creeds and Statistics of Every Christian Denomination in the United States and British Provinces (Boston, 1836), 105.

163. *JSP*, D12:456.

164. The procedures summarized in this paragraph are detailed in *GH* 18.7.1–7; 18.8.

of God unto him of the truth of the gospel, but he could not receive the *gift* of the Holy Ghost until after he was Baptized, & had he not taken this sign or ordinance upon him, the Holy Ghost which convinced him of the truth of God would have left him."[165] The Book of Mormon teaches, as do all Christian theologies, that Christ "manifesteth himself unto all those who believe in him, by the power of the Holy Ghost; yea, unto every nation, kindred, tongue, and people" (2 Nephi 26:13). Yet the *gift* of the Holy Spirit, this additional divine endowment, is to be sacramentally bestowed by the imposition of hands following baptism. "The Holy Ghost," notes James Talmage, "has frequently operated for good through persons that are unbaptized; indeed, some measure of this power is given to all mankind . . . the Holy Spirit is the power of intelligence, of wise direction, of development, of life." However, "the actual companionship of the Holy Ghost, the divinely-bestowed right to His ministrations . . . [is] given as a permanent possession only to the faithful, repentant, baptized candidate for salvation; and with all such this gift will abide, unless forfeited through transgression."[166]

The concluding phrase in Talmage's explanation points to the *ex opere operantis* character of confirmation in Mormon doctrine. One's enjoyment of the "gift of the Holy Ghost" is contingent on one's fidelity to God. For this reason, the ritual words of confirmation, echoing John 20:22, are in the imperative voice: "Receive the Holy Ghost."[167] Consistent with Mormonism's soteriological synergism, Latter-day Saints are urged to strive to live in a way that is "worthy" of the Spirit's companioning guidance and are reminded that it is Christ's atonement that "makes it possible for us to be purified and so be worthy of the companionship of the Holy Ghost."[168] Each Sunday, through their participation in the sacrament of the Lord's Supper (see chapter 10), Latter-day Saints renew their baptismal covenant to "take upon them the name of [Christ], and always remember him and keep his commandments which he has given them; that they may always have his Spirit to be with them" (D&C 20:77). Church members seek to experience the Spirit's "constant companionship," its "continual guidance and inspiration," that they believe

165. *JSP*, D9:293 (emphasis added).

166. James E. Talmage, *The Articles of Faith: A Series of Lectures on the Principal Doctrines of the Church of Jesus Christ of Latter-day Saints* (Salt Lake City: Deseret News Press, 1899), 170.

167. The confirmation officiant "states 'receive the Holy Ghost' (not 'receive the gift of the Holy Ghost')." *GH* 18.8.2.

168. Henry B. Eyring, "Priesthood and Personal Prayer," *Ensign*, May 2015, 87.

confirmation opens to them.[169] This requires committed discipleship. Joseph Smith taught that only as disciples strive to be "full of charity" and let "virtue garnish their thoughts unceasingly" would the Holy Ghost be their "constant companion" (D&C 121:45–46).

It might be asked, "In what does the 'constant companionship' of the Holy Ghost consist?" An answer frequently offered in LDS discourse is that this companionship is most often realized through what Latter-day Saints call the "promptings" or "impressions" of the Holy Spirit. Mormons believe these promptings not only steer them away from physical harm, sinful acts, and anything untoward, but also guide them toward effective, beneficial interpersonal interactions in the home, church, and community. Promptings can lead disciples to deepen family relations, promote neighborliness, and even flourish in the mundane matters of everyday life. In a sense, the "whisperings" or "leadings" of the Spirit constitute figurative fulfillment of Jesus's promise that the Spirit will "guide you into all truth" (John 16:13) and "abide with you for ever" (John 14:16). Apostle Dallin Oaks taught that the Holy Ghost can be "our comforter, our direction finder, our communicator, our interpreter, our witness, and our purifier."[170] Reflecting on what the confirmatory gift of the Holy Ghost opened for her, a Latter-day Saint convert recalled, "I felt the influence of the Holy Ghost settle upon me with greater intensity than I had ever felt before. He was like an old friend who had guided me in the past but now had come to stay."[171] This account captures something of the intimacy and permanency with which Latter-day Saints view the companioning guidance of the Holy Spirit made real and personal by the sacrament of confirmation. Such regular, personal interaction with the Holy Ghost is among the divine gifts and graces that Latter-day Saints most cherish.

169. "The gift of the Holy Ghost is the right to have, whenever one is worthy, the companionship of the Holy Ghost." *Bible Dictionary*, s.v. "Holy Ghost." *Gospel Principles* defines the gift as the "privilege" of receiving "continual guidance and inspiration from the Holy Ghost" (121). "After receiving the gift of the Holy Ghost, a person who keeps his or her covenants has the right to the constant companionship of the Holy Ghost." *Doctrinal Mastery Core Document* (Salt Lake City: The Church of Jesus Christ of Latter-day Saints, 2018), 19.

170. Oaks, "Always Have His Spirit," *Ensign*, November 1996, 61.

171. Quoted in Oaks, "Always Have His Spirit," 60.

THE EUCHARIST

Savoring the Lord's Supper

Whether known as the "Eucharist," "Holy Communion," "Lord's Supper," or simply "the Sacrament" (as Latter-day Saints prefer to call it), this special ceremonial act of Christian worship is for many the "Sacrament of sacraments," to use the words of Thomas Aquinas.[1] LDS Church president David McKay offered his assessment that "no more sacred ordinance is administered in the Church of Christ than the administration of the sacrament."[2] The common belief is that Jesus instituted this "Most Blessed Sacrament" and intended it to be practiced in perpetuity. Scholars have looked for its roots in Jewish ritual meals, such as the Passover; in Jewish sacrifices and prayer patterns; in Greco-Roman banquets and symposia; and in the practices of the Jewish sect in Qumran near the Dead Sea.[3] Whatever the Eucharist's cultural background, specific texts in the New Testament provide an account of its institution. Given the centuries of liturgical elaboration that followed, it is important to examine the scriptural foundation upon which all eucharistic practice is based. The key passages are the "Supper Narratives" in the Synoptic Gospels (Matt. 26:17–29; Mark 14:12–25; Luke 22:7–20) and Paul's report of what he "received of the Lord" regarding the practice (1 Cor. 11:23–29).[4]

---

1. Quoted in *CCC* 1211.

2. *Teachings: David O. McKay*, 34.

3. The scholarly literature on cultural parallels to the Eucharist is extensive. A helpful overview is Bryan D. Spinks, "In Search of the Meals behind the Last Supper: Cultural Background and Eucharistic Origins," in his *Do This in Remembrance of Me: The Eucharist from the Early Church to the Present Day* (London: SCM, 2013), 1–11.

4. Whereas these accounts tell little about what was said during the meal apart from the words used to institute the sacrament, the Gospel of John devotes five full chapters (13–17) to Jesus's words and deeds on this occasion. Surprisingly, though, John never mentions the breaking of bread or the sharing of the cup of wine.

The simple narrative in the Synoptics is that as Christ and the disciples "did eat, Jesus took bread, and blessed, and brake it, and gave to them, and said, Take, eat: this is my body. And he took the cup, and when he had given thanks, he gave it to them: and they all drank of it. And he said unto them, This is my blood of the new testament, which is shed for many" (Mark 14:22–24; Matt. 26:28 adds "for the remission of sins"). Luke's account is similar but shares distinctive features with Paul's report. In their accounts of the Lord's Supper, Luke and Paul share a common variation from Matthew and Mark that has proven to be highly significant in Christian history. Although it is not universally attested in the ancient manuscripts, Luke records that as the Lord distributed the bread to his disciples, he amplified the words of institution to specifically include a commemorative purpose: "This is my body which is given for you: this do in remembrance of me" (Luke 22:19). The Lukan account coincides closely with the tradition Paul received in which the memorial intent is stated twice: "Take, eat: this is my body, which is broken for you: this do in remembrance of me. After the same manner also he took the cup, when he had supped, saying, This cup is the new testament in my blood: this do ye, as oft as ye drink it, in remembrance of me" (1 Cor. 11:24–25).[5] *Anamnēsis* is the Greek word rendered as "in remembrance" in the KJV (and in other translations as "in memory," "as a memorial," or "as a reminder"). The rich connotations of *anamnēsis*, which will be explored later, allow it to be understood in ways that transcend mere intellectual recollection, and its proper interpretation and application have been part of eucharistic debates over the centuries.

General Meanings of the Eucharist

At its core, the Eucharist is intended to represent (some say re-present) Christ's sacrificial death on the cross. Participation in the Lord's Supper is a public proclamation of that redemptive reality. As Paul put it, "As often as ye eat this bread, and drink this cup, ye do shew the Lord's death till he come" (1 Cor. 11:26). The statement also indicates that the Eucharist is a sacrament that is to be repeated and celebrated perpetually "till he [Christ] come." The Gospels present the Eucharist as being instituted in the context of Jesus and

---

5. In the principal ancient manuscripts, Luke contains several other minor variations: (1) two cups of wine are shared, which is not inconsistent with the multiple sharing of cups in Jewish celebratory feasts; and (2) one of the cups (the eucharistic cup?) precedes the breaking of bread (as it does in the early, postapostolic Didache).

his disciples celebrating the annual Passover meal commemorating God's deliverance of Israel from bondage to the Egyptians. Christians see a parallel in the Lord's Supper where the eucharistic "meal" foreshadows a greater and more comprehensive liberation—deliverance from the bondage of human sin—made possible by the broken body and shed blood of Jesus Christ. Indeed, the New Testament knows Christ as the paschal Lamb slain for the sins of the world (1 Cor. 5:7; John 1:29).[6]

Another widely shared belief is that Christ's words "this is my blood of the new testament [covenant]" (Matt. 26:28; Mark 14:24) or "the new testament [covenant] in my blood" (Luke 22:20; 1 Cor. 11:25) point to the inauguration of the new covenant community made possible through the shedding of his blood. Joseph Smith revised Mark 14:24 to express the idea this way: "And he said unto them, This is in rememberence of my blood; which is shed for many, *and the new testament which I give unto you.*"[7] The somewhat ambiguous KJV wording about Christ's new covenant or "new testament" with his people being "in" or "of" his blood is understood, and often translated, to mean that his shed blood "establishes," "confirms," "ratifies," or "seals" the new testament/covenant. The notion that blood, in this case Christ's own sacrificial blood, marks the establishment of a (new) covenant would have been familiar to Jewish disciples who knew from the Torah (Exod. 24) that at Sinai "the covenant formally constituting Israel as God's people" was sealed by blood. In the Exodus account, Moses presents to his people the terms of the covenant received on the mountain, and the people assent to these terms. The next morning, Moses sets up a symbolic, ceremonial scene in which offerings are made and bulls sacrificed. He then sprinkles their blood on both the altar (representing God) and on the people, saying, "Behold the blood of the covenant which the LORD hath made with you concerning all these words" (Exod. 24:8). Later, Moses and the leaders of Israel ascend the mountain and see God "and did eat and drink" (Exod. 24:11). Jewish scholarship considers this to have been a

---

6. A popular, contemporary look at parallels between the Passover and the Lord's Supper is Brant Pitre, *Jesus and the Jewish Roots of the Eucharist* (New York: Doubleday, 2011). For a deep dive into the banqueting and meal culture of the ancient Near East as context for the Eucharist, the keenly interested might selectively consult essays in the massive, multivolume *Eucharist—Its Origins and Contexts*, ed. David Hellholm and Dieter Sanger, 3 vols. (Tübingen: Mohr Siebeck, 2017). Christians have also found other Old Testament foreshadowing of the Eucharist in the gift of manna and the blessing of bread and wine by the ancient priest-king Melchizedek (Exod. 16; Gen. 14:18).

7. *NTOB*, 352 (emphasis added).

"sacrificial meal," noting that such a meal is "a well-attested way of celebrating the establishment of a covenant."[8] Not surprisingly, many Christians see in this covenant-sealing ceremony and meal a foreshadowing of the Last Supper.[9]

The KJV's choice to sometimes render *diathēkē* as "testament" can also be understood in the way it is used in the phrase "last will and testament." Martin Luther, for instance, plays off this meaning when he writes:

> A testament, as everyone knows, is a promise made by one about to die, in which he designates his bequest and appoints his heirs. A testament, therefore, involves first, the death of the testator [Heb. 9:16], and second, the promise of an inheritance and the naming of the heir. . . . The same thing is also clearly seen in these words of Christ. . . . He names and designates the bequest when he says "for remission of sins" [and] he appoints the heirs when he says: "For you" and "for many," that is for those who accept and believe the promise of the testator.[10]

As to the nature of the new testament/covenant, Christian reflection has generally followed the interpretation in Hebrews 8–10, which glosses the promise in Jeremiah 31:31–34 of a new covenant "not according to the covenant" that God made with Israel, which they "broke," but one in which he will put his law "in their inward parts, and write it in their hearts." Hebrews considers this a new and "better" covenant and calls Christ, who brings or establishes it, a *mesitēs*. A *mesitēs* is one who acts as arbiter, agent, or go-between in arranging or ratifying an agreement or effecting a reconciliation. The term is typically translated "mediator." The polyvalence of *mesitēs* aptly captures for Christians Christ's eucharistically redemptive role in bringing a new covenant of salvation and reconciliation to humankind through his life and death. Latter-day Saint commentary concurs: "Divine covenants are ratified with a

---

8. Adele Berlin and Marc Zvi Brettler, eds., *The Jewish Study Bible*, 2nd ed. (New York: Oxford University Press, 2014), 153–54. From a Jewish perspective, "dashing the blood on the altar and on the people joins God and Israel in the covenant." Moreover, "establishing a covenant by the parties sharing blood, each other's or that of an animal, is attested in many places" in antiquity (154).

9. Another parallel noted is with the *todah* or sacrifice of thanksgiving offered in gratitude for having received some form of well-being (Lev. 7:12–15), known in the KJV as the "peace offering." "The meat of the well-being offering is eaten primarily by the offerer and his guests in a sacred meal" that binds them to each other and God. *Jewish Study Bible*, 209.

10. Martin Luther, *The Babylonian Captivity of the Church*, in *The Annotated Luther*, vol. 3, *Church and Sacraments*, ed. Paul W. Robinson (Minneapolis: Fortress, 2016), 40–41.

sacrifice. . . . Jesus Christ is both the Sacrifice and the Mediator of the new and everlasting covenant."[11] Church president John Taylor added that "the plan, the arrangement, the agreement" to have the Son of God mediate the new covenant "was made, entered into and accepted before the foundation of the world; it was prefigured by sacrifices, and was carried out and consummated on the cross."[12]

THE SACRIFICIAL NATURE OF THE EUCHARIST

Early Christians spoke quite naturally of the Eucharist as a sacrifice "because it followed the [ancient] pattern of the communion sacrifice: gifts are offered to God, consecrated by prayer, and then received back by the offerers for their consumption."[13] The New Testament regards Christ's atoning death on the cross as foreshadowed in and a fulfillment of Old Testament sacrifices and offerings. In words attributed to Paul, Christ "hath loved us, and hath given himself for us an offering and a sacrifice to God for a sweet-smelling savour" (Eph. 5:2). Hebrews develops at length Christ's role as both high priestly sacrificer *and* that which is sacrificed. Ultimately, in contrast to the assumed salvific inefficacy of the Old Testament cultus, Christ, the "great high priest" (Heb. 4:14), is "set on the right hand of the throne of the Majesty in the heavens" to serve as the "minister of the sanctuary, and of the true tabernacle, which the Lord pitched, and not man" (Heb. 8:1-2). Catholics envision this heavenly ministry as a perpetual intercession that is symbolized and actualized on earth every time a priest-officiant, *in persona Christi*, lifts up the bread and wine as a sacrificial offering to God. Catholic theology does *not* claim that this is a historical repetition of Christ's once-for-all bloody sacrifice, a "reslaying" of the Lord. It does, however, view it as a commemorative reenactment of such spiritual potency that it is almost as if it were a current event, one that is eternally present in which communicants share by participating in the Eucharist. Additionally, the Eucharist is believed to effect an ongoing propitiation of the Almighty.[14]

---

11. *DCC*, 4. See also D&C 76:69.

12. John Taylor, *An Examination . . . of the Mediation and Atonement of Our Lord and Savior Jesus Christ* (Salt Lake City: Deseret News, 1882), 171. See also apostle Boyd K. Packer's "The Mediator," *Ensign*, May 1977, 55-56.

13. Frederick C. Bauerschmidt, "The Eucharist," in *Oxford Handbook of Catholic Theology*, ed. Lewis Ayres and Medi Ann Volpe (Oxford: Oxford University Press, 2015), 284.

14. Even among Catholics, though, there have been highly technical debates. Is the Eucharist a sacrificial "oblation" or an "immolation"? Is it a "destructive" or a "constructive"

Since the time of the Reformation, in one way or another, Protestants have challenged this Catholic view of the Eucharist. At issue is whether or in what way the Eucharist should be considered a present sacrifice. To the degree that Protestants describe the Lord's Supper as a sacrifice at all (and some eschew the characterization entirely lest it detract from Christ's unique sacrifice on the cross), they do so metaphorically. The Bible speaks of a "sacrifice of praise" (Heb. 13:15) and a "sacrifice of thanksgiving" (Ps. 116:17). Participants in the Lord's Supper are viewed as offering such sacrifices of praise and thanksgiving to the Father for the gift of his Son either formally as part of the eucharistic liturgy or mentally throughout the celebration (or both). Latter-day Saints, too, stress *eucharistia* (thanksgiving) as a proper part of sacramental worship. First Presidency counselor David McKay urged church members during the Lord's Supper to "meditate . . . and silently and prayerfully express appreciation for God's goodness" in sending his Son to redeem humankind.[15] Another church leader taught that the first step toward realizing the benefits of the Lord's Supper "is to have a feeling of gratitude to Heavenly Father during the sacrament for the Atonement of His Son."[16] Many Christians, including Latter-day Saints, see the Lord's Supper as a sacrifice by considering participation in it an occasion for offering oneself "as a living sacrifice, holy and acceptable to God, which is your spiritual worship" (Rom. 12:1 NRSV). Communion is a time for renewed commitment to God, a self-offering of love, service, and obedience that constitutes a living sacrifice in imitation of the ultimate self-offering of Christ.

That Catholics see something more in the sacrificial character of the Eucharist, however, does not prevent them from also embracing these metaphorical ideas. In the words of one Catholic cardinal, "To his self-sacrifice, we join our own, our very selves."[17] For Catholics, the portion of the eucharistic ceremony known as the "offertory" or "presentation of the gifts" involves not only communicants' material offerings (typically monetary donations today) but also their spiritual gifts. As a representative of the congregation solemnly processes to the altar to deliver the sacrament's bread and wine, this can symbolize the sacrificial offering of each communicant's life to God in union with Christ's self-offering.[18]

---

sacrifice? And should it in some sense be viewed as an "additional" sacrifice? See Trent Pomplun, "Post-Tridentine Sacramental Theology," in *OHST*, 347–61.

15. McKay, *Conference Report*, April 1946, 114.

16. Don R. Clarke, "Blessings of the Sacrament," *Ensign*, November 2012, 104.

17. Cardinal Francis E. George, as quoted in Donald Wuerl and Mike Aquilina, *The Mass: The Glory, the Mystery, and the Tradition* (New York: Image, 2013), 16.

18. A popular Catholic author describes the Presentation of the Gifts in this manner:

When the priest elevates the bread and wine heavenward, it is thought that the worshipers' offerings, symbolic of their own "living sacrifice," are joined to a re-presentation (but not historical repetition) of Christ's own sacrifice.[19]

Latter-day Saints agree that sacramental worship is about personal sacrifice and consecration to God. Notes a church publication: "When you partake of the sacrament, you witness to God that your remembrance of His Son will extend beyond the short time of that sacred ordinance" and "that you are willing to take upon yourself the name of Jesus Christ and that you will keep His commandments."[20] Such personal consecration to Christ necessarily entails "that we are willing to repent of our sins."[21] Repentance, a commitment to more fully align one's life with God's will, *is* a sacrifice, since *sacrifice* literally means to "make holy." Revelation urges Latter-day Saints to offer that sacrifice of repentance and covenant renewal in conjunction with Communion on a weekly basis: "Thou shalt offer a sacrifice unto the Lord thy God in righteousness, even that of a broken heart and a contrite spirit. And . . . thou shalt go to the house of prayer and offer up thy sacraments upon my holy day. . . . For verily this is a day appointed unto you to . . . offer thine oblations and thy sacraments unto the Most High" (D&C 59:8–12).[22]

Although Latter-day Saints fully embrace figurative notions of participation in the Eucharist as a sacrifice, they almost never characterize the sacrament itself as such. Nor do they see the consecration of the sacramental elements as a priestly reenactment of Christ's sacrifice. Hebrews 9:24, a verse Catholics commonly cite in support of their notion of Christ's "heavenly sacrifice," states, "For Christ is not entered into the holy places made with hands, which are the figures of the true; but into heaven itself, now to appear in the presence of God for us." Mormons see Christ's heavenly presence "for us" more as legal advocacy than as priestly sacrifice. A revelation declares, "Listen to him who is the advocate with the Father, who is pleading your cause before him—saying:

"Ultimately, the rite symbolizes our giving of our entire lives to God in the offering of bread and wine." Edward Sri, *A Biblical Walk through the Mass: Understanding What We Say and Do in the Liturgy* (West Chester, PA: Ascension, 2015), 87.

19. "As the priest offers the gifts, so we offer ourselves and all that we have—our work, prayers, and Christian witness, our family life, our daily work, our leisure and our play. . . . In the words of the Second Vatican Council, 'these sacrifices are most lovingly offered to the Father' with the bread and wine." Wuerl and Aquilina, *The Mass*, 146.

20. *True to the Faith*, 148.

21. *Preach My Gospel: A Guide to Sharing the Gospel of Jesus Christ*, 2nd ed. (Salt Lake City: The Church of Jesus Christ of Latter-day Saints, 2023), 88.

22. This echoes Ps. 51:17—"The sacrifices of God are a broken spirit: a broken and a contrite heart."

Father, behold the sufferings and death of him who did no sin, in whom thou wast well pleased; behold the blood of thy Son which was shed, the blood of him whom thou gavest that thyself might be glorified. Wherefore, Father, spare these my brethren that believe on my name, that they may come unto me and have everlasting life" (D&C 45:3–5). Apostle Russell Nelson explained to his LDS audience that "the word *advocate* comes from Latin roots meaning a 'voice for,' or 'one who pleads for another.' Other related terms are used in scripture, such as *intercessor* or *mediator*." Nelson added that seeing Christ as "our advocate-intercessor-mediator with the Father gives us assurance of his unequaled understanding, justice, and mercy."[23]

The Presence of Christ in the Eucharist

The eucharistic controversy of longest standing deals with how best to understand Christ's "presence" in the Eucharist.[24] To some it may be surprising that the brief words—"this is my body" or "this is my blood"—could generate the voluminous literature and lengthy debates that they have, especially since most biblical scholars today doubt that they are Christ's *ipsissima verba* (his very words) in the first place. It may be helpful to describe the range of views about dominical presence by plotting them along a continuum. At one end would be the view that Christ's body is literally, physically present in the sacrament. This is sometimes referred to as the "substantialist" or "objective" view because the very substance of Christ's body, as actual object, is thought to be present in the Eucharist. On the other end of the spectrum is the idea that Christ is present only in worshipers' minds and hearts as they recall his sacrifice. This is the "subjective" view. In between, a variety of positions may be identified that partake in varying degrees of both objective and subjective characteristics. Major types of eucharistic thinking are often labeled "transubstantiation," "consubstantiation," "spiritual presence," and "memorialism." At their core, these varying positions depend on differing approaches to scriptural interpretation and distinct philosophical principles. Before examining these different typologies, it should be clarified that whatever the metaphysical subtleties of their varying notions of presence, they all affirm that Christ's "human" body, the one he received from

23. Russell Nelson, "Jesus the Christ—Our Master and More" (Brigham Young University, February 2, 1992), 4, https://speeches.byu.edu/talks/russell-m-nelson/jesus-christ-master/.

24. Accessible overviews of contrasting perspectives can be found in John H. Armstrong, ed., *Understanding Four Views on the Lord's Supper* (Grand Rapids: Zondervan, 2007), and Gordon T. Smith, ed., *The Lord's Supper: Five Views* (Downers Grove, IL: InterVarsity Press, 2008).

Mary and with which he ascended into heaven, remains in heaven during eucharistic celebrations. Even the most strictly "objective" or "substantialist" view—"transubstantiation"—holds that neither in whole nor in part is Christ's "human" body, which theologians describe as "corporeal" and "local" (meaning physically located), found on any eucharistic altar or table.[25]

Although the term "transubstantiation" did not come into common usage until the Middle Ages, notions of a real change in the substance of the eucharistic elements had been present in Christianity inchoately from the earliest centuries. The common belief was that once the bread and wine were consecrated, they truly and literally became the body and blood of Christ. Such realism was unambiguously asserted as early as the fourth century by the likes of Cyril of Jerusalem in his *Mystagogic Catechesis* and Ambrose of Milan in *On the Sacraments*. A proto-doctrine of transubstantiation may even be implicit in Justin Martyr's second-century comment to Emperor Antoninus Pius (reign, 138–161) that Christians do not receive the bread and wine "as common bread or common drink" but that after the eucharistic "word of prayer . . . that food . . . is the flesh and blood of the incarnate Jesus."[26] Nonetheless, at different times during the Middle Ages, various Catholic ecclesiastics debated the nature of Christ's presence in the Eucharist. Although some argued for a figurative, spiritual interpretation, substantialism carried the day.[27] Its most sophisticated

25. A typical substantialist characterization of the Eucharist credited to the Lutheran delegation at the 1529 Marburg Colloquy proclaims that while "Christ is truly present, that is, substantively, essentially," he is not so "quantitatively, qualitatively, or locally." Quoted in Roland H. Bainton, *Here I Stand: A Life of Martin Luther* (New York: Abingdon, 1950), 319–20. A subtly different position parses Christ's humanity so that there is a dimension to it that is ubiquitous through being suffused with divinity and therefore omnipresent upon Christ's ascension into heaven. This aspect of Christ's body can inhabit the eucharistic elements. Others make a distinction between Christ's individual, personal human nature (the corporeal body that stays in heaven) and his generic human nature that Christ shares with all humankind that mystically is present in the Eucharist.

26. Justin, *1 Apology* 66.2, as quoted in J. N. D. Kelly, *Early Christian Doctrines*, 5th ed. (New York: Harper & Row, 1978), 198. For the fourth century, see Khaled Anatolios, "Sacraments in the Fourth Century," in *OHST*, 152–53. The term "transubstantiation" was first introduced in the 1100s and officially endorsed at the Fourth Lateran Council in 1215. The term, however, simply explained "an affirmation about Christ's presence in the sacrament that was already assumed and taken for granted [in] this period." Boyd Taylor Colman, "The Christo-Pneumatic-Ecclesial Character of Twelfth-Century Sacramental Theology," in *OHST*, 205.

27. "In sacramental theology from the ninth century to the eleventh, an extended debate on the doctrine of the real presence took place as to whether the body of Christ in the Eucharist was the same as the body born of the Virgin, which suffered and died, and is now

and formidable advocate was Thomas Aquinas, who used Aristotelian philosophy to explicate transubstantiation. Aristotle viewed all material objects as composed of both "substance" and "accidents." A thing's "accidents" are its external, visible, palpable characteristics; its "substance" is its intrinsic, inner, invisible reality, its essence. Using these Aristotelian categories, Aquinas and his supporters argued that the internal, imperceptible substance of the bread and wine, not their outer accidents or appearances, were, upon consecration, metaphysically transformed into the equally invisible, infinite substance of Christ's body. The outward accidents of Christ's body, its local and corporeal character, remained unchanged in heaven, as did the bread and wine on the altar.

To assist in comprehending the rarefied distinctions involved in different theories of eucharistic presence, a series of simple formulas can be introduced. Let "A" stand for "accidents," "BW" for "bread and wine," and "CB" for "Christ's body." The outward "accidents" of the bread and wine would then be designated A_{BW}, and the accidents of Christ's body as A_{CB}. Similarly, if "S" is used to identify the "substance" of either Christ's body or the bread and wine, then the inner substance or essence of Christ's body could be depicted as S_{CB} and the "substance" of the elements prior to consecration would be S_{BW}. Thus, the accident-substance character of the bread and wine prior to consecration would be stated as A_{BW}/S_{BW}. Once transubstantiated through priestly consecration, however, the eucharistic elements become A_{BW}/S_{CB}. Note that the accidents of the bread and wine stay the same, but their inner substance has been replaced by Christ's body. During the Reformation, Protestant critics viewed such an interior, invisible transformation as metaphysically suspect. Some mocked what they considered the superstitious or magical character of the Catholic ceremony.[28]

---

risen in glory at the right hand of the Father." Mark G. Vaillancourt, "Sacramental Theology from Gottschalk to Lanfranc," in *OHST*, 187 (187–200). Prominent in the ninth-century debate were the writings of Paschasius Radbertus in support of substantialism and Ratramnus of Corbie on behalf of a symbolic interpretation. An equally significant controversy broke out in the eleventh century between Berengarius of Tours, who "spoke of the body and blood as one thing, and the sacrament of the body and blood as another" (195), and Lanfranc of Canterbury, who defended traditional eucharistic realism.

28. Later critics invoked the old (unsubstantiated) chestnut that the expression "hocus-pocus" derives from a mumbled corruption of the Latin words of consecration—"*Hoc Est Corpus Meum*" ("This is my body"). The *OED* traces this idea to the conjecture of eighteenth-century Anglican archbishop John Tillotson, who declared, "In all probability those common juggling [magic] words of hocus pocus are nothing else but a corruption of hoc est corpus, by way of ridiculous imitation of the priests of the Church of Rome in their trick of Transubstantiation." *OED*, s.v. "hocus-pocus."

Martin Luther countered transubstantiation with his theory sometimes labeled "consubstantiation." Luther believed that in the Eucharist neither the elements' accidents *nor* their substance changes, but Christ conjoins his divine substance to the elements' underlying substance. Whereas transubstantiation replaces the substance of the bread and wine with the substance of Christ's body, the two are concurrently present in Luther's view. Thus, in Luther's theory the consecrated eucharistic elements would be depicted as $A_{BW}/(S_{BW}+S_{CB})$. The divine substance of Christ's body, which Luther believed to be ubiquitous, is present "in, with, and under" the unchanged substance of bread and wine. Thus, when communicants eat the bread, they are truly eating Christ's substantial flesh along with the unchanged accidents *and* substance of the bread and wine. To justify consubstantiation, Luther invoked the age-old Christological example of iron in fire. "In red-hot iron," he reasoned, "the two substances, fire and iron, are so mingled that every part is both iron and fire." In this way, "the body of Christ [is] contained in every part of the substance of the bread."[29]

John Calvin, however, rejected a substantial presence of any kind, believing that the faithful partake of Christ "spiritually" in the Eucharist. Of his substantialist opponents, Calvin remarked, "They enclose Christ in the bread," but "we do not think it lawful for us to drag him from heaven." Rather, the manner of partaking is "spiritual because the secret power of the Spirit" is the source of "our union with Christ," which is the objective of the Eucharist. "Away with that calumny that Christ is removed from his Supper unless he lies hidden under the covering of bread!"[30] Rather than the elements containing Christ's substantial presence, the Holy Spirit imparts the nourishing and invigorating benefits of Christ's flesh and blood to communicants spiritually, not locally. In Calvin's view, Christ's "human," local body, both accidents *and* substance, remains in heaven. Thus, a Calvinian understanding of the Eucharist may be depicted as $A_{BW}/S_{BW}+C_{SP,}$ where even after consecration the bread and wine are just that but are accompanied by Christ's spiritual presence (C_{SP}) that does indeed impart his redemptive benefits to communicants.[31] Calvinian notions of spiritual presence are apparent in a number of Christian traditions influenced by Reformed doctrine. The English Book of Common Prayer, for instance, includes this priestly pronouncement at distribution: "Take and eat this in remembrance that Christ

---

29. Luther, *The Babylonian Captivity of the Church*, 35.
30. Calvin, *Institutes* 4.17.33, 31.
31. The Eucharist was the "conduit or instrumental means by which Christ and the believer communed in the Spirit." Michael Allen, "Sacraments in the Reformed and Anglican Reformation," in *OHST*, 292.

died for thee, and feed on him in thy heart by faith with thanksgiving."[32] Though seemingly figurative, Reformed eucharistic theology emphasized that the "feeding" was no less than an actual partaking of Christ.

A fully figurative understanding of "Take, eat: this is my body," however, was promoted by Swiss Reformer Huldrych Zwingli. Zwingli taught that it is the Holy Ghost, not Christ's bodily substance or even his spiritual presence in the elements, that conveys to communicants the benefits of the Eucharist. "To eat the body of Christ spiritually," writes Zwingli, sounding rather like Calvin, "is equivalent to trusting with heart and soul upon the mercy and goodness of God through Christ. . . . If I may put it more precisely, to eat the body of Christ sacramentally is to eat the body of Christ with the heart and the mind *in conjunction with* the sacrament," not by means of it, as Calvin taught.[33] Christ's presence is real, but spiritually realized apart from the elements. His presence is an attendant, accompanying influence not intrinsic to the sacramental elements themselves. "Whereas for Zwingli the Holy Spirit needs no means" to draw us to Christ's body and blood, for the other real-presence theorists it can only happen through "the very means God has ordained," namely, "in the bread and the cup."[34] Calvin felt that Zwingli's views were too psychological and downplayed the metaphysical. Calvin wanted to make room for eucharistic mystery: "By true partaking of him, his life passes into us and is made ours—just as bread when taken as food imparts vigor to the body."[35]

Zwingli was profoundly influenced in his views by two Dutch humanists—the great Desiderius Erasmus and the lesser Cornelius Hoen.[36] Erasmus was famous across Europe for works ranging from his editions of the Greek New Testament to his hermeneutical and exegetical aids to biblical study. For Erasmus, spirit trumped flesh, and the internal mattered more than the external. Applied to the sacraments, this invited communicants to look for Christ not

32. Brian Cummings, ed., *The Book of Common Prayer: The Texts of 1549, 1559, and 1662* (Oxford: Oxford University Press, 2011), 403. The additional verbiage first appeared in the 1552 revision. The quote here is from the 1662 edition.

33. Zwingli, *An Exposition of the Faith* (1531), as quoted in Spinks, *Do This in Remembrance of Me*, 275 (emphasis added).

34. Mickey L. Mattox, "Sacraments in the Lutheran Reformation," in *OHST*, 278.

35. Calvin, *Institutes* 4.17.5.

36. Bruce Gordon, *Zwingli: God's Armed Prophet* (New Haven: Yale University Press, 2021), 35, calls Erasmus "the most powerful and enduring influence on Zwingli." Amy Nelson Burnett, *Debating the Sacraments: Print and Authority in the Early Reformation* (New York: Oxford University Press, 2019), argues that Erasmus was more significant than Zwingli in providing the hermeneutical basis for those who rejected Christ's bodily presence in the Eucharist and took a figurative approach to the relevant scriptural texts.

in the physical elements of the Eucharist but in the spiritual meaning of the ceremony as one that united them as believers and recommitted them as moral soldiers for Christ.[37] Such views shaped Zwingli's thought in fundamental ways and made him susceptible to the antisubstantialist arguments presented in Cornelius Hoen's *Christian Letter on the Lord's Supper*. Key among those arguments was how Hoen, harking back to the early church fathers, contended that the "is" (*est*) in the words of institution—"this is my body"—should be understood as "signifies."[38] The bread and wine signify Christ's body; they are not identical to it, nor do they participate in it or convey it spiritually. The eucharistic elements figuratively *point* to Christ's redemption.[39] Still, in his own way, Zwingli retained a sense of divine mystery in his understanding of the sacraments. He believed that during the Lord's Supper, the Holy Ghost stirs within communicants such "a vivid consciousness of Christ" that "the events of the passion become present" and "temporal distinctions between then and now are erased, and we are with him and he with us."[40] Such Holy Ghost–generated vividness qualifies as a form of "real presence" doctrine even though Christ is "only" present in the hearts and minds of the communicants as the Spirit stirs their recollections of and reflections on Christ's redemptive sacrifice. This can be portrayed as $A_{BW}/S_{BW} + HG$ to indicate that it is the work of the Holy Ghost, not Christ's personal, spiritual presence, as Calvin thought, that is the instrument of communicating the benefits of the Eucharist.

37. Burnett, *Debating the Sacraments*, 50–76.

38. Huldrych Zwingli, *Friendly Exegesis, That Is, Exposition of the Matter of the Eucharist, Addressed to Martin Luther* (1527), in *The European Reformations Sourcebook*, ed. Carter Lindberg, 2nd ed. (Chichester, UK: Wiley-Blackwell, 2014), 116. Two years later, at the Marburg Colloquy, "Luther and Zwingli agreed on fourteen points of doctrine, but divided publicly, bitterly, and irreparably, over the single word 'is' in Christ's statement, 'for this is my body.'" Lee Palmer Wandel, ed., *A Companion to the Eucharist in the Reformation* (Leiden: Brill, 2013), 8.

39. Hoen and Zwingli were not alone in interpreting the institution narrative in this fashion. "It is striking how many of Hoen's arguments can be found in Wyclif's *Trialogus*, the Latin treatises of Taborite theologians, or the confessions of the Bohemian Brethren." Burnett, *Debating the Sacraments*, 71.

40. Linwood Urban, *A Short History of Christian Thought* (New York: Oxford University Press, 1995), 289–90. "The primary movement of memory for Zwingli is [that] the Holy Spirit takes a crucial datum from the church's past (in this case, the death and resurrection of Jesus Christ) and makes it as real to believers in the present as the bread and wine they share." David C. Steinmetz, *Taking the Long View: Christian Theology in Historical Perspective* (New York: Oxford University Press, 2011), 118. Steinmetz's entire chapter—"Christ and the Eucharist" (115–26)—is useful for understanding the sacramental theology of each of the major reformers.

It might be observed that between the various theories of eucharistic presence, particularly those considered "Calvinian" and "Zwinglian," there are distinctions without much of a difference. Each envisions the same end result in which the Eucharist provides spiritual nourishment to communicants and brings them into union with Christ and communion with each other. Each theory assumes that such benefits are conferred as a gracious, interior mystery, imperceptible to the senses. Yet, as one continues to the fully subjective end of the sacramental continuum, questions of presence almost disappear from the discussion. Zwingli, the Anabaptists, and later Baptist traditions followed the memorialist trajectory to the point of complete disengagement from any instrumentalist notion of the Eucharist per se as a channel of supernatural grace. For them, the Lord's Supper was "simply" the occasion for the accompanying, albeit gracious and efficacious, work of the Spirit. Anabaptists saw the sacrament as "a response to grace, not a means of grace." The Holy Spirit, they believed, "brings the believer and Christ together by faith, but this occurs alongside rather than through the sacramental media."[41] As Anabaptist pioneer Balthasar Hubmaier argued, the "divine presence in the Supper comes not as Christ in his divinity but as Spirit."[42] In the early 1600s, founding English Baptist John Smyth taught that the sacraments "doe not confer, and convey grace and regeneration to the participants, or communicants: but as the word preached they serve only to support and stir up the repentance, and faith of the communicants."[43] The Lord's Supper may still be considered a spiritual feast but not because of the eucharistic elements themselves. Rather, the celebration of the Eucharist serves a commemorative purpose, facilitating a spiritual *anamnēsis* (remembrance) as nourishing and revitalizing as any more metaphysical banquet. During the centuries that followed, in what one historian has called "the church's accommodation to the Enlightenment," such memorialist understandings of the Supper became ever more popular, especially in eighteenth- and nineteenth-century America.[44]

41. Allen, "Sacraments in the Reformed and Anglican Reformation," 292; George Hunsinger, "The Lord's Supper in Twentieth-Century and Contemporary Protestant Theology," in *OHST*, 410.

42. John D. Rempel, "Sacraments in the Radical Reformation," in *OHST*, 304. See Rempel's fuller study, *The Lord's Supper in Anabaptism: A Study in the Christology of Balthasar Hubmaier, Pilgram Marpeck, and Dirk Philips* (Scottdale, PA: Herald, 1993).

43. Quoted in Curtis W. Freeman, *Contesting Catholicity: Theology for Other Baptists* (Waco, TX: Baylor University Press, 2014), 317.

44. By the eighteenth century, memorialism could be found not only in Baptist traditions but also among those who embraced the "New England theology" and even among some traditional Presbyterians and Congregationalists, as well as Methodists. It was also the preferred perspective among groups that took exception to various aspects of Calvin-

MORMON MEMORIALISM AND *ANAMNĒSIS*

Although not devoid of objective accents, Latter-day Saint sacramental theology is decidedly subjectivist in nature. The phrase "real presence" is not part of Mormon parlance, and Latter-day Saints rarely discuss *how* Christ is present during the Eucharist, other than to say that through the influence of the Holy Spirit his presence can be felt in the heart and mind of the faithful communicant. Latter-day Saints have no theological reason to say with Calvin (and others), "When we have received the symbol of the body, let us no less surely trust that [Christ's] body itself is also given to us."[45] For Latter-day Saints, experiencing the Lord's presence during the sacrament is not qualitatively different than what Christ intended when he said, "Where two or three are gathered together in my name, there am I in the midst of them" (Matt. 18:20).[46] The commemorative nature of Mormon memorialism is apparent also in the church's practice of referring to the sacramental elements as "emblems" of Christ's sacrificial death. Consistent with this is a strong *ex opere operantis* interpretation, to be illustrated in due course, that highlights the requisite faith and worthiness of the communicant for the sacrament to be effective.[47] In this, at least, Latter-day Saints are in definite agreement with Calvin's declaration: "I hold that men bear away from this Sacrament no more than they gather with the vessel of faith."[48]

As with other forms of commemorative eucharistic theology, Mormon memorialism is rooted in the "this do in remembrance of me" injunctions recorded in Luke 22:19 and 1 Corinthians 11:24. Joseph Smith, in his "New Translation" of the Bible, even chose to emend the Matthean and Markan accounts of the Last Supper to make sure they included these dominical words as well.[49] Additionally, the Book of Mormon account of Christ's institution of

---

ism, such as the Unitarians. See E. Brooks Holifield, "Sacramental Theology in America: Seventeenth–Nineteenth Centuries," in *OHST*, 382–92.

45. Calvin, *Institutes* 4.17.10.

46. Baptists also tend to see the Lord's eucharistic presence as "not different in kind or degree from God's presence in ordinary faith-filled worship." Roger E. Olson, "The Baptist View," in Smith, *The Lord's Supper*, 95.

47. Parallel to early Mormon sacramental theology and practice on a number of issues such as these is the religious movement associated with Barton Stone and Alexander Campbell, which eventuated in the Christian Church (Disciples of Christ) and the Churches of Christ. See Paul M. Blowers and Byron C. Lambert, "The Lord's Supper," in *Encyclopedia of the Stone-Campbell Movement*, ed. Douglas A. Foster et al. (Grand Rapids: Eerdmans, 2004), 489–96.

48. Calvin, *Institutes* 4.17.33.

49. *NTOB*, 306–7, 351–52.

the sacrament among his New World followers has a clearly commemorative cast: "And this shall ye do in remembrance of my body, which I have shown unto you. And it shall be a testimony unto the Father that ye do always remember me. And if ye do always remember me ye shall have my Spirit to be with you" (3 Nephi 18:7). In turn, these words influenced the Latter-day Saint eucharistic prayers currently in use: "O God, the Eternal Father, we ask thee in the name of thy Son, Jesus Christ, to bless and sanctify this bread to the souls of all those who partake of it, that they may eat in remembrance of the body of thy Son, and witness unto thee, O God, the Eternal Father, that they are willing to take upon them the name of thy Son, and always remember him and keep his commandments which he has given them; that they may always have his Spirit to be with them. Amen" (D&C 20:77); and "O God, the Eternal Father, we ask thee in the name of thy Son, Jesus Christ, to bless and sanctify this wine [now, water] to the souls of all those who drink of it, that they may do it in remembrance of the blood of thy Son, which was shed for them; that they may witness unto thee, O God, the Eternal Father, that they do always remember him, that they may have his Spirit to be with them. Amen" (D&C 20:79).

Although Latter-day Saints typically do not reference or discuss the term *anamnēsis*, their vision of what remembrance entails resonates with the rich connotations of the term.[50] Remembrance is more than passive mental recollection of the events surrounding Christ's passion. Remembrance is action-oriented, not passive reception. Somewhat like Erasmus, President David McKay taught that remembrance involves one's promise to fully "enter into the fold of Christ, to cherish virtues mentioned in the gospel of Christ, to keep them ever in mind, to love the Lord whole-heartedly, and to labor, even at the sacrifice of self, for the brotherhood of man—these and all kindred virtues are associated with the partaking of the Lord's supper."[51] In short, it is to offer oneself as a living sacrifice. Church leader Cheryl Esplin taught, "As we partake of the sacrament, we witness to God that we will remember His Son always, not just during the brief sacrament ordinance. This means that we will con-

---

50. Review of the "LDS General Conference Corpus" (https://www.lds-general-conference.org) reveals that in nearly two hundred years of general conferences, the sacrament of the Lord's Supper has been referenced some 2,800 times. In hundreds of those instances, vision and advice are provided with regard to what remembrance/*anamnēsis* should entail.

51. David McKay, *Gospel Ideals, Selections from the Discourses of David O. McKay, Ninth President of the Church of Jesus Christ of Latter-day Saints* (Salt Lake City: Improvement Era, 1953), 147. See also Jeffrey Holland, "This Do in Remembrance of Me," *Ensign*, November 1995, 68–69.

stantly look to the Savior's example and teachings to guide our thoughts, our choices, and our acts."[52] In ways, the active *anamnēsis* promoted in the Church of Jesus Christ of Latter-day Saints parallels the emphasis on *anamnēsis* as dynamic retrieval and participation common in twentieth-century liturgical reform movements. As much as any Christian liturgists, Latter-day Saints in their own idiom talk about "reliving," "reenacting," "making present" Christ's atoning sacrifice to regularly reinforce their own connection to Christ and his cause. The Latter-day Saint vision of *anamnēsis* emphasizes remembrance as recommitment to covenants made at baptism to honor and imitate Christ in daily life.[53] A church manual explains to Latter-day Saints: "When you were baptized, you entered into a covenant with God. You promised to take upon yourself the name of Jesus Christ, keep His commandments, and serve Him to the end (see Mosiah 18:8–10; D&C 20:37). You renew this covenant each time you partake of the sacrament (see D&C 20:77, 79)."[54]

Mormons also make a point about active *anamnēsis* through their interpretation of the "Bread of Life" sermon in John 6, which some Christians read as foreshadowing the Lord's Supper. It has been a point of debate in Christian theology whether such statements as "whoso eateth my flesh, and drinketh my blood, hath eternal life" (John 6:54) are best understood as a reference to the Eucharist or more broadly as a metaphor for devoted discipleship in general. Memorialists like Zwingli and the Latter-day Saints lean to the latter interpretation.[55] Zwingli wrote, "His body is eaten when it is believed that it was slain for us. It is faith, therefore, not eating, about which Christ is speaking here."[56] Similarly, Bruce McConkie explained, "To eat the flesh and drink the blood of the Son of God is, first, to accept him in the most literal and full sense, with no reservation whatever, as the [Son] of the Eternal Father; and, secondly, it is to keep the commandments of the Son by accepting his gospel . . . and enduring

---

52. Cheryl A. Esplin, "The Sacrament: A Renewal for the Soul," *Ensign*, November 2014, 12. See also *True to the Faith*, 148.

53. This doctrine is not unique to the Latter-day Saints. It is shared by other memorialists as well. From a "Baptist" perspective, theologian James McClendon writes that the Lord's Supper "affirm[s] the renewal of the pledge each in baptism makes in answer to God's proclaimed word." McClendon, *Systematic Theology*, vol. 2, *Doctrine* (Nashville: Abingdon, 1994), 386.

54. *True to the Faith*, 23. See also 44.

55. A church instructional manual acknowledges both readings: Eating Christ's flesh "can mean to internalize His teachings and Atonement. It can also represent partaking of the sacrament, which the Savior would institute later." *New Testament Seminary Teacher Manual* (2016), 224.

56. Quoted in W. P. Stephens, "Zwingli on John 6:63," in *Biblical Interpretation in the Era of the Reformation*, ed. Richard A. Muller and John L. Thompson (Grand Rapids: Eerdmans, 1996), 168.

in obedience and righteousness unto the end. Those who by this course eat his flesh and drink his blood shall have eternal life."[57] McConkie supports his metaphorical interpretation with reference to 1 Corinthians 10:3–4, where Paul, speaking of Israel in Moses's day, says, "[They] did all eat the same spiritual meat; and did all drink the same spiritual drink: for they drank of that spiritual Rock that followed them: and that Rock was Christ." Apostle Todd Christofferson develops his explanation of eucharistic *anamnēsis* by way of John 6:57—"he that eateth me, even he shall live by me." To sacramentally "eat" Christ's flesh, explains Christofferson, is to commit to "live by" his will. It is "a striking way of expressing how completely we must bring the Savior into our life, into our very being," and should lead us "to consider how fully and completely we must incorporate His character and the pattern of His sinless life into our life and being." In short, "to eat the flesh and drink the blood of Christ means to pursue holiness."[58] Such declarations exemplify the Latter-day Saint attitude that genuine eucharistic *anamnēsis* entails the believer's active imitation of Christ as grateful *anamnēsis* for Christ's atoning sacrifice.

Mormon memorialism should not be misread as a complete denial of any objective quality to the Eucharist. Sacramental grace is still affirmed. Apostle Jeffrey Holland taught that through the sacraments the faithful "gain access to [God's} power. . . . At such moments we not only acknowledge His divinity, but we also quite literally take something of that divinity to ourselves."[59] The eucharistic prayers quoted above petition the Father to "bless and sanctify" the elements "to the souls of all those who" partake so "that" they may do it "in remembrance of" Christ's sacrifice and be able to "witness unto" the Father that they will "always remember [Christ]" and "keep his commandments." Careful attention to the wording of the prayers notices that the *epiklēsis* (invocation) of divine, sanctifying grace is to enable and empower communicants to remember the Lord through responsive discipleship, "that they may always have his Spirit to be with them" (D&C 20:77, 79). The objective aspect of the sacrament is also suggested in the

57. Bruce R. McConkie, *Doctrinal New Testament Commentary*, vol. 1, *The Gospels* (Salt Lake City: Bookcraft, 1965), 1:358. See also Talmage, *Jesus the Christ*, 342–43.

58. D. Todd Christofferson, "The Living Bread Which Came Down from Heaven," *Ensign*, November 2017, 36–39. That such perspectives are shared by ordinary members of the church is exemplified by the author's neighbor who remarked that when we partake of the sacrament "we are consuming His attributes, His goodness, His Love, and His righteousness. Every time we partake of the sacrament, we can, very literally become more like Him" (Mary McCann, personal correspondence).

59. Jeffrey R. Holland, *Of Souls, Symbols, and Sacraments* (Salt Lake City: Deseret Book, 2001), 27–29. Apostle David Bednar stated simply that the sacrament of the Lord's Supper is one of the ordinances "necessary to obtain access to the power of godliness." Bednar, "Always Retain a Remission of Your Sins," *Ensign*, May 2016, 61.

Book of Mormon description of Christ's celebrating Communion with his New World disciples. On that occasion, Christ explains that whoever communicates does so to the benefit of "his soul" and promises that "his soul shall never hunger nor thirst but shall be filled." The next verse reports: "Now, when the multitude had all eaten and drunk, behold, they were filled with the Spirit; and they did cry out with one voice, and gave glory to Jesus" (3 Nephi 20:8–9). Nonetheless, such expressions fall short of unambiguously proclaiming that the Lord's Supper conveys a special, extraordinary grace not obtainable elsewhere.

Still, the Latter-day Saint vision is clear that through the grace of God, the sacrament of the Lord's Supper, when properly partaken, can be a source of blessing and sanctification. Brigham Young declared that Communion is one of the sacraments "that have been instituted in order that the people may be sanctified, that Jesus may bless them and give unto them his spirit, and guide and direct them that they may secure unto themselves life eternal."[60] Young sounds like John Calvin with his emphasis on how eucharistic participation deepens and intensifies our transformative union with Christ. Calvin taught that "there cannot be a spur which can pierce us more to the quick" than Holy Communion and by which "we may repeatedly gather strength until we shall have reached heavenly immortality."[61] Apostle Melvin Ballard remarked, "I have always looked upon this blessed privilege as the means of spiritual growth, and there is none other quite so fruitful in the achievement of that end as the partaking, worthily, of the sacrament of the Lord's supper."[62] At this point, debates about Christ's presence and distinctions as to whether eucharistic grace is inherent in the elements or is external to them and whether it is spiritually conferred alongside or "inside" the sacrament tend to fade in importance. Mormon sacramental theology may be fundamentally memorialist, but it offers a definite appreciation for the divine grace associated with the sacrament of the Lord's Supper and its vital role in Christian formation.

Benefits/Effects of the Eucharist

Wherever particular Christian theologies of the Eucharist fit on the objective-subjective spectrum with regard to Christ's presence, virtually all acknowledge in *ex opere operantis* fashion that to fully receive the Eucharist's fruits or

---

60. *Journal of Discourses*, 19:92.

61. Quoted in Mary Patton Baker, "Calvin's *Praxis* of the Lord's Supper and the *Duplex Gratia* of Salvation," in *Since We Are Justified by Faith: Justification in the Theologies of the Protestant Reformation*, ed. Michael Parsons (Milton Keynes, UK: Paternoster, 2012), 96.

62. Melvin Ballard, "The Sacramental Covenant," *Improvement Era*, October 1919, 1026.

benefits requires faith and worthiness on the part of the communicant. This is implicit in Paul's counsel to "let a man examine himself, and so let him eat of that bread, and drink of that cup. For he that eateth and drinketh unworthily, eateth and drinketh damnation to himself" (1 Cor. 11:28–29). Or more positively, "Christ our passover is sacrificed for us: therefore let us keep the feast, not with old leaven, neither with the leaven of malice and wickedness; but with the unleavened bread of sincerity and truth" (1 Cor. 5:7–8). Such texts lead most Christian traditions to emphasize spiritual preparation for Communion if its benefits are to be fully realized. The Orthodox, for instance, encourage cultivating a proper disposition to receive the Eucharist through regular confession and fasting and attending vespers (evening prayer service) the night before communing. Even the Catholic Church, which maintains as strong an emphasis as any on the *ex opere operato* character of the sacraments, clearly states that while the Holy Communion irrevocably makes present the promised graces, they only "bear fruit in those who receive them with required dispositions."[63] Further, "anyone who desires to receive Christ in Eucharistic communion must be in a state of grace."[64] In fact, "to attribute the efficacy of [any of the] sacramental signs to their mere external performance, apart from the interior dispositions that they demand, is to fall into superstition."[65] Medieval Catholic theology distinguished the *res et sacramentum*—the *ex opere operato* reality of Christ's bodily presence in the consecrated elements—and the *res tantum*—the graced effect on, or spiritual benefit to, the communicant from that presence. Christ's presence in the Eucharist is unconditional, unfailing, but the fruits of that presence depend on recipients' dispositions.

Protestant traditions maintain a similar outlook. Lutherans agree with Catholics that without fail "all communicants receive the Lord's body and blood supernaturally united with bread and wine." However, "only those who [do] so in repentant faith receive the benefits of a renewal of forgiveness, strengthening along their earthly pilgrimage, and a hidden bestowal of the glory of the life to come in body and soul."[66] The Bohemian Confession of

---

63. *CCC* 1131. This is similar to the LDS view of the sacrament of confirmation (see chapter 9). The gracious gift of the Holy Ghost's companionship is definitely conferred in this ordinance, but the actualization of that companionship and its "fruits" and benefits are dependent on the attitude and actions of the recipient.

64. *CCC* 1415.

65. *CCC* 2111.

66. John R. Stephenson, "Sacraments in Lutheranism, 1600–1800," in *Oxford Handbook of Early Modern Theology, 1600–1800*, ed. Ulrich L. Lehner, Richard A. Muller, and A. G. Roeber (New York: Oxford University Press, 2016), 350.

1535 states that "when someone comes to the sacraments unworthily, he is not rendered worthy and fine by them; rather, he thereby brings a greater sin and damnation upon himself."[67] Similar statements can be found in the Westminster Confession and the Anglican Articles of Religion. Puritan insistence on a pure-body ecclesiology (see chapter 7) meant that they generally restricted the Lord's Supper to those who could provide a credible account of their regenerative, conversion experience in addition to their commitment to a Christian lifestyle, although others considered it a means of conversion.[68] Until the nineteenth century, Presbyterian elders prior to Communion service "would visit each member and examine his or her knowledge of the faith and purity of life. Those who met with the elders' approval were given a small lead token that permitted them to receive communion. The goal was a careful protection of the table from profanation by immoral or unfaithful people."[69]

The Church of Jesus Christ of Latter-day Saints is also committed to pastoral vigilance in ensuring that the Lord's Supper is not profaned. Articles and Covenants states that "previous to their partaking of the sacrament . . . members shall manifest before the church and also before the elders, by a godly walk and conversation, that they are worthy of it" (D&C 20:68–69). In ways this parallels the practice among many ecclesial bodies of ensuring that only the worthy participate in the Lord's Supper, but in practice the elders of the church have generally invited members to self-monitor. It has almost never led to formal "scrutinies" by church elders dispensing admission tokens or to encouragement for members to make a general confession of sin to the congregational leaders prior to participation. Still, a Book of Mormon passage echoing 1 Corinthians 11 presents Christ's words thus:

> And now behold, this is the commandment which I give unto you, that ye shall not suffer any one knowingly to partake of my flesh and blood unworthily, when ye shall minister it; For whoso eateth and drinketh my flesh and blood unworthily eateth and drinketh damnation to his soul; therefore if ye know that a man is unworthy to eat and drink of my flesh and blood ye

---

67. "Article 11: Of the Sacraments," *Bohemian Confession, 1535*, in *Creeds & Confessions*, 1:818.

68. E. Brooks Holifield, *The Covenant Sealed: The Development of Puritan Sacramental Theology in Old and New England, 1570–1720* (New Haven: Yale University Press, 1974), offers a long history of Puritan discourse on the meaning and practice of the sacrament of the Lord's Supper, as well as of the sacrament of baptism.

69. Mary McWhorter Tenney, *Communion Tokens: Their History and Use, with a Treatise on the Relation of the Sacrament to the Vitality and Revivals of the Church* (Grand Rapids: Zondervan, 1936), 17.

shall forbid him. Nevertheless, ye shall not cast him out from among you, but ye shall minister unto him and shall pray for him unto the Father, in my name; and if it so be that he repenteth . . . [ye] shall minister unto him of my flesh and blood. (3 Nephi 18:28–30)

This position is reiterated in the Doctrine and Covenants where church leaders are "commanded not to cast any one who belongeth to the church out of your sacrament meetings; nevertheless, if any have trespassed, let him not partake until he makes reconciliation" (D&C 46:4).

While such passages have prompted LDS general authorities to emphasize the importance of worthy participation in the sacrament, they have almost never so emphasized the damning consequences of unworthy participation that sizable numbers of Latter-day Saints have demurred from coming to the Lord's Table, as sometimes happened in response to the withering sermons of seventeenth-century Puritans. There is no equivalent in Mormonism to *Ten Sermons tending chiefly to the fitting men for the worthy receiving of the Lord's Supper* (1610) that devotes several hundred pages to detailing every aspect of proper penitential preparation. Nor is there a comparable publication to the *Treatise concerning the Lord's Supper*, by Thomas Doolittle, where the unworthy receiver of the sacrament is likened to a "Christ-murderer" and warned that on judgment day, Christ's blood will "cry out against you, instead of pleading for you." Many who listened to or read such sermons were, in the view of minister Solomon Stoddard, "scared out of Religion."[70] While the *General Handbook* of the Church of Jesus Christ of Latter-day Saints today continues to allow congregational leaders to "fence the Lord's table" (as it is expressed in other Christian traditions) from individuals guilty of major and sustained sin, the *Handbook's* directive is that "it should not be the first restriction given to a repentant person who has a broken heart and contrite spirit. However, if a person has committed serious sins, a leader may suspend this privilege for a time."[71]

Because few Latter-day Saints are involved in grievous sin, Mormon preaching emphasizes the positive side of the *ex opere operantis* principle by stressing that a gracious encounter with Christ in the Lord's Supper is affected by, if not effected by, the proper preparation and disposition of the communicant.

70. David D. Hall, *Worlds of Wonder, Days of Judgment: Popular Religious Belief in Early New England* (New York: Knopf, 1989), 156–61. For Stoddard's comment, see Hall, "New England, 1660–1730," in *Cambridge Companion to Puritanism*, ed. John Coffey and Paul C. H. Lim (Cambridge: Cambridge University Press, 2008), 148.
71. *GH* 32.8.3.

A church instructional manual explains: "The attitude with which we partake of the sacrament influences our experience with it. If we partake of the sacrament with a pure heart, we receive the promised blessings of the Lord."[72] Current advice to church members is this: "In preparation for the sacrament each week, take time to examine your life and repent of your sins. You do not need to be perfect in order to partake of the sacrament, but you should have a spirit of humility and repentance in your heart. Every week you should prepare for that sacred ordinance with a broken heart and a contrite spirit (see 3 Nephi 9:20)."[73] A proper disposition during the distribution of the sacramental elements is also considered important. This period "becomes a weekly opportunity for introspection, repentance, and rededication."[74] Modeling the ideal Latter-day Saint attitude while participating in Holy Communion is this description from apostle Howard Hunter of his experience during the administration of the sacrament: "I was troubled. I asked myself this question: 'Do I place God above all other things and keep all of His commandments?' Then came reflection and resolution. To make a covenant with the Lord to always keep His commandments is a serious obligation, and to renew that covenant by partaking of the sacrament is equally serious. The solemn moments of thought while the sacrament is being served have great significance. They are moments of self-examination, introspection, self-discernment—a time to reflect and to resolve."[75]

EUCHARIST AND THE FORGIVENESS OF SINS

The eucharistic benefit of renewed forgiveness of sins flows from one's approaching the Lord's Table with a penitent heart. This understanding reaches back to the patristic period. With quotes from Ambrose of Milan and the much later Council of Trent (1545–1563), the Catholic *Catechism* declares that

72. *Gospel Principles*, 137. Other Christian traditions, too, hold that "one must be not only a believer but a practicing believer to take of the elements. Anything less is sin." Yet, the emphasis is not so much on the threat of damnation for unworthy participation as on a lack of positive benefit. In other words, "it is quite possible to partake of the Lord's Supper and be unaffected by the experience." Millard J. Erickson, *Christian Theology*, 3rd ed. (Grand Rapids: Baker Academic, 2013), 1038, 1039. Latter-day Saints would agree.

73. *True to the Faith*, 148. Similarly, the Reformed *Manner of Celebrating the Sacrament of the Lord's Supper* declares, "We come not to this Supper to testify hereby that we are perfect and righteous in ourselves . . . all the worthiness our Lord requires is, that we truly know ourselves to be sorry for our sins, and find our pleasure, joy, and satisfaction in Him above." Baker, "Calvin's *Praxis* of the Lord's Supper," 98. For Catholicism, see *CCC* 1098.

74. *True to the Faith*, 148.

75. *Teachings: Howard W. Hunter*, 204.

"the Eucharist cannot unite us to Christ without at the same time cleansing us from past sins and preserving us from future sins." As a consequence, the faithful are encouraged to participate frequently in the Eucharist, as well as the sacrament of penance that prepares one for it. Catholic counsel is that because "as often as [Christ's] blood is poured out, it is poured for the forgiveness of sins, I should always receive it, so that it may always forgive my sins. Because I always sin, I should always have a remedy. As bodily nourishment restores lost strength, so the Eucharist . . . wipes away venial sins [everyday faults]."[76] The reformer Martin Luther did not disagree. "The 'sacrament of the altar,'" he affirmed, "offers the forgiveness of sins."[77] And Mormons concur. "Through the Atonement, Jesus has made it possible for you to be cleansed of your sins each time you take His sacrament."[78] Just as one's baptism brings initial forgiveness of sins, in the weekly sacramental renewal of the covenants made at baptism, "the Lord renews the promised remission of your sins."[79]

For Latter-day Saints, however, eucharistic pardon does not function *ex opere operato*. A current church manual notes that "merely eating the bread and drinking the water during the sacrament does not automatically qualify us to receive a remission, or forgiveness, of our sins. We must exercise faith in Jesus Christ, repent, and partake of the sacrament with real intent by always remembering Him and striving to keep His commandments. By worthily partaking of the sacrament . . . we can receive a remission of our sins."[80] Partaking of the sacrament is often described as renewing one's baptismal covenants. When the sacrament is approached with the proper disposition, declares Dallin Oaks, "the Lord renews the cleansing effect of our baptism."[81] Adds Todd Christofferson, "The bread and water become symbolic cleansing agents and the sign of our renewed covenant. It is as if we were being baptized afresh and the door once again opened for the Holy Spirit to enter."[82] Counselor in the First Presidency George Cannon put the Latter-day Saint perspective this

---

76. *CCC* 1393–1394. The Eucharist, however, "is not ordered to the forgiveness of mortal sins—that is proper to the sacrament of Reconciliation. The Eucharist is properly the sacrament of those who are in full communion with the Church." *CCC* 1395.

77. Mattox, "Sacraments in the Lutheran Reformation," 276.

78. "Baptism in the Book of Mormon," The Church of Jesus Christ of Latter-day Saints, https://www.comeuntochrist.org/blog/baptism-in-the-book-of-mormon.

79. *True to the Faith*, 147.

80. *New Testament Seminary Teacher Manual* (2016), 103.

81. Dallin H. Oaks, "The Aaronic Priesthood and the Sacrament," *Ensign*, November 1998, 38.

82. D. Todd Christofferson, "Justification and Sanctification," *Ensign*, June 2001, 24.

way: "The ordinance of baptism is instituted for the remission of sins. The sacrament of the Lord's Supper was not instituted for that purpose. Yet, when people partake of that sacrament worthily, they no doubt obtain the forgiveness of their sins on the same principle that we obtain the forgiveness of our sins whenever we confess them and repent of them."[83] Using Book of Mormon phraseology (Mosiah 4:12, 26; Alma 4:14), apostle David Bednar characterized eucharistic forgiveness as "retaining" the remission of sins associated with baptism: "The act of partaking of the sacrament, in and of itself, does not remit sins. But as we prepare conscientiously and participate in this holy ordinance with a broken heart and a contrite spirit, then the promise is that we may *always* have the Spirit of the Lord to be with us. And by the sanctifying power of the Holy Ghost as our constant companion, we can *always* retain [the baptismal] remission of our sins."[84]

The benefit of renewed forgiveness from the Lord is an aspect of sacramental participation that has had considerable popular appeal among Latter-day Saints. In one oft-quoted sermon, Melvin Ballard articulated the appeal thus:

Who is there among us that does not wound his spirit by word, thought, or deed, from Sabbath to Sabbath? We do things for which we are sorry and desire to be forgiven, or we have erred against someone and given injury. If there is a feeling in our hearts that we are sorry for what we have done, if there is a feeling in our souls that we would like to be forgiven, then the method . . . is to repent of our sins . . . and then repair to the sacrament table where, if we have sincerely repented and put ourselves in proper condition, we shall be forgiven, and spiritual healing will come to our souls.

For Ballard, this was not just a theological affirmation, it was an experiential reality. "I am a witness that there is a spirit attending the administration of the sacrament that warms the soul from head to foot; you feel the wounds of the spirit being healed, and the load being lifted. Comfort and happiness come to the soul that is worthy and truly desirous of partaking of this spiritual food."[85]

---

83. Jerreld L. Newquist, ed., *Gospel Truth: Discourses and Writings of President George Q. Cannon*, 2 vols. (Salt Lake City: Deseret Book, 1974), 2:152. See also McConkie, *Doctrinal New Testament Commentary*, 2:364, 366.

84. Bednar, "Always Retain a Remission of Your Sins," 61–62.

85. Ballard, "The Sacramental Covenant," 1026–27.

EUCHARIST AND UNION WITH CHRIST AND CHRIST'S BODY

From the beginning, the Eucharist has served as a fellowship meal, an occasion when disciples come together to break bread and renew their sense of spiritual community. It is a time to reinforce their communion and union with Christ. The apostle Paul asked, "The cup of blessing which we bless, is it not the communion of the blood of Christ? The bread which we break, is it not the communion of the body of Christ? For we being many are one bread, and one body: for we are all partakers of that one bread" (1 Cor. 10:16–17). The image of "one bread," a single loaf, is used by Paul to emphasize that believers constitute, and in the sacrament are constituted as, a single, united body, the "body of Christ" (1 Cor. 12). One of Paul's pithiest declarations is that "we are members of [Christ's] body, of his flesh, and of his bones" (Eph. 5:30). The Heidelberg Catechism expounds this idea by noting that as we partake of the Lord's Supper, we are "united more and more to [Christ's] blessed body by the Holy Spirit dwelling both in Christ and in us that, although he is in heaven and we are on earth, we are nevertheless flesh of his flesh and bone of his bone, always living and being governed by one Spirit."[86] Even groups such as the Anabaptists who do not view the church as Christ's mystical body are willing to see it as his "sacramental body." For them, as for Latter-day Saints, it is "the tangible worshipping community gathered to break bread that [is] transformed," not the sacramental elements. "Christ's presence in the meal flow[s] from his presence in the community." This visible, historical community is the body of Christ "that [takes] on form and [is] transformed in Communion."[87] For Balthasar Hubmaier, "the object of Communion becomes the community's covenant rather than the elements of bread and wine." The breaking of bread is the "outward act of the visible church focused on being rather than receiving the body of Christ."[88] These are perspectives that might be voiced in any Latter-day Saint discussion of sacramental theology.

Although Mormons do occasionally speak of the sacrament as a sign and source of ecclesial unity, historically this has not been a primary emphasis. Reference to the church as the body of Christ is common enough, but seeing the Lord's Supper as a fellowship meal designed in part to deepen a sense of community among believers following Paul's one-bread/one-body analogy has been rare. In nearly two centuries of general conference addresses, hundreds

---

86. *Creeds & Confessions*, 2:443.
87. Rempel, "Sacraments in the Radical Reformation," 299, 301.
88. Rempel, "Sacraments in the Radical Reformation," 304.

of which discuss the sacrament of the Lord's Supper, only once has 1 Corinthians 10:16–17 been quoted, and then it was not expounded.[89] The corporate dimension of the sacrament has tended to get overshadowed by attention to the personal spiritual benefits that come to the individual through worthy participation in the Supper.[90] Moreover, because Latter-day Saints almost never use the word "Communion" to refer to the Lord's Supper, nor do they physically gather at the Lord's Table to partake of the elements, natural opportunities are missed to reflect on the community-in-union character of the sacrament.[91] Still, occasional voices have been heard to affirm the Supper's communitarian nature. Church president David McKay on occasion identified a "principle associated with the administering of the sacrament"—that we "partake of this sacrament as in the bond of brotherhood, of oneness. The element of brotherhood has been associated with it always." McKay did acknowledge, though, lack of emphasis on this point in church preaching and teaching in the early twentieth century, remarking that years earlier when he was a boy in pioneer Utah, there was more stress placed on cultivating interpersonal harmony so that participation in the Lord's Supper could truly signify unity within the body of Christ.[92]

Noticeable in LDS Church literature in the most recent decades is that this communal motif may be becoming more common. Two documents from the 2010s are illustrative. The first is the revised 2018 edition of the *New Testament Student Manual*. In reference to 1 Corinthians 10:16–17, the manual explains, in standard Christian fashion, that when communicants "partake of 'one bread' (loaf) during the ordinance of the sacrament, they affirm oneness or unity not only with Christ but also with one another."[93] A second example comes from the 2019 edition of the church's widely distributed home-study scripture manual, *Come Follow Me*, which for that year focused on the New Testament.

89. Brigham Young is the one speaker who quoted this verse. See *Journal of Discourses*, 13:139.

90. Largely because of the individualist and memorialist nature of the Latter-day Saint eucharistic experience, the church does not practice closed communion. The current official policy is: "Although the sacrament is for members of the Church, nothing should be done to prevent others from partaking of it." *GH* 18.9.3.

91. The basic meaning of "communion" is "sharing or holding something in common with others" or "mutual participation." *OED*, s.v. "communion." *Koinōnia* is the underlying Greek word translated "communion" in 1 Cor. 10:16–17. Elsewhere, it is translated as "fellowship" and broadly refers to "sharing" or "participation."

92. David O. McKay, "The Significance of the Sacrament," *Improvement Era*, January 1953, 13.

93. *NT Student Manual* (2018), 370.

"Although the ordinance of the sacrament involves a personal commitment between an individual and the Lord," notes the manual, "it is also an experience we share with others." Like the college manual just cited, *Come Follow Me* specifically directs readers to 1 Corinthians 10:16–17 and invites Latter-day Saints to "think about how this sacred ordinance can help 'many' become 'one' in Christ" and how the individual might "draw strength from partaking of the sacrament with other believers."[94] Partaking of the sacrament as a congregation has the potential to unite, just as family unity can be strengthened by sharing a meal together.

If until recently among Latter-day Saints the Supper's "horizontal" dimension of communion with fellow believers has been infrequently highlighted, its vertical dimension of communion with Christ has always been at the heart of the sacrament's meaning. Participating in the Lord's Supper, wrote an early member of the First Presidency, "puts us in communion with Him who instituted the Sacrament."[95] Church leader B. H. Roberts asked rhetorically, "To what end does all this lead—this [sacramental] covenanting to take upon [us] the name of Christ; to always remember him; to keep his commandments—to what culmination does all this conduct the [communicant]? To union with God, the one thing most important."[96] Although only occasionally connected to sacramental communion, it should not be thought that the idea of churchly unity or oneness per se is unimportant to Latter-day Saints. Quite the opposite (see chapter 7). Numerous LDS scriptural passages echo the early revelation that proclaimed "if ye are not one, ye are not mine" (D&C 38:27). Yet, historically, Latter-day Saints typically have not linked that shared interest in oneness to a vision of believers gathered at the Lord's Table to jointly renew their commitment to Christ and one another.

The Sacramental Elements/Emblems

Across Christian traditions there is variety in the size, shape, and composition of the sacramental elements. In some cases, these matters have generated significant controversy. Latter-day Saints, though, have never quibbled over

---

94. *Come Follow Me—for Individuals and Families: New Testament 2019* (Salt Lake City: The Church of Jesus Christ of Latter-day Saints, 2019), 135.

95. Anthon H. Lund, *Conference Report*, April 1907, 56.

96. Roberts, *Course in Theology*, 4:121. Latter-day Saints, however, do not express this union in the common theological language about being "incorporated into" Christ. Moreover, the expression "union with Christ" is less common in LDS discourse than "union with God," the phrase used by Roberts.

whether the eucharistic bread must be wheat-based or unleavened. Nor have they worried about the substitution of water for wine. Originally, they used wine, but concern over "adulterated" commercial product prompted a revelation that told the Saints to "not purchase wine" from their "enemies" and to "partake of none except it is made anew among" (D&C 27:3–4).[97] Most crucially, the revelation added: "Behold, I say unto you, that it mattereth not what ye shall eat or what ye shall drink when ye partake of the sacrament, if it so be that ye do it with an eye single to my glory—remembering unto the Father my body which was laid down for you, and my blood which was shed for the remission of your sins" (D&C 27:2). Mormon memorialism is clearly on display in this revelation. Since the elements are not thought to carry or contain Christ in any way, their nature is less important than the remembrance they inspire. This may be why Latter-day Saints prefer the term "emblems" of the sacrament rather than "elements" of the Lord's Supper. Despite the revealed provision for using something other than wine in the sacrament, in the church's early years, Latter-day Saints did use "pure wine" of their "own make" (D&C 89:6), as opportunity permitted. They planted grape vineyards during their sojourn in Nauvoo, Illinois, and Brigham Young later called into existence the "Dixie Wine Mission" in warmer southern Utah. However, communing with water became dominant because in most places where the Mormons settled in the Great Basin, the climate was not ideal for viticulture. By the early twentieth century, communing with water had moved from being common to being normative in the Church of Jesus Christ of Latter-day Saints.

Latter-day Saints were not alone in diverging from wine consumption in the Lord's Supper. Other low-church groups in the nineteenth century that tended toward the memorialist end of the spectrum—Baptists, Brethren, and especially Methodists—began communing with unfermented grape juice rather than alcoholic wine. Influenced by the era's temperance movement, as the Latter-day Saints also may have been, Methodists decided the sacramental wine should be the less alcoholic.[98] In his *Scriptural View of the Wine Question* (1848), Moses Stuart, one of America's foremost Bible scholars in the first half of the nineteenth century, popularized the idea that although the KJV does

---

97. "The great danger for wine drinkers" at the time, writes historian Harvey Green, "was the possibility of drinking adulterated goods." Green, *Fit for America: Health, Fitness, Sport, and American Society* (New York: Pantheon, 1986), 37.

98. This history is detailed in Jennifer L. Woodruff Tait, *The Poisoned Chalice: Eucharistic Grape Juice and Common-Sense Realism in Victorian Methodism* (Tuscaloosa: University of Alabama Press, 2011). See also Betty O'Brien, "The Lord's Supper: Traditional Cup of Unity or Innovative Cups of Individuality," *Methodist History* 32 (January 1994): 79–98.

not make it clear, different terms for both fermented and unfermented wine appear in the original biblical languages. Biblical condemnations of wine, he argued, employ the Greek term for fermented wine, while Scripture's positive assessments of wine use the word for unfermented grape juice. Biblical scholars today generally find Stuart's analysis unpersuasive. At the popular level, though, temperance-sensitive Christians, including Latter-day Saints, have occasionally borrowed this "two-wine" hermeneutic to exonerate Jesus from having consumed, let alone provided (e.g., John 2), a potentially intoxicating beverage. Institutionally, however, the Church of Jesus Christ of Latter-day Saints has never endorsed the two-wine theory nor mandated the use of grape juice in the sacramental cup, despite revelatory support for "pure wine of the grape of the vine" (D&C 89:6).[99] Instead, water is the universal standard in LDS Church services. As it has turned out elsewhere, many of the churches that in the nineteenth century were concerned about alcoholic content in the eucharistic cup, by the later decades of the twentieth century, in the wake of widespread liturgical reform, reinstated communing with commercial wine. Such reforms also revived the use of the common chalice rather than the individual communion cups that became popular around the turn of the twentieth century.[100]

EUCHARISTIC LITURGIES

Little is known about how the Lord's Supper was implemented and practiced in the earliest years of Christianity. What scholars have demonstrated, though, is that rather than a single, normative rite that was faithfully followed in all regions, the early centuries witnessed varied liturgical development and elaboration. Several key eucharistic liturgies were eventually standardized in both East and West, but in recent centuries, with the global expansion and denominational proliferation of Christianity, considerable variety again exists in current eucharistic practice.[101] For instance, Christian churches vary considerably

---

99. In Methodist circles, the term "pure wine" was an appellation for grape juice. Tait, *Poisoned Chalice*, 99.

100. The individual-cup initiatives of many churches were a direct response to the secular, public hygiene movement of the late 1800s and early 1900s. The Church of Jesus Christ of Latter-day Saints continues to use individual disposable cups in its sacrament services.

101. An important scholarly milestone in the quest for the "historical Eucharist" is Hans Lietzmann's exhaustive study of the earliest sources, *Mass and Lord's Supper: A Study in the History of the Liturgy* (1926; reprint, Leiden: Brill, 1979). Although many of his conclusions have been overturned in the century since its publication, his source work remains useful,

in the frequency of their eucharistic observances. Some offer Communion as part of their regular eucharistic Mass or Communion services. Others celebrate the Lord's Supper only quarterly or even annually to ensure its specialness. All consider it central to Christian worship. Latter-day Saints are among those who see their practice as replicating that of the first Christians—"And upon the first day of the week . . . the disciples came together to break bread" (Acts 20:7). The scriptural injunction to Latter-day Saints is: each Sunday "thou shalt go to the house of prayer and offer up thy sacraments upon my holy day" (D&C 59:9).[102] In addition to all the benefits previously discussed, Mormons believe frequent participation in the Lord's Supper has a spiritually protective function. Melvin Ballard remarked that no one abandons God "and becomes an apostate in a week, nor in a month. It is a slow process. The one thing that would make for the safety of every man and woman would be to appear at the sacrament table every Sabbath day. We would not get very far away in one week. . . . The road to the sacrament table is the path of safety."[103]

Churches that include extensive ceremony and visual display in their worship services are sometimes described as "high church." High-church eucharistic services, such as the Catholic Mass, generally consist of three parts—introductory rites, the Liturgy of the Word, and the Liturgy of the Eucharist, during which congregants actually receive Holy Communion.[104] At each stage, priest and parishioners participate together in a series of scripted liturgical interactions. Introductory rites might include a formal greeting, ritual confession of sinfulness, petition for mercy, hymn or expression of praise, and prayer. These are followed by the Liturgy of the Word, which consists of scripture readings, homiletic explanation and exhortation, congregational profession of faith (usually a recitation of either the Apostles' Creed or the Nicene Creed), and the intercessory "prayers of the faithful."[105] With the Liturgy of the Eu-

---

as does his characterization of early liturgical heterogeneity. An up-to-date survey of the subject is Paul F. Bradshaw, *Eucharistic Origins* (London: SPCK, 2004).

102. The basic LDS idea is that "it is expedient that the church meet together often to partake of bread and wine in the remembrance of the Lord Jesus" (D&C 20:75).

103. Ballard, "The Sacramental Covenant," 1028.

104. For Catholics, the 2002 *Missale Romanum* is the official guide to the celebration of the Eucharist. The English translation published by the United States Conference of Catholic Bishops as *General Instruction of the Roman Missal* (*GIRM*) in 2011 "is now the single official translation for the English-speaking world" (foreword). It is the primary source for the discussion that follows.

105. Biblical passages read during the Liturgy of the Word are typically drawn from both Old and New Testaments, commonly in a multiyear cycle of readings set forth in church lectionaries (books with passages to be read during the service) and keyed to the church's

charist, the service reaches its high point. A series of prayers (the *Anaphora* or Eucharistic Prayer) are offered that include thanksgiving, acclamation, *epiklēsis* (invoking the Spirit to descend upon and transform the elements), recitation of the words of institution uttered by Jesus at the Last Supper (which constitute the consecration of the bread and wine), a ritual *anamnēsis* that announces the Eucharist as the memorial of Christ's death and resurrection, and concluding intercessory prayer and final doxology (expression of praise and thanksgiving).[106] At this point, the devout are only moments away from reception of the Holy Communion. After a few additional liturgical actions such as the recitation of the Lord's Prayer or the singing of the Agnus Dei ("Lamb of God") while the priest breaks the "bread" (host) and mingles part with the wine in the chalice, communicants solemnly proceed forward to receive the Holy Communion. Following reception of Communion, there is a formal conclusion. In the Catholic Mass, a brief period of reflective "sacred silence" occurs, and the priest pronounces a concluding prayer that "the fruits of the mystery just celebrated" may be realized in the lives of communicants.[107] The dismissal then occurs, which consists of three Latin words from which the term "Mass" is derived—*Ite, missa est* ("Go forth, the Mass is ended").[108]

Latter-day Saint Sacramental Liturgy

The eucharistic service in Catholicism and Orthodoxy, as well as in other ceremonially high churches, is rich and beautiful in its symbolism. It also stands in sharp contrast to the simplicity of low-church liturgies, such as that celebrated in the Church of Jesus Christ of Latter-day Saints. What takes place among gathered Latter-day Saints on a weekly basis follows a customary order of worship, but the individual parts of the service, with the exception of the prayer consecrating the sacramental elements, are not scripted. There is no missal or Book of Common Prayer that provides set content for the service. The LDS equivalent of introductory rites consists only of an informal welcome

---

liturgical calendar. The "Second Reading" from the New Testament usually concludes with a passage from the Gospels.

106. *General Instruction of the Roman Missal*, 78–79. The Eucharistic Prayer is "the center and summit of the entire celebration" (78).

107. *General Instruction of the Roman Missal*, 88–89.

108. The significance of the dismissal is highlighted by Pope Benedict: "These words help us to grasp the relationship between the Mass just celebrated and the mission of Christians in the world. . . . The word 'dismissal' has come to imply a 'mission.' These few words succinctly express the missionary nature of the Church." *Sacramentum Caritatis*, 51.

and announcements, followed by an opening hymn and prayer. The hymn and prayer provide the focusing moments of reverential praise included in most introductory rites, but a ritual admission of sinfulness, such as the Penitential Rite, is absent.[109] As for the Liturgy of the Word, although Latter-day Saints value the scriptures as much as any Christians, their eucharistic service is not characterized by scriptural readings. Systematic and devotional engagement with the scriptures generally takes place in one's personal study or in church instructional settings. The Latter-day Saint service includes several brief "talks" *following* Communion, but they hardly qualify as explanatory homilies. Delivered by ordinary members of the congregation as invited by their leaders, the talks are rarely theological in nature and typically light in terms of scripture quotations. They can, however, be inspirational, as through story and folksy advice speakers seek to encourage their fellow congregants to put gospel principles into practice. The closest Mormon analogue to the instructional portion of the Liturgy of the Word is actually the congregational singing of one of the church's "sacrament hymns." This takes place while the officiating priests break the bread in preparation for distribution to the congregation. Although relatively brief, Latter-day Saint sacrament hymns include many of the devotional elements present more elaborately in other eucharistic liturgies. The hymns offer *eucharistia* (thanksgiving) and acclamation for the Son's incomparable gifts. They gesture to the institution narrative and provide eloquent *anamnēsis* of the Lord's life and redemptive sacrifice. They include intercessory pleas and *epicleses*. A closer look at these sacrament hymns reveals a good deal about Mormon eucharistic theology.

In the current LDS hymnbook, just over two dozen hymns are grouped under the heading "Sacrament."[110] Of that number, four were written by Christians other than Latter-day Saints—(1) #193, Charles Gabriel's popular "I Stand All Amazed"; (2) #194, C. Frances Alexander's equally popular "There Is a Green Hill Far Away"; (3) #192, Isaac Watts's "He Died! The Great Redeemer Died," which is not as commonly included in other Christian hymnals today but is beloved by Latter-day Saints, having been included in their very first (1835) hymnal; and (4) #189, William Turton's "O Thou, Before the World

---

109. To be sure, as previously noted, an early revelation enjoins that on "the Lord's day, thou shalt offer thine oblations and thy sacraments unto the Most High, confessing thy sins unto thy brethren, and before the Lord" (D&C 59:12), but especially in the twentieth and twenty-first centuries confession is handled personally and privately rather than publicly.

110. *Hymns*, ##169–196. A new hymnbook—*Hymns—for Home and Church*—to consist of from 450 to 500 hymns is in preparation and is scheduled to be released in English, Spanish, Portuguese, and French by the end of 2026.

Began," the least well known piece from other Christian hymn writers. What these hymns share is a passionate appreciation for Christ's loving self-sacrifice that makes salvation possible. Such expressions in the four hymns just mentioned are matched in fervor by lyrics in the LDS-authored hymns. Here are some Mormon examples: "Oh, love effulgent, love divine! What debt of gratitude is mine, That in his off'ring I have part, And hold a place within his heart" (#187); "'Tis sweet to sing the matchless love of Him who left his home above; And came to earth—oh, wondrous plan—To suffer, bleed, and die for man!" (#176); and "We'll sing all hail to Jesus' name, And praise and honor give, To him who bled on Calvary's hill, And died that we might live" (#182). One LDS Church leader spoke for many when he said, "Sacred among all hymns are those that capture the sacrifice and the shedding of the blood of Jesus Christ and His infinite Atonement. My earliest memories of the healing power of the Savior are associated with sacrament hymns." In addition to worshipful devotion, he also noted that his theological "understanding of the doctrines of the Atonement is connected to the hymns," quoting as an example a stanza from "How Great the Wisdom and the Love" (#195)—"How great, how glorious, how complete, Redemption's grand design, Where justice, love, and mercy meet In harmony divine!"[111]

Many of the previously discussed aspects of Latter-day Saint sacramental theology are manifest in Mormon hymnody. For instance, seeing the Lord's Supper as the occasion for the impartation of divine grace in conjunction with sacramental participation is apparent in these lyrics: "God, our Father, hear us pray; Send thy grace this holy day. As we take of emblems blest, On our Savior's love we rest. Grant us, Father, grace divine; May thy smile upon us shine" (#170). Although remembrance is a human act, to achieve its full sacramental purpose it must be grace-empowered: "Prepare our minds that we may see, The beauties of thy grace, Salvation purchased on that tree, For all who seek thy face" (#178); and "In mem'ry of the Crucified, Our Father, we have met this hour. May thy sweet Spirit here abide, That all may feel its glowing pow'r . . . Our Father, may this sacrament, To ev'ry soul be sanctified, Who eats and drinks with pure intent, That in our Savior he'll abide" (#190). The *epiklēsis* in Mormon sacramental hymns seeks the Supper's benefits: "O Lord of Hosts, we now invoke Thy Spirit most divine, To cleanse our hearts while we partake the broken bread and wine. May we forever think of thee and of thy suff'rings sore, Endured for us on Calvary, And praise thee evermore" (#178). The Latter-day Saint perspective on the relationship between partaking of the sacrament and

111. Jay E. Jensen, "Remember and Perish Not," *Ensign*, May 2007, 12.

forgiveness of sin is captured in these lyrics: "As now our minds review the past, We know we must repent; The way to thee is righteousness—The way thy life was spent. Forgiveness is a gift from thee, We seek with pure intent. With hands now pledged to do thy work, We take the sacrament" (#169).

Not surprisingly for memorialist Mormons, many hymns promote remembrance. Here are some examples: "This sacrament doth represent His blood and body for me spent. Partaking now is deed for word That I remember him, my Lord" (#187); "As now we take the sacrament, Our thoughts are turned to thee, Thou Son of God, who lived for us, Then died on Calvary. We contemplate thy lasting grace, Thy boundless charity; To us the gift of life was giv'n, For all eternity" (#169); and "With humble heart, I bow my head, And think of thee, O Savior, Lord. I take the water and the bread, To show remembrance of thy word. Help me remember, I implore, Thou gav'st thy life on Calvary, That I might live forevermore" (#171). The vividness of *anamnēsis* that transcends mere intellectual recollection is poignantly portrayed in the lyrics of a Mormon hymn uniquely cast as Christ's words to communicants: "Rev'rently and meekly now, Let thy head most humbly bow. Think of me, thou ransomed one; Think what I for thee have done. With my blood that dripped like rain, Sweat in agony of pain, With my body on the tree, I have ransomed even thee . . . Oh, remember what was done, That the sinner might be won. On the cross of Calvary, I have suffered death for thee."[112] The hymn also commends communal harmony through mutual forgiveness: "Bid thine heart all strife to cease; With thy brethren be at peace. Oh, forgive as thou wouldst be, E'en forgiven now by me." The divine dispensation of grace is then invited: "In the solemn faith of prayer, Cast upon me all thy care, And my Spirit's grace shall be, Like a fountain unto thee." The hymn finishes with an affirmation of Christ as mediatorial advocate combined with the synergism fundamental to Mormonism: "At the throne I intercede; For thee ever do I plead. I have loved thee as thy friend, With a love that cannot end. Be obedient, I implore, Prayerful, watchful evermore, And be constant unto me, That thy Savior I may be" (#185).

Once the sacrament hymn has been sung, one of the officiating priests kneels and offers the set prayer of consecration for the bread. After the prayer, there is no formal invitation to commune and no queue of communicants lining up to receive the bread from the priests at the sacrament table. Rather,

---

112. Comparable to the reference to Christ's blood that "dripped like rain" is a stanza from Isaac Watts's hymn "He Died! The Great Redeemer Died!" There the wording is: "Come saints and drop a tear or two, For him who groan'd beneath your load: He shed a thousand drops for you, A thousand drops of precious blood." *Hymns*, #192.

the priests hand the trays of broken bread to deacons lined up in front of the table who in turn circulate through the sanctuary passing them to those seated in the congregation. This liturgical procedure of consecration and distribution is then repeated for the water (used in place of the wine). Once the trays have been returned to the priests at the sacrament table following distribution, Communion is complete. There are no post-Communion prayers or other ritual activity. The worship service now transitions to the talks, perhaps a musical number between them, and on to the closing hymn and prayer. With that, "Sacrament Meeting" is concluded.

Several observations are important here. First, the biblical words of institution are not recited before, after, or during the prayer of consecration. This helps prevent any confusion as to whether Latter-day Saints anticipate a substantial presence in the elements themselves. Next, it is noteworthy that in the wording of the prayer, the personal, plural pronoun "we" is used. This is because the priest is praying on behalf of, or acting as voice for, the entire congregation, who, as the body of Christ, are making *epiklēsis*. Although the prayer is to be offered only by ordained ministers, it is not because they possess some intrinsic power by virtue of their ordination that makes the consecration efficacious. It is simply a matter of the distribution of sacred duties among church ministers. Finally, as previously noted, the LDS eucharistic prayers draw primary attention to *anamnēsis*. What is petitioned on behalf of the communicants is that they may eat and drink in remembrance of Christ "and always remember him and keep his commandments which he has given them." Graced remembrance of the Son leads to a renewal of covenantal vows to discipleship, which makes possible that communicants "may always have his Spirit to be with them" (D&C 20:77, 79). Mormon sacramental prayers combine consecration, *anamnēsis*, and *epiklēsis*.[113]

The Eschatological Marriage Supper of the Lamb

It is appropriate in this final section to draw attention to how the Eucharist serves as a proleptic celebration of the future day when God's *basileia*—his reign, his kingdom—will be supreme. Describing the Eucharist as a "meal of

---

113. It is also worth adding that although the revealed wording of the prayers was available from the founding of the church in 1830 (see D&C 20:77, 79), it took a generation for some early Mormon converts to lay aside the practice of extemporaneous prayers of consecration common in the low-church Protestant congregations to which they had previously belonged.

the kingdom," *BEM* affirms: "The eucharist opens up the vision of the divine rule which has been promised as the final renewal of creation and is a foretaste of it."[114] Communion looks forward to an eschatological fulfillment of the petition in the Lord's Prayer that God's will be done on earth as it is in heaven. Many Christian traditions also link Jesus's Last Supper promise of a future day when he would drink the eucharistic cup "new with you in my Father's kingdom" (Matt. 26:29) with the image in Revelation of an eschatological "marriage supper of the Lamb" (Rev. 19:9). In turn, the Revelation reference is seen as a Christian appropriation of the "messianic banquet" theme found in Second Temple Judaism. This theme was itself a development of the earlier prophetic image in Isaiah 25:6–9 of Yahweh providing a banquet for the nations of the earth in what amounts to a type of coronation feast.[115] Such a feast foreshadowed in the Eucharist symbolizes the future inauguration of the Messiah's glorious reign, a time when the union of true Christians and Christ, of bride and Bridegroom, will be complete.

Of course, a tradition's eschatology is key to its interpretation of biblical texts about an end-time Eucharist and the Lamb's marriage supper. For Christian traditions that view heaven as spiritual and immaterial and disavow belief in a prior, physical millennium on earth, motifs of an eschatological Eucharist and messianic banquet are understood figuratively to depict the situation of the saved in heaven. The Catholic *Catechism*, for instance, describes the sacrament as a "pledge of the glory to come" and proclaims that "there is no surer pledge or dearer sign of this great hope in the new heavens and new earth 'in which righteousness dwells,' than the Eucharist." The sacrament anticipates the figurative "heavenly banquet" when "all the elect will be seated at the table of the kingdom."[116] Many Protestant theologies maintain a similar perspective. As only one example, in various Methodist communion liturgies the petition is heard that the Eucharist might unite God's people "until Christ comes in final victory and we feast at his heavenly banquet."[117]

Still, there has always been a chiliastic (millennialist) Christian minority who envision the marriage supper, especially when associated with the promised eschatological Communion, as an actual, material event. Early examples

114. *BEM*, 22.

115. Scott Harrower, "Eucharist," in *T&T Clark Companion to Atonement*, ed. Adam J. Johnson (London: Bloomsbury, 2017), 480–82. The "marriage supper of the Lamb" mentioned in Revelation also echoes the parables of the royal wedding feast (Matt. 22:1–14) and ten virgins (Matt. 25:1–13).

116. *CCC*, section 7 title, 1402–1405, 1344.

117. *United Methodist Book of Worship*, 38.

include patristic millenarians such as Irenaeus, who wrote that Christ "promised to drink of the fruit of the vine with His disciples, thus indicating both . . . the inheritance of the earth in which the new fruit of the vine is drunk, and the resurrection of His disciples in the flesh." Moreover, emphasized Irenaeus, "He cannot by any means be understood as drinking of the fruit of the vine when settled down with His [disciples] above in a super-celestial place; nor, again, are they who drink it devoid of flesh, for to drink of that which flows from the vine pertains to flesh, and not spirit."[118] Irenaeus's millennialism held that at the second coming, "Christ will raise the just to reign with him in his kingdom." The resurrected just will "enjoy the land promised to the patriarchs and drink the fruit of the vine" with Christ in the "eschatological banquet."[119]

Latter-day Saint theology, too, sees the Eucharist as pointing to a glorious future. John Taylor remarked that "in partaking of the Sacrament we not only commemorate the death and sufferings of our Lord and Savior Jesus Christ, but we also shadow forth the time when he will come again and when we shall meet and eat bread with him in the kingdom of God."[120] A Doctrine and Covenants revelation connects intertextually with the Bible in promising a future "supper of the house of the Lord, well prepared, unto which all nations shall be invited." The supper will be, glossing Isaiah 25:6, "a feast of fat things, of wine on the lees well refined," and is specifically said to include "the lame, and the blind, and the deaf," who will "come in unto the marriage of the Lamb, and partake of the supper of the Lord, prepared for the great day to come" (D&C 58:7–11). An earlier revelation, echoing Matthew 26:29, urged, "Marvel not, for the hour cometh that I will drink of the fruit of the vine with you on the earth and with . . . all those whom my Father hath given me out of the world" (D&C 27:5, 14).[121] From one standpoint, the essence of the Latter-day Saint proclamation to the world is: "Prepare ye the way of the Lord, prepare ye the supper of the Lamb, make ready for the Bridegroom" (D&C 65:3). Joseph Smith taught that those worthy at the second coming would "be crowned with a crown of righteousness; be clothed in white raiment; be admitted to the

---

118. Irenaeus, *Against Heresies* 5.33.1, in *ANF*, 1:562.

119. John Behr, *Irenaeus of Lyons: Identifying Christianity* (Oxford: Oxford University Press, 2013), 182–83.

120. *Journal of Discourses*, 14:185. Taylor's eschatological perspective continues as the standard LDS view today: "Thus, the sacrament not only symbolizes the Savior's Atonement but also looks forward in anticipation to the time when He will return to the earth in glory." *NT Student Manual* (2018), 83.

121. Between the two verses quoted, Joseph Smith listed by name various past prophets who would be participating in this eschatological sacrament. See D&C 27:5–13.

marriage-feast . . . and reign with Christ on the earth, where, according to the ancient promise, they will partake of the fruit of the vine new in the glorious kingdom with him."[122]

Although these statements can be understood metaphorically, and Latter-day Saints have read them in that fashion, they are also open to literal interpretation. Brigham Young remarked that the resurrected righteous would "sit down with Jesus, where he will administer [the sacrament] to them again in fulfillment of his saying to them, 'I will not drink henceforth of this fruit of the vine, until the day when I drink it new with you in my Father's kingdom.'"[123] Bruce McConkie pushed the outer limits of literalism with his interpretation that "every faithful person in the whole history of the world, every person who has so lived as to merit eternal life in the kingdom of the Father will be in attendance and will partake, with the Lord, of the sacrament."[124] Although rarely discussed in general conferences today, the idea that the Bridegroom will literally break sacramental bread with his churchly bride after he returns to earth still appears in church literature. As an example, a church scripture study manual comments thus on Doctrine and Covenants 27: "This prophecy anticipates the time when Jesus Christ will partake of the sacrament as part of the events surrounding His return to the earth in glory. . . . The Prophet Joseph Smith learned that not only will ancient prophets join together to partake of the emblems of the sacrament with the Savior but also 'all those whom [the] Father hath given [Him] out of the world.'"[125] A current sacrament hymn petitions, "When thou comest in thy glory, To this earth to rule and reign, And with faithful ones partake of the bread and wine again, May we be among the number worthy to surround the board, And partake anew the emblems of the suff'rings of our Lord" (#183).

Latter-day Saint discourse sometimes distinguishes the marriage supper of the Lamb, which it typically views as symbolic, from the eschatological Eucharist, which it often construes as a literal event. Regarding the marriage supper of the Lamb, for instance, a New Testament study manual explains, "In part, at least, the symbolism of the marriage supper refers to the coming of Christ to the earth at the outset of the great millennial day."[126] Similarly, the Doctrine

---

122. *JSP*, D3:483.

123. *Journal of Discourses*, 19:91. See also *Journal of Discourses*, 15:2.

124. Bruce R. McConkie, *Promised Messiah: The First Coming of Christ* (Salt Lake City: Deseret Book, 1978), 595.

125. *D&C Student Manual* (2017), 158. The manual also includes the statement by McConkie (159).

126. *Life and Teachings of Jesus & His Apostles Course Manual* (1979), 467. See also *New Testament: Gospel Doctrine Teacher's Manual* (1997), 194, and *NT Student Manual* (2014), 562.

and Covenants manual quoted in the previous paragraph offers the view that "the joyful reunion between the Lord and His people" at the second coming "is symbolized in the celebratory marriage feast." The Bridegroom comes to claim the faithful as his bride. Those who "keep their covenants with the Lord shall be 'arrayed in fine linen . . . the righteousness of the saints' (Revelation 19:8)," and they "will have the joy of welcoming the Lord and rejoicing with Him at His coming."[127] Whether figurative or literal, Latter-day Saints look forward with *eucharistia* (thanksgiving) to the sacramental character of the eschaton ("last," climax of history).

127. *D&C Student Manual* (2017), 355. Different figurative reflections on the Lamb's marriage supper include the idea that the "image of a feast reminds us that the gospel of Jesus Christ satisfies the spiritual, emotional, social, and physical hunger, or needs, of the entire posterity of Adam and Eve. Inviting others and preparing for this great supper is an important message of the latter days." *New Testament Seminary Student Study Guide* (2007), 175–76.

ADDITIONAL SACRAMENTS

An Abundance of Grace

This chapter completes the discussion of Christian sacraments by exploring the remainder of the seven rites recognized as sacraments by the Roman Catholic Church and Eastern Orthodox churches, indicating along the way points of convergence and divergence with Mormon doctrine. The chapter concludes with a consideration of the most distinctive sacraments of the Church of Jesus Christ of Latter-day Saints—the ordinances performed in its sacred temples.

PENANCE AND RECONCILIATION

The Latin word *poenitentia*, from which both "penance" and "penitence" are derived, is the term used in the Vulgate[1] to translate *metanoia*, the Greek New Testament term typically rendered in modern English Bibles as "repentance."[2] *Metanoia*, of course, has broad application in human experience, but the *sacrament* of penance or the "mystery of *metanoia*," as it is sometimes called in Orthodoxy, deals specifically with the problem of postbaptismal sin.[3]

1. The Latin translation of the Bible dating to the late fourth or early fifth century that became the "common" (*vulgata*) edition used in Western Christianity for over a thousand years. During the Reformation, Protestants produced their own translations, but the Roman Catholic Church adopted the Vulgate as its official Latin-language Bible at the Council of Trent in 1546. The Vulgate retained that status well into the twentieth century.

2. Reflecting the Vulgate rendering, the later Catholic Douay-Rheims English translation uses "penance" instead of "repentance." More recent Catholic versions such as the Jerusalem Bible (JB, NJB, RNJB) and the revised edition of the New American Bible (NABRE) consistently translate *metanoia* as "repentance."

3. Reliable, succinct discussions of the Roman Catholic sacrament of penance can be found in P. M. Gy, "Penance and Reconciliation," in *The Church at Prayer*, vol. 3, *The Sacraments*, ed. A. G. Martimort et al., trans. Matthew J. O'Connell (Collegeville, MN: Liturgical Press, 1988), 101–15, and David N. Power, "Sacrament and Order of Penance and Reconcil-

What happens when forgiven Christians sin again, as they inevitably will? Is forgiveness to be found? The faith of believers is that the answer is "Yes!" In the words of the psalmist, "For thou, Lord, art good, and ready to forgive; and plenteous in mercy unto all them that call upon thee" (Ps. 86:5). Theological reflection on relevant biblical texts points to contrition and confession, with their implied abandonment of sin and amendment of life, as milestones on the path to this forgiveness. "If we confess our sins, he is faithful and just to forgive us our sins, and to cleanse us from all unrighteousness" (1 John 1:9). "He that covereth his sins shall not prosper: but whoso confesseth and forsaketh them shall have mercy" (Prov. 28:13). A Doctrine and Covenants verse glosses the latter passage: "By this ye may know if a man repenteth of his sins—behold, he will confess them and forsake them" (D&C 58:43). Additionally, some traditions, including Mormonism, emphasize that when sin harms another, some form of reparation or restitution should be made. This follows Old Testament practice as well as the New Testament example of Zacchaeus the tax collector, who declared, "If I have taken any thing from any man by false accusation, I restore him fourfold" (Luke 19:8).

The Latter-day Saint doctrine of repentance is that it "includes exercising faith in Jesus Christ, having a broken heart and contrite spirit, recognizing and forsaking sin, seeking forgiveness, making restitution, and demonstrating a renewed commitment to keep the commandments."[4] The word "repent" and its derivatives appear more frequently in the Book of Mormon and Doctrine and Covenants than in the Bible. So important is repentance in Mormon doctrine that Latter-day Saints sometimes label the good news the "gospel of repentance." Moreover, early LDS ministers were told that "the thing which will be of the most worth unto you will be to declare repentance unto this people, that you may bring souls unto me" (D&C 15:6; 16:6). The reason is fundamental: "For, behold, the Lord your Redeemer suffered death in the flesh; wherefore he suffered the pain of all men, that all men might repent and come unto him. And he hath arisen again from the dead, that he might bring all men unto him, on conditions of repentance. And how great is his joy in the soul that repenteth! Wherefore, you are called to cry repentance unto this people" (D&C 18:11–14). Small wonder that one of the earliest revelatory directives to the Mormon ministry was: "Say nothing but repentance unto this generation" (D&C 6:9; 11:9).

---

iation," in *Systematic Theology: Roman Catholic Perspectives*, ed. Francis Schüssler Fiorenza and John P. Galvin, 2nd ed. (Minneapolis: Fortress, 2011), 543–58.

4. *GH* 31.1.7.

A similar commitment to promoting repentance is plainly manifest in Lutheranism. For Lutherans, "the abiding significance of baptism . . . consists in its establishment in the Christian of that life of perpetual repentance mentioned so prominently in the Ninety-Five Theses." The mark of "authentic Christian existence" is "true and daily repentance." It is "nothing less than a return to baptism, and *ipso facto* a re-appropriation of the grace once given." Regular repentance is "a recognition—indeed, an insistence—that the Christian life itself includes a Spirit-led dynamism that moves the believer ever forward toward holiness; toward, that is, the completion of the good work that was begun in one's baptism." In sum, Jesus's exhortation to "repent and believe the gospel" does not mean "that the Christian should occasionally go to the sacrament of penance, but rather that the gospel itself should initiate the Christian into a new way of life whose central identifying mark is the humility of daily repentance."[5] Such sentiments closely parallel the exhortation given to Latter-day Saints by church president Russell Nelson. "Nothing is more liberating, more ennobling, or more crucial to our individual progression," he declared, "than is a regular, daily focus on repentance. Repentance is not an event; it is a process." Because "repentance opens our access to the power of the Atonement of Jesus Christ," he concluded, "I plead with you to . . . experience the strengthening power of daily repentance."[6]

Contrition is considered by most Christians to be the beginning and heart of true repentance. The etymology of "contrition" moves back through Latin to Hebrew and denotes that which is "bruised," "crushed," or "pulverized." Thus, contrition suggests profound, painful remorse for sin. Orthodox sometimes refer to contrite repentance as the "baptism of tears."[7] It is a process that requires "struggle or pain" and comes about only through genuine "conversion and through tears, through confession of iniquities and turning away from evil."[8] Catholics also use the term "conversion" to signal that contrition implies an "interior penance" that is truly transformative. The Catholic *Catechism* defines contrition as deep "sorrow of the soul and detestation for the sin committed, together with the resolution not to sin again."[9] These are perspectives

5. Mickey L. Mattox, "Sacraments in the Lutheran Reformation," in *OHST*, 274, 271.

6. Russell M. Nelson, "We Can Do Better and Be Better," *Ensign*, May 2019, 67. In response to Nelson's counsel, a heightened emphasis on regular repentance has been apparent at general conferences, and repeated reference to the practice is made in the *General Handbook*. See, for example, *GH* 1.2.1, 16; 10.1.2; 11.1.2.

7. McGuckin, *Orthodox Church*, 304.

8. Brian A. Butcher, "Orthodox Sacramental Theology," in *OHST*, 330.

9. *CCC* 1451. The Westminster Confession describes the genuinely penitent person as

with which Latter-day Saint scripture and discourse agree, often employing the psalmic phrases "broken heart" and "contrite spirit" (e.g., Ps. 34:18) to depict the truly penitent. The Book of Mormon proclaims that Christ "offereth himself a sacrifice for sin . . . unto all those who have a broken heart and a contrite spirit; and unto none else can the ends of the law be answered" (2 Nephi 2:7). The Doctrine and Covenants promises "remission of sins unto the contrite heart" (D&C 21:9). And the *General Handbook* adds, "Mere confession and refraining from a sin for a period of time do not on their own constitute repentance. There must also be evidence of a broken heart, a contrite spirit, and a lasting change of behavior."[10] In this vein, traditional Catholic penitential manuals distinguished between contrition and "attrition," the latter being defined as sorrow for sin that was not based on the love of God but on lesser motives such as fear of punishment. "Perfect" contrition, in the Catholic view, or the "contrition of charity," is motivated by the love of God. It is an "interior repentance" that constitutes "a radical reorientation of our whole life, a return, a conversion to God with all our heart, an end of sin, a turning away from evil, with repugnance toward the evil actions we have committed."[11]

In turn, confession goes hand in hand with true contrition. The Greek word for "confession" carries connotations of an open, public acknowledgment of one's sins, and this seems to have occurred in the earliest centuries, often accompanied by public humiliation and severe penances. In time, public confession and humiliation gave way to private confession, first to God and confidentially to a priest. "I acknowledge my sin unto [God]," declared the psalmist, "and mine iniquity have I not hid. I said, I will confess my transgressions unto the Lᴏʀᴅ; and thou forgavest the iniquity of my sin" (Ps. 32:5). In time, confession to a priest took on a sacramental character and became central to the sacrament variously known as penance, reconciliation, or confession.[12] In its fullness, the sacrament consists of contrition, confession, satisfaction, and absolution. The grace believed to be conveyed through the sacrament deepens contrition, facilitates confession, strengthens resolve to

---

having a keen sense "of the filthiness and odiousness of his sins, as contrary to the holy nature and righteous law of God." Thus, he "so grieves for and hates his sins, as to turn from them all unto God, purposing and endeavouring to walk with him in all the ways of his commandments." WC 15.2.

10. *GH* (2020) 24.5.2.1. On one occasion, revelation communicated forgiveness but warned, "go your ways and sin no more; [for] unto that soul who sinneth shall the former sins return, saith the Lord your God" (D&C 82:7).

11. *CCC* 1431.

12. *CCC* 1423–1424.

make satisfaction and abandon sin, and ultimately comforts the penitent through liturgical pronouncement of absolution. Annual confession is still required of practicing Catholics and frequent confession of venial (ordinary) sins is recommended. Confession for more serious sins, typically designated "grave" or "mortal," is essential. As noted in the *Catechism*, "Christ instituted the sacrament of Penance for all sinful members of his Church: above all for those who, since Baptism, have fallen into grave sin, and have thus lost their baptismal grace and wounded ecclesial communion. It is to them that the sacrament of Penance offers a new possibility to convert and to recover the grace of justification."[13] In Orthodoxy, in addition to sacramental confession to a priest, there is an "Eastern inclination to honor the charismata [giftedness] of 'spiritual' men (and, on occasion, women) apart from any consideration of ordination." Such spiritual persons are sought out as counselors and confessors (the individual to whom one confesses), and it is thought that in some ways they have "the power to 'bind and loose' whether they [are] priests or not."[14] In Orthodox Russia, the popularity of such spiritual "elders" was particularly pronounced in the nineteenth century, as epitomized by the wise Zossima in Dostoevsky's *Brothers Karamazov*. Lacking priestly ordination, these spiritual advisers, however, do not "pronounce the prayer of sacramental absolution" and, where desired, send the penitent to a priest for that culminating rite.[15]

Although most Protestant traditions and the Church of Jesus Christ of Latter-day Saints do not practice sacramental confession, they do affirm with Orthodox and Catholics the benefit of counseling with a spiritual leader when it would help overcome sin and receive forgiveness, and they do practice their own forms of church discipline.[16] Protestants have a long history of "fraternal correction" and "mutual edification" in congregational settings, private visitations, and even in correspondence, rooted in their primarily communal interpretation of Matthew 18:15–20, a key New Testament passage on church discipline.[17] This broadened, nonsacramental approach to confession and rec-

13. CCC 1446. As "grave sins," the *Catechism* lists "for example, idolatry, murder, or adultery." CCC 1447.

14. Butcher, "Orthodox Sacramental Theology," 335–36.

15. Timothy Ware, *The Orthodox Church* (London: Penguin Books, 1964), 295–97.

16. As just one example, see Gregory A. Wills, *Democratic Religion: Freedom, Authority, and Church Discipline in the Baptist South, 1785–1900* (New York: Oxford University Press, 1997), a case study of the disciplinary practices among Georgia Baptists in the nineteenth century.

17. John T. McNeill, *A History of the Cure of Souls* (New York: Harper & Row, 1951), 163–286, passim.

onciliation reflects Protestantism's characteristic "priesthood of all believers" theology (see chapter 8) that works to supplement if not supplant the penitential role of the ordained minister. Prominent early Methodist John Fletcher voiced the common Protestant view when he wrote that making "frequent pastoral visits" to "private houses" and carrying out "vigilant inspection into families" are the foundation "upon which the discipline of the Church depends."[18]

Such perspectives are also apparent in early LDS practice. The church's founding Articles and Covenants provided for the ministerial office of "teachers," originally adult men of some experience who were to "watch over the church always, and be with and strengthen them." In particular, they were to "see that there is no iniquity in the church, neither hardness with each other, neither lying, backbiting, nor evil speaking" (D&C 20:53–54). If repentance could not be induced through persuasive fraternal ministrations, then the church's "Laws" (D&C 42) called for resolution through procedures similar to those outlined in Matthew 18:15–20 (see D&C 42:87–93). The revealed "Laws" qualified the biblical injunction "them that sin rebuke before all, that others also may fear" (1 Tim. 5:20) to state that "if thy brother or sister offend many, he or she shall be chastened before many, and if any one offend openly, he or she shall be rebuked openly" (D&C 42:90–91). However, the revelation also stressed that "If any shall offend in secret, he or she shall be rebuked in secret, that he or she may have opportunity to confess in secret . . . that the church may not speak reproachfully of him or her" (D&C 42:92). The sinner was to be delivered "unto the church" as stated in Matthew 18:17, but the definition of "church" was clarified to mean "not to the members, but to the elders. And it shall be done in a meeting, and that not before the world" (D&C 42:89). John Wesley had similar reservations about public confession and reproof and similarly redefined "church" in Matthew 18:17: "It would not answer any valuable end, to tell the faults of every particular member to the church," he remarked. "It remains that you tell it to the elder or elders of the church, to those who are overseers of that flock of Christ to which you belong."[19] In time, the LDS Church developed more elaborate disciplinary and penitential procedures, and they did so along the lines of this early concern for privacy and propriety in confession and reconciliation.

At present, LDS Church discipline is almost solely the responsibility of

18. John William [Fletcher], *The Portrait of St. Paul or, the True Model for Christians and Pastors* (New York: Kirk & Robinson, 1804), 187, 183.

19. John Wesley, "The Cure of Evil Speaking—Matthew 18:15–17 (Sermon 49)," in *Works of John Wesley*, vol. 2, *Sermons II (34–70)*, ed. Albert C. Outler (Nashville: Abingdon, 1988).

bishops and stake presidents, local pastoral officers charged with taking the oversight of the flock and serving formally and officially as their confessors. Whereas nineteenth-century church records contain many accounts of relatively minor transgressive behavior being aired before the elders of the church, bishops and stake presidents today generally deal only with more serious sin. The church's current position on penance is expressed this way: "Most repentance takes place between an individual, God, and those who have been affected by a person's sins. However, sometimes a bishop or stake president needs to help Church members in their efforts to repent."[20] The basic vision is one of spiritual rehabilitation through loving and patient ministration rather than punishment and shaming. An entire section in the church's *General Handbook* is devoted to guiding bishops and stake presidents "through the key decisions and actions necessary to help someone repent of a serious sin."[21] Confession enables sinners to "unburden themselves so they can fully seek the Lord's help in changing and healing."[22] LDS bishops and stake presidents may encourage certain spiritual exercises to assist the individual to become truly penitent and discern internally that they have been forgiven by God. To this end, the *General Handbook* offers suggestions to bishops and stake presidents in a section titled "Uplifting Activities to Help with Repenting and Building Spiritual Fortifications."[23] For severe sin, formal ecclesiastical procedures are in place for both assisting those who are truly penitent to receive the grace of divine forgiveness and disciplining the recalcitrant member. Neither for lesser nor for more serious sins, however, is absolution pronounced. Luther, on the other hand, who clung tenaciously to the sacrament of confession and absolution, taught that reformed sinners should "receive the absolution, that is, forgiveness, from the [minister] as from God himself, and by no means doubt but firmly believe that our sins are thereby forgiven before God in heaven."[24]

The right to absolve sins is an interpretation of Matthew 18:18 and John 20:23,

20. *GH* 32.0.

21. *GH* 32.0–32.17. The quote is from 32.0.

22. *GH* 32.4.1.

23. *GH* 32.8.1.

24. "Small Catechism," in *Book of Concord*, 360. "Luther's inner torment over the impossibility of knowing when sufficient had been done in [contrition and amendment of life] was only relieved by his placing full trust in absolution; as far as he was concerned, the Reformation brought about enhanced appreciation of the 'power of absolution.'" John R. Stephenson, "Sacraments in Lutheranism, 1600–1800," in *The Oxford Handbook of Early Modern Theology*, ed. Ulrich L. Lehner, Richard A. Muller, and A. G. Roeber (New York: Oxford University Press, 2016), 353.

passages which report that Christ conferred upon his apostles the "keys" to "bind" and "loose" on earth and in heaven, including specifically the power to "remit" (or "retain") sins. This authority is believed to have been passed on through apostolic succession whereby those viewed as the apostles' episcopal successors and their presbyterial collaborators sacramentally pardon or absolve sins in the name of the Lord. In the current Catholic Rite of Penance, the priest declares, "Through the ministry of the Church may God give you pardon and peace. And I absolve you from your sins in the name of the Father, and of the Son, and of the Holy Ghost."[25] In the Slavonic liturgy, popular in the East, the priest "lays his hand on the penitent's head while saying this solemn prayer of blessing that confers the grace of reconciliation: May our Lord and God, Jesus Christ, through the grace and compassion of his love for mankind, forgive you my child [*Name*] all your transgressions. And I, an unworthy priest, through the power given to me by him, do forgive and absolve you from all your sins in the name of the Father, and of the Son, and of the Holy Spirit. Amen."[26]

In the Church of Jesus Christ of Latter-day Saints, authority to pronounce divine absolution of sin, strictly speaking, is limited to the church's presiding authorities. In a Doctrine and Covenants revelation, Joseph Smith was told as president of the church: "I have conferred upon you the keys and power of the priesthood . . . and [echoing John 20:23] whosoever sins you remit on earth shall be remitted eternally in the heavens; and whosoever sins you retain on earth shall be retained in heaven" (D&C 132:45–46).[27] J. Reuben Clark Jr., twentieth-century counselor in the First Presidency, remarked, "There is in the Church . . . the power to remit sins, but I do not believe it resides in the bishops. That is a power that must be exercised under the proper authority . . . by those who hold the keys that pertain to that function."[28] Even then, added apostle Spencer Kimball, "Let it be said in emphasis that even the First Presidency and the Apostles do not make a practice of absolving sins." Kimball explained the role of the bishop or stake president in this way: "The bishop, and others in comparable positions, can forgive in the sense of waiving the penalties. In our loose connotation

25. *CCC* 1449.

26. Quoted in McGuckin, *Orthodox Church*, 305.

27. The conferred power to "remit" or "retain" sins has also been interpreted as referring to the apostles' power to bring about a remission of sins through baptism (e.g., *Teachings: Lorenzo Snow*, 54) or as the authority to excommunicate and have the action recognized in heaven (e.g., *Journal of Discourses*, 13:282; 24:93; 26:247).

28. Quoted in Spencer W. Kimball, *The Miracle of Forgiveness* (Salt Lake City: Bookcraft, 1969), 333.

we sometimes call this forgiveness, but it is not forgiveness in the sense of 'wiping out' or absolution. The waiver means, however, that the individual [again] may [fully participate] and have fellowship with the people of the Church. In receiving the confession and waiving the penalties the bishop is representing the Lord. He helps to carry the burden, relieves the transgressor's strain and tension, and [facilitates] a continuation of Church activity. It is the Lord, however, who forgives sin."[29]

To be sure, all ecclesial bodies recognize that ultimately only God forgives sins. From a Catholic perspective, "whatever actions the penitent undertakes in this sacrament [penance] would remain utterly ineffective and unrealized apart from God's absolution." The "embodied presence of the priest" to whom confession is made and who pronounces absolution from sin "is a sign that reconciliation in Christ the head is effected through reconciliation with his body the Church."[30] Orthodox practice reinforces that confessors are merely the Lord's agents in forgiving sin. "This form of language is frequent in modern Orthodox writings: confession is 'through' not 'to' a priest; absolution is 'through' not 'by' one."[31] Adds an Orthodox scholar, "It is not the bishop or priest who forgives anyone's sins, but the Lord himself who does so, in the form of the consoling word of the ordained minister who witnesses the confession of the truly repentant Christian."[32]

An added component of repentance for traditions that practice something resembling the sacrament of reconciliation is "satisfaction." In the Catholic view, "absolution takes away sin," but it "does not remedy all the disorders sin has caused." Sin may harm others, but it always "injures and weakens the sinner himself." Thus, "the sinner must still recover his full spiritual health by doing something more to make amends for the sin: he must 'make satisfaction for' or 'expiate' his sins. This satisfaction is also called 'penance.'"[33] The priestly confessor determines the deeds of satisfaction ("penances") to be performed by the sinner. In doing so, he is to "take into account the penitent's personal situation and must seek his spiritual good. It must correspond as far as possible with the gravity and nature of the sins committed. It can consist of prayer, an offering, works of mercy, service of neighbor, voluntary self-denial, sacrifices, and above all the patient acceptance of the cross we must bear. Such penances

29. Kimball, *The Miracle of Forgiveness*, 333, 332.
30. Frederick Christian Bauerschmidt and James J. Buckley, *Catholic Theology: An Introduction* (Chichester, UK: Wiley-Blackwell, 2017), 281.
31. McNeill, *Cure of Souls*, 307.
32. McGuckin, *Orthodox Church*, 304.
33. CCC 1459.

help configure us to Christ."³⁴ Penances are also to be assigned in a way that helps heal the specific sin confessed.³⁵ In Orthodox churches, "the priest may, if he thinks it is advisable, impose a penance (*eptimia*), but this is not an essential part of the sacrament and is very often omitted." When required, its purpose is to demonstrate "the earnestness of the repentance."³⁶ Repentance may also require restitution. In case of serious sins, full satisfaction in the sacrament of penance entails making restitution or reparation for harm done, and absolution is conditional on payment of this debt to the aggrieved party or parties.³⁷ Mormon doctrine also sees restitution as part of complete repentance.³⁸

The spirit of current Catholic, Orthodox, and Latter-day Saint penitential guidelines is decidedly remedial rather than punitive. The confessor, be he Catholic priest or Mormon bishop, is to serve as a spiritual physician, a healer of souls, not simply a judge handing out a courtroom sentence. The rehabilitative character of penance, however, has not always been in the forefront of Christian practice. In the early centuries, for serious sin, postbaptismal forgiveness and reconciliation with the church were allowed only once in a lifetime. Those seeking it would enter a "penitential order" that restricted privileges and required arduous penances for a period of many years, not just weeks or months. Later, the church expanded the practice of penance to cover venial as well as mortal sins. Medieval penitential handbooks, influenced by Celtic monastic practice, enumerated lengthy lists of graded sins, prescribing specific penances for each sin as a kind of "tariff" for one's transgressions.³⁹ Depending on the sin, the penitential "payment" was as light as saying a single "Our Father" prayer or fasting for a day or two. In other instances, satisfaction could be quite severe. Although the Hollywood stereotype of self-flagellation as the standard medieval penance is accurate only in rare instances, the image evokes the sense of pain and suffering that sometimes did accompany the as-

34. *CCC* 1460.

35. So, for instance, "the glutton fasts, the greedy person gives alms, the slothful person dedicates a certain number of hours to prayer and service of others." Bauerschmidt and Buckley, *Catholic Theology*, 283.

36. Ware, *Orthodox Church*, 297. The final quote is from McGuckin, *Orthodox Church*, 304.

37. *CCC* 2412, 2454, 2487.

38. *GH* 32.7.3.

39. A thorough and balanced study of penance during the later Middle Ages is Thomas N. Tentler, *Sin and Confession on the Eve of the Reformation* (Princeton: Princeton University Press, 1977). Covering the full sweep of Christian history is McNeill, *A History of the Cure of Souls*. A comprehensive, older study of penitential practices is Henry C. Lea, *History of Auricular Confession and Indulgences in the Latin Church*, 3 vols. (Philadelphia: Lea Brothers, 1896).

signed fleshly mortifications of penitential discipline. The medieval practice of labeling the requisite penances as "temporal punishments" could work at cross-purposes with the purificatory and curative intent of satisfaction that was part of its theoretical objective.

So, too, the vision of satisfactional penance as (re)training the sinner in the spiritual disciplines of discipleship could be obscured by medieval penances that had little to do with overcoming the sin(s) in question. Charitable donations or pilgrimages, for instance, could function as redemptive replacements or commutations for lengthier, more rigorous, sin-focused penances. Eventually, these alternatives evolved into the practice of granting papal "indulgences" whereby the temporal punishments due to living sinners (and the dead, who would otherwise have to suffer them in purgatory) could be waived by certain deeds done for the good of the church, including financial contributions. For a price in money or land, the requisite mortifications could even be met by third parties such as willing monks or replaced by priestly masses said on the sinner's behalf.[40] Such possibilities for penance were roundly condemned in the Protestant Reformation, most famously in Martin Luther's "Ninety-Five Theses against Indulgences." On its own initiative, as well as in response to Reformation criticism, the Catholic Church over the centuries reformed and refined its penitential system a number of times to emphasize its higher purposes and spiritual vision. Still, Protestants generally have continued to view the sacrament of penance as too focused on a human contribution to one's salvation, even if synergistically facilitated by the Spirit, and not enough on faith in what are understood to be Christ's unconditional promises of forgiveness.

Latter-day Saint practice with regard to making satisfaction for serious sin tends toward the Catholic and Orthodox end of the spectrum in that it may require the bishop or stake president to temporarily restrict a transgressor's church privileges, such as partaking of the Lord's Supper, or even withdraw the person's membership for a time.[41] The stated justifications for such maximal actions include helping a person "access the redeeming power of Jesus Christ

---

40. For a more recent account of the origin and development of indulgences, see Robert W. Shaffern, *The Penitents' Treasury: Indulgences in Latin Christendom, 1175–1375* (Scranton, PA: University of Scranton Press, 2007). For a documentary history of the doctrines of "satisfaction" and "indulgences," see Paul J. Palmer, ed., *Sacraments and Forgiveness: History and Doctrinal Development of Penance, Extreme Unction, and Indulgences* (Westminster, MD: Newman, 1959).

41. The list of "serious sins" identified in the *General Handbook* includes "violent acts," such as murder and rape, abuse, "sexual immorality," and "fraudulent acts" such as predatory financial behavior. *GH* 32.6.1.1–6.4.3.

through repentance," ensuring "the integrity of the Church," and protecting church members from potentially predatory or harmful behaviors from someone within the church fold.[42] The thinking is that in cases of the most serious sin, even though the objective is always to rehabilitate the sinner, there are additional considerations pertaining to the safety and integrity of the church that shape the sinner's path to forgiveness and reconciliation. The apostle Paul was shocked that the Christian community in Corinth allowed one of their number to remain in the church while having sexual relations with his stepmother. Paul instructed the Corinthians to excommunicate the man and thus "deliver such an one unto Satan for the destruction of the flesh, that the spirit may be saved in the day of the Lord Jesus" (1 Cor. 5:5).[43] In Paul's response, one can glimpse both a pure-body ecclesiological concern for the spiritual integrity of the church and belief that in cases such as this severe measures are necessary to "save" the man's soul. Later, Paul refers to Hymenaeus and Alexander, who made a "shipwreck" of their faith and whom he "delivered unto Satan, that they may learn not to blaspheme" (1 Tim. 1:19–20). Although the New Testament encourages compassionate, fraternal correction of misbehavior, there are instances in which maintenance of the purity of the church, as well as the rehabilitation of serious sinners, seems to have compelled ecclesial actions of distancing or separation that resemble later practices of excommunication/exclusion. In the end, saving souls has always been the *theoretical* objective of penitential practices, be they informal or sacramental, private or ecclesiastical. And most Christians would agree with Latter-day Saints that Martin Luther was right in the very first of his Ninety-Five Theses when he declared that the entire life of the Christian should be one of repentance.

ANOINTING THE SICK

Even the casual reader of the Gospels recognizes that healing the sick was a central part of Christ's earthly ministry. It was also part of what he commis-

---

42. *GH* 32.2.1–3.

43. Several early LDS revelations call for serious transgressors to be delivered to the "buffetings of Satan" (D&C 78:12; 82:21; 104:10; 132:26). The exact meaning of this gloss on Paul's imagery is uncertain, and interpretations have varied over the years. At its core, the imagery seems to depict removal from the saving and protective sphere of the Holy Spirit and the body of Christ and release into the domain of Satan. Viewing the intent of this action as remedial rather than punitive, therefore, would interpret "destruction of the flesh" figuratively and positively as a reference to the sinner purging his life of its carnality and worldliness as he comes to realize the dramatic difference between the former life he enjoyed in the Spirit and in the church and the misery and darkness he now experiences outside the fold, unshielded from the torments and buffetings of Satan.

sioned his apostles to do. Mark 6:13 reports that they "anointed with oil many that were sick, and healed them." Both Catholics and Orthodox celebrate a formal sacrament that entails anointing the sick for their blessing. Other Christians, including Latter-day Saints, practice anointing and praying for the sick, but they do so in less liturgically formal ways and sometimes with different meanings attached.[44] Virtually all, however, ground their actions in Mark 6:13 and especially in James 5:14–15—"Is any sick among you? let him call for the elders of the church; and let them pray over him, anointing him with oil in the name of the Lord: and the prayer of faith shall save the sick, and the Lord shall raise him up; and if he have committed sins, they shall be forgiven him."[45]

Few Christian groups place greater emphasis on or have a more developed doctrine of divine healing than Holiness and Pentecostal churches. Indeed, for them it is one of the pillars of the "full gospel" of Jesus Christ that proclaims him "Savior," "Sanctifier," "Healer," and "Coming King" (Pentecostals add "Spirit Baptizer" as a fifth dimension).[46] As discussed in chapter 7, Holiness and Pentecostal Christians maintain a profound belief in the perpetuation rather than cessation of the apostolic gifts of the Spirit, prominent among which is the gift of healing. Historically, Pentecostals have cast their affirmation of spiritual giftedness in an eschatological context, following Peter's use of Joel 2:28 to explain the dramatic outpouring of the Spirit in his day: "And it shall come to pass in the last days, saith God, I will pour out of my Spirit upon all flesh: and your sons and your daughters shall prophesy, and your young men shall see visions, and your old men shall dream dreams" (Acts 2:17). Early Pentecostals also cited another passage in Joel (Joel 2:23) that mentioned the Levantine harvest-related "latter rain" and invoked it as an appropriate image of the extraordinary outbreak of spiritual gifts that occurred at the turn of the twentieth century. This promised "second Pentecost" was to be even more pronounced than the "early rain" depicted in Acts 2.[47] In particular, the latter-day

44. For a broad overview, see Amanda Porterfield, *Healing in the History of Christianity* (New York: Oxford University Press, 2005).

45. Some traditions also link their ministry to the sick to Mark 6:13—"And they . . . anointed with oil many that were sick, and healed them."

46. For an extended scriptural discussion, see "The Doctrine of Divine Healing," in Guy P. Duffield and Nathaniel M. Van Cleave, *Foundations of Pentecostal Theology* (Los Angeles: L.I.F.E. Bible College, 1983), 359–416. For broad but succinct overviews of theory, history, and practice, see Kimberly Ervin Alexander, "Divine Healing: Sacramental Signs of Salvation," in *The Routledge Handbook of Pentecostal Theology*, ed. Wolfgang Vondey (London: Routledge, 2020), 257–67, and the *Dictionary of Pentecostal and Charismatic Movements*, ed. Stanley M. Burgess and Gary B. McGee (Grand Rapids: Zondervan, 1988), s.v. "gift of healing" and "healing movements" (350–74).

47. See D. William Faupel, *The Everlasting Gospel: The Significance of Eschatology in the*

"charismatic renewal of the church is strikingly signified for Pentecostals in divine healing," and "divine healing of the body is cherished globally among Pentecostal churches as vital to the blessings available in Christ."[48]

Among the "spiritual gifts" that the apostle Paul famously listed in 1 Corinthians 12 are the "gifts of healing" (1 Cor. 12:9, 28, 30). Doctrine and Covenants 46 affirmingly recapitulates the catalogue of charismata in 1 Corinthians 12 and parses "gifts of healing" as the gift of "faith to heal" and the gift of "faith to be healed" (D&C 46:20, 19). Arguably one of the most extensive and notable examples of healing in the early history of the Church of Jesus Christ of Latter-day Saints occurred in summer 1839. After being forcibly driven from their homes in a variety of locations, the Saints had settled in Illinois, along the Mississippi River at a place they eventually called "Nauvoo," which they understood as a Hebrew word for "beautiful." The place, however, was not so beautiful in the summer of 1839. Malarial fever (at the time called "ague") had seized many of the recently arrived Mormon refugees, and the situation was critical. Joseph Smith responded with a healing crusade that would live in Latter-day Saint memory for years. Smith's associate Wilford Woodruff recounted: "The power of God rested upon [Joseph] mightily, and as Jesus healed all the sick around Him in His day, so Joseph, the Prophet of God, healed all around on this occasion. . . . He commanded them in a loud voice, in the name of Jesus Christ, to come up and be made whole, and they were all healed."[49] Especially noteworthy here and in other early LDS accounts of healings is the biblical mimesis (imitation). New Testament healings are replicated both in word and deed. The Woodruff account even has Smith imitating Paul's sending out handkerchiefs to heal the sick (cf. Acts 19:11–12). It is a striking example of the organic relationship between biblical primitivism and early Mormon charismata.[50]

Development of Pentecostal Thought (Sheffield: Sheffield Academic Press, 1996). The "early" and "latter rain" are mentioned in James 5:7; Deut. 11:14.

48. Frank D. Macchia, "Pentecostal and Charismatic Theology," in *Oxford Handbook of Eschatology*, ed. Jerry L. Walls (New York: Oxford University Press, 2008), 290, 286. A classic scholarly recounting of Pentecostal healing ministries in the latter half of the twentieth century is David E. Harrell, *All Things Are Possible: The Healing and Charismatic Revivals in Modern America* (Bloomington: Indiana University Press, 1975).

49. The Woodruff account is reprinted in Grant Underwood, "Supernaturalism and Healing in the Church of Jesus Christ of Latter-day Saints," in *Religions of the United States in Practice*, ed. Colleen McDannell, 2 vols. (Princeton: Princeton University Press, 2001), 1:308–9. For additional examples of healings and discussion of the healing ministry among early Latter-day Saints, see 299–307.

50. Some Pentecostals similarly use "prayer cloths" or "anointed cloths" in their healing ministry. See J. Christopher Thomas, "Toward a Pentecostal Theology of Anointed Cloths,"

Administering to the sick was something done by women as well as men from early in the church's history until several decades into the twentieth century.[51] In his day, Joseph Smith spoke to a group of church women and emphasized that the "signs following faith" mentioned in Mark 16:17–18 "should follow all that believe whether male or female." Smith asked the women "if they could not see by this sweeping stroke" that they, too, were empowered to heal the sick. He said "there could be no more sin in any female laying hands on the sick than in wetting the face with water—that it is no sin for any body to do it that has faith."[52] Apostle Orson Pratt expounded Smith's perspective with regard to Mark 16: "It seems that the gifts here named are general gifts, intended more or less for the whole Church; not only for those in the Priesthood, but for those out of the Priesthood, for males and for females. For instance, children are often taken sick, and it is the privilege of their parents, whether they have the Priesthood or not, by virtue of this promise, to lay their hands on their sick children, and ask the Lord, in the name of Jesus, to heal them." Pratt reported that this practice was quite common in his nineteenth-century experience: "How many scores and scores of cases have there been in this Church every year since it was organized, where . . . [parents'] children have been healed through the laying on of their hands."[53]

Such experiences with healing receded into the background in the twentieth century as renewed emphasis was placed on the sacrament of administering to the sick performed by the ordained ministry.[54] This ordinance had been in place from the outset, alongside a gifts-of-the-Spirit approach to healing.

---

in *Toward a Pentecostal Theology of Worship*, ed. Lee Roy Martin (Cleveland, TN: CPT Press, 2016), 89–112.

51. As illustrated in *The First Fifty Years of Relief Society: Key Documents in Latter-day Saint Women's History*, ed. Jill Mulvay Derr et al. (Salt Lake City: Church Historian's Press, 2016), passim, and Jill Mulvay Derr, Janath Russell Cannon, and Maureen Ursenbach Beecher, *Women of Covenant: The Story of Relief Society* (Salt Lake City: Deseret Book, 1992), passim.

52. Minutes, "Female Relief Society of Nauvoo," April 28, 1842, in *The First Fifty Years of Relief Society*, 55. Nor do Mormons limit the power of the prayer of faith to Latter-day Saints alone. They recognize that people of faith in many churches experience God's healing power. The Book of Mormon declares that God "manifesteth himself unto all those who believe in him, by the power of the Holy Ghost; yea, unto every nation, kindred, tongue, and people, working mighty miracles . . . among the children of men according to their faith" (2 Nephi 26:13).

53. *Journal of Discourses*, 16:289.

54. Alexander, *Mormonism in Transition*, 291–93; Derr et al., *Women of Covenant*, 219–22, 428–32; Derr et al., *The First Fifty Years*, xxiii–xxv.

An 1831 revelation, glossing James 5:14, directed that "the elders of the church, two or more, shall be called, and shall pray for and lay their hands upon [the sick] in my name . . . [and] it shall come to pass that he that hath faith in me to be healed, and is not appointed unto death, shall be healed" (D&C 42:44, 48).[55] Although this revelation does not explicitly mention anointing with oil, as referenced in James, within a few years the practice became common.[56] Latter-day Saints use olive oil, as do Catholics and Orthodox, but they do not mix it with balsam or aromatic spices and herbs. Mormon ministers consecrate the oil prior to using it in the anointing. In Orthodoxy, oil is blessed at the beginning of the sacrament by a set liturgical prayer. Catholics also use a pre-scribed prayer of consecration in which the oil is "duly blessed" by the "bishop, or if necessary, by the celebrating presbyter himself."[57] In the Church of Jesus Christ of Latter-day Saints, anyone ordained to the Melchizedek priesthood (see chapter 8) may consecrate oil. The minister does so by a simple ceremony in which he "holds an open container of olive oil, addresses Heavenly Father as in prayer, states that he is acting by the authority of the Melchizedek Priest-hood," declares that by this action he is consecrating the oil "for anointing and blessing the sick and afflicted," and "closes in the name of Jesus Christ."[58]

In contrast to Catholic presbyters who anoint the forehead and hands with oil and Orthodox priests who anoint all the sensory parts of the body, Mormon elders are instructed to put only "a drop of consecrated oil on the person's head."[59] The actual Latter-day Saint liturgy of administering to the sick is sim-

55. As mentioned in this revelation and suggested by the plural form used in James 5, it became customary in LDS practice to have at least two elders administer to the sick. Current church policy, however, does allow for performance of the ordinance by a single elder. *GH* 18.13.1.

56. See, for instance, *JSP*, D4:165; D6:534 (this reference specifically mentions anointing with oil in conjunction with the Nauvoo healings discussed above); D7:368; H1:135; J1:112, 122. Still, some early Mormon elders had to be reminded of the importance of the anoint-ing. "When a man whose faith is right goes forth to administer to the sick," explained First Presidency member Jedediah Grant (1816–1856) in 1855, "he will anoint with oil, as well as lay on his hands and pray." Grant then added with characteristic satire, "Unless you anoint with oil, your prayers will not rise higher than the fog." *Journal of Discourses*, 2:276–77. The need for such reminders passed with time. Today, the normativity of anointing with oil is so firmly established that the current necessity is to allow for exceptions: "If consecrated oil is not available, a blessing may be given by the authority of the Melchizedek Priesthood without an anointing." *GH* 18.13.

57. *CCC* 1530.

58. *GH* 18.12.2.

59. *GH* 18.13.2. In times past, a more ample application of oil was made and sometimes on the afflicted part of the body.

ple, hardly even a liturgy. The elders place their hands on the sick person's head, call the individual by name, declare their priestly authority and representation of Christ, and announce that the oil with which they then anoint the individual's head has been specially consecrated for blessing the sick and afflicted. In a second part of the ordinance, hands are again laid on the sick person's head, and the elder who acts as voice "states that he is sealing the anointing by the authority of the Melchizedek priesthood." This verbal expression is a symbolic gesture designed to impress on the mind of the recipient that the efficacy of the anointing is certain and sure. The pronouncement is followed by "words of blessing as guided by the Spirit." The blessing is given extemporaneously and is specific to the person receiving the anointing and blessing.[60]

In Catholicism, the celebration of the sacrament begins with a Liturgy of the Word designed to "awaken the faith of the sick person and of the community to ask the Lord for the strength of his Spirit." Then, "in silence," the priests of the church lay hands on the sick and "pray over them in the faith of the Church" as an "epiclesis [petition] proper to this sacrament." Following the prayer in faith, the priest anoints the infirm with blessed olive oil.[61] In Orthodoxy, holy unction (anointing), the mystery or sacrament of healing, is sometimes known as "the seven anointings" because in its ideal form seven priests participate (although as few as one may celebrate the sacrament if need be). As designated in the rite, each priest anoints a part of the body with a cross until there have been seven anointings with the same prayer being said while each anointing takes place.[62] Prior to this, as with the Liturgy of the Word that precedes the anointing in the Roman rite, the anointings and prayers in Orthodoxy are preceded by seven other prayers, seven set readings from the Epistles, and seven designated excerpts from the Gospels "that open out the mystery of Christ's healing grace among his faithful."[63]

Such practices obviously differ from the ritually sparse procedures of the LDS ordinance of administering to the sick. Another contrast, conceptual in nature, is that both Eastern and Western rites emphasize the community dimension of the sacrament more than do Mormons, for whom the ordinance is typically a private or family matter. In the Catholic view, the sacrament is a "communal celebration," in which the "whole ecclesial community is invited to surround

---

60. *GH* 18.13.2.
61. *CCC* 1518–1519.
62. See Metrophanes Critopoulos, "Confession of Faith" (1625), 13.1–5, in *Creeds & Confessions*, 1:528–30.
63. McGuckin, *Orthodox Church*, 308.

the sick in a special way through their prayers and fraternal attention."⁶⁴ The 1972 post–Vatican II revision of the *Ordo Unctionis Infirmorum* ("Order/Rite of Anointing the Sick") "highlights the fact that it is an ecclesial sacrament and should be celebrated as an act of the church" and "asks for at least a minimal gathering of the faithful around the sick person."⁶⁵ Similarly, Orthodoxy desires that the unction be "communally experienced" so that the sacrament "moves outwards far beyond the sick person who is at the centre of the anointings to embrace and comfort also those who are wounded by the suffering of their loved one."⁶⁶ The communal element in the Church of Jesus Christ of Latter-day Saints is that congregational prayers will sometimes, and personal and family prayers will often, include petitions on behalf of those who are ill or afflicted among them. Such prayers, however, are viewed as acts of general Christian compassion, not as part of the ordinance of administering to the sick.

Also noteworthy is that Latter-day Saints do not emphasize the link between healing and forgiveness mentioned in James. Regarding the relationship between sin and sickness, the Catholic position is that "in the Church's Sacrament of Anointing of the Sick, through the ministry of the priest, it is Jesus who touches the sick to heal them from sin—and sometimes even from physical ailment. . . . The primary effect of the Sacrament is a spiritual healing."⁶⁷ Mormon belief tends to reverse that order. The LDS ordinance is primarily designed to heal from physical ailment and *sometimes* from sin. First Presidency member George Cannon referenced the famous incident in which Christ forgave the paralytic's sins and then healed him (Mark 2:1–12), and asked, "Does it follow, because of . . . this act of our Savior's, that we should set forth that our sins will be forgiven by having hands laid upon us by the Elders when we are sick? However true it may be that sins are forgiven under such circumstances, it is not for the forgiveness of sins that that ordinance was instituted. It was for the healing of the sick."⁶⁸ Still, considering the ordinance from a different perspective, church leaders have not demurred from suggesting that penitent preparation to receive the anointing of the sick *may* lead to a forgiveness of sin. Bruce McConkie explained, "The person who by

64. CCC 1517.

65. David N. Power, "Anointing of the Sick," in Fiorenza and Galvin, *Systematic Theology*, 560.

66. McGuckin, *Orthodox Church*, 307.

67. United States Conference of Catholic Bishops, "Anointing of the Sick," https://www.usccb.org/prayer-and-worship/sacraments-and-sacramentals/anointing-of-the-sick.

68. Jerreld L. Newquist, ed., *Gospel Truth: Discourses and Writings of President George Q. Cannon*, 2 vols. (Salt Lake City: Deseret Book, 1974), 2:153.

faith, devotion, righteousness, and personal worthiness, is in a position to be healed, is also in a position to have the justifying approval of the Spirit for his course of life, and his sins are forgiven him, as witnessed by the fact that he receives the companionship of the Spirit, which he could not have if he were unworthy."[69]

In the Roman Catholic and Orthodox churches, the sacrament of anointing gradually evolved from a response to ordinary sickness, which it still is in the Church of Jesus Christ of Latter-day Saints, to one reserved largely for life-threatening maladies. Particularly in the West, it became a last-rites ritual, "one intended to heal the soul from sin in preparation for death."[70] Hence, the sacrament's older, alternative designation of "extreme [last] unction." Both the term and the liturgical evolution it signifies were firmly in place by the Middle Ages. Subsequently, it was reinforced by the Council of Trent in its reaction to Protestant rejection of anointing of the sick as a sacrament (although not as a pious custom). The East, however, took longer to move in this direction and never did so to the exclusion of earlier practices. As late as the seventeenth century, an Orthodox confession stated, "We call this 'holy unction' not 'extreme unction,' for we do not wait till the sick man is dying and only then give it to him. But we use this sacrament, or sacramental rite, while we still have good hope for his recovery, and we pray God to heal him and deliver him quickly from his sickness." In this way, "it is possible to use this sacrament many times during a man's life, and not just once, just as we use a doctor's medicines whenever we are ill."[71] Ultimately, in both traditions the unction came to be viewed primarily as a sacrament for the seriously ill. A summary description of Eastern practice is that "the mystery of holy anointing (Greek: *euchelaion*, or 'prayer of the oil') is celebrated whenever an Orthodox Christian is seriously ill, mentally or physically."[72] In the West, although post–Vatican II reforms have endeavored to reclaim something of the earlier vision for the rite, official policy still states that "the sacrament of Anointing of the Sick has as its purpose the conferral of a special grace on the Christian experiencing the difficulties inherent in the condition of grave illness or old age. The proper time for receiving this holy anointing has certainly arrived when the believer begins to be in danger of death because of illness or old age."[73]

---

69. McConkie, *Mormon Doctrine*, 2nd ed., 297–98.
70. Bauerschmidt and Buckley, *Catholic Theology*, 285.
71. Critopoulos, "Confession of Faith," 13.5, in *Creeds & Confessions*, 2:530.
72. McGuckin, *Orthodox Church*, 306.
73. *CCC* 1527–1528.

Anointing and blessing practices in the Church of Jesus Christ of Latter-day Saints have also evolved, but not toward an end-of-life ordinance. Part of the evolution in Mormon practice is a result of medical advances in the past century and a half. The Latter-day Saint vision has come to be that professional medical care and priestly administrations to the sick are not antithetical. "Latter-day Saints believe in applying the best available scientific knowledge and techniques," explained Dallin Oaks. "We enlist the help of healing practitioners, such as physicians and surgeons, to restore health. The use of medical science is not at odds with our prayers of faith and our reliance on priesthood blessings."[74] Since many, even most, physical distresses today can be solved by medicine and the assistance of health-care professionals, it is logical that a broader vision of what is accomplished in the anointing of the sick has come to be articulated across Christian traditions. Defeating disease, conquering sickness, and overcoming physical ailment are viewed as only a part, and perhaps not the essential part, of the grace God bestows in the sacrament of administering to the sick. Oaks characterized God's actions in this way: "Healing blessings come in many ways, each suited to our individual needs. . . . Sometimes a 'healing' cures our illness or lifts our burden. But sometimes we are 'healed' by being given strength or understanding or patience to bear the burdens placed upon us. . . . The healing power of the Lord Jesus Christ—whether it removes our burdens or strengthens us to endure and live with them like the Apostle Paul—is available for every affliction in mortality."[75]

Orthodox doctrine also acknowledges that "a dramatic physical healing may not always occur, though it often does; but this is only one of the multitude of ways that this sacrament unfailingly confers the joy of the Lord, for the deep consolation of the sick person."[76] In fact, as the Catholic *Catechism* puts it, the restoration to health only occurs "if it is conducive to the salvation of [the] soul."[77] The apostle Paul, himself a great healer, could not be healed of his "thorn in the flesh," even though he "besought the Lord thrice, that it might depart from [him]." Instead, God replied, "My grace is sufficient for thee: for my strength is made perfect in weakness. Most gladly therefore," concluded Paul, "will I rather glory in my infirmities, that the power of Christ may rest upon me" (2 Cor. 12:7–9). Emphasizes the *Catechism*: "The first grace of this sacrament is one of strengthening, peace and courage to overcome the difficul-

74. Dallin H. Oaks, "He Heals the Heavy Laden," *Ensign*, November 2006, 7–8.
75. Dallin H. Oaks, "Healing the Sick," *Ensign*, May 2010, 47.
76. McGuckin, *Orthodox Church*, 306.
77. *CCC* 1505, 1532.

ties that go with the condition of serious illness or the frailty of old age. . . . This assistance from the Lord by the power of his Spirit is meant to lead the sick person to healing of the soul, but also of the body if such is God's will."[78]

Latter-day Saints concur that the will of God is the key component in any divine healing. Dallin Oaks clarified that even "in a circumstance where there is sufficient faith to be healed," the elders "cannot give a priesthood blessing that will cause a person to be healed if that healing is not the will of the Lord."[79] Conversely, revelation assures that "it shall come to pass that he that hath faith in me to be healed, and is not appointed unto death, shall be healed" (D&C 42:48). The Lord's appointing will is the crucial factor. "All too often," remarked one general authority, "we overlook the qualifying phrase 'and is not appointed unto death' (or, we might add, 'unto sickness or handicap')."[80] In the blessing, which typically takes up most of the time involved in the administration (the anointing and "sealing" of the anointing occupy only a minute or two), the officiator may offer words of comfort, consolation, and counsel. He may even speak a prophetic word of healing. But his words are only supplementary to the actions of anointing and sealing the anointing. "The words spoken in a healing blessing," explained Oaks, "are not essential to its healing effect. If faith is sufficient and if the Lord wills it, the afflicted person will be healed or blessed whether the officiator speaks those words or not. Conversely, if the officiator yields to personal desire or inexperience and gives commands or words of blessing in excess of what the Lord chooses to bestow according to the faith of the individual, those words will not be fulfilled." To be sure, acknowledged Oaks, "the words spoken in a healing blessing can edify and energize the faith of those who hear them, but the effect of the blessing is dependent upon faith and the Lord's will, not upon the words spoken by the elder who officiated."[81]

In sum, all Christian organizations and individuals that offer healing ministries have had to develop a theology of healing that does not guarantee restoration of health and that offers a broader vision of what God is doing through such a sacrament.[82] President Spencer Kimball remarked that "being

---

78. *CCC* 1520.
79. Oaks, "Healing the Sick," 49.
80. Lance Wickman, "But If Not," *Ensign*, November 2002, 30.
81. Oaks, "Healing the Sick," 49–50.
82. Published treatments extend beyond the confines of academic theology to address popular interest in the subject. See, for instance, Glen Berteau, *Why Am I Not Healed? (When God Promised)* (Grand Rapids: Chosen Books, 2020), and Mark Pearson, *Christian Healing: A Practical & Comprehensive Guide* (Lake Mary, FL: Charisma House, 2004). See

human, we would expel from our lives physical pain and mental anguish and assure ourselves of continual ease and comfort, but if we were to close the doors upon sorrow and distress, we might be excluding our greatest friends and benefactors. Suffering can make saints of people as they learn patience, long-suffering, and self-mastery."[83] Or as the Catholic *Catechism* expresses it, suffering can "configure us to [Christ] and unite us with his redemptive Passion."[84] Moreover, Paul encouraged his followers to focus on the bigger picture of the eternal benefit of enduring well their unhealed infirmities: "For our light affliction, which is but for a moment, worketh for us a far more exceeding and eternal weight of glory" (2 Cor. 4:17). Similarly, Joseph Smith heard the word of the Lord thus: "My son, peace be unto thy soul; thine adversity and thine afflictions shall be but a small moment. And then, if thou endure it well, God shall exalt thee on high" (D&C 121:7–8). Perhaps no liturgy more eloquently captures this broader vision than the Orthodox prayer used to consecrate the oil: "May this oil, O Lord, be an oil of gladness, an oil of sanctification, a royal vestment, a powerful breastplate, a protection against every work of the devil, an inviolable seal, joy of heart, and everlasting delight, so that all who are anointed with this oil of regeneration may become mighty against their enemies and shine brightly with the radiance of your Saints, and be without spot or wrinkle, and that they may be received into your eternal rest and win the prize of their high calling."[85]

Matrimony

Of the seven sacraments, the final two are holy orders (ordination to the ministerial priesthood) and matrimony. Because priestly ordination is discussed in chapter 8, this section will focus on matrimony. The Catholic *Catechism* expresses well what many Christian traditions consider to be the fundamental importance of matrimony: "The intimate community of life and love which constitutes the married state has been established by the Creator and endowed by him with its own proper laws. . . . Although the dignity of this institution is not transparent everywhere with the same clarity, some sense of the greatness of the matrimonial union exists in all cultures. The well-being of the individual

---

also the reprinted classic *Healing the Sick*, by T. L. Osborn (Shippensburg, PA: Harrison House, 2022).

83. Spencer W. Kimball, *Faith Precedes the Miracle* (Salt Lake City: Deseret Book, 1973), 97–98.

84. CCC 1505.

85. Quoted in McGuckin, *Orthodox Church*, 308.

person and of both human and Christian society is closely bound up with the healthy state of conjugal and family life."[86] From the creation command for man and woman to become "one flesh" (Gen. 2:24) to Scripture's many figurative references to God's relationship with his people as a marriage (e.g., Eph. 5), most biblical writings endorse the institution of marriage. LDS scripture is no different. An early revelation stated clearly: "Whoso forbiddeth to marry is not ordained of God, for marriage is ordained of God unto man" (D&C 49:15).[87] And Jesus personally sanctioned marriage both in word (Mark 10/Matt. 19) and in deed (at the wedding at Cana—John 2).

To be sure, some interpreters find Jesus's views on marriage ambivalent. While the statements above demonstrate clear support for marriage, there are also warnings about privileging conjugal and kinship ties above commitment to the kingdom (e.g., Matt. 10:35–38), and there is no record of Jesus himself having married. Likewise, the apostle Paul is thought to have been ambivalent about marriage. First Corinthians 7 has proven notoriously difficult to interpret, but the majority view is that Paul here equivocates about marriage. In the latter part of the chapter, "despite the examples of married couples [serving] as missionary apostles in the early Christian movement, such as his coworkers Prisca and Aquila, Paul argues that commitment to the work of mission favors" ascetic celibacy.[88] It is noteworthy that Joseph Smith included a similar interpretation in his emendation of 1 Corinthians 7. His amplification (in italics) of verse 29 reads: "But *I speak unto you who are called to the ministry. For* this I say, brethren, the time *that remaineth* is *but* short, *that ye shall be sent forth unto the ministry.*" Smith also intensified the contrast in verses 32–33 between the married missionary and the one who is celibate: "*I would, brethren, that ye magnify your calling.* I would have you without carefulness. For he who is unmarried, careth for the things that belong to the Lord, how he may please the Lord; *therefore he prevaileth.* But he who is married, careth for the things that are of the world, how he may please his wife; *therefore there is a difference, for he is hindered.*"[89] In Smith's rendering, missionary service is assumed to be

86. *CCC* 1603. For more on Catholic views on marriage, see Walter Kasper, *Theology of Christian Marriage* (New York: Crossroad, 1985), and Michael G. Lawler, *Marriage and Sacrament: A Theology of Christian Marriage* (Collegeville, MN: Liturgical Press, 1993).

87. This revelation addressed the beliefs and practices of the nineteenth-century religious group popularly known as "Shakers." The quoted passage has the Shaker insistence on celibacy in view.

88. Francis Schüssler Fiorenza, "Marriage," in Fiorenza and Galvin, *Systematic Theology*, 590.

89. *NTOB*, 503.

an occasional and temporary condition most effectively performed in a state of de facto celibacy. In contrast, marriage is understood to be the default and normal circumstance for men and women. Married Mormon couples have labored as missionaries on occasion in the past but increasingly have done so in recent decades as retirees have been recruited to serve. Still, the majority of LDS missionaries throughout the church's history have either been single or have served "celibately" without their spouse.

Marriage, of course, in one form or another, existed long before the birth of Christianity, and the church did not immediately consider it a sacrament. Indeed, early theologians often celebrated the spiritual superiority of ascetic, celibate singleness over the marriage state. Gradually, though, as the church became more involved with performing and regulating marriages, matrimony took on a more sacred character, and a corresponding theology of marriage developed.[90] Early on, the apostle Paul, citing Genesis 2:24, referred to the oneness of marriage as "a great *mysterion*" (Eph. 5:31–32). Later, the influential Vulgate version translated *mysterion* as *sacramentum* rather than *mysterium* (the other common Latin rendering for *mysterion*). This both reflected and reinforced the emerging sacramental character of marriage in the Christian West. In the Greek-speaking East, where the sacraments have always been referred to as "*mysteria*," marriage was viewed sacramentally (and less equivocally) at an earlier date. In Orthodoxy "there is no question of opposing a 'higher' vocation to a 'lower' one. Both monastic and married life are paths of living out the gospel."[91] Thus, Orthodox priests may be married, although they must do so before entering a priestly order. As a sacrament, marriage in East and West alike is understood to be both a sign and a conduit of grace. As a sign, marriage was (and is) thought to signify and mirror the loving union of Christ and the church. The grace of matrimony, as well expressed in the Catholic *Catechism*, "perfects the human love of the spouses, strengthens their indissoluble unity, and sanctifies them on the way to eternal life."[92] Orthodoxy

---

90. By the twelfth century, matrimony was officially designated in the West as one of the seven sacraments. An overview of this history is Jean Evanou, "Marriage," in Martimort, *The Sacraments*, 185–208. A more detailed account is John Witte Jr., *From Sacrament to Contract: Marriage, Religion, and Law in the Western Tradition*, 2nd ed. (Louisville: Westminster John Knox, 2012), which focuses on the historical interplay between different Christian perspectives and Western law.

91. Michael Plekon, "The Russian Religious Revival and Its Theological Legacy," in *Cambridge Companion to Orthodox Christian Theology*, ed. Mary B. Cunningham and Elizabeth Theokritoff (Cambridge: Cambridge University Press, 2008), 210.

92. *CCC* 1661. See also *CCC* 1641, 1648.

maintains a similar understanding of this sacramental bestowal of grace as the Holy Spirit's empowering presence, and the Orthodox marriage service symbolizes it by incorporating a crowning or coronation ceremony in which crowns of leaves and flowers or silver and gold are placed on the heads of the bride and bridegroom.[93]

Although Reformers tended to reject the traditional view of matrimony as a sacrament, many Protestant churches today "retain what may be characterized as an implicit sacramentality" regarding marriage. As a consequence, the shared "convictions about marriage among Catholic, Orthodox, and Protestant churches" are "more striking than the differences separating them over its formal sacramental status."[94] This also holds true for the Church of Jesus Christ of Latter-day Saints, even though it distinguishes between civil marriages and "temple marriage sealings." The church allows civil marriages and authorizes its clergy to perform them, but it does not consider them sacramental. A temple marriage sealing, however, is considered a sacrament or sacred ordinance. A temple marriage, as the name suggests, is performed only in Latter-day Saint temples. The key distinction between the two forms of matrimony recognized by the church is that Mormons believe that through marriages performed in one of their temples, a couple is sacramentally "sealed" together not only for the duration of earth life but everlastingly. For this reason, the temple marriage sealing is also known as "eternal marriage" or "celestial marriage."[95] The official LDS position is that "a temple sealing joins a husband and wife together for time and all eternity. Couples who are sealed in the temple are promised glory and joy throughout eternity." Latter-day Saints believe "they will receive these blessings if they are faithful to the covenants they make in the temple."[96] A temple marriage sealing is so important in the Mormon worldview that LDS scripture even states that "in the celestial glory there are three heavens

---

93. Ware, *Orthodox Church*, 301. Frederica Mathewes-Green, *An Introduction to Eastern Christianity* (Brewster, MA: Paraclete, 2015), 307–18, offers more detail on the Orthodox marriage ceremony, and the Orthodox vision of marriage in general is eloquently presented in McGuckin, *Orthodox Church*, 309–23.

94. Brent Waters, "Marriage," in *OHST*, 522, 523.

95. Usage patterns for these terms in general conference and church literature have varied over the years. In the nineteenth century, "celestial marriage" was the common designation. "Eternal marriage" was used on occasion but did not become prevalent until the twentieth century. In one of history's many small ironies, the now dominant term "temple marriage" was largely unknown in the nineteenth century, whereas today, of the three terms, "celestial marriage" is the least commonly used. See "LDS General Conference Corpus," https://www.lds-general-conference.org/.

96. *GH* 27.3.

or degrees, and in order to obtain the highest a [couple] must enter into . . . the new and everlasting covenant of [temple] marriage" (D&C 130:1–2).[97]

Originally, the new and everlasting covenant of marriage was understood to include polygamous or plural marriages. Monogamy has been the historic norm for God's people, and this is reflected in the Book of Mormon statement "there shall not any man among you have save it be one wife" (Jacob 2:27). Under certain circumstances, however, God is believed to make Abraham-like exceptions: "If I will, saith the Lord of Hosts, raise up seed unto me, I will command my people; otherwise they shall hearken unto these things" (Jacob 2:30). Joseph Smith believed he had received such an exceptional command and expounded it in a revelation dictated in 1843 (D&C 132). The revelation notes that God covenanted with Abraham that his posterity would be as innumerable as the stars, and Joseph Smith is told: "This promise is yours also, because ye are of Abraham, and the promise was made unto Abraham; and by this law [of plural marriage] is the continuation of the works of my Father, wherein he glorifieth himself. Go ye, therefore, and do the works of Abraham; enter ye into my law" (D&C 132:31–32).[98]

Doctrine and Covenants 132 stresses that plural marriage is to occur only by divine "revelation and commandment" and characterizes it as "most holy." Smith introduced this "patriarchal order of matrimony" to only a handful of his most faithful followers before his untimely death in 1844. After Smith's death, Brigham Young and the other apostles soon extended the possibility of plural marriage to all worthy and willing church members. For a variety of reasons, most did not avail themselves of the "opportunity." Nonetheless, for decades in the nineteenth century in the face of systematic legal and political opposition, most monogamous Latter-day Saints defended the practice as vigorously as their polygamous counterparts. Plural marriage, or "the Principle," as it was often called, became the key public symbol of Mormonism in the second half of the nineteenth century.[99] By the late 1880s, facing

97. Prior to the revelation that introduced eternal, temple marriage, the phrase "new and everlasting covenant" was commonly used to refer to what Latter-day Saints call the "restored" gospel of Jesus Christ. See, for instance, *JSP*, J1:72–73, 81, 105, 187, and D&C 66:2. It was considered "new" because it had been revealed anew, and it was "everlasting" because Latter-day Saints believe it was the same covenant of salvation God had made with humanity in all ages. The "new and everlasting covenant" of eternal marriage may be considered a subset of this broader covenant.

98. The word "law" is used in several ways in this revelation. In some contexts, it refers to the "law" of plural marriage. In addition to the passage quoted above, see also vv. 1–3, 61–62, 64–66.

99. LDS plural marriage is a topic of perennial interest, and a voluminous scholarly literature on the subject attests to this fact. Two widely respected monographs offer a reliable

political disenfranchisement and escheatment of church property, Latter-day Saint leaders felt compelled to curtail the practice. Revelation confirmed that monogamy was again to be the marital norm. By the second decade of the twentieth century, entering into a new plural marriage warranted excommunication from the church, and church leaders redefined "celestial marriage" to exclude polygamy.[100]

Civil marriages, even those performed by a Latter-day Saint minister, are described thus in revelation: "If a man marry him a wife in the world [civilly] . . . their covenant and marriage are not of force when they are dead. . . . Therefore, when they are out of the world they neither marry nor are given in marriage; but are appointed angels in heaven, which angels are ministering servants, to minister for those who are worthy of a far more, and an exceeding, and an eternal weight of glory" (D&C 132:15–16). This passage echoes the Gospels' account of Jesus's response to the Sadducees' question about whose wife the seven-time widow would be in heaven. Christ answered, "In the resurrection they neither marry, nor are given in marriage, but are as the angels of God in heaven" (Matt. 22:30/cf. Mark 12:25). The traditional Christian interpretation of this text is that no marriage relationship will continue beyond the grave. This has prompted a variety of related questions: Will there be no marrying in heaven because the resurrected body will be spiritual in nature? If it is material, will it be devoid of sexual organs? Will maleness and femaleness be done away with altogether?[101] Latter-day Saints, however, believe that Jesus's

---

entrée into the subject: Kathryn M. Daynes, *More Wives Than One* (Urbana: University of Illinois Press, 2008), and B. Carmon Hardy, *Solemn Covenant: The Mormon Polygamous Passage* (Urbana: University of Illinois Press, 1992). Through much of the twentieth century and into the twenty-first, LDS sensitivities surrounding plural marriage prevented it from being extensively discussed in official church venues. This changed rather dramatically in the 2010s, when the church published several candid and detailed discussions of the topic on its website. See "Plural Marriage in the Church of Jesus Christ of Latter-day Saints," https://www.churchofjesuschrist.org/study/manual/gospel-topics-essays /plural-marriage-in-the-church-of-jesus-christ-of-latter-day-saints?lang=eng.

100. An "official statement" from the First Presidency in 1933 summarized the new usage: "Celestial marriage—*that is*, marriage for time and eternity—and polygamous or plural marriage are not synonymous terms. Monogamous marriages for time and eternity, solemnized in our temples in accordance with the word of the Lord and the laws of the Church, *are* celestial marriages." "Church Section," *Deseret News*, June 17, 1933 (emphasis added).

101. Early Christian consideration of such questions is explored in Taylor G. Petrey, *Resurrecting Parts: Early Christians on Desire, Reproduction, and Sexual Difference* (New York: Routledge, 2016). Latter-day Saints join a minority of Christians who envision the perpetuation of sexual difference in the next life.

point in this passage was that marriages will not be *performed* in the next life, not that they will not exist.[102] Despite the LDS Church's emphasis on eternal marriage, civil marriages per se are not disparaged. "Marriages performed under the civic law and by ministers of other denominations are regarded as honorable and effectual so far as relates to this life," declared the First Presidency, "but in order to be effectual in the life to come such covenants must be made for eternity, such unions must be formed according to God's law and under his authority, or they will have no force or effect hereafter."[103] In sum, Mormon doctrine holds that worthy temple marriages *may* perdure into the next life, but civil marriages will not. This understanding also opens the door to the LDS practice of proxy temple marriage sealings for one's ancestors as part of the church's doctrine of "salvation for the dead" (see chapter 12).

Whatever may be the best interpretation of Jesus's reply to the Sadducees, the idea that social and kin relationships will continue in the next life has a long history in Christianity. Indeed, the expectation of a happy and lasting reunion with loved ones in heaven has been a perennial human hope. Historians of Christian eschatology have found that notions of the eternal perpetuation of marital and familial love and relationships have often coexisted with, and at times even overshadowed, classical ideas of the beatific vision and a "theocentric" heaven.[104] Eastern Orthodoxy, for instance, "has no belief corresponding to that sometimes heard in Western wedding rituals: 'Until death do you part.' Marriage is a mystery [sacrament] of the kingdom. . . . It may begin in time, but it will not end in our chronological age, for the relationship it initiates passes on as a fundamental part of the eschatological joy of the Kingdom."[105] Orthodoxy considers the traditional Western interpretation of Christ's answer to the Sadducees' question "fundamentally misguided." Although Orthodox see the mystery of marriage as symbolic of, and fulfilled by, the universal union of the elect with Christ, "such a transfigured union will not cast away that earthly experience of sacramental marriage, which it 'metamorphoses.'" Nor will that union with Christ "necessitate the dismissal of all the kin and family bonds that have been instrumental in preparing

---

102. See, for example, *NT Student Manual* (2018), 66.

103. First Presidency, "An Empire in the Deseret," *Oakland Tribune*, October 15, 1911, and *Deseret News*, November 4, 1911, in *Messages of the First Presidency*, 4:249.

104. Colleen McDannell and Bernhard Lang, *Heaven: A History* (New Haven: Yale University Press, 1988), traces oscillations throughout Christian history of the dominance of either "theocentric" (God-centered) or "anthropocentric" (human-centered) notions of heaven.

105. McGuckin, *Orthodox Church*, 319–20.

countless souls to enter it. Far from it." In ways this sounds a Mormon note, but the eschatological metamorphosis it anticipates is rooted in a rather distinct ontology. For Orthodoxy, "the two souls joined in marriage are given the potential to become spiritually bonded in a mutual hypostatic relationship which, in Christ, is unique to them."[106]

The idea of marital and familial perpetuity has been particularly strong at various times and among a variety of Christian traditions in American history. The common expectation in Victorian America was that "family members" would enjoy "rich, robust, and rewarding fellowship in their heavenly home. Pastors and laypeople" alike "frequently declared their firm hope . . . that their families would be reconstituted in heaven." Although Christians in the early twentieth century "did not accentuate family reunion and fellowship in heaven as much as their antebellum and Gilded Age predecessors," they still expected that families would be "restored" and "husbands and wives would continue to love each other."[107] For Mormonism, however, the perpetuation of marriage and family in the afterlife doesn't just happen, nor is it a universal reality. As has been explained, the heavenly continuation of marital and familial ties is only considered possible through the sealing ordinance associated with temple marriages. Even then, such marriages are considered a gateway, not a guarantee. Only the faithful who keep their temple covenants with God will realize the fullest expression of what Joseph Smith taught when he remarked that the "same sociality [relationships] which exists amongst us here will exist among us there only it will be coupled with eternal glory which we do not now enjoy."[108]

Related to marital perpetuity is the idea of marital indissolubility. Both Eastern Orthodoxy and Roman Catholicism espouse some version of a doctrine of marital indissolubility based on a straightforward reading of Jesus's response when asked about divorce. Christ explained that marriage was divinely ordained from the beginning and concluded, "What therefore God hath joined together, let not man put asunder" (Mark 10:9/Matt. 19:6). For this reason, Catholics in particular see the marital bond as "indissoluble."[109] Yet, in the face of the revolutionary social and scientific developments of the twentieth century,

---

106. McGuckin, *Orthodox Church*, 320, 321.

107. Gary Scott Smith, *Heaven in the American Imagination* (New York: Oxford University Press, 2011), 79, 148. Although the popular appeal of such family-focused, "anthropocentric" visions of heaven may have been prominent, even dominant, at times, they have never fully supplanted traditional, theocentric views of the afterlife.

108. *JSP*, D12:139. Later canonized as D&C 130:2.

109. *CCC* 1614–1615, 2364, 2382.

Christian churches, including the Roman Catholic Church, have had to adjust their policies, if not their principles, regarding marriage. The invention of "the pill," a safe and effective oral contraceptive, and the dynamic impact of "second-wave" feminism, to name two of the era's most transformative developments, prompted many ecclesial bodies to modify a number of their positions with regard to sexuality, marriage, and the family. The Roman Catholic Church attempted to work around its traditional interpretation of marital indissolubility by allowing the annulment of marriages, after which (re)marriage can take place, or by simply encouraging couples to reconcile.[110] The Latter-day Saint position with regard to marital dissolubility has been stated by Dallin Oaks: "The kind of marriage required for exaltation [the fullness of salvation]— eternal in duration and godlike in quality—does not contemplate divorce. In the temples of the Lord, couples are married for all eternity." Yet, acknowledged Oaks, "Some marriages do not progress toward that ideal." So, the church "permits divorced persons to marry again without the stain of immorality specified in the higher law [Mark 10/Matt. 19]."[111] This is similar to the stand taken by most Christian churches, including the Orthodox, where "divorce is seen as an exceptional but necessary concession to human sin."[112]

Modern trends have also influenced other aspects of marriage doctrine. What used to be a strong, nearly categorical, denunciation of "birth control" among socially conservative Christian bodies such as the Church of Jesus Christ of Latter-day Saints has yielded to the promotion of sensitive and sensible "family planning." Procreation is no longer stressed as the primary, if not sole, purpose of marriage among the Mormon faithful. Now, it is also emphasized that "physical intimacy between husband and wife" is "ordained of God" both for the "creation of children" and also "for the expression of love between husband and wife." Moreover, "the decision about how many children to have and when to

110. "An annulment does not bring about the dissolution of a marriage, but rather is a declaration, made after investigation, that no marriage bond ever existed, due to conditions existing at the time of the wedding that prevented true consent on the part of one or both of the spouses. Obviously, not all people who divorce are able to obtain an annulment, but those who do are free to marry." Bauerschmidt and Buckley, *Catholic Theology*, 304.

111. Dallin H. Oaks, "Divorce," *Ensign*, May 2007, 70. The LDS Church, like many others, has softened its views over the years on the matter of divorce and remarriage. In the beginning, remarriage after divorce was suspect unless the cause of divorce was unfaithfulness on the part of the former spouse. See Grant Underwood, "'The Laws of the Church of Christ (D&C 42): A Textual and Historical Analysis," in *The Doctrine and Covenants: Revelations in Context*, ed. Andrew H. Hedges, J. Spencer Fluhman, Alonzo L. Gaskill (Provo, UT: BYU Religious Studies Center, 2008), 133–34.

112. Ware, *Orthodox Church*, 302.

have them is extremely personal and private. It should be left between the couple and the Lord."[113] Most dramatically, in the face of the social and legal normalization of LGBTQ identity in the first decades of the twenty-first century, the Church of Jesus Christ of Latter-day Saints, like other churches, was compelled to refine its discourse about same-sex attraction and behavior. Although the LDS Church continues to affirm "that God's law defines marriage as the legal and lawful union between a man and a woman" and does not allow same-sex unions to be solemnized in either its chapels or its temples, it decries homophobia and "encourages families and [church] members to reach out with sensitivity, love, and respect to persons who are attracted to others of the same sex."[114]

Detailing the Mormon experience with the seismic societal shifts in the West since the 1950s is beyond the purview of this volume, but it would be fair to characterize the Latter-day Saint response as primarily conservative in nature.[115] In 1995, the Church of Jesus Christ of Latter-day Saints issued a major proclamation entitled "The Family: A Proclamation to the World," in which it succinctly set forth its views on issues roiling society's waters. The opening sentence declares, "We, the First Presidency and the Council of the Twelve Apostles . . . solemnly proclaim that marriage between a man and a woman is ordained of God and that the family is central to the Creator's plan for the eternal destiny of His children."[116] The proclamation goes on to affirm male and female distinctiveness, the importance of chastity before marriage and fidelity thereafter, the value of children and child rearing, and the "sacred responsibilities" that "fathers and mothers" have "to help one another as equal partners."[117] Concurrent with the promotion of "The Family," and also

---

113. *GH* 38.6.4. See also 2.1.2.

114. *GH* 38.6.16; 38.6.15. The issue of same-sex marriage has been much discussed in the Church of Jesus Christ of Latter-day Saints in the twenty-first century, and church leaders have made numerous statements on the matter. An entrée to this literature can be found in the church's website essays "Same-Sex Marriage" and "Same-Sex Attraction," ChurchofJesusChrist.org. For other issues pertaining to sexual identity, see *GH* 38.6.23 and 38.7.7.

115. A reliable introduction is Patrick Q. Mason and John G. Turner, *Out of Obscurity: Mormonism Since 1945* (New York: Oxford University Press, 2016). Also illuminating is J. B. Haws, *The Mormon Image in the American Mind: Fifty Years of Public Perception* (New York: Oxford University Press, 2013).

116. "The Family: A Proclamation to the World," Ensign, November 1995, 102. Apostle Russell Nelson went so far as to declare that the ultimate purpose for which "the earth was created and that the Lord's Church was restored [was] so that families could be sealed and exalted as eternal entities." Nelson, "Nurturing Marriage," *Ensign*, May 2006, 36.

117. The notion of marital equity continues to be a regular theme in church teaching. The current *General Handbook* underlines the point: "Being united in marriage requires a

reflecting broader societal trends, has been the ever-intensifying emphasis on the importance of women and womanhood.[118] Women's contributions to church governance and teaching, even without the possibility of ordination to the ministerial priesthood, are regularly highlighted (see chapter 8). Although "The Family" is now several decades old, it has not been materially revised and continues to be held up as the official position of the church. Undergirding it is the church's bedrock commitment to temple sealings as the indispensable sacrament that makes eternal families possible.

Additional LDS Temple Sacraments

The essential prerequisite to the sacrament or ordinance of a temple marriage sealing is the sacrament known as the "temple endowment" (or simply, "the endowment"). The *General Handbook* offers this definition of the endowment: "The word *endowment* means 'a gift.' The temple endowment is literally a gift from God through which He blesses His children." Some of the gracious gifts that Latter-day Saints believe God dispenses through the endowment include "greater knowledge of the Lord's purposes and teachings; power to do all that Heavenly Father wants His children to do," and "increased hope, comfort, and peace."[119] Reference to "power" to do the Lord's work harks back to the initial focus of endowment language in LDS scripture. Before the church was a year old, the Saints were directed to relocate to Ohio where, like Jesus's disciples of old (Luke 24:49), they were promised that they would be "endowed with power from on high" (D&C 38:32). Revelation described this as "a blessing such as is not known among the children of men, and it shall be poured forth upon their heads. And from thence men shall go forth into all nations" (D&C 39:15). These statements echo language in Acts 1:4–5 where Jesus, reiterating Luke 24:49, commands his disciples to tarry in Jerusalem until they receive "the promise of the Father" and are "baptized with the Holy Ghost." Christ further declares, "[When] ye shall receive power, after that the Holy Ghost is come upon you:

---

full partnership, sharing responsibilities. A husband and wife are equal in God's eyes. One should not dominate the other. Their decisions should be made in unity and love, with full participation of both." *GH* 2.1.2.

118. An insightful historical overview by a prominent Catholic scholar and longtime resident of Utah is Colleen McDannell, *Sister Saints: Mormon Women Since the End of Polygamy* (New York: Oxford University Press, 2019), esp. 153–71. The extensive literature on second-wave feminism and its impact on Western society as well as the specific Mormon experience with it can be accessed through McDannell's exhaustive bibliographic essay (235–79).

119. *GH* 27.2.

[then] ye shall be witnesses unto me both in Jerusalem, and in all Judaea, and in Samaria, and unto the uttermost part of the earth" (Acts 1:8). The dramatic fulfillment of this promised endowment takes place during the Jewish celebration known as Pentecost as described in Acts 2, and the remainder of the book of Acts recounts how the gospel witness began to be proclaimed outward from Jerusalem to the rest of the Roman world.

Revelation to the early Latter-day Saints clearly intended them to replicate this experience. The word of the Lord was: "Build a house, in the which house, I design to endow those whom I have chosen with power from on high; For this is the promise of the Father unto you; therefore I command you to tarry, even as mine apostles at Jerusalem" (D&C 95:8–9). Further links to Pentecost came when the house, later referred to as the Kirtland (Ohio) "Temple," was consecrated. The prayer of dedication petitioned, echoing Acts 1:8: "We ask thee, Holy Father, that thy servants may go forth from this house armed with thy power . . . [that] from this place they may bear exceedingly great and glorious tidings, in truth, unto the ends of the earth" (D&C 109:22–23).

All this, of course, will sound familiar to Christians whose particular theology of confirmation considers one of the purposes of receiving the Holy Spirit to be strengthening the individual for service and proclamation. This is especially true of Pentecostals influenced by Reformed perspectives whose doctrine of "baptism with the Holy Ghost" anticipates that the experience brings a level of spiritual empowerment for witness and ministry above and beyond (and subsequent to) reception of the Holy Ghost in conjunction with water baptism. As their name implies, Pentecostals in general seek the full spiritual profundity of the Pentecost experience, some even to speaking in tongues. The Assemblies of God, the world's largest Pentecostal denomination; the Church of God in Christ, the largest Pentecostal denomination in the USA; and the Church of God (Cleveland, TN), one of the oldest Pentecostal denominations consider speaking in tongues as the essential physical "evidence," or at least the natural consequence, of baptism in the Holy Spirit.[120]

---

120. "Assemblies of God 16 Fundamental Truths," no. 8, https://ag.org/Beliefs/Statement-of-Fundamental-Truths#8; no. 4 in "What We Believe," Church of God in Christ, https://www.cogic.org/about-us/what-we-believe/; and articles 8 and 9 of the Church of God "Declaration of Faith," https://churchofgod.org/beliefs/declaration-of-faith/. Not all Pentecostals, however, understand Spirit baptism in this way. Those strongly influenced by the Wesleyan Holiness tradition see it primarily as an experience of further sanctification subsequent to the spiritual regeneration and cleansing from sin associated with conversion. Sometimes called the "second blessing" or "entire sanctification," it is conceived of as a purifying fire that roots out the disposition to sin. A convenient overview of the various Pentecostal doc-

There are noticeable similarities in early Mormonism. The dedicatory prayer for the Kirtland Temple asked God to reprise the dramatic events detailed in Acts 2: "As upon those on the day of Pentecost," petitioned the prayer, "let the gift of tongues be poured out upon thy people, even cloven tongues as of fire, and the interpretation thereof. And let thy house be filled, as with a rushing mighty wind, with thy glory" (D&C 109:36–37). Answer to the prayer was reported in Joseph Smith's history: "A noise was heard like the sound of a rushing mighty wind, which filled the Temple, and all the congregation simultaneously arose, being moved upon by an invisible power. Many began to speak in tongues and prophesy; others saw glorious visions; and [Joseph Smith] beheld the Temple was filled with angels, which fact [he] declared to the congregation."[121] Additional dramatic outpourings of the Spirit occurred in successive gatherings of the Saints associated with the temple's dedication. The summary report in the official history exultantly declared, "It was a penticost and enduement indeed, long to be remembered . . . and the occurrences of this day shall be handed down upon the pages of sacred history to all generations, as the day of Pentecost."[122] Years later, Eliza Snow, one of the participants and a prominent woman leader, put it this way: "The ceremonies of that dedication may be rehearsed, but no mortal language can describe the heavenly manifestations of that memorable day. Angels appeared to some, while a sense of divine presence was realized by all present, and each heart was filled with 'joy inexpressible and full of glory' [1 Pet. 1:8]."[123]

Within a decade of the Kirtland experience, the endowment became a fully ritualized liturgy. The joyful, glorious sense of the divine presence continued, but the experience was no longer spontaneous as the rushing wind. Instead, the presence of the Spirit was felt through a series of ritual performances that entailed covenant making, the reception of special blessings, and the impartation of divine knowledge. Although particular actions and wording in the endowment ceremony have been refined over the years, its core components

---

trines of baptism in the Holy Spirit is John W. Wyckoff, "The Baptism in the Holy Spirit," in *Systematic Theology*, ed. Stanley M. Horton, rev. ed. (Springfield, MO: Logion, 1995), 423–55. See also Frank D. Macchia, "Spirit Baptism: Initiation into the Fullness of God's Promises," in Vondey, *The Routledge Handbook of Pentecostal Theology*, 247–56.

121. *Teachings: Joseph Smith*, 308.

122. *JSP*, J1:216. See also Steven C. Harper, "'A Pentecost and Endowment Indeed': Six Eyewitness Accounts of the Kirtland Temple Experience," in *Opening the Heavens: Accounts of Divine Manifestations, 1820–1844*, ed. John W. Welch (Provo, UT: Brigham Young University Press, 2005), 327–71.

123. Quoted in *Teachings: Joseph Smith*, 307–8.

remain, including the emphasis on receiving power from on high. Reiterating portions of the Kirtland Temple dedicatory prayer, apostle Neal Andersen recently declared, "The temple is literally the house of the Lord. I promise you as you come worthily and prayerfully to His holy house, you will be armed with His power, His name will be upon you, His angels will have charge over you, and you will grow up in the blessing of the Holy Ghost."[124] The central focus of the endowment as uniting the participant ever more profoundly to Jesus Christ has also been heightened over the years, especially in recent decades. The ordinance of the temple endowment continues to be a ritually rich, spiritually significant ceremony that lies at the heart of Latter-day Saint religiosity today and is considered one of the church's essential sacraments of salvation and "exaltation" in the next life. The endowment, therefore, merits closer examination.

The sacrament of the endowment is received in two parts. "In the first part, a person receives a preliminary ordinance called the initiatory. The initiatory is also known as the washing and anointing (see Exod 29:4–9)." The initiatory pronounces "special blessings" on the recipient "related to the person's divine heritage and potential."[125] Details of the initiatory ordinance, as with the rest of the endowment, are considered sacred and are not discussed outside the temple, but in recent decades the church has made public on its website an abundant amount of information about its temples, their purposes, and the ordinances that are performed therein.[126] While the initiatory ordinance is relatively brief, occupying only a few minutes, and is received privately and individually, the second part of the endowment lasts more than an hour and is experienced as a congregation or "company," as the group of participants is called in temple terminology. This more expansive second segment involves a symbolic reenactment of key aspects of salvation history, "including the Creation, the fall of Adam and Eve, the Atonement of Jesus Christ, the Apostasy, and the Restoration. Members also receive instruction on how to return to the Lord's presence." Punctuating the ceremony at appropriate points are occasions when the individual members of the company ceremonially covenant to obey God's laws and live the gospel. Specifically singled out for covenantal obedience are "the law of sacrifice, which means sacrificing to support the Lord's work and repenting with a broken heart and contrite spirit," and "the law of chastity, which means having no sexual activity except with those to whom

---

124. Neal A. Andersen, "Temples, Houses of the Lord Dotting the Earth," *Liahona*, May 2024, 113.

125. *GH* 27.2. All quotations in this paragraph are taken from this source.

126. See https://www.churchofjesuschrist.org/temples?lang=eng.

[one is] legally and lawfully wedded according to God's law." Additionally, endowment recipients covenant to "keep the law of consecration, which means dedicating their time, talents, and everything with which the Lord has blessed them to building up Jesus Christ's Church on the earth."[127]

For Latter-day Saints raised in the church, the endowment is typically received in young adulthood. Any worthy Latter-day Saint woman or man who is at least eighteen years of age, has been a member of the church for at least one year, and desires "to receive and honor sacred temple covenants throughout their li[fe]" may experience the endowment. Church "members who have received a mission call or are preparing to be sealed [in marriage] in the temple should receive the endowment."[128] In order to receive the endowment and subsequent marriage sealing sacraments, candidates must possess a "temple recommend" signed both by themselves and by their local church leaders, who interview them to ensure worthiness and commitment to Christ.[129] To some, LDS temple worship may seem exclusive, even elitist. The perspective of church president Russell Nelson, however, is that "the blessings of the temple are available to any and all people who will prepare themselves. . . . The Lord wants all His children to partake of the eternal blessings available in His temple. He has directed what each person must do to qualify to enter His holy house. . . . All requirements to enter the temple relate to personal holiness."[130] Because the temple ordinances are considered the capstone LDS sacraments necessary to receive "exaltation," the fullness of salvation in the afterlife, they provide an elaborate, ritual occasion for affirming the fullness of one's devo-

---

127. As with all sacraments, Latter-day Saint temple sacraments have experienced development and refinement over time. That history is viewed from different perspectives in Richard E. Bennett, *Temples Rising: A Heritage of Sacrifice* (Salt Lake City: Deseret Book, 2019), and David John Buerger, *The Mysteries of Godliness: A History of Mormon Temple Worship* (Salt Lake City: Signature Books, 1994).

128. *GH* 27.2.2. President Russell Nelson, however, urged young adults "not to wait until marriage to be endowed in the house of the Lord. Begin now," he counseled them, "to learn and experience what it means to be armed with priesthood power" received through the endowment. Nelson, "The Temple and Your Spiritual Foundation," *Liahona*, November 2021, 95.

129. Fifteen set questions are asked in all temple-recommend interviews. They are listed in *GH* 26.3.3.1 and in *Liahona*, November 2019, 121. The *General Handbook* summarizes them thus: "Temple recommend interviews allow members to demonstrate that they have a testimony [of the truthfulness of the gospel and the restored church of Christ] and are striving to obey God's commandments and follow His prophets. Priesthood leaders also affirm, through the interview, that the member is worthy." *GH* 26.3.

130. *Liahona*, November 2019, 120–21.

tion to Christ. Commitments made initially at baptism are now expected to be made with a level of maturity and understanding that anticipates lifelong collaboration with the Holy Spirit "to be conformed to the image of [God's] Son" (Rom. 8:29).

The same idea that undergirds confirmation in many Christian traditions of fostering a mature profession of, and commitment to, the faith is taken to a new level of seriousness with the temple endowment. For Latter-day Saints, preparation to make a truly informed profession of faith and earnest commitment to Christ is a lengthier, more intense undertaking than in traditions that hope to achieve this through confirmation in early adolescence. In the Church of Jesus Christ of Latter-day Saints, it is a multistaged progression that only begins in baptism at age eight and culminates in young adulthood with participation in the endowment. Remarks apostle David Bednar, the "scriptures help us understand that the process of taking upon ourselves the name of Jesus Christ that is commenced in the waters of baptism is continued and enlarged in the house of the Lord [temple]. As we stand in the waters of baptism, we look to the temple. As we partake of the sacrament, we look to the temple."[131]

Especially in recent teaching, apostles and prophets have emphasized that everything in and about the temple and temple sacraments is focused on Jesus Christ and helping individuals draw closer, and be drawn closer, to him. President Russell Nelson has been particularly emphatic on this point: "The temple lies at the center of strengthening our faith and spiritual fortitude because the Savior and His doctrine are the very heart of the temple. Everything taught in the temple, through instruction and through the Spirit, increases our understanding of Jesus Christ. His essential ordinances bind us to Him through sacred priesthood covenants. Then, as we keep our covenants, He endows us with *His* healing, strengthening power." In short, "*Everything* we believe and *every* promise God has made to His covenant people come together in the temple."[132] President Nelson's remarks prompted apostle Ulisses Soares to sum up the temple experience as "a sacred journey of learning to become higher and holier disciples of Christ."[133]

131. *Ensign*, May 2009, 98.

132. Nelson, "The Temple and Your Spiritual Foundation," 93–94. The church has produced several videos explaining how it would like its temples and temple sacraments to be understood. Useful in this regard are "Two Apostles Lead a Virtual Tour of the Rome Italy Temple," https://www.youtube.com/watch?v=dhWgPwEQQ98; "Blessings of the Temple," https://www.youtube.com/watch?v=vC4or19cLuw; and "Temples through Time," https://www.youtube.com/watch?v=Y6a1ohpWeZA.

133. Ulisses Soares, "Covenant Confidence through Jesus Christ," *Liahona*, May 2024, 17.

The temple ordinances are by far the most symbolically and liturgically rich aspects of Latter-day Saint worship. To church members accustomed to the plain, low-church style of weekly worship in the Church of Jesus Christ of Latter-day Saints, the temple sacraments provide a dramatic contrast that powerfully inducts the believer into sacred space. This reality is enhanced by the wearing of distinctive temple clothing and the use of symbolic gestures, handclasps, and names, collectively known as "signs," "tokens," and "Keywords of the Priesthood."[134] In an oft-quoted description of the endowment, Brigham Young explained that the endowment is "to receive all those ordinances in the House of the Lord, which are necessary for you, after you have departed this life, to enable you to walk back to the presence of the Father . . . and gain your eternal exaltation." Young specifically mentioned the necessity of obtaining "the key words, the signs and tokens" given in the endowment.[135] The liturgical inclusion of such signs, tokens, and key words has led some, including Latter-day Saints, to note parallels with the induction ceremonies of Freemasonry. Apostle Heber Kimball was one of the first group to receive the endowment when it was introduced by Joseph Smith. Shortly thereafter, he wrote to fellow apostle Parley Pratt, reporting that "we have received some precious things through the Prophet on the priesthood that would cause your soul to rejoice." Kimball then made this observation: "There is a similarity of priesthood in masonry."[136] Some early Saints familiar with Freemasonry imagined that the Masonic ritual was a corruption of the endowment had by God's people anciently but now restored in its original purity through revelation to Joseph Smith. One Smith associate was enthusiastic about such a supposed relationship, proposing that Freemasonry might be considered "a Stepping Stone or Preparation for . . . the true Origin of Masonry."[137] Others paid little attention to the similarities.[138]

134. Figure 7, Facsimile 2—Explanation, Book of Abraham. The Book of Abraham was published with the facsimiles of three stylized graphic depictions found on the Egyptian papyri Joseph Smith acquired in the 1830s. Facsimile 2 resembles a hypocephalus, a round funerary amulet covered with figures and text placed under the head of mummies. The "explanation" provided for Facsimile 2 in the Book of Abraham relates to Latter-day Saint theology rather than Egyptian afterlife beliefs. See *JSP*, R4:276–83.

135. *Journal of Discourses*, 2:31.

136. Kimball to Pratt, June 17, 1842, Parley P. Pratt correspondence, 1842–1855, Church History Library, The Church of Jesus Christ of Latter-day Saints.

137. Quoted in Andrew F. Ehat, "'They Might Have Known That He Was Not a Fallen Prophet': The Nauvoo Journal of Joseph Fielding," *BYU Studies* 19 (Winter 1979): 145.

138. "Of the thousands of Saints who eventually received their endowment in the Nauvoo Temple, many of whom were Masons, few ever criticized it as a plagiarism or something

Most twenty-first-century Latter-day Saints are unfamiliar and unconcerned with Masonry. While ritualistic similarities with Freemasonry are not denied by the church, the distinctly LDS religious content and intent of endowment ceremonies are emphasized. The endowment's sacred nature as a sacrament of salvation is stressed. A church website essay explains: "Masonic rituals deliver stage-by-stage instruction using dramatization and symbolic gestures and clothing, with content based on Masonic legends. The endowment employs similar teaching devices, but it draws primarily upon the revelations and inspired translations given to Joseph Smith for its content."[139] The manner in which the relationship between Masonry and the temple endowment is framed today in church literature is to suggest that Joseph Smith's prior involvement with Freemasonry "served as a catalyst for [the] revelation" that inaugurated this important new sacrament.[140] Whether or not Latter-day Saints today see Masonry as the "adulteration" of an ancient endowment ceremony, it is still common to argue for the antiquity of the endowment.[141] Moreover, such thinking is not limited to Latter-day Saints. Frank Moore Cross Jr., Emeritus Hancock Professor of Hebrew and Other Oriental Languages at Harvard University, made clear that he was neither a Mormon nor a believer in Latter-day Saint revelation. Yet, he observed, "I am both interested and delighted to see so much of ancient reli-

---

having been borrowed from the Masonic fraternity." Bennett, *Temples Rising*, 88. Among those Masonic Mormons who received the endowment and saw it as more distinctive than similar was James Adams, deputy Grand Master Mason of Illinois.

139. "Masonry," The Church of Jesus Christ of Latter-day Saints, https://www.churchofje suschrist.org/study/history/topics/masonry. The article elaborates: "Masonic ceremonies promote self-improvement, brotherhood, charity, and fidelity to truth for the purpose of making better men, who in turn make a better society. During temple ordinances, men *and women* covenant with God to obey His laws for the purpose of gaining exaltation through the Atonement of Jesus Christ" (emphasis added). In the United States at the time Joseph Smith introduced the endowment, women were not included in Masonic lodges as they soon were in the endowment ceremonies.

140. "Masonry." See also the church's brief historical essay "Temple Endowment" in its "Church History Topics" section at churchofjesuschrist.org. An article-length discussion of the relationship between Freemasonry and the endowment is Steven C. Harper, "Freemasonry and the Latter-day Saint Temple Endowment Ceremony," in *A Reason for Faith: Navigating LDS Doctrine and Church History*, ed. Laura Harris Hales (Provo, UT: BYU Religious Studies Center, 2016), 143–57. A book-length treatment is Michael W. Homer, *Joseph's Temples: The Dynamic Relationship between Freemasonry and Mormonism* (Salt Lake City: University of Utah Press, 2014).

141. The scholarly case for this belief has been made most extensively by religion professor Hugh Nibley. See, for instance, *The Message of the Joseph Smith Papyri: An Egyptian Endowment*, 2nd ed. (Salt Lake City: Deseret Book, 2005).

gious tradition, particularly biblical tradition, taken up into the religious structures and rituals of the Mormons. . . . Someone who does not know much about temples and Mormons building temples should be directed to the Bible."[142]

Part of what Cross is pointing to is the distinctive temple clothing that reflects aspects of the priestly attire described in the book of Exodus. Participation in the endowment entails wearing specially designed white, outer clothing known as "the robes of the holy priesthood." Additionally, in the initiatory portion of the endowment, participants are clothed in sacred, symbolic undergarments. The church notes that "to those outside a particular faith, [that faith's} rituals and clothing may seem unfamiliar. But for the participants they can stir the deepest feelings of the soul, motivate them to do good, even shape the course of a whole life of service. [Consider:] The nun's habit. The priest's cassock. The Jewish prayer shawl. The Muslim's skullcap. The saffron robes of the Buddhist monk." And Latter-day Saint temple attire. "Temple garments are worn by adult members of the Church who [in the sacraments of the temple] have made sacred promises of fidelity to God's commandments and the gospel of Jesus Christ." Thereafter the sacred undergarments are worn daily by the devout. "To Church members, the modest temple garment, worn under normal clothing, along with the symbolic vestments worn during temple worship, represent the sacred and personal aspect of their relationship with God and their commitment to live good, honorable lives."[143]

Church leader Anette Dennis sees the wearing of the garment as a symbolic way to respond to Paul's injunction to "put ye on the Lord Jesus Christ" (Rom. 13:14). In her personal reflections on Adam and Eve being clothed with

---

142. Quoted in the video "Why Mormons Build Temples," The Church of Jesus Christ of Latter-day Saints, https://www.churchofjesuschrist.org/media/video/2010-05-1210-why-mormons-build-temples?lang=eng&alang=eng. It should be pointed out that Cross is speaking in general terms. The Church of Jesus Christ of Latter-day Saints does not claim that the endowment and marriage sealings were performed in either the First Temple of Jerusalem (Solomon's) or the Second Temple (Zerubbabel's/Herod's).

143. "Temple Garments," The Church of Jesus Christ of Latter-day Saints, https://newsroom.churchofjesuschrist.org/article/temple-garments. Both the "garments" and the temple "robes" are displayed in a church-produced video entitled "Sacred Temple Clothing," The Church of Jesus Christ of Latter-day Saints, https://www.churchofjesuschrist.org/temples/sacred-temple-clothing. At the time the church released the video in 2014, they issued this statement: "Because there is little or no accurate information on this subject on the Internet the Church feels it important to provide this resource. The wearing of religious clothing reflects commitment and devotion to God. Latter-day Saints seek the same respect and sensitivity regarding our sacred clothing as shown to those of other faiths who wear religious vestments."

a "coat of skins" ("garment of skins," NRSV, NIV), she envisions the possibility "that an animal was sacrificed to make those coats of skins—symbolic of the Savior's own sacrifice for us." This leads her to note that "*kaphar* is the basic Hebrew word for atonement, and one of its meanings is 'to cover.'" Thus, the "temple garment reminds us that the Savior and the blessings of His Atonement cover us throughout our lives. As we put on the garment of the holy priesthood each day, that beautiful symbol becomes a part of us."[144] First Presidency member Dallin Oaks explains the importance of daily wearing the temple garment in these words: "It reminds endowed members of the sacred covenants they have made and the blessings they have been promised in the holy temple. To achieve those holy purposes, we are instructed to wear temple garments continuously, with the only exceptions being those obviously necessary. Because covenants do not 'take a day off,' to remove one's garments can be understood as a disclaimer of the covenant responsibilities and blessings to which they relate. In contrast, persons who wear their garments faithfully and keep their temple covenants continually affirm their role as disciples of the Lord Jesus Christ."[145]

Curious but respectful as most are when it comes to this subject, a chaplain at US Naval Chaplaincy School in Newport, Rhode Island, once asked a visiting LDS church leader about the significance of the "Mormon underwear." In reply, the leader inquired, "In civilian life and also when conducting the meetings in the military service you wear clerical clothing, do you not?" The chaplain said that he did. The leader continued, "I would suppose that that has some importance to you." Among other purposes, "it reminds you of who you are and what your obligations and covenants are. It is a continual reminder that you are a member of the clergy, that you regard yourself as a servant of the Lord, and that you are responsible to live in such a way as to be worthy of your ordination." The church leader then likened this to the wearing of the temple garment: "We draw something of the same benefits from this special clothing as you would draw from your clerical vestments. The difference is that we wear ours under our clothing instead of outside, for we are employed in various occupations in addition to our service in the Church." The general authority then added that "there are some deeper spiritual meanings as well, connecting the practice of wearing this garment with covenants that are made in the temple. . . . The garment, covering the body, is a visual and tactile reminder of these covenants."[146]

144. J. Anette Dennis, "Put Ye On the Lord Jesus Christ," *Liahona*, May 2024, 11.

145. Dallin H. Oaks, "Covenants and Responsibilities," *Liahona*, May 2024, 95–96.

146. *Preparing to Enter the Holy Temple* (Salt Lake City: The Church of Jesus Christ of Latter-day Saints, 2002), 20–23.

In the realm of comparison with other religious rituals and practices, additional parallels with LDS temple worship are plentiful. For instance, a number of similarities have been noticed between aspects of Catholic liturgy and Latter-day Saint temple ceremonies.[147] Orthodox have a long tradition of regarding their churches as hallowed locations where "holiness to the Lord" is the order of the day. Saint Maximus the Confessor taught that "the holy angels remain [in the building] even after the synaxis [gathered eucharistic worship] and the grace of the Holy Spirit always invisibly is present in the church. For this reason, it is a marked aspect of Orthodoxy how much the faithful love their churches, care for them with great affection, and visit them often for private prayer as well as for public services."[148] The same statement holds true for how Latter-day Saints feel about their temples. Church president Gordon Hinckley taught that the temple is "a place of personal inspiration and revelation. Legion are those who in times of stress, when difficult decisions must be made and perplexing problems must be handled, have come to the temple in a spirit of fasting and prayer to seek divine direction. Many have testified that while voices of revelation were not heard, impressions concerning a course to follow were experienced at that time or later which became answers to their prayers." Hinckley described the temple as a spiritual oasis and invited members "to leave the noise and the tumult of the world and step within the walls of a sacred house of God, there to feel His spirit in an environment of holiness and peace."[149] Hinckley's presidential successor, Thomas Monson, concurred: "As we attend the temple, there can come to us a dimension of spirituality and a feeling of peace which will transcend any other feeling which could come into the human heart. We will grasp the true meaning of the words of the Savior when He said: 'Peace I leave with you, my peace I give unto you.'"[150]

---

147. For example, see Marcus von Wellnitz, "The Catholic Liturgy and the Mormon Temple," *BYU Studies* 21 (Winter 1981): 3–35.

148. John A. McGuckin, ed., *Encyclopedia of Eastern Orthodox Christianity* (Chichester, UK: Wiley-Blackwell, 2011), s.v. "church (Orthodox ecclesiology)."

149. *Teachings: Gordon B. Hinckley*, 316–17. Apostle David Bednar, in discussing Ps. 46:10— "Be still, and know that I am God"—recounted the experience of taking a group of journalists on a prededication tour of one of the temples: "Before entering the celestial room, I explained that this particular room in the house of the Lord symbolically represents the peace and beauty of the heavenly home to which we can return after this life. I indicated to our guests that we would not speak while in the celestial room, but I would be happy to answer any questions after we moved to the next stop on the tour." Later, "one of the journalists said with great emotion, 'I have never experienced anything like that in my entire life. I did not know quiet like that existed in the world; I simply did not believe such stillness was possible.'" Bednar, "Be Still, and Know That I Am God," *Liahona*, May 2024, 28.

150. *Teachings: Thomas S. Monson*, 237–38.

Latter-day Saints experience the temples as sanctuaries of prayer and contemplation, but in one sense this is a by-product of being there to vicariously receive the ordinances of exaltation for and in behalf of the deceased. Faithful Latter-day Saints will go through the endowment ceremony perhaps hundreds of times in their lives. With the exception of the first instance in which they receive their own endowment, on each subsequent occasion they are serving as proxy recipients for those who have passed on. In this sense, temple worship is also temple service. Indeed, President Hinckley called the temple "a sanctuary of service. Most of the work done in this sacred house," he explained, "is performed vicariously in behalf of those who have passed beyond the veil of death. I know of no other work to compare with it. It more nearly approaches the vicarious sacrifice of the Son of God in behalf of all mankind than any other work of which I am aware. . . . It is a service which is of the very essence of selflessness."[151] Latter-day Saints often refer to this sacred service as the work of "salvation for the dead."[152]

Whatever their reasons for "attending" the temple, Latter-day Saints cherish it and the sacraments received there as the apex of their religious experience. Revelation characterizes the temple as "a house of prayer, a house of fasting, a house of faith, a house of learning, a house of glory, a house of order, a house of God" (D&C 109:8). "This list of attributes," emphasized President Nelson, "is much more than a description of a temple. It is a promise about what will happen to those who serve and worship in the house of the Lord. They can expect to receive answers to prayer, personal revelation, greater faith, strength, comfort, increased knowledge, and increased power. . . . The temple is the gateway to the greatest blessings God has in store for each of us." Ultimately, promised the prophet, "nothing will bolster [one's] testimony of the Lord Jesus Christ and His Atonement" more than "worshipping in the temple."[153] In short, declared President Hinckley, "These unique and wonderful buildings, and the ordinances administered therein represent the ultimate in our worship. These ordinances become the most profound expressions of our theology."[154]

151. *Teachings: Gordon B. Hinckley*, 315.

152. For a full discussion, see the section "Salvation for the Dead" in chapter 12.

153. Russell M. Nelson, "Rejoice in the Gift of Priesthood Keys," *Liahona*, May 2024, 121–22.

154. *Teachings: Gordon B. Hinckley*, 312.

Eschatology

The End of the Age and the Afterlife

In 1970, the publishing world was caught by surprise. A religious nonfiction book by an obscure evangelical author, Hal Lindsey, rapidly became a best seller. Books about prophecy had long been sold in Christian bookstores, but *The Late Great Planet Earth* was pitched to a broad, popular audience. In journalistic style, it creatively and relentlessly tied the arcane imagery of the Apocalypse of John (Revelation) and other prophetic books to the latest news headlines. Its end-of-the-world alarmism piqued the same popular appetite for the sensational as did the tabloids like *National Enquirer* with which *Late Great* shared shelf space in supermarkets. The book sold millions of copies. By the end of the 1970s, the *New York Times* called it the best-selling book of the decade. A generation later, a pair of Christian "fundamentalists"—Tim LaHaye and Jerry Jenkins—launched the even more wildly successful Left Behind series. Between 1995 and 2007, LaHaye and Jenkins produced a sixteen-volume fictional saga of how the world would spiral downward to its dramatic historical conclusion. Following the same success formula that propelled *Late Great* to the top of the charts, the Left Behind series broke all publishing records in the evangelical world. In 1998 the first four books concurrently occupied the top four slots in the *New York Times* best-seller list. Volume 10 made its debut as number one on the list. By the middle of the second decade of the twenty-first century, some seventy million copies of Left Behind volumes had been sold, several movie adaptations had been produced, and a whole array of spin-off products had been generated, from graphic novels and computer games to audiobooks and study guides.[1]

In 1975, a young psychiatrist by the name of Raymond Moody published *Life after Life*, a collection of accounts of individuals who, after being pro-

---

1. For more on the phenomena discussed in this paragraph, see Crawford Gribben, *Writing the Rapture: Prophecy Fiction in Evangelical America* (New York: Oxford University Press, 2009).

nounced clinically dead, revived and told of their experiences while being separated from their bodies. What seemed eerily noteworthy in their reports were the similarities: passing through darkness or a tunnel toward a bright light, encountering a world of beauty and peace, communication with a being of light, rapid review of one's life, and sudden return to one's body. Moody labeled these occurrences "near-death experiences" (NDEs), and a new and soon to be much-contested field of study was born. *Life after Life* quickly became a best seller and spawned a number of similar publications. Still in print in the third decade of the twenty-first century, *Life after Life* has sold well over ten million copies. Combined with the many related publications of NDEs or "out-of-body" experiences, the sales figure for such books numbers in the tens of millions.[2] All this has fostered the founding of various research entities such as the Near-Death Experience Research Foundation and the International Association of Near-Death Studies, as well as the *Journal of Near-Death Studies*. Fascination with NDEs has also generated a firestorm of criticism. A range of scholars from psychologists to neurobiologists have leaped into the fray to challenge NDE research methodologies and offer alternative explanations. The debate is far from settled.

So, what do these two publishing phenomena and their aftermaths have in common? Public fascination with the future, of course. The prophecy books focus on the future of the world; the NDEs address the future "life after life" of the individual. Significantly, these are the two main concerns addressed in the subdivision of theology known as "eschatology." Derived from the Greek *eschata* ("last things," "ultimate realities"), eschatology focuses on the "end" of both human history and individual human lives but less in the sense of a conclusion or termination and more as a "final purpose" or "ultimate objective" to which salvation history is headed.[3] All religions have an eschatological dimension, but in Christianity eschatology is especially important. As one Orthodox bishop expressed it, "Eschatology permeates the entire life of the Church: its services, sacraments and rites, its theological and moral doctrine, its asceticism and mysticism. The entire history of the Church is filled with

2. Two twenty-first-century best sellers that illustrate the popularity of this genre are John Burke's *Imagine Heaven: Near-Death Experiences, God's Promises, and the Exhilarating Future That Awaits You* (Grand Rapids: Baker Books, 2015), and Todd Burpo's *Heaven Is for Real: A Little Boy's Astounding Story of His Trip to Heaven and Back* (Nashville: Nelson, 2011), on which the Hollywood movie *Heaven Is for Real* (2014) was based.

3. For instance, theologian Frank D. Macchia titles the section of his systematic theology dealing with eschatology "Final Purpose." See Macchia, *Tongues of Fire: A Systematic Theology of the Christian Faith* (Eugene, OR: Cascade, 2023), 375–424.

eschatological expectations" and "all dogmas of faith are directly related to it."[4] A Pentecostal scholar called eschatology "the integrating theme of Pentecostal theology."[5] Such is the subject of this chapter. We begin by focusing on the end of human history and examine beliefs about the "late great planet earth."

THE "END" OF HISTORY

How will history end? The traditional answer, as proclaimed in the Apostles' Creed, is that Christ "shall come to judge the living and the dead" and consign them to their appropriate eternal state.[6] This single, climactic event is affirmed by virtually all Christians. A minority, however, including the Latter-day Saints, also anticipate a prior coming of Christ that inaugurates a thousand years of paradisiacal peace and spiritual prosperity known as "the millennium." This view has worn various labels over the years: (1) *chiliasm*, from the Greek *chilias*, meaning "thousand"; (2) *premillennialism*, because it holds that the Lord's parousia ("coming," "presence") or "second advent" occurs before, not after, the millennium; and (3) *apocalyptic millenarianism*, because it emphasizes that Christ's coming and inauguration of the millennium will bring about the destruction of the wicked and the triumph of the righteous, ideas that frequently appear in ancient apocalyptic literature.[7] Chiliasm was common in the early centuries of Christianity, but by the fifth century the church favored a figurative interpretation of Revelation 20 (where the millennium is explicitly mentioned) that discounted the idea of a literal thousand-year paradise on earth.[8] Following the Reformation, however, millenarianism

4. Bishop Hilarion Alfeyev, "Eschatology," in *Cambridge Companion to Orthodox Christian Theology*, ed. Mary B. Cunningham and Elizabeth Theokritoff (Cambridge: Cambridge University Press, 2008), 107.

5. Frank D. Macchia, "Pentecostal and Charismatic Theology," in *Oxford Handbook of Eschatology*, ed. Jerry L. Walls (New York: Oxford University Press, 2008), 261.

6. *Creeds & Confessions*, 1:669. Similar affirmations are found in all the earliest baptismal creeds and "rules of faith," including the normative Nicene and Niceno-Constantinopolitan Creeds (1:13, 44, 56–57, 61, 101, 112, 152, 159, 163).

7. For a succinct introduction to millennialism, see Timothy P. Weber, "Millennialism," in Walls, *Oxford Handbook of Eschatology*, 365–83. For more comprehensive treatment, with special focus on social-scientific and cross-cultural perspectives, see Catherine Wessinger, ed., *Oxford Handbook of Millennialism* (New York: Oxford University Press, 2011); on apocalypticism, see *Continuum History of Apocalypticism*, ed. John J. Collins, Bernard McGinn, and Stephen J. Stein (New York: Continuum, 2003).

8. See Brian E. Daley, *The Hope of the Early Church: A Handbook of Patristic Eschatology* (New York: Cambridge University Press, 1991).

experienced a modest revival and since then has been embraced by various faith communities, including the Church of Jesus Christ of Latter-day Saints. In the nineteenth century, a distinctive version of millenarianism known as "dispensational premillennialism," or simply "dispensationalism," arose and in the twentieth century became the preferred eschatology of many conservative evangelicals.[9]

The question naturally arises, "How do Christians arrive at different eschatological views?" The answer, as always, is that they do so through distinctive interpretations of the Bible rooted in contrasting hermeneutical principles. This can be readily seen by how different interpreters engage the prophetic scenario provided in the Apocalypse of John. Revelation 19 depicts a dramatic return of Christ to rout the forces of wickedness and bind Satan. This is followed in chapter 20 by a "first resurrection" of Christian martyrs and other faithful believers who live and reign "with Christ a thousand years" (vv. 6, 4). The "rest of the dead [live] not again until the thousand years [are] finished" (v. 5). At that point, "the dead, small and great, stand before God" to be judged "according to their works" (v. 12). Following this, in chapters 21 and 22, John describes his vision of the "new heavens and new earth." Millenarians who read these chapters in Revelation sequentially and literally place the second coming a thousand years prior to Christ's later return in association with the last judgment affirmed in the Apostles' Creed. As will be seen, they also tend to envision the millennium terrestrially as a new Eden.

For much of Christian history, though, the dominant eschatology has interpreted John's visions neither literally nor linearly. The "thousand years" is typically taken to represent Christ's and the saints' figurative "reign" in and through the church Christ established on earth. The millennium is thus merely a metaphor for the gospel age. Similarly, the "first resurrection" is not a bodily resurrection. It is either a reference to the spiritual rebirth of the faithful in

---

9. Dispensationalism is not a monolith. It has varied over time from earlier "classic" dispensationalism rooted in the nineteenth-century teachings of John Nelson Darby and popularized in the *Scofield Reference Bible* (1909) to the "progressive" dispensationalism promoted at the end of the twentieth century. For an influential exposition of a slightly revised classic dispensationalism, see Charles C. Ryrie, *Dispensationalism Today* (Chicago: Moody Press, 1965). For the significantly revised "progressive" dispensationalism, see Craig A. Blaising and Darrell L. Bock, *Progressive Dispensationalism: An Up-to-Date Handbook of Contemporary Dispensationalist Thought* (Wheaton, IL: Bridgepoint, 1993). For a useful history of dispensationalism, with an eye to its impact on American culture and politics, see Daniel G. Hummel, *The Rise and Fall of Dispensationalism: How the Evangelical Battle over the End Times Shaped a Nation* (Grand Rapids: Eerdmans, 2023).

which they "rise" to newness of life in Christ or it refers to the faithful deceased, such as the early Christian martyrs who reign with Christ in heaven.[10] Not surprisingly, theologians refer to this figurative reading of history's final events as *amillennialism* (nonmillennialism) because it rejects the idea of an actual eschatological millennium, especially of a terrestrial nature. A small number of those who interpret the prophecies figuratively do, however, embrace the idea of a millennium of sorts prior to the eschaton (the end, last of human history). They view it as a lengthy but indefinite period of time, not a precise thousand years. Rather than conceiving of the millennial earth as transformed into an Edenic paradise, this interpretation anticipates a continuation of ordinary life on earth with the significant exception that Christianity will prevail across the globe thanks to a great eschatological outpouring of the Holy Spirit. Because this type of eschatology, like amillennialism, maintains that Christ's physical return will occur *after* the millennium, it is sometimes labeled *postmillennialism.* One way to summarize the different Christian interpretations of how history will end is to note that premillennialists, like the Latter-day Saints, as opposed to amillennialists and postmillennialists, envision *two* parousias (one that launches and one that concludes the millennium), two physical resurrections (the premillennial "first" resurrection of the righteous and the postmillennial general resurrection), two judgments (one that determines the makeup of the first resurrection, and the final judgment of humankind at the end of time), and two eschatological transformations labeled "new heavens and new earth" (the paradisiacal renewal of the earth that constitutes the millennium and the final renovation that makes of earth an eternal heaven).[11]

The question of how millenarians relate the "new heaven" and "new earth" to the millennium requires further commentary. Since Revelation 20 gives no description of the thousand years beyond mentioning the reign of Christ and the first resurrection, premillennialists have typically looked to Old Testament prophecies picturing Israel's latter-day glory, its "messianic age," to flesh out their picture of life during the millennium. The book of Isaiah, for instance, has been a key source with its depictions in 65:17-25 and 11:6-9 of a glorious

10. Such interpretations can be found in the Catholic *Catechism* (CCC 668-682), the *Orthodox Study Bible* (OSB, 1743-1745), Augsburg Confession (*Book of Concord,* 50-51), and Calvin's *Institutes* 3.25.5.

11. Theological debate between these differing forms of millennialism can be found in Robert G. Clouse, ed., *The Meaning of the Millennium: Four Views* (Downers Grove, IL: InterVarsity Press, 1977), and Darrell L. Bock, ed., *Three Views on the Millennium and Beyond* (Grand Rapids: Zondervan, 1999).

future age. Such textual appropriation by premillennialists is facilitated by the fact that in describing the wondrous future, Isaiah 65:17 uses the same phrase—"new heavens and a new earth"—that appears in Revelation 21:1 (and 2 Pet. 3:13).[12] Latter-day Saint millenarianism also makes this connection and applies the Isaianic passages to its portrayal of the millennium. The Book of Mormon incorporates the entirety of Isaiah 11 in its text (2 Nephi 21) and later reiterates the chapter's images, interpreting them as how God will "bring about the restoration of his people upon the earth" (2 Nephi 30:8-15). A Doctrine and Covenants revelation glosses Isaiah 65 in a major passage pertaining to the millennium: "And in that day the enmity of man, and the enmity of beasts, yea, the enmity of all flesh, shall cease from before my face. And in that day whatsoever any man shall ask, it shall be given unto him. And in that day Satan shall not have power to tempt any man. And there shall be no sorrow because there is no death. In that day an infant shall not die until he is old; and his life shall be as the age of a tree" (D&C 101:26-30).[13] Predictably, many (amillennialist) Christians view these Isaianic prophecies figuratively as attempts to depict the remarkable future age of the eschatological "new creation" rather than a prior thousand years of peace and prosperity.

Part of early Mormon reflection on the millennial "new earth" centered on the "New Jerusalem." In the Bible, the term is mentioned only (twice) in the book of Revelation and is generally regarded as a figurative expression for the divine presence or the Lamb's bride (the church) in the "new earth" of the eternal state. Latter-day Saint scripture, on the other hand, uses the term repeatedly and also sets it in a latter-day or millennial context (e.g., Ether 13:3-12; D&C 45:65-71). Thus deployed, the New Jerusalem was understood as an actual brick-and-mortar city the Latter-day Saints were to build in America in preparation for the Lord's return and that would serve, along with the rebuilt old Jerusalem, as

12. Illustrative of this textual linkage among dispensational premillennialists is the fact that the *Tim LaHaye Prophecy Study Bible* (Chattanooga, TN: AMG Publishers, 2000) places its article "The New Jerusalem" (discussed in Rev. 21-22) opposite the text of Isa. 65.

13. Discussion of LDS belief about the nature of life during the millennium can be found in *Gospel Principles*, 263-67; *Doctrines of the Gospel Student Manual* (2010), 104-6; *True to the Faith*, 103-4; *Gospel Fundamentals* (Salt Lake City: The Church of Jesus Christ of Latter-day Saints, 2002), chapter 34; and "Topics and Questions," s.v. "millennium," at churchofje suschrist.org. In the early years of Mormonism, a vivid millennial imagination, especially at the popular level, anticipated aspects of the millennium that rarely if ever are voiced today and have not received official endorsement. See Grant Underwood, *The Millenarian World of Early Mormonism* (Urbana: University of Illinois Press, 1993), and, for the later nineteenth and early twentieth centuries, Christopher James Blythe, *Terrible Revolution: Latter-day Saints and the American Apocalypse* (New York: Oxford University Press, 2020).

one of Christ's two millennial "capitals."[14] Just as "Zion" was another name for the old-world Jerusalem, early Latter-day Saints applied the term as an alternate designation for their New Jerusalem. When efforts to build their material Zion at a divinely revealed location in western Missouri were thwarted by antagonists, emphasis began to be placed on a passage in the Doctrine and Covenants that declared: "This is Zion—the pure in heart" (D&C 97:21). As the church grew and began to gain an international presence in the twentieth century, the vision of building a holy people more than a single holy city gained center stage.[15] Still, Joseph Smith's 1842 affirmation "that Zion (the New Jerusalem) will be built upon the American continent" (Articles of Faith 10) remains on the books. Although currently a literal, material interpretation of Smith's declaration is common, it is possible that at some point in the future it may yield to a figurative interpretation based on Doctrine and Covenants 97:21. For the present, though, church doctrine continues to contemplate the end-time building of an actual city, even if it does regard the endeavor as having been indefinitely postponed until future revelation revives it and offers clarifying guidance.[16]

When considering premillennialism, it is important to recognize the differences in eschatological schema. A closer look at differing beliefs about the coming of the Lord as described in 1 Thessalonians 4:16–17 provides a useful example. The passage states: "The Lord himself shall descend from heaven with a shout . . . with the trump of God: and the dead in Christ shall rise first: then we which are alive and remain shall be caught up together with them in the clouds, to meet the Lord in the air."[17] For dispensational premillennialists, this passage describes

14. Isaiah 2:3 predicts that "out of Zion shall go forth the law, and the word of the LORD from Jerusalem." Rather than interpreting this as an example of Hebrew parallelism, Latter-day Saints have read it as anticipating dual millennial capitals. See *Doctrines of Salvation*, 3:69–71. Joseph Fielding Smith's interpretation has been referenced in multiple twenty-first-century church curricular materials (e.g., *D&C Student Manual* [2017], 303; *Book of Mormon Student Manual* [2009], 75; and *Doctrines of the Gospel Student Manual* [2010], 105–6).

15. Some theologians interpret New Testament references to the New Jerusalem similarly. See Robert H. Gundry, "The New Jerusalem: People as Place, Not Place for People," *Novum Testamentum* 29 (1987): 254–64.

16. See Bruce R. McConkie, *New Witness for the Articles of Faith* (Salt Lake City: Deseret Book, 1985), 597–604. See the discussion of Zion in "Divine Foreknowledge, Sovereignty, and Prophecy" in chapter 2.

17. Some read this passage as evidence that Paul expected the parousia in his own lifetime. In Joseph Smith's "New Translation" of the Bible, however, Smith emended "we which are alive and remain" to read "they who are alive at the coming of the Lord." *NTOB*, 527. Smith also made a number of modifications in the "Olivet discourse" in Matt. 24 to similarly avoid the impression that Jesus expected a first-century conclusion to history. See *NTOB*, 220, 294.

an end-time "rapture" (carrying off, transporting) of believers to heaven prior to what dispensationalists calculate through an exercise in prophetic numerology will be a seven-year period of "tribulation" preceding Christ's return. Latter-day Saints and other nondispensational premillennialists, however, do not understand the "great tribulation" discussed by Jesus in his future-facing "Olivet discourse" (Mark 13/Matt. 24) to be a fixed seven years. Nor do they embrace a pretribulation rapture. Rather, they view Paul's depiction in 1 Thessalonians of the saints (living and dead) being raised at Christ's coming as a kind of posttribulation rapture to meet him "in the air: and so shall we ever be with the Lord" (v. 17). Paul ends his description here, but theologians go on to finish the story. Some argue that the aerial rendezvous with the Lord then leads to the faithful being directly transported to heaven to begin their eternal life. Others see the passage as depicting the righteous being caught up to join the returning Lord in his triumphal descent to earth to inaugurate the millennium. This interpretation evokes the image of loyal citizens coming out to meet the visiting king and returning joyously with him to the city to begin the celebration.

While the grammar and ambiguity of Paul's letter prevent definitive interpretation, what all agree on is that Paul is seeking to give the Thessalonians hope for their deceased, that the Christian dead will indeed be resurrected and again be with their Lord. Latter-day Saint scripture echoes 1 Thessalonians in its description of a first resurrection in conjunction with Christ's coming: "For I will reveal myself from heaven with power and great glory," and "a trump shall sound both long and loud . . . and they shall come forth—yea, even the dead which died in me, to receive a crown of righteousness . . . to be with me, that we may be one" (D&C 29:11–13). The message on the great day of the Lord's return will be: "Ye saints arise and live; ye sinners stay and sleep until I shall call again" at the end of the thousand years (D&C 43:18).[18] Paul himself mentions an "order" to the resurrection. Christ is "the firstfruits; afterward they that are Christ's at his coming. Then cometh the end, when he shall have delivered up the kingdom to God" (1 Cor. 15:22–24). By interpreting this passage through the lens of Revelation 20, premillennialists, including Latter-days Saints, read a thousand-year interval into "then" in "*then* cometh the end." To preclude a prima facie reading of "then," which communicates immediacy, Joseph Smith, in his "New Translation" of the Bible, replaced "then" with "afterward," the same adverb used in the previous clause that connected

---

18. The "sinners" here mentioned are "the rest of the dead; and they live not again until the thousand years are ended, neither again, until the end of the earth" (D&C 88:101). This echoes Rev. 20:5: "the rest of the dead lived not again until the thousand years were finished."

Christ's own resurrection with the much later resurrection of those "that are Christ's at his coming."[19]

APOCALYPTICISM AND EARLY MORMONISM

In Mormonism's early years, the Latter-day Saints were sustained by a noticeably apocalyptic version of premillennialism that echoed early Christian chiliasm. The context for Christian chiliasm included self-identification as the "new Israel" in fulfillment of Old Testament prophecy and opposition to Gnostic antimaterialism. Yet, as much as any other factor, it may have been Christianity's persecuted and marginal status in the Roman Empire that disposed the faithful toward a kind of apocalyptic millenarianism. Apocalypticism is the dream of "the great reversal."[20] Growing out of a profound discontent with the status quo and seeing society and its power brokers as evil and antagonistic, apocalypticism promises that the first will be last and the last first. Power structures fully controlled by the adversary can hardly be expected to yield to the efforts of the godly. Only God can make the situation right. Thus, if the present generation is viewed as ripe in iniquity, and especially if the righteous are being persecuted, the faithful are thereby provided with assurance that all is proceeding according to divine plan, that everything is in place for the great reversal soon to be effected by Christ's return. The book of Revelation promises the destruction of the wicked and the vindication of the suffering saints. Devout Christians will literally be brought back to life and, in a dramatic inversion of social hierarchies, instead of being oppressed will sit on thrones reigning with Christ for a thousand years. When this divine recompense is thought to be imminent, the appeal to beleaguered believers is obvious.[21]

The persecution of early Latter-day Saints was likewise an incubator for the kind of apocalyptic millenarianism to which Joseph Smith and his associates regularly gave voice.[22] It is even possible in Mormon history to correlate oscillations in the intensity of the Saints' millenarian rhetoric with the way they were treated by their neighbors. For example, marked apocalyptic rhetoric followed a frustrating summer of opposition in 1830. Multiple attempts by Joseph Smith to meet with a group of recently baptized believers to confirm them had

---

19. *NTOB*, 509.
20. See John J. Collins, ed., *The Oxford Handbook of Apocalyptic Literature* (New York: Oxford University Press, 2014), and his earlier *Continuum History of Apocalypticism*.
21. On reading Revelation apocalyptically, see Adela Yarbro Collins, *Crisis and Catharsis: The Power of the Apocalypse* (Philadelphia: Westminster, 1984).
22. See Underwood, *Millenarian World of Early Mormonism*, 42–57.

been thwarted by antagonists, and Smith even had to endure the humiliation of local imprisonment and trial on trumped-up charges. Such experiences lay in the immediate background of a letter he wrote to those affected by the persecution. "Brethren," he declared, "be not discouraged when we tell you of perilous times, for they must shortly come, for the sword, famine, and pestilence [are] approaching, for there shall be great destructions upon the face of this land."[23] Several weeks later a revelation added: "For the hour is nigh, and the day is soon at hand, when the earth will be ripe; and all the proud, and they that do wickedly, shall be as stubble, and I will burn them up, saith the Lord of Hosts, that wickedness shall not be upon the earth" (D&C 29:9–10).[24] At times, the rhetoric of apocalyptic vindication was explicitly directed against the Saints' antagonists. After a particularly traumatic and destructive episode of persecution some years later, Joseph Smith attempted to comfort his followers by writing that "the time soon shall come when the son of man shall descend in the clouds of heaven" and "will have our oppressors in derision." This statement glossed Psalm 2:4–5—"the Lord shall have them in derision. Then shall he speak unto them in his wrath, and vex them in his sore displeasure." When Christ returns, noted Smith, the avenging Lord, in fulfillment of Proverbs 1:26, "will laugh at their calamity and mock when their fear comith."[25]

Such apocalyptic rhetoric, particularly its local application, is all but nonexistent in the Church of Jesus Christ of Latter-day Saints today. Societal acceptance of the church and its members has changed dramatically since the nineteenth century. As people make their peace with the world (and the world makes its peace with them), the apocalyptic dream of the "great reversal" diminishes. This happened in the early centuries of Christianity, and a similar trajectory can be traced in LDS history. Harsh "them-us" rhetoric softens, and greater inclusiveness is manifest. In short, the more abrasive features of apocalyptic millenarianism, which served the Latter-day Saints' needs in an earlier period, have quietly, perhaps unwittingly, been laid aside. None of this, though, has overturned the basic tenets of their premillennial eschatology.[26]

---

23. *JSP*, D1:176.

24. This echoes a Book of Mormon statement that God "will preserve the righteous by his power, even if it so be that the fulness of his wrath must come, and the righteous be preserved, even unto the destruction of their enemies by fire. Wherefore, the righteous need not fear; for thus saith the prophet, they shall be saved, even if it so be as by fire" (1 Nephi 22:17).

25. *JSP*, D6:363.

26. In the 1980s, apostle Bruce McConkie published *The Millennial Messiah: The Second Coming of the Son of Man* (Salt Lake City: Deseret Book, 1982). At 726 pages, it is the longest single work ever written by a Latter-day Saint on eschatological matters. What is striking is

Along with an ebb of apocalyptic rhetoric, a decline in the sense of eschatological imminence is also apparent. In the subsequent two centuries since the founding of the Church of Jesus Christ of Latter-day Saints, the amount of theological attention paid to the second coming and millennium, at least by the church's leaders, has waned considerably. A study of general conference discourses reveals that such discussion "diminished drastically after 1920."[27] Most recently, however, church president Russell Nelson has made repeated reference to the importance of preparing for the second coming of Christ, although without elaborating on its nature or specifying a timetable for its fulfillment.[28] Continuing a motivational theme voiced to the youth of the church since the mid-twentieth century by apostles and prophets, President Nelson told the youth, "Our Heavenly Father has reserved many of His most noble spirits—perhaps, I might say, His finest team—for this final phase. Those noble spirits—those finest players, those heroes—are *you!*"[29]

Like the first Christians, early Latter-day Saints tended to expect the "day of the Lord" in their own lifetimes.[30] Six months after the church was founded, a revelation declared, "Verily, verily, I say unto you, the time is soon at hand that I shall come in a cloud with power and great glory" (D&C 34:7). Indeed, many of Joseph Smith's early revelations mention that the end is "nigh," "at hand," or will "soon" come.[31] While all such declarations with regard to timing can be read relatively, as they are today, the early Saints took them largely at face

how little McConkie's millennial treatise differs from eschatological works written during Mormonism's first generations.

27. Gordon Shepherd and Gary Shepherd, *A Kingdom Transformed: Early Mormonism and the Modern LDS Church*, 2nd ed. (Salt Lake City: University of Utah Press, 2015), 194–95.

28. In his first address to the church after becoming president in 2018, Nelson remarked, "Our Savior and Redeemer, Jesus Christ, will perform some of His mightiest works between now and when He comes again" (*Ensign*, May 2018, 96). Later, in a lighthearted moment, he added, "Eat your vitamin pills. Get your rest. It's going to be exciting." Of his vision of "preparing the Church and the world for the Second Coming," his wife remarked, "he is sincere" and "really focused on that. It's pretty stunning." https://newsroom.churchofje suschrist.org/article/latter-day-saint-prophet-wife-apostle-share-insights-global-ministry.

29. See https://www.churchofjesuschrist.org/study/new-era/2018/08-se/hope-of-is rael?lang=eng#p67.

30. "Christians, in fact, have almost always looked forward to the second coming of Christ, with all that it signifies, as something 'very near, even at the gates.'" Daley, *Hope of the Early Church*, 3.

31. The phrase "come quickly" is found in D&C 33:18; 34:12; 35:27; 39:24; 41:4; 49:28; 51:20; 54:10; 68:35; 87:8; 88:126; 99:5; 112:34. Expressions that the end is "nigh" or "at hand" can be found in D&C 1:12, 35; 29:9, 10; 33:10; 34:7; 35:15, 16, 26; 39:19, 21; 42:7; 43:17; 45:37–39; 49:6; 58:4; 63:53; 104:59; 106:4; 128:24; 133:17. For statements that eschatological events will take place "soon," see D&C 29:7; 34:7; 38:8; 101:11, 98.

value. Smith's own sense of imminence, however, declined toward the end of his life.[32] A catalyst was his encounter with William Miller, the forerunner of Seventh-day Adventists, who through complex and symbolic interpretation of the prophetic books of the Bible, particularly Daniel and Revelation, concluded that the second coming of Christ would occur "about the year 1843."[33] In part, Smith rejected Miller's prediction on the grounds that too many biblical prophecies remained unfulfilled as 1843 approached. Moreover, added Smith, "I was once praying very earnestly to know the time of the comeing of the son of man when I heard a voice repeat the following 'Joseph my son, if thou livest untill thou art 85 years old [he was 37 at the time of this recounting] thou shalt see the face of the son of man, therefore let this suffice and trouble me no more on this matter.'" Smith then remarked, "I was left thus without being able to decide wether this coming referred to the beginning of the Millenium, or to some previous appearing, or wether I should die and thus see his face. I believe the coming of the son of man will not be any sooner than that time."[34] In the event, Smith was murdered the very next year at the age of thirty-eight, presumably seeing the Lord's face much sooner than his eighty-fifth birthday.

THE INTERMEDIATE STATE

Having examined beliefs about the end of human history, we turn now to a consideration of the end of individual human lives. What happens to human beings at death? Do they cease to exist or continue in some state of personal, conscious existence? The New Testament is generally read to affirm life after death, and belief in a resurrection of some kind is widely proclaimed. What New Testament authors do not detail is the condition or state of the deceased after death and prior to the resurrection. Are human souls or spirits consigned directly to heaven or hell, or do they end up in some separate, transitional "place" or state to await a later reunion with their renovated, resurrected bodies? As with other issues, because the Bible is not a work of systematic theology, its hints and ambiguities make a definitive answer elusive. Several prominent passages reflect this ambiguity. Paul writes of his "desire to depart [this life], and to be with Christ" (Phil. 1:23). Does this imply that the righteous deceased go immediately to heaven where Christ is or that they will "be with him" spir-

---

32. On the eschatological beliefs of both Joseph Smith and early Latter-day Saints generally, see Underwood, *Millenarian World of Early Mormonism*, passim.

33. William Miller, *Evidence from Scripture and History of the Second Coming of Christ about the Year 1843; Exhibited in a Course of Lectures* (Troy, NY: Kemble & Hooper, 1836).

34. JSP, J2:403-4, later canonized as D&C 130:14-17.

itually in a separate heaven-like condition (or place)? Luke famously reports Jesus's remark to the thief on the cross, "To-day shalt thou be with me in paradise" (Luke 23:43). Does "paradise" here refer to heaven and Jesus's statement about "today" prove that heaven is where penitent souls go immediately upon death? Or does "paradise" refer to a condition of interim blessedness that is heaven-like but not heaven itself? In 2 Corinthians 5:1, Paul speaks of our earthly body as the "tabernacle" (tent) that presently clothes our spirit or soul, but he declares that when it is "dissolved, we have a building of God, an house not made with hands, eternal in the heavens." Is Paul referring to a resurrected and immortal physical body or to the resurrected spiritual body of which he had written earlier (1 Cor. 15:44)? For centuries students of the Bible have differed on how best to answer these questions and interpret these passages.

Another place of contested interpretation in the New Testament is the parable of the rich man and Lazarus (Luke 16:19–31). The parable portrays an earth-life scene in which a rich man persistently ignores a starving beggar named Lazarus. Then, both men pass away. Lazarus finds himself "comforted" in "Abraham's bosom," while the rich man suffers "torments" in "hell." Although the parable's point is *not* to proclaim a particular doctrine of the afterlife but to urge the proper, generous use of riches, the story nonetheless has been read to shed light on the afterlife. Is "Abraham's bosom" a metonym for heaven where Lazarus finds himself in the eternal-state company of the pious? Or does "Abraham's bosom" identify an intermediate place or state of blessed rest and saintly association for the righteous? Is the hell (*hadēs*, in this passage) where the rich man suffers to be understood as a transitional condition until the resurrection and final judgment? Or is it depicting his eternal state of torment and fiery punishment?[35] Again, answers differ. So where do various Christian traditions come down on the perennial question of what follows death?

If one were to do a head count, it is likely that a majority of Christians, either in terms of popular belief or their tradition's formal theology, anticipate immediate entrance upon death into heaven or hell rather than to some

---

35. The latter seems less likely since Luke uses *hadēs* to identify the rich man's location rather than *gehenna*. In antiquity, the Valley of Hinnom (*gei hinnom* [Heb.] or *gehenna* [Gk.]) allegedly served at times as a cultic site for child sacrifice and at other times as a garbage dump. Although it is mentioned in the Old Testament, it is there "not associated with hell or afterlife." Later, "in the Hellenistic period, and particularly in the New Testament, the location came to be used metaphorically for hell, full of fiery torment." Alan F. Segal, *Life after Death: A History of the Afterlife in Western Religion* (New York: Doubleday, 2004), 135. See also Alan E. Bernstein, *The Formation of Hell: Death and Retribution in the Ancient and Early Christian Worlds* (Ithaca, NY: Cornell University Press, 1993).

intermediate state or place. This is so because the numerically dominant Roman Catholic Church and a significant number of Protestant denominations espouse such beliefs.[36] However, Catholics do qualify this belief by noting that transitionally and temporarily Christians will experience a postmortem period of refining penitential suffering and purification known as "purgatory." "All who die in God's grace and friendship, but still imperfectly purified," explains the *Catechism*, "are indeed assured of their eternal salvation; but after death they undergo purification, so as to achieve the holiness necessary to enter the joy of heaven. The Church gives the name Purgatory to this final purification of the elect."[37] To clarify, purgatory is *not* hell; purgatory is for Christians. Time in purgatory (and the intermediate state is still "in time," not "in eternity") varies from individual to individual, but it is always temporary and it always, upon complete purification, eventuates in entrance into heaven. Indeed, it has often been called heaven's "antechamber."[38] Once purified, Christian souls enter heaven and enjoy the "beatific vision," an "intuitive" and "face-to-face" vision of God,[39] which "will continue without any interruption and without end until the [resurrection and] last judgment and from then on forever." Thus, souls refined in purgatory "already before they take up their bodies again and before the general judgment, have been, are, and will be with Christ in heaven." In contrast, "the souls of those who die in actual mortal sin go down into hell immediately after death and there suffer the pain of hell," although they, too, will be resurrected and on judgment day "will appear with their bodies 'before the judgment seat of Christ' to give an account of their personal deeds."[40]

Eastern Orthodoxy envisions an intermediate state that is distinct from heaven or hell. Explains one Orthodox scholar, "The idea of an intermediate *state*, neither heaven nor hell, seems generally to be assumed in Orthodox belief, though to think of this state as a *place*, comparable with heaven and hell, is unusual." Also,

---

36. *CCC* 980–1060; Wayne Grudem, *Systematic Theology: An Introduction to Biblical Doctrine*, 2nd ed. (Grand Rapids: Zondervan Academic, 2020), 1005–16.

37. *CCC* 1030–1031.

38. Scholars agree that while a fully developed doctrine of purgatory did not emerge until the second millennium (see Jacques Le Goff's seminal *The Birth of Purgatory* [Chicago: University of Chicago Press, 1984]), a trajectory of teachings in that direction is discernible early on. See Isabel Moreira, *Heaven's Purge: Purgatory in Late Antiquity* (New York: Oxford University Press, 2010). Popular perceptions and misperceptions of purgatory are explored in Diana Walsh Pasulka, *Heaven Can Wait: Purgatory in Catholic Devotional and Popular Culture* (New York: Oxford University Press, 2015).

39. On the "beatific" (blessed) vision or *visio Dei* (vision of God), see Hans Boersma, *Seeing God: The Beatific Vision in Christian Tradition* (Grand Rapids: Eerdmans, 2018).

40. Denzinger 1001, 1000, 1002.

while Orthodoxy does not dismiss the possibility of some kind of postmortem purification and suffering, it does repudiate the medieval Catholic notion of a purgatorial "fire" of expiation.[41] Protestants reject purgatory's underlying premise altogether, arguing that heaven-worthy purity is a grace God monergistically bestows upon the elect at death. The statement in the Westminster Confession is typical: upon death "the souls of the righteous [are] then made perfect in holiness."[42] About as far as most Protestants are willing to go toward the concept of an intermediate state is to consider the doctrine Calvin once opposed labeled *psychopannychia*, popularly known as "soul sleep."[43] Promoted in his day by some Anabaptists, *psychopannychia* builds on "sleep" as a scriptural metaphor or euphemism for death and maintains that the soul perdures after death in unconsciousness until "awakened" at the resurrection. Although never the dominant view, the doctrine has appeared in the writings of Protestants as diverse as Anabaptists and Martin Luther, and it received renewed acceptance among such nineteenth-century groups as the Adventist churches and Jehovah's Witnesses.[44] A modern variation on this theme harks back to what many consider the early Hebrew view and envisions the human to be a psychophysical unit rather than dualistically composed of body and distinct soul. This view posits that at death the human being entirely ceases to exist until essentially re-created in the resurrection.[45]

For the Church of Jesus Christ of Latter-day Saints, in addition to relevant biblical passages, a foundational text regarding life after death is found in the Book of Mormon: "Now, concerning the state of the soul between death and the resurrection—Behold . . . the spirits of all men, as soon as they are departed from this mortal body, yea, the spirits of all men, whether they be good or evil, are taken home to that God who gave them life.[46] And then shall it come

41. Andrew Louth, *Introducing Eastern Orthodox Theology* (Downers Grove, IL: IVP Academic, 2013), 155.

42. WC 32.

43. *Psychopannychia; or, A Refutation of the Error Entertained by Some Unskilful Persons* (1534) was one of Calvin's earliest treatises. Richard C. Gamble, "Calvin's Controversies," in *The Cambridge Companion to John Calvin*, ed. Donald K. McKim (Cambridge: Cambridge University Press, 2004), 189.

44. See Bryan W. Ball, *The Soul Sleepers: Christian Mortalism from Wycliffe to Priestley* (Cambridge: James Clarke, 2008).

45. Although something like this view appears to have been held in ancient Judaism, it has been rare among Christians until the twentieth century, when developments in neuroscience prompted its reconsideration and reconfiguration as "physicalism" or "holistic dualism." See chapter 5.

46. This statement echoes Eccles. 12:7: "Then shall the dust return to the earth as it was: and the spirit shall return unto God who gave it."

to pass, that the spirits of those who are righteous are received into a state of happiness, which is called paradise, a state of rest, a state of peace," and "the spirits of the wicked, yea, who . . . chose evil works rather than good . . . shall be cast out into outer darkness" where "there shall be weeping, and wailing, and gnashing of teeth."[47] The passage then affirms that the wicked "shall remain in this state, as well as the righteous in paradise . . . until the time which is appointed of God that the dead shall come forth, and be reunited, both soul and body, and be brought to stand before God, and be judged according to their works" (Alma 40:11–14, 21).

On the surface, if one reads "paradise" as a synonym for heaven and "outer darkness" as an alternate term for hell, this passage represents a fairly standard statement of the majoritarian eschatological view that upon death and after an initial judgment, souls go either to heaven or hell to await the resurrection.[48] Although there was little discussion of Alma 40 in Mormonism's early years, in time the passage came to be understood as describing the intermediate state as a separate "spirit world" quite distinct from the eternal heaven or hell, which Latter-day Saints also understand in spatial terms. Such a view was an easy conceptualization for Mormons, who posit a similarly "located" pre-existent world of souls.[49] If our spirits "had an existence before we came here," remarked Joseph F. Smith, "we certainly shall continue that existence when we leave here."[50] Leave here to go where? Heaven? "No, not anywhere nigh there," answered Brigham Young, "but into the spirit world. Where is the spirit world? It is right here" on earth, invisible, in another dimension, a parallel universe, so to speak. "Can you see it with your natural eyes?" asked Young. "No. Can you

---

47. "Outer darkness" is a biblically uncommon phrase found only in Matt. 8:12; 22:13; 25:30. Aside from Alma 40, it is found in LDS scripture only in D&C 101:91; 133:73.

48. Similar to Alma 40 is the formative 1689 London Baptist Confession, which echoes the Westminster Confession and states that, upon death, "the souls of the righteous being then made perfect in holiness, are received into paradise, where they are with Christ . . . waiting for the full redemption of their bodies; and the souls of the wicked are cast into hell, where they remain in torment and utter darkness, reserved to the judgment of the great day." *Creeds & Confessions*, 2:646.

49. See chapter 5.

50. *Gospel Doctrine*, 40. As it was in the preexistence, "when you are in the spirit world, everything there will appear as natural as things now do," explained Brigham Young. "Spirits will be familiar with spirits in the spirit world—will converse, behold, and exercise every variety of communication with one another as familiarly and naturally as while here in [fleshly] tabernacles." This, of course, entails a continuation of "powers of motion, of thought, and . . . attributes of moral, intellectual, and sympathetic affections and emotions." *Journal of Discourses*, 7:239.

see spirits in this room? No." Yet, "If the Lord would permit it . . . you could see the spirits that have departed from this world, as plainly as you now see bodies with your natural eyes."[51] Young's apostolic colleague Parley Pratt agreed with him about the location of the world of departed souls: "The spirit world is not the heaven where Jesus Christ, his Father, and other beings dwell . . . it is here on the very planet where we were born."[52] Moreover, emphasized Pratt, in the spirit world, we continue to be "in every way interested in our relationships, kindred ties, sympathies, affections, and hopes, as if we had continued to live, but had stepped aside."[53] To be sure, belief in a proximate spirit world filled with souls interested in this life was nothing new in the nineteenth century, where spiritualism and its vision of a thin veil separating the embodied from the disembodied were taking America by storm.[54] The idea that the spirit world is "here on earth" continues to be reiterated in LDS publications today, especially as mediated through comments by Brigham Young.[55]

Emphasizing that the spirit world is not heaven has even led some church leaders to qualify the statement in Alma that upon death souls "are taken home to that God who gave them life" (Alma 40:11). First Presidency member George Cannon argued on the basis of God's omnipresence (Ps. 139:7–8) that Alma did "not intend to convey the idea that [spirits] are immediately ushered into the *personal* presence of God."[56] Some years later, apostle Joseph Fielding Smith concurred that it was a mistaken idea that "all spirits go back into the presence of God for an assignment to a place of peace or a place of punishment and before him receive their individual sentence." Rather, the statement "taken home to God" in Alma "simply means that their mortal existence has come to an end, and they have returned to the world of spirits, where they are assigned to a place according to their works with the just or with the unjust, there to await the resurrection."[57] In any case, "the fulness of the presence of the Father,

51. *Journal of Discourses*, 3:368–69.

52. Pratt, *Key to Theology*, 126.

53. *Journal of Discourses*, 1:8.

54. See Catherine L. Albanese, *A Republic of Mind and Spirit: A Cultural History of American Metaphysical Religion* (New Haven: Yale University Press, 2007), 121–254; and Bret E. Carroll, *Spiritualism in Antebellum America* (Bloomington: Indiana University Press, 1997), 16–34, 60–84.

55. See, for example, *Gospel Principles*, 241–42; *Book of Mormon Student Manual* (2009), 243; "What Happens after We Die?" *New Era*, March 2013, 28–31; and *Teachings: Brigham Young*, 279–84.

56. George Q. Cannon, "Editorial Thoughts," *Juvenile Instructor*, June 1891, 353–54 (emphasis added).

57. Joseph Fielding Smith, *Answers to Gospel Questions* (Salt Lake City: Deseret Book, 1958), 2:85.

and of His Son Jesus Christ," declared Parley Pratt, is "reserved for resurrected beings, who dwell in immortal flesh. . . . The world of resurrected beings, and the world of spirits, are two distinct spheres, as much so as our own sphere is distinct from that of the spirit world."[58] It has long been common among Latter-day Saints to argue this distinction biblically by contrasting Jesus's statement to the thief on the cross, "To-day shalt thou be with me in paradise" (Luke 23:43), with his statement three days later to Mary, "Touch me not; for I am not yet ascended to my Father" (John 20:17). The reasoning of James Talmage is typical: paradise "is not the place of final glory; for such the thief who died with Christ was assuredly not prepared, yet we cannot doubt the fulfilment of our Lord's promise that the penitent malefactor should be with Him in paradise that day; and, moreover, the declaration of the risen Savior to Mary Magdalene, three days later, that He had not at that time ascended to His Father, is proof of His having spent the intermediate time in paradise."[59]

Alma implies that the condition and "location" of the deceased in the spirit world are the result of a preliminary or partial judgment that he calls "their consignation [consignment] to happiness or misery" (Alma 40:15, 17).[60] In this, Mormon doctrine parallels other Christian eschatologies that affirm a "particular" judgment at death as opposed to the "final" or "last" judgment at the end of time. Catholics view this postmortem judgment more definitively than do Latter-day Saints. The *Catechism* states that each individual "receives his *eternal* retribution in his immortal soul at the very moment of his death, in a particular judgment that [brings] either entrance into the blessedness of heaven—through a purification [in purgatory] or immediately—or immediate and everlasting damnation."[61] Nor has Alma's envisioned assessorial "consignation" of deceased souls ever been viewed in as elaborate a fashion as some earlier forms of the Orthodox Trisagion (Thrice Holy) liturgy for the departed. In these rites, the deceased individual was understood to be involved in a six-day postmortem journey through "toll-houses" manned by supernatural gatekeepers (some-

---

58. *Journal of Discourses*, 1:9.

59. James E. Talmage, *The Articles of Faith: A Series of Lectures on the Principal Doctrines of the Church of Jesus Christ of Latter-day Saints* (Salt Lake City: Deseret New Press, 1899), 405. This contrasts with the standard Christian interpretation that the "good" thief through divine grace was truly penitent and expressed genuine, saving faith in Christ on the eve of his death. For an early example of this view, see Archbishop Theophilus of Alexandria's "Homily on the Crucifixion and the Good Thief," reproduced in Normal Russell, *Theophilus of Alexandria* (London: Routledge, 2007), 63–70.

60. Subsequent LDS discourse called this a "partial" judgment. See, for example, *Gospel Doctrine*, 565, 566; Charles W. Penrose, *Conference Report*, October 1916, 18; and *Gospel Principles*, 269.

61. *CCC* 1022 (emphasis added).

times both angelic and demonic) who examine the departed for every earthly sin and vice. The soul fortunate enough to advance beyond the tollhouses with the aid of angels and the prayers of saints and loved ones then goes on tour of heaven and hell. Following this, similar to Latter-day Saint doctrine, the soul "undergoes the particular judgement, and then is assigned to an intermediate state, a state of waiting in Paradise or Hades, provisional in comparison with heaven and hell, that await the decisions of the Last Judgement."[62]

Once the particular judgment at death takes place, how does the individual's consignment to happiness or misery play out in the intermediate state? Brigham Young believed that in the next life "good and evil spirits go together" and "inhabit one kingdom." "I know it is a startling idea," admitted Young, "to say that the Prophet and the persecutor of the Prophet, all go . . . together." But in life we "find the righteous and the wicked, all dwelling together; and when we go beyond this veil . . . we go where both Saints and sinners go; they all go to one place."[63] In expressing such a view, Young was probably influenced by Joseph Smith, who arrived at a similar conclusion through linguistics. "There has been much said," remarked Smith, "about the sayings of Jesus on the cross to the thief saying this day thou shalt be with me in paradise. The commentators or translators make it out to say Paradise but what is Paradise?" Although Smith might have noted Paul's one metaphorical link between paradise and heaven (2 Cor. 12:2–4), his intent on this occasion was strictly lexical: there "is nothing in the original . . . that signifies Paradise" is heaven. Although Smith had limited knowledge of Hebrew and even less acquaintance with Greek, he owned lexicons.[64] From them he may have learned that *ouranos*, used several hundred times in the New Testament, is the primary Greek term for heaven, whereas *paradeisos* (park, garden) appears only three times. Smith believed that what Jesus meant to communicate to the thief when he used the term "paradise" was "this day I will be with thee in the world of spirits." He "did not say Paradise" to mean "heaven."[65] For Smith, paradise was linked to other

---

62. Louth, *Eastern Orthodox Theology*, 150–51. Louth adds that "this comparatively detailed account of the fate of the soul after death . . . has never been formally defined, and rests for its authority less on the Fathers of the Church than on popular belief, supported by liturgical practice" (151).

63. *Journal of Discourses*, 3:94–95.

64. An entry in Joseph Smith's journal notes that his close associate Oliver Cowdery presented him with both a Hebrew and a Greek lexicon in November 1835 upon his return from a trip to New York City. *JSP*, J1:107.

65. *JSP*, D12:385–86. In the Book of Mormon, "paradise" consistently refers to the pre-resurrection realm of the righteous deceased (Alma 40:12–21; 2 Nephi 9:13; 4 Nephi 1:14;

terms for the world of disembodied souls: "Hades shaole paradise, spirits in prision is all one[.] It is a world of spirits, the righteous & the wicked all go to the same world of spirits."⁶⁶

Joseph Smith also made a similar point about the term "hell." "What is hell?" he asked. "It is taken from *hades* the Greek or *shaole*, the (hebrew)." Here, Smith is on more familiar footing. The "true signification" for these terms "is a world of spirits." It is the abode of the dead where "disembodied spirits all go—good bad & indifferent."⁶⁷ Although "the righteous and the wicked are together in Hades," differentiation is possible, explained Brigham Young. The righteous in paradise "are in possession of the spirit of Jesus—the power of God, which is their heaven." But it is also their "prison" because they "have not got their [resurrected] bodies yet," and "in the presence of the Father, and the Son, they cannot dwell, and be crowned, until the work of the redemption of both body and spirit is completed."⁶⁸ Joseph F. Smith later saw in vision that "the dead had looked upon the long absence of their spirits from their bodies as a bondage" (D&C 138:50; cf. 45:17). As for the wicked in the world of departed souls, "Are they happy? No. . . . They fully understand that they have persecuted the just and Holy One, and they feel the wrath of the Almighty resting upon them, having a terrible foreboding of the final consummation of their just sentence, to become angels to the devil."⁶⁹ The other way in which differentiation is likely, offered James Talmage, is that "in the intermediate state like will seek like, the clean and good finding companionship with their kind, and the wicked congregating through the natural attraction of evil for evil."⁷⁰

As time passed, however, the Mormon conception of a single society of departed spirits, albeit experiencing dramatically different psychological and

---

Moroni 10:34). Occasionally in other contexts, metaphorical reference to heaven as paradise has seemed appropriate. D&C 77:2 mentions "heaven, the paradise of God," and Joseph F. Smith later spoke of those who "dwell in heaven, or in the paradise of the just." *Journal of Discourses*, 23:173.

66. *JSP*, D12:386.

67. *JSP*, D12:386, 383. Brigham Young remarked that "though we may call it Hades or hell. It is the world of spirits, it is where Jesus went, and where we all go, both good and bad." *Journal of Discourses*, 17:142.

68. *Journal of Discourses*, 3:95.

69. *Journal of Discourses*, 3:94-95. "Now this is the state of the souls of the wicked, yea, in darkness, and a state of awful, fearful looking for the fiery indignation of the wrath of God upon them; thus they remain in this state, as well as the righteous in paradise, until the time of their resurrection" (Alma 40:14).

70. James E. Talmage, *The Vitality of Mormonism: Brief Essays on Distinctive Doctrines of the Church of Jesus Christ of Latter-day Saints* (Boston: Gorham, 1919), 262.

emotional states, faded and a more "geographically" differentiated spirit world emerged. The abode of the righteous dead came to be referred to almost exclusively as "paradise," and "spirit prison" became the term of choice for the location of all other departed souls.[71] LDS discourse sometimes uses "hell" as a synonym for "spirit prison," but more commonly it is deployed to identify a division of or condition within spirit prison where "the wicked" suffer for their unrepented sins.[72] Latter-day Saints believe that "three kinds of people" will inhabit spirit prison: (1) "those who lived good lives but did not accept the gospel"; (2) "those who never had the opportunity to hear the gospel"; and (3) "those who were wicked in this life."[73] Alma 40 does not know groups 1 and 2. It only differentiates between "the righteous" and "the wicked," consigning the latter to "outer darkness," where "weeping and gnashing of teeth" take place. Biblical interpretation typically associates these Matthean phrases with hell in the final state, and broader Mormon doctrine does not disagree. Yet Alma 40 uses them to describe the condition or place of the wicked in the intermediate state, "weeping, and wailing, and gnashing [their] teeth until the time of their resurrection" (Alma 40:13–14). To reduce confusion in current LDS teaching as to which state is in view, "spirit prison" rather than "hell" tends to be used when discussing the intermediate state.[74] That the other two of the three categories of spirit-prison inhabitants—the unevangelized and the good but unconverted souls—are not known in the Book of Mormon reflects the fact that a doctrine of "salvation for the dead" did not begin to appear until after the book's publication.

Today the notion of a socially differentiated spirit world is dominant among Latter-day Saints.[75] Teaching diagrams in several current church manuals, as well as language describing the different "parts" or "places" in the spirit world, imply a geographic separation.[76] Indeed, the spirit world is conceived in almost

71. Although "spirit prison" per se is not a scriptural term, it is derived from 1 Pet. 3:19, which says that Christ "went and preached unto the spirits in prison," and may also reflect the use of "prison" as a metaphor for the abode of the dead in Isaiah. See Isa. 24:21–22; 42:6–7; 49:8–9.

72. *True to the Faith*, s.v. "hell."

73. *Gospel Fundamentals* (2002), 196.

74. See, for example, *True to the Faith*, 46.

75. For example, *Gospel Principles* says that in the spirit world "the righteous and the wicked are separated" (243). Also quoted today is Heber Kimball's account of the near-death experience of Jedediah Grant, Brigham Young's counselor in the First Presidency: "He saw the righteous gathered together in the spirit world, and there were no wicked spirits among them." *Journal of Discourses*, 4:136.

76. See diagrams in *New Testament Seminary Teacher Resource Manual* (2003), 14, and *Doctrine and Covenants Seminary Teacher Resource Manual* (2005), 8. *Guide to the Scriptures,*

"hemispheric" terms in the popular LDS imagination. The development of Mormon thought on the "geography" of the hereafter parallels an earlier evolution in Western eschatology. As on so many other topics, Augustine, though not the first, was almost always the most articulate expounder of the theological ideas he addressed. He made the clearest distinction between "hades" as the term for the entire domain of the dead (as Joseph Smith did) and "hell" as the region where the damned suffer. Previously, Tertullian had taught that the underworld hades "is divided into two, 'the good and the bad lower places.'" Paradise is "Tertullian's name for the comfortable part of the lower-region," and "heaven and Paradise are not the same. The latter is a garden in the lower regions." Hell, on the other hand, is the "bad lower place" in the underworld. In sum, "all souls are in the lower regions until the resurrection."[77] Eventually, medieval Catholicism identified several additional "places" in the intermediate state: purgatory (already discussed); *limbus patrum* (limbo of the fathers), where the Old Testament patriarchs dwelt until liberated by Christ during his "descent to Hades"; and children's limbo, for the unbaptized infants.[78]

The question is occasionally asked if LDS theology's elaborate vision of the postmortem spirit world includes any conception resembling the Catholic doctrine of purgatory. The answer is that while Latter-day Saints are just as ready as Catholics to admit that church members die without being sin-free, exactly how this will be resolved in the next life has not been a common topic of discussion.[79] This may reflect more frequent attention to the strong exhortation in the Book of Mormon that "this life is the time for men to prepare to meet God." Therefore, "do not procrastinate the day of your repentance until the end; for after this day of life, which is given us to prepare for eternity, behold, if we do not improve our time while in this life, then cometh the night of darkness wherein there can be no labor performed" (Alma 34:32–33). Because this passage does not appear to take cognizance of the developed Mormon doctrine of the afterlife and vicarious work for the dead, subsequent interpretation has been necessary

---

s.v. "paradise," defines paradise as "that *part* of the spirit world in which the righteous spirits who have departed from this life await the resurrection of the body" (emphasis added).

77. David E. Wilhite, "Tertullian on the Afterlife: 'Only Martyrs Are in Heaven' and Other Misunderstandings," *Zeitschrift für Antikes Christentum/Journal of Ancient Christianity* 24, no. 3 (2020): 499 (490–508).

78. It may be recalled from the discussion in chapter 9 that in the aftermath of Vatican II, notions of a limbo for children have almost disappeared, and "hope" is expressed "that there is a way of salvation for children who have died without Baptism." *CCC* 1261.

79. Protestants also, for the most part, have not developed a doctrine of purgatory, although appreciation for aspects of it can be found in Jerry L. Walls's *Purgatory: The Logic of Total Transformation* (New York: Oxford University Press, 2011), and *Heaven, Hell, and Purgatory: A Protestant View of the Cosmic Drama* (Grand Rapids: Brazos, 2015).

to harmonize the two. Joseph Fielding Smith taught that "this life" in the passage should be understood to include the intermediate state and, therefore, is still part of humanity's "probationary" period during which repentance can take place. Apostle Neal Maxwell added, "We tend to overlook the reality that . . . our time of mortal trial, testing, proving, and overcoming by faith . . . will continue in some key respects into the spirit world."[80]

Still, with the Book of Mormon statement in mind that repentance should not be procrastinated, church leaders have cautioned that postmortem purification may be more difficult than personal reformation during earth life. In a much-cited address from the early twentieth century, apostle Melvin Ballard opined that because in the afterlife the spirit is unable to work together with the body, "it is my judgment that any man or woman can do more to conform to the laws of God in one year in this life than they could in ten years when they are dead." For this reason, "every man and woman who is putting off until the next life the task of correcting and overcoming the weakness of the flesh are sentencing themselves to years of bondage, for no man or woman will come forth in the resurrection" until purified from sin.[81] Will Latter-day Saints' purgatorial repentance take place in paradise? Joseph F. Smith thought not: "If we do not conform to [God's] will, obey his laws and yield to his requirements in this world, we will be consigned to [spirit prison] where we will remain until we pay the debt."[82] In the end, though, there is an exit door from spirit prison, just as there is from purgatory. Church members who have paid their penitential debt and completed their repentance will, along with the unevangelized who embrace the gospel in spirit prison, "be welcomed into paradise."[83] In the Mormon schema, the purified are admitted to the spirit-world paradise; in the Catholic scenario, they are admitted to the heavenly paradise.

Salvation for the Dead

Christians of all kinds have long wrestled with how best to understand the fate of the "unevangelized"—those who died without hearing the gospel. Various theories have been developed over the years to resolve this dilemma.[84] Of

---

80. Neal A. Maxwell, *The Promise of Discipleship* (Salt Lake City: Deseret Book, 2001), 119.

81. Melvin J. Ballard, *Three Degrees of Glory: A Discourse* (Salt Lake City, 1922), 13–15.

82. *Gospel Doctrine*, 41.

83. *Principles of the Gospel* (Salt Lake City: The Church of Jesus Christ of Latter-day Saints, 2014), 68.

84. Detailed in James Beilby, *Postmortem Opportunity: A Biblical and Theological Assessment of Salvation after Death* (Downers Grove, IL: IVP Academic, 2021), and Jeffrey A.

course, for strongly predestinarian theologies, the problem of the unevangelized does not even exist. God determined beforehand exactly who would be saved, and he sees to it that they are. The rest of humanity, never destined for salvation in the first place, simply receive the damnation their sinful rebellion against God deserves. Nondeterministic Christian theologies, however, offer a number of solutions to the problem of the unevangelized, including: (1) "universalism"—ultimately God saves everyone. (2) God saves the virtuous regardless of their religious beliefs or lack thereof. This includes morally exemplary women and men from all ages and places. (3) A slight variation of #2 focuses on religious piety and envisions the salvation of all who are God-fearing practitioners of their own religious principles.[85] Theories of this third kind recognize that non-Christian religions possess sufficient divine truth to enable their adherents to enter into a saving relationship with God or at least to prepare them to accept the gospel when it is presented to them.

A version of this latter type of thinking is Catholic theologian Karl Rahner's idea of the "anonymous Christian" that posits that Christ's grace can be found in individuals of all religions even if they are not conscious of it.[86] The official Roman Catholic position is a combination of #2 and #3 above. The Dogmatic Constitution of the Church, *Lumen Gentium*, states: "Those also can attain to salvation who through no fault of their own do not know the Gospel of Christ or His Church, yet sincerely seek God and moved by grace strive by their deeds to do His will as it is known to them through the dictates of conscience. Nor does Divine Providence deny the helps necessary for salvation to those who, without blame on their part, have not yet arrived at an explicit knowledge of God and with His grace strive to live a good life."[87] Some years before Vatican II, in response to a group of Catholic rigorists in Boston who believed that "all men are excluded from eternal salvation except for Catholics and [Catholic] catechumens," the Sacred Congregation of the Holy Office sent a letter of correction to the archbishop of Boston. It clarified that "it is not always required that [a person] be incorporated into the Church actually as a member, but it is necessary that at least he be united to her by desire and

---

Trumbower, *Rescue for the Dead: The Posthumous Salvation of Non-Christians in Early Christianity* (New York: Oxford University Press, 2001).

85. See John Sanders, ed., *What about Those Who Have Never Heard? Three Views on the Destiny of the Unevangelized* (Downers Grove, IL: InterVarsity Press, 1995).

86. See Rahner, "Anonymous and Explicit Faith," in *Theological Investigations*, vol. 16 (New York: Seabury, 1979), 52–59, and "Observations on the Problem of the Anonymous Christian," in *Theological Investigations*, vol. 14 (New York: Seabury, 1976), 280–94.

87. *Lumen Gentium*, 16, in Denzinger 4140.

longing." This desire must be "animated by [the grace of] charity." Thus, "the implicit desire can produce no [saving] effect unless a person has [the divinely imparted grace of] supernatural faith."[88]

Other theories require conscious acceptance of the gospel. Several ideas have been proposed for how this might be accomplished: (1) God is his own missionary—in all ages and places, he works through the Holy Spirit, the ministry of angels, even dreams to reveal himself and teach the gospel. In this view, communicating the good news has not been confined to God's earthly ministers. (2) Acceptance at death—this is the idea that everyone who does not hear the gospel on earth will, immediately upon death, be given the chance to accept or reject Christ. (3) Hypothetical acceptance—God saves all who *would* have accepted the gospel if they had had the chance. Since God knows what each person would do in any given situation, he knows exactly who would have chosen Christ if circumstances had permitted. This eliminates the need for any kind of afterlife evangelism whether by human or heavenly means. (4) Postmortem ministry—the unevangelized will have the opportunity in the intermediate state to hear and accept the gospel. Divine love and mercy overflow the boundary of the grave.

Because Latter-day Saint theology offers an expansive version of #4, we shall focus on that position in this section. Various biblical passages have been adduced to support such an idea, but two in 1 Peter have been particularly influential. First Peter 3:18–20 describes Christ as "being put to death in the flesh, but quickened by the Spirit: by which also he went and preached unto the spirits in prison; which sometime were disobedient, when once the longsuffering of God waited in the days of Noah." First Peter 4:6 adds: "For for this cause was the gospel preached also to them that are dead, that they might be judged according to men in the flesh, but live according to God in the spirit." Precisely what these texts mean and whether or not they should be interpretively linked have been matters of considerable debate over the years.[89] Some commentators have uncoupled the two passages, arguing that the "dead" mentioned in 4:6 refer either to the *spiritually* dead (per Augustine) or to Christians who had the gospel preached to them in life but have died (the common "judgment"

---

88. Denzinger 3869–3872.

89. Trumbower, *Rescue for the Dead*, 44, notes that these verses "have received an extraordinary amount of attention through the centuries because they might indicate that a person could die an unrepentant, unconverted sinner, yet still by saved by responding positively to the gospel in the afterlife." For a rehearsal of prominent interpretive options pertaining to these passages, see William J. Dalton, *Christ's Proclamation to the Spirits: A Study of 1 Peter 3:18–4:6*, 2nd ed. (Rome: Editrice Pontifico Istituto Biblico, 1989).

on all human beings) and now live happily according to God in the spirit. Others, in contrast, contend that "the most natural explanation is surely to connect" the "dead" in 4:6 with "the spirits in prison" in 3:19 and that 3:19 "is best taken to mean that in the interval between his death and resurrection Christ preached to the dead."[90] Elaborates another commentator: "The whole passage clearly means that Christ, as a spirit, preached to certain spirits, who had been disobedient to the end of their earthly life. This preaching took place between His death and resurrection, and its purpose was that, by hearing the gospel, these men might have an opportunity of repentance."[91]

This is a way of understanding the purpose for which Christ "descended into hell" (Hades), as mentioned in the Apostles' Creed.[92] The idea that he descended into the underworld to preach to, and liberate, the dead was advanced early in Christian history. In its support both Justin Martyr and Irenaeus quoted a verse they believed had been expurgated from Jeremiah (or Isaiah): "The Lord God remembered his dead people of Israel who lay in the graves, and he descended to preach to them his own salvation."[93] In also voicing this idea, the second-century Shepherd of Hermas added an intriguing detail that parallels the later Mormon position that during his descent Christ commissioned the righteous in paradise to carry out the evangelization of the spirit world. The Ninth Similitude (parable) depicts a scene in which it is not Christ himself who does the preaching but forty deceased Christian apostles and teachers.[94] Clement of Alexandria felt confident that if Christ "preached the gospel to those in the flesh in order that they might not be condemned unjustly, how is it conceivable that he did not for the same reason preach the gospel to those who had departed this life before his coming?"[95]

90. Charles E. B. Cranfield, "1 Peter," in *Peake's Commentary on the Bible*, ed. Matthew Black (London: Nelson & Sons, 1962), 1029. The *Orthodox Study Bible* concurs: "The dead [of 4:6] are most likely those preached to 'in prison' in Hades." *OSB*, 1687.

91. J. R. Dummelow, ed., *Commentary on the Holy Bible* (New York: Macmillan, 1909), 1046.

92. On the other hand, the *New Oxford Annotated Bible* offers the opinion that 1 Pet. 3:18–20 "is unrelated to 4:6 and the 'descent to the world of the dead' of the Apostles' Creed" (2130).

93. Justin Martyr, *Dialogue with Trypho* 72, in *ANF*, 1:235; Irenaeus, *Against Heresies* 3.20.4, in *ANF*, 1:451 (see also 4.27.2, in *ANF*, 1:499). See also Terrance L. Tiessen, *Irenaeus on the Salvation of the Unevangelized* (Metuchen, NJ: Scarecrow, 1993). In the second-century context of this argument, inclusion of the patriarchs and prophets in the economy of salvation was partially a reaction against Gnostic disparagement of the Old Testament.

94. Shepherd of Hermas, Similitude 9.16, in *ANF*, 2:49.

95. Quoted in Ralph V. Turner, "*Descendit Ad Inferos*: Medieval Views on Christ's Descent into Hell and the Salvation of the Ancient Just," *Journal of the History of Ideas* 27 (April–June 1966): 174.

A later text regarding Christ and the dead that became particularly important in Christianity is the *Descensus Christi ad inferos* ("Christ's Descent to the underworld/hell"), a portion of the apocryphal fifth-century Gospel of Nicodemus.[96] In this narrative, Christ descends into Hades, bursts open its gates, binds the devil, liberates the dead, and rises triumphant with them to paradise. In this "harrowing of hell" (as the story came to be known), an infuriated Hades chides his erstwhile ally Satan: "Turn and see that not one dead man is left in me. All that you gained through the tree of knowledge you have lost through the tree of the cross."[97] In the centuries after the *Descensus* appeared, it became deeply embedded in Christian liturgies and even artistic expression.[98] Although demurrals about the descent had occasionally been voiced in the West, the Protestant Reformation intensified such hesitations. Following Calvin, many in the Reformed tradition understood the sparse creedal phrase "descended into hell" simply as a figurative expression referring to Christ's suffering the pains of hell while on the cross.[99] John Wesley even dropped the phrase *descendit ad inferos* from his creedal revisions and interpreted 1 Peter 3:19 not as a liberating proclamation to the imprisoned

96. This text, in its several versions, may be consulted in J. K. Elliott, *The Apocryphal New Testament: A Collection of Apocryphal Christian Literature in an English Translation* (Oxford: Oxford University Press, 1993), 164–204, and Wilhelm Schneemelcher, ed., *New Testament Apocrypha*, vol. 1, *Gospels and Related Writings* (Cambridge: James Clark, 1991), 501–36. For additional discussion and contextualization, see Trumbower, *Rescue for the Dead*, 91–108, and a useful earlier study—J. A. MacCulloch, *The Harrowing of Hell: A Comparative Study of an Early Christian Doctrine* (Edinburgh: T&T Clark, 1930).

97. In the Greek version of the *Descensus*, all departed souls are released from Hades; in the Latin redactions, only the saints are. The quotation is from Elliott, *The Apocryphal New Testament*, 188. In the Latin B version, the resurrected sons of Simeon, who report these events to the Sanhedrin, testify that "We rose with Christ from hell, and he himself raised us from the dead." Schneemelcher, *New Testament Apocrypha*, 528. A resurrection of the righteous at that time is made plausible by reference to Matt. 27:52—"And the graves were opened; and many bodies of the saints which slept arose."

98. For instance, Willam Langland (1332–1386) integrated the *Descensus* into his famous fourteenth-century poem *Piers the Plowman*, and Fulbert of Chartres (d. 1028) included it in his much-performed "Ye Choirs of New Jerusalem." The "harrowing of hell" was also a popular subject of medieval art as illustrated by the woodcut of Albrecht Dürer (1471–1528) titled *The Harrowing of Hell*. See Karl Tamburr, *The Harrowing of Hell in Medieval England* (Cambridge: D. S. Brewer, 2007).

99. Calvin, *Institutes* 2.16.10. For subsequent discussion, see Peter Marshall, "The Reformation of Hell? Protestant and Catholic Infernalisms in England, c. 1560–1640," *Journal of Ecclesiastical History* 61 (April 2010): 279–98. For the Lutheran interpretation, see David V. N. Bagchi, "Luther versus Luther? The Problem of Christ's Descent into Hell in the Long Sixteenth Century," *Perichoresis* 6, no. 2 (2008): 175–200.

wicked but as the Lord executing his sentence upon them and reserving them to "the judgment of the great day."[100]

Where, then, does Mormonism come down on the matter of Christ's descent to the realm of the dead and on the idea of postmortem evangelism generally? The short answer is that Latter-day Saint doctrine interprets the relevant Petrine passages at face value. Joseph Smith considered 1 Peter 3:19-20 "an account of our Saviour preaching to the spirits in prison; to spirits that had been imprisoned from the days of Noah."[101] In Smith's amplification of Genesis 5, Enoch sees these spirits and God explains, "These which thine eyes are upon shall perish in the floods; and behold, I will shut them up; a prison have I prepared for them." Yet, in conjunction with Christ's future descent, Enoch also sees that "as many of the [penitent] spirits as were in prison came forth and stood on the right hand of God; and the remainder were reserved in chains of darkness until the judgment of the great day" (Moses 7:38, 56-57). Enoch's vision has intertextual links to Isaiah 24:22—they "shall be shut up in the prison, and after many days shall they be visited"—and Isaiah 42:7, in which the "servant" (Christ) came "to open the blind eyes, to bring out the prisoners from the prison, and them that sit in darkness out of the prison house." As Joseph Smith commented, "It is very evident from this that he not only went to preach to them, but to deliver, or bring them *out of the prison house*. . . . Thus we find that . . . those characters referred to by Isaiah, have their time of visitation, and deliverance, after having been many days in prison."[102] Another early revelation informed Smith that there was a place in heaven for the spirits that had been "kept in prison, whom the Son visited, and preached the gospel unto them, that they might be judged according to men in the flesh" (D&C 76:73).

Over the next decade, Joseph Smith's view of the redemption of the dead greatly expanded. In 1836, a revelation declared, "All who have died without a knowledge of this gospel, who would have received it if they had been permitted to tarry, shall be heirs of the celestial kingdom of God; also all that shall die henceforth without a knowledge of it, who would have received it with all their hearts, shall be heirs of that kingdom" (D&C 137:7-8). Although this sounds like a straightforward declaration of the "hypothetical acceptance" argument mentioned above (#3), subsequent reflection read "would have" accepted the gospel to mean *will* accept it when it is presented to them in the

---

100. John Wesley, *Explanatory Notes on the New Testament* (1755; reprint, London: Epworth, 1950), 882.

101. *JSP*, D9:377.

102. *JSP*, D9:377.

spirit world.[103] Latter-day Saints came to believe that preaching the gospel in the spirit world was an ongoing and necessary activity and was performed by the departed righteous in paradise. "All those who have not had an opportunity of hearing the Gospel . . . in the flesh," wrote Joseph Smith in 1838, "must have it hereafter, before they can be finally judged."[104] When this position was combined with the Mormon logic of the essentiality of baptism for salvation, it led to the beginning of proxy baptisms for the dead in 1840. Smith found support for such a practice in 1 Corinthians 15:29—"Else what shall they do which are baptized for the dead, if the dead rise not at all? why are they then baptized for the dead?"[105] In launching the practice, Smith declared that the Saints now "have the privilege of being baptized for those of their relatives who are dead, whom they believe would have embraced the Gospel if they had been privileged with hearing it, and who have received the Gospel in the spirit [world] through the instrumentality of those who have been commissioned to preach to them."[106] Shortly thereafter, Smith clarified that this ordinance was to be performed in temples (D&C 124:28–39), and today all Mormon temples have a dedicated baptismal font for that purpose.

Joseph Smith considered baptism for the dead one of the "most glorious of all subjects belonging to the everlasting gospel" (D&C 128:17). It would become even more important for the twentieth-century church as part of its grand vision of helping make Christ's sacraments of salvation and exaltation available to all who have ever lived. This led to unparalleled efforts to microfilm genealogical records and promote family history research, activities that enabled identification of the deceased who could not only vicariously receive the baptismal ordinance but could also be ritually linked ("sealed") to other family members.[107] During the latter part of the century, the church escalated construction of its temples and aggressively moved to extend to all the possi-

103. A hypothetical-acceptance reading of this revelation, however, is maintained by other churches that trace their roots to Joseph Smith, such as the Community of Christ.

104. *JSP*, D6:144.

105. The meaning of this passage is much contested. Many different interpretations are discussed in a seminal series of articles by Bernard Foschini entitled "Those Who Are Baptized for the Dead, 1 Cor 15:29." See *Catholic Biblical Quarterly* 12 (1950): 260–76, 379–88; 13 (1951): 46–78, 172–98, 276–83. Nonetheless, "despite dozens of proposed solutions, the reference itself is simply so obscure and our knowledge so limited that we cannot discern just what this rite actually involved or meant." R. P. Carlson, "The Role of Baptism in Paul's Thought," *Interpretation* 47 (July 1993): 261.

106. *JSP*, D7:470.

107. For a detailed discussion of these developments, see James B. Allen, Jessie L. Embry, and Kahlile B. Mehr, *Hearts Turned to the Fathers: A History of the Genealogical Society of*

bility of a vicarious baptism. President Spencer Kimball declared that helping to "redeem the dead" was one of the three crucial activities of the church.[108] Earlier in the century, apostle John Widtsoe explained the underlying rationale for such efforts: "The basic reason for the importance of the work for the dead, is that the Lord would save all his children. . . . The work of the Lord will not be completed until all who come on earth have had a full and fair chance to accept or reject the gospel. The power to do so remains with the dead in the spirit world, where the gospel will be preached to them."[109]

Those who accept the gospel can be linked together with their descendants and progenitors in eternal family units through the temple sealing ordinance (see chapter 11). The importance of this transhistorical family unification led Joseph Smith to declare, borrowing a phrase from Hebrews 11:40, "They without us cannot be made perfect, neither can we without our dead be made perfect" (D&C 128:15). Smith linked an obscure phrase from Obadiah 21—"saviours shall come up on mount Zion"—to this work of salvation for the dead. The Saints, he said, "become Saviors on Mount Zion by building their temples, erecting their Baptismal fonts & going forth & receiving all the ordinances . . . in behalf of all our Progenitors who are dead & redeem them that they may come forth in the first resurrection & be exhalted to thrones of glory with us." Joseph Smith then alluded to Malachi 4:5–6 and declared, "Herein is the chain that binds the hearts of the fathers to the children, & the children to the Fathers which fulfills the mission of Elijah."[110] This perspective continues to be voiced in the twenty-first century. President Thomas Monson explained, "Great service is given when we perform vicarious ordinances for those who have gone beyond the veil. . . . We expect no thanks, nor do we have the assurance that they will accept that which we offer. However, we serve, and in that process . . . we literally become saviors on Mount Zion." Monson then noted a parallel with Christ's work on the principle of vicariousness: "As our Savior gave His life as a vicarious sacrifice for us, so we, in some small measure, do the same when we perform proxy work in the temple for those who have no means of moving forward unless something is done for them by those of us here on the earth."[111] From an LDS perspective, for a loving God to extend

---

Utah, 1894–1994 (Provo, UT: BYU Studies, 1995). For the "sealing" ordinance, in particular, see chapter 11.

108. The other two were to "perfect the Saints" and "preach the Gospel." *Ensign*, May 1981, 5.

109. John A. Widtsoe, *Gospel Interpretations: Aids to Faith in a Modern Day, Being a Companion Volume to Evidences and Reconciliations* (Salt Lake City: Bookcraft, 1947), 98.

110. *JSP*, D14:105.

111. *Teachings: Thomas S. Monson*, 238.

his mercy beyond the grave and provide a postmortem opportunity for the unevangelized to accept the gospel and receive the ordinances of salvation and exaltation "justifies the ways of God to man; places the human family upon an equal footing, and harmonizes with every principle of righteousness, justice, and truth."[112]

In the aftermath of Joseph Smith's distinctive use of "saviors on mount Zion," the phrase became a popular metonym among Latter-day Saints for those receiving the sacraments for and on behalf of the deceased. This use of "saviors on mount Zion" is in no way intended to equate Christ's human instruments in his work of salvation with the Son of God himself. Latter-day Saints say with Isaiah, "O Lord, thou art our father; we are the clay, and thou our potter; and we all are the work of thy hand" (Isa. 64:8). Moreover, the Hebrew word undergirding "saviors" in the KJV translation is elsewhere rendered as "deliverers" (e.g., NIV, NASB). This fits the Latter-day Saint doctrine of salvation more clearly since the unevangelized are pictured as dwelling in spirit prison until they are "delivered" from prison by the gospel being preached to them and saving ordinances being performed on their behalf. The other way in which "saviors" or "deliverers" may be misleading is that either can be read to connote a definite outcome that overrides personal preference. Such a reading, however, would be totally inconsistent with LDS theology's profound commitment to human agency. Deceased souls are understood to have complete freedom of choice whether to hear and embrace the gospel in the spirit world and accept the ordinances vicariously performed on their behalf. No one in this world or the spirit world can be compelled or coerced to accept Christ's gift of salvation. As President Gordon Hinckley expressed it, "In the spirit world [the deceased] are free to accept or reject those earthly ordinances performed for them. . . . There must be no compulsion in the work of the Lord, but there must be opportunity."[113]

The service of earthly "saviors"/"deliverers" on behalf of the deceased is believed to be matched by the labors of those on "the other side of the veil." Brigham Young declared that "with the millions who have never heard" the gospel, "there is a mighty [preaching] work to perform in the spirit world."[114] Many a bereaving family is told that "all those who die in the faith go to the Prison of spirits to preach to the dead in body."[115] This depiction of a vast army of departed godly souls teaching the gospel to fellow spirits in prison came to

---

112. *JSP*, D9:380.
113. *Teachings: Gordon B. Hinckley*, 314.
114. *Journal of Discourses*, 4:285.
115. *JSP*, D14:487.

full fruition in the early twentieth century in an extended vision experienced by church president Joseph F. Smith.[116] Smith reported that as he meditated on 1 Peter 3:18–20 and 4:6 and pondered how Christ could have preached to myriads of deceased spirits in "the brief time intervening between the crucifixion and his resurrection . . . my eyes were opened, and my understanding [was] quickened." What Smith learned, similar to the point made in Shepherd of Hermas, was "that the Lord went not in person among the wicked and the disobedient who had rejected the truth, to teach them; But behold, from among the righteous, he organized his forces and appointed messengers, clothed with power and authority, and commissioned them to go forth and carry the light of the gospel to them that were in darkness, even to all the spirits of men; and thus was the gospel preached to the dead" (D&C 138:27, 29–30). Later the vision revealed that faithful Latter-day Saint women and men in the present who "depart from mortal life, continue their labors in the preaching of the gospel of repentance and redemption, through the sacrifice of the Only Begotten Son of God . . . in the great world of the spirits of the dead" (D&C 138:57).[117]

Such a sweeping vision of intermediate-state evangelism and the temple liturgical structure that supports it is unparalleled in Christian history. While a variety of early Christian fathers posited some degree of rescue for the dead, none did so on the Mormon scale. Moreover, after Augustine decided that posthumous salvation for non-Christians was theologically unacceptable, the door effectively closed on the possibility of such a doctrine in Catholic teaching. The current Catholic position is summarized in the *Catechism*: "Death puts an end to human life as the time open to either accepting or rejecting the divine grace manifested in Christ."[118] Where Catholic, Orthodox, and Mormon doctrines of the dead do converge is on the principle of vicariousness, the idea that certain acts of devotion and service performed by the living on behalf of the deceased can materially impact the afterlife condition of the departed. This is an old and venerable notion. Prayers and offerings for the dead date at least to the Maccabean period in the second century BC. Judas Maccabeus is said to have taken up a collection for a sin offering on behalf of fallen comrades believed to have

116. The background to this revelation is detailed in George S. Tate, "'The Great World of the Spirits of the Dead': Death, the Great War, and the 1918 Influenza Pandemic as Context for Doctrine and Covenants 138," *BYU Studies* 46, no. 1 (2007): 5–40.

117. Smith taught that women "will be fully authorized and empowered to preach the gospel and minister to the women while the elders and prophets are preaching it to the men." *Gospel Doctrine*, 581–82.

118. *CCC* 1021. Elsewhere the *Catechism* quotes John of Damascus to the effect that "there is no repentance for men after death." *CCC* 393.

died in battle because they violated Torah law. The offering "made atonement for the dead, so that they might be delivered from their sin" (2 Maccabees 12:39–45). Based on this scriptural precedent, "from the beginning the [Catholic] Church has honored the memory of the dead and offered prayers in suffrage for them, above all the Eucharistic sacrifice [mass], so that, thus purified, they may attain the beatific vision of God. The Church also commends almsgiving, indulgences, and works of penance undertaken on behalf of the dead."[119] As one historical study argues, the belief was widespread in early Christianity that "the devotional intercessions of the living could tip the balance between heaven and hell for the deceased."[120] It is still acknowledged in the Catholic Church that such "suffrages" by the earthly or "pilgrim" church can help contrite souls in purgatory "be more promptly and efficaciously purified of the punishments for sin."[121]

Although, as has been pointed out, Orthodoxy never embraced the Catholic version of purgatory, it does maintain a similar "practice of praying for the departed and even for 'those in hell.'" Vespers (evening prayer service) at Pentecost, for instance, "is based on this."[122] The popular *Liturgy of St. John Chrysostom* includes repeated prayers for the departed that "the Lord our God may establish their souls where the righteous rest."[123] Like the Latter-day Saints, the Orthodox hold that "until the Last Judgment, changes for the better are possible in the fate of any sinner. . . . Until the final verdict of the Judge is pronounced, there is hope for all the departed to enter the Kingdom of heaven."[124] Whether Catholics celebrating Eucharist for the dead, Orthodox offering prayers for the departed at vespers, or Mormons performing baptisms

119. *CCC* 1032. In the Middle Ages, many "sacerdotal and monastic acts were organized around delivering dead souls from purgatory to heaven by prayer and mass." Kevin Madigan, *Medieval Christianity: A New History* (New Haven: Yale University Press, 2015), 176. Masses and prayers for the dead were even a regular part of life for the cleric-academics and students at the renowned medieval University of Paris. William J. Courtenay, *Rituals for the Dead: Religion and Community in the Medieval University of Paris* (Notre Dame: University of Notre Dame Press, 2019).

120. Peter R. Brown, *The Ransom of the Soul: Afterlife and Wealth in Early Western Christianity* (Cambridge, MA: Harvard University Press, 2018), book jacket. Further, Brown's argument is that "early Christian doctrine held that the living and the dead, as equally sinful beings, needed each other in order to achieve redemption." This parallels Joseph Smith's sentiment expressed in the Doctrine and Covenants 128:15 that "they without us cannot be made perfect, neither can we without our dead be made perfect."

121. *CCC* 1475.

122. Alfeyev, "Eschatology," 115.

123. Louth, *Eastern Orthodox Theology*, 150.

124. Alfeyev, "Eschatology," 115.

for the dead, sacramental vicariousness is believed to help open the door to God's full presence in heaven for the deceased. This vision was eloquently expressed by Pope John Paul II: "Vicariousness" is the reality "upon which the entire mystery of Christ is founded. His superabundant love saves us all. Yet it is part of the grandeur of Christ's love not to leave us in the condition of passive recipients, but to draw us into his saving work."[125] Here is a broadly Christian version of "saviors on mount Zion." Indeed, it may be that the loving caress of vicariousness is present in many traditions. Religion scholar Robert Orsi contends that in one way or another relationships between the living and the dead are at the heart of religion itself.[126]

Resurrection

Christian traditions disagree about the nature of the resurrection body, as well as whether there will be more than one resurrection. The basic Christian affirmation expressed in the Apostles' Creed is simply belief in "the resurrection of the body." But what kind of body? If the believer's eternal destiny is thought to be the beatific vision, an unending spiritual contemplation of an immaterial Deity in a static condition outside time and space, it is challenging to see much use for a physical body. Yet, belief in *carnis resurrectionem* (lit. "resurrection of the flesh"), as it is phrased in the Apostles' Creed, means that most Christian traditions affirm the physicality of the resurrection. From the second-century Christian apologists combating antimaterialism to the Cappadocians in the fourth century and Augustine a generation later, patristic eschatology, as well as the later medieval tradition, overwhelmingly leaned toward belief in a same-body, same-flesh resurrection.[127] Roman Catholicism definitively established its view of the resurrection in a series of thirteenth-century pronouncements: "We believe in the true resurrection of this flesh that we now possess," and all "will rise again with their own bodies which they now bear."[128]

Because many Christian traditions ground their doctrine in the teachings of the early fathers, patristic expressions affirming a fleshly resurrection bear

125. John Paul II, "Bull of Indication *Incarnationis Mysterium* (November 29, 1998)," in Jacques Dupuis, *The Christian Faith in the Doctrinal Documents of the Catholic Church*, 7th ed. (New York: Alba House, 2001), 715.

126. Robert Orsi, *Between Heaven and Earth: The Religious Worlds People Make and the Scholars Who Study Them* (Princeton: Princeton University Press, 2004), 2–3.

127. Caroline Walker Bynum, *The Resurrection of the Body in Western Christianity, 200–1336* (New York: Columbia University Press, 1995).

128. *CCC* 1017, 999.

closer examination. Irenaeus's second-century *Against Heresies* strongly opposed Gnostic notions of a solely spiritual perpetuity of the human being. So did Tertullian's treatise *On the Resurrection of the Flesh*, written to oppose the antimaterialists of his day. Both men expected humans to be raised at the last day with tangible, material bodies. In *Against Heresies*, Irenaeus reasoned, "Surely it is much more difficult and incredible" for God out of nothing to have brought humanity into existence as living and thinking creatures with "bones, and nerves, and veins, and the rest of man's organi[sm] than [it will be] to reintegrate again that which had been created and then afterwards decomposed into earth."[129] Irenaeus further argued that "in the dead who were raised by Christ we possess the highest proof of the resurrection." He asked, "In what bodies did they rise again? In those same, no doubt, in which they had also died. For if it were not in the very same, then certainly those same individuals who had died did not rise again."[130] The undergirding principle was "material continuity accounts for identity."[131] For most Christians then and now, the resurrected Christ provides the prototype of humankind's resurrection bodies: "Handle me, and see," offered Jesus, "for a spirit hath not flesh and bones, as ye see me have" (Luke 24:39). Paul taught that "he that raised up Christ from the dead shall also quicken [give life to] your mortal bodies" (Rom. 8:11) and "will change our weak mortal bodies and make them like his own glorious body" (Phil. 3:21 GNT).

Central to any discussion of the nature of the resurrection body is the teaching of the apostle Paul in 1 Corinthians 15. The human body, he declared, "is sown in corruption; it is raised in incorruption. . . . It is sown a natural body; it is raised a spiritual body" (vv. 42, 44). Paul also taught that "flesh and blood cannot inherit the kingdom of God" (v. 50). As both Irenaeus and Tertullian observed, this latter passage was "the pre-eminent text within the systems of those who would deny the resurrection of the flesh."[132] But the New Testament phrase "flesh and blood" is a metaphor for mortal human beings. Christ told Peter, "Blessed art thou, Simon Barjona: for flesh and blood hath not revealed it unto thee, but my Father which is in heaven" (Matt. 16:17), and Paul himself wrote: "I conferred not with flesh and blood" (Gal. 1:16). The core of the debate was how best to understand the phrase "raised a spiritual body."

129. Irenaeus, *Against Heresies* 5.3.2, in *ANF*, 1:529.
130. Irenaeus, *Against Heresies* 5.13.1.
131. Bynum, *Resurrection of the Body*, 34.
132. D. Jeffrey Bingham, "Irenaeus Reads Romans 8: Resurrection and Renovation," in *Early Patristic Readings of Romans*, ed. Kathy L. Gaca and L. L. Welborn (New York: T&T Clark, 2005), 115.

On the surface it may seem simply to refer to a body composed entirely of spirit, but some New Testament scholars explain that the passage "does not mean that the future body will be 'spiritual' in the sense of 'immaterial.' The adjectives explain not what the body is made of but what is making it alive."[133] Augustine titled chapter 22 in book 13 of his *City of God* "Of the Bodies Which the Saints Will Have after the Resurrection, Which Will Be Spiritual, Although Their Flesh Will Not Be Changed into Spirit." Expounding the meaning of being raised a "spiritual body," Augustine noted, "Just as the spirit is not improperly called carnal when it serves the flesh, so shall the flesh rightly be called spiritual when it serves the spirit . . . with all distress, all corruptibility and all reluctance gone."[134] Jerome affirmed a physical resurrection even more forcefully: "The reality of a resurrection without flesh and bones," he declared, "is unintelligible."[135] Jerome suggested stressing to heretics that the resurrected body "will exhibit anew the hair and the teeth, the chest and the stomach, the hands and the feet, and all the other members of the body."[136]

As part of Tertullian's earlier argument for the human-like anatomy of the resurrection body, he, too, emphasized that the resurrection body, although transformed and glorified, would still have hair, eyes, and all the other normal body parts.[137] Jerome also affirmed sexual differentiation in resurrection bodies.[138] Augustine agreed that males and females would be resurrected as such with all their usual physical characteristics, though neither marriage nor sexual intercourse would occur in heaven. This would not be a problem because the transformed, resurrected, but still sexed person would be purged of

---

133. N. T. Wright and Michael F. Bird, *The New Testament in Its World: An Introduction to the History, Literature, and Theology of the First Christians* (Grand Rapids: Zondervan, 2019), 494. This, as will be seen, is also the view of the Latter-day Saints.

134. Augustine, *City of God against the Pagans*, trans. R. W. Dyson (Cambridge: Cambridge University Press, 1998), 13.22, 13.20 (pp. 566–67, 569). Augustine distinguished the prefall body and the spiritual body primarily because Adam and Eve needed nourishment and consumed food to satiate hunger and thirst. Augustine believed none of these needs would exist in spiritual bodies purged of earthly appetites.

135. Jerome, *Against John of Jerusalem* 31, in *NPNF*, 2/6:440.

136. Jerome, Letter 84, in *NPNF*, 2/6:178. Even Origen, the patristic master of spiritual interpretation, rejected the idea that the resurrection body would be ethereal. Though it would be fallen flesh no more, the features that once existed in the flesh will remain the same features in the spiritual body, but "there will be the greatest possible change for the better." Richard B. Tollinton, ed., *Selections from the Commentaries and Homilies of Origen* (London: SPCK, 1929), 233, 232.

137. Tertullian, *On the Resurrection of the Flesh* 35, in *ANF*, 3:571.

138. Jerome, Letter 108, in *NPNF*, 2/6:208, and Daley, *Hope of the Early Church*, 102–3.

lust.[139] By the seventh century, any other view was considered irrational. The profession of faith issued at the Eleventh Synod of Toledo in 675 declared: "According to the example of our head [Jesus Christ], we confess that there is a true resurrection of the flesh for all the dead. And we do not believe that we shall rise in ethereal or any other flesh, as some foolishly imagine, but in this very flesh in which we live and are and move."[140] Orthodox Christians concur: "The 'spiritual' body is not a pale shadow of the material . . . the opposite is true. The resurrection body is the fulfillment of what God intends for our present body. It is the material fulfilled, not dematerialized."[141]

So where does Mormonism come down on the nature of the resurrected body and the meaning of "spiritual body"? With its decidedly materialistic metaphysics that sees even God the Father as having a glorified body "of flesh and bones" (see chapter 1), it is hardly surprising that Latter-day Saints affirm the same for resurrection bodies. This gives added meaning to LDS use of 1 John 3:2—"it doth not yet appear what we shall be: but we know that, when he shall appear, we shall be like him." For Latter-day Saints, as for the theologians just discussed, the resurrection body is incorruptible, immortal, and glorified by God, but it also has enough continuity with the present to be described as a transformed and perfected version of one's own body of flesh and bones. As for the meaning of "spiritual body," Joseph Smith gave a different twist to 1 Corinthians 15:50 by stating, "Flesh and blood cannot [inherit the kingdom of God] but flesh and *bones* quickened by the Spirit of God can."[142] "Blood," he added, "is the part of the body that causes corruption," and "the resurrection . . . is devised to take away corruption" so that "we will be able to goe in[to] the presents of god."[143] The Book of Mormon describes the resurrection as "spirits uniting with their bodies, never to be divided" and "no more [to] see corruption." Thus, "the whole becoming spiritual" (Alma 11:45). A Doctrine and Covenants revelation sets forth LDS doctrine in this way: "For notwithstanding they die, they also shall rise again, a spiritual body." As such, they "shall receive the same body which was a natural body; even ye shall receive your bodies, and your glory shall

---

139. See *City of God* 22.17, titled "Whether the Bodies of Women Will Retain Their Sex in the Resurrection" (Dyson trans., 1144–46). Other fathers, such as the Cappadocians, believed that as the soul, like God, was genderless, so the resurrected body would be without sexual distinction.

140. Denzinger 540.

141. *OSB*, 1570.

142. *JSP*, D13:168 (emphasis added). This parallels the view of N. T. Wright quoted above. See note 133.

143. *JSP*, D14:488.

be that [celestial] glory by which your bodies are quickened" (D&C 88:27–28). President Howard Hunter taught that such views are the proper interpretation of Paul's teachings: "Our bodies after the resurrection, quickened by the spirit, shall become immortal and never die. This is the meaning of the statements of Paul that . . . 'there is a spiritual body' and 'that flesh and blood cannot inherit the kingdom of God' [1 Cor. 15:44, 50]. The natural body is flesh and blood, but quickened by the spirit instead of blood, it can and will enter the kingdom."[144] Former heart surgeon and apostle Russell Nelson remarked that, in a sense, "the Atonement of Jesus Christ became [our] *immortal creation*." Because of it "our physical bodies [can] become perfected. They [can] again function without blood, just as Adam's and Eve's did in their *paradisiacal form*."[145] This is what makes a resurrected body a "spiritual body" in Mormon doctrine.

Apart from figuring out how the resurrected "spiritual body" is also a fleshly body, theologians have had to wrestle with a number of philosophical questions and criticisms of this affirmation. From the beginning, for instance, the "chain of consumption" argument was leveled against Christian belief in the resurrection of the physical body. A man is eaten by an animal, who is eaten by another animal, and so on until it is difficult to keep track of the original parts of the individual. To that challenge, response came early from Athenian philosopher-convert Athenagoras, who in his *On the Resurrection* simply argued that the chain notwithstanding, an omnipotent God can raise humans in their own bodies.[146] Augustine later devoted a chapter in his *City of God* to arguing that "in the resurrection, the substance [elements] of our bodies, no matter how widely dispersed, will be entirely reunited."[147] Similar to Athenagoras, Augustine reasoned that it was "unthinkable that there should be any limits to the Creator's omnipotence in resuscitating and restoring to life every element of any human body that has been devoured by beasts or consumed by fire, or reduced to dust, or dissolved into liquid, or evaporated into air."[148] This has been the dominant stance throughout Christian history,

---

144. *Teachings: Howard W. Hunter*, 108. Joseph Smith once suggested that the spiritual quickening of the resurrected body would entail Spirit literally "flowing in the veins." *JSP*, D14:488. While this idea has occasionally been repeated over the years, it is not an official doctrine, and church literature today simply affirms that the resurrected body will be "quickened" or vitalized by the Spirit.

145. Russell M. Nelson, "The Atonement," *Ensign*, November 1996, 34.

146. Athenagoras, *On the Resurrection* 3–7, in *Athenagoras: Legatio and De Resurrectione*, ed. and trans. William R. Schoedel (Oxford: Clarendon, 1972), 95–107.

147. Augustine, *City of God* 22.20 (Dyson trans., 1150).

148. Gerald G. Walsh and Daniel J. Honan, ed. and trans., *Saint Augustine: The City of*

with the intent always being to maintain belief in the continuity of individual human identity. Thus, Joseph Smith stood in a long line of theologians when he declared that there is "no fundamental principle belonging to a human System that ever goes into another . . . we have the testimony that God will raise us up & he has power to do it. If any one supposes that any part of our bodies that is the fundame[n]tal parts thereof, ever [permanently] goes into another body he is mistaken."[149]

Yet if material continuity is to be adamantly affirmed, the question may be asked, "How is the equally cherished principle of bodily perfection in the resurrection to be maintained?" Augustine offered this answer: if a sculptor "has for some reason made a flawed statue, he can recast it and make it beautiful, removing the defect without losing any of the substance . . . he can simply melt down the whole and remix it, without producing any ugliness or diminishing the quantity of material. And if a man can do this, what are we to think of the Almighty Artist?"[150] God is infinitely more skilled. "There is no deformity of any human body, whether normal or exceptional or even monstrous, which He cannot so eliminate" and yet "leave the total substance intact, while the ugliness disappears."[151] With that understanding Augustine, and many who have followed him, was able to assure his readers that abnormal bodily shapes "will not exist in heaven. There, all defects will be corrected."[152] Not surprisingly, Augustine even ventured to suggest an age at which people would be resurrected. Here again Christ was considered the pattern: "All the dead will rise neither older nor younger than Christ, but at that age and vigour to which we know Christ attained. For the most learned men of the world have defined the prime of life at around the age of thirty years."[153] In sum, no feature or aspect of the resurrected body will be "incompatible with the happiness of the saints in the life to come."[154]

Although Latter-day Saint thinkers have occasionally indulged in speculation about the nature of the resurrected body, church leaders today do not

---

God, Books XVII–XXII, Fathers of the Church (Washington, DC: Catholic University of America Press, 1954), 22.20 (p. 470).

149. *JSP*, J2:343–44. See similar affirmations by Brigham Young (*Journal of Discourses*, 8:28) and John Taylor (*Journal of Discourses*, 18:333–34).

150. Augustine, *City of God* 22.19 (Dyson, 1148).

151. Augustine, *City of God* 22.19 (Walsh and Honan, 468).

152. Augustine, *City of God* 22.19 (Dyson, 1149).

153. Augustine, *City of God* 22.15 (Dyson, 1143). Ephesians 4:13 mentions the Christian goal of becoming the "perfect man" with "the stature [*hēlikia*] of the fulness of Christ." *Hēlikia* can also be translated as "age." Because Augustine rejected the idea that all would be of equal size in the resurrection, he chose to interpret *hēlikia* as "age" rather than "stature."

154. Augustine, *City of God* 22.19 (Walsh and Honan, 468).

attempt to pinpoint an age at which people will be resurrected, nor do they identify a particular body shape or morphology that will obtain in the resurrection.[155] They simply reaffirm with little elaboration the Book of Mormon declaration that "the soul shall be restored to the body, and the body to the soul; yea, and every limb and joint shall be restored to its body; yea, even a hair of the head shall not be lost; but all things shall be restored to their proper and perfect frame" (Alma 40:23).[156] The one aspect of a perfected, resurrected body that LDS teaching does emphasize is that "deformity will be removed; defects will be eliminated, and men and women shall attain to the perfection of their spirit [bodies]."[157] According to Dallin Oaks, the defects that will be eliminated include "the physical, mental, or emotional deficiencies we bring with us at birth or acquire during mortal life. Because of the resurrection, we know that these mortal deficiencies are only temporary."[158]

Last Judgment

Associated with the resurrection at the end of time is the "last" or "final" judgment. This judgment is understood to bring about the ultimate triumph of perfect, divine justice for God's creation and creatures. It is the moment when all things will be made right for the cosmos as well as for individuals. In most Christian eschatologies, the final judgment follows a single, general resurrection of all human beings. The final judgment is the occasion on which

---

155. In Mormonism's early years, Joseph Smith is reported to have said that mothers who lose a child in infancy will "have their children in Eternity . . . in its precise form as it fell in its mothers arms. Eternity is full of thrones upon which dwell thousands of children reigning on thrones of glory not one cubit added to their stature." *JSP*, D14:340. This was a controversial idea even among Joseph's closest associates. Orson Pratt later remarked, "I very much doubt whether the Prophet Joseph, at the time he preached that sermon had been fully instructed by revelation on that point." *Journal of Discourses*, 16:335. In the early twentieth century, President Joseph F. Smith reported his uncle's teaching somewhat differently: the infant child will "come up in the resurrection as a child," and the mother "will have the joy, the pleasure and satisfaction of nurturing this child, after its resurrection, until it reaches the full stature of its spirit." Joseph F. Smith, "Status of Children in the Resurrection," *Improvement Era*, May 1918, 571. Joseph F. Smith's view is the one that is shared in institutional church literature today. For instance, it is included in the 1998 *Teachings: Joseph F. Smith*, 130–32, and reiterated in Mark A. Mathews, "The Salvation of Little Children Who Die: What We Do and Don't Know," *Liahona*, July 2021, 14.

156. See, for example, "Basic Doctrines," 571; *True to the Faith*, 46.

157. *Gospel Doctrine*, 29.

158. *Ensign*, May 2000, 14.

all are then judged by God. "I saw the dead, small and great," declared John the Revelator, "stand before God; and the books were opened . . . and the dead were judged out of those things which were written in the books . . . and they were judged every man according to their works" (Rev. 20:12–13). The apostle Paul concurred: "We must all appear before the judgment seat of Christ; that every one may receive . . . according to that he hath done, whether it be good or bad" (2 Cor. 5:10). That is when "every one of us shall give account of himself to God" (Rom. 14:12), and he "will render to every man according to his deeds" (Rom. 2:6). For "God shall judge the secrets of men by Jesus Christ according to [the] gospel" (Rom. 2:16). "To those who by patiently doing good seek for glory and honor and immortality, he will give eternal life; while for those who are self-seeking and who obey not the truth but wickedness, there will be wrath and fury" (Rom. 2:7–8 NRSV).[159] LDS scripture is replete with similar declarations. The prophet Mormon reminded his people that one day, "ye must all stand before the judgment-seat of Christ, yea, every soul who belongs to the whole human family of Adam, and ye must stand to be judged of your works, whether they be good or evil" (Mormon 3:20). And the prophet Jacob counseled, "Prepare your souls for that glorious day when justice shall be administered unto the righteous, even the day of judgment, that ye may not shrink with awful fear; that ye may not . . . be constrained to exclaim: Holy, holy are thy judgments, O Lord God Almighty—but I know my guilt; I transgressed thy law, and my transgressions are mine" (2 Nephi 9:46).[160]

Some theologians consider that one's eternal destiny is largely determined at the time of the "particular" or "partial" judgment" upon death. From this perspective, the final judgment "merely" serves as a "public" confirmation of the particular judgment and the justice of God in either admitting the righteous to heaven or consigning the wicked to hell. For souls already suffering in hell, the last judgment following their end-time resurrection is more an arraignment than a trial; it confronts them with the judgment of condemnation long since determined. Similarly, whether one's theology envisions admission to heaven upon death or belief in the premillennial "first resurrection" of those who "are Christ's at his coming" (1 Cor. 15:23), these particular judgments long

159. Some theologians have wrestled with the tension between salvation by grace and judgment by works. In the sometimes-hairsplitting distinctions of the debate, it is argued that the final judgment will be in *accordance* with our works, not on the *basis* of our works. Various perspectives on the final judgment are presented in Alan P. Stanley, ed., *Four Views on the Role of Works at the Final Judgment* (Grand Rapids: Zondervan, 2013).

160. The Book of Mormon includes several poignant portrayals of judgment day. See, in particular, Alma 5:15–25; 41:3–7.

before the final judgment tend to mitigate the sense of the Great Assize at the last day. Traditional dispensationalist theology even sees the particular judgment to be *the* sole judgment for Christians and posits that the last judgment described in Revelation 20:12 pertains only to non-Christians.[161] Although not agreeing with classic dispensationalism on this point, Latter-day Saint theology does recognize that the final judgment is somewhat redundant. Bruce McConkie declared: "True all men, both the righteous and the wicked, shall be present" at the final judgment. "All shall hear the decrees. . . . But, at this late date, the judgment of the righteous dead is in fact a thing of the past." Having risen as part of the first resurrection, "having received eternal life, having entered into a glorious rest, having lived and reigned during the millennium" (or, in the Catholic view, at death having been judged worthy of heaven and having been admitted there after a period of culminating purification), all this "long antedates th[e] formal occasion when all men shall stand before the judgment bar to hear confirmed what has already been established."[162] Nonetheless, Mormonism still strongly affirms a doctrine of final judgment. In part, this is because LDS theology, as previously discussed, envisions an intermediate state in which human agency and choice continue, including the possibility of repentance. Because the spirit world is an extension of earthly "probation," final judgment must await the Final Judgment.

As with certain other Christian theologies of judgment, Latter-day Saint doctrine eschews the caricatured scene of the foreboding divine courtroom presided over by a stern and austere Almighty. "We have a loving Heavenly Father," assured Dallin Oaks, "who will see that we receive every blessing and every advantage that our own desires and choices allow." Moreover, "the Final Judgment is not just an evaluation of a sum total of good and evil acts—what we have *done*. It is based on the final effect of our acts and thoughts—what we have *become*." Disciples of Christ "qualify for eternal life through . . . a profound change of nature." That change is effected by the grace of God, but it requires a cooperative life of responsive, heartfelt discipleship. "It is not enough for anyone just to go through the motions." As Jesus taught in the Sermon on the Mount, "Not every one that saith unto me, Lord, Lord, shall enter

---

161. The note in the *Scofield Bible* for Rev. 20:12 states that the dead there judged "can only be the wicked dead" since "the redeemed" were judged and "raised from among the dead one thousand years before" (1351). See also Tim LaHaye, "The Great White Throne Judgment," in *Tim LaHaye Prophecy Study Bible*, 1401. This view is set forth (and challenged) in Stanley, *Final Judgment*, 9–62.

162. Bruce R. McConkie, *Doctrinal New Testament Commentary*, vol. 3, *Colossians–Revelation* (Salt Lake City: Bookcraft, 1973), 576–77.

into the kingdom of heaven; but he that doeth the will of my Father which is in heaven" (Matt. 7:21). "The commandments, ordinances, and covenants of the gospel," continued Oaks, "are not a list of deposits required to be made in some heavenly account. The gospel of Jesus Christ is a plan that shows us how to become what our Heavenly Father desires us to become."[163] More than an audit of one's words and deeds over a lifetime, then, judgment is a focus on the end result, a recognition of the kind of person those words and deeds have produced.

HEAVEN

Whenever and however judgment takes place, the ultimate result is the determination of one's status in the eternal state. As it turns out, the Bible actually says very little about the eternal state, and what it does say is ambiguous enough to have generated a wide range of views. Most Christian theologies affirm the existence of a future heaven or hell, but given the paucity of scriptural details, it is not surprising that the nature of these two states or realms has been much debated over the centuries. Believers have tended to fill the descriptive lacuna with their own imaginative ruminations and reflections, typically depicting life in heaven as a projection and intensification of whatever for them would constitute an ideal existence and hell as the most terrifying experience of suffering imaginable.[164] An important historical study concludes that over the years "two major images dominate theology, pious literature, art, and popular ideas. Some Christians expect to spend heavenly life in 'eternal solitude with God alone.' Others cannot conceive of blessedness without being reunited with friends, spouse, children, or relatives." The study terms these views "theocentric—'centering in God,' and anthropocentric—'focusing on the human.'" It further shows that although the two models of heaven often coexist to some degree, "one of them can generally be considered the dominant view for a given time and place."[165]

---

163. Dallin H. Oaks, "Kingdoms of Glory," *Liahona*, November 2023, 28.

164. Insightful and accessible on this topic are Segal, *Life after Death*; Bart D. Ehrman, *Heaven and Hell: A History of the Afterlife* (New York: Simon & Schuster, 2020); Gary Scott Smith, *Heaven in the American Imagination* (New York: Oxford University Press, 2011); and Lisa Miller, *Heaven: Our Enduring Fascination with the Afterlife* (New York: Harper, 2010).

165. Colleen McDannell and Bernhard Lang, *Heaven: A History* (New Haven: Yale University Press, 1988), 353–58. See also Jeffrey Burton Russell, *A History of Heaven: The Singing Silence* (Princeton: Princeton University Press, 1997), and Ulrich E. Simon, *Heaven in the Christian Tradition* (New York: Harper, 1958).

Theocentrism typically pictures heaven as a transcendent, spiritual, otherworldly realm (not a material, renovated earth) where God "resides" and heaven's inhabitants are joyously engaged in constant worship. As just one illustration of this perspective, prominent Puritan Richard Baxter emphasized in his *Saints' Everlasting Rest* that heaven consists of an "everlasting rejoicing" in God and "a perpetual singing of his high praises."[166] A theocentric heaven is the heaven of the beatific vision, the blessed brilliance of which transfixes its occupants and social relations fade from view. An anthropocentric heaven has a decidedly different orientation. "Rather than viewing heaven as the structural opposite of life on earth, it is seen as a continuation and fulfillment of material existence." Heaven is a place as much as a condition, often the renovated "new earth" of John's Apocalypse. Life in heaven is characterized by action, endeavor, and spiritual progress. "The journey to God does not end with admittance to heaven but continues eternally. Spiritual development is therefore endless." Perhaps the most prominent characteristic of the anthropocentric heaven, as its name suggests, is an emphasis on social reunion and relationships. "Social relationships, including the love between man and woman, are seen as fundamental to heavenly life and not in conflict with divine purpose."[167]

Off and on over the centuries, Christians have anticipated a continuation of social relationships in some fashion in the next life. This expectation was expressed as early as the third century when regarding heaven Cyprian wrote affectionately, "Many of our dear ones await us there, and a dense crowd of parents, brothers, children, is longing for us, already assured of their own safety, and still longing for our salvation. What gladness there will be for them and for us when we enter their presence and share their embrace!"[168] While this vision of heaven has been promulgated periodically throughout Christian history, "with the nineteenth century came the apex of the anthropocentric heaven. A wide variety of preachers, theologians, poets, and popular writers depicted heaven as a social community where the saints meet their relatives and friends" and experience "productive work, spiritual development," and "the ultimate harmony of the human and the divine."[169] Support for either an anthropocen-

---

166. Quoted in McDannell and Lang, *Heaven*, 172. McDannell and Lang found that notions of a theocentric heaven were also dominant in the writings of the early Augustine, medieval mystics, medieval scholastics, many Protestant reformers, and "much of contemporary theology" (354).

167. McDannell and Lang, *Heaven*, 183.

168. Cyprian, *On Mortality*, as quoted in Alister E. McGrath, *Christian Theology: An Introduction* (Chichester, UK: Wiley-Blackwell, 2011), 447.

169. McDannell and Lang, *Heaven*, 356–57. The authors found that the anthropocentric

tric or theocentric understanding of heaven has been found to "not depend on the level of sophistication of those presenting the image (theologians versus lay people), or time frame (early versus contemporary), or theological preference (Protestant versus Catholic)."[170] As will be seen throughout the remainder of this chapter, the Latter-day Saint vision of heaven falls squarely within the anthropocentric category.

Few aspects of an anthropocentric heaven are more pronounced in LDS discourse than the anticipation of the perpetuity of the family. What is said about interactions with loved ones in the intermediate state is only amplified when describing the joy of family associations for eternity. To be sure, as was discussed in the section on matrimony in chapter 11, eternal family togetherness is linked to faithful adherence to covenants made in the sacrament of a temple marriage sealing, but LDS discourse and literature, music and art, alike abound in blissful depictions of how the "same sociality which exists among us here will exist among us there, only it will be coupled with eternal glory" (D&C 130:2).[171] As previously noted, similar sentiments have been expressed by other American and European Christians, especially during the Victorian era.[172] Women in particular during that period articulated a vision of heaven that resolved the age-old problem of maternal loss of children by positing that the family would be a persisting reality in the afterlife.[173] What sets the Latter-day Saints apart, though, is the scope of the family reunions they hope for in heaven. Through their extensive efforts to trace family roots and vicar-

model was also advanced by the later Augustine; certain medieval authors; most Renaissance writers; eighteenth-century visionaries such as Emanuel Swedenborg; and, as mentioned, a wide variety of nineteenth-century individuals and groups (355–56).

170. McDannell and Lang, *Heaven*, 353.

171. Examples can be found in almost every relevant church publication. *The Eternal Family, Religion 200: A Cornerstone Course* (Salt Lake City: The Church of Jesus Christ of Latter-day Saints, 2015), and *Families and Temples* (Salt Lake City: The Church of Jesus Christ of Latter-day Saints, 2016) are entirely devoted to expounding the LDS doctrine of the family.

172. Among Protestants, "perceptions of heaven shifted in both Europe and America from a God-centered heaven that focused on worshipping and serving the Trinity, to a more human-centered heaven revolving around family and fellowship. . . . During the mid-nineteenth century heaven was depicted principally as a heavenly home where relationships with earthly family members were extremely important." Smith, *Heaven in the American Imagination*, 8. For details, see the chapter titled "Heaven as Home: The Victorians and Heaven, 1830–1870," 70–86.

173. Historian Ann Braude stresses the female contribution to the "familization" of heaven in *Sisters and Saints: Women and Religion in America* (New York: Oxford University Press, 2007).

iously perform the sealing ordinances for deceased ancestors in LDS temples, Mormons contemplate a vast familial throng linked together from across the ages in joyous eternal association. Where other Christians have emphasized the heavenly fellowship of all the saints—friends, fellow believers, even biblical and historical heroes of the past—as much as family, Latter-day Saint mention of such interactions, though it takes place, tends to be eclipsed by the comprehensiveness of their family-specific vision.

Another aspect of the anthropocentric vision of heaven shared by Latter-day Saints and other Christians is belief in a material heaven, typically thought to be associated with the eschatological "new heaven and new earth." Anthropocentrism's anticipation of all the productive, progressive activity and loving social relationships that God originally designed for humanity and that will be fulfilled in heaven seem to some to require a material, terrestrial venue. Rather than being utterly annihilated in the eschaton, the earth will be utterly renovated. So renovated in fact that its material relationship to the present earth may resemble the dramatic difference between our present mortal bodies and the incorruptible, "spiritual" (but still material) bodies we will have when resurrected. The Apocalypse of John endeavors to communicate this transcendent change through a variety of dramatic, even bizarre, images in its final chapters. For biblical scholars and theologians who read Revelation as depicting an anthropocentric heaven, although particular points may be debated, "what is clear" overall "is that heaven will finally be on earth."[174] As noted New Testament scholar N. T. Wright remarked, Revelation concludes "not with humans going up to heaven, but with the God of heaven coming to earth."[175]

Mormon eschatological reflection concurs. John Taylor's comments are typical: "This earth is man's eternal inheritance, where he will exist after the resurrection, for it is destined to be purified and become celestial." Taylor is here echoing a Doctrine and Covenants revelation stating that the earth "must needs be sanctified from all unrighteousness, that it may be prepared for the celestial glory; For after it hath filled the measure of its creation, it shall be crowned with glory . . . that bodies who are of the celestial kingdom may possess it forever and ever" (D&C 88:18-20). Taylor continued: "I know that this position is considered

174. Walls, *Heaven, Hell, and Purgatory*, 29.
175. Wright and Bird, *New Testament in Its World*, 840. Wright has vigorously advanced the argument for a material heaven on a renovated earth in *Surprised by Hope: Rethinking Heaven, the Resurrection, and the Mission of the Church* (New York: HarperOne, 2008), and *Revelation for Everyone* (Louisville: Westminster John Knox, 2009). A popular treatise is Randy Alcorn, *Heaven* (Chicago: Tyndale House, 2004).

strange by many, because it is generally supposed that we are going to heaven; that heaven is the final destination of the righteous; and that when we leave this world, we never return. Hence [Charles] Wesley says—'Beyond the bounds of time and space, Look forward to that heavenly place.'"[176] If the notion of a material heaven was "strange" in Wesley's eighteenth-century England, it was, as has been discussed, much less so in nineteenth-century America. Still, Latter-day Saints found the older view a suitable foil for their eschatological doctrine. One early Saint expressed his belief in satirical rhyme: "The heaven of sectarians is not the heaven for me; So doubtful its location, neither on land nor sea. But I've a heaven on the earth—the land and home that gave me birth, A heaven of light and knowledge—O, that's the heaven for me."[177] This continues to be the position of the Church of Jesus Christ of Latter-day Saints today, although it regards the celestial New Jerusalem of Revelation 21 and 22 more conventionally as "symbolizing God's presence among His people" in the "new heaven and new earth" rather than as the terrestrial, millennial capital discussed earlier in this chapter.[178]

DEGREES OF HEAVENLY GLORY

Historically, Christian theologies have assumed that only a minority of human beings will be saved in heaven. After all, the Sermon on the Mount proclaims, "Strait is the gate, and narrow is the way, which leadeth unto life, and few there be that find it" (Matt. 7:14). In recent centuries, however, cultural forces have combined to make more common the conception of a benevolent Deity with capacious designs for human salvation. As such, perceptions of hell have changed dramatically since the days of Dante.[179] The concept of universal

---

176. John Taylor, *The Government of God* (Liverpool: S. W. Richards, 1852), 38.

177. *Times and Seasons*, February 1845, 799.

178. *NT Student Manual* (2018), 566–67. For example, the "precious stones" mentioned in Rev. 21 and said to compose the city's walls and gates may "represent the Lord's followers who have been refined and made holy" (566–67). In the past, Latter-day Saint literalism tended to conflate Revelation's New Jerusalem, now consistently regarded as a celestial "city," with the millennial and material American New Jerusalem, much discussed elsewhere in LDS scripture. See, for instance, *JSP*, D5:57; *Compendium of Doctrines*, 174–75; and Orson Pratt, *New Jerusalem; or, The Fulfilment of Modern Prophecy* (Liverpool: R. James, 1949), 24. Today, LDS students are told that "the New Jerusalem spoken of in Revelation 21 is not the same city that is to be built on the American continent as part of the last days and the Second Coming of Jesus Christ (see Articles of Faith 10). It refers to the celestial kingdom." *New Testament Seminary Student Study Guide* (2007), 178.

179. Changing views of hell are explored in D. P. Walker, *The Decline of Hell: Seventeenth-Century Discussions of Eternal Torment* (Chicago: University of Chicago Press, 1964), and

salvation, though still a minority report, gets more of a hearing today than ever before.[180] As did others in his day, Joseph Smith questioned the adequacy of traditional assumptions about heaven and hell. To him "It appeared self-evident . . . that if God rewarded every one according to the deeds done in the body, the term 'heaven,' as intended for the saint's eternal home, must include more kingdoms than one."[181] He drew the same conclusion from John 14:2— "In my Father's house are many mansions."[182] On one occasion, while working on his "New Translation" of the Bible, Smith and an associate pondered the contrast in John 5:29 between "the resurrection of life" and "the resurrection of damnation." In so doing, Smith recorded, "The Lord touched the eyes of our understandings and they were opened," and an extended vision of the eternal state followed. Smith's written account of "the Vision" (D&C 76), as he called it, is just under three thousand words in length and presents a picture of a multileveled heaven consisting of varying degrees of blessedness or glory enjoyed by its inhabitants. Highlights from this significant vision invite closer consideration. First, however, it is worth noting that Smith was far from alone in propounding the idea that heaven's inhabitants experience different degrees of glory and reward.

Beginning in antiquity, works of Jewish pseudepigrapha and early Christian apocrypha such as 2 Enoch and the Ascension of Isaiah contain references to multiple heavens.[183] Patristic sources perpetuate the idea. As only one example, in an Easter sermon on the resurrection, Augustine quoted 1 Corinthians 15:41–42—"There is one glory of the sun, and another glory of the moon,

---

Isabel Moreira and Margaret Toscano, eds., *Hell and Its Afterlife: Historical and Contemporary Perspectives* (Farnham, UK: Ashgate, 2010). The lingering homiletic importance of hell in nineteenth-century America, however, is discussed in Kathryn Gin Lum, *Damned Nation: Hell in America from the Revolution to Reconstruction* (New York: Oxford University Press, 2014).

180. The definitive historical study of universalism is Michael J. McClymond, *The Devil's Redemption: A New History and Interpretation of Christian Universalism*, 2 vols. (Grand Rapids: Baker Academic, 2018). See also the briefer Thomas Talbott, "Universalism," in *Oxford Handbook of Eschatology*, 446–61; the varying positions summarized in Robin A. Parry and Christopher H. Partridge, eds., *Universal Salvation: The Current Debate* (Grand Rapids: Eerdmans, 2003); and the theological-historical argument in behalf of universalism by Orthodox scholar David Bentley Hart, *That All Shall Be Saved: Heaven, Hell, & Universal Salvation* (New Haven: Yale University Press, 2019).

181. *Times and Seasons*, August 1844, 592.

182. Smith referenced this passage a number of times. See, for instance, *JSP*, D6:551 and D12:386.

183. Adela Y. Collins, "Heaven," in *Harper's Bible Dictionary*, ed. Paul J. Achtemeier (San Francisco: Harper & Row, 1985), 377.

and another glory of the stars: for one star differeth from another star in glory. So also is the resurrection of the dead"—and remarked, "You see, glory was promised to the bodies of the saints and different degrees of glory because the merits of [people's] charity are different."[184] Indeed, the notion that all receive the same degree of glory in heaven (promoted by Jovinian and rebutted by Jerome) was condemned at synods in Rome and Milan near the end of the fourth century.[185] Later, Aquinas echoed Augustine's view, and gradations of reward in a hierarchical heaven or "degrees of glory" (*gradus gloriae*) became a common concept in the Middle Ages.[186]

During the Reformation, Protestants repudiated any notion that heavenly rewards were earned or deserved. Still, while Reformers did not consider faithful Christian discipleship the *cause* of admission to heaven, they did allow that heavenly rewards were variously distributed as the promised (and natural) *consequence* of earthly righteousness.[187] In other words, God rewards the elect with varying degrees of glory *in accordance with* their works, but not *on account of* them. In his first edition of the *Apology of the Augsburg Confession* (1531), Philip Melanchthon wrote that according to Paul (1 Cor. 3:8), "*Every man shall receive his own reward according to his own labor.* For the blessed will have reward, one higher than the other. . . . For there will be distinctions in the glory of the saints."[188] Calvin considered it "above all controversy" that "just as God, variously distributing his gifts to the saints in this world, beams upon them unequally, so there will not be an equal measure of glory in heaven."[189]

---

184. Augustine, Sermon 241.8, in *Sermons on the Liturgical Season*, trans. Mary Sarah Muldowney, Fathers of the Church (Washington, DC: Catholic University of America Press, 1959), 263.

185. For the late fourth-century controversy, see Jerome, *Against Jovinianus* 2.18–38, in *NPNF*, 2/6: 402–16.

186. Aquinas, *Summa Theologiae* 3a.Supp.93.3, and Gerald O'Collins, *A Concise Dictionary of Catholic Theology* (New York: Paulist, 1991), s.v. "glory." A version of *gradus gloriae* can be seen in Dante's *Paradiso*, which with its portrayal of ascending heavenly spheres provides a picture of God's assessment of the different kinds of lives that will determine one's distance from, or proximity to, the ultimate afterlife reward—the beatific vision.

187. See Emma Disley, "Degrees of Glory: Protestant Doctrine and the Concept of Rewards Hereafter," *Journal of Theological Studies* 42, no. 1 (1991): 77–105.

188. Philip Melanchthon, *Apology of the Augsburg Confession* 3, in *Concordia or Book of Concord: The Symbols of the Evangelical Lutheran Church*, trans. F. Bente and W. H. T. Dau (St. Louis: Concordia, 1952), 67, 66.

189. Calvin, *Institutes* 3.25.10. Protestants such as Calvin tended to conceive of heavenly rewards as different positions and responsibilities in God's eternal kingdom rather than different degrees of blessedness or greater vision of God.

And Luther, reflecting on 1 Corinthians 15:41, reasoned that "just as heavenly bodies emit varying degrees of light, so shall the risen elect enjoy varying degrees of glory, 'making each nicely distinct from the other.' These differences will be determined by our works in this lifetime, or in other words, by our progress in sanctification."[190]

Similar views were advanced in America. Eighteenth-century Congregationalist minister James Dana argued that Christ's comment about "many mansions" meant that the departed would experience "various kinds and degrees of glory" that reflected their earthly "knowledge, purity and love." A century later, famed evangelist Reuben Torrey complained that "the idea that all Christians 'will have an equally glorious eternity' . . . contradicted both the Bible and 'sanctified common sense.'" Although "we are saved by faith," he wrote, we are "rewarded according to our own works." In the same era as Torrey but at the other end of the theological spectrum from the conservative evangelist, liberal Baptist theologian William Newton Clarke "emphasized the role that virtue and works played in determining people's eternal destiny." After a period earlier in the twentieth century of limited discussion of the topic, the later twentieth century witnessed "considerable attention" being given "to the subject of heavenly rewards." A common view was that people "will be assigned different mansions and positions and have different levels of happiness depending on their earthly dedication to Christ." Christian author Tim LaHaye expressed the common sentiment that an individual's earthly discipleship would determine "the degree of his reward" in heaven.[191] "The current Catholic view on heaven is as an abode of the blessed, where (after the resurrection with glorified bodies) they enjoy, in the company of Christ and the angels, the immediate vision of God face to face. . . . There are infinite degrees of glory corresponding to degrees of merit, but all are unspeakably happy in the eternal presence of God."[192]

So, what is different about Joseph Smith's vision of a hierarchical heaven? Primarily the idea that virtually all people will eventually receive some degree of heavenly glory. Only a numerically insignificant handful of God's most intransigent opponents—designated "sons of perdition" in the Vision—will end up in hell for eternity (D&C 76:31–45). Dallin Oaks declared, "The revealed doctrine

190. Quoted in Disley, "Degrees of Glory," 104.

191. Quotations in this paragraph are from Smith, *Heaven in the American Imagination*, 56 (Dana), 149 (Torrey), 150 (Clarke), 194 (later twentieth century, LaHaye).

192. Heidi J. Hornik, "Eschatology in Fine Art," in Walls, *Oxford Handbook of Eschatology*, 648.

of the restored Church of Jesus Christ teaches that *all the children of God*—with exceptions too limited to consider here [the 'sons of perdition']—will ultimately inherit one of the three kingdoms of glory."[193] Aside from the very few sons of perdition, "all the rest shall be brought forth" in the resurrection to experience heaven in some way "through the triumph and the glory of the Lamb who was slain" (D&C 76:39). Quentin Cook noted that just as in the beginning "the vast majority of Heavenly Father's children" were "valiant in their premortal estate," so they would be "profoundly blessed following the ultimate judgment" as they enter a kingdom of glory, "the lowest of which 'surpasses all understanding,'"[194] Latter-day Saints consider this near-universalism a profound demonstration of God's "amazing" grace and the almost incomprehensible depth of his love for his children. Such a capacious view of redemption, however, can be startling if not troubling to those accustomed to seeing heaven as the abode of the relatively small number of the elect and hell, being what fallen humans deserve anyway, as what most will experience.

Not surprisingly, when Smith's Vision was first publicized, its extensive depiction of a multimansioned heaven challenged the conventional views of even some Mormon converts. Recalled Brigham Young: "When God revealed to Joseph Smith and Sidney Rigdon that there was a place prepared for all, according to the light they had received and their rejection of evil and practice of good, it was a great trial to many, and some apostatized because God was not going to send to everlasting punishment heathens and infants, but had a place of salvation, in due time, for all, and would bless the honest and virtuous and truthful, whether they ever belonged to any church or not. It was a new doctrine to this generation, and many stumbled at it."[195] On the other hand, some early Saints felt emboldened by the Vision to preach a complete *apokatastasis* (restoration) of all beings reminiscent of Origen's eschatology. This, however, went too far. "Say to the Brethren Hulits and to all others," wrote Joseph Smith to church leaders in Missouri, "that the Lord never authorized them to say that the Devil nor his angels nor the Sons of perdition should ever be restored. . . . We, therefore, command that this doctrine be taught no more in Zion [and] sanction the decission of the Bishop and his council in relation to this doctrine being a bar of communion."[196] Even though Mormonism dramatically diminished hell's domain, it was unwilling to completely do away with it.

193. Oaks, "Kingdoms of Glory," 26.
194. Quentin L. Cook, "Conversion to the Will of God," *Liahona*, May 2022, 55.
195. *Journal of Discourses*, 16:42.
196. *JSP*, D3:155. The views of Origen and other early fathers on *apokatastasis* are dis-

For the vast majority of humanity, the Vision reveals that a hierarchically structured heaven awaits them, a heaven comprised of three "kingdoms"—the *Celestial, Terrestrial,* and *Telestial.* Joseph Smith believed these three corresponded to what Paul wrote in 1 Corinthians 15:40–42 about the glory of the sun, moon, and stars. Although this passage has often been the source of theological rumination about differing degrees of heavenly glory, Smith's tripartite division of heaven into three discrete kingdoms has been less common, and naming the heavenly kingdoms, particularly the Terrestrial Kingdom and the Telestial Kingdom, is unique to Mormonism.[197] Smith considered Paul's statement about being "caught up to the third heaven" (2 Cor. 12:2) as confirmation that there are three heavens and evidence that Paul had seen the highest, or Celestial, kingdom.[198]

The Celestial Kingdom is the heavenly habitation reserved for those who accept Jesus as their savior, receive an authorized baptism, live in love and obedience to Christ's teachings, and endure in faith to the end of their lives on earth. They are the "just" who are "made perfect through Jesus the mediator . . . who wrought out [his] perfect atonement through the shedding of his own blood" (D&C 76:50–70). The Terrestrial Kingdom, likened to the moon in contrast to the sun, is said to be populated by "honorable men of the earth" who were spiritually "blinded by the craftiness of men." The inhabitants of this kingdom are those who were "not valiant in the testimony of Jesus; wherefore, they obtain not the crown over the kingdom of our God" (D&C 76:71–80). Even blatantly wicked people traditionally set aside for everlasting punishment, such as "whoremongers" and "sorcerers" (D&C 76:103–105; cf. Rev. 21:8), after expiating their own sins in the spirit-world hell until the final judgment (D&C 76:81–89, 98–106), will be resurrected with a degree of glory, albeit the least, and enter the Telestial Kingdom. A closer look at the verses in question, explains apostle Todd Christofferson, reveals that "the distinguishing charac-

---

cussed at length in McClymond, *The Devil's Redemption,* 231–320. See also John R. Sachs, "Apocatastasis in Patristic Theology," *Theological Studies* 54 (1993): 617–40.

197. Smith did not interpret "celestial [*epourania*] bodies, and bodies terrestrial [*epigeia*]" (1 Cor. 15:40) as synonyms for "heavenly" and "earthly" bodies, as is common in biblical interpretation and translation. He saw them as two different kinds of heavenly bodies, and in his "New Translation" he added a third type—"Telestial" (a Mormon neologism): "Also Celestial bodies, and bodies Terrestrial, and bodies Telestial; but the glory of the Celestial, one; and the Terrestrial, another; and the Telestial, another." *NTOB,* 509.

198. *JSP,* D12:386. Later Christians have adduced a similar division in afterlife rewards from the parable of the sower where recipients of the gospel "seed" are described as "bring[ing] forth fruit, some thirtyfold, some sixty, and some an hundred" (Mark 4:20). See, for instance, Irenaeus, *Against Heresies* 5.36.

teristic for the inhabitants of each kingdom is how they relate to 'the testimony of Jesus,' ranging from (1) wholehearted devotion [in the Celestial Kingdom] to (2) not being valiant [in the Terrestrial Kingdom] to (3) outright rejection [in the Telestial Kingdom]." Each person's eternal future hinges on his or her reaction to the "testimony of Jesus . . . the witness of the Holy Spirit that He is the divine Son of God, the Messiah and Redeemer."[199]

Understandably, some might wonder about the propriety of profoundly evil people being admitted to any part of heaven even after expiatory suffering. While a definitive explanation is elusive, part of an answer may be gleaned from two considerations. The first relates to interpretations of Jesus's declaration that "all manner of sin and blasphemy shall be forgiven unto men: but the blasphemy against the Holy Ghost shall not be forgiven unto men . . . neither in this world, neither in the world to come" (Matt. 12:31–32). Apart from this single stated exception of "blasphemy against the Holy Ghost," Jesus says that "all manner of sin," even the most heinous acts, can be forgiven, and that they can be forgiven "in the world to come" if necessary. Mormon doctrine, as previously noted, holds that not only the grievous and inveterate sinner but any unrepentant individual will need to suffer penitential justice for a period in the intermediate state. LDS revelation declares, "I, God, have suffered . . . for all, that they might not suffer if they would repent; but if they would not repent they must suffer even as I" (D&C 19:16–17). Satisfaction for sin is critical, but does it necessarily cleanse and transform the sinner's soul? To be sure, people can change; they are not static, immutable beings. But can the deepest recesses of an incorrigible evildoer's heart and mind really be transformed? Some say yes.

Influential twentieth-century Christian writer C. S. Lewis argued extensively and passionately that a loving Lord wants to radically remake *all* human beings in his own image, even the most evil ones. He seeks to turn us into "little Christs" if we will let him. Lewis puts these words into Christ's mouth: "Whatever suffering it may cost you in your earthly life, whatever inconceivable purification it may cost you after death . . . I will never rest, nor let you rest, until you are literally perfect—until my Father can say without reservation that He is well pleased with you."[200] Could, would, Christ do this even with an Adolf Hitler or Saddam Hussein? Might such a dramatic inner transformation require a thousand years or more of divine discipline, of discipling, in the intermediate-state hell of spirit prison prior to the last

199. D. Todd Christofferson, "The Testimony of Jesus," *Liahona*, May 2024, 97.
200. C. S. Lewis, *Mere Christianity* (New York: HarperOne, 1952), 202.

resurrection? Following Lewis's line of reasoning, if Christ accomplished this transforming sanctification for Hitler or Hussein, in an important sense each man would no longer be the same person who was responsible for murdering and brutalizing so many of his fellow humans. Like Dickens's misanthropic Ebenezer Scrooge, each man will "have come to see his entire earth life in the light of heaven. He will see the crimes he committed through the eyes of Christ. He will understand with full clarity the pain he caused and the wrong he did, and he will hate his sin[s], just as God does, and deeply regret ever committing [them]."[201] And he will have suffered for them, excruciatingly and at great length (D&C 19:15–18). To grant such a pardoned and Christ-purified Hitler or Hussein a modicum of heavenly blessedness in the Telestial Kingdom would be exponentially different in degree, but not in kind, from admitting a transformed Scrooge after he had become "as good a friend . . . as good a man as the good old city knew."[202]

Given Mormonism's capacious view of heaven, is there still a place for hell in the eternal state? The answer is yes, but its population is drastically reduced in comparison with what is anticipated in many Christian theologies. According to the Vision, only the very few "sons of perdition," those who never cease to make open war on God and his kingdom, "shall go away into the lake of fire and brimstone with the devil and his angels and [are] the only ones on whom the second death shall have any power" (D&C 76:36–37; cf. Rev. 20:14; 21:8). These "shall remain filthy still" (D&C 88:102; cf. Rev. 22:11) and are "vessels of wrath, doomed to suffer the wrath of God, with the devil and his angels in eternity" (D&C 76:33).[203] Because the vast majority of sinners will "only" experience hell in the intermediate state prior to the resurrection and then only until satisfaction for sin is exacted and soul-transforming purification is achieved, LDS scripture offers a revised understanding of "eternal" torment and "endless" punishment. "Surely every man must repent or suffer," begins

201. Walls, *Heaven, Hell, and Purgatory*, 152. See also Walls's discussion of evildoers and the afterlife in 93–116, 133–53.

202. Charles Dickens, *A Christmas Carol* (London, 1843), 165.

203. Although neither an official nor a consensus view, a few early Mormon leaders conceived the second death in annihilationist terms. Apostle Erastus Snow, for instance, opined, "I understand that the second death is a spiritual death. Is it meant that the spirit shall die? Each of you can draw your own conclusions . . . but I can conceive of no other spiritual death than dissolution. I understand, when applied to the mortal tabernacle, [death] alludes to the dissolution of that tabernacle. . . . I conceive that the same term is applicable to the spirit in like manner. . . . These reflections of mine I do not teach as doctrine, binding your consciences, but as views which I have of the sacred Scriptures, referring to the second death." *Journal of Discourses*, 7:358–59.

Doctrine and Covenants 19:4–12. "Nevertheless, it is not written that there shall be no end to this torment, but it is written endless torment." The difference lies in the meanings of "endless" and "eternal." "For, behold, I am endless, and the punishment which is given from my hand is endless punishment, for Endless is my name. Wherefore—Eternal punishment is God's punishment. Endless punishment is God's punishment." Thus, in this case, "endless" and "eternal" are not meant to be temporal descriptions but possessive adjectives naming the source (God) rather than the duration of the punishment.

This does not mean that the intensity of suffering in the spirit-world hell is reduced: "I revoke not the judgments which I shall pass, but woes shall go forth, weeping, wailing and gnashing of teeth, yea, to those who are found on my left hand" (D&C 19:5). The Vision describes those in hell during the intermediate state in this manner: "These are they who suffer the vengeance of eternal fire. These are they who are cast down to hell and suffer the wrath of Almighty God, until the fulness of times, when Christ shall . . . deliver up the kingdom, and present it unto the Father" (D&C 76:105–106). Although suffering in the spirit-world hell is understood to be acute, it is terminable for all but the handful of sons of perdition. Still, Doctrine and Covenants 19 justifies letting the common connotations of "eternal" and "endless" stand when used in scriptural statements about torment and damnation because of the terms' potentially sin-deterring and therefore soul-saving effect: "It is written eternal damnation; wherefore it is more express than other scriptures, that it might work upon the hearts of the children of men, altogether for my name's glory." Although the purgatorial and transformative path is painful and long in the intermediate-state hell, it eventuates in resurrection and at least some degree of heavenly glory in the Telestial Kingdom. In the Vision's rapturous portrayal of a multilevel heaven, even the glory of this lowest heavenly realm "surpasses all understanding," and its inhabitants are considered "heirs of salvation" (D&C 76:89, 88).

Eternal Life and Exaltation

Although the Vision depicts the overwhelming majority of God's children enjoying some degree of blessedness and glory in eternity, only the Lord's most faithful disciple-servants will dwell in the presence of God and his Christ forever in the Celestial Kingdom. Even in the Celestial Kingdom there is a hierarchy of reward, with "exaltation" being the highest.[204] In Mormon terminology, "exaltation" is also known as "eternal life." Admittedly, Latter-day Saint theology

---

204. *Principles of the Gospel*, 75. See also D&C 131:1–3.

applies its own distinctive meaning to "eternal life," just as it does to "eternal damnation." Because "eternal" can serve as a name for God, "eternal life" refers not just to immortality but to the very kind and quality of life that God has. The church's *General Handbook* states: "Immortality is to live forever with a resurrected physical body. Eternal life, or exaltation, is to become like God and live in His presence eternally."[205] Little wonder, then, that revelation declares: "Eternal life is the greatest of all the gifts of God" (D&C 14:7). In the KJV, *zōēn aiōnion* is commonly translated "eternal life" or "everlasting life." *Aiōnios* has a complex etymology and varying applications, but primarily it is used to denote everlastingness or existence without beginning or end. It is the closest Greek term to the English word "eternal." In the case of "eternal life" (and "eternal damnation"), however, Latter-day Saint usage is theological rather than linguistic. Theologically, Latter-day Saints distinguish eternal life from immortality.

Perhaps the most dramatic aspect of eternal life as living in God's presence and becoming like him is that eventually "exaltation means . . . godhood—the kind of life our Heavenly Father lives."[206] As often noted in this volume, Latter-day Saints consider human beings to be literal spirit children of Heavenly Father and Heavenly Mother (see chapter 5) who share a basic ontological oneness with their Parents. As such, the afterlife for God's responsive children is envisioned to be one of potentially endless progress that aeons into the future enables them to become fully like their divine Parents. This is sometimes expressed as God's children one day becoming gods themselves. Lorenzo Snow, later church president, declared: "We believe that we are the offspring of our Father in heaven, and that we possess in our spiritual organizations the same capabilities, powers and faculties that our Father possesses, although in an infantile state, requiring us to pass through a certain course or ordeal by which they will be developed and improved" throughout eternity.[207] Of this prospect, Parley Pratt rhapsodized, "The very germs of these Godlike attributes, being engendered in man, the offspring of Deity, only need cultivating, improving, developing, and advancing by means of a series of progressive changes, in order to arrive at the fountain 'Head,' the standard, the climax of Divine Humanity," and be "called a *God*."[208] This stunning possibility bears resemblance to, but is distinct from, the Eastern doctrine of theosis or deification.[209]

205. *GH* 1.1.
206. *Basic Doctrines of the Gospel*, 5.
207. *Journal of Discourses*, 14:300.
208. Pratt, *Key to Theology*, 32–33.
209. An accessible introduction to patristic teaching on theosis by one of the leading scholars in the field is Norman Russell's *Fellow Workers with God: Orthodox Thinking on*

As early as Gregory of Nyssa in the fourth century, the notion of spiritual elevation through *epektasis* (eternal endeavor or stretching forth) was being articulated in the East. *Epektasis* has been described as "unceasing progress into virtue and the knowledge of God; Christian life is about a continuous climb towards perfection whose boundaries are limitlessness. According to this teaching, the soul, being attracted to God, is in a perpetual climb towards the superior plateau of the plenitude of Grace. Man becoming Godlike, here on Earth as in eternity, involves a permanent progress and a never-ending stretch [*epektasis*]." Undergirding this lengthy process that continues throughout eternity is the doctrine that "God did not want to create man only as a being gifted with special, distinctive qualities, superior to all other created beings, but wanted to create him to become a god by Divine Grace."[210] One modern Orthodox scholar has observed that it is a "fundamental Orthodox conviction that the human vocation, or ultimate raison d'etre is to become by grace what God is by nature."[211] This echoes Maximus the Confessor from centuries before: "Humanity was created for and to this end [progressive ascent to God]. But our forefather Adam misused his freedom and . . . chose to estrange himself from the divine and blessed goal, preferring by his own choice to be a *pile of dust* (See Gen 2:7) rather than god by grace."[212] Other Christians may not speak of "deification," but they do hold the related hope, grounded in the redemptive grace of Christ, for a full restoration of the *imago Dei* in the afterlife. Origen stated the point succinctly: "The fulfillment of the likeness [to God] is reserved for the final consummation."[213] A Reformed

---

Theosis (Crestwood, NY: St. Vladimir's Seminary Press, 2009). For a more detailed and technical treatment, see Russell's *Doctrine of Deification in the Greek Patristic Tradition* (Oxford: Oxford University Press, 2004). For Western perspectives on theosis, see Jared Ortiz, ed., *Deification in the Latin Patristic Tradition* (Washington, DC: Catholic University of America Press, 2019); David V. Meconi and Carl E. Olson, eds., *Called to Be the Children of God: The Catholic Theology of Human Deification* (San Francisco: Ignatius, 2016); and Veli-Matti Kärkkäinen, *One with God: Salvation as Deification and Justification* (Collegeville, MN: Liturgical Press, 2007).

210. Liviu Petcu, "The Doctrine of Epektasis: One of the Major Contributions of Saint Gregory of Nyssa to the History of Thinking," *Revista Portuguesa de Filosofia* 73, no. 2 (2017): 774, 771.

211. John Breck, "Divine Initiative: Salvation in Orthodox Theology," in *Salvation in Christ: A Lutheran-Orthodox Dialogue*, ed. John Meyendorff and Robert Tobias (Minneapolis: Augsburg Fortress, 1992), 114.

212. Quoted in Paul M. Blowers, *Maximus the Confessor: Jesus Christ and the Transfiguration of the World* (Oxford: Oxford University Press, 2016), 218.

213. Origen, *On First Principles* 3.4.1.

theologian summarized the human story as moving from "original" image to "perverted" image to "renewed" image to "perfected" image.[214] For Orthodox, though, the perfected image is cultivated in "one endless *prokope* or advancement. Heaven is not a static place, but one where the endless joy of discovery, constantly unfolding, gives to the created order the closest experience of the infinite it can have."[215]

Historically, American Christians have often expressed similar views. Jonathan Edwards "expected the saints to grow throughout eternity in holiness, love, understanding, and happiness. 'There is eternal progress' in heaven," he wrote. Later, his grandson and Yale president Timothy Dwight agreed that the saints in heaven would continually attain "higher perfection" in "knowledge, power, and love." Charles Finney claimed that their growth in knowledge was such that eventually "they would know exponentially more than everyone in the world did collectively."[216] The notion of everlasting intellectual and spiritual growth in heaven continued to be common in the late 1800s. Ministers ranging from Henry Ward Beecher to Charles Hodge "emphasized that moral and intellectual progress occurred in heaven." In the early twentieth century, in what historians have dubbed the "Progressive Era," the idea of "personal growth and progress became as important as worship [and] contemplation . . . had been in earlier generations." Heaven's residents "would have marvelous opportunities to learn, develop their characters, and advance spiritually" as they progressed toward realizing their "divine possibilities."[217] By the later years of the twentieth century, however, Christians placed "less emphasis on personal progress in heaven," and, as it always had been, the idea was challenged by some theologians. Still, others found unappealing the notion that individuals were perfected upon entering heaven. "If the saints always remained on the same level," one minister wrote, "heavenly life would lack 'challenge, variety, and interest.'" Part of the attraction of heaven, insisted a Catholic author, is that it "will be a time for continual growth and moral progress."[218]

Latter-day Saints have little disagreement with such explanations, as far as they go. The Mormon vision of deification is rooted in the same premise of

214. Anthony A. Hoekema, *Created in God's Image* (Grand Rapids: Eerdmans, 1986), 82–96.

215. McGuckin, *Orthodox Church*, 227.

216. Smith, *Heaven in the American Imagination*, 34, 55. See also William Ellery Channing's classic 1828 sermon "Likeness to God." (Reproduced in Sydney E. Ahlstrom and Jonathan S. Carey, eds., *An American Reformation: A Documentary History of Unitarian Christianity* [Middletown, CT: Wesleyan University Press, 1985], 118–35.)

217. Smith, *Heaven in the American Imagination*, 121, 135, 143–44.

218. Smith, *Heaven in the American Imagination*, 190.

endless spiritual progress in the afterlife. Yet, as we shall see, it includes distinctive processual elements and is more dramatic in its end result. "Here then is eternal life," declared Joseph Smith in one of his most provocative sermons. "You have got to learn how to be Gods yourselves, and to be kings and priests to God, . . . by going from a small degree to another, from grace to grace, from exaltation to exaltation, until you are able to sit in glory, as [do] those who sit enthroned in everlasting power."[219] John Taylor exulted in the prospect and remarked that in the distant future when the faithful may be so "crowned, and are perfect men and women in the Lord, one in glory, one in knowledge, and one in image: they are like Christ, and he is like God: then, O, then, they are all 'Living Gods.'"[220] Of such "perfected beings," the First Presidency wrote, they "are rightly called gods, being, like the Savior, [and] possessed of 'the fullness of the Godhead bodily.'"[221]

The LDS *Guide to the Scriptures* succinctly identifies the basic components of this potential afterlife trajectory: "Men and women who are faithful in receiving the necessary ordinances [sacraments], keeping their covenants, and obeying God's commands will enter into their exaltation and become as God."[222] This statement, while true as far as it goes, omits the emphasis found elsewhere in LDS discourse on the length of time involved in this process of deification. "When you climb up a ladder," declared Joseph Smith, "you must begin at the bottom and go on until you learn the last principle." But after entering the Celestial Kingdom, still "it will be a *great while* before you have learned the last."[223] Smith's point was made even more forcefully in an official statement from the church's First Presidency early in the twentieth century: "Man is the child of God, formed in the divine image and endowed with divine attributes, and even as the infant son of an earthly father and mother is capable in due time of becoming a man, so the undeveloped offspring of celestial parentage is capable, by experience *through ages and aeons*, of evolving into a God."[224] Of course, it is possible to theorize that God could miraculously and instantaneously confer

---

219. *JSP*, D14:345–46.

220. "The Living God," *Times and Seasons*, February 1845, 809 (808–9). Taylor saw humanity's divine potential symbolized in John's vision of God's servants being sealed with the Father's name on their foreheads (Rev. 14:1; 22:4; 7:3). "'His name in their foreheads,'" commented Taylor, "undoubtedly means 'God'" (809).

221. *Improvement Era*, April 1912, 485.

222. *Guide to the Scriptures*, s.v. "man, men."

223. *JSP*, D14:330 (emphasis added).

224. "Origin of Man: By the First Presidency of the Church," *Improvement Era*, November 13, 1909, 81 (emphasis added).

the full range of divine attributes and powers on his resurrected children, but the Mormon doctrine of eternal progression implies both *epektasis* and a very long, gradual, grace-aided process of continual learning and development. From an LDS standpoint, compared to the relatively little progress toward full god-likeness that even the most grace-endowed, synergistically engaged disciple of Christ can experience on earth, deification should be seen primarily as a prolonged afterlife phenomenon. Hence its consideration in this chapter.

The expectation of a very lengthy period of postmortal progress toward godhood means that most Latter-day Saints have the same humility about the vast qualitative distance between themselves and God the Father that other Christians do. They tend to view the prospect of even an aeons-from-now deification as something almost incomprehensible given their current, limited level of God-likeness. Certainly, no Mormon prophet or apostle is on record as saying that either he himself or anyone else has climbed the ladder of god-liness here on earth to the point that he is a mere rung away from reaching godhood.[225] Moreover, when deification is discussed in LDS Church circles today, it often lacks the nineteenth-century attention to a vision of the deified exercising cosmic power or ruling over an innumerable posterity of their own procreation on worlds the deified themselves have created.[226] For pastoral reasons, the present focus is on Christian formation and spiritual growth in this life rather than on speculation about the nature of a far distant and little-understood future possibility of literal deification. Drawing on the gifts and graces of the Spirit to become *like* God, rather than to become *a* god, is the more common emphasis today.[227] To be sure, an oft-cited 1995 proclamation of the church's First Presidency and Council of the Twelve affirms that "Each

225. The Doctrine and Covenants does, however, state that Abraham, Isaac, and Jacob "have entered into their exaltation, according to the promises, and sit upon thrones, and are not angels but are gods" (D&C 132:37).

226. Prior to the birth of Mormonism, early modern interest in the vastness of the universe led some to postulate a plurality of divine beings (as well as worlds), although generally not conceived as exalted, deified human beings. Ben Franklin, for instance, in his personal "Articles of Belief and Acts of Religion" (1728), wrote, "I CONCEIVE then, that the INFINITE has created many Beings or Gods, vastly superior to Man. . . . I conceive that each of these is exceeding wise, and good, and very powerful; and that Each has made for himself, one glorious Sun, attended with a beautiful and admirable System of Planets." Nonetheless, and here Latter-day Saints would agree, "It is that particular wise and good God, who is the Author and Owner of our System, that I propose for the Object of my Praise and Adora-tion." Founders Online, https://founders.archives.gov/documents/Franklin/01-01-02-0032.

227. An important twenty-first-century document that epitomizes the humility and reverence with which the topic is currently discussed, as opposed to the triumphalist tone

[person] is a beloved spirit son or daughter of heavenly parents, and, as such, each has a divine nature and destiny."[228] Yet exactly where it will all lead in the next life is only vaguely understood and rarely discussed. Given how difficult it is, in any case, for finite mortals to truly comprehend much about the full nature of an *infinite* God, Latter-day Saints realize it is unlikely that in this present life they will ever have a very profound understanding of what it means for humans to grow into godhood. In an interview with the press, President Gordon Hinckley reportedly characterized the doctrine as "pretty deep theology that we don't know very much about."[229]

And yet, despite occasional rumors to the contrary and a lack of detailed knowledge about the process, on the eve of his accession to the church presidency, Hinckley affirmed that "the whole design of the gospel is to lead us onward and upward . . . even, eventually, to godhood." Hinckley also acknowledged, "Our enemies have criticized us for believing in this. Our reply is that this lofty concept in no way diminishes God the Eternal Father. He is the Almighty. He is the Creator and Governor of the universe. He is the greatest of all and will always be so. But just as any earthly father wishes for his sons and daughters every success in life, so I believe our Father in Heaven wishes for his children that they might approach him in stature and stand beside him resplendent in godly strength and wisdom."[230] Such an expression parallels in spirit the different imagery used by medieval mystic "Meister" Eckhart: "The seed of God is in us. Given an intelligent farmer and a diligent fieldhand, it will thrive and grow up to God whose seed it is, and, accordingly, its fruit will be God-nature. Pear seeds grow into pear trees; nut seeds into nut trees, and God-seed into God."[231]

A decade prior to Hinckley's remarks, apostle Boyd Packer delivered a general conference address entitled "The Pattern of Our Parentage" in which he expressed sentiments similar to those Hinckley would later voice. With pointed emphasis, Packer declared, "I humbly but resolutely affirm that we will not,

---

of the nineteenth century, is the church's Gospel Topics essay entitled "Becoming Like God" at churchofjesuschrist.org.

228. *Ensign*, November 1995, 102.

229. Don Lattin, "Musings of the Main Mormon," *San Francisco Chronicle*, April 13, 1997.

230. "Don't Drop the Ball," *Ensign*, November 1994, 48.

231. Eckhart, *The Aristocrat*, as quoted in *A History of Christian Theology*, ed. William C. Placher and Derek R. Nelson, 2nd ed. (Louisville: Westminster John Knox, 2013), 143. John L. Brooke, *The Refiner's Fire: The Making of Mormon Cosmology, 1644–1844* (New York: Cambridge University Press, 1994), finds similar parallels to Mormon belief in deification among the radical Christian sects and hermetic perfectionists of early modern Europe.

we cannot, stray from this doctrine. On this fundamental truth we will *never* yield!" In his strong affirmation of the LDS understanding of deification, Packer quoted approvingly a stanza from a poem composed by Lorenzo Snow. The poem alludes to Philippians 2:5–6—"Let this mind be in you, which was also in Christ Jesus: Who, being in the form of God, thought it not robbery to be equal with God." Poetically glossing this passage, Snow wrote, "A Son of God, like God to be, Would not be robbing Deity, And he who has this hope within, Will purify himself from sin." Packer added, "This thought does not fill me with arrogance. It fills me with overwhelming humility. Nor does it sponsor any inclination to worship oneself or any man." On the contrary, Packer stressed, "The Father *is* the one true God. *This* thing is certain: no one will ever ascend above Him; no one will ever replace Him. . . . We revere our Father and our God; we *worship* Him."[232] This crucial qualifier continues to be expressed in current church literature. As one instructional manual puts it, "exalted beings will continue to worship Heavenly Father in the eternities to come; He will always be our God."[233] Such expressions echo the authoritative declaration of the First Presidency from early in the twentieth century that although couples may eventually "reach the status of Godhood . . . they are still subject to Jesus Christ as their [spiritual] Father in this exalted relationship; and so we read in [D&C 76:59]: 'and they are Christ's, and Christ is God's.'"[234] They will always be subordinate and subservient to the Son of God, as he is to the Father.

By now it may be obvious that there is a fundamental difference between LDS and other Christian theories of theosis or deification. For the early Greek fathers and subsequent Orthodox theologians, theosis is essentially a synonym for what in the West is known as sanctification. One Orthodox theologian has defined theosis as "the process of the sanctification of Christians whereby they become progressively conformed to God."[235] Church fathers in the Greek East found a number of supporting scriptural images and metaphors for theosis. One of the more common was "participation in the divine nature," a phrase

---

232. Boyd K. Packer, "The Pattern of Our Parentage," *Ensign*, November 1984, 66.

233. *NT Student Manual* (2018), 541. The use of "exalted beings" as a synonym for "gods" hints at a subtle shift in rhetorical style for how the doctrine of humanity's divine potential is presented today.

234. "The Father and the Son," 939.

235. John A. McGuckin, "The Strategic Adaptation of Deification in the Cappadocians," in *Partakers of the Divine Nature: The History and Development of Deification in the Christian Traditions*, ed. Michael J. Christensen and Jeffrey A. Wittung (Madison, NJ: Fairleigh Dickinson University Press, 2007), 95. The entire *Partakers of the Divine Nature* volume is a useful collection for understanding doctrines of deification.

originating in 2 Peter 1:4. This passage was interpreted to mean that Christians "participate in" or share the divine nature through the Spirit of Christ that dwells in them. The underlying Greek word *koinōnos* is typically rendered "partner" or "associate," one with whom something is shared. It is the word used in Luke 5:10 to describe the fishing partnership between Peter, James, and John. *Koinōnia* is often translated as "fellowship" or "communion." This sense of comradeship and communal participation inherent in the *koinōnos* word group is often missed by modern users of the King James Bible (such as the Latter-day Saints) because in 2 Peter 1:4 the KJV renders *koinōnos* as "partakers." Given the evolution of the English language, "partakers" today conveys more of an idea of individual acquisition than of sharing, which was implicit in the original Greek.

As the patristic discussion of *how* Christians participate in the divine nature developed, the understanding of participation became far richer than any notion of merely basking associatively in God's reflected glory. Eastern fathers found an interpretive key in the incarnation. By becoming flesh, Christ took on fallen human nature—our human nature—precisely so he could purify and divinize it. As Gregory of Nyssa expressed it in one of his *Catechetical Orations*, when the second person of the Godhead became flesh, divinity "was transfused throughout our nature, so that our nature, by virtue of this transfusion, might itself become divine."[236] Theologians have sometimes dubbed this concept of participation in the divine nature as the "exchange formula," and early fathers from Irenaeus to Athanasius taught the doctrine using phrases like "God became man so man could become god."[237] Such expressions have surprised and impressed Mormons, who, without fully understanding them, have occasionally lifted them out of context and held them up as proof that early Christians taught the *LDS* doctrine of deification. Yet Athanasius's pithy statement does not equate with Lorenzo Snow's famous aphorism—"as God now is, man may become." The "exchange formula" signifies an exchange of characteristics and attributes, not a change in fundamental nature. Humans remain human, and God continues to be God. Christians, whether in the Greek East or Latin West, consistently upheld what they considered the unbreachable wall separating God and human beings, expressed as the onto-

236. *Great Catechism*, 25, as quoted in McGuckin, "Strategic Adaptation of Deification in the Cappadocians," 113. On the human nature Christ assumed, see chapter 3, especially note 55.

237. Athanasius's expression is from *De Incarnatione* 54:3. What he and others may have meant by it is explored in Vladimir Kharlamov, "Rhetorical Application of *Theosis* in Greek Patristic Theology," in Christensen and Wittung, *Partakers of the Divine Nature*, 117–23.

logical opposites of Creator and creature, divinity and humanity, infinite and finite, self-existent and contingent. Deification for the Eastern fathers did not grow out of any ontological potential in the soul's primal, preexistent nature as it does for Latter-day Saints but is a process of divinization by grace alone. Moreover, godly attributes are rarely viewed as detachable qualities that "cling to the human heart apart from Christ."[238] Deification is about community, not autonomy. If Christ is not present, humans are not godly. People may live moral, upright lives on their own, but true godliness exists only in Christ and is present in humans only through their participation in him.

Here the Internet might serve as a helpful analogy. Christ's divinity, his righteousness, his godly attributes are like the incomprehensibly powerful Internet. As long as we are connected to the Internet, all its wonders become available to us; we share in its power and benefits. We become infinitely knowledgeable, but not independently so. Similarly, when we become Christ's and enter into union with him, we participate in his righteousness, we become partakers of the divine nature, but we are still human. While by this connection, this union, we can truly be said to be "gods," it is not in the sense that we personally, independently, have become gods. We are not new Internets, as it were, rivals to the World Wide Web. That is beyond us. No matter how much we download from the Internet or how often we use it, there will always be a vast qualitative difference between what Google (or God) knows and what we know. Similarly, no matter how responsive we are to the indwelling Christ or how much his infusion of *caritas*, the pure love of Christ, creates certain habits of grace within us, we are still improved human beings at best, not new and separate deities. Created humanity can never become uncreated divinity. It is a matter of participation, not personal possession. For most Christians, who begin with the presupposition of an unbridgeable gulf between humanity and divinity, deification must always remain a metaphor.

Yet Mormonism boldly proclaims a different vision. As discussed earlier, Joseph Smith bridged the ontological gap between God and humanity by teaching that God, angels, and humans are the same class of being, the same "race," so to speak, except at vastly different points in their development. God was once human, and humans can become gods. This was one of the Mormon prophet's most distinctive doctrines, and one that is virtually without parallel in Christendom, East or West. In addition to its dramatic dissolution of the Creator-creature divide, the LDS doctrine of eschatological deification also

---

238. Martin Luther, *Lectures on Galatians*, quoted in Tuomo Mannermaa, *Christ Present in Faith: Luther's View of Justification* (Minneapolis: Fortress, 2005), 29.

differs from some Christian conceptions of divinization in its previously discussed eternal prolongation. Apart from Christians such as Orthodox whose vision of heaven includes perpetual spiritual progress, traditions that embrace a notion of deification tend to discuss it as an earth-life process of sanctification that leads to perfecting glorification at death or following the resurrection. For Latter-day Saints, on the other hand, sanctification during earth life only puts the Saints on their own "one-yard line" of eternal progression toward godhood. The remaining ninety-nine yards, so to speak, will require "ages and aeons" to traverse.[239] This perspective is yet another reason Mormon eschatology is more compatible with the progress-friendly nature of the anthropocentric vision of heaven than with the static perfection of the theocentric heaven.

Perhaps the most pointed manifestation of an anthropocentric depiction of heaven in Latter-day Saint eschatology as it relates to deification is the way in which marriage and family play a central role. As Joseph Smith explained, "In the celestial glory there are three heavens or degrees; and in order to obtain the highest"—the one labeled "exaltation" that potentially leads to deification—a man and a woman "must enter into . . . the new and everlasting covenant of marriage" (D&C 131:1–2).[240] For this reason, a temple marriage is sometimes called the "covenant of exaltation."[241] Even after receiving the holy sacrament of temple marriage, however, deification as the fullness of exaltation and eternal life is not assured. It is simply made possible. The reality is that "strait is the gate and narrow the way that leadeth unto the exaltation and continuation of the lives, and few there be that find it" (D&C 132:21–22). Joseph Smith remarked, "How many will be able to abide a celestial law & go through & receive their exhaltation I am unable to say but many are called & few are chosen."[242] Yet, if a married couple honors this "covenant of exaltation" and with the help

239. "Origin of Man," 81. Boyd Packer taught Latter-day Saints that "we may now be young in our progression—juvenile, even infantile, compared with Him. Nevertheless, in the eternities to come, if we are worthy, we may be[come] like unto Him." Packer, "Pattern of Our Parentage," 67.

240. As explained in chapter 11, from the time of this revelation to near the turn of the twentieth century, the new and everlasting covenant of marriage was understood to include polygamous or plural marriages. In an effort to encourage the practice of plural marriage, some nineteenth-century church leaders taught that it was essential to exaltation and that monogamous temple marriages were insufficient (e.g., *Journal of Discourses*, 20:28). Once the practice of plural marriage was officially and effectively discontinued in the early twentieth century, this doctrine was no longer advanced. Monogamous temple marriage became the gateway ordinance to exaltation.

241. *Guide to the Scriptures*, s.v. "Abrahamic Covenant."

242. *JSP*, D14:106–7.

of God's grace continues to develop toward deification, at some distant point in the eternal state, they may receive "their exaltation and glory in all things [and] then shall they be gods" (D&C 132:19–20). This, remarked apostle Robert Hales, is "the very essence of eternal life."[243] As summarized in the headnote for Doctrine and Covenants 132, "Celestial marriage and a continuation of the family unit" are what potentially and eventually make it possible for human beings "to become gods."[244] Explained apostle Russell Nelson, "In God's eternal plan, salvation is an individual matter; exaltation is a family matter."[245]

This emphasis on marriage and family inevitably raises questions for church members who are single. Years ago, President Lorenzo Snow declared, "There is no Latter-day Saint who dies after having lived a faithful life who will lose anything . . . when opportunities were not furnished him or her. In other words, if a young man or a young woman has no opportunity of getting married, and they live faithful lives up to the time of their death, they will have all the blessings, exaltation, and glory that any man or woman will have who had this opportunity and improved it. That is sure and positive."[246] This reassurance continues to be expressed in the twenty-first century. Boyd Packer observed: "For some all is not complete in mortal life, for marriage and a family of their own have passed them by. But the great plan of happiness and the laws which govern it continue after death. Watched over by a kind and loving Heavenly Father, they will not, in the eternal pattern of things, be denied blessings necessary for their exaltation, including marriage and family."[247]

243. Robert D. Hales, "The Plan of Salvation: A Sacred Treasure of Knowledge to Guide Us," *Ensign*, October 2015, 29.

244. Mormon doctrine holds that couples who eventually are deified will, like their heavenly parents, beget their own spirit offspring. An important part of the fullness of exaltation is "a continuation of the seeds forever and ever" (D&C 132:19). Without specifying the means of generation, Joseph Smith taught that by this "multiplication of Lives . . . the eternal worlds are created and occupied." *JSP*, D12:488. LDS doctrine emphasizes, however, that the creation of worlds will not take place apart from continued association with the Creator. Brigham Young acknowledged that the deified will "possess the power and the knowledge to . . . bring [worlds] into existence." But, he queried, will they do it "of themselves, independent of their Creator"? "No," he answered. "They and their Creator will always be one . . . working and operating together . . . to all eternity." *Journal of Discourses*, 2:304.

245. Russell M. Nelson, "Salvation and Exaltation," *Ensign*, May 2008, 10.

246. *Teachings: Lorenzo Snow*, 130.

247. *Ensign*, November 2003, 25. See also, Russell M. Nelson, "Celestial Marriage," *Ensign*, November 2008, 94. How these reassuring words square with the doctrine that marriages will not be performed in the afterlife is a question for which there is no official answer. Latter-day Saints for the present are left to trust an all-loving and all-powerful heavenly Father with regard to how this will unfold in the next life and to say with the Book

To a unique degree, therefore, Mormonism is a "family-centered" theology. Explained Dallin Oaks: "Our theology begins with heavenly parents, and our highest aspiration is to attain the fulness of eternal exaltation. We know this is possible only in a family relationship."[248] For this reason, Russell Nelson expressed the view that the ultimate objective of creation and the primary purpose for the church's restoration was "so that families could be sealed and exalted as eternal entities."[249] Clearly, Mormonism takes the anthropocentric model of heaven to a new level. Yet it does so firmly rooted in relationship with Christ. Church leaders emphatically stress that only a marriage and family centered in Christ and eternally drawing on his grace will ever reach exaltation or godhood. Thus, while acknowledging the characteristics of heaven that scholars have dubbed "anthropocentric," Latter-day Saints would prefer to describe their vision of eternal life as "Christocentric."

---

of Mormon prophet Alma, "Now these mysteries are not yet fully made known unto me; therefore I shall forbear" (Alma 37:11).

248. Dallin H. Oaks, "No Other Gods," *Ensign*, November 2013, 73.

249. Russell M. Nelson, "Nurturing Marriage," *Ensign*, May 2006, 36.

Afterword

At the conclusion of this lengthy theological "road trip," the author wonders where the reader has arrived in terms of how to interpret the intentionally ambiguous "among" in the book's title, *Latter-day Saint Theology among Christian Theologies*. Have the distinctives of Latter-day Saint belief loomed so large that the reader regards the Church of Jesus Christ of Latter-day Saints as a separate religion apart from Christianity? Or, have the commonalities encountered led the reader to see the church as one "among" many variants of Christianity in the world today, as part of the Christian family? Contemplating a response to these questions may be a bit like deciding whether the proverbial cup is partially full or partially empty. It is a matter of perspective. In the end, whether the reader decides that the theology of the Church of Jesus Christ of Latter-day Saints shares enough with other Christianities to be considered part of the larger Christian community will inevitably be a personal and subjective judgment. Regardless of how readers may determine the degree of the cup's fullness, they should at least know, after having read this book, that there is something in the cup!

Because for a number of the years involved in producing this volume the author has held a professorial chair committed to deepening interreligious understanding and fostering interfaith goodwill, his personal hope is that readers will conclude their theological journey with such takeaway observations as these: "I find that the beliefs and practices of the Church of Jesus Christ of Latter-day Saints coincide at more points with the convictions and confessions of other Christian bodies than I had previously realized." Furthermore, "I now comprehend more fully than before the nature of, as well as the rationale for, the distinctives of the Latter-day Saint faith." "I also see that the author, as he stated in the book's introduction, does indeed have a decided admiration for the effort and insight manifest by devoted theologians throughout Christian history." And, "In turn, this makes me more inclined to appreciate the faith of the Church of Jesus Christ of Latter-day Saints, even though it is not my own."

Sadly, in times past, this has not always been the way in which Christians have viewed each other. Diversity and complexity can prompt insecurity, which in some cases can lead to antipathy. Whatever their "reasons," ranging from social and political objections to philosophical and theological differences, some Christians have felt challenged by the beliefs and practices of other Christians. Their response has been to draw a line in the sand and declare the threatening alternative "heretical," perhaps "diabolical." Even a cursory reading of Christian history reveals startling levels of internecine vituperation and vindictiveness. Past Protestant reference to the Roman Catholic pope as the "antichrist" rather than the "vicar of Christ" is just one familiar example. During and after the Reformation, both Protestants and Catholics were sufficiently intent on denying to each other the label of authentic "Christian" that they even denied life to each other in wars of religion and executions for heresy.

One version of Christianity that suffered the negative animus of the dominant Christian establishment in early nineteenth-century America was Universalism (so named because of its more generous expectations for the eventual salvation of humankind). In comments that could resonate with any group that has ever been the object of fellow Christians' zealous efforts to construct exclusionary boundaries, a Universalist minister vented his frustration in these words:

> Many, very many, are ready to denounce as infidels all who do not adopt their creed. We are daily classed with infidels and told that we have no right to the Christian name. This is the CONSTANT talk of some preachers. UNIVERSALISTS ARE NOT CHRISTIANS—UNIVERSALISTS ARE INFIDELS. Hardly any assertions are more frequent than these—hardly any are made with so much assurance—hardly any are so industriously circulated. I know our opposers justify their course by saying we deny some of [what they consider] the essential doctrines of Christianity. . . . But who shall decide what are cardinal errors? The Catholics say that all Protestants hold to cardinal errors and will be lost. Some Protestants say the same of the Catholics. Different Protestant sects say the same of each other. . . . Would it not be well for those who declare that we are not Christians, to decide first, among themselves, what doctrines are essential to the Christian character, before they condemn us?[1]

Along with Universalism, newer Christian traditions such as Christian Science, Seventh-day Adventism, and Pentecostalism have all been vigorously

---

1. Otis Skinner, "Sermon VII: The Faith Necessary to Constitute a Christian," in *A Series of Sermons in Defence of the Doctrine of Universal Salvation* (Boston, 1842), 137, 139, 141–42.

denounced in the not-too-distant past. Even older, "mainline" churches have not escaped condemnation from Christian extremists. The "False Religions" page at jesus-is-savior.com includes in its list Roman Catholicism, Eastern Orthodoxy, Lutheranism, Episcopalianism, the United Church of Christ, and the Christian Church (Disciples of Christ). It is hardly surprising, then, that self-appointed Christian gatekeepers have periodically endeavored to deny to the Church of Jesus Christ of Latter-day Saints its perennial claim to being a Christian institution.

Happily, times have changed considerably since the earlier days of fratricidal conflict between Christian traditions. While "boundary maintenance" continues to be an activity in which many ecclesial bodies engage, most today recognize the value of Christian collegiality. Many seek some form of Christian unity, even reunification. In terms of pursuing Christian harmony, if not unity in diversity, the words of Jesus come to mind. On one occasion when his disciples attempted to restrain a man acting in Christ's name "because he followeth not with us," Jesus replied, "Forbid him not: for he that is not against us is for us" (Luke 9:49–50). History bears witness to the power of the temptation to deny fellowship to those who "follow not with us," but Jesus's response invites Christians to draw a circle to take in fellow believers of a different walk rather than dogmatically wall them out. This sentiment is well expressed in the words of Mel Robeck, a prominent Pentecostal leader in global interfaith work for over four decades: "I have found that I do my best ecumenical work when I choose to treat all people who claim to be followers of Jesus, as my sisters and brothers in Christ, as my Christian 'neighbors.' . . . In the same way, I accept any church that confesses Jesus Christ as Savior and Lord to be part of the Body of Christ. . . . Only God knows the heart of each individual, and only He has both the right and the ability to say who is or who is not a genuine follower of Jesus."[2] This book gestures toward just such a capacious conception of Christianity and collegiality for all who take upon them the name of Christ. The author's hope is that thoughtful engagement with this volume will have contributed in some small way to the irenic goal of shedding the parochial coil of an exclusivist faith for the glistening skin of inclusivist Christian discipleship.

---

2. Cecil M. Robeck Jr., *Week of Prayer for Christian Unity 2024: Two Sermons by Cecil M. Robeck, Jr.* (Alhambra, CA: Bethany Church, 2024), 23.

Birth and Death Dates of Persons Discussed

Abelard, Peter (1079–?1142)
Adams, John (1735–1826)
Ambrose of Milan (339–397)
Andersen, Neal L. (1951–)
Anselm of Canterbury (1033 or 1034–1109)
Antonov, Simeon Ivanovich (1866–1938)
Apollinarus of Laodicea (d. 382)
Aristotle (384–322 BC)
Arius (ca. 250–336)
Arminius, Jacob (1560–1609)
Athanasius of Alexandria (ca. 293–373)
Augustine of Hippo (354–430)
Baillie, Robert (1599–1662)
Ballard, Melvin J. (1873–1939)
Ballard, M. Russell (1928–2023)
Barth, Karl (1886–1968)
Basil of Caesarea (ca. 329–379)
Bateman, Merrill J. (1936–)
Bauer, Walter (1877–1960)
Baxter, Richard (1615–1691)
Bednar, David A. (1952–)
Beecher, Edward (1803–1895)
Beecher, Lyman (1775–1863)
Benson, Ezra Taft (1899–1994)
Bernard of Clairvaux (1090–1153)

Biddle, John (1615–1662)
Bonhoeffer, Dietrich (1906–1945)
Bradwardine, Thomas (ca. 1290–1349)
Brown, Hugh B. (1883–1975)
Bucer, Martin (1491–1551)
Bulgakov, Sergei (1871–1944)
Bull, George (1634–1710)
Bultmann, Rudolf (1884–1976)
Burns, J. Patout (1939–)
Bushnell, Horace (1802–1876)
Butler, Jon (1940–)
Callister, Tad R. (1945–)
Callistus (d. 222)
Calvin, John (1509–1564)
Cannon, George Q. (1827–1901)
Cassian, John (360–435)
Chadwick, Owen (1916–2015)
Christofferson, D. Todd (1945–)
Chrysostom, John (ca. 347–407)
Cicero (106–43 BC)
Clark, J. Reuben, Jr. (1871–1961)
Clarke, William Newton (1841–1912)
Clement of Alexandria (ca. 150–between 211 and 215)
Congar, Yves (1904–1995)
Cook, Quentin L. (1940–)
Cotton, John (1585–1652)
Cowdery, Oliver (1806–1850)

Cowper, William (1731–1800)

Crick, Francis (1916–2004)

Cross, Frank Moore, Jr. (1921–2012)

Cyprian (d. 258)

Cyril of Alexandria (ca. 375–444)

Cyril of Jerusalem (315?–?386)

Dana, James (1735–1812)

Darby, John Nelson (1800–1882)

Davenant, John (1572–1641)

Descartes, René (1596–1650)

Dodds, E. R. (1893–1979)

Doolittle, Thomas (1630–1707)

Dulles, Avery R. (1918–2008)

Duns Scotus, John (1266?–1308)

Dwight, Timothy (1752–1817)

Eckhart, "Meister" (ca. 1260–?1327)

Edwards, Jonathan (1703–1758)

Epicurus (341–270 BC)

Episcopius, Simon (1583–1643)

Erasmus, Desiderius (1466?–1536)

Eusebius of Caesarea (ca. 260–ca. 339)

Eusebius of Emesa (ca. 300–ca. 359)

Eutyches (ca. 378–ca. 450)

Eyring, Henry B. (1933–)

Faust, James E. (1920–2007)

Finney, Charles (1792–1875)

Fletcher, John William (1729–1785)

Florovsky, Georges (1893–1979)

Fredriksen, Paula (1951–)

Gong, Gerrit W. (1953–)

Grant, Heber J. (1856–1945)

Grebel, Conrad (ca. 1498–1526)

Gregory of Nazianzus (ca. 330–ca. 389)

Gregory of Nyssa (ca. 335–ca. 394)

Gregory of Rimini (d. 1358)

Gregory the Great (540–604)

Grotius, Hugo (1583–1645)

Hafen, Bruce C. (1940–)

Hague, William (1808–1887)

Hales, Robert D. (1932–2017)

Hammond, Henry (1605–1660)

Harnack, Adolf (1851–1930)

Hartshorne, Charles (1897–2000)

Henley, William E. (1849–1903)

Hick, John H. (1922–2012)

Hilary of Poitiers (ca. 315–ca. 367)

Hinckley, Gordon B. (1910–2008)

Hippolytus of Rome (ca. 170–ca. 235)

Hodge, Charles (1797–1878)

Hodgson, Leonard (1889–1969)

Hoen, Cornelius (ca. 1440–ca. 1524)

Hofstadter, Douglas R. (1945–)

Holland, Jeffrey R. (1940–)

Hubmaier, Balthasar (1480–1528)

Hume, David (1711–1776)

Hunter, Howard W. (1907–1995)

Isidore of Seville (ca. 560–636)

James, William (1842–1920)

Jantzen, Grace (1948–2006)

Jefferson, Thomas (1743–1826)

Jenkins, Jerry B. (1949–)

Jenson, Robert W. (1930–2017)

Jerome (ca. 347–419 or 420)

John Paul II (1920–2005)

Johnson, William B. (1782–1862)

Jovinian (340–ca. 405)

Justin Martyr (ca. 100–ca. 165)

Kearon, Patrick (1961–)

Keats, John (1795–1821)

Kimball, Heber C. (1801–1868)

Kimball, Spencer W. (1895–1985)

Küng, Hans (1928–2021)

LaCugna, Catherine (1952–1997)

LaHaye, Tim (1926–2016)

Laud, William (1573–1645)

Lee, Harold B. (1899–1973)

Leibniz, Gottfried (1646–1716)

Lewis, C. S. (1898–1963)

Lindsey, Hal (1929–)

Locke, John (1632–1704)

Lossky, Vladimir (1903–1958)

Lubac, Henri de (1896–1991)

Lucian of Antioch (ca. 240?–312)

Lund, Anthon H. (1844–1921)

Luther, Martin (1483–1546)

Marcellus of Ancyra (d. 374)

Mattison, Hiram (1811–1868)

Maxwell, Neal A. (1926–2004)

McConkie, Bruce R. (1915–1985)

McGuckin, John A. (1952–)

McKay, David O. (1873–1970)

McMurrin, Sterling M. (1914–1996)

McNemar, Richard (1770–1839)

Melanchthon, Philip (1497–1560)

Mill, John Stuart (1806–1873)

Miller, William (1782–1849)

Milton, John (1608–1674)

Molina, Luis de (1535–1600)

Moltmann, Jürgen (1926–)

Monson, Thomas S. (1927–2018)

Moody, Raymond A. (1944–)

Neiman, Susan (1955–)

Nelson, Russell M. (1924–)

Nestorius of Constantinople (d. ca. 451)

Nevin, John (1803–1886)

Oaks, Dallin H. (1932–)

O'Kelley, James (1738–1826)

Origen (185?–?254)

Orsi, Robert A. (1953–)

Owen, John (1616–1683)

Oxenham, Henry (1829–1888)

Packer, Boyd K. (1924–2015)

Packer, J. I. (1926–2020)

Pascal, Blaise (1623–1662)

Paul of Samosata (third century)

Pelagius (ca. 354–after 418)

Penrose, Charles W. (1832–1925)

Peter Lombard (ca. 1095–1160)

Pius V (1504–1572)

Pius XI (1857–1939)

Plato (ca. 428–348 or 347 BC)

Pratt, Orson (1811–1881)

Pratt, Parley P. (1807–1857)

Rad, Gerhard von (1901–1971)

Rahner, Karl (1904–1984)

Rasband, Ronald A. (1951–)

Renlund, Dale G. (1952–)

Richards, Willard (1804–1854)

Rigdon, Sidney (1793–1876)

Ritschl, Albrecht (1822–1889)

Robeck, Cecil M., Jr. (1945–)

Roberts, B. H. (1857–1933)

Romney, Marion G. (1897–1988)

Schelling, Friedrich (1775–1854)

Schleiermacher, Friedrich (1768–1834)

Schmucker, Samuel Simon (1799–1873)

Seixas, Gershom Mendes (1745–1816)

Seixas, Joshua (1802–1874)

Serapion (fourth century)

Servetus, Michael (ca. 1511–1553)

Sheldon, Gilbert (1598–1677)

Smith, Bathsheba W. (1822–1910)

Smith, George Albert (1870–1951)

Smith, Joseph (1805–1844)

Smith, Joseph F. (1838–1918)

Smith, Joseph Fielding (1876–1972)

Smyth, John (ca. 1554–1612)

Snow, Erastus (1818–1888)

Snow, Lorenzo (1814–1901)

Soares, Ulisses (1958–)

Sommer, Benjamin D. (1964–)

Sozzini, Fausto/Faustus Socinus (1539–1604)

Stendahl, Krister (1921–2008)

Stevenson, Gary E. (1955–)

Stoddard, Solomon (1643–1729)

Stone, Barton (1772–1844)
Stowe, Harriet Beecher (1811–1896)
Suárez, Francisco (1548–1617)
Talmage, James E. (1862–1933)
Taylor, Jeremy (1613–1667)
Taylor, John (1808–1887)
Taylor, Nathaniel W. (1786–1858)
Tertullian (ca. 155 or 160–after 220)
Theodore of Mopsuestia (ca. 350–428 or 429)
Theodoret of Cyrrhus (ca. 393–ca. 458)
Thomas Aquinas (1225–1274)
Tillotson, John (1630–1694)
Torrey, Reuben A. (1856–1928)
Turretin, Francis (1623–1687)
Tyndale, William (ca. 1494–1536)
Uchtdorf, Dieter F. (1940–)
Ussher, James (1581–1656)
Vanstone, William H. (1923–1999)
Vincent of Lérins (d. ca. 450)

Ware, Kallistos [Timothy W.] (1934–2022)
Watts, Isaac (1674–1748)
Webb, Stephen H. (1961–2016)
Wesley, John (1703–1791)
Whedon, Daniel (1808–1885)
Whitehead, Alfred North (1861–1947)
Whitmer, John (1802–1878)
Whitney, Orson F. (1855–1931)
Widtsoe, John A. (1872–1952)
William of Ockham (ca. 1285–?1349)
Williams, Roger (1603?–1683)
Williams, Rowan D. (1950–)
Wolfe, Tom (1930–2018)
Wood, Gordon S. (1933–)
Woodruff, Wilford (1807–1898)
Wright, N. T. (1948–)
Young, Brigham (1801–1877)
Zwingli, Huldrych (1484–1531)

BIBLIOGRAPHY

This bibliography includes only *some* of the influential sources used in preparing this volume. Additional resources are indicated in the footnotes. The sources on the abbreviations page, obviously of prime importance, are not repeated here. The bibliography also focuses primarily on relevant sources pertaining to Christian history and theology. To access the many interpretive studies of Mormon history and thought, the reader is directed to the comprehensive bibliographic database at mormonhistory.byu.edu.

Ahlstrom, Sydney E. *A Religious History of the American People.* New Haven: Yale University Press, 1972.

Albanese, Catherine L. *A Republic of Mind and Spirit: A Cultural History of American Metaphysical Religion.* New Haven: Yale University Press, 2007.

Alexander, Thomas G. *Mormonism in Transition: A History of the Latter-day Saints, 1890–1930.* Urbana: University of Illinois Press, 1986.

Allen, David L. *The Extent of the Atonement: A Historical and Critical Review.* Nashville: B&H Academic, 2016.

Allen, James B., and Glen M. Leonard. *The Story of the Latter-day Saints.* 2nd ed. Salt Lake City: Deseret Book, 1992.

Allen, Michael, and Scott R. Swain, eds. *Christian Dogmatics: Reformed Theology for the Church Catholic.* Grand Rapids: Baker Academic, 2016.

Anatolios, Khaled. *Retrieving Nicaea: The Development and Meaning of Trinitarian Doctrine.* Grand Rapids: Baker Academic, 2011.

Armstrong, John H., and Paul E. Engle, eds. *Understanding Four Views on Baptism.* Grand Rapids: Zondervan, 2007.

Arrington, Leonard J., and Davis Bitton. *The Mormon Experience: A History of the Latter-day Saints.* 2nd ed. Urbana: University of Illinois Press, 1992.

Augustine. *Selected Writings on Grace and Pelagianism.* Edited by Boniface Ramsey and Roland Teske. New York: New City, 2011.

Ayres, Lewis. *Nicaea and Its Legacy: An Approach to Fourth-Century Trinitarian Theology*. New York: Oxford University Press, 2004.

Ayres, Lewis, and Medi A. Volpe. *The Oxford Handbook of Catholic Theology*. Oxford: Oxford University Press, 2019.

Bagchi, David, and David C. Steinmetz, eds. *The Cambridge Companion to Reformation Theology*. New York: Cambridge University Press, 2004.

Bangs, Carl. *Arminius: A Study in the Dutch Reformation*. 2nd ed. Grand Rapids: Zondervan, 1985.

Barclay, John M. G. *Paul and the Gift*. Grand Rapids: Eerdmans, 2015.

Barlow, Philip L. *Mormons and the Bible: The Place of the Latter-day Saints in American Religion*. New York: Oxford University Press, 1991.

Barnes, Linda L., and Susan S. Sered, eds. *Religion and Healing in America*. New York: Oxford University Press, 2005.

Bauckham, Richard. *Jesus and the God of Israel: God Crucified and Other Studies on the New Testament's Christology of Divine Identity*. Grand Rapids: Eerdmans, 2008.

Bauer, Walter. *Orthodoxy and Heresy in Earliest Christianity*. Philadelphia: Fortress, 1971.

Bauerschmidt, Frederick Christian, and James J. Buckley. *Catholic Theology: An Introduction*. Chichester, UK: Wiley-Blackwell, 2017.

Beasley-Murray, George R. *Baptism in the New Testament*. Grand Rapids: Eerdmans, 1962.

Beeley, Christopher A. *The Unity of Christ: Continuity and Conflict in Patristic Tradition*. New Haven: Yale University Press, 2012.

Behr, John. *Irenaeus of Lyons: Identifying Christianity*. Oxford: Oxford University Press, 2013.

Beilby, James. *Postmortem Opportunity: A Biblical and Theological Assessment of Salvation after Death*. Downers Grove, IL: IVP Academic, 2021.

Beilby, James, and Paul R. Eddy, eds. *Justification: Five Views*. Downers Grove, IL: IVP Academic, 2011.

———. *The Nature of the Atonement: Four Views*. Downers Grove, IL: IVP Academic, 2006.

Bettenson, Henry, and Christ Maunder, eds. *Documents of the Christian Church*. 4th ed. Oxford: Oxford University Press, 2011.

Bonner, Ali. *The Myth of Pelagianism*. Oxford: Oxford University Press, 2018.

Boyd, Gregory A., and Paul R. Eddy. *Across the Spectrum: Understanding Issues in Evangelical Theology*. 2nd ed. Grand Rapids: Baker Academic, 2009.

Bradshaw, Paul F. *Reconstructing Early Christian Worship*. London: SPCK, 2009.

Brown, David. *Divine Humanity: Kenosis and the Construction of a Christian Theology*. Waco, TX: Baylor University Press, 2011.

Brown, Peter. *Augustine of Hippo*. Los Angeles: University of California Press, 1969.

Brown, Raymond E. *An Introduction to New Testament Christology*. New York: Paulist, 1994.

Burgess, Stanley M., Gary B. McGee, and Patrick H. Alexander, eds. *Dictionary of Pentecostal and Charismatic Movements*. Grand Rapids: Zondervan, 1988.

Burns, J. Patout, and Robin M. Jensen. *Christianity in Roman Africa: The Development of Its Practices and Beliefs*. Grand Rapids: Eerdmans, 2014.

———. *Theological Anthropology*. Philadelphia: Fortress, 1981.

Bynum, Caroline Walker. *The Resurrection of the Body in Western Christianity, 200–1336*. New York: Columbia University Press, 1995.

Callister, Tad R. *The Infinite Atonement*. Salt Lake City: Deseret Book, 2000.

Chadwick, Henry. *The Church in Ancient Society: From Galilee to Gregory the Great*. New York: Oxford University Press, 2001.

Christensen, Michael J., and Jeffrey A. Wittung, eds. *Partakers of the Divine Nature: The History and Development of Deification in the Christian Traditions*. Madison, NJ: Fairleigh Dickinson University Press, 2007.

Clouse, Robert G., ed. *The Meaning of the Millennium: Four Views*. Downers Grove, IL: InterVarsity Press, 1977.

Collins, John J., Bernard McGinn, and Stephen J. Stein. *The Continuum History of Apocalypticism*. New York: Continuum, 2003.

Crisp, Oliver D. *Approaching the Atonement: Introducing the Reconciling Work of Christ*. Downers Grove, IL: IVP Academic, 2017.

———. *Divinity and Humanity: The Incarnation Reconsidered*. Cambridge: Cambridge University Press, 2007.

———. *The Word Enfleshed: Exploring the Person and Work of Christ*. Grand Rapids: Baker Academic, 2016.

Crisp, Oliver D., and Fred Sanders, eds. *Christology, Ancient and Modern: Explorations in Constructive Dogmatics*. Grand Rapids: Zondervan, 2013.

———. *Locating Atonement: Explorations in Constructive Dogmatics*. Grand Rapids: Zondervan, 2015.

Cunningham, Mary B., and Elizabeth Theokritoff. *The Cambridge Companion to Orthodox Christian Theology*. Cambridge: Cambridge University Press, 2008.

Davies, Brian. *Thomas Aquinas's Summa Theologiae: A Guide & Commentary*. New York: Oxford University Press, 2014.

Davies, Douglas. *Introduction to Mormonism*. Cambridge: Cambridge University Press, 2003.

Davis, Stephen T., Daniel Kendall, and Gerald O'Collins, eds. *The Incarnation*. New York: Oxford University Press, 2002.

Dayton, Donald W., and Robert K. Johnston, eds. *The Variety of American Evangelicalism.* Downers Grove, IL: InterVarsity Press, 1991.

Dieter, Melvin E., Anthony A. Hoekema, Stanley M. Horton, J. Robertson McQuilkin, and John F. Walvoord. *Five Views on Sanctification.* Grand Rapids: Zondervan, 1987.

Dorrien, Gary. *The Spirit of American Liberal Theology: A History.* Louisville: Westminster John Knox, 2023.

Dulles, Avery. *Magisterium: Teacher and Guardian of the Faith.* Naples, FL: Sapientia Press of Ave Maria University, 2007.

————. *Models of the Church.* Expanded ed. New York: Image Books, 2002.

Dunn, James D. G. *Christology in the Making: A New Testament Inquiry into the Origins of the Doctrine of the Incarnation.* 2nd ed. Grand Rapids: Eerdmans, 1996.

————. *The Theology of Paul the Apostle.* Grand Rapids: Eerdmans, 1998.

————. *Unity and Diversity in the New Testament: An Inquiry into the Character of Earliest Christianity.* Philadelphia: Westminster, 1977.

Dupuis, Jacques. *The Christian Faith in the Doctrinal Documents of the Catholic Church.* 7th ed. New York: Alba House, 2001.

Ehrman, Bart D. *Heaven and Hell: A History of the Afterlife.* New York: Simon & Schuster, 2020.

Ehrman, Bart D., Michael F. Bird, and Robert B. Stewart. *When Did Jesus Become God? A Christological Debate.* Louisville: Westminster John Knox, 2022.

Eire, Carlos M. N. *Reformations: The Early Modern World, 1450–1650.* New Haven: Yale University Press, 2016.

Emery, Gilles, and Matthew Levering, eds. *The Oxford Handbook of the Trinity.* Oxford: Oxford University Press, 2012.

Erasmus, Desiderius, and Martin Luther. *Discourse on Free Will.* Translated by Ernst F. Winter. London: Bloomsbury Academic, 2013.

Erickson, Millard J. *Christian Theology.* 3rd ed. Grand Rapids: Baker Academic, 2013.

Ferguson, Everett. *Baptism in the Early Church: History, Theology, and Liturgy in the First Five Centuries.* Grand Rapids: Eerdmans, 2009.

Fiorenza, Francis Schüssler, and John P. Galvin, eds. *Systematic Theology: Roman Catholic Perspectives.* 2nd ed. Minneapolis: Fortress, 2011.

Foster, Douglas A. *A Life of Alexander Campbell.* Grand Rapids: Eerdmans, 2020.

Frend, W. H. C. *The Rise of Christianity.* Philadelphia: Fortress, 1984.

Gagliardi, Mauro. *Truth Is a Synthesis: Catholic Dogmatic Theology.* Steubenville, OH: Emmaus Academic, 2020.

Gaillardetz, Richard R. *By What Authority? A Primer on Scripture, the Magisterium, and the Sense of the Faithful.* Collegeville, MN: Liturgical Press, 1997.

Gavrilyuk, Paul L. *The Suffering of the Impassible God: The Dialectics of Patristic Thought*. Oxford: Oxford University Press, 2004.

Gerrish, B. A. *Christian Faith: Dogmatics in Outline*. Louisville: Westminster John Knox, 2015.

Givens, Terryl L., and Philip L. Barlow, eds. *The Oxford Handbook of Mormonism*. New York: Oxford University Press, 2015.

Gonzalez, Justo L. *A History of Christian Thought in One Volume*. Nashville: Abingdon, 2014.

Green, Joel B., and Stuart L. Palmer, eds. *In Search of the Soul: Four Views of the Mind-Body Problem*. Downers Grove, IL: InterVarsity Press, 2005.

Griffin, David, and James McLachlan. "A Dialogue on Process Theology." In *Mormonism in Dialogue with Contemporary Christian Theologies*, edited by Donald W. Musser and David L. Paulsen, 161–210. Macon, GA: Mercer University Press, 2007.

Grillmeier, Aloys. *Christ in Christian Tradition: From the Apostolic Age to Chalcedon*. Translated by John Bowden. 2nd ed. Atlanta: John Knox, 1975.

Grudem, Wayne. *Systematic Theology: An Introduction to Biblical Doctrine*. 2nd ed. Grand Rapids: Zondervan, 2020.

Hall, David G., ed. *Puritans in the New World: A Critical Anthology*. Princeton: Princeton University Press, 2004.

———. *Worlds of Wonder, Days of Judgment: Popular Religious Belief in Early New England*. New York: Knopf, 1989.

Hanson, R. P. C. *The Search for the Christian Doctrine of God: The Arian Controversy, 318–381*. Edinburgh: T&T Clark, 1988.

Hardy, Edward R., ed. *Christology of the Later Fathers*. Philadelphia: Westminster, 1954.

Harmless, William, ed. *Augustine in His Own Words*. Washington, DC: Catholic University of America Press, 2010.

Hart, David B. *That All Shall Be Saved: Heaven, Hell & Universal Salvation*. New Haven: Yale University Press, 2019.

Hartley, William G. *My Fellow Servants: Essays on the History of the Priesthood*. Provo, UT: BYU Press, 2010.

Harvey, Susan Ashbrook, and David G. Hunter, eds. *The Oxford Handbook of Early Christian Studies*. New York: Oxford University Press, 2008.

Hatch, Nathan. *The Democratization of American Christianity*. New Haven: Yale University Press, 1989.

Haws, J. B. *The Mormon Image in the American Mind: Fifty Years of Public Perception*. New York: Oxford University Press, 2013.

Heine, Ronald E. *Classical Christian Doctrine.* Grand Rapids: Baker Academic, 2013.

Helm, Paul, Bruce A. Ware, Roger E. Olson, and John Sanders. *Perspectives on the Doctrine of God: Four Views.* Nashville: B&H Academic, 2008.

Hengel, Martin. *The Atonement: The Origins of the Doctrine in the New Testament.* Philadelphia: Fortress, 1981.

Hick, John. *Evil and the God of Love.* Rev. ed. San Francisco: Harper & Row, 1977.

Hillerbrand, Hans J., Kirsi I. Stjerna, and Timothy J. Wengert, eds. *The Annotated Luther.* 6 vols. Minneapolis: Fortress, 2015–2017.

Holifield, E. Brooks. *Theology in America: Christian Thought from the Age of the Puritans to the Civil War.* New Haven: Yale University Press, 2003.

Holland, Jeffrey R. *Christ and the New Covenant: The Messianic Message of the Book of Mormon.* Salt Lake City: Deseret Book, 1997.

———. *Of Souls, Symbols, and Sacraments.* Salt Lake City: Deseret Book, 2001.

Holmes, Michael W. *The Apostolic Fathers.* 2nd ed. Grand Rapids: Baker Books, 1989.

Hovorun, Cyril. *Eastern Christianity in Its Texts.* London: T&T Clark, 2022.

Howard, Thomas A. *The Faiths of Others: A History of Interreligious Dialogue.* New Haven: Yale University Press, 2021.

Howe, Daniel W. *The Unitarian Conscience: Harvard Moral Philosophy, 1805–1861.* Cambridge, MA: Harvard University Press, 1970.

———. *What Hath God Wrought: The Transformation of America, 1815–1849.* New York: Oxford University Press, 2007.

Hughes, Richard T., ed. *The American Quest for the Primitive Church.* Urbana: University of Illinois Press, 1988.

Hughes, Richard T., and C. Leonard Allen. *Illusions of Innocence: Protestant Primitivism in America, 1630–1875.* Chicago: University of Chicago Press, 1988.

Hummel, Daniel G. *The Rise and Fall of Dispensationalism: How the Evangelical Battle over the End Times Shaped a Nation.* Grand Rapids: Eerdmans, 2023.

Hurtado, Larry. *Ancient Jewish Monotheism and Early Christian Jesus-Devotion: The Context and Character of Christological Faith.* Waco, TX: Baylor University Press, 2017.

Hwang, Alexander Y., Brian J. Matz, and Augustine Casiday, eds. *Grace for Grace: The Debates after Augustine and Pelagius.* Washington, DC: Catholic University of America Press, 2014.

Jacobs, Alan. *Original Sin: A Cultural History.* New York: HarperOne, 2009.

Jenson, Robert W. *Theology in Outline: Can These Bones Live?* New York: Oxford University Press, 2016.

Johnson, Adam J. *T&T Clark Companion to Atonement.* New York: Bloomsbury, 2017.

Johnson, Maxwell E. *Sacraments and Worship: The Sources of Christian Theology.* Louisville: Westminster John Knox, 2012.

Kapic, Kelly M., and Bruce L. McCormack, eds. *Mapping Modern Theology: A Thematic and Historical Introduction.* Grand Rapids: Baker Academic, 2012.

Kärkkäinen, Veli-Matti. *One with God: Salvation as Deification and Justification.* Collegeville, MN: Liturgical Press, 2007.

Kasper, Walter. *Harvesting the Fruits: Basic Aspect of Christian Faith in Ecumenical Dialogue.* London: Continuum, 2009.

——. *The Petrine Ministry: Catholics and Orthodox in Dialogue.* Translated by the Staff of the Pontifical Council for Promoting Christian Unity. New York and Mahwah, NJ: Newman, 2006.

Keating, Daniel A. *Deification and Grace.* Naples, FL: Sapientia Press of Ave Maria University, 2007.

Kelly, J. N. D. *Early Christian Doctrines.* London: MPG Books, 1950.

Koester, Helmut. *Introduction to the New Testament.* Vol. 2, *History and Literature of Early Christianity.* 2nd ed. New York: de Gruyter, 2000.

Lane, Tony. *Exploring Christian Doctrine: A Guide to What Christians Believe.* Downers Grove, IL: IVP Academic, 2014.

Lehner, Ulrich L., Richard A. Muller, and A. G. Roeber, eds. *The Oxford Handbook of Early Modern Theology, 1600–1800.* New York: Oxford University Press, 2016.

Lim, Paul C. H. *Mystery Unveiled: The Crisis of the Trinity in Early Modern England.* New York: Oxford University Press, 2012.

Lohse, Bernhard. *A Short History of Christian Doctrine: From the First Century to the Present.* Translated by F. E. Stoeffler. Philadelphia: Fortress, 1985.

Lossky, Vladimir. *Orthodox Theology: An Introduction.* Crestwood, NY: St. Vladimir's Seminary Press, 1978.

Louth, Andrew. *Introducing Eastern Orthodox Theology.* Downers Grove, IL: IVP Academic, 2013.

Ludlow, Daniel H., ed. *Encyclopedia of Mormonism.* 4 vols. New York: Macmillan, 1992.

Lum, Kathryn G. *Damned Nation: Hell in America from the Revolution to Reconstruction.* New York: Oxford University Press, 2014.

Luther, Martin. *Treatise on Good Works.* Translated by Scott H. Hendrix. Minneapolis: Fortress, 2012.

Macchia, Frank D. *Jesus the Spirit Baptizer: Christology in Light of Pentecost.* Grand Rapids: Eerdmans, 2018.

——. *Tongues of Fire: A Systematic Theology of the Christian Faith.* Eugene, OR: Cascade, 2023.

MacCulloch, Diarmaid. *The Reformation: A History.* New York: Penguin Books, 2003.

Macleod, Donald. *The Person of Christ: Contours of Christian Theology.* Downers Grove, IL: IVP Academic, 1998.

Madigan, Kevin. *Medieval Christianity: A New History.* New Haven: Yale University Press, 2015.

Madsen, Truman G. *Defender of the Faith: The B. H. Roberts Story.* Salt Lake City: Bookcraft, 1980.

———. *Eternal Man.* Salt Lake City: Deseret Book, 1966.

Markschies, Christoph. *God's Body: Jewish, Christian, and Pagan Images of God.* Waco, TX: Baylor University Press, 2019.

Mason, Patrick Q., and John G. Turner. *Out of Obscurity: Mormonism Since 1945.* New York: Oxford University Press, 2016.

Mathewes-Green, Frederica. *An Introduction to Eastern Christianity.* Brewster, MA: Paraclete, 2015.

McBrien, Richard P. *Catholicism.* San Francisco: HarperSanFrancisco, 1994.

McClymond, Michael J. *The Devil's Redemption: A New History and Interpretation of Christian Universalism.* 2 vols. Grand Rapids: Baker Academic, 2018.

McConkie, Bruce R. *Doctrinal New Testament Commentary.* 3 vols. Salt Lake City: Bookcraft, 1965–1973.

———. *A New Witness for the Articles of Faith.* Salt Lake City: Deseret Book, 1985.

McDannell, Colleen. *Sister Saints: Mormon Women Since the End of Polygamy.* New York: Oxford University Press, 2019.

McDannell, Colleen, and Bernhard Lang. *Heaven: A History.* New Haven: Yale University Press, 1988.

McFarland, Ian A. *In Adam's Fall: A Meditation on the Christian Doctrine of Original Sin.* Malden, MA: Wiley-Blackwell, 2010.

McGowan, Andrew B. *Ancient Christian Worship: Early Church Practices in Social, Historical, and Theological Perspective.* Grand Rapids: Baker Academic, 2014.

McGrath, Alister E. *Christian Theology.* 6th ed. Chichester, UK: Wiley-Blackwell, 2016.

———. *Iustitia Dei: A History of the Christian Doctrine of Justification.* 3rd ed. Cambridge: Cambridge University Press, 2005.

McGuckin, John A. *The Path of Christianity: The First Thousand Years.* Downers Grove, IL: IVP Academic, 2017.

McKim, Donald K. *Theological Turning Points: Major Issues in Christian Thought.* Louisville: Westminster John Knox, 1989.

McMurrin, Sterling M. *The Philosophical Foundations of Mormon Theology*. Salt Lake City: University of Utah Press, 1959.

———. *The Theological Foundations of the Mormon Religion*. Salt Lake City: University of Utah Press, 1965.

McNeill, John T. *A History of the Cure of Souls*. New York: Harper & Row, 1951.

Meconi, David, and Carl E. Olson. *Called to Be the Children of God: The Catholic Theology of Human Deification*. San Francisco: Ignatius, 2016.

Meyendorff, John. *Byzantine Theology: Historical Trends & Doctrinal Themes*. New York: Fordham University Press, 1974.

Minear, Paul S. *Images of the Church in the New Testament*. Philadelphia: Westminster, 1960.

Mohler, R. A. *The Apostles' Creed: Discovering Authentic Christianity in an Age of Counterfeits*. Nashville: Nelson, 2019.

Moltmann, Jürgen. *The Coming of God: Christian Eschatology*. Translated by Margaret Kohl. Minneapolis: Fortress, 1996.

Moo, Douglas J. *The Letter to the Romans*. Grand Rapids: Eerdmans, 2018.

Mouw, Richard J. *Talking with Mormons: An Invitation to Evangelicals*. Grand Rapids: Eerdmans, 2012.

———. *Uncommon Decency: Christian Civility in an Uncivil World*. Rev. ed. Downers Grove, IL: IVP, 2010.

Mouw, Richard J., and Robert L. Millet. *Talking Doctrine: Mormons and Evangelicals in Conversation*. Downers Grove, IL: IVP Academic, 2015.

Muller, Richard A. *Calvin and the Reformed Tradition: On the Works of Christ and the Order of Salvation*. Grand Rapids: Baker Academic, 2012.

Need, Stephen W. *Truly Divine and Truly Human: The Story of Christ and the Seven Ecumenical Councils*. Peabody, MA: Hendrickson, 2008.

Niebuhr, H. R., and Daniel D. Williams, eds. *The Ministry in Historical Perspective*. San Francisco: Harper & Row, 1956.

Nimmo, Paul T., and Keith L. Johnson, eds. *Kenosis: The Self-Emptying of Christ in Scripture and Tradition*. Grand Rapids: Eerdmans, 2022.

Noll, Mark A. *America's God: From Jonathan Edwards to Abraham Lincoln*. New York: Oxford University Press, 2002.

Noll, Mark A., David W. Bebbington, and George A. Rawlyk. *Evangelicalism: Comparative Studies of Popular Protestantism in North America, the British Isles, and Beyond, 1700–1990*. New York: Oxford University Press, 1994.

Norris, Richard A., Jr., ed. *The Christological Controversy*. Philadelphia: Fortress, 1980.

Numbers, Ronald L., and Jonathan M. Butler. *The Disappointed: Millerism and Millenarianism in the Nineteenth Century*. Knoxville: University of Tennessee Press, 1993.

Oakes, Edward T. *A Theology of Grace in Six Controversies*. Grand Rapids: Eerdmans, 2016.

Oberman, Heiko. *The Harvest of Medieval Theology: Gabriel Biel and Late Medieval Nominalism*. Rev. ed. Grand Rapids: Eerdmans, 1967.

O'Collins, Gerald. *Christology: A Biblical, Historical, and Systematic Study of Jesus*. Oxford: Oxford University Press, 1995.

O'Dea, Thomas F. *The Mormons*. Chicago: University of Chicago Press, 1957.

Oden, Thomas C. *Classic Christianity: A Systematic Theology*. New York: HarperOne, 1987.

————. *John Wesley's Teachings*. 4 vols. Grand Rapids: Zondervan, 2012–2014.

O'Donnell, James J. *Augustine: A New Biography*. San Francisco: HarperCollins, 2005.

Olson, Roger E. *The Mosaic of Christian Belief: Twenty Centuries of Unity & Diversity*. 2nd ed. Downers Grove, IL: IVP Academic, 2016.

O'Malley, John W. *Vatican I: The Council and the Making of the Ultramontane Church*. Cambridge, MA: Belknap Press of Harvard University Press, 2018.

————. *What Happened at Vatican II*. Cambridge, MA: Harvard University Press, 2008.

Oord, Thomas J. *The Uncontrolling Love of God: An Open and Relationship Account of Providence*. Downers Grove, IL: IVP Academic, 2015.

Ostler, Blake T. *Exploring Mormon Thought: The Attributes of God*. Sandy, UT: Kofford Books, 2001.

Ott, Ludwig. *Fundamentals of Catholic Dogma*. Translated by Patrick Lynch. 6th ed. St. Louis: Herder, 1964.

Ozment, Steven. *The Age of Reform, 1250–1550: An Intellectual and Religious History of Late Medieval and Reformation Europe*. New Haven: Yale University Press, 1980.

Paulsen, David L., and Donald W. Musser, eds. *Mormonism in Dialogue with Contemporary Christian Theologies*. Macon, GA: Mercer University Press, 2007.

Pelikan, Jaroslav. *The Christian Tradition: A History of the Development of Doctrine*. 5 vols. Chicago: University of Chicago Press, 1971–1989.

Petrey, Taylor G., Cory Crawford, and Eric A. Eliason. *The Bible and the Latter-day Saint Tradition*. Salt Lake City: University of Utah Press, 2023.

Phan, Peter C. *The Cambridge Companion to the Trinity*. Cambridge: Cambridge University Press, 2011.

Placher, William C., ed. *Essentials of Christian Theology*. Louisville: Westminster John Knox, 2003.

Placher, William C., and Derek R. Nelson, eds. *A History of Christian Theology*. 2nd ed. Louisville: Westminster John Knox, 2013.

Plantinga, Richard J., Thomas R. Thompson, and Matthew D. Lundberg. *An Introduction to Christian Theology*. Cambridge: Cambridge University Press, 2010.

Renlund, Dale G., and Ruth L. Renlund. *The Melchizedek Priesthood: Understanding the Doctrine, Living the Principles*. Salt Lake City: Deseret Book, 2018.

Robeck, Cecil M., Jr., ed. *Charismatic Experiences in History*. Peabody, MA: Hendrickson, 1985.

Roberts, B. H. *The Gospel: An Exposition of Its First Principles*. Salt Lake City: Contributor, 1888.

———. *The Mormon Doctrine of Deity*. Salt Lake City: Deseret News, 1903.

———. *The Truth, the Way, the Life*. Edited by John W. Welch. Provo, UT: BYU Studies, 1994.

Romanides, John. *The Ancestral Sin*. Translated by George Gabriel. Ridgewood, NJ: Zephyr, 2002.

Rusch, William G., ed. *The Trinitarian Controversy*. Philadelphia: Fortress, 1980.

Russell, Norman. *The Doctrine of Deification in the Greek Patristic Tradition*. New York: Oxford University Press, 2009.

———. *Fellow Workers with God: Orthodox Thinking on Theosis*. Crestwood, NY: St. Vladimir's Seminary Press, 2009.

Sandeen, Ernest R. *The Roots of Fundamentalism: British & American Millenarianism, 1830–1930*. Chicago: University of Chicago Press, 1970.

Sanders, John. *The God Who Risks: A Theology of Providence*. Downers Grove, IL: InterVarsity Press, 1998.

———. *No Other Name: An Investigation into the Destiny of the Unevangelized*. Grand Rapids: Eerdmans, 1992.

Scheck, Thomas P. *Origen and the History of Justification: The Legacy of Origen's Commentary on Romans*. Notre Dame: University of Notre Dame Press, 2008.

Schreiner, Thomas R. *Romans*. Grand Rapids: Baker Academic, 2018.

Shepherd, Gordon, and Gary Shepherd. *A Kingdom Transformed: Early Mormonism and the Modern LDS Church*. 2nd ed. Salt Lake City: University of Utah Press, 2015.

Siecienski, A. E. *The Papacy and the Orthodox: Sources and History of a Debate*. New York: Oxford University Press, 2017.

Smith, Gary S. *Heaven in the American Imagination*. New York: Oxford University Press, 2011.

Smith, Gordon T., ed. *The Lord's Supper: Five Views*. Downers Grove, IL: InterVarsity Press, 2008.

Smith, H. Shelton. *Changing Conceptions of Original Sin.* New York: Scribner's Sons, 1955.

Sommer, Benjamin D. *The Bodies of God and the World of Ancient Israel.* New York: Cambridge University Press, 2009.

Spezzano, Daria. *The Glory of God's Grace: Deification according to St. Thomas Aquinas.* Naples, FL: Sapientia Press of Ave Maria University, 2015.

Spinks, Bryan D. *Do This in Remembrance of Me: The Eucharist from the Early Church to the Present Day.* London: SCM, 2013.

Sri, Edward. *A Biblical Walk through the Mass: Understanding What We Say and Do in the Liturgy.* West Chester, PA: Ascension, 2015.

Stanglin, Keith D., and Thomas H. McCall. *Jacob Arminius: Theologian of Grace.* New York: Oxford University Press, 2012.

Stanley, Alan P., ed. *Four Views on the Role of Works at the Final Judgment.* Grand Rapids: Zondervan, 2013.

Steinmetz, David C. *Taking the Long View: Christian Theology in Historical Perspective.* New York: Oxford University Press, 2011.

Stewart, Alistair C. *The Original Bishops: Office and Order in the First Christian Communities.* Grand Rapids: Baker Academic, 2014.

Stump, J. B., and Chad Meister, eds. *Original Sin and the Fall: Five Views.* Downers Grove, IL: IVP Academic, 2020.

Sullivan, Francis A. *Magisterium: Teaching Authority in the Catholic Church.* New York and Mahwah, NJ: Paulist, 1983.

Synan, Vinson. *The Holiness-Pentecostal Tradition: Charismatic Movements in the Twentieth Century.* 2nd ed. Grand Rapids: Eerdmans, 1997.

Talmage, James E. *The Articles of Faith: A Series of Lectures on the Principal Doctrines of the Church of Jesus Christ of Latter-day Saints.* Salt Lake City: Deseret News Press, 1899.

———. *The Vitality of Mormonism: Brief Essays on Distinctive Doctrines of the Church of Jesus Christ of Latter-day Saints.* Boston: Gorham, 1919.

Taylor, John. *An Examination into and an Elucidation of the Great Principle of the Mediation and Atonement of Our Lord and Savior Jesus Christ.* Salt Lake City: Deseret News Press, 1882.

Tentler, Thomas N. *Sin and Confession on the Eve of the Reformation.* Princeton: Princeton University Press, 1977.

Thiessen, Henry C. *Lectures in Systematic Theology.* Grand Rapids: Eerdmans, 2006.

Thiselton, Anthony C. *Systematic Theology.* Grand Rapids: Eerdmans, 2015.

Thomas, J. Christopher. *A Pentecostal Reads the Book of Mormon: A Literary and Theological Introduction.* Cleveland, TN: CPT Press, 2016.

Thorsen, Don. *An Exploration of Christian Theology*. Grand Rapids: Baker Academic, 2008.

Tidball, Derek, David Hilborn, and Justin Thacker, eds. *The Atonement Debate*. Grand Rapids: Zondervan, 2008.

Torrell, Jean-Pierre. *Saint Thomas Aquinas*. Vol. 1, *The Person and His Work*. Translated by Robert Royal. Washington, DC: Catholic University of America Press, 2005.

Trumbower, Jeffrey A. *Rescue for the Dead: The Posthumous Salvation of Non-Christians in Early Christianity*. New York: Oxford University Press, 2001.

Underwood, Grant. *The Millenarian World of Early Mormonism*. Urbana: University of Illinois Press, 1993.

Urban, Linwood. *A Short History of Christian Thought*. New York: Oxford University Press, 1995.

Vermes, Geza. *Christian Beginnings: From Nazareth to Nicaea*. New Haven: Yale University Press, 2013.

Walls, Jerry L. *Heaven, Hell, and Purgatory: A Protestant View of the Cosmic Drama*. Grand Rapids: Brazos, 2015.

————, ed. *The Oxford Handbook of Eschatology*. Oxford: Oxford University Press, 2008.

Ware, Timothy. *The Orthodox Church*. London: Penguin Books, 1964.

Weaver, Rebecca H. *Divine Grace and Human Agency*. Macon, GA: Mercer University Press, 1996.

Webb, Stephen H. *Mormon Christianity*. New York: Oxford University Press, 2013.

Weber, Timothy P. *Living in the Shadow of the Second Coming: American Premillennialism, 1875–1982*. Grand Rapids: Academie Books, 1983.

Webster, John B., Kathryn Tanner, and Iain R. Torrance, eds. *The Oxford Handbook of Systematic Theology*. New York: Oxford University Press, 2007.

Widtsoe, John A. *Evidences and Reconciliations: Aids to Faith in a Modern Day*. 3 vols. Salt Lake City: Bookcraft, 1943–1951.

————. *Rational Theology: As Taught by the Church of Jesus Christ of Latter-day Saints*. Salt Lake City: General Priesthood Committee, 1915.

Wigger, John H. *Taking Heaven by Storm: Methodism and the Rise of Popular Christianity in America*. New York: Oxford University Press, 1998.

Wilcox, Miranda, and John D. Young, eds. *Standing Apart: Mormon Historical Consciousness and the Concept of Apostasy*. New York: Oxford University Press, 2014.

Wiles, Maurice F. *The Christian Fathers*. Philadelphia: Lippincott, 1966.

Wiley, Tatha. *Original Sin: Origins, Developments, Contemporary Meanings*. New York: Paulist, 2002.

Wilken, Robert L. *The Spirit of Early Christian Thought: Seeking the Face of God*. New Haven: Yale University Press, 2003.

Williams, George H. *The Radical Reformation*. Philadelphia: Westminster, 1962.

Williams, Rowan. *Arius: Heresy and Tradition*. Rev. ed. Grand Rapids: Eerdmans, 2002.

Wright, N. T. *Surprised by Hope: Rethinking Heaven, the Resurrection, and the Mission of the Church*. New York: HarperOne, 2008.

Young, Frances M., and Andrew Teal. *From Nicaea to Chalcedon: A Guide to the Literature and Its Background*. 2nd ed. Grand Rapids: Baker Academic, 2010.

Index of Authors

Abelard, Peter, 145–46
Ablabius, 56
Abraham, William J., 224n19, 253n100
Achtemeier, Paul J., 525n183
Adams, Dickinson W., 24n19
Ahlstrom, Sydney, 263n135, 535n216
Aland, Kurt, 377n102
Albanese, Catherine L., 494n54
Alcorn, Randy, 523n175
Alexander, C. Frances, 427
Alexander, Kimberly Ervin, 304n110,
   447n46
Alexander, Thomas G., 57n136, 187n35,
   307n119, 449n54
Alfeyev, Bishop Hilarion, 480n4, 510n122,
   510n124
Allen, David L., 156n52, 164n84, 165n90
Allen, James B., 2n3, 506n107
Allen, Michael, 405n31, 408n41
Ambrose of Milan, 403, 417–18
Anatolios, Khaled, 44n86, 48n101, 403n26
Andersen, Neal, 469
Anderson, Allan H., 278n32
Anderson, Neil L., 271n7
Anderson, Nephi, 195n68
Andrus, Helen Mae, 330n83
Andrus, Hyrum L., 330n83
Anselm of Canterbury, 3, 41, 84–85, 145,
   147, 156, 157, 158
Apollinarius (Apollinaris) of Laodicea,
   116–17, 118n67
Aquilina, Mike, 400n17, 401n19
Aquinas. *See* Thomas Aquinas

Arbesmann, Rudolph, 351n1
Aristotle, 56, 76–77, 246–47n82, 341, 404
Arius, 101, 107
Arminius, Jacob, 85, 221n8, 223
Armour, Rollin S., 380n114
Armstrong, John H., 360n34, 363n47,
   402n24
Arrington, Leonard J., 3n3
Athanasius of Alexandria, 91n90, 113, 136,
   138, 248, 540
Athenagoras, 515
Augustine of Hippo, 11, 20–21, 21n6, 23n16,
   34–35n53, 51n110, 74, 84, 91, 92, 119, 137,
   161, 163, 182–83, 190–91, 195, 196n71,
   199–200, 201, 202, 205, 209, 213, 220n6,
   221–23, 240, 249, 261, 266, 281, 288, 316,
   321, 352, 355, 356, 358, 369, 371n81, 377,
   499, 502, 509, 511, 513, 515, 516, 521n166,
   525–26
Aulén, Gustav, 147n23
Ayres, Lewis, 44n86, 53n116, 56n130,
   280n38, 320n45, 328n72, 357n20, 399n13

Babcock, William S., 181n13
Bagchi, David V. N., 504n99
Baillie, Robert, 310
Bainton, Roland H., 403n25
Baker, J. A., 179n8
Baker, Jacob T., 76n41
Baker, Lynne Rudder, 181n12
Baker, Mark D., 153n39
Baker, Mary Patton, 413n61, 417n73
Ball, Bryan W., 492n44

Ballard, Melvin, 44, 154, 154n43, 297, 413, 419, 425, 500, 500n81
Ballard, Russell, 15, 271n9
Barclay, John M. G., 244n75
Barlow, Philip L., 17n31, 98n121
Barrett, David, 335n97
Barrett, Matthew, 199n81
Barringer, Joshua P., 171n119
Barth, Karl, 46, 51, 112, 114n55, 274, 280, 381
Basil of Caesarea, 50
Basinger, David, 86n76
Bateman, Merrill, 174
Bauckham, Richard, 41n76, 102n10, 102n13, 365n55
Bauer, Walter, 277
Bauerschmidt, Frederick Christian, 342n116, 357n23, 399n13, 443n30, 444n35, 453n70, 464n110
Baxter, Richard, 156, 164, 521
Bayle, Pierre, 96n111
Beasley-Murray, George R., 359n31
Beatrice, Pier Franco, 377n103
Beckert, Jens, 247n82
Bednar, David, 174, 251, 412n59, 419, 471, 476n149
Beecher, Edward, 183, 196
Beecher, Henry Ward, 535
Beecher, Lyman, 257
Beecher, Maureen Ursenbach, 189n40, 449n51
Beeke, Jonathan, 146n20
Beeley, Christopher A., 48n100, 107n31, 116n60, 119n69
Behr, John, 112n47, 118n67, 182n16, 196n73, 229n38, 432n119
Beilby, James, 143n9, 153n40, 500n84
Bellarmine, Robert, 391n159
Benedict XVI (pope), 326n65
Bennett, Richard E., 470n127, 473n138
Bennion, Samuel O., 264n139
Benson, Ezra Taft, 131, 160, 217, 236, 250, 324
Bente, F., 526n188
Beradino, Angelo di, 384n132
Berengarius of Tours, 404n27
Bergera, Gary James, 56n129

Berlin, Adele, 62n2, 398n8
Bernard of Clairvaux, 146
Bernstein, Alan E., 490n35
Berteau, Glen, 455n82
Bettenson, Henry, 121n78
Betz, Hans Dieter, 180n10
Biddle, John, 46
Bingham, D. Jeffrey, 512n132
Birch, Brian D., 82n62
Bird, Michael F., 102n11, 513n133, 523n175
Bitton, Davis, 3n3
Black, Matthew, 371n81, 503n90
Blain, Jacob, 196n74, 210
Blaising, Craig A., 481n9
Bliss, Philip, 288
Bloom, Harold, 185n28
Blosser, Benjamin P., 181n15, 182n16, 193n60
Blowers, Paul M., 183n22, 381n118, 409n47, 534n212
Blumhofer, Edith W., 278n32
Blythe, Christopher James, 483n13
Bock, Darrell L., 481n9, 482n11
Boersma, Hans, 491n39
Bonhoeffer, Dietrich, 42
Bonner, Ali, 74n34
Bousset, Wilhelm, 102
Bouteneff, Peter, 205n105
Bower, Jacob, 374n93
Boyd, Gregory A., 382n122
Bozeman, Theodore Dwight, 164n85
Bradshaw, Paul F., 345n125, 373n91, 384n131, 425n101
Bradwardine, Thomas, 256n109
Braude, Ann, 522n173
Bray, Gerald, 204n100
Breck, John, 534n211
Brettler, Marc Zvi, 62n2, 398n8
Brightman, Edgar S., 95n110
Bringhurst, Newell G., 4n5
Brink, Gert van den, 148n26
Bromiley, Geoffrey W., 378n104, 381n117
Brooke, John L., 538n231
Brown, David, 126n91, 127n92
Brown, Hugh B., 28
Brown, Peter R., 510n120

Browning, Robert L., 390n155
Bruce, Barbara J., 220n6
Brunner, Emil, 191
Bucer, Martin, 226n27, 240n64, 389–90
Buckley, James J., 342n116, 357n23, 443n30, 444n35, 453n70, 464n110
Buerger, David John, 211n124, 470n127
Bulgakov, Sergei, 168
Bull, George, 223, 244–45
Bultmann, Rudolf, 180
Burgess, Stanley M., 289n61, 304n108, 335n97, 447n46
Burke, John, 479n2
Burkert, Walter, 366n57
Burnett, Amy Nelson, 390n154, 406n36, 407n37, 407n39
Burns, J. Patout, 202n92, 210n120, 262, 384n132
Burpo, Todd, 479n2
Bushnell, Horace, 249
Butcher, Brian A., 374n92, 376n100, 389n149, 437n8, 439n14
Butler, Jon, 308
Bynum, Caroline Walker, 511n127, 512n131

Caldwell, Patricia, 290n66
Callister, Tad R., 172n125, 174, 260n124
Calvin, John, 14, 31n38, 40n71, 67, 70–71, 84, 89–90, 91–92, 125n88, 140, 147–48, 163, 165, 168, 202, 222, 241, 246, 316–17, 363, 364n48, 381, 405, 406n35, 408–9n44, 409n45, 409n48, 413, 492, 504, 526
Campbell, Alexander, 162n79, 364n49, 364n51, 375, 409n47
Canedy, Ardel, 199n81
Cannon, Donald Q., 185n28
Cannon, George Q., 55, 227n30, 267n147, 332, 418–19, 452, 494
Cannon, Janath Russell, 449n51
Capes, David B., 102n13
Cappon, Lester J., 34n48
Caragounis, Chrys C., 333n90
Carey, Jonathan S., 535n216
Carlson, R. P., 506n105
Carroll, Bret E., 494n54
Carson, D. A., 90n89

Casiday, Augustine, 222n13
Cassian, John, 21, 265, 266, 267
Cessario, Romanus, 353n8
Chadwick, Henry, 57n132, 182n18, 193n59, 203n98
Chadwick, Jabez, 47
Chadwick, Owen, 253n101, 265–66, 266n143, 266n145
Chamberlin, William Henry, 186n34
Channing, William Ellery, 535n216
Chappell, Paul G., 305n112
Cherbonnier, Edmond, 29n35
Chrisman, Miriam Usher, 226n27
Christensen, Michael J., 539n235, 540n237
Christofferson, D. Todd, 158–59, 242n68, 279–80, 362n42, 412, 418n82, 529–30
Clark, Alan J., 306n116
Clark, Elizabeth A., 21n9, 181n14
Clark, J. Reuben, Jr., 132, 337–38, 442
Clarke, Don R., 400n16
Clarke, James, 222n14
Clarke, William Newton, 527, 527n191
Clarkson, John F., 281n40
Clement of Alexandria, 203, 503
Clifford, Anne M., 192n54
Clouse, Robert G., 482n11
Cobb, John B., Jr., 82n61, 96n112
Cochrane, Arthur C., 363n45
Cohen, Shaye J. D., 340n112
Cole, Graham A., 154n44
Collins, C. John, 199n81
Collins, John J., 480n7, 486n20
Colman, Boyd Taylor, 403n26
Congar, Yves, 280
Cook, Gene R., 216n3
Cook, Quentin L., 286, 314n29, 347n133, 528
Cooper, John W., 180n11
Copan, Paul, 63n3
Cotton, John, 310
Coulter, Dale M., 252n97, 288–89, 289n61
Courtenay, William J., 510n119
Cowdery, Oliver, 69, 158, 297, 330–31, 496n64
Cowper, William, 71, 72
Cragg, Gerald R., 223n18

Craig, William Lane, 63n3, 86n76, 143n9
Cranfield, Charles E. B., 503n90
Crawford, Cory, 16n30
Crick, Francis, 178–79
Crisp, Oliver D., 31n38, 66n16, 102n11, 114n55, 126n91, 138n143, 143n9, 148n26, 149n27, 152n38, 153n40
Critopoulos, Metrophanes, 451n62, 453n71
Cross, Frank Moore, Jr., 473
Cross, Richard, 112n47
Cummings, Brian, 235n50, 406n32
Cunningham, Mary B., 75n38, 205n105, 458n91, 480n4
Cyprian of Carthage, 147n23, 201, 220n6, 321, 373n90, 387–88, 391, 521n168
Cyril of Alexandria, 117, 118–19n69, 120, 121, 204
Cyril of Jerusalem, 403

Daley, Brian E., 115n58, 138n142, 480n8, 488n30, 513n138
Dalton, William J., 502n89
Daly, Emily Joseph, 351n1
Dan, Robert, 45n91
Dana, James, 527
Daniel-Hughes, Carly, 193n61, 194n62
Danker, Frederick William, 268n2, 351n2, 359n32
Dante Alighieri, 208n113
Darby, John Nelson, 481n9
Dau, W. H. T., 526n188
Davenant, John, 164, 165n90
Davies, Brian, 23n14, 41n74
Davies, Douglas, 167n99
Davies, Matthew R., 307n120
Davis, Stephen T., 152n38, 218n5
Davis, Thomas J., 224n22
Davison, Andrew, 160n67
Dawson, Robert D., 112n49
Daynes, Kathryn M., 461n99
Dayton, Donald W., 273n12, 289n60
Deane, S. N., 157n54
Deferrari, Roy, 110n40
Delumeau, Jean, 232n47
Dennis, Anette, 474–75
Dennis, J. Anette, 475n144

Denzinger, Heinrich, 84n69, 368n69, 371n81, 387n148, 491n40, 501n87, 502n88, 514n140
Derr, Jill Mulvay, 97n117, 189n40, 349n140, 449n51, 449n54
Descartes, René, 33
Dickens, Charles, 531
Dickson, David, 279n35
Dieter, Melvin E., 289n60
Dillstone, F. W., 146n17
Disley, Emma, 526n187, 527n190
Dodds, E. R., 284
Doolittle, Thomas, 416
Dostoevsky, Fyodor, 439
Doyle, Dennis M., 280n38
Drecoll, Volker, 228n33
Drummelow, J. R., 503n91
Duffield, Guy P., 447n46
Duffy, Eamon, 320n46
Dulles, Avery, 285, 294n82
Dunn, James D. G., 102n11, 143n8, 218n5, 239n59, 277n25
Duns Scotus, John, 256n109
Dunzl, Franz, 49n105
Dürer, Albrecht, 504n98
Durling, Robert M., 208n113
Dwight, Timothy, 535
Dyson, R. W., 513n134

Eck, Johannes, 240n64
Eddy, Paul R., 143n9, 153n40, 382n122
Edwards, Jonathan, 148, 232, 535
Ehat, Andrew F., 472n137
Ehrman, Bart D., 33n47, 102n11, 520n164
Eichrodt, Walther, 179n8
Eilers, Kent, 45n89
Eire, Carlos M. N., 380n115
Elgat, Guy, 76n41
Eliason, Eric A., 16n30
Elliott, J. K., 504n96, 504n97
Ellis, Mark A., 173n127, 238n57
Embry, Jessie L., 506n107
Emery, Gilles, 44n86, 46n95
Engberg-Pedersen, Troels, 43n83
Engle, Paul E., 360n34, 363n47
Epicurus, 90

Episcopius, Simon, 223
Erasmus, Desiderius, 73, 406
Erickson, John H., 374n92
Erickson, Millard J., 141n2, 417n72
Ernst, Cornelius, 235n51
Eskenazi, Tamara Cohn, 349n139
Esplin, Cheryl, 410–11, 411n52
Eusebius of Caesarea, 110n40, 111, 116
Eusebius of Emesa, 136
Eutyches, 121
Evanou, Jean, 458n90
Evans, Ernest, 49n104, 59n141
Evans, Joseph W., 90n89
Eyring, Henry, 70n26, 251n95, 288, 393n168

Fahlbusch, Erwin, 274n17
Fairweather, Eugene T., 146n18, 157n56
Falls, Thomas B., 110n39, 203n99, 229n36
Fancher, G., 47
Farris, Joshua R., 179n9
Farrow, Douglas B., 137n140
Faupel, D. William, 447n47
Faust, James, 173–74, 231n44
Fee, Gordon D., 218n5
Ferguson, Everett, 372n88, 373n90,
    378n107, 384n132, 387n144, 387n146,
    387n147
Fiddes, Paul S., 146n21, 150n33
Finke, Roger, 308n2
Finney, Charles, 256–57, 535
Fletcher, John William, 289n60, 440n18
Flew, Anthony, 75n36
Flint, Thomas, 86n76
Florovsky, Georges, 334
Fluhman, J. Spencer, 464n111
Flynn, Gabriel, 280n38
Foord, Martin, 222n14
Foschini, Bernard, 506n105
Foster, Douglas A., 409n47
Franchot, Jenny, 313n21
Franklin, Ben, 537n226
Fredriksen, Paula, 181
Freedman, David Noel, 301n100
Freeman, Anthony, 179n7
Freeman, Curtis W., 408n43
Frend, W. H. C., 355n18

Fretheim, Terence E., 349n139
Friedrich, Gerhard, 301n100

Gabriel, Andrew K., 335n98, 335n99
Gabriel, Charles, 151n35, 427
Gabriel, George, 199n83
Gaca, Kathy L., 512n132
Gaillardetz, Richard R., 329n77
Galadza, Peter, 357n24, 376n100, 389n149
Galvin, John P., 192n54, 199n79, 436n3,
    457n88
Gamble, Richard C., 492n43
Ganssle, Gregory E., 35n54
Gaskill, Alonzo L., 464n111
Gathercole, Simon J., 102n12
Gause, R. Hollis, 335n99
Gaustad, Edwin S., 374n93
Gavrilyuk, Paul L., 43n83, 118n69, 247n84,
    363n47
Geach, Peter T., 90n89
Geffert, Bryn, 247n86, 247n87
Gentner, Dedre, 8n9
George, Francis E., 400n17
Gibbs, Josiah M., 63n5
Gilbert, Sidney, 352n3
Givens, Fiona, 43n84
Givens, Terryl L., 43n84, 98n121, 183n20
Godfrey, Audrey M., 97n117, 187n35
Godfrey, Kenneth W., 97n117, 184n26
Goetz, Ronald, 41n77
Goggin, T. A., 236n53
Goldberg, Elkhonon, 179n7
Goldhill, Simon, 35n54
Golitzin, Alexander, 22n9
Gong, Gerrit, 286
González, Justo L., 121n77
Gordon, Adoniram Judson (A. J.), 305
Gordon, Bruce, 406n36
Gottstein, Alon Goshen, 192n56
Grant, Heber, 170
Grant, Jedediah, 450n56, 498n75
Greaves, Richard L., 164n84
Grebel, Conrad, 380n115
Green, Harvey, 423n97
Green, Joel B., 149n31, 153n39, 179n9,
    180n11

Green, John C., 307n121
Gregg, Robert C., 136n137
Gregory of Nazianzus, 50, 51, 112–13n50, 118–19n69, 144n13
Gregory of Nyssa, 47n98, 50, 53n116, 56, 91n90, 138, 144, 204–5, 534, 540
Gregory of Rimini, 256n109
Gregory the Great, 145
Grensted, Laurence W., 145n14, 167n96
Gribben, Crawford, 478n1
Griffin, Carl W., 22n10
Griffin, Clifford S., 274n14
Griffin, David Ray, 82n61, 82n63, 91n94
Grobel, Kendrik, 180n10
Groh, Dennis E., 136n137
Groothuis, Douglas, 177n2
Gropper, Johann, 240n64
Grotius, Hugo, 148
Grow, Matthew J., 313n21
Gruchy, John W. de, 42n81
Grudem, Wayne, 178n3, 491n36
Guelzo, Allen C., 148n27
Gumerlock, Francis X., 222n13
Gundry, Robert H., 484n15
Gunkel, Herman, 192n55
Gunter, W. Stephen, 224n20
Gunton, Colin E., 150n33
Gy, P. M., 435n3

Hafen, Bruce, 175
Hafen, Marie K., 175n136
Hague, William, 311
Haight, Roger, 199n79
Haldon, Charles, 24n17
Hales, Laura Harris, 473n140
Hales, Robert, 543
Hall, Christopher A., 41n75
Hall, David D., 291n68, 416n70
Hall, Stuart G., 50n106
Hallstrom, Donald L., 27n29
Halton, Charles, 45n89
Halton, Thomas P., 110n39
Hamer, John C., 4n5
Hammond, Henry, 223
Hampton, Stephen, 223n18, 245n78
Hanson, R. P. C., 44n86, 107n30, 116n61, 137n140, 188n39

Hardy, B. Carmon, 461n99
Harnack, Adolf von, 24n20, 304n108
Harower, Scott, 431n115
Harper, Steven C., 468n122, 473n140
Harrell, Charles R., 195n65
Harrell, David E., 448n48
Harrison, Alan, 24n19
Harrison, Nonna Verna, 75n38, 206n107
Hart, David Bentley, 107n29, 525n180
Hartley, William G., 299n91, 343n120
Hartshorne, Charles, 42, 42n80, 82n60
Harvey, Susan Ashbrook, 115n58, 200n84, 372n87
Hasker, William, 73n32, 85n70
Hatch, Nathan, 224n22, 227n28, 309n4
Haws, J. B., 1n1, 465n115
Haykin, Michael A. G., 149n28
Hayward, John, 391n162
Heather, Peter, 50n106, 320n46
Hedges, Andrew H., 464n111
Hegel, Georg Wilhelm Friedrich, 27n29
Heine, Ronald E., 54n121, 195n70
Heitzenrater, Richard P., 252n96
Heller, Clarence N., 316n33
Hellholm, David, 362n41, 397n6
Helm, Paul, 35n54, 40n71, 85n74
Helmer, Christine, 21n7
Hendrix, Scott H., 263n134
Hengel, Martin, 143n8
Henley, William, 263–64
Hera, Marianus Pale, 47n98
Hick, John, 91n90, 93
Hilary of Poitiers, 188
Hilborn, David, 143n9
Hill, Edmund, 182n19
Hilton, John, III, 170n116, 171n119
Hinckley, Bryant S., 44n85
Hinckley, Gordon B., 5, 28, 36, 131n114, 189, 271n7, 327, 476, 477, 508, 538
Hinlicky, Paul R., 40n70
Hippolytus of Rome, 49, 49n104, 115n57, 221
Hodge, Charles, 114, 381, 535
Hodgson, Leonard, 52–53, 53n115
Hoekema, Anthony A., 535n214
Hoen, Cornelius, 406, 407

Index of Authors

Hofstadter, Douglas, 7
Holifield, E. Brooks, 24n20, 224n23, 248n88, 249n92, 375n94, 379n109, 381n120, 409n44, 415n68
Holland, Jeffrey, 48, 48n102, 98, 133, 156, 161, 172n125, 260, 271n9, 352, 353n11, 410n51, 412
Holmes, Michael W., 373n90
Holmes, Stephan R., 149n30, 153n40
Holyoak, Keith J., 8n9
Homer, Michael W., 473n140
Honan, Daniel J., 515n148
Hooker, Thomas, 165
Hornik, Heidi J., 527n192
Horton, Stanley M., 468n120
Hovorun, Cyril, 124n84
Howison, George H., 186n34
Hubmaier, Balthasar, 408, 420
Huggard, E. M., 96n115
Hughes, Anthony, 265n142
Hughes, Philip Edgcumbe, 378n104
Hughes, Phillip, 114n55
Hughes, Richard T., 309n5
Hume, David, 90
Hummel, Daniel G., 481n9
Humphries, Thomas, 357n20
Hunsinger, George, 408n41
Hunter, David G., 116n58, 200n84, 372n87
Hunter, Howard W., 98, 125, 174, 174n130, 333–34, 367n64, 417, 515
Hurtado, Larry, 102n10, 102n12
Hwang, Alexander Y., 222n13
Hyde, Emily K., 170n116

Iannaccone, Laurence R., 308n2
Insole, Christopher J., 20n4
Irenaeus, 51, 137, 167, 200, 203, 210, 278, 432, 512, 540
Isidore of Seville, 356

Jagger, Peter J., 390n155
Jaki, Stanley L., 192n55
James, William, 79n50, 86n77
Jamison, A. Leland, 263n135
Jantzen, Grace, 42
Jaques, John, 185n29
Jenkins, Jerry, 478

Jenkins, Philip, 116n59
Jenkins, Thomas E., 111n43
Jensen, Alexander S., 73n32
Jensen, Jay E., 428n111
Jensen, Richard L., 299n91
Jensen, Robin M., 202n92, 373n91, 384n132
Jenson, Robert, 44, 143–44, 191, 202n94
Jeremias, Joachim, 377n102
Jerome, 182n17, 209, 513, 526n185
Jewett, Paul K., 379n112
John Chrysostom, 41, 81, 203–4, 221, 236, 378
John of Damascus, 509n118
John Paul II (pope), 252, 275–76, 511
Johnson, Adam J., 148n26, 149n29, 154n44, 431n115
Johnson, Keith L., 126n91
Johnson, Luke Timothy, 107n27
Johnson, Maxwell E., 353n6, 359n30, 372n87, 384n131, 386n141, 387n148, 389n150
Johnson, Todd, 335n97
Johnson, William B., 149
Jowers, Dennis W., 67n16
Julian of Eclanum, 201n88
Justin Martyr, 54, 64n7, 107, 110, 111, 203, 229, 387, 403, 503

Kadane, Matthew, 46n93
Kane, Robert, 73n32
Kant, Immanuel, 46
Kärkkäinen, Veli-Matti, 534n209
Kasper, Walter, 243n73, 322n52, 323n53, 323n54, 323n55, 347n131, 457n86
Kaufman, Gordon D., 24n18
Kavanagh, Aidan, 386n141, 390n155
Kearney, Richard, 24n19
Kearon, Patrick, 159
Keating, Daniel, 247n84
Keats, John, 93
Keener, Craig S., 303n107
Kelly, J. N. D., 47n98, 144n13, 196n73, 403n26
Kendall, Daniel, 218n5
Kesich, Lydia, 168n103
Kharlamov, Vladimir, 540n237
Kimball, Edward L., 88n82

Kimball, Heber, 170, 472, 498n75
Kimball, Spencer, 88, 97–98n118, 187n36, 213, 318, 326, 331–33, 338–39, 350n143, 442–43, 455–56, 507
Kirby, James E., 224n19, 253n100
Kittel, Gerhard, 301n100
Knafl, Anne K., 19n2, 20n4, 57n133
Koester, Helmut, 277n25
Kokinovet, Boicho N., 8n9
Kolb, Robert A., 237n56, 241n65
Konstan, David, 35n54
Koskela, Douglas M., 363n47
Krailsheimer, A. J., 177n1
Krausmuller, Dirk, 136n138
Küng, Hans, 277, 292, 346n127

Laborde, Lucas, 389n152
LaCugna, Catherine, 52, 52n114
LaHaye, Tim, 478, 519n161, 527, 527n191
Laing, John D., 86n75
Lamb, Matthew L., 353n8
Lamberigts, Mathijs, 200n84, 202n93
Lambert, Byron C., 409n47
Lampe, G. E., 351n1
Land, Stephen J., 278n32, 335n99
Lanfranc of Canterbury, 404n27
Lang, Bernhard, 462n104, 520n165, 521–22n169, 521n166, 522n170
Langland, William, 504n98
Lanooy, Rienk, 218n5
Lattin, Don, 538n229
Laud, William, 221n8, 223
Law, William, 242n69
Lawler, Michael G., 457n86
Lea, Henry C., 444n39
Lebet, Benjamin, 179n7
LeDoux, Joseph, 179n7
Lee, Harold, 284
Lee, Samuel, 110n40
Leff, Gordon, 256n109
Leflow, Brian, 41n74
Le Goff, Jacques, 491n38
Lehmann, Hartmut, 273n12, 273n13
Lehner, Ulrich L., 46n93, 273n12, 391n159, 414n66, 441n24
Leibniz, Gottfried, 96

Leinsle, Ulrich G., 256n109
Le Saint, William P., 147n23, 287n57
Levering, Matthew, 44n86, 46n95, 223n16, 353n8
Lewis, C. S., 80, 140, 530
Liddell, H. G., 359n32
Lietzmann, Hans, 424n101
Lillback, Peter A., 165n88
Lim, Paul C. H., 45n90, 416n70
Lin, Paul J., 23n16
Lindberg, Carter, 320n47, 407n38
Lindsey, Hal, 478
Little, James A., 12n17, 229n35
Locke, John, 46
Lockshin, Martin I., 349n139
Lombard, Peter, 163, 342n116, 352–53
Long, Stephen A., 223n16
Lossky, Vladimir, 168
Louth, Andrew, 22n9, 183n22, 199n80, 354n12, 492n41, 496n62, 510n123
Lubac, Henri de, 280
Lucar, Cyril, 66n16
Lugioyo, Brian, 226n27
Luibheid, Colm, 253n101, 266n143
Lum, Kathryn Gin, 525n179
Lund, Anthon H., 186–87, 187n35, 422n95
Lundberg, Matthew D., 122n80
Luther, Martin, 14, 43, 67, 74–75, 163, 202, 214–15, 220–21, 222, 234, 240, 241, 262–63, 268–69n2, 317, 345, 366, 384, 398, 405, 441, 445, 527, 541n238
Lynch, Michael J., 163n83
Lynch, Patrick, 353n7

Maas, Eduard van der, 335n97
Macchia, Frank D., 94n105, 154n41, 154n42, 252n97, 278n32, 448n48, 468n120, 479n3, 480n5
MacCulloch, J. A., 504n96
Mackintosh, Hugh, 114n55
Macleod, Donald, 114n55
Madigan, Kevin, 510n119
Madsen, Truman G., 98n121, 187n36
Madueme, Hans, 199n81
Mannermaa, Tuomo, 541n238
Manscill, Craig K., 307n120

Marcel, Pierre-Charles, 378n104
Marcellus of Ancyra, 136, 137
Marcion of Sinope, 115n58
Maritain, Jacques, 90n89
Markos, Louis, 20n3
Marks, John, 192n56
Markschies, Christoph, 20n2
Marsden, George M., 257n116
Marshall, Peter, 504n99
Martimort, A. G., 435n3
Martin, Luther H., 366n60
Martin, Moses, 293n76
Marty, Martin, 308
Martyn, Louis, 239n61
Mason, Patrick Q., 465n115
Matheson, Peter, 240n64
Mathewes-Green, Frederica, 459n93
Mathews, Mark A., 517n155
Matthews, Robert J., 17n31
Mattison, Hiram, 47, 47n96, 168n100
Mattox, Mickey L., 406n34, 418n77, 437n5
Matz, Brian J., 222n13
Matz, Robert J., 41n76
Maunder, Chris, 121n78
Maximus the Confessor, 476, 534
Maxwell, Neal, 38, 87, 156, 174, 500
May, Gerhard, 62n3
McCall, Thomas H., 85n70, 92n95
McClear, Ernest V., 205n103
McClendon, James, 411n53
McClymond, Michael J., 525n180, 529n196
McConkie, Bruce R., 12n17, 60, 88, 106,
    129, 130, 133n121, 134, 135, 155n46, 160,
    169, 171–72, 197, 206n110, 232n46,
    249–50, 313n24, 334n92, 338, 365, 411–12,
    419n83, 433, 452–53, 484n16, 487n26,
    488n26, 519
McCormack, Bruce Lindley, 126n91
McCready, Douglas, 101n9
McDannell, Colleen, 448n49, 462n104,
    466n118, 520n165, 521–22n169, 521n166,
    521n167, 522n170
McDermott, Gerald, 133n119
McDonald, Brett, 53n117
McFarland, Ian A., 30n37, 198n78, 200n86
McGee, Gary B., 289n61, 335n97, 447n46

McGinn, Bernard, 480n7
McGoldrick, James E., 222n15
McGowan, Andrew B., 371n81, 384n129
McGrath, Alister E., 52n114, 146n19,
    190n48, 239n61, 521n168
McGuckin, John A., 118n66, 247n85, 268n1,
    275, 334, 335, 335n100, 348n135, 391n160,
    437n7, 443n32, 451n63, 453n72, 454n76,
    456n85, 459n93, 462n105, 463n106,
    476n148, 535n215, 539n235, 540n236
McGuinness, Philip, 24n19
McInroy, Mark, 27n29
McKay, David, 124, 258–59, 284n48, 395,
    400, 410, 421
McKenna, Stephen, 51n110
McKim, Donald K., 492n43
McLachlan, James M., 76n41, 98n121,
    186n34
McLoughlin, William G., 256n111
McMullin, Keith, 160n70
McMurrin, Sterling M., 13n18, 39n68, 95,
    187n36
McNeill, John T., 439n17, 443n31, 444n39
McPartlan, Paul, 320n45, 360n34
Meconi, David V., 534n209
Medley, Samuel, 140n2
Mehr, Kahlile B., 506n107
Meister, Chad, 203n96
Melanchthon, Philip, 221, 240n64, 378–79,
    526
Merkle, Benjamin R., 45n91
Mesle, C. Robert, 42n80
Meyendorff, John, 204n101, 323n53, 534n211
Meyer, Donald, 224n22
Meyers, Carol, 349n139
Miles, Richard, 355n18
Mill, John Stuart, 48–49, 49n103, 95
Miller, Lisa, 520n164
Miller, Michael J., 256n109
Miller, Perry, 164n86, 164n87
Miller, William, 489, 489n33
Milton, John, 46
Minear, Paul S., 269n3
Mogila, Peter, 66n16
Moiser, Jeremy, 232n47
Molina, Luis de, 85–86

Molnar, Paul, 44, 44n87
Moltmann, Jürgen, 42, 43n82, 275
Monson, Thomas, 171, 476, 507
Moo, Douglas J., 125n88
Moody, Raymond, 478–79
Moore, Jonathan D., 165n91
Morales, Isaac A., 359n31
Moreira, Isabel, 491n38, 525n179
Morgan, Edmund S., 290n66, 310n11,
310n12, 310n14
Morris, George Q., 213n129
Morris, Rudolph E., 292n74
Morris, Thomas V., 86n76
Mortimer, Sarah, 148n26
Moulton, Arthur, 284n48
Mozley, John, 147n22
Muldowney, Mary Sarah, 526n184
Muller, Richard A., 273n12, 391n159,
411n56, 414n66, 441n24
Mullins, R. T., 35n54
Muntzer, Thomas, 380n115
Murphy, Nancey, 180n11
Musser, Donald W., 82n63

Neiman, Susan, 95
Nelson, Derek R., 41n73, 538n231
Nelson, Nels L., 186n34
Nelson, Russell M., 100, 142–43n7, 155n45,
158, 175, 176n139, 209n117, 228n31,
293–94, 319, 336, 347n133, 348–49, 350,
402, 437, 465n116, 470, 471, 477, 488, 515,
543, 544
Nestorius of Constantinople, 120
Nettles, Thomas J., 363n47
Nevin, John, 308
Newquist, Jerreld L., 55n125, 332n87,
419n83, 452n68
Newton, John Henry, 71n30
Nibley, Hugh, 473n141
Nicholson, Eric, 232n47
Nimmo, Paul T., 126n91
Nissinen, Martti, 339n110
Noldeke, Theodor, 192n55
Noll, Mark A., 257n115, 258n117, 374n93
Norris, Richard A., Jr., 107n25, 117n62
Novenson, Matthew V., 102n10
Nutt, Roger W., 223n16

Oakes, Edward T., 253n101
Oaks, Dallin, 77, 93, 154n42, 161–62, 173,
174, 267n147, 313–14, 348, 394, 418, 454,
455, 464, 475, 517, 519, 520, 527–28, 544
Oberman, Heiko Augustinus, 355n17,
357n22
O'Brien, Betty, 423n98
O'Collins, Gerald, 110n40, 218n5, 252n99,
526n186
O'Connell, Matthew J., 435n3
O'Connell, Robert J., 195n71
O'Dea, Thomas F., 256n110
Oden, Thomas C., 224n19
O'Donnell, James J., 200n85
O'Kelley, James, 309
Oliphint, K. Scott, 112n48
Olson, Carl E., 534n209
Olson, Roger E., 382n121, 409n46
O'Malley, John W., 321n49, 322n51, 326n64
O'Neill, John C., 63n3
Oord, Thomas Jay, 96n113
Origen of Alexandria, 20, 40n72, 41, 48,
64n7, 91n90, 112, 138, 144, 162n78, 181, 182,
191, 193, 194, 195–96, 197, 200–201, 202,
220n6, 229, 244, 513n136, 528, 534n213
Orsi, Robert, 9, 511
Ortiz, Jared, 534n209
Osborn, T. L., 456n82
Ostler, Blake T., 39n68, 87n78, 98n121,
186n32
Ott, Ludwig, 353n7
Oulton, John Ernest Leonard, 203n98
Outler, Albert C., 224n20, 252n96, 258n118,
440n19
Owen, John, 156
Oxenham, Henry, 167

Packer, Boyd, 56–57, 155–56, 173, 283,
399n12, 538–39, 542n239
Packer, J. I., 152
Page, Meghan D., 145n15
Palmer, Paul J., 445n40
Palmer, Stuart L., 180n11
Pannenberg, Wolfhart, 281
Papandrea, James L., 49n105
Parker, J. H., 145n16
Parry, Donald W., 98n121

Parry, Robin A., 525n180
Parsons, Michael, 413n61
Parsons, Wilfrid, 201n89
Partridge, Christopher H., 525n180
Parvis, Sara, 136n138
Pascal, Blaise, 177
Pasquato, Ottorino, 384n132
Pasulka, Diana Walsh, 491n38
Patterson, Paul A., 22n9
Paulsen, David L., 22n10, 43n84, 53n117, 76n41, 82n62, 82n63, 98n121, 189n43
Pearson, Mark, 455n82
Pecknold, Chad C., 389n152
Pelagius, 74
Pelikan, Jaroslav, 136n136, 140n2, 144n11, 200n85, 201n90, 253n101, 321n48
Penrose, Charles W., 12n17, 170n117, 187n35, 311, 495n60
Perrin, Nicholas, 361n37, 361n38, 373n89
Petau, Denis, 391n159
Petcu, Liviu, 534n210
Peters, John Leland, 253n100, 289n60
Peterson, Daniel C., 98n121
Peterson, Michael L., 83n64
Petrey, Taylor G., 16n30, 21n7, 461n101
Phan, Peter C., 46n95
Phelps, W. W., 65n14
Phillips, L. Edward, 384n131
Pinegar, Rex D., 318n40
Pinnock, Clark H., 82n61, 85n70, 86n76
Pirnat, Antal, 45n91
Pitre, Brant, 397n6
Placher, William C., 24n17, 41n73, 43n82, 538n231
Plantinga, Cornelius, Jr., 56n130
Plantinga, Richard J., 122n80
Plato, 20, 64, 129n102, 152, 181
Plekon, Michael, 458n91
Polkinghorne, John, 42n78
Pollmann, Karla, 191n52, 228n33
Poloma, Margaret M., 307n121
Pomplun, Trent, 357n23, 391n159, 400n14
Pope, Robert G., 291n67
Porterfield, Amanda, 447n44
Power, David N., 435n3, 452n65
Pratt, Orson, 34, 36, 38, 55, 64, 128, 135,

158, 161, 170, 195n67, 242–43, 244, 449, 517n155, 524n178
Pratt, Parley, 27, 64n8, 107–8, 123, 139, 159, 161, 162, 231n43, 304, 472, 494, 495, 533
Price, Richard, 191n52
Prince, Gregory, 284n48
Pulido, Martin, 189n43

Quain, Edward A., 351n1

Rad, Gerhard von, 192
Radbertus, Paschasius, 404n27
Radde-Gallwitz, Andrew, 49n104
Rahner, Karl, 46, 52, 235, 501n86
Ramelli, Ilaria, 35n54
Rasband, Ronald, 70, 72
Ratramnus of Corbie, 404n27
Reed, Roy A., 390n155
Reeves, Michael, 199n81
Regev, Eyal, 290n64
Reid, J. K. S., 222n14
Rempel, John D., 380n114, 382n121, 408n42, 420n87, 420n88
Renlund, Dale, 189, 259, 350n143
Renlund, Ruth Lybbert, 350n143
Rettig, John W., 356n19
Richards, Franklin D., 12n17, 229n35, 295n87
Richards, Legrand, 312n19
Richards, Willard, 227, 228, 229n35
Richardson, Cyril, 44–45n88
Riches, Aaron, 120n76
Richie, Tony, 278n32
Ricks, Stephen D., 98n121
Rigdon, Sidney, 295, 364n52, 390–91
Ringe, Sharon, 239n60
Ritschl, Albrecht, 24n20, 240n63
Roberts, B. H., 12n17, 49n103, 55–56, 87, 90, 95, 104, 123, 128, 129, 135, 138, 151–52, 171, 186, 187n35, 193n58, 209n115, 295, 313, 370, 422
Robertson, John, 148n26
Robinson, Joseph E., 155n47
Robinson, Paul W., 317n37, 366n58, 398n10
Roeber, A. G., 273n12, 391n159, 414n66, 441n24
Romanides, John, 199n83

Rombs, Ronnie J., 196n71
Romney, Marion G., 171n121, 214n132
Rosemann, Philipp W., 59n142
Rowley, H. H., 371n81
Ruloff, C. P., 96n114
Rusch, William G., 56n130, 107n30
Russell, Jeffrey Burton, 520n165
Russell, Norman, 495n59, 533n209
Russell, William R., 222n15
Ruthven, Jon Mark, 304n108
Ryrie, Charles C., 481n9

Sachs, John R., 529n196
Salter, Martin, 378n105
Sanders, Fred, 66n16, 152n38
Sanders, John, 83n64, 84n67, 501n85
Sandmel, Samuel, 7
Sanger, Dieter, 397n6
Santer, Mark, 133n121
Saum, Lewis O., 69n20
Scheck, Thomas P., 144n12, 162n78, 201n87, 202n91, 244n76
Schelling, Friedrich, 76
Schleiermacher, Friedrich, 46, 281
Schlesinger, Arthur M., Jr., 224n22
Schmucker, Samuel Simon, 224–25, 258
Schneemelcher, Wilhelm, 504n96, 504n97
Schoedel, William R., 515n146
Schreiner, Thomas R., 125n87, 153n40
Schüssler Fiorenza, Francis, 24n18, 192n54, 199n79, 436n3, 457n88
Scott, Mark S. M., 195n70
Scott, Richard, 187n36
Scullion, John J., 192n55
Segal, Alan F., 490n35
Servetus, Michael, 45
Sexton, Jason S., 44n87
Shaffern, Robert W., 445n40
Shakespeare, William, 94
Sharp, Carolyn J., 339n110
Sheldon, Gilbert, 223
Shepherd, Gary, 488n27
Shepherd, Gordon, 488n27
Shields, Steven L., 4n5
Shuster, Marguerite, 96n114, 97n116
Siecienski, A. Edward, 323n53

Silano, Giulio, 59n142, 163n82
Simon, Ulrich E., 520n165
Simonetti, Manlio, 333n90
Smith, Gary Scott, 263n137, 463n107, 520n164, 535n216, 535n217, 535n218
Smith, George Albert, 315
Smith, Gordon T., 402n24
Smith, H. Shelton, 205n104
Smith, James Ward, 263n135
Smith, Joseph, 2, 4, 7, 13–14, 16, 20, 25, 26, 28, 29, 31–32, 33, 37, 43, 47, 54, 59–60n143, 63–64, 68, 69, 71, 78, 79, 87, 88, 99, 104, 108, 109, 123, 130–31, 134, 151, 160, 164, 165, 166, 184, 185, 192–93, 203, 209, 225, 227, 230, 232, 238n58, 243, 244, 254, 273n11, 284, 293, 294, 295, 297, 301n98, 302, 309, 310–11, 312, 318–19, 325, 330, 333, 338, 340–41, 349, 355, 360, 365, 366, 369, 370, 371, 379–80, 382, 392–93, 397, 432–33, 442, 449, 456, 457–58, 460, 468, 472, 484, 484n17, 486–87, 488–89, 496–97, 505–7, 514, 515n144, 516, 517n155, 525, 527–29, 536, 541, 542–43
Smith, Joseph Fielding, 12n17, 37, 55, 69, 109n38, 127, 134, 135, 158, 171, 184, 185n27, 186–87, 191, 195, 325n60, 331n85, 350, 358, 362, 368, 484n14, 493, 494, 497, 500, 509
Smith, Mark S., 19n2, 198n77
Smith, Timothy L., 273n12, 274n14, 289n62
Smyth, John, 408
Snow, Eliza R., 189n40, 468
Snow, Erastus, 114, 124, 130, 531n203
Snow, Lorenzo, 36, 128–29, 190, 533, 540, 543
Soares, Ulisses, 471n133
Socinus, Faustus, 148
Sommer, Benjamin, 19
Souter, Alexander, 387n143
Spencer, John H., 309n6
Spencer, Orson, 15
Spezzano, Daria, 247n83, 259n123
Sri, Edward, 401n18
Stackhouse, John G., Jr., 133n119
Staker, Mark L., 306n115
Stang, Charles M., 117n64, 119n71
Stanglin, Keith D., 85n70, 92n95

Stanley, Alan P., 518n159
Stark, Rodney, 308n2
Stavrou, Theofanis G., 247n86, 247n87
Steely, J. E., 102n10
Stein, Stephen J., 8n10, 480n7
Steinmetz, David C., 407n40
Stendahl, Krister, 8–9, 240n62, 371n81
Stephens, W. P., 411n56
Stephenson, John R., 414n66, 441n24
Stevenson, Gary, 337
Stewart, Alistair C., 299n93
Stewart, Robert B., 102n11
Stjerna, Kirsi I., 75n35
Stoddard, Solomon, 416
Stoever, William K. B., 249n91
Stone, Barton, 375, 409n47
Stowe, Harriet Beecher, 110–11
Strawbridge, Gregg, 379n113
Strom, Jonathan, 273n12, 273n13
Stuart, Moses, 423–24
Stump, J. B., 203n96
Stuy, Brian H., 227n30
Suárez, Francisco, 85–86
Sullivan, Francis A., 329n77
Sutherland, Keith, 179n7
Swedenborg, Emanuel, 522n169
Sweeney, Douglas A., 148–49n27, 224n22
Swinburne, Richard, 53n115
Synan, Vinson, 289n60

Talbott, Thomas, 525n180
Taliaferro, Charles, 179n9
Talmage, James, 11, 12n16, 57n134, 77, 81, 85, 92, 104n17, 106, 109, 127, 132, 168, 169, 171, 229n35, 230, 393, 495, 497
Tamburr, Karl, 504n98
Tamez, Elsa, 239n60
Tanner, Kathryn, 6n7, 102n11, 146n21, 200n86
Tapsell, Grant, 221n9
Tate, George S., 509n116
Taylor, Barbara Brown, 9n11
Taylor, Brian K., 190n47
Taylor, Jeremy, 223, 242n69
Taylor, John, 100, 108, 113, 151, 168, 172–73,

255, 290, 295–96, 300, 313n22, 314, 334, 399, 432, 516n149, 523–24, 536
Taylor, Mark C., 24n18
Taylor, Nathaniel W., 205, 257, 258
Tenney, Mary McWhorter, 415n69
Tentler, Thomas N., 444n39
Tertullian, 49, 50, 111, 147n23, 193, 200, 287, 304n108, 351n1, 384, 387, 499, 512, 513
Teske, Roland J., 201n88, 249n90, 261n128
Thacker, Justin, 143n9
Theodore of Mopsuestia, 120, 133
Theodoret of Cyrrhus, 120
Theokritoff, Elizabeth, 75n38, 205n105, 458n91, 480n4
Theophilus of Alexandria, 495n59
Thomas, John Christopher, 304n110, 306n116, 331n84, 448n50
Thomas à Kempis, 242n69
Thomas Aquinas, 22, 23, 29–30n36, 39, 41, 82, 83, 89, 91, 92, 119n73, 157, 166–67, 247n82, 259, 321, 341–42, 391n159, 404, 526
Thompson, John L., 411n56
Thompson, Mark D., 222n14
Thompson, Thomas R., 122n80
Thornhill, A. Chadwick, 41n76
Thornton, Allison K., 145n15
Thorp, Malcolm R., 299n91
Tibbs, Eve, 75n38
Tidball, Derek, 143n9, 149n29, 153n40
Tiessen, Terrance L., 503n93
Tillotson, John, 223, 404n28
Tipson, Baird, 165n89
Tobias, Robert, 534n211
Toland, John, 24n19
Tollinton, Richard B., 513n136
Tomlin, Graham, 379n108
Torjesen, Karen Jo, 21n7, 195n70
Torrance, Alan, 52n112
Torrance, Alexis, 50n107
Torrance, Iain R., 6n7, 102n11, 146n21, 200n86
Torrance, Thomas F., 112n48, 114n55
Torrell, Jean-Pierre, 30n36, 157n55
Torrey, Reuben, 527
Toscano, Margaret, 525n179

Trakatellis, Demetrius C., 54n123, 107n26
Trembelas, Panagiotis, 357n24
Trostyanskiy, Sergey, 391n160
Trumbower, Jeffrey A., 500–501n84, 502n89, 504n96
Trussel, McKenna Grace, 170n116
Turcescu, Lucian, 50n107
Turner, H. E. W., 144n13
Turner, John G., 465n115
Turner, Max, 303n107
Turner, Ralph V., 503n95
Turner, Rodney, 211n124
Turretin, Francis, 31, 147–48
Turton, William, 427–28
Twomey, D. Vincent, 136n138
Tyacke, Nicholas, 221n9, 245n78
Tyndale, William, 141, 164

Uchtdorf, Dieter, 175, 216–17, 266–67, 293, 294
Underwood, Grant, 16n30, 448n49, 464n111, 483n13, 486n22, 489n32
Urban, Linwood, 407n40
Uro, Risto, 366n60
Ussher, James, 167

Vaillancourt, Mark G., 404n27
Van Cleave, Nathaniel M., 447n46
Van Kuiken, Jerome, 114n55
Vanstone, William, 95
Vermes, Geza, 107n28
Vickers, Jason, 363n47, 383n126
Vidu, Adonis, 58n140
Vodney, Wolfgang, 447n46
Volpe, Medi Ann, 280n38, 320n45, 328n72, 399n13
Voltaire, 96–97n115
Vondey, Wolfgang, 252n97, 278n32, 289n61, 335n98

Wacker, Grant, 278n32
Wainwright, Geoffrey, 283n45, 360n34
Wainwright, William J., 181n112
Walker, D. P., 524n179
Walker, Ronald W., 2n3
Walls, Jerry L., 75n36, 224n20, 448n48, 480n5, 499n79, 523n174, 527n192, 531n201

Walsh, Gerald G., 515n148
Walsh, Liam G., 359n30, 386n141
Wandel, Lee Palmer, 407n38
Warch, Richard, 302n103
Ward, Keith, 42n78
Ware, Bruce A., 373n89, 444n36, 459n93, 464n112
Ware, Kallistos (Timothy), 278, 278n29, 283, 374n92, 439n15
Waters, Brent, 459n94
Watts, Isaac, 110, 427, 429n112
Weaver, Rebecca Harden, 253n101
Webb, Stephen H., 26, 28n32, 37n60, 99, 139n144
Weber, Timothy P., 480n7
Webster, John, 6n7, 11n14, 30n37, 40n70, 52n112, 102n11, 146n21, 200n86
Weinandy, Thomas, 41n76, 114n55
Weingart, Richard, 146n20
Weir, David A., 164n84
Weiss, Andrea L., 349n139
Welborn, L. L., 512n132
Welch, John W., 87n78, 186n33, 468n122
Wellnitz, Marcus von, 476n147
Wenham, Gordon, 62n1, 63n5
Wenk, Matthias, 303n107
Wesley, Charles, 524
Wesley, John, 14, 224, 241, 251–52, 258, 263, 288n60, 440, 504–5
Wessinger, Catherine, 480n7
Westerfield Tucker, Karen B., 383n126
Westermann, Claus, 192n55
Whedon, Daniel, 257, 258
Wheelock, Cyrus, 130n110
White, Ellen G., 131n110
White, Morton, 224n22
White, Thomas Joseph, 223n16, 357n24
Whitehead, Alfred North, 42, 42n80
Whitmer, John, 4n5, 300n95
Whitney, Orson, 130, 259–60, 264–65, 311–12
Whittaker, David J., 2n3
Whittier, John Greenleaf, 305
Wickham, Lionel, 113n50
Wickman, Lance, 455n80

Widtsoe, John A., 12n17, 36–37, 77, 80, 159n66, 186, 325n60, 507
Wilcox, Brad, 175n134
Wilcox, Miranda, 313n23
Wiles, Maurice F., 46n93, 113n51, 115n56, 119n70, 133n121
Wiley, Tatha, 199n82
Wilhite, David E., 499n77
Wilken, Robert L., 54n120
William of Ockham, 256n109
Williams, George H., 46n92
Williams, Roger, 309–10
Williams, Rowan, 101n9, 277
Williams, Thomas, 157n54
Wills, Gregory A., 439n16
Wilson, James R., 148n25
Winston, David, 63n3
Winter, Ernst F., 73n33
Wirthlin, Joseph, 171n121
Witte, John, Jr., 458n90
Wittung, Jeffrey A., 539n235, 540n237
Wolfe, Tom, 178
Wood, Gordon S., 16, 309n9
Wood, Jacob W., 389n151
Wood, Laurence W., 289n60
Wood, Susan K., 357n23, 360n34

Woodruff, Jennifer L., 423n98
Worrall, A. S., 62n3
Wright, Conrad, 46n93
Wright, David F., 360n34, 373n89
Wright, N. T., 154–55, 274–75, 513n133, 514n142, 523
Wright, Robert, 284n48
Wuerl, Donald, 400n17, 401n19
Wyckoff, John W., 468n120
Wyon, Olive, 191n51

Yang, Eric T., 152n38
Yarbro Collins, Adela, 486n21, 525n183
Yarn, David H., Jr., 338n107
Young, Brigham, 65, 69, 159, 209–10, 212–13, 214, 227, 228, 229n35, 255, 294n81, 378n106, 413, 421n89, 433, 472, 493–94, 496, 497, 498n75, 508–9, 516n149, 528, 543n244
Young, Frances, 62n3
Young, John D., 313n23

Zachuber, Johannes, 50n107
Zafirovski, Milan, 247n82
Zizioulas, John, 322n52
Zwingli, Huldrych, 164, 316, 406–7, 408

Index of Subjects

Aaron, 339
Aaronic/Levitical Priesthood, 342–43, 350.
  See also priesthood
ablution, 362
Abraham, 16, 70, 154, 191, 197, 231n43, 243,
  460
Abraham's bosom, 490
accommodationism, 20
Adam: evil and, 93; the fall and, 198–215;
  freedom of, 73–74; humanity of, 513n134;
  in image of God, 197–98; lament of,
  206; as living soul, 179; mourning by,
  208; nobility of, 211; obedience of, 207;
  postlapsarian, 206; sacrifice of, 142, 167;
  temptation of, 76
Adams, John, 24
adoption, spiritual, 367
adversity, uses of, 94
advocate, Jesus Christ as, 401–2
African Methodist Episcopal Church, 383
Agabus, 301n100
age of accountability, 161–62, 203, 381–82
age of Methodism, 224–25
Alexander, 446
Alexander, Thomas G., 186n32
Alexandria, church of, 322
Alma, 233–34, 238, 248, 249, 262
American Academy of Religion, 1
American Baptists, 374
amillennialism (nonmillennialism), 482.
  See also eschatology
Anabaptists, 374, 380, 408
analogical language, 22, 23

analogy, 22
anamnēsis (in remembrance), 396, 409–13
Ancient of days, 206
Anglican Articles of Religion, 415
Anglicans, Anglican Communion, 297,
  308, 323, 354
Anna, 301n100
anointed cloths, 448n50
anointing/anointing of the sick: as last-
  rites ritual, 453; oil for, 450; overview of,
  446–56; practice of, 387–88; as sacrament, 354; seven anointings, 451. *See also*
  healing
anonymous Christian, 501
antecedent causes, 196
anthropology, 5
anthropomorphism, 22
Antioch, 115, 322
Antiochene, 120–21
anti-Trinitarianism, 45, 46–47
Antonius Pius (emperor), 403
apocalyptic millenarianism, 480. *See also*
  eschatology
apocalypticism, 486–89. *See also* eschatology
Apollinarianism, 116–17
apophatic theology, 23
apostasy, 291, 310–11, 313
apostles, 297–98, 300–301. *See also specific
  persons*
Apostles' Creed, 11n15, 99, 481, 503, 511
apostolicity, 296–307
apostolic succession, 296–98
Apostolic Tradition, 384

Aquila, 457
Area Seventies, 343n119
Arminian Confession, 173
Arminianism, 223–24
Assemblies of God, 467
atonement: application of, 163; benefits of,
418; blessings of, 151; in *Christus Victor*
theory, 144–45; empowerment through,
174; as eternal, 296; from the fall, 160–61;
governmental theory of, 148; as healing
medicine, 165; history of, 143–50; as immortal creation, 515; as infinite, 157–63,
174, 296; as intimate, 174; kaleidoscopic
theory of, 149; LDS distinctives regarding, 172–76; LDS perspectives on, 150–57;
legal understanding of, 147–48; limited
nature of, 163–66; love and, 146; in moral
influence/moral exemplar theory, 145;
obedience and, 254; objective dimensions of, 145–46, 150–57; overcoming
through, 174; overview of, 141–42; penal
substitution theory for, 149, 156; power
of, 175; as propitiation, 152; reconciliation
and, 141; redemption through, 161n76;
for remission of sins, 365; resurrection
from, 161; saving benefits of, 164, 165;
shortcut phrases regarding, 175–76; sin
debt and, 156; subjective dimensions of,
145–46, 150–57; substitutionary, 147; sufficiency-efficacy distinction of, 163; term
usage, statistics of, 150; types of, 143–50
attrition, 438
authoritative teaching, 327–33
Azusa Street revival, 303n107

baited fishhook analogy, 144
baptism: as act of justification, 363; biblical
records of, 360n35; catechumenate and,
384; ceremony for, 392; child baptism
(pedobaptism), 377–78, 379–80, 383;
for church unity, 285; circumcision
and, 378–79; confirmation and, 386–94;
conversion and, 291; for the dead, 372,
506–7, 510–11; forgiveness of sins and,
362–65; as fundamental, 369; good works
and, 262; holiness and, 291, 379–80;

Holy Spirit's role in, 365, 386, 387n146;
imagery regarding, 361, 363–64; by
immersion, 373, 374–75; inclusion and,
378; incorporation into Christ and his
body, the church, 360–62; infant, 201–2,
203, 373, 377, 380–81, 382; by Jesus Christ,
356; justification through, 242n71, 364;
mode of, 372–77; Mormon mode of,
375–76; necessity of, 368–72; overview of,
359–60; pedobaptism (child baptism),
377–78, 379–80, 383; persons qualified
for, 377–83; preparation/requirements
for, 383–86; relationship image in, 361;
repentance and, 362, 437; requirements
for, 291; as sacrament, 354; salvation
and, 364, 368; sanctification and, 248;
as sealed document, 363–64; spiritual
rebirth and, 365–68; symbolism of, 361;
trine immersion, 373–74; validity of, 356
Baptism, Eucharist, and Ministry (BEM),
359, 363, 365, 375, 390, 431
Baptists, 408, 409n46, 423
Barnabas, 301n100
beginning, humankind in the, with God,
183–88
Benevolent Empire, 274
Benjamin (king), 233, 248, 262
Bible, 4, 15, 16–17. *See also* Scripture
binding and loosing, 317
birthright inclusion, 378
bishop of Rome, 320
bishops: absolution of sin and, 442–43; in
Catholic Church/Catholicism, 322–23,
326; conference of Holy Spirit by, 388;
discipline by, 440–41; function of, 326; in
Orthodox Christianity, 297, 322; role of,
297, 299
blood, 397, 398n8. *See also* Eucharist
"Body of Christ, The" (song), 279
Bohemian Confession of 1535, 414–15
Book of Common Prayer, 405–6
Book of Mormon: description of, 15; function of, 16; overview of, 15–16; purposes
of, 100; relationship with the Bible, 15.
See also Index of Scripture
Book of Mormon (musical), 1

born again, 220, 249–50
boundary maintenance, 4
Brethren, 423
building the kingdom, 273–74, 275–76. See also kingdom of God

calling(s), 231–39, 238n57, 344, 347
Callistus (pope), 49
canonization, 331–32
Canons of Dordt, 223
Cappadocians, 50–51
Carthage, 387
cataphaticism, 25
Catechism of the Catholic Church: on baptism, 368; on communion of the saints, 280; on contrition, 437; on creation, 66; on death, 509; on the Eucharist, 417–18, 431; on evil, 91; on God, 76; on healing, 454–55; on the Holy Spirit, 391; on infallibility, 328; on judgment, 495; on justification, 364; on matrimony, 456–57, 458; on penance, 439; on power of the keys, 317; on purgatory, 491; on the sacraments, 353, 356n19; on salvation, 260–61; on suffering, 456
catechumenate, 384
Catholic Church/Catholicism: anointing of the sick in, 450, 451–52, 453, 454–55; on atonement for the dead, 509–10; bishops in, 322–23, 326; church as, 292–96; contraception and, 464; contrition and, 438; conversion and, 437; counseling and, 439; Decree on Ecumenism (Unitatis Redintegratio) (Vatican II), 283, 328; defined, 292; Dogmatic Constitution Lumen Gentium of, 321–22, 337, 389; ecclesial leadership of, 320; Eucharist and, 399–401, 414; on good works, 261; on grace, 260–61; human freedom viewpoint of, 75; infallibility of, 329–30, 337; intermediate state in, 499; on Jesus's suffering, 167; on keys of the kingdom, 317; laity discernment in, 337; liturgies of, 425–26, 476; Liturgy of the Word of, 425, 451; magisterium, 327–30; marital indissolubility and, 463–64; Mass of, 425–26;

Morman viewpoint of, 312–13; ordination in, 341; penance and, 442; penitential system of, 445; on postmortem judgment, 495; priesthood in, 345–46; purgatory in, 491–92; revelation viewpoint of, 335–36; Rite of Penance, 442; rivalries in, 276–77; sacraments of, 341, 354, 356; salvation and, 260–61, 501–2; sanctification and, 252; on Satan, 93; supreme/extraordinary magisterium of, 328–29; unity in, 282–83; Vatican II, 321; Vulgate, 435n1. See also Roman Catholic Church
Catholic International Theological Commission, 337
Catholic Rite of Penance, 442
causality, 76–77
Celestial Kingdom of heaven, 529–30, 532–33, 536
celestial marriage, 459–60, 461. See also matrimony
celibacy, 457–58
chain of consumption, 515
Chalcedonian Christology, 122
chaos, creation versus, 62–63
charismatic renewal movement, 334–35
children: age of accountability of, 161–62, 203, 381–82; baptism (pedobaptism), 377–78, 379–80, 383; in eternity, 517n155; sin and, 213. See also baptism; infants
children of God, 367–68
chiliasm, 480, 486
chrism, 387
chrismation, 387–88
Christian, defined, 3–4
Christian Church (Disciples of Christ), 375
Christian discipleship, 252, 258
Christianity, 3–4, 276–77. See also specific types
Christlikeness, 250
Christology, 5, 101n7, 122–25
Christus Victor theory, 144–45
church: apostasy of, 310–11, 313; as apostolic, 296–307; as body of Christ, 278; as bride of Christ, 361; as Catholic, 292–96; as Christianity, 276; communion of the saints and, 280; competition of, 308;

conflict in, 309; denominations of, 308; discipline in, 440–41; diversity of, 279; dual application of, 269; ecumenism in, 284; evil and, 313; the gathering and, 286; as holy, 286–92; as Icon of the Trinity, 278; images for, 269–70; incorporation into, 360–62; interfaith dialogue in, 283–84; as invisible/hidden, 280–82, 310; as kingdom of God, 270–76; membership, 278, 386n139; Nicene-Constantinopolitan affirmation of, 276; as one, 276–86; overview of, 268–70; persecution of, 287; as pilgrim people, 288; protecting integrity of, 291n69; on rock of revelation, 336; routing of, 310; sacrament performance in, 354–55; salvation and, 220; support for, 308; as temple of the Holy Spirit, 278; unity of, 277–78, 282–83, 285
Church of God (Cleveland, TN), 467
Church of God in Christ, 467
Church of Jesus Christ of Latter-day Saints: activism of, 275; claim of, 311; conferences of, 10; as conservative, 465; contrasts of, 312; Council of, 298; defined, 269; diversity of, 279; expansion of, 2; general authorities of, 10; as God's earthly kingdom, 271; humanitarian and relief efforts of, 275; as inclusivist, 314; interfaith dialogue in, 283–84; language style changes of, 70; open canon of, 336; ordination in, 338; origin of, 2, 4, 46; primacy of, 324; reformation of, 311; Scripture of, 14–15; statistics regarding, 4; terms of, 5. *See also* Mormonism
Church of the Nazarene, 289
Cicero, 84
circumcision, 378–79
civil marriages, 459, 461–62. *See also* matrimony
Claremont Graduate University, 1
Clarke, Wycom, 97n117
classical theism, 106
clothing, temple, 474–75
commitment, sacraments of, 354
common consent doctrine, 338
common sense realism, 205

communicatio idiomatum (exchange/sharing of properties), 118, 120
communion, defined, 421n91. *See also* Eucharist
communion of the saints, 280, 294–95
comparison, value of, 7
compassion of God, 43
compatibilism, 75
Compendium of the Doctrines of the Gospel (Richards and Little), 12n17
confession, 438–39, 441
confirmation, 354, 386–94
Congregationalists, 308, 408n44
Constantinople, church of, 322
consubstantiation, 402, 405
Continental Anabaptists, 374
contraception, 464–65
contrition, 233, 233n48, 437, 438–39
conversion, 233–34, 248, 251, 251n95, 257
conviction, 232
Copenhagen Cathedral, 318
Cornelius, 360n35, 392–93
cosmogony, 64
cosmology, 32
Council of Antioch, 48
Council of Chalcedon, 116n59, 117–18, 120, 121, 137
Council of Constance, 321
Council of Nicaea, 101
Council of the Twelve Apostles. *See* Quorum of the Twelve Apostles
Council of Trent, 242n67, 368, 371n81, 417–18, 435n1, 453
counseling, 439
covenant, 378, 378n106, 398–99, 398n8
covenant of exaltation, 542–43
covenant of redemption (*pactum salutis*), 163
creatio ex nihilo, 62
creation: chaos *versus*, 62–63; curse on, 208; *ex nihilo*, 62; the fall and, 197–215; God's sovereignty over, 67; overview of, 61–66; purpose of, 61; redemption and, 61–62; reorganization of matter in, 65; Smith's insertion regarding, 194; in state of journeying, 66

creationism, 181
Crispus, 360n35
Croall Lectures, 52–53
crucifixion of Jesus Christ: agony in, 167–68; foreshadowing of, 399; Garden of Gethsemane and, 167–69, 170–72; God's anger and, 152–53; God's suffering in, 154; LDS distinctives regarding, 172–76; as outweighing sin, 157; passion of Jesus Christ in, 166–72; purpose of, 140; as ransom payment, 144; redemption in, 140; redemptive mission of, 158; satisfaction theories of, 147; significance of, 140, 143, 149, 174; sufficiency-efficacy distinction of, 163; veil tearing at, 159. *See also* atonement; Eucharist
cult, 340n112
curse, 208
Cyrus (Persian ruler), 73, 76

Daniel (prophet), 206, 271n7
daughters of Philip, 301n100
Day of Pentecost, 360n35, 386–87
deacons, 300
dead/death: acceptance at, 502; baptism for, 372, 506–7, 510–11; freedom of choice of, 508; incarnation and, 211–12; intermediate state and, 489–500; purification following, 500; redemption for, 507; ritual linkage of, 506–8; salvation for, 500–511; sealing ordinance for, 506–8; sin and, 211; spiritual, 212
debt, 147–48
debtor-creditor analogy, 155–56
Decius (emperor), 287
Decree on Ecumenism (*Unitatis Redintegratio*) (Vatican II), 283
dedication, infant, 383
deification, 247n84, 534, 535–36, 539–43
deliverance, 234
demons, 93
determinism, 74, 85
Didache, 373, 387
disability, law and, 162n79
disciples, 297–98, 441–42, 446–47
discipleship, 252, 258

discipline, church, 440–41, 446
disobedience, 77, 78
dispensationalism, 481
divine embodiment, 19–24, 25–30
divine impassibility, 39–44
divine investiture of authority, 57–58
divine otherness, 29
divine providence, 66. *See also* providence
divine simplicity, 39–44
divinity, 56, 106
divorce, 464
Dixie Wine Mission, 423
docetism, 115–16
Doctrine and Covenants, 15n21, 17, 331n85. *See also Index of Scripture*
Doctrines of Salvation (Smith), 12n17
dogma, 328n71
Dogmatic Constitution, 321–22, 501
donatism, 355–56
Donatists, 355–56
Descensus Christi ad inferos ("Christ's Descent to the underworld/hell"), 504
dualist/dichotomist anthropology, 178, 179
dyotheletism (two-wills-ism), 123

Eastern Orthodoxy. *See* Orthodox Christianity
Easter Proclamation, 207n112
Ebionism, 115–16
ecclesiology, 5
Eckhart, "Meister," 538
economy/economic, defined, 51n111
ecumenism, 284
Einstein, Albert, 197
ekklēsia (summoned assemblage of people), 268–69. *See also* church
Ekthesis, 123–24n84
elders, 299, 301n99, 450–51
election, 222–23, 225–31
elements, principles of, 64
Elizabeth (queen), 320
Elohim, 108, 109–10, 131. *See also* God
emotions, 40, 41. *See also specific emotions*
endowment, 466–77
endurance to the end, doctrine of, 251
English Baptists, 374

Enlightenment, 24, 205
Enoch, 43, 77, 285–86, 505
Episcopalians, 308
equivocal language, 22
Esau, 196, 228–29, 230
eschatology: amillennialism (nonmillennialism), 482; apocalyptic millenarianism, 480; apocalyptism, 486–89; chiliasm, 480, 486; defined, 5, 479; degrees of heavenly glory, 524–32; dispensationalism, 481; early Mormonism and, 486–89; the "end" of history and, 480–86; eternal life, 532–44; exaltation, 532–44; final judgment, 495; final/last judgment, 517–20; first resurrection and, 481; intermediate state, 489–500; marriage supper of the Lamb and, 430–34; millenarianism, 480–81; millennium in, 272, 480, 481–82; near-death experiences (NDEs) and, 479; new heaven and new earth, 481, 482–83, 523; New Jerusalem, 483–84; outer darkness, 493; paradise, 490, 493, 495, 496–97, 499; postmillennialism, 482; postmortem purification in, 500; premillennialism, 480, 484–85; providence and, 66; publications regarding, 478–79; public fascination regarding, 479; rapture, 485; resurrection of the body, 511–17; salvation for the dead, 500–511; second coming of Jesus Christ, 88, 432–33, 484, 488; soul sleep (psychopannychia), 492; spirit world, 493–95, 498–99; tribulation, 485; viewpoint variations regarding, 481. *See also* heaven; hell
eternal law, 152
eternal life, 261, 532–44
eternal marriage, 459–60. *See also* matrimony
eternity/eternal, defined, 35
Ethiopian eunuch, 360n35
Eucharist: *anamnēsis* (in remembrance) of, 396, 409–13; baptismal covenant renewal in, 393; behavior during, 400, 415–17; benefits of, 400, 408, 413–17; biblical references regarding, 395–96; blood in, 397, 422–24; bread in, 422–24; Bread of

Life and, 411–12; as commemorative, 408; communion through, 421–22; consubstantiation, 402, 405; as converting ordinance, 291; effects of, 413–17; elements/emblems of, 422–24; eschatological marriage supper of the Lamb and, 430–34; *ex opere operantis* fashion of, 413–14; as foreshadowing, 397; forgiveness of sins and, 417–19; formulas regarding, 404; frequency of, 424–25; general meanings of, 396–99; holiness and, 412; Holy Spirit in, 406, 407, 408; hymns regarding, 427–30; Latter-day Saint sacramental liturgy of, 426–30; liturgies of, 424–26; memorialism, 402; in the Middle Ages, 403–4; Mormon memorialism and, 409–13, 423; new covenant and, 397–98; overview of, 395–96; participants as worthy receivers of, 357–58n26; preparation for, 417; presence of Christ in, 402–8; as propitiation, 399; purpose of, 396, 408; as sacrament, 352, 354; as sacrifice, 400, 401; sacrificial nature of, 399–402; significance of, 352; spiritual presence, 402; subjective view of, 402; substantialist/objective view of, 402; testament in, 398; transubstantiation, 402–4; union with Christ and Christ's body, 420–22; unity through, 280; unworthiness and, 415–16; wine/juice in, 422–24
evangelical covenant (*pactum evangelicum*), 163
evangelism of fear, 232
evangelization, in intermediate state, 165
Eve: evil and, 93; the fall and, 197–215; freedom of, 73–74; humanity of, 513n134; mourning by, 208; nobility of, 211; sacrifice of, 142; sin of, 209; temptation of, 76
evil, 90–98. *See also* sin(s)
evolution, 179
exaltation, 210, 219, 532–44
exchange formula, 540
exclusivism, 314
excommunication, 317, 446
exculpation, 92
ex opere operantis, 355–58, 393, 413–14

ex opere operato, 355–58, 418
expiation, 154–55

faith, 242–43, 244, 246, 254
fall, the, 160–61, 197–215, 234n50, 256, 260
family, in heaven, 522–23
"Family, The: A Proclamation to the World," 465–66
family planning, 464–65
fear, evangelism of, 232
Fielding, Mary, 97n117
Fifth Ecumenical Council, 119
final/last judgment, 495, 510–11, 517–20
First Cause, God as, 61, 76
First Presidency: apostles in, 298; declaration of, 103, 303; on *Elohim*, 131; function of, 324, 325–27; on God, 132; on heavenly Mother, 189; on *imago dei* (image of God), 189, 193n58; on intelligences, 187; as magisterium, 327–33; proclamation of, 65, 157–58, 327, 537–38; on spirits, 111; on spiritual rebirth, 367; titles of, 302
"first resurrection," 481
Fletcher, John, 440
foreknowledge, 82, 84–90, 228, 229n35, 230
foreordination, 231n42
forgiveness: of Adam and Eve, 207; elements of, 244; Eucharist and, 417–19; from God, 443; healing and, 452–53; heaven and, 530; overview of, 362–65; repeated, 436
Forgiveness Sunday, 206
fortunate fall, doctrine of the, 207
Fourth Lateran Council, 23, 403n26
free agency, 210
freedom, 72–77, 84–86
Freemasonry, 472–73
free will, 224, 225–26, 227, 229
fullness of the gospel, 293

garden of Eden, 198
Garden of Gethsemane, 167–69, 170–72
gathering, the, doctrine of, 286
gender, defined, 194
General Authority Seventies, 343n119
General Handbook (Latter-day Saints): on baptism, 376; on endowment, 466; on eternal life, 533; on keys of the kingdom, 319; on marriage, 465–66n116; on ordinances, 352; on other faiths, 314; on prebaptismal catechesis, 385; on priesthood, 311, 348; on repentance, 438, 441; on temple endowment, 470n129
gift, defined, 394n169
gift-giving, 244
gift of the Holy Ghost, 392–93. *See also* Holy Spirit
glorification, 231
glory, degrees of, in heaven, 524–32
Gnosticism, 137
God: analogy regarding, 22; anger of, 153, 154; anthropomorphic nature of, 57; attributes of, 30–33; body of, 192–93; cataphaticism regarding, 25; characteristics of, 22; chasm regarding, 20; as coeternal, 185; commitments of, 164; compassion of, 43; as in conflict with evil, 95; creation and, 61–66; curse from, 208; dependence on, 267; distrust of, 96; divine otherness of, 29; divinity of, 106; as *Elohim*, 108, 131; emotions of, 40, 41; as enfleshed man, 26; as eternal, 95; eternal law and, 152; as Father, 27, 35–36, 57, 70, 95, 107, 153; as First Cause, 61, 76; foreknowledge of, 82, 84–90, 228, 229n35, 230; goodness of, 92, 261; *imago dei* (image of God) of, 189–94, 200, 534, 535; intervention by, 82; Jesus's distinction from, 103, 108–9, 122–23; Jesus's relationship with, 107; as judge, 517–20; as justice, 152; limitations of, 83; love of, 41, 153, 154; metaphor regarding, 22; middle knowledge of, 85–86; as missionary, 502; omnipotence of, 31, 32; omnipresence of, 31, 32, 494–95; omniscience of, 31, 32, 38, 84–86; passion of, 41; perfection of, 36, 38; personages of, 25; as personal, 27; persuasive power of, 82; predetermination by, 76, 501; presence of, 28, 533; procreation of, 190; progression and, 34–39; providence and, 66–70, 72–73, 87; purposes of, 70; reign of, 270n5; relationship with, 27,

191; resourcefulness of, 84; revelations from, 332, 502; righteousness of, 195–96; rule of, 68, 73, 107, 148; salvation and, 52; as source of unity, 278; sovereignty of, 67, 72–83, 86–90, 148; spiritual corporeality of, 25–26n24; suffering and, 42–44, 154; superintendence of, 70; as Supreme Judge, 148; temporality of, 35; time and, 34–39; trustworthiness of, 39; understanding, 23; vulnerability of, 42; weeping by, 77; will of, 72, 84; worthiness of, 42; wrath of, 154; as *YHWH*, 108. *See also specific aspects*

Godhead, defined, 55

goodness, of humanity, 214

gospel, 293, 295, 502

Gospel, The (Roberts), 12n17

Gospel Principles, 12n17

governmental theory of atonement, 148–49

grace: anonymous Christian and, 501; collaboration with, 251; cooperation of, 238; enabling from, 234–35, 238, 263; essentiality of, 254–55; as gift, 217; God's supply of, 165; help from, 266; Holy Spirit and, 236; hope in, 267; impacts of, 438–39; irresistible, 226; as ladder, 260; light of Christ and, 235–36; power of, 215; prevenient, 235; primacy of, 235; priority of, 235; redemption through, 161; regeneration and, 249; salvation and, 221, 267, 518n159; for saving faith, 165; sin and, 92; for souls, 235; statements regarding, 216–17; terms for, 216; word of God and, 237–38; working with, 238; works and, 253–67

Great Awakening, 248

Great Commission, 304, 359, 378

Great Schism, 321

Gregory I, 320

Guide to the Scriptures: on afterlife, 536; on atonement, 161; on election, 231; on God, 32; on light of Christ, 235n52; on "omnis," 32; on spiritual rebirth, 367

guilt culture, 232

hard-heartedness, 80–81

healing: faith for, 455; forgiveness and, 452–53; instances of, 306; in ordained ministry, 449–50; overview of, 446–56; sacraments of, 354; story of, 448; through medical assistance, 454; will of God and, 455; words spoken in, 455. *See also* anointing/anointing of the sick

heaven: anthropocentric views of, 520, 521–24, 542–44; assumptions regarding, 263n137; Celestial Kingdom of, 529–30, 532–33, 536; degrees of glory in, 524–32; description of, 521; family in, 522–23; following purgatory, 491; mansions in, 527; marriage in, 461–62; overview of, 520–24; personal progress in, 535; relationships in, 462–63; in rich man and Lazarus parable, 490; Smith's view regarding, 29, 134; Telestial Kingdom of, 529–30, 531, 532; Terrestrial Kingdom of, 529–30; theocentric views of, 520–21. *See also* eschatology

heavenly Mother, 188–89

Heidelberg Catechism, 363, 420

hell: description of, 493, 498, 499, 531–32; geography of, 499; Jesus descending into, 503–5; kinds of persons in, 498; obsession with, 232; overview of, 497; in rich man and Lazarus parable, 490; as spirit prison, 498, 500. *See also* eschatology

hermeneutic, defined, 20n5

heterogeneity, 221

Hezekiah (king), 89

history, end of, 480–86

Hitler, Adolf, 530–31

holiness: baptism and, 291, 379–80; of the church, 286–92; defined, 287; forms of, 291–92; process of, 250; pursuit of, 290; sanctity and, 288; as tangible, 290

holistic dualism, 492n45

Holocaust, 96

Holy Spirit: anointing and, 387–88; baptism and, 365, 386, 387n146; benefits of, 394; companionship of, 393–94; confirmation and, 386–94; enticing from, 236; in the Eucharist, 406, 407, 408; gifts from, 392–93; grace and giftings from, 344;

guidance of, 334–35; holiness from, 288; impressions of, 394; indwelling of, 246, 387, 388; at ordination, 341; outpouring of, 275; power from, 129–30; promptings of, 394; renewal through, 246; sanctification and, 246, 248; sanctity through, 288; as soul of unity, 278; speaking in tongues and, 467; vivification by, 357

hope, in grace, 267

human agency, 70, 77–83, 88, 89

humanitarianism, 275

humanity: attributes of, 124; as in the beginning with God, 183–88; body of, 178; as children of God, 367–68; choices by, 76; as coeternal, 185; constitution of, 177–80; dual nature of, 124; earthly bodies of, 490; as enemy of God, 236; evolution of, 179; the fall and, 197–215; freedom of, 72–77, 84–86; as God's spirit children, 78–79; goodness of, 214; greatness of, 177; *imago dei* (image of God) and, 189–94; impulses of, 124; intelligences and, 185–88; in intermediate state, 489–500; as literal sons and daughters of God, 27; nature of, 197–215; original sin and, 125; personal growth of, 535; preexistentialism and, 194–97; redemption need of, 112; responsibility of, 266; resurrection of, 511–17; seeds of divinity of, 214; soul of, 178, 180–83; spirit of, 178, 188–89; total depravity of, 202; wretchedness of, 177

Hussein, Saddam, 530–31

Hymenaeus, 446

hymns, for the Eucharist, 427–30

hypostasis, 50

hypothetical acceptance, 502, 505–6

hypothetical universalism, 163, 165

identity, in Christ, 361

illumination, sacraments of, 354

imago dei (image of God), 189–94, 200, 534, 535

immanent, defined, 51n111

impressions of the Holy Spirit, 394

incarnation of Jesus Christ: death and, 211–12; mystery of, 118; overview of, 111–15; purpose of, 114–15, 540; redemptive purpose of, 113; terms regarding, 112

inclusivism, 314

infants: baptism of, 201–2, 203, 373, 377, 380–81, 382; dedication of, 383; dependence of, 247–48; in eternity, 517n155. *See also* children

initiation, 354, 359n30, 372n87

initiatory, 469

Innocent I (pope), 387n148

Innocent III (pope), 320, 357n21

intelligences, 184, 185–88

interfaith dialogue, 283–84

intermediate state, 489–500. *See also* eschatology

International Association of Near-Death Studies, 479

Internet analogy, 541

"Invictus" (Henley), 263–64

Irenaeus, 126n90

Isaac, 154

Israel, 80, 81

Israelites, 142

Israelite theology, 19

Jacob, 196, 228, 230

James (apostle), 325n58

Jefferson, Thomas, 24, 34

Jehovah's Witnesses, 492

Jeremiah, 231n42

Jerusalem, church of, 322

Jesus Christ: as administrator of sacraments, 358; as advocate, 401–2; as *archēgos* of human salvation, 134; ascension of, 137–39; atonement from, 254, 365, 418, 515; baptism and, 48, 135, 240, 356, 369–70, 371; as begotten, 105, 106; as Bread of Life, 411; cleansing by, 287; as coeternal, 185; conjunction of natures of, 120; creation through, 61; death of, 120; dependence on Holy Spirit by, 129–30; distinction from God, 103, 108–9, 122–23; divine investiture of authority on, 58; divinity of, 54, 58, 101, 102, 105, 115–22; dual consciousness of, 122, 124; earth life of, 126–36; empathy of, 114; emptying of, 126, 127; enemies of, 119; estates of, 101; as eternal God, 103; as first, 105; as forerunner, 115; as founder of unity, 278; fullness of, 135–36, 251; glorification of, 31, 137–39; God's relationship with, 107; as Good Shepherd, 317; as great high priest, 399; growth and development of, 129; as head of the church, 278; healing by, 120; heavenly presence of, 401–2; in hell, 503–5; holiness through, 288; humanity of, 115–22; as humanity's Elder Brother, 105; hypostatic union of, 118, 120; "I have come" sayings of, 102–3; imitation of, 144; incarnation of, 111–15, 118; incorporation into, 360–62; as Jehovah of the Old Testament, 108, 110–11; joint tenancy of, 117; judgment by, 480; justification through, 245; kenosis of, 126–36; on keys of the kingdom, 315–19; on kingdom of God, 270; LDS Christology regarding, 122–25; as Logos, 103–4; on marriage, 461; as *mesitēs*, 398; ministry of, 143, 346; natures of, 115–22; obsession with, 100–101; omniscience of, 127–28; passion exclamations of, 124; passion of, 166–72; paternity of, 131–32; perfection of, 136; personages of, 25; personal relationship with, 220; power of, 129–30; prayer of, 103; preexistence of, 101–11; presence of, in the Eucharist, 402–8; priesthood of, 340; *prokopē* of, 126–36; as prophet, 301n100; as propitiation, 142n6; proving by, 115; psychological unity of, 117; reception of, 135; as reconciler, 140, 142; redemption through, 209, 366; reign of, 270n5; as representative, 112; resurrection of, 137–39; as revealer of God, 140; revealing to, 128–29; as ruler, 140; sacraments instituted by, 353–54; sacrifice of, 144, 152, 154, 225, 258, 340, 346, 399, 438; salvation through, 218, 260, 265; as Savior, 144; as second Adam, 112, 113, 198; second coming of, 88; Sermon on the Mount of, 73, 519–20, 524; significance of, 143; sinlessness of, 115, 125; on spiritual rebirth, 365; as substitute for sin, 157; suffering of, 43–44, 118, 166–72; surrender of, 170; sympathy of, 114; as teacher, 303; as temple, 116; testimony of, 142; title of, 130; union with, 247–48; veiling of, 127–28; victory of, 133; will of, 48; as the Word, 102, 104; worship of, 44, 99, 107. *See also* incarnation of Jesus Christ

Jews, restoration of, 73, 76

Job, 68, 203

John (apostle), 102, 325n58

John the Baptist, 301n100, 365, 370, 371–72

Joint Declaration on the Doctrine of Justification (JDDJ), 245–46, 261

Jonah, 89

Joseph, 76

Joseph (husband of Mary), 239–40

Joseph Smith Papers, The (JSP), overview of, 13–14n20

Journal of Near-Death Studies, 479

Judas, 76, 356

Judas Barsabbas, 301n100

Judas Maccabeus, 509–10

jurisdiction, of private revelation, 336

justice, 148, 152, 153

justification: *admirabile commercium* (wonderful exchange) and, 240–41, 245, 246; baptism and, 242n71, 364; contradiction of, 244; defined, 143; effective aspect of, 240; by faith, 242–43; faith and works in, 254; overview of, 239–45; regeneration and, 248; righteousness and, 240, 241; salvation and, 241; as sanctification, 245–53; by works, 243, 259

kaleidoscopic theory of atonement, 149

kenoticism, 126–36

keys of the kingdom, 315–19, 324–25

kingdom of God, 270–76, 371n85

kingdom of heaven, 272–73

King Follett Sermon, 185

Kirtland (OH) temple, 467, 468–69

koinōnos, 539n235

Landmark Baptists, 375

language, types of, 22

last/final judgment, 495, 510–11, 517–20

Late Great Planet Earth, The (Lindsey), 478

Latter-day Saints. *See* Church of Jesus Christ of Latter-day Saints
law court, language of, 151
law of chastity, 469–70
law of sacrifice, 469
"Laws," sin resolution and, 440
lay priesthood, 339. *See also* priesthood
Lazarus, 490
Lectures on Faith, 26n24, 32
Left Behind book series (LaHaye and Jenkins), 478
Lehi, 94
Levi, 201
Levi, tribe of, 339, 349
LGBTQ identity, 465
liberal theology, 215
Libertarians, 74
Life after Life (Moody), 478–79
light of Christ, 235–36
liturgy, 354, 424–30
Liturgy of the Word, 425, 427, 451
logos, 103–4
Logos Christology, 104, 105
London Baptist Confession, 493n48
Lord's Supper. *See* Eucharist
love, 42, 190–91, 217
Lucian of Antioch, 116
Lucifer. *See* Satan
Lucius, 301n100
Lumen Gentium, 321–22, 337, 389, 501
Luther, Martin, 73n33, 492
Lutheran Augsburg Confession, 368
Lutheran Church/Lutheranism, 297, 323, 414, 437
Lutheran–Roman Catholic Commission on Unity, 346
Lutheran World Federation, 245
Lydia, 360n35

magisterium, 327–33
Manaen, 301n100
Manichaeism, 90–91
manifestations, 306–7
mansions, in heaven, 527
Marburg Colloquy, 403n25, 407n38
marriage. *See* matrimony

marriage supper of the Lamb, 430–34
Mary Magdalene, 495
Masonry, 472–73
matrimony: annulment, 464; celestial, 459–60, 461; civil, 459, 461–62; deification and, 542–43; divorce and, 464; eternal, 459–60; in heaven, 461–62; indissolubility of, 463–64; Jesus's views regarding, 457; LGBTQ identity and, 465; monogamy, 460, 542n240; overview of, 456–66; plural, 460–61, 542n240; polygamy, 460; relationship image in, 361; as sacrament, 354; temple marriage sealings, 459, 462
matter, 33–34, 65
medicine, healing through, 454
Melchizedek, 201, 340, 397n6, 450
Melchizedek Priesthood, 342, 343, 350. *See also* priesthood
mercy, 148, 153
mesitēs, 398
metaphor, 23, 218, 316
metaphysics, 22–23n13, 33
Methodism, 323, 408n44, 423, 431
Miaphysitism (one-nature-ism), 121
Michael "the Archangel," 206, 208
Michelangelo, 197
Middle Ages, 510n119
middle knowledge of God, 85–86
millenarianism, 480–81. *See also* eschatology
millennium, 272, 480, 481–82. *See also* eschatology
ministerial appointments, 302
ministerial priesthood, 339–44. *See also* priesthood
miracles, 305
missionaries, 301, 315, 347–48, 386, 457–58
modalist, 49
modernism, 215
Molinism, 85–86
Monarchianism, 49
monergism, 219, 222, 224
monogamy, 460, 542n240. *See also* matrimony
Monophysitism (one-nature-ism), 121, 123

monotheletism (one-will-ism), 123n84
moral influence/moral exemplar theory, 145
Mormon, defined, 4
Mormon Doctrine (McConkie), 12n17
Mormon Doctrine, Plain and Simple (Penrose), 12n17
Mormonism: biblical restorationism of, 272; doctrine in, 10–11; early, 486–89; literature regarding, 12–13; preached theology in, 10; public attention on, 1. *See also* Church of Jesus Christ of Latter-day Saints; *specific doctrines*
Mormon memorialism, 409–13, 423
Mormon studies, development of, 1
Mormon Zion, 88–89
Mosaic covenant, 397–98
Moses, 65, 191, 197, 339, 397
Mozart, Wolfgang Amadeus, 197
myth, defined, 198

"Naming and Blessing Children," 383
naturalistic theism, 81–82
natural law, age of accountability and, 162n78
Nauvoo healings, 448, 450n56
Nauvoo Temple, 472–73n138
Nazis, 96
Near-Death Experience Research Foundation, 479
near-death experiences (NDEs), 479
Nebuchadnezzar, 271n7
Nestorianism, 121
new covenant, 398
New Haven theology, 205
new heaven and new earth, 481, 482–83, 523. *See also* eschatology
New Jerusalem, 483–84, 524n178
New Testament, and length comparisons, 15n21. *See also Index of Scripture*
New World Zion, 286n56
Nicene-Constantinopolitan creed, 335, 362–63
Nicene Creed, 49–50, 101
Nicodemus, 365, 376n100
Nineveh, 89

Ninth Similitude parable, 503
Noah, 368n71

obedience, 217, 244, 246, 254
oil, for anointing, 450
Olivet discourse, 484n17, 485
omnipotence of God, 31, 32
omnipresence of God, 31, 32, 494–95
omniscience of God, 31, 32, 38, 84–86
oneness, 276–86
ontology, 26–27
openness theology, 82–83
ordained ministry, 341, 449–50
ordinances: defined, 352; *ex opere operantis* and, 355–58; *ex opere operato* and, 355–58; priesthood authority regarding, 358; promise of grace in, 358; requirements for, 355. *See also* sacraments
ordination, 302, 338, 344, 354
Orthodox Christianity: anointing of the sick in, 450, 451, 452, 453, 454; on atonement for the dead, 510–11; bishops in, 297, 322; on the church, 283, 476; confession and, 439, 443; counseling and, 439; divine guidance in, 334–35; governance of, 322; human freedom viewpoint of, 75; intermediate state in, 491–92; on Jesus's suffering, 168; on keys of the kingdom, 317–18; marital indissolubility and, 463–64; matrimony and, 458–59, 462–63; on Old Testament theophanies, 110; priesthood in, 348n135; providence view in, 66; repentance and, 437; sacraments of, 354, 357; on sin, 205; on spiritual body, 514; traditions of, 334, 336; Trisagion (Thrice Holy) liturgy of, 495–96; on works, 262
outer darkness, 493

pactum evangelicum (evangelical covenant), 163
pactum salutis (covenant of redemption), 163
paradise, 490, 493, 495, 496–97, 499
parallelomania, 7
parents, 381, 385
Pascal, Blaise, 24

Paschal Mystery, 353

passion, 41, 166–72

pastors, 298–99, 300, 440–41

Paul (the apostle), 4, 15, 213; baptism of, 360n35, 364; on baptism, 360, 361, 365–66, 378; on the church, 278–80, 287, 294; conversion of, 364; eschatology and the afterlife, 485, 489, 526, 529; and the Eucharist, 412, 414, 446, 448; on faith and works, 243–45, 255n108; on the fall, 198–99, 211; on human agency *versus* God's control of human choices, 76, 81, 196; on Jesus as "the Lord of glory," 119; martyrdom of, 320n45; on matrimony, 457–58; ministry of, 387n142; on offices in the church, 298, 300n94, 302n102, 303; on prophecy, 336–37; and resurrection of the body, 512, 525–26; and the sacraments, 358, 454, 456; on salvation, 217–18, 227

Paul of Samosata, 116

peace offering, 398n9

Pearl of Great Price, 17, 331n85. *See also Index of Scripture*

pedobaptism (child baptism), 377–78, 379–80, 383. *See also* baptism

Pelagianism, 266

Pelagians, 74, 200, 256

penal nonsubstitution, 148

penal substitution theory, 148, 149, 156

penal theory of atonement, 147

penance: confession and, 438–39; financial contributions and, 445; overview of, 435–46; penitential order of, 444–45; as sacrament, 354; satisfactional, 444–45

Pentecost, Day of, 360n35, 386–87

Pentecostalism, 331, 334–35, 381, 447–48, 467–68n120

perfectionism, 252

persecution, 287, 486

personage, defined, 25, 25n23

personal revelation, 336–37

personal righteousness, 210

Peter (apostle), 116n61, 242, 296–97, 299n92, 300n94, 315–16, 320n45, 325n58, 333, 386–87, 512

Pharaoh, 80, 81

Pharisees, 270

Philip, 387

Philip, daughters of, 301n100

Philippian jailor, baptism of, 360n35

Photinus, 21

physicalism, 180, 492n45

Pietists, 273

Pius V (pope), 320

Pius XI (pope), 282

Platonism, 24, 138, 181–82

pluralism, 314

plural marriage, 460–61, 542n240. *See also* matrimony

Polish Protestantism, 45

polygamy, 4–5n6, 460. *See also* matrimony

popes, overview of, 319–27. *See also specific persons*

postmillennialism, 482

postmortem ministry, 502

postmortem purification, 500

praise, 400

prayer, 83, 103

prayer cloths, 448n50

Preach My Gospel handbook, 385

prebaptismal catechesis, 384–85

predestination, 222, 228, 229, 501

predetermination, 76

pre-earth council, 79–80

preexistentialism, 181, 182, 183, 193, 194–97

premillennialism, 480, 484–85. *See also* eschatology

presbyter, 299

Presbyterians/Presbyterian church, 323, 408n44, 415

priesthood: Aaronic/Levitical Priesthood, 342–43, 350; absolution from sin and, 443; of all Christians, 344–50; authority in, 347; calling and preparation of, 229n35; common, 350; confession to, 443; defined, 339, 347, 348; function of, 339, 343–44; keys, 319; lay, 339; Melchizedek, 342, 343, 350; ministerial, 339–44; ordinances and, 358; ordination and, 342; overview of, 339–44; robes of, 474–75

primacy, 319–27

primary causation, 75–76
Primary organization, 385
Prisca, 457
prisca theologia (theology of the ancients), 371
Priscillianism, 182
progression, 34–39
Progressive Era, 535
promptings of the Holy Spirit, 394
prophecy, 86–90, 307
prophet-president, 324–25
prophets, 298, 300, 301–2, 319–27, 330–31. *See also specific persons*
propitiation, 152, 154–55
Proposition 8 (California), 1
Protestantism: breaking away in, 280; on heaven, 526; penance and, 445; priesthood in, 345, 440; rivalries in, 276–77; sacraments of, 354
providence: appeal of doctrine of, 70–72; eschatology and, 66; overview of, 66–70; problem of evil and, 90–98; salvation and, 66; suffering and, 90–98; will of God and, 72–73
psychopannychia (soul sleep), 492
purgatory, 491–92. *See also* eschatology
purification, 362, 500
Puritans, 290–91, 415

Quakers, 220
Quorum of the Twelve Apostles: on atonement, 157; authority of, 343n119; declaration of, 103, 303; function of, 298, 324, 326–27; on God, 65; on image of God, 189; as magisterium, 327–33; proclamation of, 327, 537–38; on prophets, 302; on spirits, 111; statement by, 325–26; titles of, 302

ransom, payment of, 144
rapture, 485. *See also* eschatology
rationalism, 205
Rational Theology (Widtsoe), 12n17
rebirth, 248
reciprocity, 244
reconciliation, 141, 142, 144, 215, 435–46

redemption: in atonement, 161n76; centrality of, 140; creation and, 61–62; in crucifixion of Jesus Christ, 140; for the dead, 507; defined, 143; need for, 112; through ascension of Jesus Christ, 137; through grace, 161; through incarnation, 113; through Jesus Christ, 209, 366; as universal, 163
reformation, 290, 311
Reformation: atonement and, 147, 156; baptism in, 374; Bible translation in, 435n1; body of Christ and, 270; challenges in, 45; doctrinal statement of, 76; documents of, 137; faith and works and, 262; impacts of, 276; justification and, 240; predestination and, 222; total depravity and, 202
regeneration, 248, 249, 257
Relief Society, 349
repentance: availability of, 215; baptism and, 362, 437; conditions of, 172; confession and, 438–39; contrition and, 437; defined, 89n85, 401, 436; holiness and, 290; process of, 162–63; rehabilitation and, 441, 446; as sacrifice, 401; satisfaction and, 443–44
reproduction, after the fall, 209
resistance, purpose of, 98
restoration, 294, 311
resurrected body, nature of, 516–17
resurrection, first, 481
resurrection of Jesus Christ, 137–39, 143, 161, 485
resurrection of the body, 511–17
revelations, 331–32, 333–39
revivals, 248
revocation, 88
rich man and Lazarus, parable of the, 490
Rigdon, Sidney, 338n109
righteousness, 195–96, 210, 239, 240, 241
Ripheus, 208n113
Rite of Christian Initiation of Adults (RCIA), 385
robes, 474–75
rock of revelation, 333–39
Roll of Preparatory Members, 383

Roman Catholic Church: anointing of the sick in, 453; on apostleship, 311; on bishops, 326; laity in, 337; leadership of, 320; Lutheran World Federation and, 245; marital indissolubility and, 463–64; proclamation of, 293; on resurrection of the body, 511; sacraments of, 435; on unity, 282. *See also* Catholic Church/Catholicism

Romney, Mitt, 1

routinization of charisma, 307

Sabellianism, 49

sacraments: church performance of, 354–55; compromising of, 356; defined, 351–52, 353; as distinct, 353–54; dual character of, 357; *ex opere operantis* and, 355–58; *ex opere operato* and, 355–58; of Latter-day Saints, 354; ordination requirement of, 354; participants as worthy receivers of, 357n26; Paschal Mystery and, 353; priesthood authority regarding, 358; as signs, 352–53; spiritual fruitfulness and, 357; symbolic nature of, 352; as worship, 401. *See also* ordinances; *specific sacraments*

sacrifice: and Adam and Eve, 142, 207n111; Eucharist and, 399–402; of Jesus Christ, 144, 152, 154, 225, 258, 399, 438; of praise, 400; reconciliation and, 142; repentance as, 401; of thanksgiving, 400

Sadducees, 461, 462

salvation: acceptance of, at death, 502; Adam and, 207; baptism and, 364, 368; calling and, 231–39; church and, 220; conscious acceptance of the gospel for, 502; covenant of, 164; for the dead, 500–511; divine plan and purposes of, 221–25; election and, 222, 225–31; factors for, 259; God's involvement with, 52; grace and, 221, 267, 518n159; help toward, 283; hypothetical acceptance, 502, 505–6; images regarding, 218; individuals for, 221–25; instrumental cause of, 259; justification and, 241; light of Christ and, 235–36; meritorious cause of, 259;

metaphors for, 218; obedience and, 244; overarching issues regarding, 219–21; overview of, 217–19; path to, 259; personal character of, 220; predestination and, 222; providence and, 66; public beliefs regarding, 263n137; sanctification and, 241; sovereignty-freedom debate and, 74; statements regarding, 216–17; synergism of, 255; through atonement of Jesus Christ, 161, 260, 265; traditions regarding, 220; *via salutis* of, 219; works and, 259. *See also* soteriology

Samaria, 360n35, 387, 390

sanctification: for all, 530–31; conversion and, 251; cooperation with God in, 289; entire, 253; justification as, 245–53; perfectionism and, 252; process of, 246–47, 250; purpose of, 542; pursuit of, 261; requirements for, 248; salvation and, 241; spiritual rebirth and, 248; surrender and, 253; synergism and, 289; theosis and, 539–40

sanctity, holiness and, 288

Satan: binding of, 481; buffetings of, 446n43; casting down of, 79–80; disobedience and, 78; evil and, 92–93; the fall and, 76, 207; proposal of, 83; rebellion of, 79; releasing to, 446n43

satisfaction: for crime, 143; as debt payment, 147–48; penal, 147; in penance, 444–45; repentance and, 443–44; for sin, 156, 530–31; theories of, 147

Saul at Antioch, 301n100

saviors on Mount Zion, 507–8, 511

Scripture, 4, 14–18, 237–38

sealing ordinance, 506–8

secondary causation, 75–76

second coming of Jesus Christ, 88, 432–33, 484, 488. *See also* eschatology

Second Great Awakening, 224–25

Seixas, Gershom Mendes, 63

Seixas, Joshua, 63

self-determination, 224, 229

self-flagellation, 444–45

Serapion, "Abba," 21

Sermon on the Mount, 73, 519–20, 524

seven anointings, 451
Seventh-day Adventists, 489
sexual reproduction, 209
Shakers, 457n87
Shepherd of Hermas, 503, 509
signs, in the temple, 472
Silas, 301n100
Silouan the Athonite, St. (Simeon Ivanovich Antonov), 206
Simeon, 301n100
Simon (sorcerer), 387
Simon the Pharisee, 217
sinners, defined, 485n18
sin-offering, 202
sin(s): absolving, 441–42; children and, 213; consequences for, 287; contrition for, 233; death and, 211; as endemic, 125; Eucharist and forgiveness of, 417–19; excommunication and, 446; the fall and, 198–215; forgiveness of, 362–65, 436, 452–53, 530; grace and, 92; hereditary, 199; hyper acute awareness of, 232; infant baptism and, 201–2, 203; original, 125, 198–99, 200–201; pardon for, 239; payment for, 444; physical transmission of, 205; preexistence of, 196, 196n74; punishment for, 148; rehabilitation from, 441, 446; remission of, 242, 442n27; resolution for, 440; satisfaction for, 156, 443–44, 530–31; serious, 445–46; sorrow for, 233; total depravity and, 202, 205; transmission of, 202n94; wiping out of, 146. *See also* evil
Smith, Bathsheba W., 350
Smith, Emma, 382
Smith Joseph: Book of Mormon, loss of, 87; call of, 309; death of, 2, 489; influence of, 4; keys of the kingdom to, 318–19; "King Follett Sermon" of, 185; ordination of, 297; origin of, 2; persecution of, 486–87; prayer of, 109; revelation of, 68, 71, 88, 338; suffering by, 71; translation work of, 7, 13–14, 16; vision of, 25, 525, 528–29; William Miller and, 489
Smith, Joseph, teachings of: on absolution of sin, 442; on afterlife, 108, 160; on age of accountability, 382; on angels and

humans, 541; on apostasy, 310–11; on baptism, 360, 365, 369, 370, 371, 379–80, 382; on baptism for the dead, 506–7; on the Book of Mormon, 16; on calling, 232, 238n58; on the church, 309, 312; on church leadership, 325; on circumcision-baptism analogy, 379; on creation, 63–64; on crucifixion of Jesus Christ, 151; on election, 225, 227; endowment and, 472; on eternal life, 536; on eternity, 517n155; on Eucharist, 397; on evangelists, 301n98; on the fall, 209; on family, 123; on fullness of the gospel, 293; on gifts of the Holy Ghost, 392–93; on glory, 165; on God, 25, 26, 28, 31–32, 37, 43, 60n143; on the gospel, 295; on grace, 254; on healing, 449; on heaven, 29, 134, 525, 527–29; on hell, 497; on human agency, 78, 79; on *imago dei* (image of God), 192–93; on intelligence, 184; on intermediate state, 496; on Jesus Christ, 37, 99, 104, 130–31, 166, 370, 371; on justification, 243, 244, 254; on kingdom of God, 295; on kingdom of heaven, 273n11; on law, 164; leadership of, 302; on magisterium, 330; on matrimony, 457–58, 460, 542–43; on matter, 33; on Olivet discourse, 484n17; on ordinances, 355; on outpouring of the Holy Spirit, 468; on paradise, 496–97; on physicality of God, 20; on predestination, 230; on the priesthood, 340–41; on profession, 302; on providence, 68, 69, 71; on redemption of the dead, 505–6; on Relief Society, 349; on religious views, 284; on rock of revelation, 333; on second coming of Jesus Christ, 432–33, 488–89; on signs, 449; on sin, 203; on spirit prison, 505; on spiritual body, 514, 515n144, 516; on spiritual rebirth, 366; on suffering, 456; on the Trinity, 47, 54; on the truth, 294; on works, 243; on Zion, 484
Smith, Joseph, Sr., 87
Snow, Lorenzo, 36, 190
Socinianism, 45
sola scriptura, 45, 374–75

sons of perdition, 165, 531
sons of Simeon, 504n97
sorrow, for sin, 233
soteriology: calling and, 231–39; defined, 5; individual-communal continuum regarding, 219–20; justification and, 239–45; overarching issues regarding, 219–21; overview of, 216–17; salvation defined in, 217–19. *See also* salvation
soulmaking, 93–94, 98
souls: conforming by, 193–94; as corporeal, 111; creation of, 235; defined, 178; development of, 105–6; eternal life and, 534; as God's literal children, 255–56; grace and, 235; *imago dei* (image of God) and, 190; memory of, 190; origin of, 180–83, 188; progression of, 196; rational, 178; responsiveness of, 197; spiritual suffering of, 167; transferring of, 179; understanding of, 190; viewpoints regarding, 193
"Soul's Captain, The" (Whitney), 264–65
soul sleep (psychopannychia), 492
Southern Baptist Convention (SBC), 323, 375
sovereignty of God, 72–83, 86–90, 148
Sozzini, Fausto (Faustus Socinus), 45
sparrows, 72
speaking in tongues, 467
Spinks, Bryan D., 395n3
spirit birth, 105–6
spirit bodies, 193
spirit prison, 498, 500, 503, 505. *See also* hell
spirit(s): birth of, 188–89; creation of, 194–95; defined, 178; development of, 197; as distinct entity, 180; overview of, 33–34
spiritual adoption, 367
spiritual blindness, 81
spiritual body, 513, 514–15
spiritual death, 212
spiritual giftedness, 303–7, 447
spiritual manifestations, 306–7
spiritual rebirth, 248, 365–68
spiritual rehabilitation, 441, 446
spiritual warfare, 92–93

spirit world, 493–95, 498–99, 506
stake presidents, 440–41
Stephen the Martyr, 25
Stoicism, 193
suffering: benefits of, 456; God and, 42–43; in hell, 532; of Jesus Christ, 43–44, 118, 166–72; as penance, 444–45; providence and, 90–98; purpose of, 98; Satan's role in, 92–93
surrender, 253
synergism, 255, 257, 263, 289
Synod of Toledo, 514
systematic theology, 6n7

tabernacle, earthly bodies as, 490
Talmage, James, 85n71, 85n72
teacher, role and function of, 302–3, 440
Telestial Kingdom of heaven, 529–30, 531, 532
temple: clothing in, 472, 474–75; liturgy of, 109; in Mormon Zion, 88–89; overview of, 477; service in, 477; significance of, 476; signs in, 472; tokens in, 472; veil of, 159; worship in, 476
"Temple cult," 340n112
temple endowment, 466–77
temple marriage sealing, 459–60, 462, 542–43. *See also* matrimony
temptation, 210
Terrestrial Kingdom of heaven, 529–30
testament, defined, 398
testimony, 251
Tetrarchy, 287
thanksgiving, 400
theocentrism, 520–21
theodicy, 90, 98
theology, 3, 5, 6
theosis, 539–40
thief on the cross, 495
Thompson, Mercy Fielding, 97n117
Thorvaldsen, Bertel, 100
time, 34–39
tokens, in the temple, 472
tongues, gift of, 306
Topical Guide to the Scriptures, 272
total depravity, 202, 205

traducianism, 181
transubstantiation, 402–4
tribulation, 485. *See also* eschatology
trichotomism, 178
Trinitarian Controversy, 44
Trinitarianism, 52–53
Trinity, 44–60, 107, 278
Trisagion (Thrice Holy) liturgy, 495–96
True to the Faith, 12n17
truth, embracing, 294
2000 Baptist Faith and Message, 323

Uchtdorf, Dieter, 190
unevangelized, 372, 500–511
Unitarianism, 45, 409n44
unity, 277–78, 282–83, 285
universalism, 223, 501
University of Virginia, 1
univocal language, 22
Utah, 271–72, 286
Utah State University, 1

Valley of Hinnom, 490n35
veil, of the temple, 159
vicariousness, 511
Vincent of Lérins, 292

virtue, heavenly reward and, 527
visible saints, 290–91
vocation, sacraments of, 354
Vulgate, 435n1

Waldensian Confession, 91
washing and anointing, 469
Wesley, John, 252–53
Wesleyan-Holiness movement, 288–89
Westminster Confession, 76, 415, 493
will, 48, 190–91, 196, 226
will of God, 72, 84
women, 344, 350, 509n117, 522–23
works: faith and, 243; grace and, 253–67;
    heavenly reward and, 527; intent of, 261–
    62; judgment by, 518n159; justification by,
    243, 254, 259; merit of, 261; reward for,
    261, 526; salvation and, 259
World Council of Churches (WCC), 285
World of Being, 20
worship, 42, 44, 83, 401

YHWH, 108. *See also* God

Zacchaeus, 436
Zion, 285–86, 289–90, 484
Zoramites, 226, 227

INDEX OF SCRIPTURE

OLD TESTAMENT

Genesis

1:1	61, 62
1:1–2	65
1:1–2:4	194
1:1–3	63
1:26	54, 59, 192
1:27	21
2:5–25	194
2:7	179, 534
2:24	457, 458
3:22	54
5	285, 505
5:1	192
14:18	342, 397n6
17:12	379
18:14	32
22	154
25:23	228

Exodus

3:13–15	102
4:21	80n54
6:3	108
7:3	80n54
7:13	80n54
8:15	80n54
8:19	80n54
8:32	80n54
9:12	80n54
10:1	80n54
10:20	80n54
10:27	80n54
11:10	80n54
14:4	80n54
14:8	80n54
14:17	80
16	397n6
19:5–6	346
19:6	349
24	397
24:1	342n119
24:8	397
24:9–10	342n119
24:11	397
29:4–9	469
34:6–7	33

Leviticus

7:12–15	398n9
11:44–45	288

Numbers

11:16–17	342–43n119
11:24–25	342–43n119
23:19	28

Deuteronomy

2:30	80
28–30	73

Joshua

11:20	80

1 Chronicles

16:34	33

Nehemiah

9:6	67n17

Job

42:2	68

Psalms

2:4–5	487
32:5	438
34:18	438
45:7–8	54
51	213
51:17	401n22
82	60n143
83:18	108
86:5	436
89:14	33
103:17–18	33
110:1	54
116:17	400
139:7–8	494
139:7–12	32
145:8	153
145:9	67n17

Proverbs

8:22–31	54
16:33	73
28:13	436

Ecclesiastes

12:7	492n46

Isaiah

2:3	484n14
11	483
11:6–9	482
24:5	310
24:21–22	498n71
24:22	505
25:6	432
25:6–9	431
38:1–5	89
42:6–7	498n71
42:7	505
45:1	73
49:8–9	498n71
55:8–9	23
63:17	80
64:8	508
65	483
65:17	483
65:17–25	482

Jeremiah

1:5	231
18:7–8	89
18:9–10	89
31:31–34	398

Ezekiel

18:31	256

Daniel

2:34–35	271
2:44	271n7

Hosea

11:9	28

Joel

2:23	447
2:28	447

Amos

3:7	332

Jonah

3:4	89

Zechariah

12:10	137
14:20	290

Malachi

4:5–6	507

NEW TESTAMENT

Matthew

1:20	131
3:11	362, 365
3:15	240, 370
3:16	386
5–7	73
5:48	73, 252
6:8	32
6:9	189
7:14	524
7:21	520
8:12	493n47
10:29	72
10:29–30	70
10:35–38	457
12:31–32	530
15:9	312
16	317
16:13–19	315
16:17	512
16:18	333
18	317
18:15–20	439, 440
18:17	440
18:18	316, 441
18:20	409
19	464
19:6	463
19:14	378
20:16	231n44
21:11	301n100
22:1–14	431n115
22:13	493n47
22:14	231n44
22:30	461
24	484n17, 485
25:1–13	431n115
25:30	493n47
26:17–29	395
26:28	365, 396, 397
26:29	273n10, 431, 432
27:52	504n97
28:18	135
28:19	359, 373, 378

Mark

1:4	362
1:10	386
2:1–12	452
4:20	529n198
6:2–4	301n100
6:13	447
10	464
10:9	463
10:14	378
12:25	461
13	485
14:12–25	395
14:22–24	396
14:24	397
16	304
16:15	378
16:15–18	304
16:16	368
16:17–18	449

Luke

2:36–38	301n100
2:46	131
2:52	133
3:3	362
3:16	365
3:22	386
5:10	540
6:13	298

7:16	301n100	14:16	394	16:30–33	360n35
7:26	301n100	15:5	260	17:28–29	28
7:36–50	217	15:19	287	17:29	188
10:1	343n119	16:13	394	18:8	360n35
10:17	343n119	17	47	19:4	362
16:19–31	490	17:5	103	19:6	387n142
17:20–21	270	17:6	166	19:11–12	448
17:21	271	17:21	361	20:7	425
18:16	378	17:23	361	20:28	300n94
19:8	436	17:26	361	21:9	301n100
22:7–20	395	18:36	270	21:10–14	301n100
22:19	396, 409	19:30	169	22:16	363, 364
22:20	397	20	317		
22:43–44	167n98	20:17	107, 495	**Romans**	
22:44	167	20:22	393	1:5	246
23:43	490, 495	20:23	316, 441, 442	1:20	55n126
24:39	137, 512	21:16	299n92	1:24	81
24:49	466	21:25	9	1:26	81
				2:6	518
John		**Acts**		2:7–8	518
1	104, 105	1:4–5	466	2:16	518
1:1–2	185	1:6	270n4	2:28–29	358
1:2	183	1:8	467	3:25	142n6, 154
1:3	58, 61	2	447, 467, 468	3:28	243
1:9	235, 236	2:17	447	4	244
1:12	58	2:33	139	4:2	243
1:12–13	367	2:37–41	360n35	4:4–6	243
1:14	111	2:38	242, 362, 387	4:5	241
1:16	235	2:38–39	378	4:16	243, 254
1:29	397	2:42	268	5:11	141
2	424, 457	4:12	218	5:12	198, 204, 211
3:3–5	365	4:32	47n99	5:13	162n78
3:5	250, 368, 369, 386	7:55–56	25	5:14	198
3:16	153, 154	8	390	6:3–11	245, 361
3:34	130	8:12	360n35	6:4	366, 373
4:23–24	34n52	8:17–19	387	6:23	204
4:24	34	8:35–38	360n35	8:3	114n55
5:29	525	9:17–18	360n35	8:11	512
6:44	237n55	10:47–48	360n35	8:14	368
6:54	411	11:27–28	301n100	8:16	188
6:57	412	13:1	268, 301n100	8:17	368
6:65	237	13:24	362	8:28	71
8:58	102	13:48	226	8:28–29	228
10:29	33	15:32	301n100	8:29	105, 247, 471
12:40	80	16:14–15	360n35	8:29–30	230
14:2	525	16:15	377	9	81

9:10–15	196	15:22	161	1:11	67n17, 69
9:13	230	15:22–24	485	1:20–21	139
9:18	80n55	15:23	518	2:8–9	258
10:17	237	15:29	372, 506	2:19–20	298
11:26	73, 227	15:40	529n197	4:5	277
11:28	227	15:40–42	529	4:6	33
12:1	346, 400	15:41	527	4:11	298n90, 299
13:14	474	15:41–42	525	4:11–14	298
14:12	518	15:42	512	4:13	252, 334
		15:44	490, 512, 515	4:23–24	366
1 Corinthians		15:45	198	5	457
1:2	269	15:50	512, 514, 515	5:2	399
1:10	280			5:26–27	287
1:16	377	**2 Corinthians**		5:30	420
1:24	238n58	1:21–22	389	5:31	361
1:26	238n58	4:16	249	5:31–32	458
2:8	119	4:17	456		
2:16	253	5:1	116n61, 490	**Philippians**	
3:8	526	5:1–4	180	1:23	489
5:5	446	5:10	518	2:5–6	539
5:7	397	5:17	251, 287, 366	2:6–8	127n93
5:7–8	414	5:18–20	141n4	2:9	136
6:11	363	5:21	240	2:10–11	139
7:12	330	6:1	251	2:12	258, 260
7:14	379, 380	8:1	268	2:12–13	76, 255n105
7:29	457	8:23	300	2:25	300
7:32–33	457	12:2	529	3:20–21	139
10:12	267n147	12:2–4	496	3:21	512
10:16–17	420, 421, 422	12:7–9	454	4:2	280
11	415–16	12:9	255n105	4:8	294
11:23–29	395				
11:24	409	**Galatians**		**Colossians**	
11:24–25	396	1:4	144	1:10	258
11:25	397	1:16	512	1:17	67n17
11:26	396	2:8	300	1:19	130
11:28–29	414	3:8	295	1:27	352
12	420, 448	3:26	366	2:8	24
12:4	278	3:27	361, 366	2:9	134n125
12:9	448	3:28	367n61	2:11–12	378
12:13	278, 360	4:4–5	366	2:12	373
12:20	278	4:6	367	2:14	239
12:27	360	5:6	220	3:14	366
12:28	303, 448				
12:30	448	**Ephesians**		**1 Thessalonians**	
14	301	1:10	61	1:6	386n139
14:32–33	337				

4:16–17	484	**James**		3:20	236	
4:17	485	1:22	347	7:3	536n220	
		2:17	244	12	79	
1 Timothy		2:18	242	14:1	536n220	
1:19–20	446	2:20	260	15:3	33	
2:4	221, 222, 293	2:24	244	17	312	
2:5	340	5:14–15	447	19:7–9	246	
4:4	61			19:8	434	
4:14	302n102	**1 Peter**		19:9	431	
5:20	440	1:8	468	20	480, 485	
6:20	327	1:15–16	288	20:4	481	
		2:5	346	20:5	481, 485n18	
2 Timothy		2:9	346	20:6	481	
1:14	327	3:18–20	502, 509	20:12	481, 519	
3:5	312	3:19	503	20:12–13	518	
		3:19–20	505	20:14	531	
Titus		3:21	361, 363, 368n71	21	524	
2:14	258	3:22	139	21–22	483n12	
		4:6	502, 503, 509	21:1	483	
		5:1–2	300n94	21:8	529, 531	
Hebrews		5:2	299n92	22	524	
1:3	50n108, 139, 193n58			22:4	536n220	
2:10	133	**2 Peter**		22:11	531	
2:17	113, 142n6	1:4	540	22:18–19	332	
2:18	113	1:10	232			
4:13	84	1:14	116n61	**BOOK OF MORMON**		
4:14	399	3:9	221n10			
4:15	41, 113	3:13	483	**1 Nephi**		
6:1–2	387			9:6	68	
6:20	342	**1 John**		11:16	112n48	
7:17	342	1:9	246, 436	11:26	112n48	
8–10	398	2:2	154, 158–59	11:33	169	
8:1–2	399	2:20	337	13–14	313	
8:6	340	2:27	337	13:2–6	312	
9:15	340	3:2	514	13:26–29	312	
9:24	401	3:4	151	14	312	
10:22	363	4:3	116n58	15:35	272	
11:40	507	4:8	27	19:10	120	
12:2	218	4:10	154	19:13	120	
12:9	188			22:17	487n24	
12:14	246, 288	**Jude**				
12:22	285	14	286	**2 Nephi**		
12:23	134			2	78	
12:24	340	**Revelation**		2:2	71	
13:15	400	3:14	105	2:7	151, 233, 438	

2:8	245	**Book of Jacob**		5:13	238	
2:11	94, 210	2:27	460	5:14	252	
2:13	94	2:30	460	5:15–25	518n160	
2:15–16	94	4:4–5	142	5:24	272n10	
2:16	78, 210	6:4	272n10	5:25	273n11	
2:22	211n126			5:26	252	
2:23	94	**Book of Omni**		5:28	252, 273n11	
2:24	32	1:26	253	5:33–34	225	
2:25	209			5:37	232n45	
2:27	164	**Words of Mormon**		5:50–51	273n11	
4:17–19	213	1:3–7	87	5:62	362n43	
4:26–28	213	1:7	87n81	6:2	362n43	
9:6	212			7:9	273n11	
9:8	33	**Book of Mosiah**		7:10	131	
9:8–9	93n101	2:20–21	68	7:11–12	114, 173	
9:13	496n65	3:5	103	7:14	273n11, 362n43, 366	
9:16	93n101	3:7	168	7:21	272n10	
9:18	272n10	3:8	103	7:24	262	
9:20	37	3:11	162n79	7:25	273n11	
9:21	159	3:16	162	8:10	362n43	
9:23	272n10, 369n72	3:18	218	9:12	272n10	
9:25–26	162n79	3:19	213, 214n132, 236, 237	9:25	273n11	
9:46	518	3:21	162	9:27	362n43	
9:53	33	4:1–2	233	10:6	232	
10:23	226	4:5	233	10:20	273n11	
10:25	272	4:12	419	11:37	273n11	
21	483	4:26	419	11:40–41	166	
24:27	68	5:2	248, 249, 262	11:45	514	
25:13	272n10	5:7	248	13:3–5	229n35	
25:23	266	5:15	248	13:14–19	342n117	
25:26	101	7:27	103	16:16–17	236	
26:12	103	7:28	103	19:35	360	
26:13	393, 449n52	8:5	103	26:10–14	238	
30:8–15	483	13:28	142	26:35	32	
31:5	370	18:8–10	411	29:17	272n10	
31:7	369	18:10	361	31	227	
31:9	370	21:35	361	31:5	237	
31:13	361, 365n53	25:21–22	269	31:16–17	226	
31:16	248	26:22–23	362	34:9	158	
31:17	360	27:25–26	249, 367	34:10	158	
31:17–18	248	27:27–29	233	34:14	142	
31:20	248			34:32–33	499	
31:21	272n10	**Book of Alma**		34:36	273n10	
33:1	237	4:14	419	36:12–13	234	
33:12	272n10	5:12	249	36:16–20	234	
				38:15	273n10	

39:9	273n10	11:23–28	375n97	4:19	273n10
40	493n47	11:32–34	369	12:27	255n105
40:7–14	178	11:33	273n10	13:3–12	483
40:11	494	11:36	47n99	15:34	273n10
40:11–14	493	11:38	273n10, 369		
40:12–21	496n65	11:39	333n91	**Book of Moroni**	
40:13–14	498	12:20	273n10	6:3	361
40:14	497n69	14:21	273n10	6:4	383
40:15	495	18:5	360	7:6–9	262
40:17	495	18:7	410	8:8	162
40:21	493	18:28–30	415–16	8:8–23	382
40:23	517	18:32	292	8:9	203
40:25–26	273n10	19:13	365n53	8:14	203
41:3–7	518n160	20:8–9	413	9:6	273n10
41:4	273n10	26:21	360	10:21	273n10
42:15	151, 153	27:5	361	10:24	305
42:22	151	27:19	273n10	10:26	273n10
42:25	151	28:2–3	273n10	10:32	253
48:19	362n43	28:8	273n10	10:34	497n65
49:30	362n43	28:10	273n10		
		28:40	273n10	**DOCTRINES AND COVENANTS**	
Book of Helaman				1:12	488n31
3:24	362n43	**4 Nephi**		1:30	311
3:26	360	1:14	496n65	3:1–3	68
3:30	273n11	1:15–17	286n56	6:3	273n10
3:33	281	1:17	273n10	6:9	436
3:35	253			6:13	273n10
4:11	281	**Book of Mormon**		6:37	273n11
5:17	362	3:20	518	10:52–56	281
5:19	362n43	7:7	273n10	10:55	273n11
5:32	273n11	7:10	365n53	11:3	273n10
12:4	212	8:22	68	11:9	436
13:5	87	9:9	33	11:15	333n91
13:37	93n101	9:12	209	11:30	367n62
14:30–31	165, 226	9:19	305	12	32
		9:23	369	12:3	273n10
3 Nephi		9:29	365	14:3	273n10
1:23	362n43			14:7	533
7:23–26	364n52	**Book of Ether**		15:6	273n11, 436
7:26	362n43	3:6	193	16:6	273n11, 436
9:17	142, 367n62	3:12	33	18:5	333n91
9:19	142	3:14	111	18:11–14	436
9:19–20	233n49	3:15–16	193	18:15–16	273n11
9:20	365n53, 417	3:16	111	18:21	361
9:21	142	4:18	369	18:22	369

18:25	273n11	27:3–4	423	39	32n44
18:31	255n105	27:4	273n10	39:3–4	367
18:44	273n11	27:5	432	39:15	466
18:46	273n11	27:5–13	432n121	39:19	273n11, 488n31
19:1–3	32	27:12–13	297	39:21	488n31
19:4–12	532	27:14	432	39:23	390
19:5	532	28:1–5	331	39:24	488n31
19:15–18	531	28:2	324	41:4	488n31
19:16–17	530	28:7	324	42	440, 464n111
19:17	119	28:8	331	42:7	488n31
19:18	166, 167	29:5	271n8	42:12	293
19:31	365n53	29:7	225n26, 488n31	42:44	450
20	332, 343n120	29:9–10	487, 488n31	42:45	280
20:4	254	29:11–13	485	42:48	450, 455
20:8–9	293	29:28	93n101	42:87–93	440
20:12	33	29:36–37	80, 93n101	42:89	440
20:17	30, 33	29:39	94n106	42:90–91	440
20:25	369	29:42	212	42:92	440
20:29	273n10	29:47	162	43:10	271n8
20:30–33	242	33:6	225n26	43:17	488n31
20:31	253	33:10	273n11, 488n31	43:18	485
20:35	332	33:11	365n53	45:1	271
20:37	361, 364n52, 411	33:12–13	333n91	45:3–5	402
20:38–44	300n95	33:15	390n158	45:8	367n62
20:41	390n158	33:18	488n31	45:17	497
20:53–54	440	34:3	367n62	45:37–39	488n31
20:65	338	34:7	488	45:65–71	483
20:68–69	415	34:12	488n31	46:4	416
20:70	383n127	35:2	367n62	46:19	448
20:71	381	35:5–6	391	46:20	448
20:72–74	375	35:9	305	49:6	488n31
20:75	425n102	35:15	488n31	49:13–14	390n158
20:77	393, 410	35:16	488n31	49:15	457
20:79	99, 410, 411, 412,	35:17	293	49:20	286
	430	35:26	488n31	49:28	488n31
20:84	269	35:27	271n8, 488n31	50:35	271n8
21:2	324	36	32	51:20	488n31
21:6	324	36:2	358	52:10	390n158
21:9	170, 438	38–39	32	53	26
22:1–4	376	38:2	38n65	53:6	352n3
24:13–14	306	38:8	488n31	54:4	88
25:1	367n62	38:9	271n8	54:6	88
26:1	269	38:15	271n8	54:10	488n31
26:2	338	38:27	286, 422	58:2	273n11
27	433	38:32	466	58:4	94, 488n31
27:2	423	38:35	286	58:7–11	432

58:27–28	256	76:103–105	529	93:38	161
58:43	436	76:105–106	532	94:3	271
59:8–12	401	77:2	194, 497n65	95:5–6	231n44
59:9	425	77:14	352n3	95:8–9	467
59:12	427n109	78:12	446n43	97:21	286, 484
59:21	69	78:18	271n8	98:3	71
60:7	288	82:7	438n10	99:5	488n31
62:9	271n8	82:10	164	101:11	488n31
63:4	331, 337	82:21	446n43	101:26–30	483
64:4	271n8	82:24	271n8	101:65	273n11
65:2	318	84	343n120	101:78	78
65:3	432	84:4–5	88	101:91	493n47
65:5–6	272	84:20	353	101:98	488n31
65:53	488n31	84:38	273n11	101:100	273n11
66:2	460n97	84:46–47	236	102:11	326
68:2	302	84:58	273n11	104:10	446n43
68:8–10	304	84:63	300n95	104:59	488n31
68:9	369	84:64–72	304	105:33–37	231n44
68:25	385	84:74	273n11	106:3	273n11
68:27	381	84:76	271n8	106:4	488n31
68:35	488n31	88:7–13	32	107	343n120
72:1	271n8	88:12–13	33	107:2–4	342n117
74:3	379	88:15	178	107:6	342
74:4	380	88:18–20	523	107:8	342
74:6	380	88:27–28	515	107:14	342
74:7	380	88:41	31, 32	107:18	342
76	160, 525	88:74	271	107:20	342
76:3	68	88:78	303	107:25	344
76:24	66	88:101	485n18	107:34	344
76:31–45	527	88:102	531	107:34–35	343n119
76:33	531	88:126	488n31	107:38	343n119, 344
76:36–37	531	88:127	302	107:39	301n98
76:39	165, 528	89:6	423, 424	107:54–55	208
76:43	165	90:6	324	107:56	208
76:50–70	529	90:16	271	107:80	325
76:52	390n158	93:8	104	107:91–92	302
76:59	539	93:12–13	134	109:8	477
76:71–80	529	93:13	251	109:22–23	467
76:73	505	93:15–17	135	109:29	109
76:75	108	93:16–17	134	109:33	109
76:77	108	93:19–20	134	109:34	109
76:81–89	529	93:20	235	109:36–37	468
76:88	532	93:21	184	109:42	109
76:89	532	93:29	64, 184	109:43	109
76:94–95	134	93:31–32	78	109:47	109
76:98–106	529	93:33	64	109:72	271

109:77	30, 33	132:19–20	543	5:10–11	207
110:3–4	109	132:21–22	542	5:11	209
112:29	369	132:26	446n43	5:12–15	208
112:34	488n31	132:31–32	460	5:27	208
116:1	208n114	132:37	537n225	5:56	208
117:8	208n114	132:45–46	318, 442	5:57	208
121:7–8	456	132:49	273n11	5:58	208, 295
121:34–40	231n44	132:61–62	460n98	6:48	209, 212
121:36–37	341	132:64–66	460n98	6:51–68	371n83
121:45–46	394	133:17	488n31	6:53	207
122:5–7	71	133:73	493n47	6:53–54	204
122:9	68, 71	136:41	271n8	6:55	94n106, 161, 213
124	343n120	137	331	6:62	207
124:28–39	506	137:7–8	505	6:64–66	365n53
124:49	88	137:10	382	6:64–68	367n62
124:51	88	138	331	7:11	371n83
124:126	325	138:27	509	7:18	47n99
124:133–134	352n3	138:29–30	509	7:18–19	286
124:144	338	138:35	170	7:32	77, 78
128:8	318	138:50	497	7:36–37	78
128:15	507, 510n120	138:57	509	7:38	505
128:17	506			7:56–57	505
128:20	297	**PEARL OF GREAT**		8:23–24	371n83
128:24	488n31	**PRICE**			
130:1–2	460			**Book of Abraham**	
130:2	522	**Book of Moses**		2:8	70
130:14–17	489n34	1:32	104	3	186
130:18–19	184	1:33	65	3:18	185
130:20–21	164	1:35	65	3:18–23	185
131:1–2	542	1:38	65	3:19	105
131:1–3	532n204	1:39	37, 66	3:21	185
131:7	33	2:1	65	3:22	185
131:7–8	180	2:26	60	3:23	185
132	460, 543	4:1	79	3:24	65, 115
132:1–3	460n98	4:3–4	79	3:25	79
132:5	164	4:6	76	3:28	79
132:7	358	5:4–5	207	4:1	65
132:15–16	461	5:5	207n111	4:26	60
132:19	543	5:7–8	207n111